Studies in the History of Law and Justice

Volume 4

The purpose of this book series is to publish high quality volumes on the history of law and justice.

Legal history can be a deeply provocative and influential field, as illustrated by the growth of the European universities and the ius commune, the French Revolution, the American Revolution, and indeed all the great movements for national liberation through law. The study of history gives scholars and reformers the models and courage to question entrenched injustices, by demonstrating the contingency of law and other social arrangements.

Yet legal history today finds itself diminished in the universities and legal academy. Too often scholarship betrays no knowledge of what went before, or why legal institutions took the shape that they did. This series seeks to remedy that deficiency.

Studies in the History of Law and Justice will be theoretical and reflective. Volumes will address the history of law and justice from a critical and comparative viewpoint. The studies in this series will be strong bold narratives of the development of law and justice. Some will be suitable for a very broad readership.

Contributions to this series will come from scholars on every continent and in every legal system. Volumes will promote international comparisons and dialogue. The purpose will be to provide the next generation of lawyers with the models and narratives needed to understand and improve the law and justice of their own era.

The series includes monographs focusing on a specific topic, as well as collections of articles covering a theme or collections of article by one author.

More information about this series at http://www.springer.com/series/11794

Ramses Delafontaine

Historians as Expert Judicial Witnesses in Tobacco Litigation

A Controversial Legal Practice

Springer

Ramses Delafontaine
FWO Fellow at Ghent University
Ghent, Belgium

ISSN 2198-9842 ISSN 2198-9850 (electronic)
Studies in the History of Law and Justice
ISBN 978-3-319-14291-3 ISBN 978-3-319-14292-0 (eBook)
DOI 10.1007/978-3-319-14292-0

Library of Congress Control Number: 2014959180

Springer Cham Heidelberg New York Dordrecht London

Printed on acid-free paper

Springer International Publishing AG Switzerland is part of Springer Science+Business Media (www.springer.com)

To Mama, Papa, and Selket.
For their faith and love.

Foreword by Alain Wijffels

Historical Evidence in Court: A Challenge for Lawyers and Historians

Ramses Delafontaine's book on the role of historians as expert witnesses in tobacco litigation in the United States is an important and useful work. It is important, because it touches upon some fundamental issues of both historical and legal methodology, which have been emerging during the last few decades and are therefore still novel and which both lawyers and historians are still largely unfamiliar with. It is also useful, firstly in a more theoretical sense, because it shows clearly how these issues have evolved and can at present be defined; it is also useful in a more practical sense, because its main vantage point, the implications of tobacco production, commercialisation and consumption, as reflected in legal proceedings, is far from being an open-and-shut case, and may well be regarded as paradigmatic for many other comparable issues which our societies are only beginning to face and address. On a more personal note, I also believe that it is very fortunate that a talented young historian, who belongs to a generation who have come to age after the events and developments which have generated the cases under review, is casting a fresh twenty-first-century view on such aspects of the heritage of – to a large extent – the twentieth century.

The latter remark is, I realise, highly subjective and controversial. It may therefore warrant a brief explanation. As a comparative legal historian, I have had the opportunity to teach to undergraduate and graduate students (mostly law students) during four decades in different European countries. Several years ago, I reached the conclusion – which is strongly opposed by most of my colleagues and contemporaries – that my generation has been witnessing a deep fault-line in Western culture. Some of the features of those fault-lines are not controversial and, on the contrary, fairly widely accepted. Thus, one can claim that until a generation or two ago, the two cultural pillars which had jointly supported Western culture as it grew in the Second Middle Ages and Early-Modern Times, Christianity and the study of classical (Roman-Greek) Antiquity, had provided the main intellectual references, moral values and even artistic framework of Western culture. At least as explicit references, those two pillars have by now largely vanished. I doubt whether at a deeper, structural level, those foundations are still recognisable in our Western societies. Observing the changes in almost half a century of successive intakes of students (including my own generation), together with the changes in my own field, legal studies, and the adjacent humanities and social sciences, I believe that, in the West, all aspects of our culture, whether the arts or public governance, and even scholarship, are more and more based on a different anthropology than the one which still prevailed in my own days as a student. Of course, as an adept of the *longue durée* in history, I have to recognise much further back in history features from which the present changes can be traced. The ideals and expectations of the Enlightenment, for example, have in many respects taken some two centuries to become more generally implemented in Western societies, but, as that implementation has become reality, the eighteenth-century rationalist concept of man has also been subverted. Legal changes in most Western societies reflect that subversion. Both in civil and in common law jurisdictions, the eighteenth century witnessed a new approach to rights and liberties and their assertion in written constitutional documents, but beyond the classical liberal civil rights and liberties, it was not until the late twentieth century that the impact of human rights was felt in all areas of the law – with significant differences between European countries, and between Western Europe and the United States. That general impact of human rights echoes changes which have profoundly transformed traditional branches of the law, and fostered entirely new legal branches. Few areas of the law had been so comprehensively integrated into a legal theory as contract law (at an earlier stage in the civil law tradition than in the common law tradition), and that theoretical foundation is to be found in most nineteenth-century codifications, in case law and in most of nineteenth-century and twentieth-century legal doctrine. However, from the late nineteenth century onwards, the law of employment (labour law), followed by the law of the welfare state, and even more recently by consumers' protection law, as well as countless amendments on particular points of the balance of interests between contracting parties in various types of contracts, have all contributed to a whole new practical approach to contracting – even if we have not reached yet a corresponding metamorphosis of the underlying legal theory. It is one of the characteristics of legal history that traditional rituals and formulas can survive long after the original interests they were intended to protect have become obsolete. The new development of class actions, often in order to offer a more adequate and effective procedural protection to the same interests as those developed in different areas of substantive law, should also be regarded as a feature of legal transformation in our time. Delafontaine discusses several cases of class actions and the conflicts of interests which they reflect. At the same time, class actions tend to highlight the more general social relevance of the effects of tobacco consumption, and thus raise further questions on the historical context in which that consumption has been encouraged during the previous century.

The issue of the periods of limitation ('extinctive prescription', in a more civil-law minded terminology) may at first sight appear to be a more technical adjustment of the law. However, it is closely linked to the general developments I just referred to. The classic approach to the limitations of actions was inspired by both practical and social-economic considerations, focusing mainly on private interests. The practical considerations implied that responsible citizens were deemed to look diligently after their interests, and that it was not in the interest of justice to extend too long the possibility of introducing an action when the claimant had failed to keep watch over his property and interests. The social and economic considerations made it possible to differentiate between various interests, although here, too, practical factors played a role. Typically, the protection of an action relating to land and real estate was allowed for a longer period than actions relating to chattels and personal property. In the law of torts, a distinction was sometimes made between the time of the tortious act, the time when the damage was effective, and the time when the damage was discovered or should have been discovered by the claimant in tort. In later Roman law and in Medieval canon law, the periods taken into account (e.g., in the case of acquisitive prescription, which may act as a bar to the action of the former owner) were substantially extended when public interests (such as Crown or Church property) were at stake, and in some cases, the common rules on prescription were even put aside. By the time the nineteenth-century codifications of private law were enacted, the individual *citoyen* was usually bound by comparatively strict periods of limitation, except when landed property was involved or bad faith of the other party had played a role. During the twentieth century, those strict periods with regard to actionable interests were relaxed on different grounds. In criminal law, particular heinous crimes committed during the (second world) war or against humanity were exempted from the general system of limitation. Considerations of general welfare, public health and sometimes higher standards of morality on particularly sensitive issues also contributed to generate a tendency to introduce longer periods of limitation in civil cases. Long-time exposure of employees to toxic substances (as for example in the asbestos related cases), or the delayed realisation of long-term repressed mental and physical harm (as in cases of child abuse) have made it necessary to adjust both substantive and adjective law in order to protect more effectively such interests. Arguably, there is more than a mere adjustment of the law here at stake. These issues not only affect newly protected interests which, by their nature, can only be identified and assessed over a long period of time, they are also driven by a fundamentally new understanding and concept of a human being's essential *persona*. As with human rights, one can recognise a shift towards giving primarily protection to human dignity, whereby patrimonial considerations tend to be accessory – an analysis which will inevitably be gainsaid by anyone adopting as a matter of principle a more pessimistic view on human nature. One does not, however, need to be a cynic to acknowledge that the shift has also been inspired and supported by considerations with regard to the social and economic costs of various types of harm developed over an extended period of time. Moreover, in several cases of legal proceedings where historical expertise has been called upon, the claimants are not the direct victims of the harm, but relatives and sometimes descendants of the original victim. The extension of liability so as to protect these new claimants' interests creates fresh legal issues with regard to (for example) causality and proximity. The great diversity of cases means that it is not easy to establish a common test for answering the question, how long a past harm may continue to be considered as an interest which ought to be protected by the law, especially since the interests at stake and the claims have sometimes more a symbolic than a pecuniary value. The question is all the more complex because in some instances (for example when descendants claim works of art taken by the nazis from their ancestors who perished in the Holocaust), both moral and patrimonial interests are at stake. In France, the recurring debate on the recognition of the 'Armenian genocide', or the recognition of France's responsibilities in crimes committed during the Algerian war of independence, show that a political interest may be kept alive for several generations after the events. In such cases, it is perhaps inevitable that the standards for a continuing need of historical research and reassessment may at times appear at odds with the standards required from an historian as an expert witness during a trial. As the reader of this book will find out, the involvement of historical expertise in litigation where the interests amount to very considerable sums is not consistently conducive to the image of independent critical historical research. It remains to be seen how, in future, historians will deal with the revision of earlier research when that earlier research has supported an established res judicata or, more generally, any settled case law.

For many reasons, the issues raised by litigation against the tobacco industry are bound to fascinate public opinion at large. The tobacco industry is big business, and it has become global business, part of everyday life both in industrialised and in developing countries. It affects both the individual's well-being and social welfare. In several Western countries, the use of tobacco has become a topic of controversy, with increasing bans on tobacco consumption in public places, and more recently also a tendency to advocate its ban in the private sphere. Thus, the issue of tobacco is increasingly frequently intersecting with issues of other drugs, whether still widely socially acceptable (such as alcohol and some pharmaceutical substances) or mostly prohibited (several categories of recreational drugs). The constant pressure on the legalisation of the private detention and use of prohibited drugs is in many ways at odds with the growing official and social intolerance of tobacco consumption. Changing attitudes in the West towards tobacco consumption are a fairly recent reaction in contrast to the culture of glamour which had come – not least in the visual arts – to be associated with smoking. In spite of systematic health warnings, rising taxes, restrictions on smoking in public places and a much wider acknowledgement of the risks and inconvenience of tobacco consumption, smoking remains very much part of our day-to-day environment, even among young generations. The debate about banning or not banning smoking is linked to the cultural shifts briefly sketched above, though as it befits a complex issue, the divide between smokers and non-smokers does not altogether coincide with the distinction between those who hold on to a traditional Western anthropology and those who tend to be on the side of the new anthropological paradigms which are transforming Western societies.

These developments around tobacco consumption mean that in our own *Zeitgeschichte*, this is a topic standing at the crossroads of several historical approaches: it touches – without being comprehensive – to social and economic history, the *histoire des mentalités*, cultural history, gender history, material history and history of art. Increasing regulation and legislation, but also litigation, have also brought the topic into the province of legal history.

While the main focus of Delafontaine's book is on forensic history, with a special emphasis on the role of historians in legal proceedings related to actions against tobacco companies, the author also provides a very legible survey of the underlying theoretical foundations of historical research which are being challenged by the historians' involvement in such proceedings. He also records a variety of litigation on different issues, where the historians' expertise has been called upon. Thus, one of the most original features of this book is to present the issue of historical evidence in American tobacco-related litigation in a wider context, which will contribute to a better understanding of the issues at stake among both historians and lawyers.

Alain Wijffels

Preface

He dated and cross-dated, pedigreed and triple-pedigreed, compared, noted, connoted, wove, strung, sorted, selected, inferred, calendared and counter-calendared for ten hours a day. And, because this sudden and new light of Love was upon him, he turned those dry bones of history and dirty records of misdeeds into things to weep or to laugh over as he pleased. His heart and soul were at the end of his pen, and they got into the ink. He was dowered with sympathy, insight, humour, and style for two hundred and thirty days and nights; and his book was a Book.

Rudyard Kipling

Historians and legal scholars have civil responsibilities to use their knowledge in such a way that others may benefit from it. Historians who are working as expert judicial witnesses engage in a controversial legal practice in order to defend their research and their historical truth. There exists an inherent strength in just historical narrative and facts, which has the power to withstand those who seek to alter the past for personal gain in the present and the future. The civil engagement through social advocacy and personal courage displayed by some historians in tobacco litigation deserves our admiration. This book seeks to incite academic and public debate on the involvement of historians in tobacco litigation. The forensic form of history represents an opportunity for historians and the legal profession to honour the truth, to defy those who threaten it, and defend those seeking it.

I plan to continue my research on forensic history under the project title "*The Judge and The Historian*", with special attention to the involvement of historians as expert judicial witnesses in tobacco litigation. There is still so much to discover.

Ghent, Belgium
October 31, 2014

Ramses Delafontaine

Acknowledgments

Nam et secundas res splendidiores facit amicitia
et adversas partiens communicansque leviores.

For friendship adds a brighter radiance to prosperity
and lessens the burden of adversity by dividing and sharing it.

Marcus Tullius Cicero

This book is the product of an unremitting interest in history.

I have spent many hours behind my desk and my computer, nevertheless, my research has been a unique journey through history, law, and the World Wide Web, a journey which has also literally brought me to the other side of the world. History *is* and *remains* my passion.

My research has been a work of multiple years, during which I repeatedly found that I could count on a lot of helping hands. I want to thank the following people who have advised me and supported me in writing this book:

First of all, I want express my deepest gratitude to my supervisor Prof. Dr. Berber Bevernage from Ghent University. Professor Bevernage has granted me from early on in this project a freedom of research and a level of independency which I initially did not deserve as it was solely based on his faith in my promise that I would deliver. He has offered me feedback, advice, and support whenever I was in need of any. He has inspired me through his own research, his hard work, and his activities as a founder of *the International Network for Theory and History*. I could not have wished for a better guide through the final year of my training as an aspirant historian. It gives me great pleasure that I have four years ahead of me as a Ph.D. candidate during which I will be able to discuss plenty more with my Virgil along the way.

During the preparation of this book, I have been able to rely on Prof. Dr. Dr. Wijffels for advice, help, and continued support for my research and my book. He has, through his own work and especially by coining the term ‘forensic history’, inspired me to a great extent while writing this book. I would further like to convey my greatest gratitude to Prof. Wijffels for writing such an eloquent foreword to this book.

I thank Springer for presenting me with the opportunity to publish my work on an international scale. I thank the series editors, Prof. Dr. Georges Martyn of Ghent University and Prof. Dr. Mortimer Sellers of the University of Baltimore for their guidance and help. I thank Neil Olivier for his work on this project. I would also like to thank Diana Nijenhuijzen for answering all of my e-mails and questions without delay and always ending on a happy note.

I also want to thank William Wanbaugh for ploughing through this manuscript with a sharp eye and an even sharper pencil in order to make sure that no Dutch words found their way into this book. He has done a herculean work in reviewing this book for which he has my deepest thanks.

I wish to acknowledge the help provided by Prof. Dr. Antoon De Baets from the University of Groningen, Dr. Vladimir Petrovic of the Institute for Contemporary History in Belgrade, Predrag Dojcinovic of the International Criminal Tribunal for the former Yugoslavia, Dr. Mike Lawson from Morgan, Angel & Associates, Prof. Dr. Randy Bergstrom of UC Santa Barbara University, Prof. Dr. David Hollinger from Berkeley University, Prof. Dr. Paul Sutter from the University of Colorado, and Rick Shenkman of George Mason University. They have all taken the time to answer my questions or requests and have provided key insights for my research. A special thanks goes to attorney and lecturer in law at Columbia Law School, Nathan Schachtman, for his willingness to discuss legal topics as well as extralegal subjects. I am furthermore grateful for the information provided by attorney and law professor Bill Childs and his work on expert witnesses in general. I thank Prof. Dr. Michelle Hamilton from the University of Western Ontario, the Canadian Social Sciences and Humanities Research Council, and the National Council on Public History for providing me with funds to travel to the NCPH yearly conference of 2013 held in Ottawa, it has been an eye-opening experience.

I am indebted to the following experts for their comments on my work and their replies on my questions: Prof. Dr. Robert Proctor from Stanford, Prof. Dr. Louis Kyriakoudes from the University of Southern Mississippi, and Prof. Dr. John Burnham from Ohio State University.

Furthermore, I would like to acknowledge and offer special thanks to all those who have proofread this book. Its magnitude would have simply been too much without the help of the following people:

Korneel, who has demonstrated his outstanding skill as a philologist.
Bart, for his wit and linguistic prowess.
Christoph, who sacrificed hours of well-deserved sleep to read my latest revisions.
Fons, for his unrelenting critique and support for my work.
Selket, who spent many sunny hours of her spare time to correct my work on tobacco related issues.
Matthijs, for his aid in constructing the website.
And all the other people who have aided in revising previous versions of the manuscript: Femke, Eva, Loonis, Arne, Joske, and Justine.

Most of all, I want to thank my parents who through their unconditional love and support, and their own hard work, have provided me with a compass that points to the stars.

To all, I extend my sincerest gratitude and I wish you all the best of luck. You have been part of something special in my life.

Ghent, Belgium
October 31, 2014

Ramses Delafontaine

Abstract

This book presents a comparative and systematic analysis of a controversial form of legal practice: litigation-driven history. Theoretical historians argue that societies are challenged by haunting pasts. By confronting and seeking answers to painful memories, nations all over the world seek to repair historical wrongs. The courtroom is one of the arenas where society is looking for solutions in order to address a troublesome past. Historians are brought before the judge as expert witnesses to testify and render their opinion on historical events. Despite the fact that historians have been actively aiding Justitia since the 1950s, Clio's appearance in court is still considered problematic by the legal profession. Some legal scholars have argued that historians, who are involved in forensic history, should limit themselves to preliminary historical research and present facts to lawyers and judges so that they may judge them. Based on a comparative analysis of European and American examples and a systematic analysis of the involvement of historians in tobacco litigation in the American civil justice system, using qualitative and quantitative methods, this book concludes that the forensic form of history has the potential to defend history in court and to procure more historically informed judgements. Furthermore, by historicizing the forensification of history, historians and legal scholars are challenged to critically reflect on the basic theories and methods by which they practice their profession. The final goal of this book is to discuss and present the courtroom as a performative and fact-making theatre and to redefine the forensification of history.

Contents

List of Tables

Chapter 1
General Introduction

We are like dwarves standing on the shoulders of giants. We see more and farther than our predecessors, not because of the acuteness of our sight or the stature of our body, but because we are carried aloft and elevated by the magnitude of giants.

Bernard de Chartres

Abstract In this general introduction to the book I lay out the three-part structure of my research of historians serving as expert judicial witnesses in tobacco litigation. The first part introduces the concept of *Clio's Modern Paradox* and the issues it implies for historians in court. The second part gives a general introduction to forensic history. By discussing several European and American examples I revaluate the term forensic history as conceived by Alain Wijffels. In the third part of the book I present the results of my research on the involvement of historians in tobacco litigation in the United States of America.

The title of this book indicates an ambitious project: I will make a historical inquiry into the controversial legal practice wherein historians testify as expert witnesses in court. The book has been constructed in three parts in order to deliver respectively a theoretical framework, a comparative overview of European and American litigation, and a systematical analysis of the historian as an expert witness in tobacco-related court cases in the United States of America. The first part constructs a theoretical framework of the relationship between history and law as a basic background for the other two parts of this book. The second part discusses the European and American experience of expert witnessing. The third and final part aims to give an overview of the involvement of historians in tobacco-related litigation, through a systematic analysis based on a qualitative as well as a quantitative approach. My research also aims to discuss and present the courtroom as a performative and fact-making theatre. As a conclusion, I redefine the forensification of history.

History and law go back a long way. While on the one hand, the disciplines of history and law are considered similar, they are on the other hand also considered distinctly different. Furthermore, although the connection between the two exists; it

R. Delafontaine, *Historians as Expert Judicial Witnesses in Tobacco Litigation*, Studies in the History of Law and Justice 4, DOI 10.1007/978-3-319-14292-0_1

is considered an illicit one by legal scholars as well as historians.[1] Despite the fact that both history and law are bound by the past, the practitioners of both professions have their doubts on the similarity and compatibility of the legal and historical disciplines. In fact, the arguments between both disciplines have generally focused on their irreconcilability. This belief in the incompatibility of history and law has come under a lot of pressure in recent decades. Since World War II, historians have increasingly been called into the courtroom to testify.[2] During the second half of the twentieth century, historians have served in court as expert witnesses in five main categories of forensic historical practice. (1) Historians have been active in the transnational justice movement, which is based on the legal models by which the tribunals of Nuremberg and Tokyo were organized. (2) Furthermore, historians have appeared as expert witnesses in post-World War II and post-Holocaust trials. (3) The third category in which historians have testified is comprised of Holocaust denial trials. (4) In Commonwealth countries, historians have been called upon to testify in indigenous peoples-related litigation. (5) In addition, historians have testified at an exponential rate in US civil litigation.

Although historians testify in court at an increasing rate, the legal profession has its doubt on their involvement. There are plenty of theories on this incompatibility.[3] Legal scholars stress the idea that history is unable to prove and present reliable historical facts. The historical discipline often lacks the ability to defend itself in court against such charges. Furthermore, lawyers succeed at portraying the historical profession as a useless and untrustworthy profession. The ease by which the judge or the jury members often accept these accusations to be true is troublesome. It indicates that the discipline of history has a problem with her public image. The historical profession tends to be viewed as an esoteric activity in an ivory tower or dusty archive, instead of being perceived as an important intellectual study which offers critical reflection on society. This is curious since theoretical historians François Hartog, Reinhart Koselleck, and Berber Bevernage argue that our society is very much concerned with the past; and with amending the historical wrongs of haunting pasts.[4] Not only is our society concerned with the past in order to

[1] Kelly, Alfred. 1965. Clio and the Court: An Illicit Love Affair. *The Supreme Court Review*, 119–158.

[2] Jones, Harriet, Östberg Kjell, and Randeraad Nico. 2007. *Contemporary History on Trial*. New York: Manchester University Press.

[3] See Richard Wilson's article in which he analyses different theories on the alleged incompatibility of legal and historical narratives. Wilson, Richard. 2005. Judging History: The Historical Record of the International Criminal Tribunal for the Former Yugoslavia. *Human Rights Quarterly* 27, 908–942. Vladimir Petrovic also examined this incompatibility-thesis at length in his doctoral dissertation. Petrovic, Vladimir. 2009. Historians as Expert Witnesses in the Age of Extremes. http://www.etd.ceu.hu/2009/hphpev01.pdf. Accessed 31 Oct 2014.

[4] Hartog, François. 2003. *Régimes d'historicité: présentisme et expérience du temps*. Paris: Seuil. & Koselleck, Reinhart. 2004. *Futures Past: On the Semantics of Historical Time*. New York: Columbia University Press. & Bevernage, Berber. 2012. *History, Memory, and State-Sponsored Violence*. New York: Routledge.

remediate historical wrongs, but our society is also orientated towards the past in a lot of cultural events, such as remembrance initiatives, in the construction of national identities, in heritage related issues, through a rising number and increasing popularity of historical museums, and much more.[5] I have called this incongruity, with on the one hand the popularity of the past, and on the other hand the social legitimacy problem of the historical discipline, Clio's Modern Paradox. In the first part of this book I identify three key developments that have contributed to the creation of Clio's Modern Paradox. The first part of this book serves as a theoretical framework for part II and III, which are empirical inquiries of historians working as expert judicial witnesses. Explaining Clio's Modern Paradox is imperative to understand the prejudice, that exists within the legal profession and with the general public which historians have to face in court.

The second part of my research compares the European and American experience of forensic history. The first chapter discusses examples of interactions between law and history that are often wrongfully defined as types of expert witnessing, such as the Dreyfus affair, the Nuremberg and Tokyo tribunals, and *amicus curiae* briefs. Thereafter, I review the European experience with historians as expert witnesses in court. I examine the Eichmann trial, the German post-Holocaust trials, the French Vichy trials, and the Holocaust denial trials of Zündel and Irving. These interactions of history and law have played a dominant role in shaping the preconceptions among historians and legal scholars on the incompatibility of history and law. Most European cases are very political and polemic and have called the appearance of historians as experts into question. Yet, there are also examples of a fruitful interaction, for example the Ludwigsburg paradigm. I contrast these European examples with American civil litigation, where historians have been involved in a wide range of cases. Similar to the European examples, historians and lawyers tend to remember the problematic examples of expert witnessing, and forget that the interaction does work in other instances. I discuss *Brown v. Board of Education*, the Sears case, and a lead paint toxic tort case. In addition, I present a practical guide to expert witnessing, which gives a unique and systematic overview of the consecutive steps expert witnesses go through before testifying in court. Addressing and comparing problems identified in both European and American litigation-driven history allows me to reassess the proposal by legal historian Alain Wijffels to limit the involvement of the historian to that of a historical fact provider for the court and not that of an opinionated witness.[6] I will argue, in contrast to Wijffels, that it is essential that historians can testify in court when engaging in forensic history.

---

[5]Public historians Rosenzweig and Thelen argue in their book on the popular uses of history in American daily life that Americans make the past part of their daily routine. Rosenzweig, Roy, and Thelen, David. 1998. *The Presence of the Past: Popular Uses of History in American Life*. New York: Columbia University Press. French historian Pierre Nora has examined the significance of historical landscapes for the construction of the French identity. See the multivolume work of Pierre Nora: Nora, Pierre. 1984–1992. *Les lieux de mémoire*. Vol. 1, 2, and 3. Paris: Gallimard.

[6]Wijffels, Alain. 2001. *History in Court: Historical Expertise and Methods in a Forensic Context*. Leiden: Ius Deco.

The last and third part of the book seeks to provide an analysis of one genre of US civil litigation in which historians have been particularly active, namely tobacco litigation. In order to come to conclusions that are not based on anecdotal evidence, I conduct a four-part analysis of the involvement of historians in tobacco litigation: (1) What do historians testify on? (2) When have they testified in court? (3) How have they presented their research results in court? (4) Who were the historians who were and are active in tobacco litigation? By analysing these four elements I come to a systematic overview of the involvement of historians in tobacco litigation. I strengthen the examination of these four elements with a qualitative and quantitative analysis. The qualitative approach focuses on the records of the trial experience of five historians in the landmark case *US v. Philip Morris et al.*. In conclusion of this qualitative analysis, I argue that the courtroom is a performative and fact-making theatre. My quantitative analysis has produced a list of 50 historians who have been active in 314 cases of tobacco litigation. After confronting the behaviour of these five expert witnesses with the code of ethics proposed by Belgian historian Antoon De Baets and after finding throughout my quantitative research that very few experts–and mostly those in service of the plaintiffs–have openly discussed their involvement in tobacco litigation; I identified transparency as the biggest problem with the involvement of historians in tobacco litigation. Because, as we speak [October, 2014], there are historians testifying in tobacco cases, I argue that reflection on their involvement is of an acute nature. I have made an attempt at contributing to that debate by making 50 witness profiles of these historians and their involvement in tobacco litigation freely accessible online.[7]

My research aims to be interdisciplinary and has drawn from a wide range of secondary sources from legal scholars as well as historians. The theoretical part of this work is particularly inspired by Carlo Ginzburg, the famous Italian historian, and by the American legal scholar and Judge Richard Posner, the most frequently cited legal scholar of the twentieth century. For the European cases, I draw upon the book by Alain Wijffels and the doctoral dissertation of Vladimir Petrovic, who has worked as a researcher at the Dutch Institute for War, Holocaust and Genocide Studies (NIOD). The section on American civil litigation, on the other hand, is based on the examination of a wide array of personal accounts. The construction of the practical guide to expert witnessing, included in this book, led to the discovery of a number of new and unpublished materials on expert witnessing by historians. The tobacco cases are discussed through two epic works on tobacco history: *The Cigarette Century* by Allan Brandt and *Golden Holocaust* by Robert Proctor. Both monographs are the product of litigation-driven historical research. In addition, I have gone through a body of trial records that are provided by specialized online databases. These trial records offer an excellent opportunity to test the idea of the courtroom as a performative and fact-making theatre.

[7]See all the witness profiles online at: http://www.thejudgeandthehistorian.ugent.be. Accessed 31 Oct 2014. Disclosure: website made and maintained by the author.

As a conclusion to this book, I offer a reassessment of the concept of the forensification of history. The epilogue to this book presents a five-point proposal with basic principles expert witnesses should adhere to when they engage in a forensic form of history.

Bibliography

Bevernage, Berber. 2012. *History, memory, and state-sponsored violence*. New York: Routledge.

Hartog, Francois. 2003. *Régimes d'historicité: présentisme et expérience du temps*. Paris: Seuil.

Harriet, Jones, Kjell Östberg, and Nico Randeraad. 2007. *Contemporary history on trial*. New York: Manchester University Press.

Kelly, Alfred. 1965. Clio and the court: An Illicit love affair. *The Supreme Court Review* 1965: 119–158.

Koselleck, Reinhart. 2004. *Futures past: On the semantics of historical time*. New York: Columbia University Press.

Nora, Pierre. 1984–1992. *Les lieux de mémoire*. Paris: Gallimard.

Petrovic, Vladimir. 2009. *Historians as expert witnesses in the age of extremes*. Unpublished doctoral dissertation, presented at the Central European University, Budapest.

Rosenzweig, Roy, and David Thelen. 1998. *The presence of the past: Popular uses of history in American life*. New York: Columbia University Press.

Wijffels, Alain. 2001. *History in court: Historical expertise and methods in a forensic context*. Leiden: Ius Deco.

Wilson, Richard. 2005. The historical record of the international criminal tribunal for the former Yugoslavia. *Human Rights Quarterly* 27: 908–942.

Part I
History and Law

You know, all of us have an instinctive judgment that we make. You meet a person, you say, "I trust this person. I don't trust this person. I find her interesting. I don't find him interesting." Whatever. You make these quick judgments. That's the way you get through life. And, judges do the same thing. And, I suppose there's nothing wrong with that if it's just a beginning point. But, after you make a judgment, you then must formulate the reason for your judgment into a verbal phrase, into a verbal formula. And then, you have to see if that makes sense, if it's logical, if it's fair, if it accords with the law, if it accords with the Constitution, if it accords with your own sense of ethics and morality. And, if at any point along this process you think you're wrong, you have to go back and do it all over again. And that's, I think, not unique to the law, in that any prudent person behaves that way.

[...]

Lawyers, judges, law professors talk all the time about stare decisis. If you want to say something important, we use Latin because it makes it sound more important. Stare decisis means that you're bound by what previous judges have decided, unless it's very wrong and very important, and then you have to depart from that precedent and that's a major event in the law. But essentially, you're bound by stare decisis. When I went on the court, I thought, "Well, this is not very interesting. It's antiquarian. It's like historical research." I thought I'd be like a scientist putting together an explanation for an experiment that had failed, and I go back and say, "Well, you did this wrong or you did that," and I was interested in it because I love the law, but I thought it was rather limiting. I was quite mistaken. Really, the dynamic of being bound by precedent, the so called stare decisis, is very forward-looking, because it teaches you that you will be bound by what you do. You're the first person that will be bound by what you do, and if you're on a court which reviews other courts, they will all be bound by what you do. So, there is really a very forward-looking dynamic to judging. You must ask yourself, to the extent that you can without being imprecise, "How will my judgment play out in the future?" And, there's a lot of looking out the window in that job.[1]

American Supreme Court Justice Anthony Kennedy

[1]Interview with Supreme Court Justice Anthony Kennedy for *The Academy of Achievement*. The transcript and video excerpts can be found here http://www.achievement.org/autodoc/page/ken0int-3. Accessed 31 Oct 2014.

Chapter 2
Introductory Theoretical Remarks on the Alleged Problematic Nature of the Interaction of History and Law

He who loves practice without theory is like the sailor who boards ship without a rudder and compass and never knows where he may cast.

Leonardo Da Vinci

Abstract This first part of the book is of a theoretical nature. The first chapters introduce the concept of *Clio's Modern Paradox. Clio's Modern Paradox* explains why history and historians, from a theoretical point of view, are conceived as controversial in the courtroom. By discussing certain issues from theoretical history in an interdisciplinary context of law and history, I lay the theoretical groundwork in which I will discuss forensic history.

In the first part of this book I discuss the theoretical issues that have burdened historians and history in the courtroom. Litigation often encompasses more than only the historical facts and events relevant to the case addressed in the courtroom. Social credibility and legitimacy of the historical craft influences how the testimony of the expert historian is valued in court and determines the impact it has on the judge or the jury. As American historian Richard Golsan points out during his discussion of two French Vichy-related trials wherein historians were involved as expert witnesses; "History itself, with a capital "H", was, effectively, put on trial."[1] Why is it that historians serving as expert witnesses in court, not only have to defend their own research and credentials, but also the validity of their discipline? Why have lawyers often succeeded in convincing the judge or the jury that history and historians are not bringing anything valuable to the courtroom to aid the trier of fact?

I begin this first part of the book with an inquiry into the reasons why history is vulnerable to theoretical and epistemological attacks on its constitution as an autonomous field of knowledge. In order to research this, I present a minor overview

[1] Golsan, Richard. 2000. *Memory and justice on trial. The Papon affair*, 13. New York: Routledge.

R. Delafontaine, *Historians as Expert Judicial Witnesses in Tobacco Litigation*, Studies in the History of Law and Justice 4, DOI 10.1007/978-3-319-14292-0_2

of theoretical history[2] since the nineteenth century in which I discuss three major developments which have contributed to the theoretical weakness of historians and their research in court: (1) The first reason is the unattainable but still influential traditional interpretation of Ranke's adage on objectivity.[3] (2) Secondly, I argue that theoretical history has failed to rebut postmodern relativism.[4] (3) The third and final reason is my claim that the historical profession suffers from a lack of theoretical conceptualization.[5] When historians are questioned about the epistemological basis of their profession in court, lawyers are merely repeating the general sentiment in society towards the historical craft, namely that there is little social appreciation for the historical discipline.[6] I claim that this is rather paradoxical, since our society is very concerned with the past.[7] Intriguingly, the past itself is very popular, whereas the historical discipline and historians themselves are not popular. This negative relation between the past and the historical discipline is what I call *Clio's Modern Paradox*.

---

[2]Dutch historian Jan Romein described "theoretical history" as follows: "theoretical history aims at bridging the gap that divides the cautiously objective technique employed to ascertain the isolated facts of history, and the arbitrarily subjective method by which these facts are assembled into a picture of the past." Romein, Jan. 1948. Theoretical History. *Journal of the History of Ideas* 9, 54. I will define "theoretical history" following Romein, adding that "theoretical history" also discusses how historians *should* conduct their research. Another source for my definition of historical theory is the Dutch theoretical historian Chris Lorenz who defined "theory of history" as follows: "Theory of history consists of 'the philosophical examination of all aspects of our descriptions, beliefs, and knowledge of the past' and is both descriptive and normative." See Lorenz, Chris. 2011. History and Theory. In *The Oxford History of Historical Writing, Vol. 5*, ed. Daniel Woolf and Axel Schneider, 13–35. Oxford: Oxford University Press, 28. I have defined "theoretical history" in this book as follows: "The theories used by historians to discuss how their craft is functioning and how it should function." All other definitions described in this introduction are predominantly drawn from American historiography. I allow this Americanization of my theoretical discussion because of the fact that litigation-driven history is a predominantly American matter.

[3]The traditional interpretation of Ranke's adage is consequentially described as "positivist objectivity." In this book, "positivist objectivity" is defined as: "The conviction that facts can be presented as they have actually happened in the past, without any interference of the historian or his methods." I will argue in favour of an intersubjective objectivity, which I interpret as follows: "Objectivity of an intersubjective nature demands that historians publish their research in order to let their peers determine whether the historian has been objective or not. Objectivity is therefore essentially a shared idea between fellow historians on what professional historical research is comprised of."

[4]In this book I define "postmodern relativism" as follows: "Those postmodern historical philosophical assumptions that deny any relation between fact and historical narrative."

[5]Under "theoretical conceptualization" I understand: "The definition in clear terms of assumptions and analytical tools that are common in historical practice, such as epistemological concepts, concepts on objectivity, causality, narrative, temporality, spatiality, and ethics, shared by the majority of the historical profession."

[6]I define "the historical discipline" as: "The professional research of history that is practiced and taught in predominantly academic but also public environments."

[7]"The past" is understood in this book as follows: "The past is a much broader term than history; "the past" does not only encompass history but also memory, remembrance, and heritage."

Law and all legal institutions have an increasingly important role to play in our democratic and litigious society as well as in our daily lives.[8] Judge Posner wrote in his introduction of *Law and Literature* that: "Law so permeates American life that all of us should take an interest in it."[9] Social norms and other non-legal regulation have been gradually displaced by legal regulation.[10] Laws are based on the social norms they replace, most of which are of a historical nature.[11] How has the study of law convinced the general public that law can generate truthful knowledge and therefore is at liberty to judge them? Which developments have contributed to the fact that law has become so important in society, while the historical discipline has slowly disappeared into a peripheral social role? This dichotomy is very interesting, since history and law fundamentally share the same object of study: human conduct and the irregularity bound to it.[12] The relationship between law and history has, moreover, always been a close one. The Italian historian Carlo Ginzburg called the relationship of history and law intricate and yet ambiguous.[13] American historian Richard Wilson wrote that "[l]aw and history are inextricably linked and share similar methods and aims."[14] If both studies are so alike, why are expert historians treated with such hostility in the courtroom by the legal profession. In order to find the answer(s) to this question, I retrace the developments that shaped Clio's Modern Paradox.

Theory has not been central to studies of historians as expert witnesses in court. Most literature on the subject does not offer a theoretical frame on the issues that arise with historians serving as experts. Ignorance has been the foremost reason for the opposition with which history is met by the legal profession in court. In order to diminish these prejudices amongst historians and lawyers alike, I draw from an interdisciplinary body of works from noted historians and legal scholars to offer a heterogeneous overview on the topic. In general, I use the works written by the famous Italian historian Carlo Ginzburg, who has published on the relationship between law and history in: *History, Rhetoric, and Proof* and *The Judge and the*

[8]I define "the law" in this book as: "A body of legal rules and standards that have been the result of research [the study of law] and practice [legal doctrine and advocacy] with the aim to regulate social interaction as best as possible."

[9]Posner, Richard. 2009. *Law and Literature*. Cambridge: Harvard University Press, XVI.

[10]Posner, Eric. 2002. *Law and Social Norms*. Cambridge: Harvard University Press, 8.

[11]Posner, as n. 10, 8.

[12]Generally, law is equated with advocacy but law is also legislation and legal doctrine. Legislators, judges, and legal scholars try to study human conduct in order to regulate and maintain ways of social interaction which allow the greatest happiness for the greatest number of people.

[13]Ginzburg, Carlo. 1999. *The Judge and the Historian: Marginal Notes on a Late-Twentieth-Century Miscarriage of Justice*. Trans. A. Shugaar. London: Verso, 4.

[14]Wilson, Richard. 2005. Judging History: The Historical Record of the International Criminal Tribunal for the Former Yugoslavia. *Human Rights Quarterly* 27, 917.

Historian: Marginal Notes on a Late-Twentieth-Century Miscarriage of Justice.[15] Ginzburg's arguments are put to work to counter, on the one hand the positivist idea of history and history as a science,[16] and on the other hand to defend historical theory against postmodern relativism. To discuss law, I focus on the works of the American Federal Judge and noted legal scholar Richard Posner. Posner is an international authority on the theory of law and the most cited legal scholar of the twentieth century. In this theoretical part of my work, I have incorporated Posner's *How Judges Think* and *Law and Literature.*[17] These core works are reinforced with articles and books written by a broad array of theoretical historians and legal scholars. Moreover, I give special attention to public history and historians and lawyers who have studied or even participated in expert witnessing or criminal tribunals.

My research aims to be interdisciplinary by examining research from the historical profession as well as from the study of law. By discussing perspectives of legal scholars and historians on the same subjects, I can compare the issues brought forward by the two disciplines when they meet in court, thereby creating a more nuanced picture of the controversial practice of expert witnessing. I analyse the developments in theoretical history which have made the historical discipline so vulnerable for epistemological attacks in court. By challenging the generalizations that rule the debate amongst historians and legal scholars on the incompatibility of history and law, I will be able to propose theorized answers to a polemic debate. This theoretical part aims to be generally applicable to all cases I discuss in the rest of this work, which is why I refrain from encumbering this theoretical part with references to specific cases of expert witnessing. Casuistry will mark parts II and III of the book. This theoretical introduction will help frame the general setting of the historian's entrance into the courtroom on a meta-level.

Bibliography

Ginzburg, Carlo. 1999a. *History, Rhetoric, and Proof.* Hanover: University Press of New England.

Ginzburg, Carlo. 1999b. *The Judge and the Historian: Marginal Notes on a Late-Twentieth-Century Miscarriage of Justice.* Trans. A. Shugaar. London: Verso.

Golsan, Richard. 2000. *Memory and justice on trial. The Papon affair*, 13. New York: Routledge.

Lorenz, Chris. 2011. History and theory. In *The Oxford history of historical writing*, vol. 5, ed. Daniel Woolf and Axel Schneider, 13–35. Oxford: Oxford University Press.

[15]Ginzburg, Carlo. 1999. *History, Rhetoric, and Proof.* Hanover: University Press of New England. & Ginzburg, as n. 13.

[16]I define the contemporary dominant idea of "science" in this book as follows: "Intellectual disciplines that research "natural" objects through testable and objective [neutral, impartial] methods or general laws which allegedly produce absolute and usable facts."

[17]Posner, Richard. 2008. *How Judges Think.* Cambridge: Harvard University Press. & Posner, as n. 9.

Posner, Eric. 2002. *Law and social norms*. Cambridge: Harvard University Press.
Posner, Richard. 2008. *How judges think*. Cambridge: Harvard University Press.
Posner, Richard. 2009. *Law and literature*. Cambridge: Harvard University Press.
Romein, Jan. 1948. Theoretical history. *Journal of the History of Ideas* 9: 53–64.
Wilson, Richard. 2005. The historical record of the international criminal tribunal for the former Yugoslavia. *Human Rights Quarterly* 27: 908–942.

Chapter 3
Clio's Modern Paradox Unraveled

Papa, explique-moi donc à quoi sert l'histoire.
Dad, can you tell me what the purpose of history is?

Marc Bloch

Abstract This theoretical chapter explains the theoretical issues in historiography behind *Clio's Modern Paradox*. I have defined three core problems that explain history's vulnerability in court on an epistemological level. An introduction into these issues helps us understand why historians and most expert witnesses tend to cling to their alleged objectivity and why historians would do well to leave it behind.

As I remarked in the introduction, the past is more alive than ever in today's society. Public historians Rosenzweig and Thelen noted the following remark in their study dedicated to the popular uses of history in American daily life: "there is clearly an enormous and growing public interest in history, manifest in museum attendance, historically oriented tourism, participation in festivals, and even the media-driven excesses of nostalgia and commemoration of recent historical periods."[1] Rosenzweig and Thelen give the past a central role in daily routine: "Americans ... make the past part of their everyday routines and turn to it as a way of grappling with profound questions about how to live."[2] Noted French historian Pierre Nora has drawn attention in his work *Les lieux de mémoire* to the popularity of historical landscapes which have historical significance for French national history and identity.[3] Just as Nora, British historian Raphael Samuel also defines these historical landscapes as important sources of unofficial knowledge, popular memory, and identity.[4] From a more theoretical perspective, historians

[1] Rosenzweig, Roy, and Thelen, David. 1998. *The Presence of the Past: Popular Uses of History in American Life*. New York: Columbia University Press, 3.

[2] Rosenzweig and Thelen, as n. 1, 18.

[3] See the multivolume work of Nora, Pierre. 1984–1992. *Les lieux de mémoire*. Vol. 1, 2, and 3. Paris: Gallimard.

[4] Samuel, Raphael. 1994. *Theatres of Memory. Vol. 1: Past and Present in Contemporary Culture*. London: Verso, 11, 39.

R. Delafontaine, *Historians as Expert Judicial Witnesses in Tobacco Litigation*,
Studies in the History of Law and Justice 4, DOI 10.1007/978-3-319-14292-0_3

François Hartog and Reinhart Koselleck, have argued that the temporal orientation of our society is situated towards the past, while Berber Bevernage emphasizes the presentness of the past and the continued influence of mass atrocities in the present.[5] At the inaugural conference of the *International Network for Theory of History* (INTH) in Ghent in July 2013, François Hartog gave a lecture in which he argued that identity, memory, and heritage were drawing the past into the present. Moreover, he stated that "[m]emory in public space has pushed out history" and "the past is no longer passing away."[6]

Ironically, the historical discipline, despite the popularity of the past, does not receive much praise from the general public as a field of knowledge, nor from their academic colleagues. This is what I call *Clio's Modern Paradox*. How has this paradox come into existence? For centuries the social elite; politicians, lawyers, soldiers, priests, ambassadors and so forth, had been historians as well. Historical writing was a well-regarded and respectable activity for the higher classes. This was before the professionalization of history. As a professionalized field in the nineteenth century, history was a matter of national importance. Historians constructed historical master narratives which formed the basis of unity and identity in national states. A history professor in nineteenth-century Germany was a respected member of the national elite.[7] An American history professor in 1890 made five times the salary of an unskilled labourer; by 1940 that ratio had dropped to less than two to one.[8] Simultaneously with their salaries, historians saw their social influence diminish as well. Despite that the past was steadily playing a larger role in society, historians lost social influence.[9] How did this downfall of Clio come to pass?

First of all there is a need for self-criticism. I argue that certain developments in theoretical history of recent decades are equally responsible for Clio's fall from grace as the outside pressures laid upon the discipline to be scientific or useful. The internal reasons for the decline of social influence of the historical profession are threefold. The first reason has been the fervent striving of historians to make

---

[5]Hartog, François. 2003. *Régimes d'historicité: présentisme et expérience du temps.* Paris: Seuil. & Koselleck, Reinhart. 2004. *Futures Past: On the Semantics of Historical Time.* New York: Columbia University Press. & Bevernage, Berber. 2012. *History, Memory, and State-Sponsored Violence.* New York: Routledge.

[6]For more information on INTH, see http://www.inth.ugent.be. Accessed 31 Oct 2014. For more information on the conference, see http://www.inth.ugent.be/?page_id=2927. Accessed 31 Oct 2014. Notes on Hartog's lecture are with the author. The quote from Hartog, is similar to what Dutch Historian Chris Lorenz has argued: "the pastness of the past" has lost its 'evidential' quality and has been replaced by a "haunting past." Lorenz, Chris. 2010. Unstuck in Time. Or: the Sudden Presence of the Past. In *Performing the Past. Memory, History and Identity in Modern Europe*, ed. Karin Tilmans, Frank van Vree, and Jay Winter, 67–102. Amsterdam: Amsterdam University Press, 68.

[7]Novick, Peter. 1998. *That Noble Dream. The "Objectivity Question" and the American Historical Profession.* New York: Cambridge University Press, 22–23.

[8]Novick, as n. 7, 170.

[9]Novick, as n. 7, 185.

history into a science. Ethan Kleinberg, the executive editor of the academic journal *History and Theory*, declared in a lecture he gave at the 2013 inaugural conference of the *International Network for Theory and History* in Ghent that this quest to be scientific by historians was "the holy grail of history."[10] Secondly, theoretical history has failed to rebut and defend itself against postmodern relativism. In some cases theoretical history's attention and energy is being engulfed by marginal trends which have no relevance in the real world. The third has been the failure of theoretical history to provide the theoretical conceptualization on which a study of history is built. Theoretical historians have not strived to define basic theoretical concepts of the study of history in a systematic and consensual manner. These three internal reasons, making history into a science, theoretical radicalization, and lack of theoretical conceptualization have influenced the historical profession in a reciprocal manner.[11] These developments have culminated in a historical profession under epistemological attack in court, hard-pressed and troubled to defend its position as a valuable and autonomous field of knowledge. The following chapter discusses these problematic developments.

3.1 Theoretical Historical Developments

As mentioned above, I concentrate on three reasons for *Clio's Modern Paradox*: (1) the quest to make history into a science, (2) the postmodern radicalization of parts of theoretical history and (3) the lack of systematic theoretical conceptualization. In order to better understand how history as a field is valued by the legal profession, it is worthwhile to discuss the role of these three elements in the development of the historical profession as we know it today.[12] I analyse these key developments in theoretical history in a chronological manner. I begin my overview where most surveys of theoretical history start, namely with Ranke and German nineteenth-century historical writing. At the start of the First World War, our survey leaves Germany for France, and I discuss some of the innovations brought to the historical profession by the French Annales Schools. I consider the influence of the linguistic turn and the wave of post-modernism which has dominated theoretical history since the 1970s. Thereafter, following the fall of the Berlin Wall and the end of the Cold

[10]See n. 6 for more information on INTH and the conference, cfr. supra. Notes on Kleinberg's lecture are with the author.

[11]These terms were defined in Part I, Chap. 2: Introductory Theoretical Remarks on the Alleged Problematic Nature of the Interaction of History and Law, cfr. supra.

[12]I have to note that I am working with certain generalizations, the simplicity of which harms many individual and idealistic efforts from within both the legal and the historical profession, which have tried to discourage the use of those general abstractions. Those singular efforts are unfortunately the exceptions that confirm the rule that historians and legal practitioners think about one another in complete and often ignorant generalities.

War, I turn to public history, a predominantly American matter. Finally, I come to a conclusion on Clio's Modern Paradox and its relevance to litigation-driven history.

3.1.1 The Ghost of von Ranke

Leopold von Ranke surely is one of the most cited historians of the last two centuries. His often repeated adage, that historians shall write history "wie es eigentlich gewesen" [as it actually happened], "is equally known as it is worn out."[13] Intriguingly, Ranke is often misquoted as having written: "wie es eigentlich gewesen [*ist*]"(as it actually [has] happened). This small but relevant difference reveals an interesting element in the dominant interpretation of Ranke's dictum. The traditional principles derived from Ranke are that historical documents open up to historians. Through rigorous use of critical-philological techniques historians are able to reveal the true past. According to this view, the ideal historian can show the past "as things have actually happened." This impartial and fact-finding historian does not construct history but merely presents it as he discovered it in primary historical documents. This ideal type became a guiding star for generations of historians.

Yet, Ranke's omission of the final word "ist" suggests that Ranke did not mean that historians should interpret texts without adding any meaning to the facts. Instead, historians Iggers, Novick, and Evans argue that Ranke intended to urge historians to interpret the past and show its essential [eigentlich] meaning.[14] So it was not only Ranke's intention to search strictly for the facts, but also to find its inner meaning, to interpret historical facts.[15] Adding "ist" instructs historians to find historical facts as they have happened. Without "ist", historians interpret historical facts for the sake of their meaning, what they are. Adding "ist" also alters the meaning given to the word "eigentlich". With the addition of "ist", "eigentlich" means factual, without "ist", "eigentlich" signifies essential or inner. The interpretation of Ranke proposed by Evans, Novick, and Iggers instructs historians to interpret rather than being the objective medium through which historical facts reach us.

Furthermore, Ranke wrote the comment in a book on the history of the Latin and Teutonic peoples, not an essay of some sort on theoretical history.[16] Adding to the

---

[13]Lorenz, Chris. 2008. *De constructie van het verleden.* Amsterdam: Boom. English Edition: Lorenz, Chris. 2007. Construction of the Past: An Introduction to the Philosophy of History. Amsterdam: Boom Publishers.

[14]Novick, as n. 7, 21–31. & Iggers, Georg. 2011. *The Theory and Practice of History. Leopold von Ranke.* New York: Routledge, xix–xx. & Evans, Richard. 2000. *In Defence of History.* London, Granta Books, 14–15.

[15]Novick, as n. 7, 21–31. & Iggers, as n. 14, xix–xx. & Evans, as n. 14, 14–15.

[16]The book is an overview of the Roman and Germanic peoples around the time of Columbus's discovery of America entitled "Geschichte der Romanischen und Germanischen Völker von 1494 bis 1514."

previous arguments that he has no major work on theoretical history,[17] leads Iggers, Novick, and Evans to argue that all in all Ranke was more of a romantic and idealist historian than a nineteenth-century positivist, as he is commonly conceived.[18] Considering these combined arguments, I am inclined to concur with Evans, Novick, and Iggers, and interpret Ranke's dictum accordingly. Ironically, there is a distinct possibility, to me, that Ranke wrote down his comment without a lot of theoretical foresight at all.

Whatever may be the truth of it, there is one thing certain about Ranke's adage. Its legacy has made an indelible mark on the historical profession that still weighs heavily on the discipline today. *Heavily* because Ranke's intellectual inheritance was determined, as it happens in most cases, by his followers. Overall historians in the nineteenth century adhered to the first interpretation of Ranke's dictum that allowed historians to claim that they worked with objective knowledge. Yes, there was discussion whether history was nomothetic or idiosyncratic, but each side in this debate believed that historians were able to objectively mine for facts in historical documents. Why did historians in a rare moment of uniformity choose to believe that what Ranke meant to say was that historians should be objective scientists, as if historians were chemists in the laboratory of history?[19]

3.1.2 The Professionalization of History & Science as the New Intellectual Gold Standard

During the nineteenth century, the field of history underwent a series of developments which are categorized as the professionalization of history. The historical discipline firmly established itself in universities, publishing its own journals, and building its own theoretical framework to sustain and legitimize a historical episteme. Notwithstanding the epistemic fact that historical facts were not similar to the objectives of the natural sciences, the historical profession sought to jump on the bandwagon of the success attained by the sciences. For history to be identified as a science there was one key element to be claimed: objectivity.

Historians were caught in a general appraisal for the natural sciences and its proclaimed ability to render objective and reliable knowledge through natural laws sustained by empirically deduced facts. The traditional interpretation of Ranke's dictum now became fully accepted. If historical facts could be deduced from texts "as they actually had happened", historians were able to claim positivist objectivity. Mary Furner dubbed this choice which presented itself at the end of the nineteenth century as "the crisis of professionalization of American Social Sciences."

---

[17] Ranke's 400-year historical overview of the Roman papacy is considered to be his greatest work.

[18] Novick, as n. 7, 21–31. & Iggers, as n. 14, xix–xx. & Evans, as n. 14, 14–15.

[19] Evans, as n. 14, 17–18. I am thinking, for example, of historians like Hippolyte Taine, Auguste Compte, Charles Seignobos, Victor Langlois, and Carl Lamprecht.

According to Furner, positivist objectivity was chosen and institutionalized as a safe choice.[20] This choice was not self-evident.[21] German theoretical historian Iggers writes that "central to the process of professionalization was the firm belief in the scientific status of history."[22] The scientific model of the natural sciences therefore played an important role in the professionalization of history. According to Iggers, knowledge is defined in terms and ideas borrowed from the natural sciences.[23]

A majority within the historical profession clearly had the ambition to make history into a science. According to the traditional interpretation of Ranke's remark, facts were deductible from texts. So the historical discipline remained objective. Novick describes this choice: "[h]istorical professionalization was offered as a standardized technique, a means of operationalization and an appropriate mode of discourse at the grace of the authority of the sublime norm of objectivity."[24] The historical discipline remained a unique, idiosyncratic, and explanatory endeavour but stayed firmly convinced of its own ability to be objective.[25]

Thus, regardless of their independent objectives, the historical discipline was required to be scientific. The historical discipline tried to leave its connection with literature and art to join up with the successful natural sciences.[26] I argue that the idea of the broader contemporary public is that the scientific model of the natural sciences can give abstract and therefore useful facts. Useful in the sense that they can help create a more efficient society [economically speaking]. Today, knowledge is most useful when it can be abstracted in general norms which can be tested and applied. All other disciplines of knowledge are valued in proportion to the amount of mathematics used in their field. The more numbers a study encompasses, the more "testable" a hypothesis is, the more scientific and therefore the more reliable a discipline seems to be. What we need to take from this is that knowledge, in contemporary terms, has been very narrowly defined as an image of empiricist and positivist ideas about knowledge. I believe this challenges historians to define their profession in a different manner; yet, in contrast, generations of historians have tried to make history into a science.[27]

---

[20]Furner, Mary. 1975. *Advocacy & Objectivity: A Crisis in the Professionalization of American Social Science, 1865–1905*. Lexington: The University Press of Kentucky.

[21]There were clear alternatives formulated by Rickert as well as Dilthey. Both argued in favour a separate categorization of different kinds of studies. See Iggers, Georg. 1983. *The German Conception of History: The National Tradition of Historical Thought from Herder to the Present.* Middletown: Wesleyan University Press.

[22]Iggers, Georg. 1997. *Historiography in the Twentieth Century: from Scientific Objectivity to the Postmodern Challenge.* Middletown: Wesleyan University Press, 2.

[23]Iggers, as n. 22, 2.

[24]Novick, as n. 7, 53.

[25]Lorenz, as n. 13, 251–253.

[26]Novick, as n. 7, 40.

[27]Lorenz, as n. 13, 253.

3.1.3 The Three-Headed Annales & Postmodern Headaches

After the Second World War the French *Annales*, a field changing historical periodical, did not diminish the historian's firm belief in positivist objectivity. The French *Annales* changed the historical profession in many other ways, by adding new subjects and fields. The first *Annales* introduced history from below, switching historiography's focus from kings and politicians, wars and states, to working men and women, and to economic and social evolutions instead of political ones. These new subjects, especially when concerning periods after the French revolution, would often draw on extensive administrative documents. By using new tools as computers, historians in some fields became historical statisticians.[28] Or how Emmanuel Le Roy Ladurie announced it in 1967: "L'historien de demain sera programmeur ou ne sera plus" (The historian of tomorrow will be a computer programmer or will no longer exist).[29] The second *Annales*, under Fernand Braudel, returned to covering law models, many of them with a Marxist inspiration. But it also knew great historical works in microhistory, l'histoire événementiel (history of events), and the history of mentalities. The greater discussion in the *Annales* focussed on the nomothetic or ideographic nature of the historical profession mirroring the *Methodenstreit (method dispute)* at the end of the nineteenth century in Germany. The *Annales* has challenged the historical discipline in its theory and practice, but it had not lacked confidence in the positivist idea of history.

Generations of historians had described the historical discipline as a positivist project. History was a field in the image of the natural sciences yet without universal laws. There were of course historians who had different views. Nietzsche, Droysen, and Huizinga, for example, delivered severe criticism on the positivist idea of historical objectivity. According to Dutch theoretical historian Chris Lorenz, they remained a small and rather insignificant movement within the historical discipline.[30]

Postmodernism revived lingering criticism in historiography. A variety of scholars, influenced by the greater developments in the postmodern intellectual sphere, trusted a key element of historical writing upon the theoretical agenda which, though central to the entire enterprise, had been left out of most grand schemes in historical theory: that of language and the historian's relationship with it.

I perceive the heritage of postmodernism in historiography as follows: historians, almost in unanimity, acknowledge the indispensable insights postmodernist thinking has had on historical writing. But most historians will also tell you that postmodernism: "went too far." Let me elaborate further on this rather straightforward declaration. The works of Barthes, Mink, Ankersmit, and Hayden White all argued that the nature of language was to some extent subjective. If historians

[28]For example: in cliometrics.

[29]Le Roy Ladurie, Emmanuel. 1973. *Le territoire de l'historien*. Paris: Gallimard, 14.

[30]Lorenz, as n. 13, 250.

acknowledged this subjectivity of historical discourse, they had to withdraw their claim of engaging in an objective positivist enterprise. The historian was rendered unable to mine historical documents for facts and convert them into neutral facts. Even his instruments [his mind and primary sources] were not impartial. Put differently: if Foucault was right, that words and language in total are human constructs, which have the power to control and limit our thoughts, was the historical profession then truly lost, as British historian Keith Jenkins would have us believe?[31] With all the best intentions in the world, the historian was doomed like Sisyphus to never reach the intellectual nirvana of positivist objectivity.[32] The destruction by postmodernism of the epitome of the historian as an impartial reader of the past, made it impossible for the historical discipline to retain its would-be scientific character.

Historians, like Hayden White, claimed that historical narratives are histories on their own, with no relation to the real past, at the most with links to other texts. His work *Metahistory* from 1973, studied the modes of emplotment which, according to White, were used by historians to construct their historical texts, their metafiction.[33] White wanted historical writing to become more of an aesthetic enterprise, devoid of the claims on objectivity and more receptive to the social expectations of historians and history.[34] Postmodernism has constructed a barrier between historical theory and history.[35] The problem is that postmodern relativism so drastically separates historical research from the real past that historians cannot, for example, prove that the *Shoah* happened or cannot defend "the past" from Holocaust deniers.[36]

In short postmodernism relativism left historians with a severe headache. The postmodern critique made important and valid points. It demonstrated that a single master narrative, a unitary history was not tenable, that "history was marked not only by continuity but also by ruptures."[37] But with the destruction of objectivity the whole of the historical profession was questioned. The historian and positivist objectivity, along with other theoretical conceptualizations as epistemology, causal-

[31]Jenkins, Keith. 2009. *At the Limits of History. Essays on Theory and Practice.* New York: Routledge, 57–62.

[32]Novick, as n. 7, 154.

[33]White, Hayden. 1996. The Burden of History. *History and Theory* 5, 111–112, 127–134.

[34]While I concur with White that historians should be more involved in their communities and should listen to the needs of society, and I applaud his rejection of positivist objectivity, I do not agree with his postmodern relativism on the relationship of the representation of history by the historical discipline and historical facts.

[35]Breisach, Ernst. 2003. Narrativist History in the Poststructuralist Mode. In *On the Future of History. On the postmodernist Challenge and its Aftermath*, ed. Ernst Breisach, 72–88. Chicago: University of Chicago Press, 78–80.

[36]For a discussion of the Holocaust denial trials, see Part II, Sect. 6.2. A Third Wave: Irving v. Evans: Holocaust Denial in Court, cfr. infra.

[37]Iggers, as n. 22, 13.

ity, temporality, spatiality, ethics, and truth had to be re-examined.[38] The most common answer historians came up with was to incorporate the valuable lesson of moderate postmodernism: "language is not neutral, it is constructed by power relations" into the introductions of their historical research, without really letting it influence their research or historical practice. Notwithstanding the valuable insights of the linguistic turn, historians and the historical profession did not give up their belief in positivist objectivity.[39]

British historian Raphael Samuel remarks in his *Theatres of Memory* that it was only after "some twenty years or more" that the works of White and other postmodern historical theorists had started to disturb the tranquillity of professional historians.[40] Novick makes a similar argument "that there was a clear will to repress dissident historiography, but there simply was little dissidence to suppress."[41] Iggers came to the same conclusion in his examination of the most recent 20 years of theoretical history: "..., while historians became much more guarded in their belief in the authority of science, they nevertheless worked with the conviction that the historian dealt with a real and not an imagined past ... ."[42] This demonstrates the resilience of positivist objectivity. By agreeing almost collectively to honour positivist objectivity, the works of historians resulted "... in a convergent, celebratory historiography, which in turn promoted confidence in the objectivity of the work produced."[43]

At the eve of the new millennium theoretical history was in bad shape and the historical profession found itself in similar conditions. Historian Carlo Ginzburg, who describes the current form of historiography as "a ménage à trois of literary theory, anthropology and history, with rather ambiguous products as the result."[44] According to Ginzburg the historical profession left itself open to attack from cynics and critics without any proper response by still adhering to positivist objectivity without any substantial defence against or alternative for postmodernism relativism. Ginzburg continued his argument and stated that "[t]he contiguity between history and rhetoric has pushed aside the one between history and proof."[45] Instead of using the lessons of the linguistic-turn to redefine its theoretical conceptualizations and reinvent the historical craft in a way that is fundamentally different from the ideal of the sciences, historians stayed loyal to the idea of the historical profession as a science. The historical discipline all of a sudden could not prove anything, and the

---

[38] Iggers, as n. 22, 13.

[39] Iggers, as n. 22, 14–16.

[40] Samuel, as n. 4, 429.

[41] Novick, as n. 7, 332.

[42] Iggers, as n. 22, 14–16.

[43] Novick, as n. 7, 320.

[44] Ginzburg, Carlo. 1999. *History, Rhetoric, and Proof.* Hanover: University Press of New England, 71.

[45] Ginzburg, as n. 44, 1.

only answer that was provided was: "but we really remain objective."[46] Historians chose to let the ghost of von Ranke hit them on the head once again.

3.1.4 Descending the Ivory Tower

In 1978, a new historical journal rolled of the presses for the first time. It was called *The Public Historian*. After a year it was sponsored by the National Council on Public History, which was founded in 1979.[47] The journal aimed to become a platform for the rising number of historians who had found work in the private sector, in other words outside the walls of academia.[48] What is public history: "[i]n its simplest meaning, public history refers to the employment of historians and the historical method outside of academia: in government, private corporations, the media, historical societies and museums, even in private practice."[49]

Due to economic hardship historians were seeking jobs in government, in business and also with law firms. Public historians found themselves in non-traditional work environments which posed new theoretical and ethical problems.[50] Historians had to find a balance between professional ethics on the one hand and harder-to-make deadlines and the expectations of employers and other private market-like conditions on the other hand. Another essential part of public history is an attempt to communicate with the broader public and find ways to incorporate other non-academic forms of historical knowledge. Public historian David Thelen calls this communication "a Participatory Historical Culture."[51] Historian Raphael Samuel argued in favour of a similar "social form of knowledge", which is the result "of a thousand different hands."[52] For many public historians, going outside of the university meant to achieve something "real" and liberation from a "lifetime of

[46]Novick describes how American historians have continued to stay loyal to the traditional concept of objectivity. See Novick, as n. 7, 132–134, 208, 239, 249, 299.

[47]Public history is predominantly only institutionalized in America. Only in the last decade has it been finding solid ground at European Institutions. See, for example, the Institute for Public History at the University of Ghent: http://www.ipg.ugent.be. Accessed 31 Oct 2014. [In Dutch]

[48]Johnson, Wesley. 1978. Editor's Preface. *The Public Historian* 1, 4–10.

[49]Kelley, Robert. 1978. Public History: Its Origins, Nature and Prospects. *The Public Historian* 1, 16.

[50]Graham, Otis. 1979. Historians and the World of (Off-Campus) Power. *The Public Historian* 1, 35–37. Graham has been the editor of the public historian for 8 years while simultaneously serving as an expert witness for tobacco companies. See Expert Witness Profile No. 17, Otis Graham.

[51]Rosenzweig and Thelen, as n. 1, 190. Rosenzweig makes a similar argument on 177.

[52]Samuel, as n. 4, 8.

at least perceived contemporary irrelevance" on the campuses.[53] Public historians stress the importance of "applicable history or knowledge".[54]

Many historians [often academic] and people from outside the profession were sceptical about the public turn in history and accused public historians of "selling history."[55] When Novick discussed the movement of public history, he remarked that "[t]he objectivity question was a sore point with public historians, and their programmatic writings returned to it again and again, almost always with a defensive tone."[56] A "tu quoque-argument" was created, which stated that both 'kinds' of historians were equally objective.[57] The questions of ethics, truth, and objectivity are closely linked and public historians continuously try to show that academics and public historians are not that different.[58] As Public Historian Carl Ryant remarked in *The Public Historian* of 1986, the problem for public historians is not to produce good history, "only how best to achieve that end."[59] Many academics were and are convinced that public historians do not practice their profession in the same manner as they do. Although academic historians acknowledged the fact that they were themselves not entirely objective, academics were surely more objective than public historians. It would be difficult to deny that public historians are under distinct pressure to give up their professional ethics. But academics are equally coming under more and more comparable pressure themselves. Pressures to produce higher valued publications and write on trendy subjects to ensure tenure are as compelling as contractual obligations faced by public historians. Promotion and funding play their role both inside and outside the university. As we shall see, regarding historians as expert witnesses in tobacco litigation, the big pay checks from the tobacco industry lured academics and non-academics alike.[60]

3.1.5 Conclusions on Clio's Modern Paradox

Through a discussion of developments in theoretical history, this part of my research has come up with three major problems which have contributed to the current state of affairs in the historical discipline. (1) There exists a strong will among

[53]Graham, as n. 50, 40.

[54]Graham, Otis, and Reed, Lindsey. 1990. Editor's Corner. *The Public Historian* 12, 7–8.

[55]See for a rebuttal by a public historian of these critics: Shallat, Todd. 1978. We Who Would Sell History? *The Public Historian* 1, 81–82.

[56]Novick, as n. 7, 514.

[57]Novick, as n. 7, 516.

[58]Ryant, Carl. 1986. The Public Historian and Business History: A Question of Ethics. *The Public Historian* 8, 33–34, 36–38.

[59]Ryant, as n. 58, 38.

[60]See Part III, Sect. 16.3.1. Advocacy, cfr. infra.

historians, following general trends in the entire intellectual enterprise of the last two centuries, to mould their field of knowledge into a science. Because history has to be a science, its practitioners have to be objective in a positivist manner. This kind of objectivity is legitimated by the traditional interpretation of Ranke's dictum. It remains a task to discredit the idea of positivist objectivity with historians even today, because positivist objectivity is perceived as a strength of the historical profession rather than a weakness. This urge for an objective historical science has created a reciprocal relation with the second problem. (2) The second issue is situated in postmodern relativism. The basic assumptions of the linguistic-turn were valuable for historical theory. Radically cutting the relationship between fact and narrative is simply folly, as Carlo Ginzburg has noted several times. Denying the ability of historians to prove or to present historical fact has had negative consequences on the legitimacy of the historical discipline in academic and especially public environments. (3) Thirdly, historical theory has failed to provide systematic definitions of its fundamental conceptualizations which can be commonly accepted in the historical discipline. Without clear definitions of theoretical concepts used in current practice on epistemology, causation, objectivity, narrative, temporality, spatiality, and ethics, historians cannot expect to successfully explain and legitimize their practice to academics or the general public. Although these defined concepts will minimize to a certain extent the diversity and complexity of history, I think it is vital to have some basic definitions written down and standardized.

These preliminaries may have seemed elaborate for a book on forensic history, but the point I wish to make is a general one. Throughout this book there are examples of cases where historians were faced with the problematic nature of historical objectivity. Furthermore, the American legal rules on expert witness testimony are dominated by Popperian ideals of objectivity and science. These expectations exist within the legal profession, but history has the privilege of seeing reality in shades of grey instead of black and white. The judge has to argue in favour of a single version of the truth, a historian never has to. This small introduction should serve as a theoretical background against which attacks in court by lawyers on the foundations of the historical profession should be placed in context to. Let us now enter the courtroom.

Bibliography

Bevernage, Berber. 2012. *History, memory, and state-sponsored violence*. New York: Routledge.

Breisach, Ersnt. 2003. Narrativist history in the poststructuralist mode. In *On the future of history*, ed. Ernst Breisach, 72–88. Chicago: University of Chicago Press.

Evans, Richard. 2000. *In defence of history*. London: Granta Books.

Furner, Mary. 1975. *Advocacy & objectivity: A crisis in the professionalization of American social science, 1865–1905*. Lexington: The University Press of Kentucky.

Ginzburg, Carlo. 1999. *History, rhetoric, and proof*. Hanover: University Press of New England.

Graham, Otis. 1979. Historians and the world of (Off-Campus) power. *The Public Historian* 1: 34–40.
Graham, Otis, and Lindsey Reed. 1990. Editor's corner. *The Public Historian* 12: 7–8.
Hartog, Francois. 2003. *Régimes d'historicité: présentisme et expérience du temps*. Paris: Seuil.
Iggers, Georg. 1983. *The German conception of history: The national tradition of historical thought from Herder to the present*. Middletown: Wesleyan University Press.
Iggers, Georg. 1997. *Historiography in the twentieth century: From scientific objectivity to the postmodern challenge*. Middletown: Wesleyan University Press.
Iggers, Georg. 2011. *The theory and practice of history. Leopold von Ranke*. New York: Routledge.
Jenkins, Keith. 2009. *At the limits of history. Essays on theory and practice*. New York: Routledge.
Johnson, Wesley. 1978. Editor's preface. *The Public Historian* 1: 4–10.
Kelley, Robert. 1978. Public history: Its origins, nature and prospects. *The Public Historian* 1: 16–28.
Koselleck, Reinhart. 2004. *Futures past: On the semantics of historical time*. New York: Columbia University Press.
Ladurie, Emmanuel Le. Roy. 1973. *Le territoire de l'historien*. Paris: Gallimard.
Lorenz, Chris. 2010. Unstuck in time. Or: The sudden presence of the past. In *Performing the past. Memory, history and identity in modern Europe*, ed. Frank van Vree, Karin Tilmans, and Jay Winter, 67–102. Amsterdam: Amsterdam University Press.
Nora, Pierre. 1984–1992. *Les lieux de mémoire*. Paris: Gallimard.
Novick, Peter. 1998. *That noble dream. The "Objectivity Question" and the American historical profession*. New York: Cambridge University Press.
Rosenzweig, Roy, and David Thelen. 1998. *The presence of the past: Popular uses of history in American life*. New York: Columbia University Press.
Ryant, Carl. 1986. The public historian and business history: A question of ethics. *The Public Historian* 8: 31–38.
Samuel, Raphael. 1994. *Theatres of memory. Vol. 1: Past and present in contemporary culture*. London: Verso.
Shallat, Todd. 1978. We who would sell history? *The Public Historian* 1: 81–82.
White, Hayden. 1996. The burden of history. *History and Theory* 5: 111–134.

Part II
Historians as Expert Witnesses

Who controls the past controls the future.
Who controls the present controls the past.
All history was a palimpsest, scraped clean
and reinscribed exactly as often as was necessary.
George Orwell, from 1984.

Chapter 4
Introduction Part II

There is a higher court than courts of justice, and that is the court of conscience. It supersedes all other courts.

Mahatma Gandhi

Abstract In this second part of the book, I examine the interactions between history and law that have spurred Belgian legal historian Alain Wijffels to coin the term *forensic history*. Wijffels concentrated the conclusions of his work *History in Court* on post-Holocaust trials and Holocaust denial trials (Wijffels, Alain. 2001. *History in Court: Historical Expertise and Methods in a Forensic Context.* Leiden: Ius Deco). These brought him to a rather negative conclusion on the involvement of historians in the courtroom. In order to reassess Wijffels' term, I will compare the examples he discussed with examples from American litigation-driven history.

The first chapter of this second part of the book gives an overview of examples of interactions between law and history which are often considered to be examples of expert witnessing. Yet, as we shall see, not every time historians are involved in legal proceedings are they functioning as expert witnesses. For example, historians who work as legal consultants have a different role from expert witnesses. Historians who are involved in judicial procedures because of their skills in paleography represent another separate distinction. The unique element that defines expert witnessing is that the expert is allowed to give an opinion based on his factual historical research. The Dreyfus affair, the Nuremberg and Tokyo tribunals, and *Amicus Curiae* briefs are all important examples of interactions between law and history that are often wrongfully categorized as expert witnessing. These interactions are different but they are certainly related to expert witnessing. Many problems that come up when historians testify in court are also perceived in other interdisciplinary engagements between both disciplines. Due to the influence those similar problems and previous interactions have had on the reception of expert witnessing by the legal and historical profession, I have chosen to examine them here in the first chapter. By doing so, I am able to present clearer boundaries of what the expert witness does in court.

The following chapters furnish European and American instances in which historians have acted as expert witnesses. The chapters also delve further into the

R. Delafontaine, *Historians as Expert Judicial Witnesses in Tobacco Litigation*,
Studies in the History of Law and Justice 4, DOI 10.1007/978-3-319-14292-0_4

practicalities historians have to adjust to when they become and serve as expert witnesses. A second chapter is an inquiry into the post-World War II trials and the Holocaust denial trials in which historians have served as expert witnesses. The former topic discusses the Eichmann trial, the German Frankfurt-Auschwitz trials, the Ludwigsburg trials, and the French Vichy trials. The latter category examines the Zündel trials and the famous *Irving v. Lippstadt* trial. The third chapter gives an overview of the historian's participation in the American courtroom. Furthermore, the chapter discusses a step by step guide to the practice of expert witnessing in the United States. This practical guide goes over every step of the process based on information found in personal accounts of expert witnesses. In addition, the chapter discusses how Federal Rules of Evidence (FRE) have shaped the way in which expert evidence is presented in American courts. By comparing American litigation-driven history with European examples, I revaluate Wijffels' conclusions on the forensic form of history.[1] This comparative approach through the discussion of American and European examples allows me to further nuance and reflect upon certain problems brought up when historians enter the courtroom. Moreover, I continue to rely on the theoretical cadre from the first part of this book.

Again, I draw from a distinctly interdisciplinary body of research. Legal scholars and historians alike have taken great interest in the interactions of history and law in court. I mainly use legal historian Alain Wijffels' book *History in Court: Historical Expertise and Methods in a Forensic Context*, to fully understand his concept of "forensic history." Furthermore, I employ the research done by Vladimir Petrovic, a Serbian historian who has worked at the Dutch NIOD institute [Dutch Institute for War, Holocaust and Genocide Studies]. He has presented his work in his doctoral dissertation *Historians as Expert Witnesses in the Age of Extremes.*[2] For the American overview, I have researched personal accounts of historians who have worked as expert witnesses. Much material has been published in the American journal *The Public Historian*. These articles are of a more empirical nature and are ideal to contrast the more theoretical European discussions on the forensic context of history. Furthermore, I have been able to collect considerable information on the practical phases of expert witnessing through reports of expert witnesses on their experiences. In addition, I have procured research material on so-called "grey zones" of interactions between law and history, through personal correspondence with expert witnesses, enabling a privileged and surprising look into the controversial practice of expert witnessing by historians in the American judicial system.

Wijffels' book is on the whole dismissive of the notion of letting historians onto the "turf" of lawyers.[3] His argument is that the discipline of history has to sacrifice core values of its craft in order to adjust to the legal environment of the courtroom. Is it truly so that "forensic history has failed?", as Wijffels suggests.[4] I intend to

---

[1] Wijffels, Alain. 2001. History in Court: Historical Expertise and Methods in a Forensic Context. Leiden: Ius Deco.

[2] Petrovic, Vladimir. 2009. Historians as Expert Witnesses in the Age of Extremes. http://www.etd.ceu.hu/2009/hphpev01.pdf. Accessed 31 Oct 2014.

[3] Wijffels, as n. 1, 11, 16.

[4] Wijffels, as n. 1, 244.

find out the reasons that have led Wijffels to that pessimistic conclusion. I do this by discussing the problems brought up by both European and American examples of historians testifying as expert witnesses. The main problems on both sides of the Atlantic are advocacy, the fact that history is judged in the courtroom, the idea that when historians do not agree in court they have not been objective in their research, a lack of peer review, and the sense that historians behave in an unethical manner in court. Those five problems are discussed at length and strengthened with examples throughout the chapters. Aided by the theoretical discussion I have completed in the first part of my research and the comparative analysis in this second part of the book, I revaluate the idea of forensic history.

Bibliography

Petrovic, Vladimir. 2009. *Historians as expert witnesses in the age of extremes*. Budapest: Central European University.

Wijffels, Alain. 2001. *History in court: Historical expertise and methods in a forensic context*. Leiden: Ius Deco.

Chapter 5
Modern Interactions of Law and History

The fact that internal law does not impose a penalty for an act which constitutes a crime under international law does not relieve the person who committed the act from responsibility under international law.

Second Nuremberg Principle

Abstract This chapter considers three different forms of interdisciplinary practices of law and history that are similar to expert witnessing but remain distinctly different. I discuss the French Dreyfus affair, the Nuremberg and Tokyo tribunals, and the legal *amicus curiae* briefs written by historians. These different interactions of law and history provide an introduction to the field of forensic history and its controversial nature.

This chapter examines a selection of cases in which history and law have interacted in court. There exists a tendency among researchers, who discuss historians serving as expert witnesses, to wrongfully identify every interaction between law and history as an example of expert testimony by historians.

The French Dreyfus affair provides a good example of such a misconception. I argue that the Dreyfus trials were about paleography or the forensic assessment of documents rather than about expert witnessing. Essential in the definition of expert testimony is the expert's ability to give an opinion, based on expert knowledge and research, in order to aid the trier of fact. Other examples of wrongfully labelling the interaction between law and history as an event where historians have served as expert witnesses, have been the Nuremberg and Tokyo tribunals. While the trials were major events in the history of the twentieth-century, historians did not give any testimony. Although historians did not serve as experts, the Nuremberg trials remain very important as the cradle of criminal and international tribunals where historians and history are still playing a major role.[1] Furthermore, I analyse one other form of

[1]Due to time and research limitations, I have not examined the transnational justice movement in this book. The transnational justice movement has a literature of its own, separate from that of expert witnessing.

R. Delafontaine, *Historians as Expert Judicial Witnesses in Tobacco Litigation*, Studies in the History of Law and Justice 4, DOI 10.1007/978-3-319-14292-0_5

interaction between law and history that I do not categorize as expert witnessing, namely, the legal briefs or *amicus curiae* briefs that historians present to judges in the hope of historically informing their judgment. This chapter thus gives three instances that are often conceived of as examples of expert witnessing, but who are in fact examples of other interactions between law and history. By examining these instances we are confronted with general problems that arise when history and law come together. Problems that are also characteristic for the practice of expert witnessing. Furthermore, considering what borders on the practice of expert witnessing aids us in determining the demarcation lines of what judicial use of expert witness testimony by historians consists of.

5.1 The Dreyfus Affair: Paleography

Historical works on the role of the historian as an expert witness often start with the French Dreyfus case.[2] The affair spans two decades and reminds us of a strong anti-Semitic current apparent in the French establishment at the turn of the twentieth century. In 1894, captain Alfred Dreyfus, a French artillery officer of Jewish origin, was accused of leaking secret information of the French general staff to the German military. Dreyfus was tried for treason before a military tribunal and sentenced to life in prison. The swiftness with which Dreyfus was convicted, gave rise to questions. Soon doubt arose about the conclusiveness of the evidence and the overall fairness of the trail Dreyfus had received.

Dreyfus' conviction was based on the assumption that Dreyfus was the author of treasonous documents that had been intercepted. The court had enlisted experts to study those texts. A police investigator and a manuscript expert of the French national bank soon came to the conclusion that Dreyfus was the author of the documents. A group of intellectuals, among them not only the novelist Emile Zola, but also historian Charles Seignobes, and sociologist Emile Durkheim, demanded a re-examination of the documents.[3] In 1899, under increasing national and international pressure, the French government allowed the Dreyfus case to be reopened and the documents re-examined. After studying the letters, the French historian Émile Molinier argued, based on his professional knowledge as a historian, that the documents were not written by Dreyfus. Dreyfus' sentence was reduced to

[2]Petrovic, Vladimir. 2009. Historians as Expert Witnesses in the Age of Extremes. http://www.etd.ceu.hu/2009/hphpev01.pdf. Accessed 31 Oct 2014, 57–62. & Wijffels, Alain. 2001. *History in Court: Historical Expertise and Methods in a Forensic Context*. Leiden: Ius Deco, 10. & Dumoulin, Olivier. 2003. *Le rôle social de l'historien: de la chaire au prétoire*. Paris: Albin Michel, 167.

[3]It was because of the Dreyfus scandal that Zola wrote his famous pamphlet *J'accuse*.

10 years. Eventually, and because of unrelenting criticism, the French government cleared Dreyfus of any blame, after which he was released and reinstated in the military in 1906.[4]

It is not surprising that some historians have argued that ever since the Dreyfus affair historians "were occasionally needed for services by using their skills to reveal false documents and to authenticate legal evidence."[5] Historians announced with a certain amount of pride that they had undone "a miscarriage of justice."[6] The Dreyfus case is an example in which historians had "defeated" anti-Semitism. Although, in the end, Dreyfus had been imprisoned for 12 years and anti-Semitism stayed in France only to recur under the Vichy-regime during World War II, the case is continuously cited in the literature on historians serving as expert witnesses as a tribute to the virtue of the historian in court.

In contrast, I argue that the case is an example of a historian who used his ability to authenticate historical documents. Falsifying historical sources is a basic and essential element of professional historical practice. When Molinier argued that the documents were not written by Dreyfus, he had studied the documents aided through one of the auxiliary disciplines of history: namely paleography. Along with numismatics, archaeology, diplomatics and other fields, paleography aids historians in determining whether a historical document constitutes a falsum.[7] Determining the authenticity of a historical document is something very different from what an expert witness does in court. Experts give an opinion based on their own research of a historical subject to aid the trier of fact.[8] This opinion is based on years of study on a certain subject not on the falsification of a single document. To conclude therefore, like Petrovic, that the so-called forensic form of history started with the Dreyfus affair is too straightforward.[9]

5.2 The Nuremberg and Tokyo Tribunals: The Birth of International Tribunals

The Nuremberg and Tokyo tribunals[10] are two of the most important legal events in twentieth-century history. Both were held shortly after World War II and were designed by the Allied forces to prosecute the perpetrators of certain mass atrocities

[4]Cahm, Eric. 1996. *The Dreyfus Affair in French Society and Politics*. London: Longman, 211. For more information on the Dreyfus case see http://www.dreyfus.culture.fr/en/. Accessed on 31 Oct 2014.

[5]Petrovic, as n. 2, 59.

[6]Petrovic, as n. 2, 61.

[7]These auxiliary disciplines are also called Clio's laboratory.

[8]An example of testimony by an expert witness: is an opinion given on "the common knowledge" of the dangers of smoking with the American public between 1950 and 1980.

[9]Petrovic, as n. 2, 12.

[10]Formally called the International Military Tribunal for the Far East.

during World War II. As much as these trials were about historical events, their legacy helped shape the historical narrative on the war and those events themselves. The Nuremberg and Tokyo trials are illustrations of cases in which history itself was made and remade in court. Furthermore, especially the Nuremberg trials form a cradle for international human rights, international tribunals, and the transnational justice movement. The Nuremberg tribunal, in contrast to the Tokyo tribunal, did not only have to confront the act of aggressive war and the crimes of war committed by the German military as a whole, but also the Nazi design to root out the Jewish people. There also played a peculiar legal issue in Nuremberg. Which was that technically, the Nazis had not committed any crimes according to German law. Following the legal principle *nulla poena sine lege* (no penalty without a law), the defendants argued that they could not be convicted for crimes which had legally not existed when they were committed. To overcome this problem, the prosecutors responded that there exists a form of legal awareness, which is founded on historical principles, apparent among all civilized peoples, which incriminates certain atrocities even without written laws. This argumentation is called "the Nuremberg clause" and is written into the second section of article seven of the European Convention on Human Rights and article fifteen of the International Covenant on Civil and Political Rights.[11] Although the Nuremberg clause represents an infringement of standard practice in international law, the Nuremberg trials left an important mark on the charters of human rights of Geneva and the United Nations.

According to the German historian Erich Haberer "Nuremberg succeeded in delivering justice within limits. But it failed to capture the true nature of the Nazi state and the Holocaust."[12] For the Allied forces that had in fact not been the true purpose of the tribunal. American chief prosecutor, US Supreme Court Justice Robert Jackson, was asked by a British judge on the Nuremberg tribunal, Lord Justice Lawrence, what the goal of the Nuremberg trials was. Jackson answered that the tribunal was established to educate the German people about the war. The trials legitimated the prosecution and the punishment of the German leaders and proved to the world that the German war had been illegal and unjust.[13] American legal scholar Michael Osiel noted that the importance of the tribunal of Nuremberg was its impact on collective memory and on national histories.[14] Historian Ian Buruma writes that the Nuremberg tribunal was not so much about representing the historical facts as

---

[11]For article seven of the ECHR see http://www.echr.coe.int/Documents/Convention_ENG.pdf, 11. Accessed 31 Oct 2014. & For article fifteen of the ICCPR see http://treaties.un.org/doc/Publication/UNTS/Volume%20999/volume-999-I-14668-English.pdf, 177. Accessed 31 Oct 2014.

[12]Haberer, Erich. 2005. History and Justice: Paradigms of the Prosecution of Nazi Crimes. *Holocaust and Genocide Studies* 19, 493.

[13]Buruma, Ian. 1994. Het loon van de schuld: herinneringen aan de oorlog in Duitsland en Japan. Trans. T. Davids. Amsterdam, Atlas, 152. English Edition: Buruma, Ian. 1994. The Wages of Guilt: Memories of War in Germany and Japan. New York: Farrar, Straus & Giroux.

[14]Osiel, Mark. 2012. *Mass Atrocity, Collective Memory and the Law*. New York, Transaction Publishers, 6–9, 97–100. & Osiel, Mark. 1995. Ever Again: Legal Remembrance of Administrative Massacre. *University of Pennsylvania Law Review* 144, 609, 622, 636.

accurately as possible as it was a political process and a moral, pedagogic lesson.[15] The German-born American lawyer Robert Kempner argued that the Nuremberg trials were "the greatest historical lecture in world history."[16] For the Tokyo trials, Buruma is even harsher and writes they were an example of apologetic revisionism, a history lesson, a failure, an absurd ritual, and finally a rigged political process which undermined the European idea of justice.[17] In conclusion, the tribunals of Nuremberg and Tokyo are criticized for forcing history into a political straightjacket in court.

The Nuremberg and Tokyo tribunals did not call upon historians as expert witnesses because both tribunals were more in the business of making history than letting history aid the trier of fact.[18] The legacy of the post-war tribunals is thus twofold. First of all, the tribunals influenced how the war would be remembered to such an extent that they became important historical events themselves with their own topic in historiography.[19] Secondly, the Nuremberg trials are an important moment for the transnational justice movement. The concept of prosecuting perpetrators of mass atrocities in Nuremberg has been a precedent for tribunals of a national or an international character. Nuremberg was the starting point of handling historical injustices and their possible repair in court.[20] Contemporary examples of such tribunals are: the International Criminal Tribunal for the former Yugoslavia, the International Criminal Tribunal for Rwanda, the Special Court for Sierra Leone, the Special Tribunal for Lebanon, the Extraordinary Chambers in the Courts of Cambodia, the South African Truth and Reconciliation Commission, and other tribunals in Latin-America to confront the atrocities committed by dictatorial regimes. In contrast with Nuremberg, these tribunals are much less about delivering a convincing history lesson than about confronting and understanding a difficult and complex past in a nation's history. Their goal is to amend and strengthen national bounds. Overall, these tribunals wish to prosecute and prevent mass atrocities. For this difficult task these tribunals use the services of historians as expert witnesses.[21]

[15]Buruma, as n. 13, 153–154.

[16]Quoted in Buruma, as n. 13, 152.

[17]Buruma, as n. 13, 171–174, 182–183. The problem for the Tokyo tribunal was that the Japanese had agreed to peace on the condition that the institution and the person of the Emperor and his family were not to be harmed. The Tokyo trials thus lacked the ability to prosecute some of those who were directly responsible for the war.

[18]Petrovic, as n. 2, 110, 136.

[19]Petrovic, as n. 2, 100.

[20]Literary critic Shoshana Felman, quoted in Petrovic, as n. 2, 110.

[21]As I mentioned earlier, I will not be discussing the transnational justice (TNJ) movement because this book has to be limited in size. For the TNJ movement see the works of American historian Richard Wilson. A general article on the subject by Wilson is Wilson, Richard. 2005. Judging History: The Historical Record of the International Criminal Tribunal for the Former Yugoslavia. *Human Rights Quarterly* 27, 908–942.

5.3 The Amicus Curiae Brief: The Webster Case

The *amicus curiae* brief is a legal figure already established in Roman law which found its way into common law. The *amici curiae* (friends of the court) have the opportunity to write the court about a case to introduce legal arguments relevant to the case by which the judge could render a more impartial and informed judgment.[22] Historians have used such briefs to ensure a correct interpretation of historical facts relevant to litigation.[23] For example, historian David Rosner together with other scientists wrote a brief to the US Supreme Court considering the *Daubert v. Merrell Dow Pharm. Inc.* case, the verdict of which established a new rule for expert testimony.[24] Another example of an *amicus curiae* brief by historians is a brief that was signed by over 281 historians and that was filed with the US Supreme Court in the case of *Webster v. Reproductive Health Services*.[25]

The Webster case of 1989 considered the right of individual states, in this case, the state of Missouri, to impose restrictions on the use of state funds, facilities, and employees in performing, assisting with, or counselling on abortions. This restriction had been considered forbidden under *Roe v. Wade*, a landmark case from 1973. The discussion on abortion or the reproductive rights of women divided and still divides the American nation in a pro-choice camp and a pro-life camp. Public historians wanted to aid the court's decision with a historical perspective on the subject of abortion in American history. The fact that 281 historians had signed an *amicus brief* with a version of American history they all agreed upon, raised enough questions for public historians to organize a round table discussion in the summer issue of *The Public Historian* of 1990.

The Webster *amicus* brief had been an initiative of the pro-choice lawyers. Sylvia Law, professor of law, medicine, and psychiatry at New York University School of Law, helped draft the brief together with several historians.[26] After multiple

---

[22]For a short introduction to the legal term of *amicus curiae* see http://www.law.cornell.edu/cfr/text/28/68.17. Accessed 31 Oct 2014.

[23]Larson, Jane, and Spillenger, Clyde. 1990. "That's Not History": The Boundaries of Advocacy and Scholarship. *The Public Historian* 12, 34. In the spring of 2013 the Organization of American Historians (OAH) filed an amicus brief in *Perry v. Hollingsworth*, a case which sought to deny gay couples the right to marry in the State of California. For more information see http://www.oah.org/about/reports/reports-statements/20130501_oah-amicus-brief. Accessed 31 Oct 2014. I only discuss one example here from the Webster case, but there are many more legal briefs written by historians.

[24]See Part II, Sect. 7.3.6.3. The Daubert Standard: Popper & The Judge as Gatekeeper, cfr. infra. See also note 152 in Edmond, Gary. 2002. Whigs in Court: Historiographical Problems with Expert Evidence. *Yale Journal of Law & Humanities* 14, 173.

[25]Law, Sylvia. 1990. Conversations between Historians and the Constitution. *The Public Historian* 12, 11.

[26]Law, as n. 25, 11.

versions and discussions, the brief was eventually filed in the form of a nineteen-page report.[27] Historians had different motives to write and eventually sign the brief. In her article, Sylvia Law writes that historians were concerned that history was used in court by judges and lawyers to strengthen their legal arguments without much regard for historical truth. A common used phrase by legal practitioners to back up historically based arguments is for example: "Our history and traditions tell us that . . . "[28] Sylvia Law stated that another reason why historians joined the project was that they wanted to avoid a verdict which was not historically informed.[29] For the two historians who were the main writers of the brief, Jane Larson and Clyde Spillenger, their brief also served to mobilize public opinion on the subject.[30]

All contributing historians to the round table discussed the problem of advocacy. That the adversarial system provoked partisanship was acknowledged by all authors who had joined the round table.[31] Historians should stay objective, many of the involved historians argued.[32] Furthermore, historians had to remain faithful to the complexity of history.[33] The authors of the brief were fairly confident that they had succeeded in writing a brief that was different from major historical works but that was still based on facts and maintained the professional credibility of the subscribers of the brief.[34] Law wrote that advocacy had not precluded truth from their brief.[35] James Mohr, who had also signed the brief, argued that the amicus brief was "a balanced and credible report."[36] Another co-signer of the brief Michael Grossberg, wrote that the brief upheld "the professional standards of the historical practice."[37] According to Grossberg, the Webster brief avoided being merely "law office history."[38] Both Sylvia Law and Michael Grossberg argued that avoiding this "law office history" was far easier when writing a brief than when serving as an

---

[27]Law, as n. 25, 15–16. The final draft of the *amicus* brief was added to *The Public Historian*: Spillinger, Clyde, Larson, Jane, and Law, Sylvia. 1990. Brief of 281 American Historians as Amici Curiae Supporting Appellees. *The Public Historian* 12, 57–75.

[28]Law, as n. 25, 12.

[29]Law, as n. 25, 14.

[30]Larson and Spillenger, as n. 23, 35.

[31]Law, as n. 25, 13–14. & Larson and Spillenger, as n. 23, 36–40. Mohr, James. 1990. Historically Based Legal Briefs: Observations of a Participant in the Webster Process. *The Public Historian* 12, 19–20.

[32]Mohr, as n. 31, 25.

[33]Larson and Spillenger, as n. 23, 40.

[34]Larson and Spillenger, as n. 23, 40, 43.

[35]Law, as n. 25, 14.

[36]Mohr, as n. 31, 25.

[37]Grossberg, Michael. 1990. The Webster Brief: History as Advocacy, or Would You Sign It? *The Public Historian* 12, 48.

[38]Grossberg, as n. 37, 48. Quoting from A. Kelly's work about his contribution as a historian to the *Brown v. Board of Education* case: Kelly, Alfred. 1965. Clio and the Court: An Illicit Love Affair. *Supreme Court Review*, 123.

expert witness.[39] Not all historians involved were so enthusiastic about the result. Mohr and Freedman, although they had signed the brief, wrote they did not entirely agree with all of the aspects of the report.[40] Both argued that the final document was political and written in a technical vocabulary to fit legal arguments.[41]

The general idea of the brief was that the historical attitude on abortion in the United States had changed from time to time and from place to place. In her assessment of the Webster brief, historian Wendy Chavkin wrote that the historical consensus on abortion was strongly influenced by the commercial needs of the medical profession.[42] Neither side could really use history to strengthen their arguments. America had not been pro-choice or pro-life during its entire history. Eventually the Supreme Court decided to allow the states to make laws limiting state funds going to public information and community counsel on abortion. The final decision of the judges did not use any historical arguments.[43] The judicial opinion by the US Supreme Court had not followed the historical argument made by the pro-life camp, namely that America historically had been opposed to abortion. The Webster brief had achieved its goal by preventing the use of wrongful historical argumentation in the final opinion by the judges. Grossberg concluded that "[t]he historians' brief to the Webster case is the statement of 400 [unconfirmed number] historians who no longer wish to evade the responsibilities of their craft to inform the present."[44]

Although the legal briefs are a different kind of interaction between law and history than expert witnessing; the authors of these briefs experienced similar problems like advocacy, which most of them unsurprisingly solve by claiming they have remained objective.

Bibliography

Buruma, Ian. 1994. *Het loon van de schuld: herinneringen aan de oorlog in Duitsland en Japan.* Trans. T. Davids. Amsterdam: Atlas.

Cahm, Eric. 1996. *The Dreyfus affair in French society and politics.* London: Longman.

Chavkin, Wendy. 1990. Webster, health, and history. *The Public Historian* 12: 53–56.

Dumoulin, Olivier. 2003. *Le rôle social de l'historien: de la chaire au prétoire.* Paris: Albin Michel.

Edmond, Gary. 2002. Whigs in court: Historiographical problems with expert evidence. *Yale Journal of Law & Humanities* 14: 123–175.

---

39 Law, as n. 25, 14. & Grossberg, as n. 37, 46.

40 Freedman, Estelle. 1990. Historical Interpretation and Legal Advocacy: Rethinking the Webster Amicus Brief. *The Public Historian* 12, 28, 32. & Mohr, as n. 31, 25.

41 Freedman, as n. 40, 29. & Mohr, as n. 31, 25.

42 Chavkin, Wendy. 1990. Webster, Health, and History. *The Public Historian* 12, 54–56.

43 Law, as n. 25, 14.

44 Grossberg, as n. 37, 52.

Freedman, Estelle. 1990. Historical interpretation and legal advocacy: Rethinking the Webster Amicus brief. *The Public Historian* 112: 27–32.
Grossberg, Michael. 1990. The Webster brief: History as advocacy, or would you sign it? *The Public Historian* 12: 45–52.
Haberer, Erich. 2005. History and justice: Paradigms of the prosecution of Nazi crimes. *Holocaust and Genocide Studies* 19: 497–519.
Kelly, Alfred. 1965. Clio and the Court: An illicit love affair. *The Supreme Court Review* 1965: 119–158.
Larson, Jane, and Clyde Spillenger. 1990. "That's not history": The boundaries of advocacy and scholarship. *The Public Historian* 12: 33–43.
Law, Sylvia. 1990. Conversations between historians and the constitution. *The Public Historian* 12: 11–17.
Mohr, James. 1990. Historically based legal briefs: Observation of a participant in the Webster process. *The Public Historian* 12: 19–26.
Osiel, Mark. 1995. Ever again: Legal remembrance of administrative massacre. *University of Pennsylvania Law Review* 144: 463–704.
Osiel, Mark. 2012. *Mass atrocity, collective memory and the law*. New York: Transaction Publishers.
Petrovic, Vladimir. 2009. *Historians as expert witnesses in the age of extremes*. Budapest: Central European University.
Spillinger, Clyde, Jane Larson, and Sylvia Law. 1990. Brief of 281 American historians as Amici Curiae supporting appellees. *The Public Historian* 12: 57–75.
Wijffels, Alain. 2001. *History in court: Historical expertise and methods in a forensic context*. Leiden: Ius Deco.
Wilson, Richard. 2005. The historical record of the international criminal tribunal for the former Yugoslavia. *Human Rights Quarterly* 27: 908–942.

Chapter 6
The Globalization of the Historian as an Expert Witness

In my soul and conscience, I believe that an historian cannot serve as a "witness," and that his expertise is poorly suited to the rules and objectives of a judicial proceedings.

Henry Rousso

Abstract I start this chapter by determining five separate waves of historical expert testimony. Of these five I discuss two categories of predominantly European trials where historians have been active as expert judicial witnesses. These categories consist of the Eichmann trial, the German Frankfurt-Auschwitz Trials, and the Ludwigsburg Paradigm, the French Vichy trials, and the Holocaust denial trials like *Irving v. Lipstadt*.

After World War II, historians have served as experts in a multitude of legal cases in different countries. This globalization of the historian as an expert witness is traditionally divided into five categories. I have already referred to the first category of transnational justice. The second category of expert witnessing is the collection of all the post-Holocaust and post-World War II litigation in Israel, Germany, and France. For these three countries, these trials were as much about individuals as they were about national history and the role their country or people had played during the war. This category has had a major impact on the perception and reception of the forensic form of history by the legal as well as the historical profession. A third category is that of Holocaust denial litigation. The most famous examples are the British case *Irving v. Lipstadt* and the lesser-known Zündel trials in Canada. In many European and Commonwealth countries the denial of the Holocaust is penalized. This is also a category comprised of litigation which has had an important influence on the concept of the judicial use of expert historical testimony. The litigation which is presently going on in former Commonwealth countries like Australia, Canada, and New Zealand define a fourth category. Historians serve as expert witnesses in post-colonial trials concerning the rights of native peoples. These cases are litigated because of land rights, water rights, rights to raw materials, and reparation of historical wrongs. Historians have testified on native peoples' history in specially established tribunals and normal civil litigation. Most famous are the Waitangi

R. Delafontaine, *Historians as Expert Judicial Witnesses in Tobacco Litigation*, Studies in the History of Law and Justice 4, DOI 10.1007/978-3-319-14292-0_6

tribunal in New-Zealand, the *Delgamuukw v. British Columbia* case in Canada and *Mabo v. Queensland* in Australia.[1] A fifth and final category, is a broad category that comprises all civil American litigation where historians are involved in, ranging from land and water rights cases, indigenous peoples litigation, tobacco litigation, racial discrimination cases, gender related litigation, environmental cases, toxic tort litigation, etc.. Expert witnessing by historians is an established, institutionalized, and growing practice in America. The litigation-driven history in the US has an influence on the American historical profession as a whole due the number of historians involved. This is the category that has the most bearing on and relevance to historical practice today.

In this book, I examine the second, third, and fifth wave of expert witnessing in the twentieth century. The second and third waves have had a distinct impact on the general discourse on the interaction between history and law in Europe and the United States. Several cases were highly political and had polemic aftermaths. This controversial nature is very apparent in Wijffels' selection of cases. He discussed the German Frankfurt-Auschwitz trials and the French Vichy trials, and the infamous Irving trial. The Ludwigsburg trials are not examined by Wijffels' work, thereby leaving an important part of the German post-World War II litigation out of the picture. I have added these trials to my own limited overview to ensure a more balanced review of this second wave. I use the fifth wave of expert witnessing to make a comparison with the examples from the second and third wave. By comparing the European and American categories of expert witnessing, I can reassess Wijffels' concept of the forensic context of history.

6.1 The Second Wave: Post-Holocaust and Post-World War II Litigation

These trials are criminal cases against individuals who were accused of committing crimes against humanity during World War II or during the Shoah. In Germany, France, and Israel these trials were more than a judgment on the crimes of an individual. These trials were historical lessons of a psychological and a pedagogical nature. For France and Germany the cases aspired to come to terms with a difficult and shameful period in the nation's history. I divide this category further into three topics. I begin with an analysis of the Israeli example from 1961: the trial of SS-officer Adolf Eichmann. Secondly, the German Frankfurt-Auschwitz trials and the Ludwigsburg paradigm are discussed. Subsequently, I go into the French tripartite Papon, Barbie, and Touvier. All three categories have had a significant impact on the way European and American historians and lawyers perceive the interaction of their fields.

[1] However, I do not discuss these trials because of their small influence on the idea of forensic history as developed by Wijffels and also because of the limits in time and space of my research.

6.1.1 Eichmann in Jerusalem

On the 21st of May 1960, a plane carrying Adolf Eichmann landed in Israel. He had been captured by Mossad operatives in Argentina a couple of days earlier.[2] Eichmann had been a high-ranking SS officer during World War II. He had been responsible for the administration of the transportation of the Jews to the extermination camps. For his role in the Shoah, the Israelis had brought Eichmann to Israel to be tried in an Israeli court. Ben-Gurion, the Israeli prime minister at the time, had clear intentions for the trial. The Eichmann trial needed to become the living recreation of a national and human disaster. Ben-Gurion wanted to retell and rewrite the legacy of Nuremberg in the Eichmann trial.[3] While the former had been about an unjust war and about crimes against humanity–not only those committed against the Jewish people–, the latter would concentrate solely on crimes committed against the Jewish people.[4]

Historians seem to agree that the trial played out how Ben-Gurion had intended it. Serbian historian Vladimir Petrovic concluded that the Eichmann trial had revised history and had indeed stressed the uniqueness of the Holocaust.[5] Both Georgi Verbeeck and the Canadian historian Michael Marrus acknowledged the didactical role the Eichmann process had played in shaping Jewish public memory of the war and the Shoah.[6] Marrus went even further when he suggested that the process was more dramatic than it was judicial.[7] Hannah Arendt, the famous political theorist of Jewish descent who herself had fled to the United States from Europe reported the Eichmann trial for *The New Yorker*.[8] On these articles and her experience of the trial Arendt based her famous book *Eichmann in Jerusalem: A Report on the Banality of Evil.* In the book Arendt argued that the Eichmann trial had become

[2]Eichmann was tried under the rarely applied passive personality principle, which allows a state to prosecute foreign nationals who committed crimes against its citizens abroad. Eichmann's lawyers unsuccessfully attempted to discredit the employed passive personality principle. Moreover, they argued that Israel held no jurisdiction over Eichmann, according to international law. For the trial records see http://www.nizkor.org/hweb/people/e/eichmann-adolf/transcripts/Sessions/Defence-Submission-01-05.html & http://www.nizkor.org/hweb/people/e/eichmann-adolf/transcripts/Sessions/Defence-Submission-01-08.html. Accessed 31 Oct 2014.

[3]Ben-Gurion quoted in: Osiel, Mark. 1995. Ever Again: Legal Remembrance of Administrative Massacre. *University of Pennsylvania Law Review* 144, 507.

[4]Ben-Gurion quoted in: Osiel, as n. 3, 507.

[5]Petrovic, Vladimir. 2009. Historians as Expert Witnesses in the Age of Extremes, 199. http://www.etd.ceu.hu/2009/hphpev01.pdf. Accessed 31 Oct 2014.

[6]Marrus, Michael. 2000. L'historien et l'Holocaust dans le prétoire. In *Le génocide des Juifs entre procès et histoire, 1943–2000,* ed. Florent Brayard, 25–55. Brussels: Éditions Complexe, 27. & Verbeeck, Georgi. 2001. The 'Auschwitz-Lie' in Germany: Political Reactions and Legal Measures. In *History in Court: Historical Expertise and Methods in a Forensic Context,* ed. Wijffels, Alain, 133–160. Leiden: Ius Deco, 149.

[7]Marrus, as n. 6, 40.

[8]*The New Yorker* is an American news magazine.

a show trial where Eichmann's physical presence was the only thing that helped the audience remember that Eichmann was on trial and not history. Eichmann had become peripheral in his own trial, according to Arendt.[9] American legal scholar Mark Osiel writes that the Eichmann trial created a national saga and a national story which repaired the broken band between history and the Jewish people.[10] Not surprisingly the history proposed by the Eichmann trial was a populist version of Jewish history, consisting of recurrent versions of the legend of David against Goliath, of respectively brave resistance and barbaric repression.[11] Furthermore, the Eichmann trial created a new collective memory of the Holocaust for the newly established Jewish nation but also on an international level.[12] The Eichmann trial has created much political sympathy for the Jewish people and their suffering during World War II.[13]

"I appear here as a witness, not an eyewitness or a jurist, but as a historian", Salo Baron said when he took the stand to testify at the Eichmann trial.[14] Baron was the only historian who appeared as an expert witness during the trial. Similarly to Arendt, Baron had fled Europe from his Polish hometown to America. In America, Baron continued his academic career and institutionalized Jewish history as a field in American faculties of history. It was in his capacity as an expert on Jewish history that Baron was called upon to testify against Eichmann.[15] Rather than giving a historical overview of Eichmann's crimes, Baron's testimony explained the general context of the Nazi genocide of the Jews.[16] Baron was questioned by counsel for the defence who tried to attack his testimony on an epistemological level. Eichmann's German lawyer Dr. Robert Servitius attempted to discredit Baron's testimony by directing attention to what Arendt called "the murky issues of philosophy of history."[17] Hannah Arendt condemned the mixture of the task of the historian and the judge, an issue that was also addressed during the proceedings in court.[18] For Arendt it was wrong to have Baron testify on the Holocaust in general because it drew attention away from Eichmann's person, who was actually on trial. Arendt argued that the story of the Eichmann trial should have been that a person like Eichmann, a bureaucrat without special pathological signs of being a psychotic

---

[9]Arendt, Hannah. 1976. *Eichmann in Jerusalem: A Report on the Banality of Evil.* Harmondsworth: Penguin Books.

[10]Osiel, as n. 3, 473.

[11]Osiel, as n. 3, 618.

[12]Osiel, as n. 3, 619.

[13]Osiel, as n. 3, 644.

[14]Quotation from Salo Baron from the trial record, accessed via: http://www.nizkor.org/hweb/people/e/eichmann-adolf/transcripts/Sessions/Session-012-04.html. Accessed 31 Oct 2014.

[15]Petrovic, as n. 5, 120.

[16]Petrovic, as n. 5, 122.

[17]Petrovic, as n. 5, 122–123.

[18]Petrovic, as n. 5, 124.

murderer, had played such an important role in the organization and planning of the extermination of millions of people, or what Arendt called: *the banality of evil in the person of Adolf Eichmann.*[19] Eventually the court's decision was not greatly influenced by the testimony given by Baron.[20] Hannah Arendt concluded that the Eichmann trial had failed to deliver a fair trial for Eichmann. "[t]he purpose of the trial is to render justice, and nothing else", Arendt wrote disillusioned.[21] Adolf Eichmann was sentenced to death and hanged on the 31st of May 1962. The Eichmann trial became an example of how history and the testimony of a historian as an expert witness could be used for political purposes in the courtroom.

6.1.2 The Frankfurt-Auschwitz Trials and the Ludwigsburg Paradigm

Just as Ben-Gurion had felt that it was necessary to reinterpret the history of World War II and the Holocaust, West Germany started a series of trials, known as the Frankfurt-Auschwitz trials, to address anew Germany's responsibility in the Shoah. Historians have played a considerable role in these legal cases.[22] Expert historians were primarily recruited from *The Institute for Contemporary History* in Munich.[23] They were there to sketch as clearly as possible a picture of the historical and political landscape in which each individual crime on trial had taken place. Historians were needed to provide a general background to enable the judges to consider the actions of the individual in their historical context.[24]

The first of many trials started in 1963, when 22 officers and guards who had worked at Auschwitz were put on trial.[25] Like the Eichmann trial and the Nuremberg tribunal, the Frankfurt-Auschwitz trials had a pedagogic purpose.[26] The testimonies of historians were used to provoke public debate.[27] As much as the German trials were about changing and constructing public memory, they produced excellent historical research that is still part of the historiography on the Holocaust

---

[19]Arendt, as n. 9, 262. & Douglas, Lawrence. 2000. Régenter le passé: le négationnisme et la loi. In *Le génocide des Juifs entre procès et histoire, 1943–2000*, ed. Florent Brayard, 213–242. Brussels: Éditions Complexe, 227.

[20]Petrovic, as n. 5, 124–125.

[21]Arendt, as n. 9, 263.

[22]Petrovic, as n. 5, 31–32. For example: the historians Martin Broszat, Hans Buchheim, Hans-Adolf Jacobsen, Helmut Krausnick, and Jürgen Kuczynski.

[23]Petrovic, as n. 5, 128.

[24]Petrovic, as n. 5, 129–130, 133.

[25]Petrovic, as n. 5, 127.

[26]Petrovic, as n. 5, 118.

[27]Petrovic, as n. 5, 133.

and World War II.[28] The judges frequently cited and used the witness reports in their judgments.[29] Again attempts were made by, among others, legal scholar Ernst Forsthoff to undermine historians as expert witnesses by making the argument that the historical profession contemporized its knowledge in court and was therefore irrelevant. "History was rewritten every few years by a new generation of historians; hence, it had no legal value, which allowed it to be admitted to the courtroom", Forsthoff argued. According to Forsthoff, history was not based on solid facts as opposed to legal facts that were treated in the courtroom.[30] For Forshoff, in the Frankfurt-Auschwitz trial "justice had become beholden to the expert historian and history turned into a forensic historicism."[31]

In 1958, an institution was formed in the German town of Ludwigsburg to investigate the crimes of the German national socialists through historical research and documentation. It was called the *Zentrale Stelle der Landesjustizverwaltung zur Aufklärung Nationalsozialistischer Verbrechen* or the *Central Agency of the State Judicial Administration for the Investigation of National Socialist Crimes*.[32] In the litigation that was initiated as a consequence of newly uncovered evidence, historians played an important role as expert witnesses in collaboration with jurists.[33] Historian Erich Haberer called that corporation and the results it produced "the paradigm of Ludwigsburg."[34] The Ludwigsburg paradigm was a "reciprocally beneficial relationship" between historians and lawyers.[35] Haberer argued that the Ludwigsburg paradigm had succeeded in demystifying "the Nazi genocide", because the historical testimonies, based on solid historical research, were able to change the defendants from monsters into ordinary men and women.[36] This de-demonization had been the problematic issue, which according to Hannah Arendt had been absent in the Eichmann trial.[37] When in 1990, the 80-year-old Josef Schwammberger, who had been an SS officer active in Poland, was brought to trial, he was expected to be the last person to answer in court for his crimes during the Holocaust.[38] However, the trials had not seen their last act, for in 2008, 90-year-old Josef Scheungraber was convicted for war crimes committed in Tuscany

[28]Haberer, Erich. 2005. History and Justice: Paradigms of the Prosecution of Nazi Crimes. *Holocaust and Genocide Studies* 19, 505. & Petrovic, as n. 5, 118, 135.

[29]Petrovic, as n. 5, 131.

[30]Haberer, as n. 28, 509.

[31]Quoted in Haberer, as n. 28, 509.

[32]Petrovic, as n. 5, 138.

[33]Petrovic, as n. 5, 226.

[34]Haberer, as n. 28, 510.

[35]Haberer, as n. 28, 508–510.

[36]Haberer, as n. 28, 505.

[37]Arendt, as n. 9, 286–302.

[38]Petrovic, as n. 5, 139.

during World War II.[39] Altogether, in total there were 6,500 German criminal cases tried concerning crimes committed during the Holocaust or World War II.[40] The German post-Holocaust and post-World War II litigation shows that, although at first the Frankfurt-Auschwitz trials had tried to create a politically informed version of the German experience in World War II, interdisciplinary cooperation in the Ludwigsburg paradigm had procured excellent historical research and more just judgments for individuals involved in mass atrocities.

6.1.3 Dealing with a Troublesome Past: Vichy in Court

France has known three landmark court cases concerning World War II. These three have many things in common, but the most striking common feature has to be the enormous political influence on the trials and their theatrical character. The Papon trial is the best known of the three, not in the least because the trial lasted for 15 years, from 1983 to 1998, making it the longest trial in modern French history, according to French historian Annette Wieviorka.[41] Another factor for the resonance the Papon trial got in French society was the fact that after his career as a senior police official in the Vichy regime, where he had actively supported the German operations and also collaborated to transport French Jews to extermination camps, Papon had been a high official in the post-war French government. He had functioned as the police chief of Paris after the war and later as a minister of budget under president Giscard d'Estaing.[42] Papon was sentenced to 10 years in prison.[43] He was released in 2002. Papon died a free man in 2007. The second trial discussed is the Barbie trial. Klaus Barbie was a German SS officer who had been head of the Gestapo in Lyon during the war. He had earned himself the nickname: "The Butcher of Lyon."[44] While spending most of his post-war years working for American secret agencies, Barbie moved to Bolivia. In 1983, he was arrested and extradited to France, where he was indicted for his war crimes. The trial started in 1987 and

[39]Petrovic, as n. 5, 139. The Simon Wiesenthal Center continues to demand that the last living perpetrators of crimes connected to the Shoah should be arrested and tried. In 2013, a campaign under the title Operation Last Chance II hung up posters with the title "Spät aber nicht zu spät" (Late but not too late) in German cities to encourage the general public to corporate with the search of Nazi War Criminals. Rewards were promised up to €25,000. For more information on this campaign see http://www.wiesenthal.com/site/apps/nlnet/content2.aspx?c=lsKWLbPJLnF&b=4441467&ct=13224167#.Uw0YreN5Oxo. Accessed 31 Oct 2014.

[40]Petrovic, as n. 5, 139.

[41]Wieviorka, Annette. 2000. La France et le crime contre l'humanité. In *Le génocide des Juifs entre procès et histoire, 1943–2000*, ed. Florent Brayard, 113–132. Brussels: Éditions Complexe, 113.

[42]Wijffels, as n. 6, 270. & Petrovic, as n. 5, 215, 221.

[43]Petrovic, as n. 5, 223. & Wieviorka, as n. 41, 128.

[44]Petrovic, as n. 5, 216.

Barbie was sentenced to life in prison. He died in prison in 1991. Paul Touvier, the protagonist of the third Vichy trial, was, according to Wieviorka, only of a secondary level in the Vichy apparatus when compared to Papon.[45] Nonetheless, the Touvier trial had a significant impact on French national debate on the Vichy-era. Touvier was the first Frenchmen to be tried and convicted for crimes against humanity.[46] He had been ordered to kill seven Jewish hostages near Lyon in 1944 as retaliation for the murder of a high-ranking member of the Vichy administration. His trial began in 1994. In 1995, Touvier was convicted to serve a life sentence. Touvier expressed remorse for his deeds. He died in prison in 1996. There could have been a fourth similar trial. René Bousquet, who had also been a police chief under the Vichy regime, was accused of crimes against humanity in 1991, but shortly before his trial he was shot and killed in 1993. Historians have been active players in these trials as expert witnesses as well as in the public debate that surrounded them.

The French Vichy trials proved to be an insurmountable task for the already strained relationship between law and history, according to Henry Rousso.[47] Historians were asked to testify in all three cases. American historian Robert Paxton testified in both the Papon and Barbie trial. French historian Henry Rousso was asked to testify both in the Papon and Touvier trial. He refused twice. Since, Rousso has devoted an extensive amount of publications to the defence of his choice. Rousso wrote an eloquent letter to the court who presided over the Papon case.[48] Rousso declared: "I refuse to be used, not for my knowledge but for my position." Another problem according to Rousso was what he called *The Vichy Syndrome*, which became the title for a book he later published. In his book Rousso quoted Emmanuel Le Roy Ladurie on the subject. According to Le Roy Ladurie, the prosecution of Paul Touvier had turned into "the subject of enormous media attention and the vehicle for a debate on the legitimacy and activities of the Vichy regime, becoming popularly identified as a trial of the Vichy government."[49] This issue was very problematic for Rousso because there was an individual's fate to consider in all three cases.[50] This phenomenon is especially apparent in the case of Touvier who, despite his low rank, became a scapegoat for the crimes of the Vichy regime.[51] American historian Richard Golsan described the Touvier trial as a trial for the remembrance of the Vichy regime. Touvier became "a character out of a

---

[45]Wieviorka, as n. 41, 123.

[46]Papon was still appealing his case in court and would only be convicted in 1998.

[47]Rousso, Henry. 2000a. Juger le passé? Justice et histoire en France. In *Le génocide des Juifs entre procès et histoire, 1943–2000*, ed. Florent Brayard, 262–287. Brussels: Éditions Complexe, 283.

[48]Rousso, Henry. 2000b. Letter to the president of the Bordeaux Assizes Court. In *The Papon Affair: Memory and Justice on Trial*, ed. Richard Golsan, 193–194. New York: Routledge.

[49]Rousso, Henry. 1994. *The Vichy Syndrome: History and Memory in France since 1944*. Trans. A. Goldhammer. Cambridge: Harvard University Press, 210.

[50]Petrovic, as n. 5, 223.

[51]Petrovic, as n. 5, 220–221.

novel."[52] The depersonalized character of the Touvier trial bears much similarity with the Eichmann trial and the first Frankfurt-Auschwitz trials.

In the case of Barbie, who had personally tortured and killed several victims, the purpose of the trial was somewhat different than reckoning with the Vichy past. For Rousso, the Barbie trial was all about the revenge on history by those who had suffered.[53] Osiel quotes the French philosopher Finkielkraut who agreed with Rousso when he described the Barbie trial as "an unpaid debt with truth."[54] Osiel went even further when he wrote that the Barbie and Touvier trials were attempts to blame someone else other than the French themselves. In Barbie's case, this was easy since he was not French but German. Touvier, in contrast, was presented as a simple tool in German hands.[55] Papon, as a fully autonomous Frenchman, had been convicted for collaborating with the Germans in the Holocaust. The important difference was that Papon, in contrast to Barbie and Touvier, had not killed anyone personally, so he was sentenced to 10 years in prison, while Touvier and Barbie had to spend the remainder of their life behind bars because they had personally committed murder.

Rousso had more reasons to refuse to serve as an expert witness. According to Rousso some crimes against the French resistance could no longer be prosecuted due to the statutes of limitations. Osiel agreed with him on this and argued that due to the statutes of limitations, Barbie and Touvier could be convicted only for their crimes against humanity.[56] The trials thus stressed the crimes connected to the Holocaust and reduced the significance of their other crimes, for example those against the French Resistance.[57] Another problem with the Touvier trial and an important point for Rousso to refuse to participate, was the changed judicial role in which historians were to testify. Instead of going on the stand as expert witnesses who gave their general opinion on the historical context to aid the trier of fact, historians were asked to serve as regular witnesses. The reason behind this choice was an attempt from the court to have historians witness about the personal actions of Touvier rather than the general background in which Touvier had committed his crimes.[58] After he had testified in the Touvier trial, American historian Robert Paxton outlined the

[52]Golsan, Richard. 1996. *Memory, the Holocaust and French Justice: The Bousquet and Touvier Affairs*. Hanover: University Press of New England, 28–29. This remark is very similar to the issues Hannah Arendt had with the Eichmann trial.

[53]Rousso, as n. 49, 171.

[54]Osiel, as n. 3, 531.

[55]Osiel, as n. 3, 581.

[56]The statutes of limitations determine the maximum time after which a crime can no longer be prosecuted. The time differs depending on which crime is concerned. In some countries the ability to initiate litigation for crimes against humanity is not limited. For more information on the legal term of statutes of limitations see http://www.law.cornell.edu/wex/statute_of_limitations. Accessed 31 Oct 2014.

[57]Rousso, as n. 49, 160–161. & Osiel, as n. 3, 546.

[58]Petrovic, as n. 5, 220.

general context of the Vichy era again at the Papon trial. According to Petrovic, the experts occasionally contradicted each other from time to time which was considered problematic by the courts.[59] French historian Jeanneney stated in his bundle of essays on the Vichy trials that the historian had to be superior to a normal witness because he had to give a context, an interpretation of a period, a logic of a time rather than a set of facts.[60] Rousso had no intention to join such a biased enterprise and abandon part of his freedom of speech and analysis.[61]

Furthermore, history itself was again on trial, according to Wijffels.[62] In the Papon trial, historical theory was attacked by defending legal counsel. The defence lawyers argued that history was not suitable for judging, something which the expert witnesses were certainly doing. History remained "a fluid matter", Papon himself added.[63] For Wijffels, the Papon case showed that in court, there was a difference between the notion of proof in law and in history. The former was clear, the latter blurred.[64]

The Papon trial employed historians at different stages. A first group of historians did pre-trial work collecting all the facts that were relevant or needed extra attention. Wijffels argues that this first procedure was crucial. Since this pre-trial process is not public, the historians could remain more objective, according to Wijffels. The pre-trial phase has a major impact on the final story due to the selection and prioritization of elements in the historical narrative that is constructed with its judicial application in mind. Consequentially, it is very important for Wijffels that historians remain, particularly in that initial phase, as impartial as possible. The second stage was the testimony given by the expert historian. For Wijffels that part did the most harm to historical truth. Wijffels argues to confine the involvement of historians to the fact-finding phase.[65] We return to his proposal in the concluding chapter of this second part of the book.[66]

The Vichy trials received enormous media and political attention and became a major part of public memory of the Vichy past of the French nation.[67] In historiography several historians debated the outcome of the trials and the role of the historical discipline in it. As could be expected after his refusal to serve as an expert witness, Rousso was a very prominent participant in this debate together with other

[59] Petrovic, as n. 5, 222. The historians active in these three cases were: Azzema, Amoroux, Baruch, Bergès, Burrin, Druon, Lacouture, Paxton, Remond, Steiner, Streim.

[60] Jeanneney, Jean-Noël. 1998. *Le passé dans le prétoire: l'historien, le juge et le journaliste.* Paris: Seuil, 71.

[61] Petrovic, as n. 5, 226.

[62] Wijffels, as n. 6, 36, 301.

[63] Quoted in Petrovic, as n. 5, 222–223.

[64] Wijffels, as n. 6, 275–278.

[65] Wijffels, as n. 6, 271–272, 301.

[66] See Part II, Chap. 8: A Reassessment of Wijffels' Concept of Forensic History, cfr. infra.

[67] Osiel, as n. 3, 471. & Wijffels, as n. 6, 299–300. & Petrovic, as n. 5, 224–225.

critics such as the French historians Jeanneney and Dumoulin. All three had clear objections to the role historians had played in the Vichy trials. Jeanneney argued that there had been great confusion in the French legal system to the manner in which historians had to testify. In his book *Le passé dans le prétoire: l'historien, le juge et le journaliste* (*The Past in Court: the Historian, the Judge, and the Journalist*), Jeanneney explains that this confusion had unfavourable consequences for the historians in court. The French legal conditions precluded historians from doing any proper historical work.[68] Alain Wijffels quotes the French legal scholar Henri Angevin, who wrote that the French legal system was not fit to apply historical testimony and that judges, furthermore, did not prevent historians from making statements about the accused and his character. Historians should come to court to give information, according to Angevin, not to judge.[69] Another critical work on the appliance of history in the court room is that of Olivier Dumoulin. In his *Le rôle social de l'historien: de la chaire au prétoire (The Social Role of the Historian: from the Academy to the Courtroom)*, Dumoulin presents a critical overview of French litigation in which historians had functioned as experts. Concerning the Vichy trials, Dumoulin was critical of the considerable influence the adversarial paradigm had exerted. The application of a common law-inspired practice had encouraged both parties to bring their own expert witnesses, a wicked novelty, according to Dumoulin, which harmed historical truth and the historical discipline.[70] Wijffels agrees with Dumoulin and concludes that the Vichy trials had no significant contribution to historical knowledge.[71]

Rousso's objections and refusal and those of like-minded historians were met with counterarguments from other prominent French historians among them François Bédarida. In his *The Social Responsibility of the Historian*, Bédarida wrote: "[a]fter the radical critique of the 1960s, which destroyed the certainties, buried the utopias and disassembled the beliefs, a return of the values of humanism, morals, and meaning since the 1980s has been witnessed. To be sure, historians have their part in that recasting of intellectual life. They must continue to confront the imperatives of the present."[72] Bédarida himself had played a role in the Touvier trial.[73] In *Histoire, critique et responsabilité,* Bédarida discusses the ideas of Paul

[68]Jeanneney, as n. 60, 13–16.

[69]Quoting Henri Angevin from his *La pratique de la Cour d'assises*. See Wijffels, as n. 6, 272.

[70]Dumoulin, Olivier. Dumoulin 2003. *Le rôle social de l'historien: de la chaire au prétoire*. Paris: Albin Michel, 11.

[71]Wijffels, as n. 6, 296.

[72]Bédarida, François. 1994. *The Social Responsibility of the Historian*. Oxford: Berghahn, 6. Bédarida refers to postmodern historical theory which the first part of this book discussed see Part I, Sect. 3.1.3. The Three-headed Annales & Postmodern Headaches, cfr. supra.

[73]Bédarida, François. 2003b. L'Affaire Touvier et l'Église: spectroscopie d'un historien. In *Histoire, critique et responsabilité,* ed. Gabrielle Muc and Michel Trebitsch, 269–287. Bruxelles: Éditions Complexe. The book was edited in honour of Bédarida, who passed away in 2001, and is filled with his own essays and contributions from several other historians. Rousso wrote several essays and the introduction.

Ricoeur on memory and history in a legal context.[74] Bédarida's text discussed the relationship of memory and history and how that tension is felt in court cases were historians serve as expert witnesses.[75] Wijffels quotes Rousso in an interview in which he also acknowledges the presence of the contradiction of memory and academic history in court.[76] The article Bédarida wrote refers to Ricoeur's major work *Histoire et vérité*.[77] Therein, Ricoeur expressed his resolution that historians were bound by a conviction to find the truth and convey these truths as a mediator: "un médiateur entre l'événement et l'histoire, comme un gardien du temps" (a mediator between the event and history, as a guardian of time).[78] For Bédarida history was about the truth, "vérité" while memory was about loyalty or "fidélité."[79] He argued that there was a clear epistemological difference between the two. For Bédarida memory had reigned in the Vichy trials.

Petrovic concluded that the Vichy trials proved that the French courts had not been ready for historians serving as expert witnesses.[80] Wijffels came to the same conclusion. To him French legal scholars had badly defined the role of the historians in court.[81] The Vichy trials of Papon, Barbie, and Touvier had succumbed to external pressure from the media and politics. This delivered, a certain kind of justice, as Golsan and Rousso remarked: the Touvier trial was against forgetting the crimes committed in World War II and aimed at reaffirming the belief in democratic values.[82] For historians as well as for legal scholars, the Vichy trials represented a failed interaction of law and history.[83] Yet, as the following citation from the son of one of the victims of Touvier explains, not all had gone wrong with the Vichy Trials: "[m]y father was not judged by anyone. He was arrested, thrown five hours later against a wall, and assassinated. ... I am happy to find myself in front of a court that is democratic, engaged in an adversarial debate where everyone can

[74]François, Bédarida. 2003a. Une invitation à penser l'histoire: Paul Ricoeur, la mémoire, l'histoire et l'oubli. In *Histoire, critique et responsabilité,* ed. Gabrielle Muc and Michel Trebitsch, 249–267. Brussels: Éditions Complexe.

[75]François, Bédarida. 2003c. Les responsabilités de l'historien <<expert>>. In *Histoire, critique et responsabilité,* ed. Gabrielle Muc and Michel Trebitsch, 289–298. Brussels: Éditions Complexe.

[76]Wijffels, as n. 6, 295.

[77]Ricoeur, Paul. 2001. *Histoire et vérité.* Paris: Seuil.

[78]Bédarida, as n. 74, 251, 257.

[79]Bédarida, as n. 74, 257, 266. Evans quotes Rousso to make a similar distinction, see Evans, Richard. 2002. History, Memory, and the Law: the Historian as Expert Witness. *History and Theory* 41, 334.

[80]Petrovic, as n. 5, 219.

[81]Wijffels, as n. 6, 23.

[82]Golsan, as n. 52, 42. & Rousso, Henry. 1996. Reflections. In *Memory, the Holocaust and French Justice: The Bousquet and Touvier Affairs*, ed. Richard Golsan, 155–169. Hanover: University Press of New England, 169.

[83]Wijffels, as n. 6, 298–301.

speak, anything can be said, even by the accused."[84] In the end, the Vichy trials became another example of how history in court could be used for political means. Because of their wide coverage in the French media, and the great response to the trials in the French public debate, the Vichy trials influenced French, European, and American historians and legal scholars to think of expert witnessing by historians as a controversial practice.

6.1.4 *Conclusions on the Post-War Judgment of History in Court*

Almost all authors mentioned above agree that these trials were show trials. Especially the Eichmann trial and the French Vichy trials were grand dramatizations aimed at constructing a collective memory.[85] Petrovic calls these show trials a form of judicial memory making.[86] The trials had a pedagogic agenda which was set by extralegal factors, predominantly political ones.[87] Rousso also called the French trials show trials.[88] Defence counsel for Barbie, Jacques Vèrges, was correct, according to Osiel, when he observed that the trials were "an event."[89] For Douglas, the Eichmann trial and the French Vichy trials failed to do justice to history and the character of the Holocaust. It was problematic for Douglas to represent the Holocaust in court.[90] Alain Wijffels was clearly not enthusiastic about these trials. He called the testimonies of the experts in the Holocaust trials examples of the forensic form of history. The courts had demanded facts from historians, so that judges could judge those facts–as in the Latin adage: *Da mihi facta, dabo tibi ius*. But the contrary had happened with forensic history in post-war trials according to Wijffels. He states that a wrong conception of history had been institutionalized. History had been allowed to judge in court, which, for Wijffels, was the job of the law.[91] Despite this critique, Petrovic argued that the dominant belief that law and history were incompatible had been broken through this wave of Holocaust-related

[84]Quoted in Osiel, as n. 3, 704.

[85]Osiel, as n. 3, 687. & Frei, Norbert. 2000. Le retour du droit en Allemagne: La justice et l'histoire contemporaine après l'Holocaust – un bilan provisoire. In *Le génocide des Juifs entre procès et histoire, 1943–2000*, ed. Florent Brayard, 57–77. Brussels: Éditions Complexe, 58–62. & Douglas, as n. 19, 213.

[86]Petrovic, as n. 5, 118.

[87]Douglas, as n. 19, 213, 225–226.

[88]Quoted in Petrovic, as n. 5, 225.

[89]Quoted in Osiel, as n. 3, 678–679.

[90]Douglas, as n. 19, 237.

[91]Wijffels, as n. 6, 299–301.

litigation.[92] Petrovic argued, in contrast to Wijffels, that historians were necessary in the courtroom to paint a general historical context to place individual historical crimes in perspective.[93]

Petrovic had analysed national trends in a comparative manner. He concluded that by 1990 German lawyers and historians were cooperating to find the truth, while in France, historians, led by Rousso, were still discussing the controversy of expert testimony by historians.[94] Erich Haberer laid the comparative basis for Petrovic's study in his article *History and Justice: Paradigms of the Prosecution of Nazi Crimes*, in which he discusses two paradigms of Nazi crimes prosecution.[95] The first one was the Nuremberg paradigm, which could also be called the Eichmann, Papon, Barbie, or Touvier paradigm. For Haberer, these trials had didactic and pedagogical purposes. They all had a common plan: to "select Nazi documents ahistorically and exclude nearly all witnesses, which was aimed at making the evidence conform to preconceived ideas of Nazi criminality."[96] Subsequently Haberer discussed the German trials which employed an individualized history in the spirit of "Ludwigsburg historiography."[97] Browning agreed that the Ludwigsburg paradigm shift presents a re-conceptualization of the Nazi genocide. According to Browning research was now focused on "what actually happened on the ground."[98]

According to Haberer, justice did not suffer in the Ludwigsburg paradigm because of its reliance on historical expertise and history was not compromised because its practitioners served as expert witnesses. On the contrary for Haberer, expert reports were precise and meticulously researched, reaching a level of research that exceeded normal academic demand, because the reports had to have the "standards of proof, relevance, interpretation and documentary provenance and expertise" which had to "meet the scrutiny of defence counsels as well as those of prosecutors."[99] The reports constructed in the Ludwigsburg paradigm are considered models of historical research and have withstood the test of time.

I conclude this topic on the post-World War II and post-Holocaust trials with two preliminary attempts to reformulate the concept of forensic history by citing Browning and Haberer. Christopher Browning wrote in Friedländer's work on the problematic representation of Nazism and the Holocaust that "[t]he lawyer and the historian often ask different questions and meet different levels of proof. ... Nonetheless, the historical study and judicial investigation of the Holocaust have been inextricably intertwined, as historians and lawyers have used the fruits of one

---

[92]Petrovic, as n. 5, 137, 141.

[93]Petrovic, as n. 5, 136.

[94]Petrovic, as n. 5, 226.

[95]Haberer, as n. 28, 497–519.

[96]Haberer, as n. 28, 491–492.

[97]Haberer, as n. 28, 507–508.

[98]Quoted in Haberer, as n. 28, 508.

[99]Haberer, as n. 28, 509.

another's labours."[100] Haberer concluded his article on the post-Holocaust litigation as follows:

> In short, then, the paradigmatic Ludwigsburg and post-Ludwigsburg trials discussed here did not undermine the credibility of judges and historians. Both observed the rules and discourse of their respective professions and neither blurred the distinction between justice legally applied and truth historically defined. ... Here the "idea of proof" was the touchstone of the shared concepts of the critical ascertainment of facts and the clarification of contemporary conditions and circumstances. For this reason alone, the judge and the historian had much in common, despite the different requirements and objectives of justice and history. ... their common efforts provided us with a solid basis of information which can be considered beyond a reasonable doubt. This hard core evidence on the crimes of the Third Reich, offered by its criminals, its victims and its documentation, constitutes the irreducible testimony of this murderous past.[101]

The German Ludwigsburg trails had shown that even a subject as ungraspable as the Shoah could render justice in a criminal court if historians and lawyers were able to work together and share their research openly. Both Browning and Haberer have expressed great confidence in expert witnessing by historians, if historians and lawyers are prepared to engage in a constructive cooperation. As we shall see in American litigation-driven history, a very close relationship and constructive corporation between lawyers and historians is essential for the success of expert witnesses in court. On the other hand this close partnership forms a dangerous road to advocacy on the part of the expert witness. Yet, mutual understanding of professional standards attributes to a better collaboration between legal counsel and the expert witness, thereby adjusting expectations on the side of the lawyers in the fact-creating ability of an expert historian.

6.2 A Third Wave: Irving v. Lipstadt: Holocaust Denial in Court

The Belgian law of the 23rd of March 1995 states in its first article that the crime described as the denial, manifest minimization, attempt to justify or the approval of the genocide during World War II committed by the German National-Socialistic regime will be punished with a sentence of maximum one year of imprisonment.[102]

---

[100]Browning, Christopher. 1992. German Memory, Judicial Interrogation, and Historical Reconstruction: Writing Perpetrator History from Postwar Testimony. In *Probing the Limits of Representation: Nazism and the Final Solution*, ed. Saul Friedländer, 22–36. Cambridge: Harvard University Press, 34.

[101]Haberer, as n. 28, 510. A part of the quotation from Haberer was inspired on the arguments of Historian Dick de Mildt.

[102]An additional fine is possible, the minimal punishment is 8 days of imprisonment. Belgian law on Holocaust denial see http://www.ejustice.just.fgov.be/cgi_loi/change_lg.pl?language=nl&la=N&cn=1995032331&table_name=wet. Accessed 31 Oct 2014. [In Dutch].

The circumstances under which the previous described crime is committed are met when the statement can be accessed by a number of people, either privately or publicly.[103] Belgium is not the only country where denying the Holocaust is a crime. Other European countries like Germany, France, Spain, Holland, Switzerland, Austria, Poland, Lithuania, Slovakia, the Czech Republic, and Hungary have penalized the denial of the Shoah.[104] Non-European countries like South-Africa, Canada, New-Zealand, and Israel have similar legislation. The European Additional Protocol to the Convention on Cybercrime of 2003, which deals with the criminalization of acts of a racist and xenophobic nature committed through computer systems penalizes in its sixth article "the denial, gross minimization, approval or justification of genocide or crimes against humanity."[105] The United States, where freedom of speech is protected by the first amendment of the American constitution, has no law penalizing such denials.

These laws aim to prevent the minimization or denial of the horrors of the Holocaust. Several historians have taken the stand as expert witnesses in these trials but some have also sat in the bench of the accused. I discuss two examples, the Zündel trials and the Irving trials, the latter even more infamous than the former. Despite the greater significance of the Irving trial, I examine the trials chronologically because of Irving's earlier involvement in the Zündel trials. Zündel, a German Holocaust denier who lived in Canada from 1958 to 2000, has been convicted twice of Holocaust denial. Zündel had broken the Canadian law on Holocaust denial by printing and distributing pamphlets like "Did six million Jews really die?"[106] The services of historian Raul Hilberg, an absolute authority on the Holocaust, were hired by the prosecutors to prove the existence of the Holocaust.[107] The defence lawyer Douglas Christie attacked Hilberg's credibility as a researcher and questioned the quality of his evidence. Defence counsel pushed Hilberg to produce scientific evidence of the existence of the gas chambers in Auschwitz, thereby asserting the epistemological relativity of historical evidence and engaging in a general debate on the theory of history which often focused on nihilistic trends within the field.[108] During the trial, both parties strengthened their ranks. While the defence attained the support of two noted Holocaust deniers; namely Robert Faurisson and David Irving, the prosecution added historian Christopher Browning

---

[103]Article 1 of the law of 23/05/1995 is governed by the conditions of article 444 of the Belgian Penal code. Belgian Penal Code see http://www.ejustice.just.fgov.be/cgi_loi/change_lg.pl?language=nl&la=N&table_name=wet&cn=1867060801. Accessed 31 Oct 2014. [In Dutch].

[104]Some countries incriminate denial of genocides and crimes against humanity. Others punish denial of respectively Nazi and Soviet crimes.

[105]Article 6 of The European Additional Protocol to the Convention on Cybercrime can be consulted via http://conventions.coe.int/Treaty/en/Treaties/Html/189.htm. Accessed 31 Oct 2014.

[106]Douglas, as n. 19, 215. & Petrovic, as n. 5, 265.

[107]Petrovic, as n. 5, 265. The historians involved in the Zündel trials were Christopher Browning, Robert Faurisson, Raul Hilberg, David Irving, and Mark Weber.

[108]Petrovic, as n. 5, 265–266.

to their team.[109] Zündel was convicted twice, but in the end both trials were overturned by the Canadian Supreme Court on the grounds that the law by which Zündel was convicted was unconstitutional.[110] Zündel was extradited to Germany where he was arrested and indicted for inciting racial hate. The German trial lasted from 2006 to 2007. Zündel was convicted to 5 years of imprisonment.[111]

One of the most famous–or infamous–defamation trials against a historian has been the 1996 trial *Irving v. Penguin Books Limited, Deborah E. Lipstadt.* In her book *Denying the Holocaust* which debated the increasing attacks on the Holocaust as a historical fact, Lipstadt had named Irving as one of the most dangerous spokespersons of Holocaust denial.[112] Irving claimed that Lipstadt had given him offense and had harmed and stained his professional reputation as well as his personal honour.[113] So it was up to Lipstadt and her publisher to prove that Lipstadt's accusations were not aimed at insulting Irving but resulted from historical research that had proven Irving's historical opinions were wrong. In one cunning move, Irving succeeded in turning the tables and made his opponent prove that the Holocaust really had happened.[114] Unsurprisingly, the trial became centred as much on methods of historical argumentation as on facts about the Shoah.[115]

The defence hired the services of five expert witnesses, among whom Richard Evans and Christopher Browning were the most well-known scholars. Irving defended himself as an expert historian. Soon *Irving v. Lipstadt* developed into a trial neither about victims nor about perpetrators, but into a trial in which history itself was judged and made.[116] The trial was about history as a field of knowledge, about its methods and its flaws.[117] The whole event resembled something of a historical conference on historical theory with Richard Evans and David Irving in a pivotal role. The report which Evans, who had scrupulously dissected the works of Irving, presented to the court stated that Irving had made minor and major distortions in his works on the Holocaust.[118] Evans went even further and argued that Irving was not a historian, who generally interprets the past and seeks the truth, but had been

[109]Petrovic, as n. 5, 267.

[110]Petrovic, as n. 5, 257.

[111]Petrovic, as n. 5, 267 & The verdict of the trial can be consulted via: http://www.nizkor.org/hweb/people/z/zundel-ernst/supreme-court/1992-preliminary-version.html. Accessed 31 Oct 2014.

[112]Lipstadt, Deborah. 1993. *Denying the Holocaust: The Growing Assault on Truth and Memory.* New York: Free Press, 161, 180–181.

[113]Wijffels, as n. 6, 304. & Petrovic, as n. 5, 268. & Marrus, as n. 6, 41.

[114]Wijffels, as n. 6, 28–29.

[115]Wijffels, as n. 6, 29. The historians active in *Irving v. Lipstadt* were: Christopher Browning, Watt Cameroon, Richard Evans, Hajo Funke, John Keegan, Peter Longerich, and Robert Van Pelt.

[116]Petrovic, as n. 5, 269. & Wijffels, as n. 6, 29, 319.

[117]Wijffels, as n. 6, 318–319, 321–322.

[118]Wijffels, as n. 6, 311.

selective and tendentious.[119] For Evans, Irving was an ideologue who searched the past for arguments that fitted his own political project. The historian's concern, by contrast, was with the past. Evans concluded that "That is why, in the end, Irving is not a historian."[120] A 300-page verdict by the judge, filled with academic vocabulary and very theoretically informed, favoured the defendants.[121] Irving's career and reputation were badly damaged.[122] In 2005, Irving was arrested in Austria for Holocaust denial. He has been banished from the country after a short period of jail time.

Afterwards, several historians had strong reservations about the use of history in court and the penalization of Holocaust denial. Christopher Browning, echoing one of the arguments Rousso had made for not participating as an expert witness, said he found it problematic to testify about historical events when an individual's fate hung in the balance.[123] Despite his moral conundrum, Browning eventually served in both the Zündel and the Irving case. Florent Brayard concluded that the normative character of the law had impaired the probability to grasp the historical complexity of the Holocaust.[124]

According to Wijffels, bringing Holocaust denial into the courtroom was the wrong method of dealing with the issue.[125] Not only because of the fact that the difference between good and bad historiography was essentially being judged, but also because of the enormous media attention the trial received.[126] The trial lasted for 232 days, during which David Irving was a protagonist, because not only was he crossed-examined but he was also allowed to make closing statements.[127] Lipstadt herself argued that it was in essence wrong to limit the freedom of speech even for Holocaust deniers. She claimed that the illegal character would turn historical revisionism into a forbidden fruit, which would be so much more intriguing. Furthermore, Holocaust denial litigation gives deniers a public forum. The courtroom functions as an important medium where the discussions about the denial of the existence of the Holocaust give credit to and acknowledge the subject.[128] A similar argument was made by legal scholar Robert A. Kahn concerning the Zündel trials.[129] Brayard rather cynically remarked that the Holocaust denial trials were

[119]Petrovic, as n. 5, 270.

[120]Petrovic, as n. 5, 270.

[121]Petrovic, as n. 5, 271–273.

[122]Wijffels, as n. 6, 330–331.

[123]Quoted in Petrovic, as n. 5, 4.

[124]Douglas, as n. 19, 215–216, 237–238.

[125]Wijffels, as n. 6, 22.

[126]Petrovic, as n. 5, 273.

[127]Wijffels, as n. 6, 314.

[128]Lipstadt, as n. 112, 1–29. & Petrovic, as n. 5, 258.

[129]Quoted in Osiel, as n. 3, 542, note 303.

worth millions of dollars in publicity value.[130] Another point of criticism is the limitation of the freedom of speech. The only legitimate claim Zündel and Irving made was that they were repressed in their right to freedom of speech.[131] After the conclusion of the trial Lipstadt remained opposed to this limitation of freedom of speech.[132] Noam Chomsky, the famous American political theorist, made an even more outspoken statement for freedom of speech when he wrote the preface of noted Holocaust denier Robert Faurisson's *Mémoire en défense.*[133]

French historian François Bédarida argued that the revisionist interpretation of the genocide by the Nazis is, at best, an illogical and loose form of reasoning, nothing more than a simplistic historical conspiracy theory.[134] The problem for the historical discipline is that it confronts the historical profession with its dubious basic conceptions of objectivity and the harm done by the more extreme postmodern historical theories.[135] Historian Hayden White declared that the Holocaust is so unique that it needs its own models of representation. White's claim that "[t]here is an inexpungible relativity in every representation of historical phenomena",[136] has made it challenging to debunk the myths of Irving and Zündel, and other Holocaust deniers.[137] For Bédarida, the principle of truth, the object of historical interpretation and construction can resist the fiction of an overall too enthusiastic critical method.[138] Rebutting the claim by White and others that there was no connection between historiography and reality, was the idea behind the book Richard Evans wrote after his testimony in the Irving trial. He titled his work *In the Defence of History.*[139] Evans, considering his tribulations as an expert witness, concluded that a historian was able to tell the truth without falling into the trap of straightforward advocacy. History, for Evans, had quite similar standards of proof as law; both are able to prove beyond a reasonable doubt.[140] Holocaust denial trials

---

[130]Marrus, as n. 6, 42.

[131]Petrovic, as n. 5, 258.

[132]Petrovic, as n. 5, 258.

[133]Petrovic, as n. 5, 257.

[134]Bédarida, as n. 75, 290–291.

[135]Bédarida, as n. 75, 292, 294.

[136]White, Hayden. 1992. Historical Emplotment and the Problem of Truth. In *Probing the Limits of Representation: Nazism and the Final Solution*, ed. Saul Friedländer, 37–53. Cambridge: Harvard University Press. See our discussion on postmodern historical theory in Part I, Sect. 3.1.3. The Three-headed Annales & Postmodern Headaches, cfr. supra.

[137]Bédarida, as n. 75, 294.

[138]Bédarida, as n. 75, 295.

[139]Evans, Richard. 2000. *In Defence of History.* London, Granta Books.

[140]Evans, as n. 79, 330. Historians have had second thoughts about penalizing Holocaust denial. By giving a really marginalized group the opportunity to broadcast their ideas in court to a much higher number of people than they normally could reach, more harm than good was done. The nineteenth article of the Universal Declaration of Human Rights of 1948 which reads as follows: "[e]veryone has the right to freedom of opinion and expression; this right includes freedom to

were, despite their problematic characteristic, that is that historical method is judged in court, successful in discrediting Holocaust denial and its exponents.

I have now discussed the most important European examples of expert witnessing which have contributed to the image of expert witnessing as a forensic form of historical research, as described by Wijffels. I now start my discussion on the American form of litigation-driven history.

Bibliography

Arendt, Hannah. 1976. *Eichmann in Jerusalem: A report on the banality of evil*. Harmondsworth: Penguin.

Bédarida, François. 1994. *The social responsibility of the historian*. Oxford: Berghahn.

Bédarida, François. 2003a. Une invitation à penser l'histoire: Paul Ricoeur, la mémoire, l'histoire et l'oubli. In *Histoire, critique et responsabilité*, ed. Gabrielle Muc and Michel Trebitsch, 249–267. Brussels: Éditions Complexe.

Bédarida, François. 2003b. L'Affaire Touvier et l'Église: spectroscopie d'un historien. In *Histoire, critique et responsabilité*, ed. Gabrielle Muc and Michel Trebitsch, 269–287. Brussels: Éditions Complexe.

Bédarida, François. 2003c. Les responsabilités de l'historien <<expert>> In *Histoire, critique et responsabilité*, ed. Gabrielle Muc and Michel Trebitsch, 289–298. Brussels: Éditions Complexe.

Browning, Christopher. 1992. German memory, judicial interrogation, and historical reconstruction: Writing perpetrator history from postwar testimony. In *Probing the limits of representation: Nazism and the final solution*, ed. Saul Friedländer, 22–36. Cambridge: Harvard University Press.

Douglas, Lawrence. 2000. Régenter le passé: le négationisme et la loi. In *Le génocide des Juifs entre procès et histoire, 1943–2000*, ed. Florent Brayard, 213–242. Brussels: Éditions Complexe.

Dumoulin, Olivier. 2003. *Le rôle social de l'historien: de la chaire au prétoire*. Paris: Albin Michel.

Evans, Richard. 2000. *In defence of history*. London: Granta Books.

Evans, Richard. 2002. History, memory, and the law: The historian as expert witness. *History and Theory* 41: 326–345.

Golsan, Richard. 1996. *Memory, the Holocaust and French justice: The Bousquet and Touvier affairs*. Hanover: University Press of New England.

Haberer, Erich. 2005. History and justice: Paradigms of the prosecution of Nazi crimes. *Holocaust and Genocide Studies* 19: 497–519.

hold opinions without interference and to seek, receive and impart information and ideas through any media and regardless of frontiers." should not be diminished in any way. For the Universal Declaration of Human Rights, see http://www.un.org/en/documents/udhr. Accessed 31 Oct 2014. Freedom of speech is absolute, even when it comes to the Shoah. Should the memory of other genocides also be protected by a law? For example, in France a law was confirmed under former President Nicolas Sarkozy which forbade the denial of the Armenian genocide. I think this is the wrong path to take. Holocaust denial and similar theories are met with sufficient resistance in a democratic society by the strength of historical research, the sense of truth and justice in society as a whole to keep Holocaust denial from becoming anything more than what it essentially is: a marginal political theory, not history.

Jeanneney, Jean-Noël. 1998. *Le passé dans le prétoire: l'historien, le juge et le journaliste*. Paris: Seuil.

Lipstadt, Deborah. 1993. *Denying the Holocaust: The growing assault on truth and memory*. New York: Free Press.

Marrus, Michael. 2000. L'historien et l'Holocaust dans le prétoire. In *Le génocide des Juifs entre procès et histoire, 1943–2000*, ed. Florent Brayard, 25–55. Brussels: Éditions Complexe.

Norbert, Frei. 2000. Le retour du droit en Allemagne: La justice et l'histoire contemporaine après l'Holocaust – un bilan provisoire. In *Le génocide des Juifs entre procès et histoire, 1943–2000*, ed. François Brayard, 57–77. Brussels: Éditions Complexe.

Osiel, Mark. 1995. Ever again: Legal remembrance of administrative massacre. *University of Pennsylvania Law Review* 144: 463–704.

Petrovic, Vladimir. 2009. *Historians as expert witnesses in the age of extremes*. Budapest: Central European University.

Ricoeur, Paul. 2001. *Histoire et vérité*. Paris: Seuil.

Rousso, Henry. 1994. *The Vichy Syndrome: History and Memory in France since 1944.* Trans. A. Goldhammer. Cambridge: Harvard University Press.

Rousso, Henry. 1996. Reflections. In *History, the Holocaust, and French justice: The Bousquet and Touvier affairs*, ed. Richard Golsan, 155–169. Hanover: University Press of New England.

Rousso, Henry. 2000a. Juger le passé? Justice et histoire en France. In *Le génocide des Juifs entre procès et histoire, 1943–2000*, ed. Florent Brayard, 262–287. Brussels: Éditions Complexe.

Rousso, Henry. 2000b. Letter to the president of the Bordeaux Assizes court. In *The Papon affair*, ed. Richard Golsan, 193–194. New York: Routledge.

Verbeeck, Georgi. 2001. The 'Auschwitz-Lie' in Germany: Political Reactions and Legal Measures. In *History in Court: Historical Expertise and Methods in a Forensic Context*, ed. Wijffels, Alain, 133–160. Leiden: Ius Deco.

White, Hayden. 1992. Historical emplotment and the problem of truth. In *Probing the limits of representation: Nazism and the final solution*, ed. Saul Friedländer, 37–53. Cambridge: Harvard University Press.

Wieviorka, Annette. 2000. La France et le crime contre l'humanté. In *Le génocide des Juifs entre procès et histoire, 1943–2000*, ed. Florent Brayard, 113–132. Brussels: Éditions Complexe.

Wijffels, Alain. 2001. *History in court: Historical expertise and methods in a forensic context*. Leiden: Ius Deco.

Chapter 7
Litigation-Driven History

Gentlemen of the jury, there are three kinds of liars, the common liar, the damned liar and the scientific expert.

An American Attorney

Abstract In this chapter I discuss a selective list of American examples of historians serving as expert judicial witnesses. The chapter reviews the earliest mentions and debate of expert witnessing at the end of the nineteenth century, after which it turns to *Brown v. Board of Education*, the Sears case, and an example from toxic tort litigation. The following topic discusses a practical guide to expert witnessing in the American judicial system for historians. Legal as well as extralegal aspects are considered and elaborated on through examples from personal reports from former experts. Considerable attention is devoted to the Daubert ruling and rule 702 of the Federal Rules of Evidence which have envisioned the Judge to perform a gatekeeping role when reviewing expert testimony. In a final part of the chapter, I discuss the issues which are responsible for making expert witnessing into a controversial practice.

The term litigation-driven history finds its origin in the United States. Public and academic historians have increasingly been called upon to serve as expert witnesses in court. The historical research those experts do in preparation of their court report and possible deposition and testimony in court, is called litigation-driven history. The website of the *American Historical Association* (AHA) lists the possibilities for historians to work in a legal related environment under the rather unfortunate chosen name: historians as advocates.[1] Legal companies, lawyers, companies, or private persons hire expert historical knowledge to aid them in court. The practice of expert witnessing is not a recent one. The first topic of this chapter examines a short history of expert witnessing in the US and the late arrival of historians in the courtroom. The second part of this chapter addresses the diversity of subjects on which historians testify in court. I go over them thematically with several

[1]The list of the AHA via http://www.historians.org/pubs/free/careers/advocate.htm. Accessed 31 Oct 2014.

R. Delafontaine, *Historians as Expert Judicial Witnesses in Tobacco Litigation*, Studies in the History of Law and Justice 4, DOI 10.1007/978-3-319-14292-0_7

examples of different cases and expert historians who served as witnesses. These two topics introduce several practical and theoretical problems expert historians face in American courtrooms. These issues will be discussed at the end of the second part of this book. Furthermore, I discuss the practical manner by which historians prepare their testimony and the legal setting in which it is given. The legal rules of evidence for expert witnesses are also addressed, since they have a great influence on the expert's report. Moreover, these legal rules inform us of how the legal profession defines scientific knowledge or what kind of witness testimony judges expect in court. After this chapter I confront the different elements through which the European experience of expert historical testimony differs from the American experience.

7.1 Expert Witnessing Through the Ages

Common law has a far-reaching tradition of letting experts testify in court to help the judge or the jury understand "expert knowledge." The often cited American Judge Learned Hand wrote an article in 1901 in which he discussed common law cases involving expert witnesses as far back as the year 1345.[2] In this article he stated that: "[n]o one will deny that the law should in some way effectively use expert knowledge wherever it will aid in settling disputes. The only question is as to how it can do so best."[3] Historian Christopher Hamlin discussed expert witnessing in the Victorian age from 1860 until 1885. Hamlin concluded that modern legal problems concerning the expert witness's testimony troubled Victorians as well.[4]

The first problem raised by Victorians is that of objectivity or its antonym advocacy. Hamlin describes how lawyers and judges doubted the ability of expert witnesses to present disinterested science. In other words, they doubted expert knowledge would be without bias or preconceptions.[5] A person who sold his credibility to the highest bidder was not compatible with the norms and methods of science in the Victorian age.[6] Expert scientists were demanding fees that exceeded regular witness fees, which increased suspicion about their intents when coming to

[2]Judge Hand described cases from 1345, 1494, 1555, 1620, 1645, and 1678 see Hand, Learned. 1901. Historical and Practical Considerations Regarding Expert Testimony. *Harvard Law Review* 15, 40.

[3]Hand, as n. 2, 40.

[4]Hamlin, Christopher. 1986. Scientific Method and Expert Witnessing: Victorian Perspectives on a Modern Problem. *Social Studies of Science* 16, 485.

[5]Hamlin, as n. 4, 486–487.

[6]Foster, William. 1897. Expert Testimony, Prevalent Complaints and Proposed Remedies. *Harvard Law Review* 11, 170–171. & Hamlin, as n. 4, 488.

court.[7] There was a serious risk, Judge Hand declared, that the expert could become the "hired champion of one side."[8] Another epitome concerning expert witnesses is provided by legal scholar Gary Edmond, who writes that at the beginning of the twentieth century expert witnesses were considered "cash crazed hired guns."[9] Or as historian Morgan Kousser's frequently quoted title puts it: "Are Expert Witnesses Whores?"[10] Judge Foster, who wrote an essay in 1897 on the practice of expert testimony, quoted a lawyer who addressed the jury as follows: "Gentlemen of the jury, there are three kinds of liars, the common liar, the damned liar and the scientific expert."[11] The fear that an expert witness would distort evidence to support the claims of his employer is a concern that is as active today as it was at the end of the nineteenth century.[12] In conclusion, from the very beginning of the practice expert witnesses performed a controversial legal practice.

A second problem was the existence of apparent disagreements between experts in court. Edmond, who discussed expert witnessing at the beginning of the twentieth century, wrote that debate amongst experts was considered problematic to identify reliable knowledge in court.[13] Such discussions amongst scientists were considered to be not scientific. Because, lawyers reasoned, if both experts were objective and made use of the correct methods, then both would have to come to the same conclusion.[14] Not much has changed as G. Jones, an independent historian who works as an expert witness, declared at the 2013 National Council of Pubic History (NCPH) conference in Ottawa: "judges and advocates don't like disagreements or contradictions."[15] This is, according to Hamlin, a naïve idea of scientific method. Dissent is not the nemesis of science, if anything "the conflict of strong opinions is central to the progress of science."[16] Or as Judge Foster put it about a hundred years ago: "men may honestly differ in opinion."[17] Hamlin concludes that science is presented unrealistically by lawyers and that the adversary procedure is not alien to science. Edmond agrees with Hamlin's conclusion when he argued that judges and

---

[7] s. n. 1909. Witnesses. Experts. Compensation Exceeding Regular Fee. *Harvard Law Review* 22, 235–236.

[8] Hand, as n. 2, 53.

[9] Edmond, Gary. 2002. Whigs in Court: Historiographical Problems with Expert Evidence. *Yale Journal of Law & Humanities* 14, 123–124.

[10] Kousser, Morgan. 1984. Are Expert Witnesses Whores? Reflections on Objectivity in Scholarship and Expert Witnessing. *The Public Historian* 6, 5–19.

[11] Foster, as n. 6, 169.

[12] Edmond, as n. 9, 171–172.

[13] Edmond, as n. 9, 170.

[14] Hamlin, as n. 2, 485, 504.

[15] Ms. Jones gave her presentation on April 19, 2013 at the conference of public history in Ottawa. Based on notes of the author.

[16] Hamlin, as n. 2, 504.

[17] Foster, as n. 6, 173.

lawyers have always used "a priori" images of science.[18] Around 1900, good science was presented as a strictly positivist pursuit. In legal terms, science had been defined in a similar manner.[19] Proper scientific practice produced results that were reliable and could be tested. Judges and lawyers had, according to Edmond, a clear-cut idea what the difference was between "good" and "bad" science. At the beginning of the twentieth century different kinds of knowledge were divided into valuable evidence and invaluable evidence.[20] This chapter will confirm that the three main problems Hamlin identified for expert witnessing at the end of the nineteenth century, namely the concern for biased expert evidence, the adverse attitude towards the existence of disagreements between experts, and the unrealistic conception of science as a whole have remained problematic for expert witnesses in court, not in the least for historians.

Judge Foster provided some alternative forms of expert witnessing. For example, he argued to allow the court to appoint its own expert. This idea has become a legal option with the introduction of the American Federal Rules of Evidence (FRE) in 1975. Although the option is extant and is legal, it is almost never used by judges.[21] Another possible alternative can be found in a legal brief from 1896, which argues in favour of an institutionalized committee of experts, permanently paid be the state.[22] According to Hamlin, Victorians proposed to draft ethical codes for those scientists who served as expert witnesses. Judge Foster similarly called for an ethical code that would have a preventive effect on the supposed bias that existed with experts in favour of their employer.[23] Judge Hand wrote that another solution would be to allow the judge to impose general principles of interpretation on the jury, concerning the expert's testimony.[24] Judge Foster said that above all, expert witnesses should look to themselves and be pure of heart and just, when they try to represent the truth.[25] Edmond names an extra incentive for experts to present the truth: not only does the expert present the facts of the case; he or she also defends himself and his

---

[18]Edmond, as n. 9, 130.

[19]We will revisit this subject when discussing the Federal Rules of Evidence and the Daubert Standard for expert witnessing, see Part II, 7.3.6.3. The Daubert Standard: Popper & the Judge as Gatekeeper, cfr. infra.

[20]Edmond, as n. 9, 154–163, 166–169.

[21]See rule 706 of the FRE http://federalevidence.com/downloads/rules.of.evidence.pdf, 31–32. Accessed 31 Oct 2014.

[22]s. n. 1896. Expert Medical Testimony, *Harvard Law Review* 10, 305–306.

[23]Hamlin, as n. 4, 490. & Foster, as n. 6, 171. I discuss the advantages of ethical codes on several occasions see in particular: Part III, 5.4. Confronting Ethics with De Baets, cfr. infra.

[24]Hand, as n. 2, 50, 57–58. As we shall see this has become legally possible when the US Supreme Court rendered a verdict in *Kumho Tire Co. v. Carmichael* allowing the judge as a gatekeeper to impose certain rules of interpretation concerning expert testimony on the jury. See Part II, Sect. 7.3.6.3. The Daubert Standard: Popper & the Judge as Gatekeeper, cfr. infra.

[25]Foster, as n. 6, 186.

profession, risking his own reputation and that of his colleagues.[26] In conclusion, in spite of the alternatives that have been proposed, the problems with expert witnesses that bothered lawyers and judges more than a hundred years ago have remained relevant today.

7.2 An Introduction to Historians as Expert Witnesses in American Courts

Historians are active as expert witnesses in a rising number of cases in a wide variety of subjects. Especially since the 1950s, historians have become active in various legal proceedings.[27] The first instances where historians were involved in litigation were civil rights cases, such as the *Brown v. Board of Education* case from 1954. Although no historian appeared as a witness at the trial, historians were involved as consultants. Another important case is the *Equal Opportunity Commission v. Sears, Roebuck and Co.* from 1984, in which two historians took to the stand for opposing parties. Both Brown and Sears are the most famous examples of interaction in the American courtroom of law and history. Both cases are generally referred to when American historians discuss the subject of expert witnessing in the US. Yet there are many more examples. Historians have been experts in litigation concerning creationism,[28] industrial pollution,[29] land rights of indigenous peoples,[30] superfund site research,[31] water rights of indigenous peoples,[32] voting rights,[33] tobacco tort

---

[26]Edmond, as n. 6, 145.

[27]Rothman, Hal. 1993. Historian v. Historian: Interpreting the Past in the Courtroom. *The Public Historian* 15, 39.

[28]Bolton, Charles. 1982. The Historian as Expert Witness: Creationism in Arkansas. *The Public Historian* 4, 59–67.

[29]Quivik, Frederic. 2004. Of Tailings, Superfund Litigation, and Historians as Experts: *U.S. v. Asarco, et al.* (the Bunker Hill Case in Idaho). *The Public Historian* 26, 81–104. & Rothman, as n. 27, 39–53.

[30]Rothman, as n. 27, 39–53. & See the Complex Litigation blog of Frederic Joseph Aaronson LCC http://www.josephnyc.com/blog/?blogID=372. & http://josephnyc.com/blog/?blogID=1239. Accessed 31 Oct 2014.

[31]Cantelon, Philip, Ryan, Henry, Stern, Carole, and Gagen, Joseph. 1991. Performing a Superfund Site History: Time and Money Well Spent. *Toxics Law Reporter*, 595–600.

[32]See Historian Michael Brescia's account on http://www.statemuseum.arizona.edu/research/historian_as_expert_witness.shtml. Accessed 31 Oct 2014.

[33]Kousser, as n. 10, 5–19. & Neuenschwander, John. 2002. Historians as Expert Witnesses: The View from the Bench. *The Organization of American Historians Newsletter* 30. https://archives.iupui.edu/bitstream/handle/2450/6017/A2010_11-016_Box13_OAH_Vol30No3_August2002.pdf?sequence=2. Accessed 31 Oct 2014.

litigation,[34] historical jurisdiction over rivers,[35] lead paint poisoning toxic tort litigation,[36] other consumer product tort litigation, and many more issues. I first examine the Brown and Sears cases because of their significance to the American experience of the interaction between law and history. After which, I discuss a case where historians have testified as experts in lead paint poisoning toxic tort litigation to give an example of a general and normal practice of expert witnessing in the US. In a third part, I describe the practical steps a historian goes through as an expert witness in preparation of his or her expert report and court testimony.

7.2.1 *Brown v. Board of Education*

The Brown case is commonly referred to as landmark case of the US Supreme court from 1954. A young black girl named Linda Brown, was not allowed to enrol in a public school just around the corner of her home. Because of that, the child had to go to a black public school more than a mile away. The issue was taken to court. The lower courts ruled that this was constitutional, following the then accepted legal standard of "separate but equal" education.[37] The US Supreme Court's revolutionary ruling on the case considered state sponsored segregation in public schools to be unconstitutional under the Fourteenth Amendment.[38] The court ruled unanimously –9 to 0- in favour of the upheaval of the *de jure* racial segregation.[39] Brown is often seen as one of the moments that sparked the mass civil rights movement of the 1950s and 1960s.[40]

The case was rife with historical argumentations, although no historian took the stand. Historians were only active as consultants in the case. Historian Alfred H. Kelly, at the time a professor of history at Wayne State University, played an important role in the construction of the historical narrative of the US Supreme Court's decision in Brown. Under the elegant title "*Clio and the Court: An Illicit Love Affair*", Kelly reported his experiences as a consultant for *the National*

---

[34] See part III of this book, cfr. infra.

[35] Becker, Carl. 1982. Professor for the Plaintiff: Classroom to Courtroom. *The Public Historian* 4, 68–77. & Soifer, Paul. 1983. The Litigation Historian: Objectivity, Responsibility, and Sources. *The Public Historian* 5, 47–62. Both were experts on the same case; namely *The Miami Conservancy District v. Alexander*. They witnessed for opposing sides.

[36] Rosner, David, and Markowitz, Gerald. 2009. The Trials and Tribulations of Two Historians: Adjudicating Responsibility for Pollution and Personal Harm. *Medical History* 53, 271–292.

[37] Petrovic, Vladimir. 2009. Historians as Expert Witnesses in the Age of Extremes, 152. http://www.etd.ceu.hu/2009/hphpcv01.pdf. Accessed 31 Oct 2014.

[38] Petrovic, as n. 37, 153–154.

[39] Petrovic, as n. 37, 166. & For the verdict in *Brown v. Board of Education* see http://www.law.cornell.edu/supremecourt/text/344/141. Accessed 31 Oct 2014.

[40] Petrovic, as n. 37, 150–151.

Association for the Advancement of Colored People.[41] Kelly begins his essay with a historical overview of the instances the US Supreme Court used history to legitimate its decisions, by interpreting the US Constitution as a historical document as early as the year 1787–the same year the US constitution had been drafted.[42] This created a sort of law-office history, whose relevance was decided by judicial fiat, and thus according to the legal or political needs of the judges which shifted from time to time.[43] History is used by the US Supreme Court "to maintain rather than break constitutional continuity", Kelly wrote.[44] When the court diverts from the precedent, it can simply argue that it has "rediscovered" the true meaning of the constitution just as "the Fathers proclaimed."[45]

The Brown case was no different, Kelly writes. The NAACP filed an *amicus curiae brief* which was "a piece of highly selective and carefully prepared law-office history."[46] The brief "manipulated history in the best tradition of American advocacy, carefully marshalling every possible scrap of evidence in favour of the desired interpretation and just as carefully doctoring all the evidence to the contrary, either by suppressing it when that seemed plausible, or by distorting it when suppression was not possible."[47] Kelly admitted that "his professional integrity was in conflict with his personal feelings about a burning political issue."[48] Another historian, C. Vann Woodward also played an important role in drafting the NAACP's brief.[49] The NAACP's brief directly influenced the court's decision in Brown.[50] Kelly concluded that "[t]he object of this process is not objective truth, historical or otherwise, but advocacy, i.e. the assertion of a client's interests."[51] Kelly's account is a disturbing example of how historical consultancy can fall into the trap of advocacy. However understandable in Kelly's, Vann Woodward's, and Franklin's case and how comprehensible their motives were, their role signifies the power of historical distortion in court.[52] The Brown case is a clear example of advocacy, of

[41]Kelly, Alfred. 1962. An Inside Story: When the Supreme Court Ordered Desegregation. *U.S. News & World Report* 5, 86–88.

[42]Kelly, Alfred. 1965. Clio and the Court: An Illicit Love Affair. *The Supreme Court Review*, 119–120.

[43]Kelly, as n. 42, 122–123.

[44]Kelly, as n. 42, 127.

[45]Kelly, as n. 42, 129.

[46]Kelly, as n. 42, 144.

[47]Kelly, as n. 42, 144.

[48]Soifer, as n. 35, 51–52.

[49]Franklin, John. 2004. To and from Brown v. Board of Education. *Washington History* 16, 12. John Franklin was the third historian working with the NAACP for *Brown v. Board of Education.*

[50]Kelly, as n. 42, 155.

[51]Kelly, as n. 42, 156.

[52]For an extended read on the Brown case by a Pulitzer prize-winning author see: Kluger, Richard. 2004. *Simple Justice. The History of Brown v. Board of Education and Black America's Struggle for Equality*. New York: Vintage.

historical research without peer review or publication, of open partisanship, and of a historian inspired by his own morality, but without adhering to the ethics of professional historical research. Despite all those reservations, Petrovic writes that the Brown case was an important moment for "the legitimization of historians' legal contribution."[53] The danger of justifying this kind of abuse of history through historical consulting for the "right" moral ethics, lies in the fact that the "right" moral ethics represent a very loosely defined term which can as easily be used by a racist as by civil rights activists. It is therefore important that historians, certainly those active in consulting, are subjected to a minimum of ethical rules through an ethical code.[54]

7.2.2 *Equal Employment Opportunity Commission v. Sears, Roebuck and Co.*

The case brought in 1984 against Sears, a big American retail company, by the Equal Employment Opportunity Commission [EOOC], accused Sears of conducting a female unfriendly employment policy on a national level. The EEOC argued that the low number of females, who held high sales positions with a commission in the company, was a consequence of the sexual discrimination policies conducted within Sears. The procedures took several years, from 1984 till 1986. In the end Sears was acquitted.[55]

Both parties hired the services of a historian as an expert witnesses. The defence recruited theoretical historian Rosalind Rosenberg. The plaintiff needed its own expert to counter Rosenberg's testimony and enlisted historian and feminist Alice Kessler-Harris to their cause.[56] In her personal account, Kessler-Harris writes that she was asked to "rebut her [Rosenberg's] testimony."[57] Rosenberg based her testimony on the research of other scholars, among them that of Kessler-Harris. Kessler-Harris herself, in contrast, based her testimony predominantly on her own research.[58] Rosenberg argued that it was natural for women to be less attracted to stressful and very demanding jobs.[59] To Kessler-Harris the argument

---

[53]Petrovic, as n. 37, 170.

[54]I refer to Part III, Sect. 14.4. Confronting Ethics with De Baets, cfr. infra.

[55]Hall, Jacquelyn, and Cooper, Sandi. 1986. Women's History Goes to Trial: EEOC v. Sears, Roebuck and Company. *Signs*, 11, 753–756. & Milkman, Ruth. 1986. Women's History and the Sears Case. *Feminist Studies* 12, 380.

[56]Jellison, Katherine. 1987. History in the Courtroom: The Sears Case in Perspective. *The Public Historian* 9, 9–10.

[57]Kessler-Harris, Alice. 1987. Equal Employment Opportunity Commission v. Sears, Roebuck and Company: A Personal Account. *Feminist Review* 25, 46.

[58]Milkman, as n. 55, 376. & Jellison, as n. 56, 11.

[59]For the written testimony of Rosenberg see Hall and Cooper, as n. 55, 757–766.

Rosenberg made was a self-fulfilling prophecy. Kessler-Harris maintained that only a discrimination policy within Sears could account for the lack of women in corporate top functions.[60] The Sears case soon became cause for controversy in the historical community. The discussion escalated onto a national level, "with articles in *The New York Times* and editorials in *The Washington Post*."[61] The debate was twofold according to historian Katherine Jellison: the first issue was that the testimony of Rosenberg was, to some historians, an immoral act that harmed the feminist movement; the second problem concerned the general role of the historian as an expert in the courtroom.[62]

When the trial had finished and the verdict had been rendered, both experts had different ideas about testifying in court. Kessler-Harris became a severe critic of the historian's role in the courtroom. She especially had objections to the capacity of the judge to use her historical research in whatever way he liked. Testifying was too political and was ultimately about utilitarian purposes, according to Kessler-Harris.[63] Historian Ruth Milkman who discussed the Sears case, argued that historians should be "self-conscious in their formulations, keeping firmly in view the ways in which their work can be exploited politically."[64] Rosenberg, by contrast, accepted expert witnessing as a valuable activity for historians. "Historical truth and morality had a place in the courtroom", Rosenberg argued. Furthermore, she gave a counterargument to Kessler-Harris' objections by stating that: "the political implications of expert testimony differ little from those of historical scholarship in general."[65]

The Sears case had a "profound impact on the outlook of historical expert witnessing in the United States."[66] The case raised questions about the use and abuse of history in court. Some historians argued that historians should refuse to testify in court, to prevent the distortion of history because of the "improbability of being faithful to both the demands of their profession and the needs of the lawyer calling on them to testify."[67] Especially the "objectivity question" was discussed at length. How could historians "remain dispassionate observers of historical truth despite their participation in legal proceedings?"[68] In general, the Sears case and the controversy that surrounded it had made historians aware of the dangers of testifying in court.

---

[60]Novick, Peter. 1998. *That Noble Dream. The "Objectivity Question" and the American Historical Profession.* New York: Cambridge University Press, 502–510. & Kessler-Harris, as n. 57, 53–54, 56–62. For Kessler-Harris' written testimony see Hall and Cooper, as n. 55, 767–779.

[61]Kessler-Harris, as n. 57, 46, 50–51.

[62]Jellison, as n. 56, 12–17. & Kessler-Harris, as n. 57, 46, 50–51.

[63]Kessler-Harris, as n. 57, 64–66. & quoted in Jellison, as n. 56, 18.

[64]Milkman, as n. 55, 394–395.

[65]Quoted in Jellison, as n. 56, 18–19.

[66]Petrovic, as n. 37, 199.

[67]Quoted in Petrovic, as n. 37, 199.

[68]Rosner and Markowitz, as n. 36, 275.

7.2.3 Toxic Tort Litigation: Lead Paint Toxic Tort Litigation

In an article with the alliterative title: *The Trials and Tribulations of Two Historians,* David Rosner and Gerald Markowitz describe their experiences during two trials, in 2005 and 2007, as expert witnesses on lead paint.[69] The litigation concentrated on the question whether the lead paint industry knew they sold a toxic product to their customers and if so, when they became aware of this. If the industry had continued to sell a product they knew constituted a health hazard, the lead paint companies could be held liable for negligence. Historians were hired to determine exactly when the companies became aware of the danger of their products.[70] For Rosner and Markowitz their experience was as much a personal as a professional experience. When confronted with the gratitude of the victims they defended, the historians wrote: "It made us realize that history does matter."[71]

Their work in the archives produced a book, entitled *Deceit and Denial: the Deadly Politics of Industrial Pollution.*[72] The book discussed the role of the lead paint industry in creating a public health tragedy. The book was based "literally on hundreds of thousands of pages of company documents."[73] Amongst them many internal documents of the industry which had become available because of the lawsuits.[74]

The history of lead poisoning presented in court by Rosner and Markowitz did not only provoke discussion about the facts of the case but also about the historical métier itself. Both experts were attacked by lawyers of opposing counsel for not being objective.[75] Furthermore, there were discussions about the epistemological status of historical facts.[76] Lawyers tried several tactics which have been termed as tactics of "agnotology" by historian and expert witness in tobacco trials Robert Proctor. Agnotology is the study of misleading and providing inaccurate information to create doubt and ignorance about veritable knowledge.[77] The defence counsel used such tactics to convince the jury and the judge that the lead paint industry was not aware of the dangers of their product, although scientific research had

[69]Both have testified in cases on lead paint and silicosis litigation.

[70]Wiener, Jon. 2005. Cancer, Chemicals and History. *The Nation*, February 7. Via http://www.thenation.com/article/cancer-chemicals-and-history. Accessed 31 Oct 2014.

[71]Rosner and Markowitz, as n. 36, 279–280. Toxic tort cases on lead paint have many things in common with tobacco litigation which I discuss in part III of my research.

[72]Another book of Rosner and Markowitz, which was also based on their trial research, is *Deadly Dust*, which discusses the history on silicosis, commonly known as miners' asthma.

[73]Rosner and Markowitz, as n. 36, 282.

[74]Rosner and Markowitz, as n. 36, 282. The same has happened in tobacco litigation. See Part III, Chap. 13 Tobacco Litigation, cfr. infra.

[75]Rosner and Markowitz, as n. 36, 275–276.

[76]Rosner and Markowitz, as n. 36, 288–291.

[77]I discuss this further in part III of my research, see Part III, Sect. 13.4.3. Game III: The Third Wave of Tobacco Litigation. & Sect. 14.2.1.1. Deposition, cfr. infra.

already proven that lead paint was unhealthy. The only goal for the defence was to prove there was "doubt" about the certainty of the scientific evidence linking lead paint and disease. If there had been doubt, the industry would have been able to avoid its liability. Historians Rosner and Markowitz were hired to testify that there was no controversy and that the industry had continued to sell their dangerous product despite of the scientific evidence. Rosner and Markowitz had played an important role in the trail to prove that the lead paint industry had been negligent.

A very vocal opponent of Rosner and Markowitz is the New York-based lawyer and experienced toxic tort litigator Nathan Schachtman.[78] In an article which also had an alliterative title; *On Deadly Dust and Histrionic Historians*, Schachtman discussed what he called: "[t]he intrusion of historians into the litigation process."[79] Schachtman's article accuses the historical report of Rosner and Markowitz of being: "tendentious" and "devoid of any empirical support."[80] To him both historians were "advocates and agents of chance" by expressing "biased viewpoints."[81] Schachtman's main argument is that "historians will usually be inappropriate witnesses because they do not contribute anything beyond what trial lawyers may accomplish through competent proofs and argument to the trier of fact."[82] He continues this idea further on his blog where he titles one text concerning historian's expert witnesses as follows: "How testifying historians are like lawn-mowing dogs."[83] Schachtman elaborates on his title as follows: "[a]n historian testifying as an expert witness is a bit like a dog cutting your lawn – You don't care whether the dog mows in a straight line, or cuts too high or too low, or even whether the dog rakes up after cutting. Dogs should not be cutting the grass at all."[84] He continues with the following after Rosner and Markowitz had addressed his accusations in several academic articles: "Caution! Suggesting that historians should not serve as expert witnesses may cause the dog to bite."[85] However entertaining the article and certainly the blog posts by Schachtman may be, his opinion represents

[78]Mr. Schachtman maintains a blog on his website see http://schachtmanlaw.com/blog. Accessed 31 Oct 2014. Schachtman is also a lecturer at law at Columbia Law School in New York.

[79]Schachtman, Nathan. 2003. On Deadly Dust And Histrionic Historians: Preliminary Thoughts On History And Historians As Expert Witnesses In Products Liability Cases. *Mealey's Litigation Report: Silica* 2, 2.

[80]Schachtman, as n. 79, 1.

[81]Schachtman, as n. 79, 2–3.

[82]Schachtman, as n. 79, 2.

[83]Schachtman, Nathan. 2010. How Testifying Historians are Like Lawn-Mowing dogs. http://schachtmanlaw.com/how-testifying-historians-are-like-lawn-mowing-dogs. Accessed 31 Oct 2014.

[84]Schachtman, as n. 83.

[85]Schachtman, as n. 83.

the general way lawyers think about historians as expert witnesses.[86] Lawyers need historical facts to strengthen their rhetoric, and the historical profession is presented as having a fact finding objective and as a positivist enterprise, which legitimates the historical facts lawyers need.[87] When they do not need historical argumentation, lawyers argue to keep history out of the courtroom. Schachtman goes even further and suggests that lawyers without any historical training or experience can do the job of the historian.

After reviewing earlier versions of this book Schachtman wrote a new blog post responding to my discussion of the topic of historians as expert witnesses.[88] In his piece *Historical Histortions,* another alliterative title, Schachtman elaborates further on his overall stance on historians serving as expert witnesses. In reaction to my claim that he suggests that lawyers can do the job of historians he notes the following:

> "Given their training and skills in documenting and recounting narratives, lawyers do, indeed, often do the job of historians, and they often do it very well. Of course, lawyers are often guided, inspired, and assisted by professional historians. Sometimes that guidance is necessary. Lawyers' narratives, unlike historians', are also subject to judicial control in the form of evidentiary rules about speculation, relevance, reliability, authentication, and trustworthiness."[89]

Furthermore, Schachtman confirmed he did not think that the skill sets for the two disciplines were so different.[90] Yet Schachtman nuanced his position when he wrote that: "Ramses Delafontaine is wrong, however, to opine that my rants against Rosner and Markowitz suggest that I have ruled out any role for historians in litigation."[91] Schachtman gives an example from *In re: Welding Rod Prods. Liab. Litig.*, a case on welding fume in which historian Lisa K. Walker served as an expert witness and played a positive role according to Schachtman. Having fortified his position with more case law Schachtman concludes in favour of a limited use of expert witnesses to present historical narratives in judicial proceedings.[92]

---

[86]See also a more post by Schachtman: Schachtman, Nathan. 2010. Courting Clio: Historians and Their Testimony in Products Liability Litigation. http://schachtmanlaw.com/courting-clio-historians-and-their-testimony-in-products-liability-litigation. Accessed 31 Oct 2014. & Schachtman, Nathan. 2010. Counter Narratives for Hire. http://schachtmanlaw.com/counter-narratives-for-hire. Accessed 31 Oct 2014. & Schachtman, Nathan. 2010. Narratives & Historians for Hire. http://schachtmanlaw.com/narratives-historians-for-hire. Accessed 31 Oct 2014. I spoke earlier of these generalizations used by legal practitioners and historians to depict each other in Part I, Chap. 2: Introductory Theoretical Remarks on the Alleged Problematic Nature of the Interaction of History and Law, cfr. supra.

[87]Rosner and Markowitz, as n. 36, 286.

[88]Schachtman, Nathan. 2014. Hysterical Histortions. http://schachtmanlaw.com/hysterical-histortions. Accessed 31 Oct 2014.

[89]Schachtman, as n. 88.

[90]Personal correspondence with the author.

[91]Schachtman, as n. 88.

[92]Schachtman, as n. 88.

Rosner and Markowitz were not only challenged by Schachtman, they were also personally harassed by the chemical companies they witnessed against. Their book *Deceit and Denial* was subpoenaed as well as every reviewer of it, demanding that they turned over all the documents they had used in preparing their book.[93] The all-out attack by the industry provoked reactions from the academic world. Wilthey, director of University of California Press at the time, declared that she had never heard of reviewers being subpoenaed before.[94] In *The Nation*, historian Jon Wiener wrote an article on the attacks on Rosner and Markowitz. His piece begins as follows: "Twenty of the biggest chemical companies in the United States have launched a campaign to discredit two historians who have studied the industry's efforts to conceal links between their products and cancer."[95] The expert who was recruited by the industry, historian Philip Scranton of the Rutgers University, claimed that *Deceit and Denial* did not live up to professional expectations.[96] Scranton accused Rosner and Markowitz of having "violated the AHA's and NCPH's guidelines in six specific areas."[97] Legal attempts to silence and limit the freedom of research of historians who work as expert witnesses are not limited to Rosner and Markowitz, as we shall see when discussing tobacco litigation.[98]

The "trials and tribulations" of Rosner and Markowitz expose the risks historians take when they testify in court. Their experience also shows that professional historical investigation can prove historical facts, even beyond a reasonable doubt, and defend itself against close scrutiny. Transparency, making research documents available, publication of research, peer review, and so forth are the parameters to test whether historians have conducted their research in a professional manner. Rosner and Markowitz succeeded in making it possible for their peers to review their work. They published a book on their research, *Deceit and Denial*, which has its own website with extra and easy accessible information.[99] Furthermore, the litigation has made many internal industry documents researchable, not only for the expert witnesses themselves but also for other researchers.[100] The free accessibility

---

[93]Rosner and Markowitz, as n. 36, 284.

[94]Guterman, Lila. 2004. Peer Reviewers are Subpoenaed in Cancer Lawsuit Against Chemical Companies. *The Chronicle of Higher Education*, November 19.

[95]Wiener, as n. 70.

[96]Rosner and Markowitz, as n. 36, 289. & Wiener, as n. 70.

[97]Rosner, David, and Markowitz, Gerald. 2004. The Chemical Industry's Attack on Historians. *George Mason University's History News Network*, December 5. http://hnn.us/articles/8730.html. Accessed 31 Oct 2014. Scraton has been on the payroll of the tobacco industry at least since 2002, when his affiliation with Japan Tobacco had been uncovered after he had written a pamphlet attacking the WHO anti-tobacco campaign. According to the *British Medical Journal*, Scranton had told "Japan Tobacco that he was good value for money." See Kmietowicz, Zosia, and Ferriman, Annabel. 2002. Pro-Tobacco Writer Admits He Should Have Declared an Interest. *BMJ* 324, 257.

[98]See Part III, Sect. 15.6. The Tobacco Companies v. Robert Proctor, cfr. infra.

[99]See http://www.deceitanddenial.org. Accessed 31 Oct 2014.

[100]See the database with the Chemical Industry's Archives http://www.chemicalindustryarchives.org/search/default.asp?stemming=Yes&cmd=start&request=&i=vinyl&search=GO. Accessed 31 Oct 2014.

of documents, publications of research results, and peer review allows other historians and researchers to consider if Rosner's and Markowitz's testimony was objective. This kind of control from within the historical discipline or intersubjective objectivity, can only be provided if expert witnesses let other historians review their work and their sources, something that is not always the case as we shall see when discussing the expert witnesses who are hired by tobacco companies.

7.3 A Guide to the Practice of Expert Witnessing by Historians

In this topic I give a short overview of the consecutive steps taken by historians before they testify in court. By discussing the way historians prepare for court, we can better understand the construction of historical knowledge in the courtroom. The different phases that are analysed are: consulting, recruitment of the expert witness, and the preparation of the expert report. Furthermore, I discuss the interactions between historians and lawyers. I also analyse three possible ways in which historians can testify in court, namely through direct testimony, cross-examination, and a possible redirect. After which, I discuss the rules of evidence that are applicable to expert testimony. Examining how these rules have developed and why, will enable us to understand how expert testimony is currently defined in the legal discipline.

This chapter is based on a wide array of articles from legal scholars as well as historians. I chiefly discuss personal accounts from historians who have testified as expert witnesses in American courts. In addition, certain phases of the expert witnessing experience are based on unpublished information, on presentations that were given at the session on litigation-driven history at the NCPH conference in Ottawa in April 2013, and furthermore on personal information obtained through informal sources. Not much is published on the pre-trial phases. This is because lawyers try to minimize the paper trail, since there is a risk that opposing counsel will subpoena a document that was used to prepare the expert report. This legal concern creates "grey-zones" in the expert witnessing practice, yet through personal accounts I have been able to present a minimal framing of these interactions. This practical introduction to expert witnessing, allows us to further determine the influences or restraints the legal environment has on historical research and discourse. The chronology of expert witnessing will also serve to better understand the role historians play as expert witnesses in tobacco litigation.

7.3.1 Consulting

Consulting is the first step in the litigation process. In most cases where history comes to court, historians are active as consultants. Only in a small number of cases do historians actually testify. For example, the historian Alfred Kelly, as we mentioned earlier when we discussed *Brown v. Board of Education*, played a very important role in the case, but solely as a consultant not as an expert witness.[101] Generally, historians or specialized companies are contacted to collect and organize documents for a case. The criteria by which the selection of relevant documents is done, is often not made by the consultants themselves, but by lawyers or by the historical expert who is going to testify. The job of historical consultants is thus to find and list documents that answer to the criteria demanded by their client. Furthermore, the consultant also constructs a basic chronology of the historical events that are important to the trial. When original documents cannot be brought to court, they have to be scanned. Original files have to be copied numerous times, because adding labels, like a number or a code, to the documents is considered problematic by legal counsel. Consultants should always have original copies at their disposal. The court demands original and primary documents as evidence. Labels distort such authenticity.

Concurrently set up with the research for primary documentation are databases which contain primary documents digitalized and directly linked with other databases which contain the characteristics of the documents or other historical relevant information for the litigators. Those characteristics are, among others: the physical location, the author(s), the date, and the physical constitution of the document. To make it easier for their clients to use the databases and select important historical material, historical consultants use key words, tombstone information [which contains information on the document], digital colour labelling, and, if necessary, a small synthesis is added. Furthermore, each source also has a unique entry in the database. This systematic handling of documentation makes it easy for clients to rapidly access any possible information on a document, allowing them to reference each document easily in their witness report or legal argumentation. Databases can also show gaps in the historical research, and therefore have the ability to prevent inconsistencies in the witness report. It is also an easy basis for drafting the obligatory affidavits, which list the historical documents witnesses or lawyers are going to use in court. Historical consulting happens in a digital world. Digital compatibility with the clients, to prevent the loss of information, is also very important.

Stuart Manson, the president of Public History Inc., a Canadian historical consulting firm, argued that consulting was a specific kind of historical research.[102] In the exposé he gave at the conference on Public History in Ottawa in April 2013 under the title *Knowing Your Public in Litigation Research: Specialized Client Requirements and Products, Mr. Mason explained the manner in which his product is created.*[103] The consultant gets his order from the client to look for historical

[101] See Part II, Sect. 7.2.1. Brown v. Board of Education, cfr. supra.

[102] The website of Public History Inc. can be visited via http://www.publichistory.ca. Accessed 31 Oct 2014.

[103] Mr. Mason gave his presentation on April 19, 2013 at the annual meeting of the National Council on Public History in Ottawa. Based on notes of the author.

documents on a subject. The client can give extra parameters like a date or an author for example. The only thing the consultant does is selecting the documents that fulfil the prerequisites demanded by the client. These selected historical sources are the product of historical consulting. Mason argued *that his product was very objective, since the* digital client-historian-product relationship exists with almost no decision making by the historians who do the research. Manson declared that historical consulting is a format unlike historical writing, very forward and direct, with a high standard of objectivity and impartiality, because their product was very well referenced and without interference in the research of the personal preferences of the consultant.

The comment above shows how dominant traditional objectivity still is with historians and lawyers. Notwithstanding the fact that Mr. Mason's company will probably deliver top-notch historical work, which will indeed enable clients to build a very well referenced historical argumentation, their product is only objective in a certain positivist meaning of the word. There is already a subjective and very definitive choice when the client demands a selection of certain historical sources to construct his narrative. Thereby, the client will demand only those sources that best fit his arguments. Furthermore, the client-consult relationship is not one-sided. An historical consultant advises lawyers on which sources will best suit their argument and which documents have the most historical authority. All of these decisions have a very distinct influence on the end-product. Consulting, as any other form of historical knowledge production, is subjective and can only be kept in check with the implementation of ethical codes. Traditional Rankean objectivity remains, to some, not only an intellectual point of view, but is even stressed as a selling point.[104]

7.3.2 Recruitment of the Expert Witness

Another intriguing stage in the historian's road to court is his recruitment by clients, mostly law firms. I make a distinction between historical firms which offer expert witnesses and historians who are hired as an individual. Most individual historians, who are not connected to a firm, are academics, but many academics are also employed at historical firms. On the one hand, these academic historians are enlisted by law firms for their erudition, impressive scholarship, and publications on the subject; in short: expert knowledge. On the other hand, high social standing and the fame of their institutions definitely plays a dominant role as well when recruiting experts. This is a point of criticism on the expert witnessing system. Another issue is that high profile experts demand big pay checks.[105] This becomes problematic

[104] See Part I, Sect. 3.1.1. The Ghost of von Ranke, cfr. infra.

[105] See Expert Witness Profile No. 10, Elizabeth Cobbs Hoffman. & See Expert Witness Profile No. 14, Peter English. & See Expert Witness Profile No. 20, Jon Harkness. & See Expert Witness Profile No. 30, Kenneth Ludmerer. & See Expert Witness Profile No. 31, James Kirby Martin. &

for the equal arms principle in litigation. A party can be faced with a serious disadvantage, when they lack the resources to hire an authority on the historical subject that plays an important role in the litigation, while the other party does have those means. Judges and jury alike are more impressed by an academic from Yale or Harvard than from a small local university. This censure is judgmental, yet the same is true for hiring lawyers. New York or Chicago based law firms have more means and experience than a local law firm. Big law firms have dozens of aids and highly qualified lawyers. Top lawyers have a great advantage since their efficiency is high as repeat players. Repeat players are lawyers or law firms who specialize in one specific kind of litigation, for example tort litigation.[106] Expert witnessing, in a way, favours those parties in litigation who are well funded.

But this does not mean a party with limited means cannot hire an expert witness. Some historians will, while others won't, become a hired gun. Historians have their academic careers and reputations to consider, and working for some industries might put those reputations into question with their colleagues. Other historians have ethical reservations about witnessing in general or about testifying in favour of certain individual clients or companies. Historians are sometimes idealistic and join up with the lesser paying side, as we have seen in the previous topic with Rosner and Markowitz and others.[107] Some historians have demands of freedom of research or other preconditions which the client will not be willing to meet. Historians react in very different ways to proposals to testify in court, and every one of them should consider very carefully if they want to take the risk.

The way individual historians are recruited mostly happens through informal networks. Sometimes it can be important that the opposing party does not know that lawyers are looking for expert witnesses. Having a highly esteemed academic historian as an expert witness can be a big asset in court, especially when the opposing party has not bothered to bring their own expert witnesses. Furthermore, expert witnesses have to be trustworthy. In the preliminary tactical conversations, the historian might become disillusioned or might disagree with the tactics of counsel

See Expert Witness Profile No. 36, Robert Norrell. & See Expert Witness Profile No. 39, Robert Proctor. & See Expert Witness Profile No. 40, Randy Roberts. See Expert Witness Profile No. 42, David Sansing. & See Expert Witness Profile No. 44, Michael Schaller. & See Expert Witness Profile No. 50, Theodore Wilson. All these historians have acknowledged to have made more than $500,000 for their work as an expert witness in tobacco litigation. See Appendix II, Table 6. Remuneration, cfr. infra.

[106]Lawyer T. Grossman is good example of such a repeat player. He has defended tobacco companies on multiple times in court and has been listed in *the Chambers USA guide* to leading lawyers of 2012 in tobacco defence, see his website at http://www.jonesday.com/tgrossman. Accessed 31 Oct 2014. Grossman is a partner in the Jones Day law firm, which has been hired on multiple occasions by tobacco companies. See the work of American legal scholar Marc Galanter on the subject of repeat players. Galanter, Marc. 1974. Why the "Haves" Come Out Ahead: Speculations on the Limits of Legal Change. *Law & Society Review* 9, 95–160.

[107]We will examine other examples in the third part of my research when I discuss historians who are involved in tobacco litigation. See Part III, Chap. 16: Historians in Tobacco Litigation, a Conclusion, cfr. infra.

and withdraw his or her participation. Some historians will demand these talks before actually committing. Although they will try not to, lawyers will have to give the historian in question a sneak peak at their legal strategy, and how they wish to incorporate the historical argumentation. All of this revolves around historians being contacted through their personal networks, certainly in high profile cases. The fact that this recruitment happens very informally and through personal e-mail and telephone conversations, makes the recruitment phase of expert witnesses very hard to research.

In contrast to the informally recruited historians, others have made expert witnessing into a full-time job. There are historians who can simply be hired from the net.[108] Although it is hard to determine how frequently this happens. Some historians work individually as consultants, but most have found work in firms or have founded their own small firms that offer historical consultation or expert witnessing. In contrast to my previous example, Public History Inc., most companies combine ligation-driven historical research and expert witnessing. Historical Associates Incorporated (HAI), a firm that offers historical research and analyses for litigation, is an example of the latter.[109] Most of the published articles on their website read as marketing advertisements.[110] This is not surprising because historical consulting firms are part of the free market. They have to compete with other companies and stress their selling points. Another example comes from historian David Rosner, whom I mentioned earlier.[111] He received "an odd e-mail" from "the Round Table Group", a consulting firm that specialized in providing experts from various disciplines for testimony in court. The company sought to add historians to their "consortium of several thousand professors."[112]

It is interesting to examine how these firms praise the value of historical testimony in court. History Associates Inc. points to three key advantages of working with historians as expert witnesses. The first is the ability of historians to find critical historical information. An article from Reis and Wiseman, two historians who work at HAI, describes this benefit as follows: "[f]rom the beginning of the litigation process, professional historians can assist lawyers in framing the historical issues central to prosecuting or defending a claim and can assist counsel by serving as an early warning system if the historical facts do not comport with a lawyer's theory of

[108]See, for example, the site of the Round Table Group which contacted David Rosner: http://www.roundtablegroup.com/experts. Accessed 31 Oct 2014. The group has now merged with two other companies: Silicon Valley Expert Witness Group and Jury Verdict Research. They now form the Thomson Reuters Expert Witness Services. There new website is https://trexpertwitness.com. Accessed 31 Oct 2014.

[109]The website of History Associates Inc. can be found at http://www.historyassociates.com/services/historical-research. Accessed 31 Oct 2014.

[110]For a list of their articles http://www.historyassociates.com/services/historical-research/historical-research-articles-and-presentations. Accessed 31 Oct 2014.

[111]See Part II, Sect. 7.2.3. Toxic Tort Litigation: Lead Paint Toxic Tort Litigation, cfr. supra.

[112]Rosner and Markowitz, as n. 36, 273.

a case."[113] Such a modus operandi is not compatible with positivist objectivity, yet that objectivity still remains a selling point. The statement that: "[h]istorians pursue objectivity", is amply used by Reis and Wiseman.[114] The second selling point is thus that historians present authentic facts. Lastly, according to History Associates Inc., historians know how to synthesize historic information into well-documented and compelling stories. In conclusion, according to the article, historians deliver a reliable and convincing history. Historians "are trained to convey their findings within the defined scope of their research in plain language and to defend those findings under close scrutiny. Professional historians are well qualified to serve as consulting and testifying experts", Reis and Wiseman argue.[115] Another article by historian Michael Reis praises the skills of the historian to "locate smoking guns when others can't."[116] For Reis it was clear that: "[h]istorians unearth and make sense of the relevant past in the hunt for the evidence that shapes and sometimes makes the case."[117]

This commercially inspired discourse is normal in public history, but may seem strange to academic historians. Consequently, questions arise about historians who become hired guns and public historians who abuse history to fit the needs of their customers.[118] Therefore it is important that universities, historical associations, and the consulting firms themselves adopt ethical codes. The most important players are the historical associations and the universities. They should make sure the codes are generally accepted and enforced. Adhering to such an ethical code should be a precondition for joining any historical association. If the historical community as a whole commits to these basic ethical preconditions of the historical craft, then the historians who won't will be marginalized, leaving them with a distinct disadvantage when competing with historians who have committed to these codes. If these codes are broadly accepted in the historical community and the codes are amply enforced by the historical associations, these codes will be respected by judges, lawyers, and employers alike. Codification of ethical rules is no new idea, other free professions like lawyers and doctors have the same kind of systems to guard their basic ethical rules.[119] Codification and reflection on those rules are a condition sine qua non for successful and professional historical research in the public and academic sphere. Another element that can help to maintain standards of ethical and methodical

---

[113]Reis, Mike, and Wiseman, Dave. 2011. The Historian's Valuable Role as Expert and Advisor in Environmental Litigation. *The Environmental Litigator* 22, 12.

[114]Reis and Wisman, as n. 113, 12.

[115]Reis and Wisman, as n. 113, 13.

[116]Reis, Mike. 2003. Searching in the Past: Dusty Documents that may Prove the Case can be Found by Historians. *Legal Times* 26, 1.

[117]Reis, as n. 116, 2.

[118]I argue that there is a distinct possibility this is happening, as we shall see with the tobacco cases. Without any codified ethical rules in the historical profession or considerable reflection on public history within the academic environment, public history can easily be used and abused.

[119]Novick, as n. 60, 185.

historical research is employment of both public and academic historians as expert witnesses for the same project. Reflection and discussion between academic and public historians can construct and guard a responsible manner in which litigation-driven history can thrive.

7.3.3 Preparing the Witness Report

After the basic stages of consulting and preliminary research, the preparation of the expert report and the testimony begins. Consulting might have been done by a separate firm, but most firms combine both the fact-finding process and the preparation for the testimony. In a presentation entitled *The Closest Scrutiny: Aspects of Researching Native American History,* given at the Annual meeting of the National Council on Public History in Ottawa, in April of 2013, historian Michael Lawson presented the methods used to prepare an expert report.[120] Lawson, who holds a Ph.D. in American history from the University of New Mexico, is a partner at Morgan Angel & Associates, a Washington-based company specializing in litigation-driven history.[121]

Lawson especially stressed the intensive level of scrutiny to which expert reports are subjected, even more than traditional peer review and editorial process in academic contexts. Journals check the style and substance of the text, the reasonability of interpretations and conclusions, and whether the author's sources are properly cited. Review of the actual sources in the footnotes is nothing like traditional academic review, according to Lawson. In the litigation environment, Lawson continued, every word and punctuation mark in an expert report is subject to close scrutiny and may be challenged by opposing counsel and their experts. The same is true for every source cited in a report, since the expert must provide copies of every document or publication cited, as supplementary exhibits. Any mistake made in the text or in a citation has the potential of lessening the expert's credibility or even destroying it.[122] Opposing counsel may argue that if the expert could make one mistake in a report, there may be other mistakes that render the entire report suspect. Knowing your audience is very important in court, realizing that opposing lawyers will do anything to discredit the expert witness or his work has to be kept in mind at all times during the construction of a witness report.

To meet such close scrutiny historical firms like Morgan Angel, have adopted operation manuals with standard procedures to ensure the needed level of

[120]Text of the presentation of Mr. Lawson is with the author.

[121]The website of Morgan Angel & Associates can be reached via http://www.morganangel.com. Accessed 31 Oct 2014.

[122]Colton, Craig. 2006. The Historian's Responsibility in Litigation Support. *The Public Historian* 28, 111.

accuracy.[123] The manual demands that all researchers keep a research log, citing and describing all materials they review, whether they use the documents or not. The company also uses a coding system that requires the encoding of every document on the back of every page, not on the front side because the court sees that as a problem to the authenticity of the document. The code tells the name of the researcher who found the document, the date, and the page number. A secondary encoding consists of the physical location of the document, a complete citation, and a brief description. The advantage of the system is uniformity, easy referencing and fast retrieval of sources when new copies need to be made. All of these data are entered into a secured server which is not linked to the World Wide Web. Every single document is then labelled and scanned into another digital database, which is then linked to a secure database. To ensure compatibility with lawyers' databases and working methodologies, documents are given Bates numbers. The Bates system was designed by Edwin G. Bates in the late nineteenth century in order to promote his invention of the Bates Automatic Numbering Machine. It has since become the standard method used by lawyers to place identifying numbers and/or date/time-stamps on images and documents.[124] Historical firms have to be digitally compatible with their clients. The databases can be researched with specially developed software for full-text searches of sometimes hundreds of thousands of documents. This systematic organization allows the construction of witness reports that can withstand even the harshest scrutiny.

The process by which an expert report is made is divided into different stages. The expert designated to make the report, constructs his testimony using the tools we previously discussed to access primary sources with all relevant information at hand. Footnotes can be directly linked to a digital document, which makes reports more user-friendly for readers in the fact checking process, for lawyers and clients alike. When a draft is finished, two other members of the research staff, who are working on other projects, will go over the report. While one person is reading the report, the other person will check its sources. Not only the sources and citations are checked but also whether the interpretations of the author are reasonable, objective, and credible. Some reports are double checked, each time by different editors. Fact checking of expert reports is a tedious process and might take weeks. The fact checking thus involves dozens of eyes, also those of the client, before the report is finalized.

In general, the historical reports filed in court are extremely well documented and are examples of very thorough and professional historical research, despite the fact that these reports are the products of the interaction of legal counsel and historians,

---

[123] The Operations Manuel of Morgan Angel & Associates is with the author.

[124] For more information on the Bates system, see http://edison.rutgers.edu/NamesSearch/glocpage.php3?gloc=CK300&. Accessed 31 Oct 2014. It is also used in the databases which contain the internal documents of the tobacco industry, and also in those databases that provide depositions and testimonies from tobacco litigation. See Part III, Sect. 13.4.3. Game III: The Third Wave of Tobacco Litigation, cfr. infra.

and are thus constructed to fit legal strategies. Canadian historian and expert witness Arthur Ray eloquently described the practice as: "Ransacking historical documents for useful and relevant documents."[125] Historians are looking for every scrape of evidence they can get their hands on. This juristic pressure ensures that expert reports turn into well referenced documents full of historical evidence. In addition, the expert report becomes a legal document open to scrutiny by opposing counsel. Historians and their firms cannot produce a one-sided product because of the risk of being discredited by opposing counsel and historians. Historical firms need new clients in the future and will therefore not engage in apparent abuse of historical facts. Similarly, the individual historians will not risk losing his professional status, which is his most important marketing asset, by tempering with historic evidence. This kind of reasoning shows that economic issues not always drive public historians "to sell themselves", on the contrary. The prospect of attracting customers in the future is another element that forces expert witnesses to remain within the limits of professional historical research.[126] Should the appliance of ethical codes be enforced by historical associations and universities, then the cost of abusing history in favour of the clients would only increase, resulting in even less abuse or tendency to abuse historical facts. There is no single version of history, there exists no single master narrative; on the contrary, there are many truths in history. If historians disagree in court, that does not mean that one or both of them are abusing history. Based on their historical research, historians come to different conclusions, which may lead them to support one party or the other in a court case. This is how the adversarial system successfully works. Two historical narratives are offered, and in most cases the judge will find that the truth lies somewhere in the middle.

7.3.4 The Collaboration with Lawyers

This part of the expert witnessing process is shrouded in a veil of uncertainty. Lawyers have an important influence on litigation-driven history. Legal counsel wants historical arguments that fit their legal reasoning. It should be the historian's job to stand up to overreaching intrusion by lawyers into the liberty of research of historians and their conclusions on their research. Lawyers and historians begin with "in-depth meetings" to determine a research strategy. Afterwards, they stay in

[125] Comment made at the NCPH conference in Ottawa in April 2013 where Ray presented his topic *The 'Expert is the Evidence:' Theories and Facts as Evidence*. Arthur Ray is professor emeritus of the University of British Columbia who has served in multiple Canadian court cases on native Indian rights as an expert witness.

[126] The precondition is that other historians are aware of their testimony. Peer review should be essential in ethical codes. Otherwise there is little or no repercussion for overstepping professional boundaries in testimony. This is exactly what is happening with historians working as expert witnesses for the tobacco companies in tobacco litigation. See Part III, Sect. 16.3.3. Transparency, cfr. infra.

"close contact" so that "significant discoveries by the historians can be promptly reported" and "changes in the legal strategy are reflected in the research strategy of the historians."[127]

Lawyers refrain as much as possible from using documents, e-mail, faxes, and other means of communications that leave a paper trail, to avoid the risk of being subpoenaed for these documents. Historian Susan Gray, who is an associate professor at the University of Arizona and has served in multiple Great Lakes Indian treaty-rights cases as an expert witness, explained that she "spent hours and hours on the phone with lawyers."[128] Calling is championed over all other means of communication. Keeping written communications and notes to a minimum is an important extralegal strategy.[129]

Other information on the relationship between lawyers and historians is found in personal accounts of expert witnesses. Historian Charles Bolton, who testified as an expert in a case concerning creationism, wrote that lawyers sent him "a pack of documents" to research and that he, in addition, did some research of his own.[130] Historian John Burnham, who served as expert witness for the tobacco industry, reports that "[t]he lawyers decide how to try a case, not the experts."[131] The limited amount of documentation on these interactions is problematic for historians who want to research this important element of the expert witness work, yet it is understandable from a legal point of view.

7.3.5 *Witnessing*

7.3.5.1 The Deposition

When the consulting phase is over and the witness report is finished the historian prepares to defend his report in court. Firstly, the report is filed with the court, so it becomes available for opposing parties.[132] The next step is the deposition. The deposition is an interrogation by opposing counsel of the deposed [the expert witness], who is assisted by his own party's legal counsel. A court reporter [no

---

[127]Cantelon, Ryan, Stern, and Gagen, as n. 31, 596–597.

[128]Informal conversation with the author at the NCPH annual meeting in Ottawa in April 2013. She has served in *US v. Michigan State* as an expert witness. For more information see http://www.justice.gov/enrd/4543.htm. Accessed 31 Oct 2014.

[129]Klein, Robert, Lott, Leslie, and Rojas, Jose. 2007. Expert Witnesses: When Are They Necessary and Does Daubert/Kumho Make a Difference? *IP Litigator* 13, 8.

[130]Bolton, as n. 28, 61.

[131]Burnham, John. 2010. In Defense of Historians as expert Witnesses: A Rebuttal to Jon Wiener. *George Mason University's History News Network*, April 1. http://hnn.us/articles/124924.html. Accessed 31 Oct 2014.

[132]For a short introduction to the legal term of disclosure see http://www.law.cornell.edu/wex/disclosure. Accessed 31 Oct 2014.

judge is present] takes the oath of the deposed and notes everything that is said. The inquiry becomes part of the general trial record. The deposition is part of the discovery process by which each party can obtain evidence from opposing parties. It is meant to gain clarification and additional information. Another goal is to identify weaknesses in the experts' report or their qualifications as an expert. Some depositions can take only a few hours, others may continue for several days. The discourse in a deposition is formal, yet not as technical as testimony on trial. Expert witnesses try and are instructed to answer in clear formulations and in the shortest possible manner to questions by lawyers.

Questioning usually begins with a short introduction by opposing counsel on the rules of the deposition. One of those rules is that the deposed should not try to add meaning to his arguments by hand gestures or facial expressions, because they are not recorded by the trial reporter, even when the deposition is videotaped. Thereafter, the questioning starts. Questions can be asked in a seemingly random order, covering subjects ranging from professional or even personal matters to the expert report itself. Questions can also discuss a single word or a single citation from the witness report. Lines of questioning can be abandoned, to be returned to hours later, when the witness is expected to be tired and bored, and thus more inclined to let down his or her guard.

Testifying is a very stressful time for experts since lawyers try to pinpoint a weak point in the report or the professional reputation of the historian. "They could see how I responded to praise, intimidation, or other approaches and thereby learn what kind of witness I would make in court", wrote historian and expert witness Frederic Quivik.[133] Rosner and Markowitz wrote that they would "never forget [their] first deposition." They believed the whole thing could hardly last "more than a few hours." "But such was not the case." More than 20 lawyers had come to take their deposition at the New York Plaza Hotel:

> Each of us was grilled for several days from nine in the morning to five at night [sic] with defendants' lawyers going into virtually every aspect of our book, from its footnotes to its index and pagination. What were our sources for the statement on, for example, page 45? Could we provide the document that was the basis for the statement on another page? Was one reference to a point enough to "prove" that this quote represented a fair cross-section of the population? What were our credentials? How did we work together? Did we walk through the work together? Where did we live? What languages were spoken in my neighbourhood? Who did we vote for in the last election? Which magazines did we read? What organizations did we belong to? Virtually no aspect of our academic or personal lives was off-bounds in the free-for-all that seemed to have no end.[134]

[133]Quivik, as n. 29, 97. Quivik describes his deposition at 97–98. In Quivik's case, a lawsuit brought by the Department of Justice against Asarco for polluting a river, opposing counsel tried to exclude his testimony claiming that his testimony was "uniformed by any of scientific disciplines that would qualify one to offer a credible expert opinion on the movement of tailings in watershed." See page 98. Quivik's testimony was admitted by the court. See page 99.

[134]Rosner and Markowitz, as n. 36, 278–279.

Defending counsel can aid the historian during the deposition only in a limited number of ways. For example, after a question is asked and before the witness answers, counsel may raise objection to the question. Generally, objection is raised by counsel to advise the expert to answer the question carefully or to show their discontent with the formulation of the question or the subject of the question. Since there is no judge present at the deposition, who can overrule or sustain the objection, the objection is noted by the court reporter and may later be used to exclude certain evidence by a motion *in limine*.[135] It is possible that after the deposition, opposing counsel may try to exclude certain parts of the witness report, or even the entire witness report. In exceptional occasions, opposing counsel tries to exclude an expert witness from testifying.[136] The outcome of several depositions may also lead parties to believe that they have a reasonable idea of how the case is going to play out in court and how it will be judged. According to that belief, parties may wish to settle to avoid further costly litigation.[137]

7.3.5.2 Trial Testimony: Direct Examination, Cross-Examination, and Redirect Examination

If it comes to a trial, the expert witness can be demanded to appear in court to defend his expert report. A historian can be put on the stand as often as three times. The most common one is the direct examination.[138] This is a testimony in which the lawyers of the witness's own party can ask questions which the witness answers, providing historical evidence and argumentation which are in accordance with their own legal strategies.

Another possible instance in which the expert may have to testify is cross-examination. Under cross-examination, the expert witness is questioned by opposing counsel. The main goal for the lawyer is to discredit the expert or his report.[139] To neutralize an unfavourable testimony a lawyer may use any arguments he deems appropriate concerning the historian's professional career and his work. These questions can be inspired by statements made by the expert during the deposition. Lawyers can concentrate on a single citation or word, because one small mistake can be used to discredit the entire work of the historian with the judge or the jury. To undermine a witness's credibility, there are three important strategies. A first tactic is pursued to show the "lacking or questionable qualifications" of the expert witness.

[135] Klein, Lott, and Rojas, as n. 129, 7.

[136] Exclusion of testimony and evidence involves the Federal rules of evidence 401, 402, & 403, see http://www.law.cornell.edu/rules/fre. Accessed 31 Oct 2014. The rules concentrate on the relevance, competence, and probative value of the expert testimony.

[137] For a short introduction to the legal term of the deposition, see: http://www.law.cornell.edu/wex/deposition. Accessed 31 Oct 2014.

[138] Klein, Lott, and Rojas, as n. 129, 7–8.

[139] Klein, Lott, and Rojas, as n. 129, 8.

A second tries to discredit the witness by showing there exists "bias, prejudice or motive" for the expert witness's testimony. A third possibility compares "prior inconsistent statements" made by the witness that are inconsistent with his current expert testimony.[140]

Many historians share a fear of being left open to "complete testimonial evisceration on cross-examination."[141] Historian and expert witness Morgan Kousser remarked that nobody wants to look "foolish or contradictory" on the stand.[142] Expert witness and historian Carl Becker vividly recalls his experience under cross-examination: "I had neglected to read several important pages in the book, and now I was paying the price for sloth!"[143] David Rosner also lived through the cross-examination. He was on the stand for an entire morning. "Numerous objections and challenges were made by the defence attorney as he sought to undermine our book [Deceit and Denial] and David's testimony on behalf of the client. Sentences were picked out of long monologues that David had given in attempts to answer complex questions with answers longer than "yes" or "no". It was a strange experience."[144]

A third possible form of testimony an expert witness can be subjected to is the redirect. Redirect examination offers legal counsel of the expert witness's own side the opportunity to clarify or reformulate damaging arguments that have been brought up in the cross-examination.

The discourse that is used by lawyers and historians during witnessing is legal and formal. Lawyers try to trick historians into answering questions in a way that will be harmful to their own historical report. Historians attempt to answer questions with a simple "yes" or "no", to avoid saying anything that may later be used against them. Lawyers often ask the experts to reformulate their answer, in the hope of confusing them. Legal strategy can also mean a full-out attack on the entire historical profession or on the historical research methods used by the witness. Certainly in jury trials, the manner in which the expert can defend himself and his work against these attacks has a great influence on the overall acceptance by the judge and the jury of the historian's witness report. The transparency of the trial phase of the litigation-driven historical research also assures that advocacy, when met with professional historical reports, can be unmasked as such. Cross-examination is a form of scrutiny that is unthinkable of in the academic environment, but which has, in most litigation, despite the legal discourse and format, been an effective way to identify and ensure extremely well prepared and documented historical reports. Many products of litigation-driven history are considered top-notch works in their fields.

[140]Klein, Lott, and Rojas, as n. 129, 9.

[141]Colton, as n. 122, 112.

[142]Kousser, as n. 10, 16.

[143]Becker, as n. 35, 75.

[144]Rosner and Markowitz, as n. 36, 279.

7.3.6 Rules of Expert Witnessing: From Frye to Daubert

7.3.6.1 The Expert Witness

There is a difference between a normal witnesses and expert witness in legal terms. Normal witnesses are eyewitnesses or character witnesses. Information which is given in testimonies should come from the witnesses' own experience. If their testimony is not based on events they themselves witnessed, the evidence should be excluded. This is the so-called prohibition on hearsay evidence.[145] For historians, this direct link with the events of their testimony would form a problem. Most historians have no direct contact with their research object. Therefore, the legal figure of the expert witnesses is much more suited for the historian's testimony. The expert witness aids the judge and the jury in understanding aspects of the case which are, for those who are not familiar with the subject matter, not comprehensible without further explanation. Expert witnesses can give an opinion or an interpretation, which is prohibited for other witnesses.[146] Like the normal witnesses, the experts are granted witness immunity against possible prosecution by the opposing party concerning their testimony.[147] This immunity assures that expert witnesses are not discouraged from testifying under the assurance that they are not risking liability actions. That same immunity also protects the witnesses against malcontent clients seeking to blame the experts for the outcome of the case. A counterargument to the witness immunity of the experts is that civil liability of expert witnesses might discourage improper testimony. Nonetheless, grave distortions are limited because experts can still be held liable for perjury.[148] It is interesting to discuss the expert-witness rules, because it tells us more about the kind of knowledge the legal field wants to see in the courtroom and how they have defined expert knowledge. I now review the legal rules on expert-witness evidence.

7.3.6.2 The Frye Standard

The Frye Rule was established in 1923, following the decision in *Frye v. United States*. The case discussed the admissibility of the polygraph test as a method for providing reliable legal evidence. Expert witnesses were called to court and testified on the subject. The judgment argued a rule for expert testimony which can be summed up as follows: scientific evidence produced by expert witnesses should be

[145]Evidence is hearsay when it is not directly gathered by the witness.

[146]For a short introduction to the legal term of the expert witness see http://www.law.cornell.edu/wex/expert_witness. Accessed 31 Oct 2014.

[147]Masterson, Leslie. 1998. Witness Immunity or Malpractice Liability for Professionals Hired as Experts? *The Review of Litigation* 17, 394, 399–403, 413.

[148]Masterson, as n. 147, 414.

based on scientific methods that are generally accepted and established within their professions.[149] The court formulated their rule as follows:

> The rule is that the opinions of experts or skilled witnesses are admissible in evidence in those cases in which the matter of inquiry is such that inexperienced persons are unlikely to prove capable of forming a correct judgment upon it, for the reason that the subject matter so far partakes of a science, art, or trade as to require a previous habit or experience or study in it, in order to acquire a knowledge of it. When the question involved does not lie within the range of common experience or common knowledge, but requires special experience or special knowledge, then the opinions of witnesses skilled in that particular science, art, or trade to which the question relates are admissible in evidence.[150]

The Frye ruling created a standard. The judge has the sovereign right to decide to which degree the facts of the case correspond with a standard. In the case of the Frye standard, the phrasing "generally accepted methods" was interpreted very broadly. This open interpretation created a risk, because it was unclear where experimental methods stopped and institutionalized practices began. There was no clear line that determined the latter from the former. The loose interpretation of "generally accepted methods" ensured that the standard was not able to exclude so-called "junk science" from the courtroom. For legal scholars, the Frye standard was an "ultraorthodox ruling."[151] Experts were often described as "mercenaries, prostitutes, or hired guns, or as witnesses whose opinions are sold to the highest bidder."[152] As more and more expert witnesses began entering the courtrooms, legal scholars came up with stricter rules.

7.3.6.3 The Daubert Standard: Popper & the Judge as Gatekeeper

In 1975, the Federal Rules of Evidence were introduced as a code of rules concerning the admissibility of evidence and witnesses.[153] The rules on the opinions of expert testimony are addressed in article VII, rules 702, 703, 704, and 705 of the FRE. It was rule 702 that especially altered the Frye standard. It asked the court to only allow expert testimony that will "assist the trier of fact to understand the evidence or determine a fact in issue."[154] The rule stipulated four elements the court had to keep in mind when examining the admissibility of expert evidence.

---

[149] For a short introduction to the Frye rule see http://www.law.cornell.edu/wex/frye_standard. Accessed 31 Oct 2014.

[150] For the judgment in Frye v. United States see http://www.law.ufl.edu/_pdf/faculty/little/topic8.pdf, 1. Accessed 31 Oct 2014. The Frye rule is still used in some American states but has been replaced by the Daubert rules at the Federal level and in most states.

[151] Klein, Lott, and Rojas, as n. 129, 5.

[152] Masterson, as n. 147, 395.

[153] The FRE can be consulted here http://federalevidence.com/downloads/rules.of.evidence.pdf. Accessed 31 Oct 2014.

[154] Masterson, as n. 147, 396, 413–414.

Rule 702. Testimony by Expert Witnesses
A witness who is qualified as an expert by knowledge, skill, experience, training, or education may testify in the form of an opinion or otherwise if:

(a) the expert's scientific, technical, or other specialized knowledge will help the trier of fact to understand the evidence or to determine a fact in issue;
(b) the testimony is based on sufficient facts or data;
(c) the testimony is the product of reliable principles and methods; and
(d) the expert has reliably applied the principles and methods to the facts of the case.[155]

Rule 703 of the FRE sets the limits for the materials an expert witness may use in his or her testimony. FRE 703 allows the use of facts and data from secondary sources.[156] Rule 704 discusses the standard that an opinion can embrace an ultimate issue.[157] The rule explicitly prohibits this in certain instances in criminal cases.[158] FRE 705 allows the expert to give his opinion without first disclosing all the underlying facts and data. If a motion is filed, the expert can be required to disclose those facts and data during cross-examination.[159] Rule 702 of the FRE made the courts themselves responsible to exclude any expert who brought junk science into the courtroom.[160] Only evidence that helped the trier of fact would be allowed in court. Despite the new rules, which offered four parameters to qualify expert opinion as admissible, judges continued to work with a broad interpretation of the Frye ruling. One legal scholar declared that, when it concerned expert witnessing, judges had a "let it all in" mentality.[161] A 1993 Supreme Court case, *Daubert v. Merell Dow Pharmaceuticals* meant the formal end of the Frye standard on the federal level. The Daubert standard further defined rule 702 of the FRE. The Daubert standard wanted the judge to play the role of the gatekeeper, as it is popularly called.[162] The US Supreme Court wanted judges to consider four factors:

---

[155] Rule 702 of the FRE see http://federalevidence.com/downloads/rules.of.evidence.pdf, 30. Accessed 31 Oct 2014.

[156] Rule 703 of the FRE see http://federalevidence.com/downloads/rules.of.evidence.pdf, 30. Accessed 31 Oct 2014.

[157] An ultimate issue is a fact that has to be accepted–recognized as real–for a claim or defence to prevail. Crimes are legally defined, and if one of the properties of a crime is not accepted as a fact by the court, then it cannot rule there has been a crime. For example, one of the constitutional elements of the crime murder is that the accused had the premeditated intention to kill another person. When the accused has accidently killed a person, there is no intentional element, so there will be no murder verdict.

[158] Rule 704 of the FRE see http://federalevidence.com/downloads/rules.of.evidence.pdf, 31. Accessed 31 Oct 2014.

[159] Rule 705 of the FRE see http://federalevidence.com/downloads/rules.of.evidence.pdf, 31. Accessed 31 Oct 2014.

[160] For an example of such an attempt see Quivik, as n. 29, 98–99. Another example can be found in Rothman, as n. 27, 43.

[161] Masterson, as n. 147, 397.

[162] For a short introduction to the legal term of the Daubert Standard see http://www.law.cornell.edu/wex/Daubert_standard. Accessed 31 Oct 2014.

(1) Did the expert use a theory or technique that has widespread acceptance within a relevant scientific community?
(2) Has the theory or technique used by the expert been subject to peer review and publication?
(3) Whether the theory can and has been tested.
(4) Is the known error rate acceptable?[163]

The Frye standard of "general acceptance" had now been replaced by the "general helpfulness" standard of Daubert.[164] The Daubert standard focused heavily on the testability of a hypothesis or method. The US Supreme Court wanted the courts to play a gatekeeping role which only allowed scientific knowledge into the courtroom which was based on scientific method. In *Kumho Tire Co. v. Carmichael*, the US Supreme Court argued that the Daubert standard applied to all expert testimony.[165] Furthermore, the Kumho judgment made gatekeeping an obligation and a requirement for all trial judges. It also emphasized testing of the expert's evidence. Sound and objective science was the new standard for admissible evidence by expert witnesses.[166] It was the court's ambition to exclude any testimony based on subjective belief or unsupported speculation, in order to avoid irrelevant testimony and those experts "who bend their science in the direction from which their fee is coming."[167]

The Daubert Standard aimed to exclude junk science and became applicable to all expert testimony after the Kumho ruling. The standard addressed the question whether a witness would be permitted to testify; "it did not address how the witness's testimony will be evaluated and weighed by the jury."[168] A solution came with the Kumho ruling which explicitly allowed the judge to "instruct the jury about how to translate the expert's opinion about risk factors into legal conclusions . . . "[169]

Daubert has been negatively received in the legal community. Especially because the Daubert rules are applicable to all expert evidence, has the Daubert standard been ill received. The vocabulary of Daubert shows us that the standard was constructed with the natural sciences in mind. Words like data, facts, science, good science, and the idea that hypotheses should have an acceptable error rate [that it

---

[163]Klein, Lott, and Rojas, as n. 129, 5.

[164]Masterson, as n. 147, 398.

[165]For the ruling in Kumho see http://www.law.cornell.edu/supremecourt/text/97-1709. Accessed 31 Oct 2014.

[166]Klein, Lott, and Rojas, as n. 129, 5.

[167]Klein, Lott, and Rojas, as n. 129, 5.

[168]Givelber, Daniel, and Strickler, Lori. 2006. Junking Good Science: Undoing Daubert v. Merrill Dow Through Cross-Examination and Argument. *American Journal of Public Health* 96, 33.

[169]Edmond, Gary, and Mercer, David. 2002. Conjectures and Exhumations: Citations of History, Philosophy and Sociology of Science in US Federal Courts. *Law and Literature*, 14, 325. & Givelber and Strickler, as n. 168, 36. As we saw earlier, Judge Learned Hand had advocated the introduction of this legal tool at the beginning of the twentieth century. See Part II, Sect. 7.1. Expert Witnessing Through the Ages, cfr. supra.

can be tested] have all been based on the image of the natural sciences.[170] Gary Edmond and David Mercer, two legal scholars, wrote an article in which they examine "the circumstances in which a version of Sir Karl Popper's philosophy of science became US law."[171] To Edmond and Mercer, Daubert's criteria: falsifiability of the technique, peer review and publication, rate of error of a technique, and general acceptance of that technique, reflected a high degree of confidence by the majority of the US Supreme Court in the "Popperian inspired model of the scientific method."[172]

A strong dissenting opinion was voiced by Judges Rehnquist and Stevens. They both acknowledged the gatekeeping responsibility of the judge, but they were "at a loss to know" how judges were to falsify theories and methods they hardly understood.[173] "Rather than represent the sudden appearance of Popper (and the others) as an attempt to engage with or accommodate the history, philosophy and sociology of science, judicial reference to such work seems to operate as synecdoche for an implicitly proper and comprehensive representation of science and its processes", Edmond and Mercer argued.[174] The authors further wrote that the Kumho decision is a "self-supporting legal test potentially applicable to all expert opinion evidence."[175] In another article, Edmond stated that the gatekeeping criteria for justices are based on particular and simplistic models of science.[176] Difficulties in court soon arose when the application of falsification failed as a meaningful demarcation criterion in tort cases.[177] Causal relations, for example in tobacco litigation, involve epidemiological evidence, which has had difficulty proving beyond the level of a reasonable doubt, in a legal sense, that cigarettes are the only cause of a person's lung cancer.[178] The testability condition did also become problematic when old and new research methods clashed in court and gave different results based on the same facts and data. To Mercer and Edmond, the incompatibility of the Daubert standard with scientific disagreement is linked to the vigorous implementation of the theories of Karl Popper without taking into account other works on scientific theory, such as *The Structure of Scientific Revolutions* by Thomas Kuhn.[179]

---

[170]For my discussion on the monopoly of the natural sciences on the idea of knowledge, see Part I, Sect. 3.1.2. The Professionalization of History & Science as The New Intellectual Gold Standard, cfr. supra.

[171]Edmond and Mercer, as n. 169, 309.

[172]Edmond and Mercer, as n. 169,310–313.

[173]Edmond and Mercer, as n. 169, 313–314.

[174]Edmond and Mercer, as n. 169, 317.

[175]Edmond and Mercer, as n. 169, 317.

[176]Edmond, as n. 9, 175.

[177]Edmond and Mercer, as n. 169, 320.

[178]Givelber and Strickler, as n. 168, 34–35.

[179]Edmond and Mercer, as n. 169, 320–321. Edmond and Mercer refer to the American philosopher of science Thomas Kuhn, who argued that science does not progresses in a linear way but through

The ideas on science by Karl Popper were translated into law, defining, after the ruling in Kumho, also non-scientific forms of evidence.[180] Legal scholars Edmond and Mercer remarked that the study of law would have trouble presenting its own knowledge under the Daubert standard. It would be very problematic to calculate the error-rate of a legal standard. In their article, Edmond and Mercer wrote: "law will be presented [and allowed and succeed to be presented] as an activity quite different from science."[181] This is only normal because its object of study is entirely different from that of the natural sciences. But why is history not allowed the same privileges? With the decision in Daubert, and furthermore in Kumho the US Supreme Court has "naively embraced Popper as an apparently practical means of identifying reliable expertise."[182] By codifying Popper's vision on science, the Court has put into law the supposed criteria to distinguish good expert knowledge from bad expert knowledge. "The questions of whether the sciences are meaningfully unified, or falsification reconcilable with the other three criteria, and the value of non-Popperian philosophies of science are controversial issues which are simply not addressed", according to Mercer and Edmond.[183] The Kumho ruling made "the transformation of Popperian "falsifiability" into a legally acceptable image of not only scientific, but also technical and specialized knowledge complete."[184] Another legal scholar who has extensively published on expert witnessing and the Daubert rule, David Caudill, argued in an article from 2002 that the Daubert rule represents an "idealized version of science." Daubert presents science in "cognitive terms, as if theory, experiment, and publication ... are its [only] constitutive elements." He argues that this is because "we [the legal profession] don't think of science as rhetorical."[185] This is a very important explanation of why history is met with determined resistance in court. Although the law operates under its own rules, it does not allow other disciplines who come into court to deviate from its limited idea of scientific knowledge.

On his blog, New York based lawyer Gregory Joseph, who has been a lawyer in litigation concerning land rights of natives peoples, asked the question: "How can historians possibly satisfy Daubert?"[186] His solution was to determine whether the expert witness helped the trier of fact or not, considering that the other Daubert factors were far from applicable. In a more theoretical blog post, Joseph states:

---

periodic revolutions, or paradigm shifts, which altered the nature of scientific inquiry. See Kuhn, Thomas. 2012. *The Structure of Scientific Revolutions*. Chicago: University of Chicago Press.

[180]Edmond and Mercer, as n. 169, 326.

[181]Edmond and Mercer, as n. 169, 341.

[182]Edmond and Mercer, as n. 169, 339.

[183]Edmond and Mercer, as n. 169, 329.

[184]Edmond and Mercer, as n. 169, 343.

[185]Caudill, David. 2002. Scientific Narratives in Law: An Introduction. *Law and Literature* 14, 269.

[186]For the "Complex Litigation Blog" of Mr. Joseph see http://www.josephnyc.com/blog/?blogID=372. Accessed 31 Oct 2014.

"[t]here is no way to "test" whether the experts' testimony concerning the historical understanding of the treaties is correct. Nor is it possible to establish an "error rate" for historical experts."[187] History can simply not be tested like the natural sciences. Judges would do well to concentrate on another element of the Daubert standard, namely, whether the historical research has been peer reviewed and published. As we shall see further on during the discussion on the involvement of historians in tobacco litigation, this fundamental part of historical practice is completely ignored by many experts.

7.4 Preliminary Conclusions on the Historian as an Expert Witness in American Courts

This chapter has introduced a number of important American cases where historians were active as expert witnesses, as well as an inquiry into the practical and legal aspects of serving as an expert in court. Since the last decades of the nineteenth century, expert witnessing has stirred controversy in the courtroom. When historians began testifying, they were faced with issues like objectivity and advocacy, the desirability of disagreements among experts, attacks on the epistemology of expert testimony, the fact that history is judged in court, and the necessity of ethical codes. I now discuss these problems while keeping my introductory remarks on the theoretical aspects of the interaction of law and history in mind.

The idea of positivist objectivity, as I described it in part I, continues to trick historians.[188] Many historians are convinced that leaving positivist objectivity will be devastating for the credibility and objectivity of the historian. It is startling that, despite all postmodernist historical theory some historians maintain that they can objectively function in the same manner as a scientist in his laboratory.[189] Positivist objectivity is presented as a selling point by consultants, as the solution for partisanship and advocacy.[190] Objectivity is maintained, although historians know better.[191] Even while knowing that positivist objectivity does not exist, historians have to stick with it, according to historian and Judge Neuenschwander.[192] The following quote from historian and expert witness Hal Rothman is a typical example

[187]For another example on the "Complex Litigation Blog" of Mr. Joseph see http://josephnyc.com/blog/?blogID=1239. Accessed 31 Oct 2014.

[188]See Part I, Sect. 3.1.1. The Ghost of von Ranke, cfr. supra.

[189]See for example: Colton, as n. 122, 111. & Martin, Brian. 2002. Working With Lawyers: A Historian's Perspective. *The Organization of American Historians Newsletter* 30. https://archives.iupui.edu/bitstream/handle/2450/6017/A2010_11-016_Box13_OAH_Vol30No2_May2002.pdf?sequence=3. Accessed 31 Oct 2014. & Soifer, as n. 35, 48–49.

[190]Colton, as n. 122, 111. & Kousser, as n. 10, 6 & 12–14. & Becker, as n. 35, 72.

[191]Neuenschwander, as n. 33.

[192]Neuenschwander, as n. 33.

of this kind of reasoning: "credibility and perception of objective analysis, however unfashionable in some quarters, is an important part of maintaining the position of historians in the courtroom."[193] On the same page in his article, Rothman declares that "[i]n reality, of course, it [objectivity] is merely a more nuanced and evaluated form of interpretation. Yet other disciplines fail to display the illusion of objectivity in the manner in which historians are so successful."[194] Lawyers gladly join this tactic of presenting the historical discipline as objective when it serves their own ends. This usually happens when they have recruited a historian as an expert witness. When confronted with an opposing historian, lawyers turn to the task of demystifying the notion of positivist objectivity. They only have to read a couple of basic works of historical theory of the past fifty years in order to do this. This pragmatic approach displayed by lawyers is apparent in Schachtman's argumentation. On the one hand, he argues that historians should just deliver the facts to the lawyers, while, on the other hand, he denies historians the possibility of a historical episteme that can deliver useful facts in the courtroom.[195] Even when lawyers present history as an objective positivist enterprise, judges should know better.[196]

Historians have proposed different ideas to solve the advocacy problem. Some historians use the tu quoque-argument to argue that academics are equally impartial or biased–an argument Novick noted to be legion in the domain of public history.[197] Or should historians instead just "plead guilty for advocacy",[198] and simply give in to the accusations and admit that expert witnesses "join a company"?[199] I argue that historians should not do any of the foregoing. Historians should acknowledge that their craft is one of interpretation. Maintaining the positivist idea of objectivity hurts the study of history more than it benefits her. Clio is not objective; the judge, the lawyer, the jury, and the historian know this. A better form of objectivity forces itself upon historians–one that is intersubjective in nature. Intersubjective objectivity means that those historians work according to the highest ethical and professional standards of the study of history. These parameters can be encoded, as in De Baets' proposal for an ethical code for historians, and can be controlled by peer review, publication of research results, and open access to primary sources.[200] I cannot see how lawyers and judges would object to such a practice, one so similar to that of their own craft.

---

[193]Rothman, as n. 27, 51.

[194]Rothman, as n. 27, 51.

[195]Schachtman, as n. 79, 3–5.

[196]Rosner and Markowitz, as n. 37, 276–277.

[197]Kousser, as n. 10, 19. & Novick, as n. 60, 516. See also Part I, Sect. 3.1.4. Descending the Ivory Tower, cfr. supra.

[198]Soifer, as n. 35, 50.

[199]Rothman, as n. 27, 51.

[200]See Part III, Sect. 14.4. Confronting Ethics with De Baets, cfr. infra.

As we have seen, there are practical and legal conditions to testifying in court that directly influence the expert to maintain his professional and ethical standards. To keep his credibility, the historian is obliged to deliver an extremely thorough historical report. As we have seen in the previous parts of this chapter, historians go through great effort to obtain historical research of a high level. No historian wants to be called a liar while on the stand, let alone be exposed to be one during cross-examination. Historians cannot risk being discredited, not in the least for their own sake, but also for the sake of counsel's legal strategy and the client. When a party's own expert witness is excluded or discredited, this will negatively affect the chances of winning their case. Great abuse of history is furthermore neutralized by the adversarial nature of the court. When historians serve on both sides they will fear the ability of the other historian to find distortions in their own witness report.

Other historians found it problematic to see their colleagues disagree in court.[201] Again, this is a consequence of history being portrayed as a science. If historians are objective, and their methods are correct, how would it then be possible for them to come to opposing opinions based on the same facts? According to Rothman, due to the adversarial position in which they testify, both experts cancel each other out, which ensures that neither the judge nor the jury will consider either one of the testimonies.[202] Kousser metaphorically described the proceedings in the adversarial process as follows: "[A]n Invisible Hand guides the process toward the maximum production of truth."[203] I do not agree with the pessimism of Rothman, nor do I concur with the optimism of Morgan Kousser either. The verdict is influenced by many factors; legal and extralegal. The fact whether the judge or the jury will follow the testimony of the expert witness depends on many factors, of which the ability to survive cross-examination is an important one. The adversarial process is fair because it gives voice to multiple interpretations of the past, leaving it to the judge or the jury to decide which one they found most convincing.

History is restricted by the legal straightjacket of the court environment in another manner, namely by the fact that lawyers set the research scope and focus the historical investigation.[204] Lawyers play a very big role in constructing the expert reports. The role of legal counsel is often difficult to research because of their fear of being subpoenaed for any documents concerning their involvement. This so-called "law office history" can limit expert historians in their research. Yet, now I will also use the "tu quoque-argument", which is so often used by public historians, by asking the question: Are academic historians not faced with similar problems? When writing a research project, do historians not think about the possibilities of funding and publication, thereby letting their research be determined by "non-academic" factors? Again, the solution lies with the enforcement of ethical codes

---

201 See the remarks by Edmond and Hamlin, Part II, Sect. 7.1. Expert Witnessing Through the Ages, cfr. supra.

202 Rothman, as n. 27, 45.

203 Kousser, as n. 10, 15.

204 Colton, as n. 122, 111.

and transparency of research. If a majority of historians has the same standards when constructing their historical research, then there is no problem for expert witnesses and litigation-driven history.[205]

Historians have made another objection about expert witnessing. It has been voiced by historian and expert witness Charles Bolton, when he wrote that the expert cannot "control exactly how his testimony will be used or if it will be used."[206] Kessler-Harris expressed a similar sentiment after her experience in the Sears trial.[207] The counterargument is that any historical work can be used by anyone or can be interpreted in different ways. When historians conduct a historical inquiry and publish their results, they can only try to argue in favour of their interpretation. It would be dreadful if no one was allowed to discuss different argumentations or interpretations. The problem is that, in court there has to be "a final judgment." The court's decision is final in that individual case, after all appeals have been exhausted. A judgment is final in one case, but law is a dynamic discipline. When influenced by social developments, the study of law changes its idea about certain subjects. For example, with their decision in *Brown v. Board of Education*, the US Supreme Court changed legal theory on segregation.[208] The alternative for historians is to refuse to let their historical research be judged in court. Refusing to testify means to leave history in the hands of lawyers. Lawyers, like Schachtman, continue to argue that in most cases do not need help from historians to incorporate history in court.[209] In the following chapters it will become very clear that when it comes to history; lawyers, judges, and justice can use all the help they can get from historians.

There are also more personal reasons for historians to become experts in court. Many historians describe their service in court as a way to make themselves and history useful and meaningful by aiding victims and justice.[210] In their article, Rosner and Markowitz described the most meaningful moment of their trial experience as follows:

> [...], the most meaningful moment came during a recess when he [Rosner] had the chance to speak with the worker who had been made ill by the silica dust and his family. This migrant told of his life, his family and his children. His wife invited David to dinner at their home. It was clear that the testimony made on his behalf was extremely important to the children who kept thanking David for coming to Texas "for their father." They had translated for him throughout David's testimony and they conveyed his deep gratitude. The testimony had affirmed the man's experience and let his own family know that his experience was

[205]See Part III, Sect. 14.4. Confronting Ethics with De Baets, cfr. infra.

[206]Bolton, as n. 28, 66.

[207]Kessler-Harris, as n. 57, 64–66.

[208]For the Brown case see Part II, Sect. 7.2.1. Brown v. Board of Education, cfr. supra.

[209]For my discussion on Schachtmans' argumentation see Part II, Sect. 7.2.3. Toxic Tort Litigation: Lead Paint Toxic Tort Litigation, cfr. supra.

[210]Bolton, as n. 28, 66. & Martin, as n. 189. & Johnson, Leland. 1983. Public Historian for the Defendant. *The Public Historian* 5, 65–76. & Rosner and Markowitz, as n. 36, 274–275.

> meaningful. This alone, it seemed was worth the extraordinary pain that the day in court had cost him. We cannot convey how moving this occasion was. It made us realize that history does matter.[211]

Another example comes from historian and expert witness Carl Becker, who wrote enthusiastically that he, like his fellow academic historians had "lived on Mount Olympus."[212] But when his party had won the case, Becker was overcome with a more down to the earth emotionality:

> Right had triumphed. Intellect had prevailed. I was a good historian. I had made the facts serve the cause of humanity against the ambitious bureaucrats, the faceless men of monolithic government. I had survived a foray into a world of real controversy, of real issues. Other historians might deal with musty facts and abstract interpretations of meaningless events-but not Becker![213]

Although Becker intentionally caricaturized his statement, I argue that there is nothing wrong with a historian who believes in his cause and can aid it in court with professional knowledge.

In conclusion the practice of historians as expert witnesses is based on thorough historical research.[214] Expert reports are prepared more meticulously than standard academic historical research.[215] Furthermore, historians should remain firmly convinced of their ability to prove and use their skills and knowledge.[216] Proof made up of historical documents and the historical record constitutes a powerful legal argument.[217] In addition, historical research for litigation has procured funds for historical inquiry that would otherwise not exist.[218] The practical guide into expert witnessing has shown how, in the best circumstances, close interaction between lawyers and historians produces reliable historical research which can survive the closest scrutiny in the courtroom. Every historian who served as an expert witness should be able to conclude as Becker did: "I would remain satisfied that I had used my sources accurately and fairly. I had not sent Clio into the streets to turn a trick."[219]

---

[211] Rosner and Markowitz, as n. 36, 279–280.

[212] Becker, as n. 35, 76.

[213] Becker, as n. 35, 68.

[214] Quivik, as n. 29, 103.

[215] Kousser, as n. 10, 17.

[216] Bolton, as n. 28, 67.

[217] Rosner and Markowitz, as n. 36, 282.

[218] Colton, as n. 122, 115.

[219] Becker, as n. 35, 77.

Bibliography

Becker, Carl. 1982. Professor for the plaintiff: Classroom to courtroom. *The Public Historian* 4: 68–77.

Bolton, Charles. 1982. The historian as expert witness: Creationism in Arkansas. *The Public Historian* 4: 59–67.

Burnham, John. 2010. In defense of historians as expert witnesses: A rebuttal to Jon Wiener. *George Mason University's History News Network,* April 1.

Cantelon, Philip, Henry Ryan, Carole Stern, and Joseph Gagen. 1991. Performing a superfund site history: Time and money well spent. *Toxics Law Reporter* 5: 595–600.

Caudill, David. 2002. Scientific narratives in law: An introduction. *Law and Literature* 14: 253–274.

Colton, Craig. 2006. The historian's responsibility in litigation support. *The Public Historian* 28: 111–115.

Edmond, Gary. 2002. Whigs in court: Historiographical problems with expert evidence. *Yale Journal of Law & Humanities* 14: 123–175.

Edmond, Gary, and David Mercer. 2002. Conjectures and exhumations: Citations of history, philosophy and sociology of science in US federal courts. *Law and Literature* 14: 309–365.

Foster, William. 1897. Expert testimony, prevalent complaints and proposed remedies. *Harvard Law Review* 11: 169–186.

Franklin, John. 2004. To and from Brown v. Board of education. *Washington History* 16: 12.

Galanter, Marc. 1974. Why the "haves" come out ahead: Speculations on the limits of legal change. *Law & Society Review* 9: 95–160.

Givelber, Daniel, and Lori Strickler. 2006. Junking good science: Undoing Daubert v Merrill Dow through cross-examination and argument. *American Journal of Public Health* 96: 33–37.

Guterman, Lila. 2004. Peer reviewers are subpoenaed in cancer lawsuit against chemical companies. *The Chronicle of Higher Education,* November 19.

Hall, Jacquelyn, and Sandi Cooper. 1986. Women's history goes to trial: EEOC v. Sears, roebuck and company. *Signs* 11: 751–779.

Hamlin, Christopher. 1986. Scientific method and expert witnessing: Victorian perspectives on a modern problem. *Social Studies of Science* 16: 458–513.

Hand, Learned. 1901. Historical and practical considerations regarding expert testimony. *Harvard Law Review* 15: 40–58.

Jellison, Katherine. 1987. History in the courtroom: The sears case in perspective. *The Public Historian* 9: 9–19.

Johnson, Leland. 1983. Public historian for the defendant. *The Public Historian* 5: 65–76.

Kelly, Alfred. 1962. An inside story: When the supreme court ordered desegregation. *U.S. News & World Report* 5: 86–88.

Kelly, Alfred. 1965. Clio and the court: An illicit love affair. *The Supreme Court Review* 1965: 119–158.

Kessler-Harris, Alice. 1987. Equal employment opportunity commission v. Sears, Roebuck and company: A personal account. *Feminist Review* 25: 46–69.

Klein, Robert, Leslie Lott, and Jose Rojas. 2007. Expert witnesses: When are they necessary and does Daubert/Kumho make a difference? *IP Litigator* 13: 1–11.

Kluger, Richard. 2004. *Simple justice. The history of Brown v. Board of education and black America's struggle for equality.* New York: Vintage Books.

Kmietowicz, Zosia, and Annabel Ferriman. 2002. Pro-tobacco writer admits he should have declared an interest. *British Medical Journal* 324: 257.

Kousser, Morgan. 1984. Are expert witnesses whores? Reflections on objectivity in scholarship and expert witnessing. *The Public Historian* 6: 5–19.

Martin, Brian. 2002. Working with lawyers: A historian's perspective. *The Organization of American Historians Newsletter* 30.

Masterson, Leslie. 1998. Witness immunity or malpractice liability for professionals hired as experts? *The Review of Litigation* 17: 393–418.
Milkman, Ruth. 1986. Women's history and the sears case. *Feminist Studies* 12: 375–400.
Neuenschwander, John. 2002. Historians as expert witnesses: The view from the bench. *The Organization of American Historians Newsletter* 30.
Novick, Peter. 1998. *That noble dream. The "objectivity question" and the American historical profession*. New York: Cambridge University Press.
Petrovic, Vladimir. 2009. Historians as expert witnesses in the age of extremes. Budapest: Central European University.
Quivik, Frederic. 2004. Of tailings, superfund litigation, and historians as experts: U.S. v. Asarco, et al. (the bunker hill case in Idaho). *The Public Historian* 26: 81–104.
Reis, Mike. 2003. Searching in the past: Dusty documents that may prove the case can be found by historians. *Legal Times* 26: 1–2.
Reis, Mike, and Dave Wiseman. 2011. The Historian's valuable role as expert and advisor in environmental litigation. *The Environmental Litigator* 22: 12–14.
Rosner, David, and Gerald Markowitz. 2004. The chemical industry's attack on historians. *George Mason University's History News Network*, December 5.
Rosner, David, and Gerald Markowitz. 2009. The trials and tribulations of two historians: Adjudicating responsibility for pollution and personal harm. *Medical History* 53: 271–292.
Rothman, Hal. 1896. Expert medical testimony. *Harvard Law Review* 10: 305–306.
Rothman, Hal. 1909. Witnesses. Experts. Compensation exceeding regular fee. *Harvard Law Review* 22: 235–236.
Rothman, Hal. 1993. Historian v. historian: Interpreting the past in the courtroom. *The Public Historian* 4: 39–53.
Schachtman, Nathan. 2003. On deadly dust and histrionic historians: Preliminary thoughts on history and historians as expert witnesses in products liability cases. *Mealey's Litigation Report: Silica* 2: 1–6.
Soifer, Paul. 1983. The litigation historian: Objectivity, responsibility, and sources. *The Public Historian* 5: 47–62.
Wiener, Jon. 2005. Cancer, Chemicals and History. *The Nation,* February 7.

Chapter 8
A Reassessment of Wijffels' Concept of Forensic History

Da mihi facta, dabo tibi ius.
Give me the facts, and I will give you the law.

Latin Proverb.

Abstract In this concluding chapter of the second part of the book, I compare the conclusions from the previous chapters on the European and American experiences with the controversial practice of historians serving as expert judicial witness. My aim is to counter the argument made by Wijffels that historians should limit their involvement to providing historical facts for lawyers instead of testifying in court.

This second part of my research has given an overview of both European and American litigation in which historians have served as expert witnesses. By examining the cases on which Wijffels drew to establish forensic history, we have come to a better understanding of his concept. The American examples in Chap. 7 have served as a comparative angle to the European examples given in Chap. 6. This comparative method allows us to discuss the problems that have presented themselves when historians testify in court from different perspectives and based on multiple examples of expert witnessing. Bearing those illustrations in mind, I now aim to examine the five characteristics that, according to Wijffels, define the problematic constitution of forensic history. Drawing from the illustrations examined in this second part of my research, I argue that Wijffels' conclusions on forensic history should be reassessed.

Wijffels gives five points that present contrasting features between a forensic history and normal historical [academic] debate. In the first place, he argues that there is less possibility for debate in court than within the protective walls of the academic society.[1] Wijffels' second and third point are related to his first argument. The second issue Wijffels defines is that the position of the expert witness differs from that of independent research in an academic situation. Whereas his third point stresses that the purposes of direct and cross-examination are of a different

[1] Wijffels, Alain. 2001. *History in Court: Historical Expertise and Methods in a Forensic Context.* Leiden: Ius Deco, 320.

R. Delafontaine, *Historians as Expert Judicial Witnesses in Tobacco Litigation*,
Studies in the History of Law and Justice 4, DOI 10.1007/978-3-319-14292-0_8

nature than normal academic debate. The fourth reason is that historians are faced with a time factor that is much more constraining than in academic environments. While his last point is similar to the objections made by historian Kessler-Harris who testified in the Sears case, namely that the judge has the power to adjudicate historical reports filed by expert witnesses and consequently make a single and final interpretation of a historical event.[2]

I reduce Wijffels' five-point scheme to a three-point scheme, on the grounds that his first three reasons are very much alike, each stressing one element of the same argument, namely that academic debate and research differs from that of the adversarial debate in court and from litigation-driven history. The first issue I discuss is thus that the forensic context of history differs from normal historical academic debate and research. The second argument I tackle is about the time pressure that is different for historians who are called upon as expert witnesses, while the third problem I review is about the power of the judge to make a judgment on historical facts.

I concur partially with Wijffels' first argument. It is clear that the forensic context constraints the historical debate because of legal preconditions. The question is: to what extent is history forced into a legal straightjacket? On the one hand, the phase during which experts have to testify in court formalizes the way historical research is presented. The depositions, the direct examination, redirect and certainly cross-examination are not normal forms of historical debate. On the other hand, on multiple occasions in litigation-driven history historians have contributed to historiography and historical research. Such examples are: German historical research under the Ludwigsburg paradigm, the books published by Rosner and Markowitz based on their work in lead paint toxic tort litigation, the work of Evans and other historians in the Irving trial, the publication of internal industry documents which would have been non-accessible to historical research if it had not had been for litigation, the extra funding for research projects because of litigation, and so forth.

Moreover, Wijffels does not take into account that there are many safeguards to ensure that historians stay true to their professional standards. Expert witnesses put their professional reputation at stake with every trial.[3] As Paul Soifer remarked: "[t]here are no friendly lawsuits; litigation is an adversary process in which the opposition is portrayed as the implacable enemy."[4] The dangers of being discredited during testimony and cross-examination by lawyers from opposing counsel is on the one hand not an event the expert witness looks forward to, on the other hand the cross-examination assures that expert reports are extremely well-documented and meticulously researched historical inquiries. The report is a document that is not written in legal vocabulary and is excellent historical research because

[2] Wijffels, as n. 1, 21, 36, 320–325.

[3] Kousser, Morgan. 1984. Are Expert Witnesses Whores? Reflections on Objectivity in Scholarship and Expert Witnessing. *The Public Historian* 6, 6. & Becker, Carl. 1982. Professor for the Plaintiff: Classroom to Courtroom. *The Public Historian* 4, 76.

[4] Soifer, Paul. 1983. The Litigation Historian: Objectivity, Responsibility, and Sources. *The Public Historian* 5, 49.

it has been prepared to face such unacademically scrupulous examination in court. Furthermore, the historian is under oath when presenting his report. Grave distortions of history can thus be liable to perjury actions. When a person's fate hangs in the balance, in criminal trials, the expert witness will also be more careful when testifying. Historical reports in general are examples of reliable historical practice because of all the risks that are involved when the report is characterized by advocacy: loss of credibility, possible exclusion from testimony, damaging the litigants chances of winning the case, risks for the professional standing of a historian, litigation risks of perjury, scrutiny by opposing counsel and the opposing expert, negative repercussions at the university, or the company where the expert is employed or when the expert is an individual consultant: loss of possible future clients, and many others reasons. Even zeal to defend the argumentation of one's own side does not preclude impartial historical research, as long as it happens according to the standards of the historical discipline.

Wijffels also discussed that the Papon trial had two stages in which historians had been active. In the first stage, historians had functioned as consultants and in the second stage, they had testified. Wijffels describes with aversion how the historian is questioned under cross-examination.[5] For him, "the cross-examination also showed the limitations of the expert's mission and findings."[6] Wijffels argues that historians should assist the investigation of the judge more as a fact deliverer than as an expert who gives his opinion.[7] Ideally for Wijffels, the historian as a forensic expert should only be active as a consultant without appearing on trial. Wijffels described the witnessing phase for expert historians as follows: "To lawyers (and others), history may be 'another country',[8] but conversely, historians appearing in court may equally find that in spite of their expert status, the rules applied by forensic practitioners in order to assess their reasoning and opinions are a far cry from those which prevail on their home turf."[9]

The counterargument to Wijffels' proposition is that limiting historical expertise to consulting would mean a self-fulfilling prophecy of all the problems Wijffels argues exist in "the forensic form of history." The reason for this is, as historian and president of History Associates Inc. Brian Martin wrote: "[t]he consulting part of expert witnessing is protected by attorney-client privilege. While everything that happens in court is not."[10] Limiting experts to the first stage of consulting would mean that the historical investigation would be unreviewable and inaccessible

---

[5]Wijffels, as n. 1, 271–273, 301.

[6]Wijffels, as n. 1, 284, 315–316.

[7]Wijffels, as n. 1, 301.

[8]Wijffels refers to the work by historian David Lowenthal: Lowenthal, David. 1999. *The Past is a Foreign Country.* Cambridge: Cambridge University Press.

[9]Wijffels, as n. 1, 11, 16.

[10]Martin, Brian. 2002. Working With Lawyers: A Historian's Perspective. *The Organization of American Historians Newsletter* 30. https://archives.iupui.edu/bitstream/handle/2450/6017/A2010_11-016_Box13_OAH_Vol30No2_May2002.pdf?sequence=3. Accessed 31 Oct 2014.

by peers. Many important historical documents would remain closed for other researchers. Lawyers try to limit all possible documentation and records to avoid subpoenas.[11] This is an excellent environment for partisanship to thrive. As I have discussed, all the imperatives for historians and their clients to be truthful and work according to the standards of their profession are situated at the expert witnessing level; in the adversarial system. The work of a testifying expert is only open to examination by the adversary during the proceedings in court.[12] Transparency is *the* key element in ensuring a professional and just historical testimony. Peer review and publication ensure good historical research, and the consequent application of ethical codes and professional standards, limiting historical forensic activity to the confinements of the basements of legal companies would have extremely dire consequences for the quality of litigation-driven history.

As much as the adversarial system inclines experts to give in to advocacy, there are enough elements in the judicial system that force historians to remain true their professional standards.[13] Kousser noted that every historian who testifies in court is confronted with a variation of the "Faustian quandary: should one compromise with evil, and, if so, how far?"[14] I argue that the Faustian dilemma is inescapable; advocacy is inescapable in any form of historical research, the courtroom forms no exception. That does not imply that is impossible to bring reliable historical knowledge into the courtroom, as historian Charles Colton concluded: "[i]t is possible to stand firm against pressure, and the historian must select that option."[15] In the end "the bench looks for the same qualities that are required of all experts: appropriate specialization, thorough research, and conclusions that are well supported by the record", judge and historian Neuenschwander noted.[16]

The second argument Wijffels makes about time, is relevant in some cases, in other examples of litigation less so. Just as in the academic environment, historians are sometimes under pressure to finish an article before the deadline for a call of papers ends, so too, do expert witnesses sometimes have to work under a great deal of stress to meet their deadlines. Issues about time are more appropriate to argue that historians should stick to testifying about a subject they are specialized in.[17]

---

[11]See Part II, Sect. 7.3.4. The Collaboration with Lawyers, cfr. supra.

[12]Martin, as n. 10.

[13]Those standards should be codified to be more effective and testable by the peers of expert witnesses, see for example Part III, Sect. 14.4. Confronting Ethics with De Baets, cfr. infra.

[14]Kousser, as n. 3, 18.

[15]Colton, Craig. 2006. The Historian's Responsibility in Litigation Support. *The Public Historian* 28, 113.

[16]Neuenschwander, John. 2002. Historians as Expert Witnesses: The View from the Bench. *The Organization of American Historians Newsletter* 30. See https://archives.iupui.edu/bitstream/handle/2450/6017/A2010_11-016_Box13_OAH_Vol30No3_August2002.pdf?sequence=2. Accessed 31 Oct 2014.

[17]Bolton, Charles. 1982. The Historian as Expert Witness: Creationism in Arkansas. *The Public Historian* 4, 66.

It is more credible to judges when academic historians working as experts have published on the subject and have experience in the area, as opposed to an expert who started his research on the subject of his testimony only 6 months before the trial.[18] Time constraints are a problem in litigation-driven history, but they are not bigger or more problematic than in any other form of the historical profession.[19] If anything, lawyers and clients who decide to invest in hiring a historian as an expert witness will want to make sure, in their own interest, that their witness has had enough time and funds to do his job and create an adequate expert report.

Wijffels' third point, that history is judged in the courtroom, is an issue we already discussed in the previous chapter, as it was voiced by multiple historians as an argument against testifying. The legal discipline is not static but dynamic, influenced in its theories and practices by social changes. Ranieri writes: "Legal history demonstrates that the law cannot reverse fundamental, long-term social and economic transformations which a society has undergone."[20] The individual case champions one historical account above the other, while the next trial might break with this so-called *stare decisis*. The Brown case offers a great example of how official legal custom changed its vision on racial segregation from one day to the next.[21] Just as in the historical discipline, the study of law reinterprets its views on the past. In other words, in law as in history, wrong and right change over time, but history will always be judged. The historians who serve as an expert witnesses are not asked to judge in their testimony. Experts give an opinion on the general historical context of what they truly believe happened. Judging should be left to the legal profession, but it is the task of the historical discipline to historically inform and protect the verdict from abuse of historical facts.

Another counterargument to the advice of Kessler-Harris for historians "to stay away from the courtroom in order to evade that history will be judged", is that history already played a role in court long before historians began testifying as expert witnesses. As described in Kelly's article on the Brown case, the US Supreme Court used historical arguments to legitimate its decisions without the appearance of any historian as an expert witness.[22] As *Brown v. Board of Education* clearly shows, lawyers and judges use history whether or not historians are involved. Schachtman's argumentation even goes a step further when he stated that the skill sets of historians and lawyers were not that different. Schachtman clearly sought

---

[18]Kousser, as n. 3, 18, 16.

[19]Another example of "the tu quoque-argument" between public and academic historians. See Part I, Sect. 3.1.4. Descending the Ivory Tower, cfr. supra.

[20]Ranieri, Filippo. 2001. The Restoration of Private Ownership in the Former GDR: The German Courts Between Legal History, Legal Doctrine and Legal Policy. In *History in Court: Historical Expertise and Methods in a Forensic Context,* ed. Alain Wijffels, 161–202. Leiden: Ius Deco, 195–196.

[21]For the Brown case see Part III, Sect. 7.2.1. Brown v. Board of Education, cfr. supra.

[22]Kelly, Alfred. 1962. An Inside Story: When the Supreme Court Ordered Desegregation. *U.S. News & World Report* 5, 119–120.

to limit the involvement of historians as expert witnesses to a minimal level.[23] As Dirk Heirbaut, professor of legal history at Ghent University, writes: "Lawyers need history, the kind of history which is ready made for use in legal argumentation or the kind of history that adds legitimacy to new laws." For Heirbaut the "history of law is useful for jurists to write history in to their own agenda from which historical truth is the first victim."[24] The task of a lawyer is not to present history truthfully, it is their job to be an advocate and to win the case. Judges use historical arguments to strengthen their judicial opinions. American legal scholar Robert Gordon made the argument that it was obvious for the legal profession to keep going back to history as "law derives its authority from things that happened in the past."[25] Historians should not leave Clio in those hands, but take the stand and aid the trier of fact with historical research. There are other ways to inform the court of historical arguments. For example, in the Webster case we discussed in the first chapter, the legal arguments based on historically misinformed narratives were used by the state of Missouri's legal counsel in an attempt to convince the Supreme Court that America's history showed that the general sentiment of the public had always been against abortion. The Webster *Amicus Curiae* brief procured a verdict without those false historical argumentations, thereby preventing the court from basing its verdict on wrong historical reasons. Witnessing is an even a stronger manner by which truthful historical facts can be presented before the court.

Why is Wijffels disappointed about the forensic form of history? On multiple occasions, Wijffels' conclusions can be best described by quoting the title of an article which was contributed to Wijffels' book by historian Matthew Mirow; *The Failure of Forensic History*.[26] Wijffels' negative view seems a consequence of the cases he discusses. His book discussed the French Vichy trials, an Australian example of a Holocaust trial: namely the case of Berezowsky, and also the Kennewick Man, and the Irving case. All these cases are characterised by a polemic and a political nature. Moreover, none of these court cases were based on a

[23]See my discussion on Schachtman's remarks in Part II, Sect. 7.2.3. Toxic Tort Litigation: Lead Paint Toxic Tort Litigation, cfr. supra.

[24]Translated from Dutch from Billiet, Bouke, Cassiman, Pieter, and Vanspeybrouck, Mathieu. 2002. *Het verleden in het heden en de plaats van de historicus in de maatschappij van vandaag.* [The Past in The Present and the Place of the Historian in Society of Today.] Ghent: Academia Press, 131, 139. See a similar argument in Mohr, James. 1990. Historically Based Legal Briefs: Observations of a Participant in the Webster Process. *The Public Historian* 12, 21.

[25]Gordon, Robert. 1996. The Past as Authority and as Social Critic: Stabilizing and Destabilizing Functions of History in Legal Argument. In *The Historic Turn in the Human Sciences,* ed. Terrence McDonald, 339–378. Ann Arbor: University of Michigan Press, 340.

[26]Wijffels, as n.1, 31–32. The case concerned was the "the Kennewick man." "The Kennewick man" was the name given to the skeletal remains of a prehistoric man. His remains were found on the bank of the Columbia River in Kennewick, Washington in 1996. The case revolved around the fact whether scientific research could be done on the remains, while Native American Tribes claimed that the Kennewick Man was one of their ancient ancestors. The case was decided in 2004 in favour of the scientists.

standardized and systematic strategy to which the expert witness is subjected, as under the Ludwigsburg paradigm or in general in the American civil courtroom.

The Kennewick Man was considered a very political case and evidently a case concerning an exceptional subject. The article by Mirow in Wijffels' book on the Kennewick Man does not represent an assessment of the case that offers much information to base a whole argumentation of forensic history on. The article discusses the case while it is only a year underway. Thus without a verdict in the case, Mirow concludes that the Kennewick case demonstrated the limits of "forensic history." While the article is based on such limited grounds, Wijffels used the Kennewick Man case as an example for all American "forensic history."[27]

The Australian example in Wijffels' book was one of the first cases in Australia concerning post-Holocaust litigation. The Berezowsky case even had to invite witnesses, lawyers, and experts from Europe, especially from Germany, because there was so little precedent in Australia on post-Holocaust trials.[28] The expert witness historian for the prosecution, Jonathan Steinberg then a Cambridge professor, described the preparation for the trial as follows "[t]he professional expertise, the attention to detail, the sheer hard work and high standards, that went into the preparation ... nothing I had done in my professional life hitherto had been as demanding."[29] Yet according to Australian historian David Fraser, the Berezowsky case provides the best example in the Australian war crimes trials in which the role of a historical expert witness was experienced as the application of "historical imagination and method to missing facts."[30] Again Wijffels had added another example of a case were the legal system had not provided the necessary tools for expert witnessing similar to the problems faced by historians in the French Vichy-trials.

Wijffels ends his book with a description of the Irving case, which he called a good example to base his conclusions on.[31] This statement is already problematic, since the Irving case can hardly be seen as a normal example of expert witnessing. As discussed, the Irving trial was more about historiography itself than about a historical event. This problematic situation was created by a law prohibiting holocaust denial, rather than the forensic interaction of law and history.

---

[27]Mirow, Matthew. 2001. The Kennewick Man, Identity, and the Failure of Forensic History. In *History in Court, Historical Expertise and Methods in a Forensic Context,* ed. Alain Wijffels. Leiden: Ius Deco, 241–266. The article on the Kennewick Man is available online via http://papers.ssrn.com/sol3/papers.cfm?abstract_id=1590289. Accessed 31 Oct 2014.

[28]Fraser, David. 2010. *Narrating the Holocaust in Australian War Crimes Trials.* Lincoln: University of Nebraska Press.

[29]Steinberg, Jonathan. 2001. The Historian in Court: Expert Witness in an Australian War Crimes Trial. In *History in Court, Historical Expertise and Methods in a Forensic Context,* ed. Alain Wijffels, 203–240. Leiden: Ius Deco, 234.

[30]Fraser, as n. 28, 151.

[31]Wijffels, as n. 1, 333.

In addition, Wijffels' argumentation in his conclusions is based on the Irving trial and the French Vichy trials, with multiple references to and quotations from Rousso's objection to testify.[32] While he had at the beginning of his book complained about an overrepresentation of German cases in the expert witness debate, Wijffels himself gives an unequal amount of importance to the French cases and the Holocaust denial cases.[33] At times, he seems even averse to the historical discipline. When we look at the inside flap of his book, we read: "May they always remember that Clio is the teacher of all evil, and Themis's servants both her most sedulous and her most mercurial disciples."[34] Moreover, Wijffels seems to suggest that historians intrude upon the turf of lawyers, describing the courtroom as the latter's "turf" and "home turf"[sic].[35] These elements put the intent of his work, which he expressed as follows "[t]his volume is therefore not so much a contribution to some theory of the relationship between History and Law, but rather it hopes to offer some insight into the questions raised when professional historians meet professional lawyers on the latter's turf, i.e. in the course of legal proceedings", in a somewhat grey-area of partisanship; the very accusations Wijffels makes against expert witnesses.

In conclusion, Wijffels' idea about the failure of the formal forensic form of history is based on examples that are especially polemic and that have been unable to stick to the standards of historical research, which many other cases prove is possible when history and law meet in court. Wijffels writes in reflection at the end of his book that "[t]he recurrent incidents inside and outside the courtroom ensured that the historians' appearances, [. . .] were from the start dragged into partisan debates expressed at the trial and throughout the extensive press coverage."[36] This is of course true for the few examples he discussed. If Wijffels had discussed the Ludwigsburg paradigm instead of a single Australian case about one Holocaust crime, he might have come to very different conclusions. Wijffels continues his line argument when he writes on page 300:

> the forensic demand to the historian – and even more that of the media – was not so much for an historical reasoning, but rather for 'facts', somehow it the simplified and unsophisticated 'da mihi factum' tradition. What distinguishes the historian from a non-historian is, however, his understanding that an historical fact is always a fact about which an historical statement is being made. This elementary rule of historical criticism is perhaps the most ignored or underestimated feature of history-writing among non-historians, and the Papon case . . .[37]

According to Wijffels, historians give opinions on historical facts, while the court demands "truth facts." On the next page, Wijffels continues his line of argument

---

[32] Wijffels, as n. 1, 299–301, 331–335.

[33] Wijffels, as n. 1, 9–11.

[34] Wijffels, as n. 1, dedication.

[35] Wijffels, as n. 1, 11, 16.

[36] Wijffels, as n. 1, 300.

[37] Wijffels, as n. 1, 300.

and states that during the Vichy trials historians were judging rather than providing facts to the court. According to him the Vichy trials illustrated "only too sharply how, in the context of legal proceedings, such a fundamental misunderstanding [of the historical discipline] can be institutionalized."[38] Again, this is largely true for the cases he discussed. To conclude and generalize, like Wijffels, that all forms of forensic history have failed is overstretching the relevance of his examples.

For me, the formal format of history in a forensic context did fail in some cases, such as the Eichmann trial, most of the Frankfurt-Auschwitz trials, and the French Vichy trials. However, in the greatest number of cases it did not fail, for example in the Ludwigsburg paradigm [which compromises over 6,500 cases], which received so much praise from Erich Haberer. The Holocaust denial trials, although this kind of litigation is not desirable, showed that expert witnesses against Zündel and Irving succeeded in discrediting both Holocaust deniers. I further think of Mark Rosner and David Markowitz's battle against the lead paint industry, and other examples where thorough historical research made a difference in court. I will, by discussing the involvement of historians in tobacco litigation in the US, give a different interpretation of the forensic appliance of history in court. To distance myself from Wijffels' formal form of forensic history, I will call my concept the forensification of history.[39] Transparency and interdisciplinary cooperation between lawyers and historians are *a condition sine qua non* for a truthful appearance of Clio in Themsis' chambers. If Clio enters the courtroom under such conditions, she presents herself in the form of the best examples which historical research has to offer. Historians have, in a forensic context, presented historical facts which have aided Themsis to judge more justly.

Bibliography

Bolton, Charles. 1982. The historian as expert witness: Creationism in Arkansas. *The Public Historian* 4: 59–67.

Colton, Craig. 2006. The Historian's responsibility in litigation support. *The Public Historian* 28: 111–115.

Fraser, David. 2010. *Narrating the Holocaust in Australian war crimes trials*. Lincoln: University of Nebraska Press.

Gordon, Robert. 1996. The past as authority and as social critic: Stabilizing and destabilizing functions of history in legal argument. In *The historic turn in the human sciences*, ed. Terrence McDonald, 339–378. Ann Arbor: University of Michigan Press.

Kousser, Morgan. 1984. Are expert witnesses whores? Reflections on objectivity in scholarship and expert witnessing. *The Public Historian* 6: 5–19.

Martin, Brian. 2002. Working with lawyers: A historian's perspective. *The Organization of American Historians Newsletter* 30.

[38] Wijffels, as n. 1, 301.

[39] See Chap. 18, Final Conclusion, cfr. infra.

Mirow, Matthew. 2001. The Kennewick Man, identity, and the failure of forensic history. In *History in court, historical expertise and methods in a forensic context*, ed. Alain Wijffels, 241–266. Leiden: Ius Deco.

Mohr, James. 1990. Historically based legal briefs: Observation of a participant in the Webster process. *The Public Historian* 12: 19–26.

Neuenschwander, John. 2002. Historians as Expert Witnesses: The View from the Bench. *The Organization of American Historians Newsletter* 30.

Ranieri, Filippo. 2001. The restoration of private ownership in the former GDR: The German courts between legal history, legal doctrine and legal policy. In *History in court: Historical expertise and methods in a forensic context*, ed. Alain Wijffels, 161–202. Leiden: Ius Deco.

Soifer, Paul. 1983. The litigation historian: Objectivity, responsibility, and sources. *The Public Historian* 5: 47–62.

Steinberg, Jonathan. 2001. The historian in court: Expert witness in an Australian war crimes trial. In *History in court, historical expertise and methods in a forensic context*, ed. Alain Wijffels, 203–240. Leiden: Ius Deco.

Wijffels, Alain. 2001. *History in court: Historical expertise and methods in a forensic context*. Leiden: Ius Deco.

Part III
Tobacco Wars

To watch someone that you love very much die a slow miserable death,
suffocating day by day, is a very unpleasant thing.
And to know exactly what caused it.
And then when you hear the denials of the cigarette
companies that they had never caused the illness or
death of a single American citizen, having sat there
and watched my mother suffocating.
Having the doctors tell me and describe for me exactly what caused it.
How it caused it and what it was doing to her.
It makes you very angry.
At least it made me very angry.
And when I get angry, I try to get even, if it is legitimate to do so.[1]

Ron Motley, Attorney for Plaintiffs in Tobacco Litigation, 1998.

[1]Brandt, Allan. 2007. *The Cigarette Century. The Rise, Fall and Deadly Persistence of a Product that Defined America.* New York: Basic Books. See the entire interview with Motley at http://www.pbs.org/wgbh/pages/frontline/shows/settlement/interviews/motley.html. Accessed 31 Oct 2014.

Chapter 9
Introduction Part III

> *... over the course of more than 50 years, Defendants lied, misrepresented, and deceived the American public, including smokers and the young people they avidly sought as "replacement smokers," about the devastating health effects of smoking and environmental tobacco smoke ...*
>
> *Judge Gladys Kessler (2006)*

Abstract In this part of the book I present my research on the involvement of historians as expert judicial witnesses in tobacco litigation in the American legal system. I have made a quantitative and qualitative analysis which has allowed me to give a broad overview of those historians involved. With historians testifying for the tobacco industry remaining silent about their involvement while making hundreds of thousands of dollars through delivering doubtful historical research on the actions committed by the tobacco companies which Judge Kessler described as *over the course of more than 50 years, Defendants lied, misrepresented, and deceived the American public*; forensic history in tobacco litigation remains a controversial practice.

In this third part of the book, I combine the conclusions of the previous parts of this book on historians as expert judicial witnesses with a case study of historians who have participated in tobacco litigation in the US. This third part aims to give an elaborate overview of that interaction between law and history based on four fundamental questions: (1) What did historians testify about in court? (2) When have historians testified in court? (3) How did they testify? (4) Who were these historians? To find the answers to these questions, I have conducted a quantitative and a qualitative analysis of the involvement of professional historians in tobacco litigation. My research is furthermore informed by an extensive read of the literature on the history of tobacco litigation and an examination of personal accounts of historians involved in tobacco trials.

The quantitative analysis has been based on earlier lists detailing the involvement of historians in tobacco litigation made by the historians Robert Proctor and Luis Kyriakoudes. I have updated these lists with more information on the historians

R. Delafontaine, *Historians as Expert Judicial Witnesses in Tobacco Litigation*, Studies in the History of Law and Justice 4, DOI 10.1007/978-3-319-14292-0_9

as well as on their activities for the tobacco industry. This quantitative analysis has resulted in an overview of 50 historians in 314 cases.[1] Furthermore, I have compiled 50 expert witness profiles which offer a short overview of these historians and their activity in tobacco litigation, with direct links to their own websites.[2] This overview has been placed online with the aspiration of ensuring more transparency in tobacco litigation and debate amongst legal scholars and historians on the subject.[3] The qualitative analysis examines how historians testify in court. I have studied the trial records of the landmark case *US v. Philip Morris et al.* from 2002 in which five historians testified as expert witnesses. Two historians testified for the United States Government and three came to court in the service of the defence, the tobacco industry. I have made a discourse analysis of this case. I discuss in the following paragraphs how I have addressed each of the four questions mentioned above.

(1) The first three chapters present the history of the cigarette and the tobacco industry. These chapters have been based on works that are in part the product of litigation-driven history: *The Cigarette Century* by Allan Brandt and *Golden Holocaust* by Robert Proctor. Both authors have worked as expert witnesses in *US v. Philip Morris et al.* These books are examples of very well-documented and thorough historical research. Historians such as Brandt and Proctor have researched the history of the tobacco industry and its product through internal industry documents-which have become available as a result of tobacco litigation-, marketing ads in movies, television series, other forms of product placement, radio ads, billboard ads, ads in newspapers and magazines. Brandt and Proctor have also researched medical and scientific journals from the 1890s onward to determine when the scientific community was convinced of the moral health hazards of smoking. Furthermore, by researching the secret documents of the industry, historians have uncovered in great detail how tobacco companies created a controversy which polluted the scientific community with studies paid for by the industry that claimed more research was needed to determine if smoking was linked to disease. Moreover, the tobacco companies continued to aggressively market their product as a desirable commodity, while the industry itself knew far better than anyone else how dangerous smoking was. Historians also uncovered how, through lobbying, the industry evaded regulation and government oversight.

On these subjects, expert historians have testified and are testifying in court. Those historical arguments make up the core of tobacco litigation, because if the tobacco companies had committed a fraud against the American public, then they were negligent in the deaths of hundreds of thousands of smokers.

[1]See Appendix III, cfr. infra.

[2]See Appendix I for all 50 expert witness profiles and Appendix II for a schematic overview, cfr. infra.

[3]See all the expert witness profiles online at http://www.thejudgeandthehistorian.ugent.be. Accessed 31 Oct 2014. Disclosure website created and maintained by the author.

Experts deliver expert reports to the courts on their research of the history of tobacco. These reports are almost never published nor made available for other researchers. In tobacco litigation, I have not found any expert except Proctor who has made one of his expert reports available online.[4] Due to the lack of available expert reports, I have deemed it wise to present the history of the tobacco industry and their product in these first chapters in order to enable the reader to get a sense of the factual and historical aspects of the expert reports. Depositions and the actual testimony on trial also engages in discussion on factual elements of the report, but all in all these are limited to the controversial parts which we will discuss at length in the following chapters. Chapter 10 discusses the rise of the cigarette as a socially accepted product, detailing seven key developments. Chapter 11 examines the scientific discovery of the health hazards of smoking from the 1930s onward. Chapter 12 reports how the tobacco industry created a "scientific controversy" about the dangers of smoking, while unrelentingly promoting their product as safe and fashionable and lobbying politicians in Washington to avoid any regulation of their product.

(2) After having established what historians testify about, I go into the three consecutive waves of tobacco litigation in which historians have been active. From the early 1950s, smokers sued the tobacco companies in order to retrieve compensation for the cost of their treatments for tobacco-related disease. Only by the end of the 1980s were the first historians hired as expert witnesses. There are three waves of tobacco litigation. The first wave, from 1950 to 1994, comprises 800 individuals suits filed against the tobacco industry, without a single final ruling in favour of the plaintiffs. A second wave started when, in 1994, the attorney generals of Mississippi and Minnesota decided to sue the tobacco companies for the costs which their states had made in treating tobacco-related diseases. These cases eventually settled in 1998 with what is known as the Master Settlement Agreement (MSA). The American Federal Government also sued the tobacco industry for similar reasons in 1999. This is the federal landmark case *US v. Philip Morris et al.* The case was tried in 2002 and the final verdict from 2006 convicted the tobacco companies for fraud against the American people. After these legal battles with the government, a third wave of tobacco litigation began. This third wave is currently underway and comprises individual suits, third party suits, and class action suits. Historians are very active in these cases. These three successive waves and the legal tactics applied in it are discussed in Chap. 13. A quantitative analysis has provided much needed information on the historians' involvement. Each case discussed in this part of my research

[4]Robert Proctor, expert for the plaintiffs, has made his expert report from *US v. Philip Morris et al.* available: http://jpsl.org/archives/tobacco-and-health-expert-witness-report-filed-behalf-plaintiffs-united-states-america-plaintiff-v-philip-morris-inc-et-al-defen. Accessed 31 Oct 2014, as well as his expert report for the plaintiffs in *Ironworkers v. Philip Morris*: see http://legacy.library.ucsf.edu/tid/vmm56c00. Accessed 31 Oct 2014.

provides the names and manner of the engagement of historians.[5] In addition, a general analysis is made of the participation of historians in each wave.

(3) A third question revolves around the issue of how these historians present the history of the cigarette and its industry in court. Supported by the practical guide to expert witnessing I presented in the second part of this book, I can now detail every stage of their involvement. I have taken into account that a majority of the witnesses working for the tobacco companies do not publish on their activities in court and that some documents are protected by court order or attorney-client privilege. It has been my intent to describe the trial which I analyse, the landmark case *US v. Philip Morris et al.* from 2002, from the experiences of historians who served as expert witnesses in the trial. Allan Brandt, professor of history of medicine, had a key role in this trial. His book delivers a personal account on his tribulations in court. Brandt was deposed and questioned under cross-examination, and played a pivotal role in the legal strategy of the Department of Justice (DOJ).

Furthermore, I have made a discourse analysis of the depositions of all five historians involved as well as of the actually on-trial testimony by Brandt in Chap. 14. The discourse analysis concentrates on three questions (1) Is the historical discipline itself attacked by lawyers? (2) In what manner do the lawyers try to discredit the expert witness? (3) What kind of arguments are used; technical [historical arguments], formal, legal, or sociotechnical.[6] The trial records I examine can be found online in databases which have been constructed to allow inquiries into the industry's secret memo's and internal documents and also in the trial records of tobacco litigation.[7] This chapter gives an impression of historians willing to defend their historical research not in the trenches, but in the open and under oath while on the witness stand and under heavy fire from opposing counsel, who does not shrink from using legal and extralegal strategies to completely eviscerate the expert witness and the expert's testimony.

(4) A final goal of this part of my research has been to determine who has participated in tobacco litigation as a historical expert witness. I have found 50 historians who have been active in 314 cases. The results of my inquiry can be found at the end of my research in Appendices I, II, and III. Appendix I is a list of 50 expert witness profiles.[8] Appendix II presents an overview of, among other issues, the institutions where experts hail from, the number of cases individual experts are active in, and their estimated remunerations.[9]

[5] See the expert witness profiles in Appendix I, cfr. infra.

[6] Concept by legal scholar David Caudill, sociotechnical arguments are a combination of technical and extralegal rhetorical strategies. See Caudill, David. 2005. Sociotechnical Arguments in Scientific Discourse: Expert Depositions in Tobacco Litigation. *The Review of Litigation* 24, 1–2.

[7] For a discussion on these databases, see Part III, Sect. 13.4.3. Game III: The Third Wave of Tobacco Litigation, cfr. infra.

[8] See Appendix I, cfr. infra.

[9] See Appendix II, cfr. infra.

Appendix III offers tables on the involvement of historians as expert judicial witnesses in tobacco litigation as well as a list with Westlaw references.[10] The witness profile gives general information on the historian, in addition to his or her tobacco-related activity.[11] Basic information consists of the name of the historian, the historian's professional occupation, the institution where the historian is currently employed, a direct link to a personal website, and a short biography. Furthermore, the level of education is addressed [all the historians involved had a Ph.D., except for consultant John Drobny[12]], the historian's fields of research, and their major publications. In relation to tobacco litigation, I have added the number of cases in which the historian in question has participated and a table which details in chronological order the name of the case, the year of the trial, and the manner in which the witness was involved in the case. I have compiled this list by elaborating on previous lists and by researching The Tobacco Deposition and Trial Testimony Archive (DATTA), which can be found online.[13] In addition, I have researched historians and cases via the legal database Westlaw.[14] This quantitative analysis has allowed me to transcend a level of anecdotal discussion and haphazard name calling, which is frequent in most articles concerning expert witnesses on tobacco,[15] and to present a systematic overview of the involvement of historians in tobacco litigation. In every case discussed, I have added the historians involved and referred to their respective witness profiles. This has provided an inquiry in which the involvement of historians in tobacco related litigation has really been able to connect the individual dots end lose ends which plague all areas of litigation-driven history because of legal tactics to minimize the paper trail of the involvement of legal counsel and the historian. When the historian is deposed or testifies, records of the proceedings in which the expert witness is concerned become easier to retrieve.[16]

[10]See Appendix III, cfr. infra.

[11]For the Standard Expert Witness Profile with extra explanation see Expert Witness Profile No. 0.

[12]See Expert Witness Profile No. 13, John Drobny.

[13]To consult to DATTA go to http://legacy.library.ucsf.edu/action/search/basic. Accessed 31 Oct 2014. This is the search engine of The Legacy Tobacco Documents Library, which comprises all the online available internal documents of the tobacco industry and the judicial documents of tobacco litigation. I have furthermore made use for compiling these profiles from different internet databases, namely the TDO, DATTA, LTDL, and also the lists on expert witnessing compiled by Childs, Kyriakoudes, and Proctor, and also the CVN Law School database of court videos. See for more information on my quantitative research and its results: Part III, Chap. 17: Final Conclusion on the Involvement of Historians in Tobacco Litigation, cfr. infra.

[14]Most profiles offer Westlaw references to trial records from tobacco litigation.

[15]I discuss the debate on the involvement of historians in tobacco litigation in Part III, Chap. 15: Debates: Reflections in Academic and National Media. I have reviewed articles from academic journals as well as from newspapers such as *The New York Times*.

[16]I have made the argument that historians should testify in court and act not only as fact-finders, in contrast with what Alain Wijffels has proposed: namely to limit the involvement of the historian to the fact-finding process before the trial. See: Part II, Chap. 8: A Reassessment of Wijffels' Concept

In addition, this approach of combining a qualitative and a quantitative approach has allowed me to make a schematic overview of all historians involved with their basic information.[17] Through the examination of those schematics and results of my qualitative inquiry into the landmark case *US v. Philip Morris et al.*, I have procured conclusions on the involvement of expert witnesses in tobacco litigation on the subjects of (A) advocacy, (B) ethics, and (C) transparency, which I discuss in Chap. 16. (A) As we have seen in the first and second part of this book, objectivity and its antithesis advocacy are problematic issues in the historical discipline and this controversial subject becomes even more problematic when historians engage in litigation-driven history. In tobacco litigation, the argument is made that historians become hired guns. This accusation is not farfetched, as some historians who testified in tobacco litigation made over half a million dollars for their litigation-related work. (B) After a qualitative analysis of *US v. Philip Morris et al.*, I put the *Code of Ethics*, drafted by Belgian historian Antoon De Baets into practice. In his book *Responsible History* from 2009, De Baets presents a twenty-article long *code of ethics* for historians.[18] The proposed code lists the rights as well as the duties of historians. Furthermore, De Baets proposes a definition of "the abuse of history." I use his definition and his *code of ethics* to determine, based on my qualitative examination of the involvement of the five historians who served as expert witnesses in *US v. Philip Morris et al*, whether these historians conducted historical research in an ethical manner. I examine whether they transgressed any articles of the code proposed by De Baets and whether they abused history according to the definition of De Baets. (C) The most significant problem with the involvement of historians in tobacco litigation is the lack of transparency. As a conclusion, I argue that these three interconnected problems can be addressed by the historical community through the collective application of ethical codes such as the one by De Baets.

In order to continue the interdisciplinary approach of my research, I discuss articles from legal scholars as well as from historians. As mentioned before, the books by Brandt and Proctor are woven through this part of my research because of the heavy involvement by both authors with the subject. Furthermore, because of the easy accessibility of the industry's archives and the litigation-related documents, I had access to an enormous amount of primary sources. The trial records, especially, offered hundreds of pages of court transcripts for my discourse analysis on the landmark case *US v. Philip Morris et al.*

In conclusion, this third part of the book presents an overview of the practice of expert witnessing by historians in tobacco litigation. By presenting the forensic

of Forensic History, cfr. supra. The opportunity to review the litigation-driven work by historians in tobacco litigation is solely possible because of these publically accessible trial records.

[17] See Appendices II and III, cfr. infra.

[18] De Baets, Antoon. 2009. *Responsible History*. New York: Berghahn Books.

practice of history in tobacco litigation in four basic characteristics; namely, *what*, *when*, *how*, and *who*- while informed, detailed, and cross-referenced with the results of a quantitative and qualitative approach, I will have arrived at a legitimate point to define my concept of the forensification of history in the final conclusion of this book.

Bibliography

Caudill, David. 2005. Sociotechnical arguments in scientific discourse: Expert depositions in tobacco litigation. *The Review of Litigation* 24: 1–56.

De Baets, Antoon. 2009. *Responsible history*. New York: Berghahn Books.

Chapter 10
A History of Tobacco

You must have a cigarette. A cigarette is the perfect type of a perfect pleasure. It is exquisite, and it leaves one unsatisfied. What more can you want?

Oscar Wilde (1891)

Abstract In this first chapter on the historical aspects of the testimony of expert historians in tobacco litigation, I discuss the origin and rise of the tobacco industry and its product. There are seven key developments which I review here: flue-curing, safety matches, mechanization, the oligopolistic structure of the industry, World War I, taxation, and aggressive advertising campaigns. Their combined dynamic introduced, what Brandt has called: "The Cigarette Century."

In this chapter, I present an elementary history of tobacco.[1] After the discovery of America, tobacco products soon conquered the known world. Chewing tobacco, pipe tobacco, and cigars were introduced to the world from the sixteenth century onward. It was only in the first decades of the twentieth century that cigarettes became the number one tobacco product. In explaining the impressive triumph of the cigarette, I identify seven key developments which led to the almost inherent presence of cigarettes in social practices throughout the twentieth century. For this chapter I drew from two field defining works; *The Cigarette century* by Allan Brandt and *Golden Holocaust* by Robert Proctor. Both works are extremely thoroughly documented. These books are the products of litigation-driven historical research. Brandt and Proctor have served as expert witnesses in tobacco litigation. The research both historians have done has been used as part of their witness testimony in court. A book review in the British medical journal *The Lancet* stated that: "[t]*he Cigarette Century* is a model for the writing of engaged history: should others follow it, it would not be the worst thing for medical history."[2] While in the

[1] For a visual history of cigarettes, see the website of *the Tobacco Atlas,* a project by the *World Lung Foundation* http://www.tobaccoatlas.org/uploads/Images/PDFs/TA4_pdf_history.pdf. Accessed 31 Oct 2014.

[2] Gilman, Sander. 2007. A Smoking Century. *The Lancet* 369, 1594.

R. Delafontaine, *Historians as Expert Judicial Witnesses in Tobacco Litigation*, Studies in the History of Law and Justice 4, DOI 10.1007/978-3-319-14292-0_10

same journal Proctors work was described as "Proctor's morally engaged historical analysis represents a damning indictment of the US tobacco industry and its well-paid accomplices."[3] By addressing the history of the cigarette here, I can more clearly demonstrate which historical evidence in tobacco litigation historians like Brandt and Proctor bring to the courtroom as expert witnesses.

10.1 The Early History of the Nicotiana Tabacum

Before the cigarette there was tobacco.[4] The tobacco plant is native to all of the Americas and has been smoked, chewed, snorted, and drunk for hundreds or even thousands of years.[5] Long before Columbus and other Europeans went ashore the newly discovered continent, tobacco had been domesticated and cultivated by Native Americans. The Mayans and the Toltecs smoked pipes and rolled tobacco leaves together to smoke. Tobacco played a critical role in their religious and healing practices. Depending on the manner in which it was used, tobacco could produce hallucinogenic experiences.[6] No one knows whether there were any diseases caused by smoking in the pre-Columbian Americas.[7] Spanish explorers testified to having seen natives smoke dried leaves or smoking tobacco from a pipe. The conquistadors brought tobacco back home with them and introduced it in Europe. Especially tobacco's possible medical advantages and its ability to alter the psychic state of its users, received a lot of attention.[8] The active and addictive substance in tobacco; nicotine was named after Jean Nicot. He was a French diplomat and consul to the King of France, who brought the plant from Portugal to his fatherland in 1559.[9] Nicot described tobacco oil to be a powerful toxin.

Soon after it was brought to the continent, tobacco became a European commodity.[10] Within a century after Columbus' voyage, tobacco was grown around the globe.[11] Especially the Portuguese, with their globally connected network of trade posts, made tobacco into a top notch commercial commodity which secured its global spread. Brandt remarks: "Although the health implications of this traffic

---

[3]Hall, Wayne. 2012. A Historian's Indictment of the US Tobacco Industry. *The Lancet* 379, 1091.

[4]Brandt, Allan. 2007. *The Cigarette Century. The Rise, Fall and Deadly Persistence of a Product that Defined America.* New York: Basic Books, 19.

[5]Proctor, Robert. 2012. *Golden Holocaust: Origins of the Cigarette Catastrophe and the Case for Abolition.* Berkeley: University of California Press, 27.

[6]Goodman, Jordan. 1993. *Tobacco in History: the Cultures of Dependence.* London: Routledge, 3–5.

[7]Proctor, as n. 5, 27.

[8]Brandt, as n. 4, 20.

[9]Proctor, as n. 5, 27.

[10]Goodman, as n. 6, 167.

[11]Goodman, as n. 6, 51–55.

were widely noted from the earliest contact, it would have been impossible to predict that tobacco would produce a pandemic three centuries later."[12]

Some Europeans were disgusted by the habit of smoking. In 1604, King James I of England wrote a treatise titled *A Counter-Blaste to Tobacco*. In this essay, the King declared his disgust for the "vile costume of tobacco taking." In what now seems an unheeded warning,[13] the king continued: "a custom loathsome to the eye, hateful to the nose, harmful to the brain, dangerous to the lung."[14] In addition to his outcry, the king announced a substantial tax on tobacco products, thereby setting a precedent for future governments.[15] Notwithstanding opinions such as these, demand for tobacco rose sharply, and by the end of the seventeenth century half of the adult male population in England was smoking.[16] Other Europeans countries saw the same trends.[17] The rising demand for tobacco helped shape the character of the American colonies.[18] Although growing tobacco was a very difficult and a risky process which took 15 months to complete, it remained the most profitable of crops for American settlers.[19]

Tobacco consumption continued to rise and new production methods were researched and altered to meet growing demands. Pipe tobacco, chewing tobacco, and rolled cigars became widespread. "By the nineteenth century tobacco and its products were deeply embedded in the new nation's [the United States] social experience–in its commerce, its labour, its leisure, and its social ritual–all before the cigarette became the dominant form of tobacco consumption."[20] Charles Dickens, on a tour through the United States in 1842, was struck by the ever-present habit of chewing tobacco. He observed that everyone had accepted this "filthy custom."[21] All three forms of smoking gained popularity. Cigar smoking became a powerful symbol of social authority and of power.[22]

[12]Brandt, as n. 4, 21.

[13]Brandt, as n. 4, 21.

[14]King James I. 1604. *Counter-Blaste to Tobacco*. Robert Barker: London. http://www.gutenberg.org/files/17008/17008-h/17008-h.htm. Accessed 31 Oct 2014.

[15]See Part III, Sect. 1.2.6. Taxation, cfr. infra.

[16]Goodman, as n. 6, 60.

[17]Goodman, as n. 6, 61–70.

[18]Brandt, as n. 4, 21.

[19]Brandt, as n. 4, 22.

[20]Brandt, as n. 4, 25.

[21]Dickens, Charles. 1874. *American notes; Pictures from Italy*. London: Chapman and Hall, 130–131.

[22]Brandt, as n. 4, 25.

10.2 The Shift to Cigarettes

Although cigarettes had been around for centuries, they had never been popular. Lacking the means for more expensive tobacco products, cigarettes were a cheap commodity for the urban poor and young. Brandt argues that the shift towards a cigarette oriented tobacco industry came about through radical changes of production means, which in turn led to changes of tobacco consumption patterns.[23] Proctor concurs with Brandt that cigarettes were not "terribly popular until the early decades of the twentieth century."[24] Until the nineteenth century tobacco use caused only limited health effects, but the shift towards cigarettes proved to be "far more popular and far more injurious."[25] In explaining the triumph of the cigarette, Proctor points out eight crucial events, six of which I shall elaborate on in this chapter, namely: flue-curing, matches, mechanization of manufacturing, World War I, taxation, and mass marketing.[26] The other two reasons, (1) manipulation of knowledge and (2) manipulation of tobacco chemistry, were not added to this chapter because they partially describe the policy of tobacco companies when cigarettes had already become a dominant tobacco product, which is the subject of the following chapter and another important element in assessing the alleged negligence claims made in tobacco litigation against the tobacco industry.[27] In addition and following Brandt, I added one more reason; namely the oligopolistic structure of the tobacco industry. This overview on the origin of the cigarette and the tobacco industry offers historical characteristics of a product and an industry that defined America. Furthermore, this historical overview explains the origins of health-problems caused by smoking, which are also addressed in tobacco litigation. Moreover, by examining a short genealogy of the tobacco industry, we will better understand the industry's legal tactics in court.

10.2.1 The Invention of Flue-Curing[28]

Tobacco had to be dried before it could be used. Open fires proved unpredictable and hard to control. By the middle of the nineteenth century large furnaces with iron piping were used in combination with charcoal instead of wood to dry the

[23]Brandt, as n. 4, 25.

[24]Proctor, as n. 5, 28.

[25]Proctor, Robert. 2004. The Global Smoking Epidemic: A History and Status Report. *Clinical Lung Cancer* 5, 372.

[26]Proctor, as n. 5, 29.

[27]In an article from 2004 Proctor also distinguishes between the first six and the latter two events. See Proctor, as n. 25.

[28]Proctor, as n. 5, 28.

tobacco leaves. This modus operandi was named flue-curing. Flue-curing produced enough heat and could be carried out under controllable conditions.[29] The danger of fire was reduced and the tobacco was no longer exposed to smoky fumes that could wreck the taste. But as Proctor notes, the most important consequence of the flue-curing process was achieved in smokability. Bright tobacco, tobacco dried by flue-curing tasted much milder when smoked. The process increased the sugar content. Sweeter and more flavourful cigarettes are milder and thus better inhalable. Tobacco companies continued to research and develop cigarettes that were more comfortable to inhale. This *American blend* would revolutionize smoking.[30]

According to Proctor, "[i]t is hard to overestimate the impact of this innovation."[31] Proctor's statement expresses the fact that until that point in history smokers rarely inhaled into the lungs but rather only into the mouth and nose. Up until the 1950s American epidemiologists asked on their survey forms: "Do you inhale?"[32] The smoke of flue-cured tobacco was easily inhaled into the lungs, producing a more profound level of addiction.[33] Brandt comes to the same conclusion: "[n]icotine addiction was born in the serendipitous marriage of bright tobacco and flue-curing."[34] The deadly health effects of drawing smoke and nicotine into the lungs prompted Brandt to the following conclusion: "[t]his physiological process would create a mass industry and a consequent epidemic of tobacco-related diseases."[35] Proctor goes one step further when he argues that "[f]lue curing may well be the deadliest invention in the history of modern manufacturing."[36]

10.2.2 Matches[37]

Not until the nineteenth century were matches with a controlled phosphorus burn devised.[38] Before matches or lighters, smokers needed a pre-existing flame or some kind of tinderbox. Matches allowed "the making of fire to become mobile, convenient, and ubiquitous."[39] White phosphorus matches were invented in the 1830s, but these were very dangerous. These matches caught fire when a person

[29]Brandt, as n. 4, 24.
[30]Proctor, as n. 5, 33–34.
[31]Proctor, as n. 25, 372.
[32]Proctor, as n. 5, 32.
[33]Proctor, as n. 25, 372.
[34]Brandt, as n. 4, 24.
[35]Brandt, as n. 4, 24.
[36]Proctor, as n. 5, 34, 561.
[37]Proctor, as n. 5, 28.
[38]Proctor, as n. 5, 36.
[39]Proctor, as n. 5, 28.

was unaware and caused poisonous fumes and rotting teeth.[40] Safety matches were soon developed, these could only be ignited using a specially prepared surface on the box. This advancement limited the risk of accidental fire. Safety matches were easily produced in large numbers. Furthermore, they demanded little skill to light cigarettes with great speed and convenience. These innovations were essential to the rise of cigarettes as an immensely popular product.[41] The twentieth century saw the proliferation of fire-making devices, like the liquid-fuel metallic lighter. These lighters were rapidly mass produced, making it even easier to light *a stick* whenever and wherever you wanted.[42]

10.2.3 Mechanization of Cigarette Manufacturing[43]

Cigarettes were hand rolled by cigarette rollers up until the first years of the 1880s. These workers produced around 500 to 1,500 cigarettes a day.[44] Despite several patents on automated cigarette-rolling machines, hand rolling remained the only process reliable enough for commercial cigarettes. A young Virginian inventor, named James Bonsack designed an automated cigarette rolling machine in 1881. It required three human attendants, but it produced over 200 cigarettes every minute.[45] The next machine Bonsack designed, produced over 100,000 cigarettes on a daily basis, multiplying the daily production rate of traditional hand rollers by 200.[46]

The cost of production fell, and soon machines replaced hand rollers throughout the industry.[47] The Bonsack machine did not fare well with the cigar industry, which was at the time a much older and more successful industry than the cigarette business.[48] Cigars were far more difficult to produce with a machine, due to the fact that cigars are rolled in leaves instead of paper.[49] At the beginning of the twentieth century, companies from other nations followed the American example and designed better and faster devices. British, French, and German machines soon rivalled American designs. By the turn of the century tobacco rolling machines produced 500 cigarettes per minute.

---

[40] Proctor, as n. 25, 372.

[41] Proctor, as n. 5, 37.

[42] Proctor, as n. 5, 37.

[43] Proctor, as n. 5, 28.

[44] Proctor, as n. 5, 40.

[45] Brandt, as n. 4, 27.

[46] Proctor, as n. 25, 372.

[47] Proctor, as n. 5, 39.

[48] Brandt, as n. 4, 30.

[49] Proctor, as n. 5, 39.

This evolution put the cigarette rollers at a serious disadvantage. In the 1930s cigar rollers in Germany protested against this mechanization out of fear for their jobs. The Nazi government responded with legislation which banned the use of machinery in cigar factories. The cigar industry returned the favour by supporting the Nazi party. The Sturmzigarette the storm troopers' own brand and their chief source of income, also remained hand rolled.[50] After the war, production followed rising consumption rates. In 1976, the Molins Mark 9 produced 5,000 cigarettes per minute, the Molins Mark I had been the first in 1926 to produce over a 1,000 cigarettes per minute. By 1998, the Lorillard's machine produced 16,400 cigarettes per minute. The absolute state of the art cigarette-rolling machine is called the G. D. 121 P, which has an output of 20,000 cigarettes per minute.[51] Rapid production and lowered costs were the benefits of mechanization for the tobacco industry. In addition, machines made it possible to add additives to tobacco products. Many of these can be regarded as toxic or poisonous. As we shall see in the following chapters, tobacco companies have stressed that smoking is an adult choice. It is the consumer's choice to smoke, fully aware of the health hazards attributed to smoking. Cigarettes are presented by the industry as if they were an unalterable and natural part of human custom. Proctor remarks that historians, policy makers, or even tobacco control experts have heeded little attention to the way in which cigarettes are produced. "That, of course, is precisely how the industry wants it: all the burden of 'choice' is put on the smoker, while none on the manufacturer."[52] The history of the mechanization tells us a whole other story; the way in which cigarettes are produced and which additives are used, are the responsibility of the industry itself. The manner in which cigarettes are produced and to what extent the industry uses additives, like heightened nicotine levels, are important issues in tobacco litigation. This is just one of the historical insights on the cover-up administrated by the tobacco companies that historians have brought to the courtroom as expert witnesses.[53]

10.2.4 The Oligopolistic Structure of the Tobacco Industry[54]

Brandt describes another and no less important innovation by James Duke, the first cigarette producer to completely replace his hand rollers by Bonsack machines. Using his strategy of aggressively undercutting the selling-price of his competitors on the one hand and the continuous mechanization of his production process on the other hand; Duke claimed a dominant position in the American tobacco industry in

[50] Proctor, as n. 5, 42.

[51] Proctor, as n. 5, 37.

[52] Proctor, as n. 5, 43.

[53] Proctor, as n. 5, 42–43.

[54] A market condition in which sellers are so few that the actions of any one of them will materially affect price and have measurable impact on its competitors.

the final decades of the nineteenth century. Duke also sought to expand the company abroad, establishing companies in countries like Canada, Australia, Britain, Japan, and China.[55] Thereby laying the foundations of a global tobacco industry. In his quest to make a more efficient and profitable company, Duke convinced most other tobacco companies to join him in a trust that would be known as the American Tobacco Company. In 1890, the newly formed Tobacco Company could claim a virtual monopoly, controlling almost 90 % of all cigarettes sales in the United States.[56] The consolidation of the Tobacco Trust transformed the tobacco industry from a collection of small family-companies into a conglomerate of a few players, Big Tobacco was born.

During times of economic downturn at the beginning of the twentieth century, the US Congress and US federal courts sought to limit the power of corporate capitalism. In 1907, the Department of Justice indicted American Tobacco for violation of the Sherman Act.[57] The American Tobacco Company not only controlled 80–90 % of all cigarettes sales, but also 75–85 % of sales of all other sorts of tobacco products, with the exception of the cigar business. American Tobacco was one of the three largest companies in the United States, together with US Steel and Standard Oil. When the Department of Justice filed a lawsuit against American Tobacco, accusing the company of being in violation of the Sherman Act, the federal court that initially heard the case banned the company from interstate trading until competitive conditions were restored. In May 1911, the US Supreme Court ordered the dissolution of the American Tobacco Company. That very same day, the Supreme Court also ordered the breaking up of the Standard Oil Trust.[58] The court described how the ruthless design of the trust erected a perpetual barrier for any other company that wished to enter the tobacco trade. The court found that the trust had an injurious restraint on commerce and trade.[59] For 8 months American Tobacco and the attorney general and other court judges negotiated a settlement. The settlement that was agreed upon was tagged by assistant attorney general Jim McReynolds, who was the chief prosecutor of the case, as a: "subterfuge fit only for the scrapheap."[60]

What McReynolds meant was that although on paper the Tobacco Trust had been dissolved, the major players in the industry remained in control of the dominant positions in the market. One commentator at the time, Louis Brandeis, called the

---

[55]Brandt, as n. 4, 34–37.

[56]Brandt, as n. 4, 31–34.

[57]The Antitrust Act of July 2, 1890, 15 U.S.C. §§ 1–7, also called the Sherman Antitrust Act. http://www.justice.gov/atr/public/divisionmanual/chapter2.pdf. Accessed 31 Oct 2014.

[58]Brandt, as n. 4, 39.

[59]U.S. Supreme Court, *United States v. American Tobacco Co.*, 221 U.S. 106, 193 (1911). http://supreme.justia.com/cases/federal/us/221/106/case.html. Accessed 31 Oct 2014.

[60]Brandt, as n. 4, 40–41. Settling and extralegal strategies are favourite tactics of the tobacco industry as we shall see; for example in Part III, Sect. 13.2.2. The Master Settlement Agreement & Part III, Sect. 13.4.2. Game II: The Second Wave of Tobacco Litigation, cfr. infra.

settlement "[a]n illegal trust legalized."[61] Brandt arrives at the same conclusion: "[d]issolving the monopoly merely put an oligopoly in its place."[62] The tobacco industry became almost impossible to enter for new competitors because of its oligopolistic structure. Another reason why it was so difficult for new companies to compete with established tobacco companies was: consumer loyalty. Smokers were and still are very loyal customers. Many smokers stick to one brand during their entire life. Entering the market for smaller tobacco companies was "like picking a number at roulette."[63] After the settlement, three major tobacco companies remained: the American Tobacco Company, Liggett & Meyers, and R.J. Reynolds. Even during the Great Depression the big three were not threatened by so-called cheapies, cigarettes that were made from very low-quality tobacco.[64] Only one company would be added to this dominant trio; namely Philip Morris.[65] Philip Morris entered the ranks of the Big Three in 1933 as an independent company that had arisen from the debris of the old American Tobacco Trust. Its most famous brand was the Marlboro cigarette.[66]

The boundless ambitions of Duke and other cigarettes producers gave rise to a tobacco industry controlled by a few players. Utterly exploiting the critical link between mass production and mass consumption and fully aware of the highly addictive properties of their product, the industry strived to achieve the global and impressive potential of their product.[67] Mechanization and addiction are key factors to explain why cigarettes have become one of the most lucrative products ever sold. Proctor quotes Warren Buffet on the subject explaining his takeover of R.J. Reynolds: "I'll tell you why I like the cigarette business. It costs a penny to make. Sell it for a dollar. It's addictive."[68]

Economists have called the structure of the industry: oligopolistic.[69] Sloan et al. argue that the oligopolistic structure of the industry allowed it to better defend itself against shocks from harmful litigation.[70] This oligopolistic structure of the tobacco industry accounts for what Brandt has described as an industry marked,

[61] Brandt, as n. 4, 41. Similar sentiments were common after the settlements by the tobacco industry in the 1990s, see Part III, Sect. 13.2.2. The Master Settlement Agreement, cfr. infra.

[62] Brandt, as n. 4, 40–41.

[63] Brandt, as n. 4, 93.

[64] Ten cent cigarettes. See Brandt, as n. 4, 93.

[65] Brandt, as n. 4, 41–42.

[66] Brandt, as n. 4, 95.

[67] Brandt, as n. 4, 42–43.

[68] Proctor, as n. 5, 42.

[69] Sloan, Frank, Trogdon, Justine, and Mathews, Carrie. 2005. Litigation and the Value of Tobacco companies. *Journal of Health Economics* 24, 427–429.

[70] We will come back to this topic at a later point in this book. See Part III, Sect. 13.3.2. Smaller Cases, cfr. infra.

despite "intense competition among manufacturers", by "their intimate collusion."[71] The industry's astounding ability for conspiring will become more apparent in the following chapters on the tobacco industry's history and its litigation strategies.[72]

10.2.5 World War I[73]

At the beginning of the twentieth century smoking was widely recognized as a dirty habit, typical for disreputable men and boys.[74] Just like alcohol consumption, tobacco use was seen as an unhealthy way of life and as an immoral one. For those reasons an anti-tobacco crusade was organized. Many US states adopted legislation to prohibit the sale of cigarettes to minors or banished the sales of cigarettes altogether.[75] In 1914, Henry Ford published a widely circulated essay under the title *The Case Against the Little White Slaver.* Therein Ford vowed not to hire smokers because of their loose morals and untruthful behaviour.[76] Despite this active opposition, cigarette sales kept on soaring. Several opinion makers and newspapers complained about the ever present veil of smoke now common in public places like subways and restaurants. One health reformer noted: "[s]moking has become so nearly universal among men, the few non-smokes are practically ignored and their rights trampled upon."[77]

An important turning point for the opposition against smoking was the First World War.[78] In the military, the cigarette, like alcohol, had been considered as a product which undermined military discipline. In 1907, the Navy Surgeon General, General Presley Morion Rixey, recommended that sailors under the age of 21 be prohibited from smoking. This idea met with fierce resistance among young sailors.[79] When World War I came, the moral dangers of cigarette smoking to discipline seemed frivolous when faced with the horrors of the European battlefield. When asked what the nation could do to assist in the war, American general Pershing demanded only two things from the home front: "[y]ou ask me what we need to

[71]Brandt, as n. 4, 42.

[72]See, for example: Part III, Sect. 13.4.1. Game I: The First Wave of Tobacco Litigation, cfr. infra.

[73]Proctor, as n. 5, 28.

[74]Brandt, as n. 4, 45.

[75]Brandt, as n. 4, 46–47.

[76]Ford, Henry. 1914. *The Case Against the Little White Slaver.* Vol. I-IV. Detroit: Henry Ford. http://babel.hathitrust.org/cgi/pt?id=mdp.39015071599628;page=root;view=1up;size=100;seq=1;orient=0. Accessed 31 Oct 2014.

[77]Brandt, as n. 4, 48.

[78]Proctor, as n. 25, 372.

[79]Brandt, as n. 4, 50–51.

win this war. I answer tobacco, as much as bullets."[80] Soldiers received cigarettes systematically as part of their rations. Cigarettes relaxed the mind and calmed the spirit. Cigarettes became known as *the friends in the trenches*. Even the Red Cross handed them out.[81] Cigarettes became symbols of brotherhood, and donating cigarettes to the army became an act of patriotism. Advertisers came up with slogans like: "When our boys light up, the Huns will light out."[82] When Germany signed the Treaty of Versailles in 1918, millions of American soldiers brought their addiction home with them.

10.2.6 Taxation[83]

I have already remarked that King James I of England, in addition to his treatise *A Counter-Blaste to Tobacco,* issued a tax on tobacco.[84] Proctor argues that taxation is one of the most important factors behind the rise of the cigarette. Since cigarettes are easily to count, homogeneous, and always in demand, as a consequence of addiction, governments started to depend on cigarette sales as a source of revenue. For example, in the 1880s the revenue of the federal Government of the United States constituted for nearly one third of taxes on tobacco.[85] In the 1930s, one twelfth of the total income of the German government was coming from tobacco taxes. Half of the activities of the Nazi Brownshirts [Sturmabteilung] were financed with the profits from their own cigarette brand; which was called the Sturmzigarette.[86]

Even today tobacco taxes remain an important source of revenue for modern nations. Proctor names China, Japan,[87] Greece, and Brazil as countries where tobacco taxes make up for 2–10 % of the national revenue. There is a striking co-dependency between tobacco manufacturers and certain governments. Furthermore, there exists a conflict of interest between public health officials who want to curtail tobacco use on the one hand, and on the other hand governments who want to keep cigarette sales going based on short-sighted economic considerations, regardless of what is best for their people's health.[88]

---

[80] Brandt, as n. 4, 51.

[81] Proctor, as n. 25, 372–373.

[82] Brandt, as n. 4, 52–53.

[83] Proctor, as n. 5, 28.

[84] See Part III, Sect. 10.1. The Early History of the Nicotiana Tabacum, cfr. supra.

[85] Proctor, as n. 25, 373.

[86] Proctor, Robert. 1999. *The Nazi War on Cancer.* New York: Princeton University Press, 234–237.

[87] Japan is a special case because the Japanese government is itself a leading tobacco manufacturer. The same goes for China, where in addition one third of all the cigarettes made in the entire world are produced.

[88] Proctor, as n. 25, 373.

10.2.7 Mass-Marketing Techniques[89]

Few industries have been able to promote their product as successfully as the tobacco companies have done. The tobacco industry has successfully used mass-marketing to present cigarettes as an inherent part of the American way of life. American tobacco companies have spent billions of dollars on ads in newspapers, ads in popular magazines, radio ads, billboard posters, movie ads, product placement in movies and sitcoms, the hiring of celebrities to promote their product, and even sky writing.[90] Brands like R.J. Reynolds's Camel, Liggett & Myers's Chesterfield, and the American Tobacco Company's Lucky Strike became national American icons. Cigarettes were featured in movies wherein cinema stars smoked and blew smoke rings on the big screen. Cigarettes were everywhere in the public domain after World War I.[91] By the early 1930s, tobacco companies were spending unprecedented sums on advertising and all enlisted professional marketing experts.[92] Mass marketing and tobacco would stick together. Americans, in the decades after World War II, were constantly confronted with the symbols of these almost mythical brands.[93] Popular slogans as: "They're Toasted"[94] for Lucky Strike and "More doctors smoke Camels"[95] for the Camel brand, were well-known. Popular television shows in the 1950s and 1960s were brought to their audiences by Marlboro, Lucky Strike, and Winston.[96] Even *The Flintstones* smoked and declared their love for Winston cigarettes.[97]

Tobacco advertisements were aimed at young people. The cigarette became a symbol for adolescence.[98] Advertisement agencies succeeded in portraying smoking as symbols of masculinity as well as a symbol of beauty, glamour, and female sexuality. Some local communities penalized public establishments who allowed

---

[89]Proctor, as n. 5, 28.

[90]Proctor, as n. 25, 373.

[91]Brandt, as n. 4, 54–56.

[92]Brandt, as n. 4, 89.

[93]In his introduction "The Camel Man and Me", Brandt describes how he was fascinated as a seven year old boy by the Camel billboard looming above Times Square in New York city. "The Camel Man blew endless perfect smoke rings into the neon-lit night sky." Brandt, as n. 4, 1–5.

[94]Brandt, as n. 4, 70.

[95]Brandt, as n. 4, 105.

[96]Proctor, as n. 25, 373.

[97]Log on to YouTube and type in search words as "tobacco ads 1950" or "tobacco ads Flintstones." If you continue to broaden your search a little, you will be amazed by the amount and variety of adds featuring several notable actors, for example John Wayne and Sylvester Stallone. The same goes for pictures of tobacco ads that can be found with a Google search. One particular example features Ronald Reagan in an ad for Chesterfields.

[98]Brandt, as n. 4, 56.

women to smoke.[99] Female smokers broke another sex taboo and marketing campaigns actively sought to capitalize on this. Women were seen as an untapped market. Tobacco commercials led the charge to do away with taboos on women's rights.[100] Young women were soon fighting for the equal right to smoke. Cigarettes were "torches of freedom" for women. One ad man working for the industry cried out against his subordinate: "[t]hey're [women] smoking indoors. But damn it, if they spend half the time outdoors and we can get'em to smoke outdoors, we'll damn near double our female market."[101] The cigarette proved a divisive element in the struggle for gender equality, Brandt notes.[102] Cigarettes marketers also tried to take advantage of "the cult of personality" which emerged in the 1920s.[103] Tobacco marketing was innovative and very successful to target those groups that had the greatest potential: children and adolescents. These groups were extra-sensitive for the portrait of success and sex marketing companies painted around cigarettes. Young people were not only most easily influenced, they held the greatest commercial potential. Adults had less years left to smoke, while kids had a whole life of smoking in front of them. The tobacco companies had to constantly find "replacement smokers", since their costumers died because of their own product.[104]

In the years after World War I, the cigarette came under attack from many anti-tobacco groups who saw smoking as a symbol of unhealthy and amoral habits. Also the practice of nationwide marketing campaigns by the tobacco industry to influence consumer behaviour, raised questions. What if this powerful tool was used to bend consumer culture to antisocial ends?[105] In some instances these questions were not ungrounded. One analyst, who wrote in 1936 on the cigarette market, noted the following on tobacco advertising: "[t]he public must be given ideas as to what it should like, and it is quite surprising sometimes how the public is sold on what might look, in sales conference, like the brainchild of a demented person."[106] But the more the cigarette was attacked, the more popular it became.

---

[99] Brandt, as n. 4, 57–65.

[100] Brandt, as n. 4, 80–88.

[101] Brandt, as n. 4, 80.

[102] Brandt, as n. 4, 65.

[103] Brandt, as n. 4, 72.

[104] The term "replacement smokers" is an actual term used be the tobacco companies in their internal documents. For example, an internal tobacco industry document from 1984 which discussed the importance of younger adult smokers, stated that: "Younger adult smokers are the only source of replacement smokers." Burrows, Diane. 1984. Younger Adult Smokers: Strategies and Opportunities. LTDL. Bates Number: 505458066/8160. http://legacy.library.ucsf.edu/tid/bot15d00. Accessed on 31 Oct 2014. See also Brandt, as n. 4, 387–388, 503. The term was also used in the final verdict in the case *US v. Philip Morris et al.*, in which Judge Kessler convicted the tobacco companies for fraud against the American public, see Part III, Sect. 14.3. The Final Judgment by Judge Kessler, cfr. infra. For the verdict see http://www.library.ucsf.edu/sites/all/files/ucsf_assets/FinalOpinion_full_version.pdf. Accessed 31 Oct 2014.

[105] Brandt, as n. 4, 75.

[106] Brandt, as n. 4, 77.

To conclude this topic on the industry's marketing techniques, I give a final example of the success of tobacco's mass marketing success: the Marlboro Cowboy. The Marlboro man and his Marlboro country symbolized a mythic time of simple pleasures.[107] Brandt notes: "[r]arely, if ever, had marketing so brilliantly combined American values, traditions, and symbols with a promotional message. The campaign created a visual shorthand for the motivation for, and meaning of, smoking in an age of technology, science, risk, and disease. It offered images rich in denial and escapism, in reassurance and immortality. The Marlboro cowboy would find an enduring place at the American campfire."[108] The industry had succeeded to "reorient the-American- culture on behalf its product."[109] The cigarette had become "phenomenally popular, deeply embedded in social interactions, and the basis of an enormously successful and powerful business enterprise."[110]

10.3 The Rise of a Deadly Product

In the year 1900, 27 % of tobacco consumers smoked cigarettes. By 1952, a stunning 81 % of tobacco users smoked cigarettes.[111] As early as 1889, a cigarette critic gave an explanation for this remarkable success: "[w]hatever its merits and demerits, one thing is certain-namely, that there is an ever increasing subjection to the influence of this narcotic, whose soothing powers are requisitioned to counteract the evil effects of the worry, overpressure and exhaustion which characterize the age in which we live."[112] Cigarettes had successfully been marketed as a form of conspicuous consumption.[113]

I have now listed seven key elements that have contributed to the rise of the cigarette, namely flue-curing, safety matches, mechanization, the oligopolistic structure of the industry, World War I, taxation, and aggressive advertising campaigns. All these developments made the cigarette into the number one tobacco product. Moreover, cigarettes became an accepted and natural part of social behaviour. Cigarettes were available for both sexes, all races, all ages, and all nations. By the

[107]Starr, Michael. 1984. The Marlboro Man: Cigarette Smoking and Masculinity in America. *Journal of Popular Culture* 17, 45, 54–57.

[108]Brandt, as n. 4, 264.

[109]Brandt, as n. 4, 67.

[110]Brandt, as n. 4, 67.

[111]Brandt, as n. 4, 97.

[112]Brandt, as n. 4, 99.

[113]Brandt, as n. 4, 100.

middle of the twentieth century the so-called "cult of the cigarette" had conquered the whole world.[114] Although critics remained, an ever expanding industry knew its time had come: "the cigarette century had arrived."[115]

Bibliography

Brandt, Allan. 2007. *The cigarette century. The rise, fall and deadly persistence of a product that defined America*. New York: Basic Books.
Gilman, Sander. 2007. A smoking century. *The Lancet* 369: 1593–1594.
Goodman, Jordan. 1993. *Tobacco in history: The cultures of dependence*. London: Routledge.
Hall, Wayne. 2012. A historian's indictment of the US Tobacco Industry. *The Lancet* 379: 1091.
Proctor, Robert. 1999. *The Nazi war on cancer*. New York: Princeton University Press.
Proctor, Robert. 2004. The global smoking epidemic: A history and status report. *Clinical Lung Cancer* 5: 371–376.
Proctor, Robert. 2012. *Golden Holocaust: Origins of the cigarette catastrophe and the case for abolition*. Berkeley: University of California Press.
Sloan, Frank, Justine Trogdon, and Carrie Matthews. 2005. Litigation and the value of tobacco companies. *Journal of Health Economics* 24: 427–447.
Starr, Michael. 1984. The Marlboro Man: Cigarette smoking and masculinity in America. *Journal of Popular Culture* 17: 45–57.

[114]Brandt, as n. 4, 100.

[115]Brandt, as n. 4, 19, 67, 101, 260.

Chapter 11
Tobacco and Health: Towards a Contemporary Perspective

The boy who smokes cigarettes need not be anxious about his future, he has none.

David Starr Jordan (1915)

Abstract This second chapter on the history of the tobacco industry and its product tackles the discovery of health hazards associated with smoking. I have given extra attention to the difficulty that scientists have had with presenting smoking as the single cause of cancer or disease. This issue has allowed the tobacco companies to claim that there was a scientific controversy on the subject which needed further research in order to be conclusive. The chapter furthermore considers the 1964 Surgeon General Report on smoking. Lastly this second chapter covers the industry's ability to evade litigation and government oversight through well-funded lobbying networks.

While the previous chapter focused on the rise of the cigarette as a commodity, I now examine the history of the discovery of the health problems caused by cigarette smoking. Where diagnosing lung cancer had been a "once in a lifetime experience" for doctors at the end of the nineteenth century, it became alarmingly more frequent in the first decades of the twentieth century. During the 1940s and 1950s, epidemiologists found that there existed a causal link between lung cancer and smoking. In subsequent decades, medical scientists would identify even more cancers and diseases directly linked to smoking. Further research on nicotine revealed it was extremely addictive. The health risks linked to cigarette smoking and its addictive nature have had disastrous impacts on public health around the globe. Rather ironically, public health and smokers aren't the only victims of cigarettes. Every year, the tobacco companies lose millions of customers due to the deadly nature of its own product. The tobacco industry continues their search for a safer and a healthier cigarette which, until further notice, has yielded no significant success.

R. Delafontaine, *Historians as Expert Judicial Witnesses in Tobacco Litigation*, Studies in the History of Law and Justice 4, DOI 10.1007/978-3-319-14292-0_11

11.1 The Discovery of Tobacco Health Hazards

There is not one tobacco hazard, there are many. Already in the eighteenth century, pipe smoking was linked to cancer of the lip. Cancer of the mouth and throat was added to that list in the nineteenth century.[1] By 1946, medical scholars found that lung cancer cases had tripled in the last three decades.[2] Lung cancer had been very rare in the early years of the twentieth century. Scientific literature on the subject was scarce. When the number of instances of lung cancers had augmented, medical scholars debated on various possible causes. In 1923, the German Society for Pathology identified several probable causes for the rising number of lung cancers, including asphalt dust and tar emissions from newly paved roads, exposure to chemical warfare in the World War I, air pollution, the growing popularity of cigarettes, increased exposure to X-rays, and even interracial marriages.[3] In the 1940s, American researchers on cancer argued whether the steep rise in the instances of lung cancer was not simply "an artefact of new technical abilities to clearly diagnose diseases previously invisible to both medical science and public health?"[4] A British epidemiologist, Richard Doll, who reflected in an interview taken in 1991 on his work from 1948 on lung cancer, explained that it was not logical to link the rise of instances of lung cancer to smoking as "[c]igarette smoking was such a normal thing and had been for such a long time that it was difficult to think that it could be associated with any disease."[5] At the time, Doll would have "put his money" on the tarring of roads or the exhausts of motor cars, to explain the rising instances of lung cancer after World War II. This anecdote by Doll is an example of how the cigarette had already been institutionalized in daily life by the middle of the twentieth century. The unquestioned use of cigarettes made the product an unlikely suspect to account for a rising number of lung cancer diagnoses.

Nonetheless, there were some dissident voices. American newspapers reported several times during the first decades of the twentieth century on young men being destroyed by the poisonous effects of nicotine or the carbon monoxides of cigarette smoke.[6] Many physicians and surgeons warned about the negative physical and mental effects of smoking cigarettes.[7] Even when combined with moral arguments on the degenerate consequences of smoking, the anti-tobacco movement faced a seemingly insurmountable task. Consumption of the cigarette rose thanks to

[1]Proctor, Robert. 1999. *The Nazi War on Cancer.* New York: Princeton University Press, 234–237.

[2]Brandt, Allan. 2007. *The Cigarette Century. The Rise, Fall and Deadly Persistence of a Product that Defined America.* New York: Basic Books, 106.

[3]Proctor, Robert. 2004. The Global Smoking Epidemic: A History and Status Report. *Clinical Lung Cancer* 5, 374.

[4]Brandt, as n. 2, 122.

[5]s.n. 1991. Conversation with Sir Richard Doll. In *British Journal of Addiction* 86, 368.

[6]Brandt, as n. 2, 106–107.

[7]Brandt, as n. 2, 107–114.

the industry's mass-marketing techniques and nicotine's addictiveness. "The very popularity of the cigarette typically was cited as medical reassurance. How could the cigarette be dangerous if so many millions of Americans used it regularly without any apparent consequences?"[8]

Hermann Rottmann, a German physician, who researched the causal link between lung cancer and smoking, is generally credited with being the first scientist to have linked lung cancer with tobacco use. Though not correct in his explanation, Rottmann observed that women working in tobacco factories were more likely to get lung cancer. He thought the tobacco dust caused the cancer. The simple truth is that these workers had easy access to cigarettes and therefore became chain-smokers. This led to higher disease rates.[9] In the 1930s, statistical research on both sides of the Atlantic showed that patients with lung cancer were very often smokers. Although Brandt remarks that: "[i]t was one thing to suggest that smoking might harm susceptible individuals, and quite another to claim that it caused serious disease."[10] Studies were afraid to answer the causation question with "yes" or "no". Much was still uncertain. Individual variation seemed to have great influence. The elusiveness of this causal link prompted questions on some of the deepest issues in science. "How do we know?", "[a]re there alternate ways of knowing?" and "[w]hat constitutes proof?"[11]

A German physician and researcher, named Robert Koch, established a set of postulates to identify causal organisms in 1884. Koch singled out four postulates to serve as a fundamental basis to determine causality in instances of infection. His four postulates to determine such an organism were that it could be: (1) identified, (2) isolated, (3) grown in culture, and (4) utilized to induce disease. This model was met with negative criticism from physicians, including Koch himself. Although he himself was diagnosed as being infected with the tubercle bacillus, he showed no signs of the disease of Tuberculosis whatsoever.[12] By the 1950s, medical science understood that chronic diseases had to be explained through multicausal schemes. The value of Koch's postulates lies in the fact that it made other, more abstract approaches to causality seem outdated. In addition, it opened the door for more modern forms of epidemiological methods.[13]

---

[8]Brandt, as n. 2, 114.

[9]Proctor, as n. 3, 373.

[10]Brandt, as n. 2, 118.

[11]The historical answers to these causality questions are of significant importance in tobacco litigation and are therefore an important part of the testimony historians bring to court. Defining the moment when the scientific community accepted the causal connection between smoking cigarettes and lung cancer and other diseases is essential to determine the liability of the tobacco industry. Brandt, as n. 2, 118. See also the topic on tobacco tactics in litigation; Part III, Sect. 13.4.1. Game I: The First Wave of Tobacco Litigation, cfr. infra.

[12]Brandt, as n. 2, 119.

[13]Brandt, as n. 2, 120–121.

Doering and Lombard, two pioneering American epidemiologists, concluded in an article, which was published in 1928 in *The New England Journal of Medicine*, that "heavy smoking had some relation to cancer in general."[14] Frederick Hoffman, a statistician who analysed smoking as a cause of cancer, brought out a report in 1931. He described difficulties in testing these links and attributed them to test-subjects who had only recently switched to cigarettes as a preferred form of tobacco consumption. Smokers also had difficulty with remembering the amounts of cigarettes they smoked.

These methodological difficulties did not hold Hoffman from concluding that he was "strongly inclined to think that the increase [in lung cancer] is directly connected with the much wider spread of cigarette smoking habits." One of these habits, according to Hoffman, included the inhaling of the smoke into the lungs.[15] Hoffmann remained fairly mild in his advice to smokers. He urged smokers to smoke with moderation.[16] During the 1930s, the relationship between smoking and health hazards was an unresolved medical debate and it would remain so for another two decades.[17] Obstacles concerning methodology in epidemiology would remain problematic to assess the link between smoking and cancer in a conclusive manner until the late 1940s.[18]

In the 1930s and 1940s, Proctor argues, three important sources of evidence were established to link smoking to lung cancer. (1) The first is epidemiology, where cancer rates among smokers and non-smokers were compared.[19] These epidemiological studies further allowed patients to be ordered according to age, sex, occupation, and so forth. Studies could be styled in both a prospective and retrospective manner. The results of these studies linked smokers to lung cancer. One study by the English epidemiologists Doll and Hill arrived at a p value of 0.00000064. In other words the statistical significance (p), or the possibility that the relationship between smoking and lung cancer was merely coincidental, was less than one in a million.[20] American colleagues of Doll and Hill came to the same conclusion.[21] (2) A second method involved animal experiments. In these "mouse painting" experiments, backs of mice were shaved and smeared with tobacco tars. These mice soon developed tumours.[22] These findings gave strong

[14]Brandt, as n. 2, 123–124.

[15]As we have discussed earlier, inhalation had become easier with cigarettes because of the invention of flue-curing, see Part III, Sect. 10.2.1. The Invention of Flue-Curing, cfr. supra.

[16]Brandt, as n. 2, 125.

[17]Brandt, as n. 2, 124.

[18]Brandt, as n. 2, 125.

[19]Proctor, as n. 3, 374.

[20]Brandt, as n. 2, 138.

[21]Brandt, as n. 2, 131–134.

[22]Proctor, as n. 3, 374.

support to the epidemiological studies of Doll and Hill.[23] (3) A third line of survey comprised studies in cellular pathology. During autopsy, doctors found that precancerous changes in lung tissues were directly associated with exposure to tobacco smoke. By the mid-1950s, these three complementary sources of evidence - epidemiology, animal experiments, and pathologic evidence- had shown a clear and strong association between lung cancer and individual tobacco use.[24]

Still, many researchers were not convinced of a definite causal link between smoking and lung cancer.[25] The problem with epidemiological studies was that some form of bias from the researchers or unexpected variables could obscure the certainty of the causal relation. Arguments of bias and statistical manipulation were not easily countered.[26] Statisticians like Joseph Berkson and Sir Ronald Fisher observed that the flawed memory of patients could not serve as a basis for causal explanation.[27] Professor emeritus of surgery Evarts Graham of Washington University,[28] who had quit smoking, attributed much of this scepticism to the fact that many medical professionals themselves still smoked and were therefore blind or unwilling to acknowledge the association.[29] Critics, of whom the tobacco industry was the most vocal, warned against a headlong acceptance of the merely statistical relation between smoking and lung cancer. A statistical relation should not be accepted as a definite cause, the cigarette companies argued.[30] Was a statistical relationship enough to explain such a complex non-infectious chronic disease as lung cancer? Could statistical correlation proof that A was the sole active cause of B? Doll and Hill and their American counterparts Wynder and Graham continued to produce study after study with a complex amount of variables which demonstrated the causal relationship between smoking and cancer. Still critics persevered in asserting that no single study could conclusively demonstrate a causal relationship between smoking and cancer.[31] The issue of the "causal conundrum" was rather humorously addressed by Evarts Graham in *The Lancet* of 1954:

> We find that many thoughtful people believe that our experimental results bring to the statistical studies additional convincing evidence of an aetiological [causal] relation between

[23]Brandt, as n. 2, 147.

[24]Proctor, as n. 3, 347. Brandt arrives at a similar conclusion: Brandt, as n. 2, 148, 153.

[25]Brandt, as n. 2, 128–129.

[26]Brandt, as n. 2, 142.

[27]Brandt, as n. 2, 142–143.

[28]Dr. Evarts Graham performed the first successful pneumonectomy –the total removal of a cancerous lung- in 1933. Although he had quit smoking, five decades of smoke inhaling caught up on him. In 1957 the man, who had stood at the centre piece of epidemiological research on the causal relationship between smoking and cancer, passed away due to bronchogenic carcinoma; more commonly known as lung cancer. Brandt remarks rather cynical: "[i]n the end, he became yet one more data point in the lethal history of smoking." Brandt, as n. 2, 131, 157.

[29]Brandt, as n. 2, 156–157.

[30]Brandt, as n. 2, 139–140.

[31]Brandt, as n. 2, 140–141.

excessive cigarette-smoking and bronchogenic carcinoma. There are others, however, who remain unconvinced. These 'die-hards' state that so far no proof of the relation has been presented. One must grant that indeed no absolute proof has been offered. But what sort of proof is called for? To satisfy the most obdurate of the die-hards it would be necessary to take the following steps:

1. Secure some human volunteers willing to have a bronchus painted with cigarette tar, perhaps through a bronchial fistula.
2. The experiment must be carried on for at least twenty or twenty-five years.
3. The subjects must spend the whole period in air conditioned quarters, never leaving them even for an hour or so, in order that there may be no contamination by a polluted atmosphere.
4. At the end of the twenty-five years they must submit to an operation or an autopsy to determine the result of the experiment.

I will say to those who wish to volunteer for such an experiment, 'please form a queue to the right; no crowding please.'[32]

Although the convincing epidemiological evidence was generally accepted by mid-twentieth century, dissenting voices remained. During several decades the industry maintained there was a scientific controversy on the causal relation between tobacco and lung cancer. I will return to this subject in the next chapter.[33]

11.2 The Reports of the Surgeon General

By the 1950s, chronic diseases had overtaken contagious and infectious diseases as the major cause of death in the largest part of the Western world. The identification of cigarettes as major health hazards was a critical turning point in the history of public health policy. Public health policies would shift their attention from infection control to non-communicable diseases.[34] This refocus of public health policy immediately caused questions on the nature of public health. Was it the task of public health institutions to regulate personal behaviours? Who would decide which habits were unhealthy? Up until then public health authorities had only been active in the control of communicable diseases, where their involvement was in the clear interest of the nation's well-being. All other aspects of a person's health had been the well-guarded provenance of the medical profession.[35] The different focus of public health officials sparked resistance and defiance by the medical profession against actions on tobacco use by the public health sector. Doctors accused the public health sector of handling beyond its own boundaries and within those of the medical profession.

---

[32]Graham, Evarts. 1954. Remarks on the Aetiology of Bronchogenic Carcinoma. *The Lancet* 263, 1307.

[33]See Part III, Sect. 3.3.1. The Tobacco Controversy: A Careful Construction, cfr. infra.

[34]Brandt, as n. 2, 211.

[35]Brandt, as n. 2, 211–212.

Despite these tensions on professional border lines, a study group on smoking and health was organized in 1956. The commission was formed on the initiative of the U.S. Surgeon General, Leroy Burney. Members of the American Cancer Society, the National Heart Institute, the National Cancer Institute, and the American Heart Association met regularly to discuss the evidence on smoking and lung cancer. Epidemiological findings, animal studies, and pathological and histological studies all added evidence to strengthen the causal relationship.[36] The Surgeon General declared that the data on smoking and disease was convincing: "[t]he sum total of scientific evidence establishes beyond reasonable doubt that cigarette smoking is a causative factor in the rapidly increasing incidence of human epidermoid carcinoma of the lung."[37] He furthermore declared that "there is increasing evidence that excessive cigarette smoking is one of the factors which can cause lung cancer."[38]

The Public Health Service (PHS) assessed its own role in informing physicians, who were generally confused on what to tell their patients about smoking. The PHS was divided on whether to "put the message out" or to "avoid a missionary statement." Notwithstanding compelling demands for action from members of the National Cancer Institute, the PHS assigned itself a limited role in the discussion on smoking, in an attempt not to overstep their role vis-à-vis physicians.[39] The *Journal of the American Medical Association* (JAMA) published a defence of clinical authority: "[n]either the proponents nor the opponents of the smoking theory have sufficient evidence to warrant the assumption of an all-or-none authoritative position. Until definitive studies are forthcoming, the physician can fulfil his responsibility by watching the situation closely, keeping courant of the facts, and advising his patients on his appraisal of those facts."[40] The squabble on professional territory with the *American Medical Association* (AMA) and the PHS, prevented the PHS to act against the dangers of smoking early on and in a decisive manner.[41] The AMA, afraid to lose any professional domain, was furthermore against a congressional proposal to label tobacco products. "The answer that will do most to protect public health lies not in labelling ... but in research", explained F. Blasingame, chief executive of the AMA.[42] The following year the AMA *Education*

[36]Brandt, as n. 2, 212–213.

[37]Brandt, as n. 2, 213.

[38]Burney, Leroy. 1957. For Release in p.m. Newspapers. LTDL. Bates Number: HT0038152/8153. http://legacy.library.ucsf.edu/tid/ihm1aa00. Accessed 31 Oct 2014.

[39]Brandt, as n. 2, 214–216.

[40]Talbott, John. 1959. Smoking and Lung Cancer. *The Journal Of the American Medical Association* 171, 2102. LTDL. Bates Number: HT0002460/2460. http://legacy.library.ucsf.edu/tid/ovi3aa00. Accessed 31 Oct 2014.

[41]Brandt, as n. 2, 218.

[42]Blasingame, Francis. 1964. Full Text of AMA Letter of Testimony to F.T.C. *Journal of the American Medical Association* 188, 31. LTDL. Bates Number: 2058214825–2058214826. http://legacy.library.ucsf.edu/tid/upp47h00. Accessed 31 Oct 2014.

Research Fund received funding from the tobacco industry. The initial grant of $10 million assured the tobacco companies of the fervent endorsement of the medical association. And so even the AMA maintained that further research was necessary on the tobacco controversy.[43] The tobacco industry had found an unlikely ally in the *American Medical Association.*

In the following years pressure was building on the PHS to organize a commission on the matter of lung cancer and smoking. In the spring of 1962, President Kennedy was asked in a national press conference to comment on the idea. Kennedy was clearly not prepared for the question and his answer was unusually hesitant:

> Reporter: Mr. President, there is another health problem that seems to be causing growing concern here and abroad, and I think this has largely been provoked by a series of independent scientific investigations, which have concluded that cigarette smoking and certain types of cancer and heart disease have a causal connection.
>
> I have two questions. Do you and your health advisors agree or disagree with these findings, and secondly, what if anything should or can the Federal government do in the circumstances?
>
> President Kennedy: The a – That Matter is sensitive enough and the stock market is in sufficient difficulty – [laughter] – without my giving you -a- an answer which is not based on complete information, which I don't have, and therefore perhaps we could – I would be glad to respond to that question in more detail next week.[44]

Two weeks later, Kennedy's Surgeon General Luther Terry, a PHS veteran, announced the establishment of a committee fully equipped to investigate the controversy on smoking and health.[45] The committee would have ten members. Terry proved also politically adequate when he included smokers as well as non-smokers in the committee. In addition, independent researchers and others who were involved with the tobacco industry were selected. The way the committee was selected, pre-emptively neutralized possible attacks of bias simply because the committee was compromised of members who represented both sides of the debate on the health risks of smoking.[46] The selection process also ensured the presence of a variety of disciplines, confirming the notion that the determination of causality required a wide variety of medical and scientific perspectives.[47] The assignment of the U.S. Surgeon General's Advisory Committee was clear: to determine the "nature and magnitude of the health effects of smoking."[48] The final document the committee presented had to be scientifically impeccable, while still politically

[43]Brandt, as n. 2, 249.

[44]Personal transcription of *Transcript of the President's New Conference on Foreign and Domestic Matters.* 24/05/1962, 9. http://www.jfklibrary.org/Asset-Viewer/Archives/JFKPOF-056-007.aspx. Accessed 31 Oct 2014. An audio file is available on http://www.jfklibrary.org/Asset-Viewer/Archives/JFKWHA-100.aspx. Accessed 31 Oct 2014. The question concerning tobacco health hazards and the role of the Federal government is discussed from 21:09 to 22:00.

[45]Brandt, as n. 2, 219.

[46]Brandt, as n. 2, 219–220.

[47]Brandt, as n. 2, 220–221.

[48]Brandt, as n. 2, 221.

acceptable. President Kennedy was cautious not to alienate Southern Congressional delegations.[49] In spite of any political goals, the committee was allowed to shape clear guidelines for public health policy in the years to come. Essentially, it all came down to this single question: "[I]s smoking harmful?"[50] The outcome of the Committee could have brought the scientific controversy on the health risks of smoking to a rest.

The diverse scientific training and temperament of the committee members created a working atmosphere where tension was constant.[51] Three members smoked during meetings.[52] Louis Fieser, a noted chemist from Harvard, smoked up to four packs a day.[53] Another member of the committee, Maurice Seevers, could not accept the addictive nature of nicotine. Although the evidence lay right in front of him, he concluded that nicotine was not addictive by prevailing definitions. Seevers argued that cigarettes had no comparable social pathologies to alcohol, marijuana, or heroin. In preserving the committee's indispensable unanimity, the committee agreed to follow Seevers' interpretation.[54] It would take another 34 years before the *Surgeon General's Report of 1988* would declare that the addictive nature of smoking was caused by nicotine.[55]

As I have described, the term "causal" was of crucial importance in the cigarette controversy. The committee proceeded to define specific approaches to reach a causal conclusion and to further acknowledge the complexity of causal processes in the medical science.[56] The committee members sought criteria suited to divide cause from factor or associated determinant. The committee concentrated on one important question: whether smoking increased an individual's chance of developing a potentially life-threatening disease.[57] The group decided, noting that complexities were recognized, to use words like "a cause" or "a major cause" or "a significant cause," or "a causal association" in certain conclusions about smoking

---

[49]Brandt, as n. 2, 219. These Southern Democrats were concerned about the votes of tobacco farmers and the support of tobacco companies.

[50]Brandt, as n. 2, 222.

[51]Brandt, as n. 2, 223.

[52]*Press Conference by Surgeon General's Committee on Smoking and Health.* 11/01/1964, 6. LTDL. Bates Number: 690000006/0043. http://legacy.library.ucsf.edu/tid/kag33f00. Accessed 31 Oct 2014.

[53]Fieser was diagnosed with lung cancer in 1965. After his recovery he became a fervent anti-smoker. In an open-hearted letter to the other members of the committee he admitted that: "My case seems to me more convincing than any statistics." http://tobaccodocuments.org/profiles/fieser_lewis_f.html. Accessed 31 Oct 2014. & Brandt, as n. 2, 229.

[54]U.S. Department of Health, Education, and Welfare, Public Health Service, Office of the Surgeon General. 1964. *Smoking and Health: Report of the Advisory Committee to the Surgeon General of the Public Health Service,* 32. http://profiles.nlm.nih.gov/ps/access/NNBBMQ.pdf. Accessed 31 Oct 2014.

[55]Brandt, as n. 2, 223.

[56]U.S. Department of Health, as n. 54, 21.

[57]Brandt, as n. 2, 226–227.

and health, to affirm their conviction on the causal link between smoking and disease.[58] Furthermore, the report identified five principles to assess the causality problem. "Consistency of the association, strength of the association, specificity of association, temporal relationship of associated variables and coherence of the association" were the five criteria used to arrive at a rational and consistent scientific explanation.[59] The strength of the associations was undeniable and the consistency of the findings led to a definitive answer of the essential question: "[c]igarette smoking is a health hazard of sufficient importance in the United States to warrant appropriate remedial action", the committee concluded.[60] The report listed the dangers and over fourteen directly related diseases.[61] For example, in regard to lung cancer the report stated that: "[c]igarette smoking is causally related to lung cancer in men; the magnitude of the effect of cigarette smoking far outweighs all other factors."[62] The final conclusion of the report left no room for doubt: "... it is the judgment of the Committee that cigarette smoking contributes substantially to mortality from certain specific diseases and the overall death rate."[63]

On the 11th of January 1964, a press conference was held to convey the findings of the committee to the American public. When the Surgeon General was asked what he would advise his patients on smoking, Terry responded that if an individual wished to continue smoking, despite the findings of the report, that person should be well aware that he or she was subjecting himself/herself to "a definitive health risk."[64] One of the last questions was aimed at Hundley, the Assistant Surgeon General: "Did you in your consideration – did you come upon any scientific approach that had promises of eliminating the health hazards involved in smoking cigarettes?"[65] The answer was "No."

Several committee members had changed their views on tobacco, prompting some to quit smoking entirely or to switch to "safer" variants.[66] By contrast, the tobacco industry would not come to any acts of repentance. On the contrary, it continued to deny that there was any sufficient evidence. Despite their efforts, the authority of the *Surgeon General's Report* pushed the tobacco industry into a corner.[67] More remarkable, as we shall see in the following chapter, the industry had

[58]U.S. Department of Health, as n. 54, 21, 30–31.

[59]U.S. Department of Health, as n. 54, 182, 182–185.

[60]U.S. Department of Health, as n. 54, 33.

[61]U.S. Department of Health, as n. 54, 33–40.

[62]U.S. Department of Health, as n. 54, 37.

[63]U.S. Department of Health, as n. 54, 31.

[64]*Press Conference by Surgeon General's Committee on Smoking and Health*. 11/01/1964, 10–11. LTDL. Bates Number: 690000006/0043. http://legacy.library.ucsf.edu/tid/kag33f00. Accessed 31 Oct 2014.

[65]*Press Conference by Surgeon General's Committee on Smoking and Health*, as n. 64, 36–37.

[66]Brandt, as n. 2, 229–230.

[67]Brandt, as n. 2, 230–231.

already and independently come to the same conclusions as the *Surgeon General's Report*, yet the tobacco industry's official position on the subject of smoking and health issues had remained unchanged.

Brandt calls the *Surgeon General's Report of 1964* a "pivotal" document in the history of public health.[68] The PHS sent out 350,000 copies all over the United States. Lacking the funding for the establishment of any significant programs, the report did provide the Surgeon General's office with the necessary authority to counter tobacco companies and the scientific controversy on tobacco health hazards. In the following years, the surgeons general's reports would have a major impact on any issue of public health.[69] In addition, the report created a scientific model to pinpoint, in a systematic and coherent manner, a causal relationship in medical science.[70] Brandt calls it "a signal contribution not only to the history of the cigarette but to the history of public health."[71]

The findings of the *Surgeon General's Report* had little direct results on public health policy. The Federal Trade Commission (FTC) had jurisdiction only to investigate the industry's marketing campaigns. If an ad was found to be misleading, the FTC ordered its cessation. Though a nuisance for the industry, it was a very costly and time-consuming activity for the FTC. If an ad campaign was examined by the FTC, and it was declared unfit, the tobacco companies would just modify or abandon the ad, to replace it with a new or an even bolder alternative.[72]

The FTC pursued labelling of tobacco products through an Act of Congress. But the Federal Cigarette Labelling and Advertising Act of 1965 (FCLAA) that emerged from Congress bore "the fingerprints of the tobacco industry." A newly founded lobbying organization, the Tobacco Institute had done an excellent job lobbying the congressional committee. In 1958, the Tobacco Institute had been founded by the tobacco companies. It was located just a few blocks away from the US Supreme Court. It quickly became one of Washington's most powerful and effective political lobbies.[73] The Institute and its lobbyists played a defining role in the way tobacco products were "regulated." The final FCLAA of 1965, a weak bill and a good example of the ability of the Tobacco Institute to influence legislation, left the labelling of tobacco products up to the tobacco companies themselves. In addition, any regulation of tobacco advertising was prohibited by the FCLAA for 4 years.[74] Brandt notes that the "FCLAA marks one of American history's most impressive examples of the power of special interests to shape

[68]Brandt, as n. 2, 237.

[69]Brandt, as n. 2, 237–239.

[70]Brandt, as n. 2, 227–228, 239.

[71]Brandt, as n. 2, 239.

[72]Brandt, as n. 2, 243.

[73]Brandt, as n. 2, 251, 276–277.

[74]Brandt, as n. 2, 256.

congressional action."[75] Moreover, the FCLAA "clearly shows that the industry possessed a systematic strategy and a capacity to further its interests irrespective of the public good."[76] Some government agencies even avoided having anything to do with the tobacco industry. The Consumer Product Safety Commission (CPSC) voted to keep cigarettes out of their jurisdiction. Agencies like the CPSC "understood that tobacco regulation would easily test the limits of their already limited authority."[77] The inability of the Federal government to regulate tobacco products showed how deeply the tobacco industry had "penetrated the economic and financial structures of American industry, media, and politics."[78]

Another example of the industry's political and lobbying prowess is the *Cigarette Advertising Code* of 1964. The code was drafted as a ban on advertising aimed at youngsters under 21 years old. These advertisements continued to state that the health dangers of smoking were unproven. The ads, furthermore, concentrated on the association of smoking and virility. These ads with the "virility" theme were made to hook adolescents on smoking. The code set forth fines of up to $100,000 when advertisements were crossing the line trying to influence young customers.[79] No such fine was ever issued.[80] Its enforcement was left up to a neutral third party, which had no real power to enforce the rules. This system of self-regulation was an ideal situation for the industry.[81] Whenever they felt the code was annoying, it would simply be ignored. But to the public, the code was presented as a "scrupulous program of self-regulation."[82] In 1970, the industry abandoned the code. Warren Braren, who had been fired from his position as head of the Code Authority's New York office, became one of the earliest whistle-blowers to turn on the tobacco industry. Braren testified during congressional hearings which discussed the renewal of the FCLAA in 1969. Braren's testimony was an embarrassment for the tobacco companies.[83] Despite Braren's testimony, and further regulations like, the Fair Labelling and Packaging Act from 1966, the Controlled Substances Act of 1970, the Consumer Product Safety Act of 1972, and the CPSC Amendments bill from 1975, cigarette sales were not regulated in a way that harmed them. The drafting of these laws was very closely monitored by the tobacco industry and the Tobacco Institute

[75] Brandt, as n. 2, 257.

[76] Brandt, as n. 2, 258. Brandt remarks, and I will address this in a later chapter, that other industries have looked at the tobacco industry "to utilize legislation and regulation in their own interests." See Part III, Chap. 16: Historians in Tobacco Litigation, a Conclusion, cfr. infra.

[77] Brandt, as n. 2, 273–274.

[78] Brandt, as n. 2, 260, 276–277.

[79] *Cigarette advertising Code.* 1964, 8. LTDL. Bates Number: TI17932021-TI17932029. http://legacy.library.ucsf.edu/tid/qfu09a00. Accessed 31 Oct 2014.

[80] Brandt, as n. 2, 259.

[81] See also 12.1. The Tobacco Controversy: A Careful Construction, cfr. infra.

[82] Brandt, as n. 2, 261.

[83] Brandt, as n. 2, 259–261.

to assure the explicit exclusion of its product.[84] The tobacco companies often referred to the prohibition of alcohol in the US from 1920 until 1933–which turned into a fiasco–to motivate a more hands-off approach in the regulation of tobacco products.[85] This strategy of self-regulation left more freedom for the industry.[86] The government itself was not entirely against this policy, considering its dependence on taxes on tobacco sales.[87]

Another important consumer-protecting government agency, The Food and Drug Administration (FDA), was also not allowed to regulate tobacco products. The tobacco companies had shown their political ingenuity, by excluding their product from the overview of the FDA. The Pure Food and Drugs Act of 1906 put tobacco products outside of the control of the FDA. Proctor reports that the industry had fought hard in Congress for its exclusion.[88] When in 1938, the bill was reinforced, tobacco companies again escaped the FDA's jurisdiction.[89] By the 1950s, there still was virtually no government oversight on tobacco products. In the end tobacco products were added to the authority of the FDA in 2009. The Bureau of Alcohol, Tobacco, and Firearms (ATF) had been responsible for the collection of tobacco taxes since 1952 when it was designated as the responsible government institution to keep an eye on tobacco products. This overview was much weaker than what the FDA could have potentially exercised.[90] The ATF remains, up until today, widely known for its inefficiency and corporate-tied executives.[91]

The Surgeon General's Report of 1964 was followed by more reports on tobacco. In the 1960s, the 1964 report was reworked three times. The following decade, eight reports were issued. In the 1980s, a new report was published every year. The reports also discussed new forms of cigarette smoking, like smokeless tobacco or involuntary smoking. The Surgeon General presented a national status report on

[84] Brandt, as n. 2, 273.

[85] Brandt, as n. 2, 242.

[86] Brandt, as n. 2, 258.

[87] See Part III, Sect. 10.2.6. Taxation, cfr. supra.

[88] Proctor, as n. 3, 373.

[89] Brandt, as n. 2, 242.

[90] Proctor, as n. 3, 373.

[91] Due to recent public shootings – 2012–2013–2014 – in the United States, the ATF has met with considerable criticism. From 2006 to 2011 the ATF had been without an appointed director as the United States Senate had neglected to confirm a candidate. The ATF is reported to be antiquated in its daily operations also because its daily operations are extremely regulated. These restrictions on the effectiveness of the ATF are the product of the influence lobby groups working for the NRA, the tobacco industry, and so forth have on the American legislative body. See Goodle, Erica, and Stolberg, Sheryl. 2012. Legal Curbs Said to Hamper A.T.F. in Gun Inquiries. *The New York Times,* December 25. http://www.nytimes.com/2012/12/26/us/legislative-handcuffs-limit-atfs-ability-to-fight-gun-crime.html?pagewanted=1&_r=1&ref=us. Accessed 31 Oct 2014. Also see Schmidt, Michael. 2013. Obama Tells Senate That It's Time to Confirm A.T.F. Director. *The New York Times*, January 16. http://www.nytimes.com/2013/01/17/us/politics/obama-urges-senate-to-confirm-todd-jones-as-atf-director.html. Accessed 31 Oct 2014.

passive smoking to the United States Congress in 1986. Two years later the addictive nature of nicotine would finally be addressed in another report. The 1990s and 2000s produced 11 more reports on the health risks of tobacco use. Apart from the traditional general status reports, some surveys concentrated on the prevention of smoking habits among youngsters, the health consequences of second-hand smoke, the use of tobacco products amongst women, and the cigarette use among racial or ethnic minority groups. *The Surgeon General's Report* on smoking and public health from 2012 focuses on the tobacco use among youth and young adults. The Report from 2014 focuses on 50 years of research on the health hazards connected with smoking. To quote the surgeons general's website: "The reports of the Surgeon General on tobacco have alerted the nation to the health risk of smoking and have transformed the issue from one of individual and consumer choice to one of epidemiology, public health, and risk for smokers and non-smokers alike."[92]

As this chapter has shown, the tobacco industry was fervently committed to keeping the scientific controversy alive. The tobacco companies continued to claim that there was no causal link between smoking and diseases. Whether by bribing the medical profession, lobbying in Washington, or aggressive marketing techniques, the tobacco companies left no stone unturned to maintain that their products were not dangerous. Despite the fact that the tobacco industry was very much aware that the overall scientific conclusion from the early 1950s onwards was that smoking was a considerable health hazard. The following chapter addresses how the tobacco industry used scientists to create and maintain the idea of a tobacco controversy on the one hand, while on the other hand, the industry enlisted the help of marketing companies to continue to aggressively promote their product while denying its unhealthy and addictive character.

Bibliography

Blasingame, Francis. 1964. Full text of AMA letter of testimony to F.T.C. *Journal of the American Medical Association* 188: 31.

Brandt, Allan. 2007. *The cigarette century. The rise, fall and deadly persistence of a product that defined America.* New York: Basic Books.

Graham, Evarts. 1954. Remarks on the aetiology of bronchogenic carcinoma. *The Lancet* 263: 1305–1308.

Proctor, Robert. 1999. *The Nazi war on cancer.* New York: Princeton University Press.

Proctor, Robert. 2004. The global smoking epidemic: A history and status report. *Clinical Lung Cancer* 5: 371–376.

Proctor, Robert. 2012. *Golden Holocaust: Origins of the cigarette catastrophe and the case for abolition.* Berkeley: University of California Press.

s.n. 1991. Conversation with Sir Richard Doll. *British Journal of Addiction* 86: 365–377.

Talbott, John. 1959. Smoking and lung cancer. *The Journal of the American Medical Association* 171: 2102.

[92]Surgeon General Initiatives on Tobacco see http://www.surgeongeneral.gov/initiatives/tobacco/index.html. Accessed 31 Oct 2014.

Chapter 12
The Tobacco Industry and Its Tactics

> *Doubt is our product, since it is the best means of competing with the "body of fact" that exists in the mind of the general public.*
>
> Brown & Williamson Tobacco Company (1969)

Abstract In this third and final chapter on the history of the tobacco industry and its product, I discuss the role the Hill & Knowlton marketing company played in creating a deception of the general public. The Frank Statement, the Tobacco Industry Research Committee, the Tobacco Institute, mass-marketing techniques, and extensive lobby-work were all part of a strategy to lead the American public to believe that there still existed a scientific controversy on smoking despite the fact that the tobacco companies' own scientists had convincing evidence to the contrary. These tactics by the tobacco industry are key elements of the testimony of expert historians in tobacco litigation today.

The discovery by medical scholars of a clear causal link between smoking and disease alarmed the tobacco industry. In the decades following 1950, tobacco companies devised strategies that would question the health impact of smoking. These elaborate tactics allowed the industry to escape liability while continuing its destructive business. In the following chapter, I address two particular strategies: The first was the construction of a scientific controversy by hiring industry-friendly scientists who would produce research funded by the tobacco industry, which questioned the causal link between smoking and disease. I discuss the legacy of the tobacco industry's incentivized "scientific research." For decades the tobacco companies have used science to further a myth of controversy surrounding cigarette smoking and lung cancer or other respiratory diseases. A second strategy of the tobacco industry has already been referred to in the previous chapters: that of mass-marketing. I discussed it as one of the seven essential steps taken in the rise of the cigarette.[1] To further defend their product, the industry added a third tactic to their scheme. Tobacco companies reinforced their marketing relations strategy with huge lobbying networks. This powerful system was well funded and influenced

[1]See Part III, Sect. 10.2.7. Mass-Marketing Techniques, cfr. supra.

R. Delafontaine, *Historians as Expert Judicial Witnesses in Tobacco Litigation*, Studies in the History of Law and Justice 4, DOI 10.1007/978-3-319-14292-0_12

politicians, news reporters, legislators, jurors, advocates, doctors, and the general public on a national, state, and local level. The Tobacco Institute and its influence has already been referred to in the previous chapter.[2] Both of these strategies have been active components in the construction of the cigarette controversy.

This chapter focuses on the creation of and the efforts to maintain a scientific controversy on smoking by the tobacco companies while simultaneously conducting an enormous marketing campaign and lobbying strategy to convince the public of the controversy's existence. Furthermore, this is a very important issue in tobacco litigation and the expert testimony of historians.

12.1 The Tobacco Controversy: A Careful Construction

In the early 1950s, the tobacco industry was faced with a serious threat to its future. Scientific research that linked smoking and cancer created a potential disaster for the tobacco companies.[3] However, the tobacco companies were determined to offer a collective response to save its industry. They had succeeded in constructing the best possible image of their product for over half a century, and now that fragile creation was at risk. The tobacco industry mounted an unprecedented public relations campaign, which claimed to be supported by "scientific research."[4] This strategy "required intrusions into scientific process and procedure."[5] The tobacco companies hired scientists of their own to counter the results from medical research, which reported at an augmenting rate that smoking cigarettes was unhealthy. Titles like "Smoking a Cause of Cancer.", "Cigarettes and Cancer.", "Cigarette Hangover.", "Beyond any Doubt." and "Fresh Hope but Hard Reality: Cubebs or Coffin Nails." fuelled public anxiety that smoking was dangerous.[6] In 1952, *Reader's Digest*, the most widely circulated American periodical at the time, published a piece under the title "Cancer by the Carton." The article referred to numbers disclosed by Dr. Alton Ochsner, a former president of the American Cancer Society, who did research on the health effects of smoking. His figures indicated that in only one decade, from 1938 to 1948, the number of lung-cancer deaths had increased by 144 %.[7]

---

[2]See Part III, Sect. 11.2. The Reports of the Surgeon General, cfr. supra.

[3]Brandt, Allan. 2007. *The Cigarette Century. The Rise, Fall and Deadly Persistence of a Product that Defined America.* New York: Basic Books, 159.

[4]Brandt, as n. 3, 160.

[5]Proctor, Robert. 1996. *Cancer Wars: How Politics Shapes What We Know and Don't Know About Cancer.* New York: Basic Books, 101–132.

[6]Brandt, as n. 3, 161, reference 9, 528. & Kluger, Richard. 1997. *Ashes to Ashes: America's Hundred-Year Cigarette War, the Public Health, and the Unabashed Triumph of Philip Morris.* New York: Vintage Books, 152.

[7]Norr, Roy. 1952. Cancer by the Carton. *Reader's Digest*, December, 7–8. LTDL. Bates Number: TIMN0105705/5707. http://legacy.library.ucsf.edu/tid/bcm92f00. Accessed 31 Oct 2014.

The industry tried to appease rising public concerns with health warranties in advertisements. Eventually, these assurances would come back to haunt the tobacco companies in litigation decades later.[8]

On December 14th 1953, the CEO's of the tobacco companies attended a meeting in the Plaza Hotel in New York City. Representatives from the tobacco industry felt the growing pressure from health advocates and the general public. On top of these problems, several industry scientists had confirmed in internal documents that there was a causal link between smoking and cancer.[9] The meeting at the Plaza Hotel was organized to handle these dangers collectively.[10] Rivalry was put aside for the sake of common interest, even at the risk of being faced with another antitrust investigation.[11] Paul Hahn, president of the American Tobacco Company in 1953, responded in a press release to the American public: "I feel a statement of reassurance to the public should be made. What the public wants to know about is whether it is true that smoking has been proved to contribute to the incidence of lung cancer. The fact, of course, is that it has not been so proved."[12] The definition of "definitive proof" would remain a very important issue in the cigarette controversy.[13] T.V. Hartnett, president of Brown & Williamson at the time, stated in an internal memorandum the importance of "challenging these findings [scientific research that argued there was a link between smoking and cancer] ethically and effectively without rancour-to win friends rather than to create enemies." Hartnett further outlined two approaches that would dominate the industry's strategy for the coming years: cancer research and public relations would make up both sides of the same coin. The public relations offices of the tobacco industry had to anticipate handling "significantly negative research results, if, as, and when they develop", according to Hartnett in 1953.[14]

The next day –December 15th 1953-, executives from tobacco companies met with John W. Hill. As president of the public relations firm Hill & Knowlton, Hill already had a long and lucrative relationship with the tobacco companies. Hill worked with the tobacco industry since the 1930s. He had also been involved with liquor and chemical industries, who had also faced health issues with their products in the past. Until then, mass-marketing had been tobacco's tool to bend

[8]Brandt, as n. 3, 163.

[9]Proctor, Robert. 2004. The Global Smoking Epidemic: A History and Status Report. *Clinical Lung Cancer* 5, 374.

[10]The univocal reaction of the industry on the Readers Digest article is a perfect example of the oligopolistic structure of the industry. See Part III, Sect. 10.2.4. The Oligopolistic Structure of the Tobacco Industry, cfr. supra.

[11]Brandt, as n. 3, 165.

[12]American Tobacco. 1953. *Press Release*. 26/11/1953, 1. http://tobaccodocuments.org/ness/6746.html. Accessed 31 Oct 2014.

[13]Brandt, as n. 3, 164.

[14]Hartnett, Timothy. 1953. *Memorandum from T. V. Hartnett*. 15/12/1953, 1–4. LTDL. Bates Number: CORTI0015611/5614. http://legacy.library.ucsf.edu/tid/kvl30c00. Accessed 31 Oct 2014.

social convention and mores on cigarettes. Hill now also used it to distort and deny important scientific data.[15] Hill himself had stopped smoking in the 1940s due to health reasons. The tobacco industry decided to enlist the services of Hill and his company in order to help shape their collective response.[16] Hill argued that the final result would depend on strict collective and collaborative action from the tobacco companies. He also identified two key elements of the industry's response. (1) Public confidence could not be achieved by advertising, which is by definition self-interested. (2) Secondly, and crucial to the whole scheme, the tobacco companies had to assert authority over the scientific research on the health hazards of cigarette smoking. Science had the distinct advantage that it had a reputation of disinterestedness.[17] The moral value of science in American culture had to be used by the tobacco companies. Since the industry was now threatened by science, the tobacco companies had to 'secure' science.[18] The public relations work could leave no fingerprints in its scrupulous behind-the-scenes management of media.[19] Simply conducting ad hominem attacks aimed at researchers or full-out denial of the statistical coincidence would only alienate the public, Hill realized.[20] Therefore, Hill's strategy concentrated on engineering a controversy, which questioned the causal link between smoking and disease. The industry's own tobacco research would insist that there were always two sides to a story and further research was needed for conclusive evidence.[21]

The following weeks, Hill's company and tobacco executives acted in crisis mode in order to further shape the strategic answers on the current threat. Hill concluded that the tobacco industry had to become a major sponsor of medical research. This offered several advantages. The tobacco companies could control research agendas and the results could be presented as independent scientific work. Science and the information it produced were to meet the goals of the public relations strategy.[22] With the assistance of Hill, the tobacco industry reacted to the health issue as a united front. Their collaboration would persist for almost five decades after 1953.[23] This understanding amongst tobacco companies is also known as "the Gentleman's agreement."[24]

15Brandt, as n. 3, 166.

16Goss, Bert. 1953. *Background Material on the Cigarette Industry Client.* 15/12/1953, 1–5. LTDL. Bates Number: TIOK0034094/4098. http://legacy.library.ucsf.edu/tid/ufu91f00. Accessed 31 Oct 2014.

17Brandt, as n. 3, 166–167.

18Brandt, as n. 3, 170.

19Brandt, as n. 3, 167.

20Brandt, as n. 3, 167, 250.

21Brandt, as n. 3, 167.

22Brandt, as n. 3, 169.

23Brandt, as n. 3, 169.

24Brandt, as n. 3, reference 29, 529.

On the 4th of January 1954, the tobacco industry published a "Frank Statement." The statement was published as an advertisement in 448 American newspapers in 258 cities. Hill and his team offered the American public a first taste of the tobacco industry's new public relations strategy. The text read as follows:

We accept an interest in people's health as a basic responsibility, paramount to every other consideration in our business.
We believe the products we make are not injurious to health.
We always have and always will cooperate closely with those whose task it is to safeguard the public health.[25]

The Frank Statement also questioned the validity of the scientific research linking cancer to smoking cigarettes. To clarify the controversy, the tobacco companies announced the creation of *the Tobacco Industry Research Committee* (TIRC). This independent institution funded by the industry would contribute to the "scientific research" already underway at individual tobacco companies.[26] The immediate goal of the Frank Statement was to silence the criticism on the industry and its product. In the long run, the statement served as a guide for industry scientist and advocates. Reactions to the statement, and thanks to expert scheming by Hill & Knowlton, were fairly positive. The industry was credited by several newspapers for creating the TIRC.[27] In an article from 2002, health advocates assessed the promises made by the industry in the Frank Statement from 1954. They convincingly showed that the tobacco industry had failed to inform the public about the health risks of their product.[28] Brandt concludes: "[i]f the tobacco companies had but followed their own explicit commitments, the history of the cigarette might be distinctly different."[29] All the internal memos, documents, and records which show the strategies used by the tobacco companies to create the controversy would later be used against the industry in tobacco litigation.

The TIRC was, since its creation, devoted to Hill's public relations goals.[30] Proctor assigns several purposes to the TIRC. First and foremost the TIRC was used to provide "reassurance research." It gave the impression that the industry was concerned about the health of its consumers. In reality, the TIRC had no projects directly relating to research on smoking and lung cancer.[31] In April 1954,

[25]Tobacco Industry Research Committee. 1954. *A Frank Statement to Cigarette smokers.* 04/01/1954. LTDL. Bates Number: 6017454. http://legacy.library.ucsf.edu/tid/qxp91e00. Accessed 31 Oct 2014.

[26]Tobacco Industry Research Committee, as n. 25.

[27]Brandt, as n. 3, 171.

[28]Cummings, Michael, Morley, Christopher, and Hyland, Andrew. 2002. Failed Promises of the Cigarette Industry and its Effect on Consumer Misperceptions about the Health Risks of Smoking. *Tobacco Control* 11, 111–114.

[29]Brandt, as n. 3, 172.

[30]Brandt, as n. 3, 172.

[31]Proctor, as n. 9, 374.

the TIRC distributed a paper titled: "A Scientific Perspective on the Cigarette Controversy."[32] The document was sent to over 200,000 persons in the medical community and to the general media. The paper was extremely well referenced and touched every argument that could be made against the causal relation between lung cancer and smoking. The arguments that were made in the paper included: the inconclusiveness of research up until that moment, the dangers of attributing much value to observations made in research of mice and tobacco tars, the invalidity of autopsy results, etc.. This and other published documents were everything but scientific; they were part of the marketing strategies of the TIRC. These publications were accompanied with widespread and fair media coverage, thanks to the well-oiled relations of the Hill & Knowlton marketing company.[33] Accordingly, the TIRC was led not by scientists but by business men, who wished that the TIRC supported the claim that there was no conclusive evidence to link smoking and disease.[34] In its recruitment of researchers, the TIRC actively looked out for known sceptics of the link between lung cancer and cigarette smoke. The scientific advisory board of the TIRC was filled with scientists who held a priori assumptions on the evidence.[35] The TIRC was a major propaganda weapon in service of the tobacco industry.[36] Until this day, "[t]he TIRC marks one of the most intensive efforts by an industry to derail independent science", according to Brandt.[37]

Meanwhile, the tobacco companies also continued their own research. Claude Teague, a researcher at R.J. Reynolds, concluded in February 1953, after reviewing epidemiologic studies and animal studies, that: "[s]tudies of clinical data tend to confirm the relationship between heavy and prolonged tobacco smoking and incidence of cancer of the lung."[38] In September 1953, the American Tobacco Company had also started experiments on mice. The tar-painted mice were reported to show, what the industry described as "biological activity." In other words, the mice developed tumours. The company's president was informed of the results, but they were never made public.[39] Another scientist at R.J. Reynolds confirmed Teague's findings several years later in 1964. In an internal report, tobacco scientist Rodgman wrote: "[s]ince it is now well-established that cigarette smoke does contain several polycyclic aromatic hydrocarbons, and considering the potential and

[32]Hill & Knowlton. 1954. *A scientific Perspective on the Cigarette Controversy*. 03/05/1954, 21. LTDL. Bates Number: 961008152/8172. http://legacy.library.ucsf.edu/tid/wye21a00. Accessed 31 Oct 2014.

[33]Brandt, as n. 3, 195.

[34]Brandt, as n. 3, 173, 181.

[35]Brandt, as n. 3, 184, 218.

[36]Proctor, as n. 9, 374.

[37]Brandt, as n. 3, 185.

[38]Teague, Claude. 1953. *Survey of Cancer Research with Emphasis upon Possible Carcinogens in Tobacco*. 02/02/1953, 23. LTDL. Bates Number: 519198674–519198696. http://legacy.library.ucsf.edu/tid/jyb77a00. Accessed 31 Oct 2014.

[39]Proctor, as n. 9, 374.

actual carcinogenic activity of a number of these compounds, a method of either complete removal or almost complete removal of these compounds from smoke is required."[40] Other former secret documents show that the industry had accepted that there were dangerous carcinogens in cigarette smoke and sought ways to eliminate them from tobacco smoke.[41] One confidential memo from 1954 stated that "[o]ur objective is to determine all chemical constituents of smoke, and to develop means of removing any which are considered harmful."[42] By acknowledging the existence of these harmful carcinogens in cigarette smoke and by researching strategies to remove them, the tobacco industry did in fact acknowledge that smoking was harmful, although they never went public with this information.[43] On the contrary, despite the worrying results of their own research, tobacco companies continued to give reassurances about the safety of their products to consumers by claiming that the scientific evidence was inconclusive.[44] Proctor remarks that were it not for the forced release of internal industry documents by recent litigation, these pertinent facts would probably still be hidden from the public.[45] By hiding the results of their own research from the general public, the tobacco industry kept the scientific controversy on smoking alive.

Wakeham, another industry scientist at Philip Morris, led a research-project on medically acceptable cigarettes. His aim was to develop a cigarette without the cancer-causing effects of cigarette smoke but with the same psychological effects of nicotine.[46] The development of this low-health risk cigarette would require: "[t]ime, money and unfaltering determination."[47] While industry scientists like Teague, Rodgman, and Wakeham had accepted and noted, in multiple internal industry documents, that there was a causal link between smoking and cancer, the TIRC continued to send out press release after press release denying any sound scientific proof of such causality.[48]

[40]Rodgman, Allan. 1964. *The Analysis of Cigarette Smoke condensate.* 12/02/1964, 56–63. LTDL. Bates Number: 504912643/2713. http://legacy.library.ucsf.edu/tid/kyv35d00. Accessed 31 Oct 2014.

[41]Brandt, as n. 3, 200.

[42]Dupuis, R. 1954. Confidential Memo to George Weisaman and Parker McComas. 31/03/1954, 1. LTDL. Bates Number: 2022239347. http://legacy.library.ucsf.edu/tid/etx74e00. Accessed 31 Oct 2014.

[43]Brandt, as n. 3, 200.

[44]Brandt, as n. 3, 199.

[45]Proctor, as n. 9, 374. The different waves of litigation against the tobacco industry will be addressed in the following chapter, see Part III, Chap. 13: Tobacco Litigation, cfr. infra.

[46]Wakeham, Helmut. 1959. An Opinion on Cigarette Smoking and Cancer. 22/09/1959, 1–2. LTDL. Bates Number: 3990224608/3990224609. http://legacy.library.ucsf.edu/tid/nqs82i00. Accessed 31 Oct 2014.

[47]Wakeham, Helmut. 1961. Wakeham Presentation to R&D Committee, New York Office. 15/11/1961, 1. LTDL. Bates Number: 2501200235/0238. http://legacy.library.ucsf.edu/tid/mvx88d00. Accessed 31 Oct 2014.

[48]Brandt, as n. 3, 202.

The TIRC had a special interest in influencing doctors through their propaganda. By sending physicians all over the country pamphlets, like the one from April 1954, the TIRC tried to convince physicians that there was a tobacco controversy. A periodical distributed by the TIRC, *Tobacco and Health Research*, was mailed free of charge to 340,000 American doctors, scientists, surgeons, dentists, and medical school faculty staff.[49] Each of these brochures were designed for public-relations purposes, not for scientific information. Insufficient evidence remained the industry's main argument. Rendering doubt about the dangers of smoking cigarettes was its main goal. The tobacco industry maintained that evidence was "scant."[50] The importance of influencing doctors lay in the fact that the opinion of one doctor could potentially influence the opinions of an exponential number of patients.[51] With rising health concerns, slogans as "[m]ore doctors smoke camels", tried to reassure consumers about the safety of cigarettes.[52]

Other articles, meant for a more lay public, were widely distributed in popular magazines. Proctor lists some titles of pamphlets that appeared around the mid-1960s: "Lung Cancer Rare in Bald Men.", "Rare Fungus Infection Mimics Lung Cancer.", "28 Reasons for Doubting Cigarette-Cancer link.", and "Nicotine Effect is Like Exercise." Some tens of thousands of copies were going out to the media, opinion leaders, tobacco industry suppliers, tobacco farmer groups, and others with an interest in the industry.[53] In January 1968, *True Magazine* published an article titled "[t]o smoke or not to smoke, that is still the question."[54] Its author, Stanley Frank, stated that there was "absolutely no proof that smoking causes human cancer."[55] Frank did not disclose that he was working for Hill & Knowlton and the TIRC.[56] After being republished several times, the article was reported to have reached over three million Americans. Free copies had been sent out to scientists, educators, government officials, and opinion makers. None of these editions mentioned that its author had been paid by the tobacco industry.[57] As I already mentioned in the previous chapter, the controversy also succeeded in dividing the PHS, the FTC, and AMA into a kerfuffle on professional boundaries.[58] Jack Anderson and Drew Pearson, two journalists, called the AMA-

---

[49]Proctor, as n. 9, 374–375. Brandt reports 500,000 issues. See Brandt, as n. 3, 197.

[50]Cummings, Michael, Brown, Anthony, and O'Conner, Richard. 2007. The Cigarette Controversy. *Cancer Epidemiology, Biomarkers & Prevention* 16, 1072.

[51]Brandt, as n. 3, 197.

[52]Brandt, as n. 3, 243.

[53]Proctor, as n. 9, 375.

[54]Glantz, Staton, Slade, John, Bero, Lisa, Hanauer, Peter, and Barnes, Deborah. 1998. *The Cigarette Papers*. Berkeley: University of California Press, 179–180.

[55]Proctor, as n. 9, 375.

[56]Glantz, Staton, Slade, John, Bero, Lisa, Hanauer, Peter, and Barnes, Deborah, as n. 54, 179.

[57]Proctor, as n. 9, 375

[58]Cfr. Supra, see Part III, Sect. 11.2. The Reports of the Surgeon General. See the discussion between the Public Health Service and the American Health Association.

tobacco connection: "the weirdest lobbying alliance in legislative history ... The doctors were more concerned about Medicare, which they fancied as a threat to their fees, than about the threat to the nation's lungs."[59] The TIRC continued to fuel the feud and succeed in driving potential allies apart.

The TIRC also tried to influence members of the Surgeon's General Advisory Committee.[60] Members were invited to meetings and corresponded with staffers of the TIRC for advice and counsel. Little, head of TIRC, tried to gain influence on an informal basis with some members of the committee. One member, Peter Hamill, was very impressed by Little and argued that Little should be admitted to help the committee. Hamill was put on medical leave when the *Surgeon General's Report* was nearing its completion. Little and Hamill met again afterwards in the TIRC headquarters in New York. Hamill expressed his disappointment in the final report and declared that he did not believe in any specific effect of tobacco use in causation of various diseases.[61] Little concluded later in a confidential TIRC note: "I have a strong feeling that this is a man of whom we probably can and should make use."[62]

A second *Frank Statement* was circulated within the tobacco industry by 1958. Although never published, its very existence proves the continued use by the industry of the idea that there was "not enough research."[63] The document candidly proclaimed that: "[t]he cause of cancer remains as much a mystery as ever."[64] Although medical evidence was piling up and was increasingly convincing, Hill & Knowlton were relentless in their quest to create a controversy.[65] The TIRC had echoed the same declarations for over a decade. There was need for more research, before anyone could conclude with full certainty that smoking caused lung cancer.[66]

By the 1960s, the industry had succeeded in creating and firmly establishing the "cigarette controversy."[67] This had prompted some historians to claim that there was a real controversy on the relation of smoking and lung cancer.[68] The controversy and its creation are important subjects for historians who testified in tobacco litigation. Central questions in court to determine possible fraud by the tobacco industry were: "[h]ow independent was the research done by the TIRC?", and "[h]ow real was the

[59]Brandt, as n. 3, 249–250.

[60]Cfr. Supra, see Part III, Sect. 11.2. The Reports of the Surgeon General.

[61]Brandt, as n. 3, 225–226.

[62]Little, Clarence. 1964. *Confidential Memorandum: Meeting with Dr. Peter V. V. Hamill on April 29*. 29/04/1964, 2. LTDL. Bates Number: HK0441013/1014[DUP1]. http://legacy.library.ucsf.edu/tid/dfx10a00. Accessed 31 Oct 2014.

[63]Brandt, as n. 3, reference 110, 533.

[64]Philip Morris. 1958. *Another Frank Statement to Smokers*. 12/12/1958, 3. LTDL. Bates Number: 1005104253/4255. http://legacy.library.ucsf.edu/tid/ifh48d00. Accessed 31 Oct 2014.

[65]Brandt, as n. 3, 197.

[66]Brandt, as n. 3, 197–198.

[67]Brandt, as n. 3, 183, 204.

[68]Brandt, as n. 3, reference 71, 531.

tobacco controversy?"[69] By explaining the trajectory of the research on tobacco, expert historians have demonstrated the negative impact tobacco funded research has had on scientific debate.[70]

Brandt argues that the industry's tactic of creating a controversy served the tobacco industry well on four fronts. (1) Primarily and particularly in the first decades after *the Frank Statement,* the scientific uncertainty offered the public a strong rationale to keep on smoking and to start smoking. (2) Secondly the "we do not know for sure approach" offered legal protection in consumer liability cases. Accusations of negligence would be much harder to prove if the tobacco industry had never assured that their products were healthy. Nor did the tobacco companies declare that their product was unhealthy. Cigarettes were successfully marked as part of an adventurous lifestyle. Cigarettes were products for people who did not want to play by the rules. (3) Thirdly, the industry evaded regulation by implementing "safety measures" of its own rather than being forced by the government, something which probably would have happened if there had been no doubt on the public health dangers of smoking. According to the tobacco companies, fitting regulations could only be implemented if they were based on the results of conclusive scientific research. If the problems were uncertain, what policy could be helpful? The industry argued that implementing regulation based on uncertain scientific evidence would not aid consumers or the tobacco companies.[71] (4) A final reason why the controversy aided the tobacco industry, according to Brandt, was that the scientific controversy offered a moral defence to sell a life-threatening product.[72]

By 1961, total sales of cigarettes had risen from 369 billion in 1954 to 488 billion in the USA. Per capita consumption was at an all-time high of 4,318 cigarettes a year in 1965, where it was -only- 3,344 in 1954.[73] One commentator noted: "[t]obacco products pass across sales counters more frequently than anything else – except money."[74] Since 1954, the year that Hill & Knowlton began their public-relations campaign for the tobacco industry, the tobacco companies had expanded their market despite very poor prospects. The tobacco industry had been stabilized and was thriving. Hill knew he had achieved success. In an internal report of 1962, he provided proof that his marketing strategies had worked: "[f]rom time to time, man-on-the-street interviews ask about the smoking question. In almost every one of these, there will be a quotation that is almost an exact paraphrase of some statement

[69]See Part III, Sect. 13.4. Tobacco Tactics in Court: Legal Game Theory, cfr. infra.

[70]Brandt, as n. 3, 183.

[71]Brandt, as n. 3, 247.

[72]Brandt, as n. 3, 198, 211.

[73]Brandt, as n. 3, 202.

[74]Greenberg, D. S. 1964. *Tobacco: After Publicity Surge, Surgeon General's Report Seems to Have Little Enduring Effect. Science* 145, 1021. Bates Number: 503241522/1523. LTDL. http://legacy.library.ucsf.edu/tid/nrn18c00. Accessed 31 Oct 2014.

issued for the tobacco accounts."[75] In other words, Hill had succeeded in planting doubt in consumers' minds about the health hazards of cigarette smoking, despite significant scientific consensus.[76] The tobacco industry attempted to sustain, for as long as possible, the idea that the causal link between smoking and several types of cancer and other respiratory diseases was "unproven."[77]

A number of articles that appeared in the *New England Journal of Medicine* of 1961 can serve as another and striking example of the success of the industry's public-relations strategy. Wynder, a noted epidemiologist on tobacco-related diseases, and Little, head of the TIRC, both contributed to the same issue of the journal. Wynder asked his critics for help with his conclusion:

> Of those who will not accept existing evidence, I should like to know what evidence would be acceptable. If one criticizes epidemiology for being statistical, if one criticizes animal research for being unrelated to the human problem and if one criticizes chemical identification of carcinogens as not have any bearing to human disease, I should like to ask if there is a form of evidence that would be accepted as being conclusive. If it were humanly possible we would at once set up a study that could yield such evidence. If it is humanly impossible, it is not a constructive kind of suggestion that would advance scientific knowledge.[78]

Little retaliated by stating that "much more research was necessary to make a definitive and sound conclusion."[79] He answered that "Lung cancer, indeed all cancer, is a challenge, an unsolved problem. Its epidemiology will probably long be an open question." Little's answer evaded the question put forth by Wynder: whether Little knew a form of science which would deliver conclusive evidence.[80] The same issue featured an editorial on the subject entitled: *The Great Debate*. The author of the piece, Joseph Garland, wrote that "[e]ach individual must choose his own course, whether to woo the lady nicotine or abjure the filthy weed, while the search for truth continues."[81] Eight years earlier, in 1953, Garland had come to a different conclusion on smoking. He then wrote, in the same journal, that previous scientific

[75]Hill, John. 1962. *Smoking Health and Statistics: the Story of the Tobacco Accounts*. 26/02/1962, 35. LTDL. Bates Number: HKC000001-HKC000038. http://legacy.library.ucsf.edu/tid/xtq56b00. Accessed 31 Oct 2014.

[76]Brandt, as n. 3, 202.

[77]Brandt, as n. 3, 106.

[78]Wynder, Ernst. 1961. An Appraisal of the Smoking-Lung-Cancer Issue. *New England Journal of Medicine* 264, 1240. LTDL. Bates Number: 501861161/1166. http://legacy.library.ucsf.edu/tid/zmy29d00. Accessed 31 Oct 2014. This statement is similar to that of Graham in *The Lancet* of 1954, see Part III, Sect. 11.1. The Discovery of Tobacco Health Hazards, cfr. supra.

[79]Brandt, as n. 3, 206.

[80]Little, Clarence. 1961. An Appraisal of the Smoking-Lung-Cancer Issue. *New England Journal of Medicine* 264, 1245. http://tobaccodocuments.org/lor/00325384-5388.html. Accessed 31 Oct 2014.

[81]Garland, Joseph. 1961. The Great Debate. *New England Journal of Medicine* 264, 1266. http://tobaccodocuments.org/lor/00325389.html. Accessed 31 Oct 2014.

research had provided "an association between cigarette smoking and lung cancer so strong as to be considered proof within the everyday meaning of the word."[82] In 8 years the industry had succeeded through a campaign of disinformation to turn the point of view of an editor of the *New England Journal of Medicine,* which was, and still is, one the most renowned and respected medical journals in the world. Garland had been convinced of the causal link between smoking and disease in 1953, however by 1961 Garland argued that that causal connection remained unsolved. It is fair to say that, as Brandt concludes; "[t]he tobacco industry had gotten its money's worth from Hill & Knowlton."[83]

After the publication of the Surgeon General's Report of 1964, the industry maintained its attempts to create controversy. The tobacco industry decided to stick with the tactics adopted in 1953, as one internal memo explains: "there is no proof that tobacco causes disease; disparage and attack all studies indicating such a relationship; support basic research on cancer largely unrelated to the hypothesis that smoking and cancer are linked; and support research on alternative theories of carcinogenesis."[84] After the Surgeon General's Report, the TIRC had been unmasked as a public relations enterprise for the tobacco industry. As a consequence, its name was changed in 1964 to the less obvious Council for Tobacco Research (CTR), although its main goal: to create controversy, remained the same.[85] In 1968 the 15-year-old collaboration between Hill & Knowlton and the tobacco companies came to an end. Nonetheless, the industry continued to question scientific evidence, although tobacco officials knew this strategy had seen its best days. The controversy was losing credibility fast. Leaked internal documents revealed discussions on the industry's tactics to create a controversy, which only hastened the process.[86] Continuing these tactics would also increase liability or even put the tobacco industry at risk of being accused of fraud.[87] The reverse argument was also considered. Leaving the controversy would imply admission of health risks and would in turn pose even higher litigation dangers.[88] Many options were discussed, but really coming to terms with the truth was not one of them. Maintaining controversy continued to be the industries' main strategy but some additional tactics were added.[89]

---

[82]Garland, Joseph. 1953. Cancer of the Lung. *New England Journal of Medicine* 249, 465. LTDL. Bates Number: 2018018568/2018018569. http://legacy.library.ucsf.edu/tid/iwt88h00. Accessed 31 Oct 2014.

[83]Brandt, as n. 3, 207.

[84]Brandt, as n. 3, 231.

[85]Brandt, as n. 3, 188.

[86]Brandt, as n. 3, 234, 265–266.

[87]Brandt, as n. 3, 234, 265–266.

[88]Brandt, as n. 3, 252.

[89]Brandt, as n. 3, 231–237.

One of those new tactics concentrated on promoting filters. This innovation acknowledged some of the results of the Surgeon General's Report. There were indeed some "not-healthy" elements in smoke. But the filters would successfully clean the smoke in such a manner that it would no longer be "unhealthy" for the moderate smoker. The filters were introduced with the claim that they reduced tar and nicotine elements in a cigarette.[90] In 1954, only 10 % of all cigarettes had filters, by the mid-1970s 90 % of cigarettes sold in the United States were "filtered."[91] Despite the hype over filtered cigarettes, there was no actual technology for the removal of unhealthy carcinogens from cigarette smoke.[92]

Again it was Claude Teague who discovered that when the pH value in filters was changed, the colour of the filter would change during smoking.[93] He recommended changing the pH levels so the filters darkened while the cigarettes were being smoked. Teague concluded: "[w]hile the use of such colour change material would probably have little or no effect on the actual efficiency of the filter tip material, the advertising and sales advantages are obvious."[94] Two other tobacco executives noted: "the illusion of filtration is as important as the fact of filtration."[95] And so the idea of a safer cigarette was sold to consumers. Marketing a safer cigarette did not mean the tobacco companies acknowledged that there was anything as a dangerous cigarette.[96] The filtered cigarettes were aggressively marketed, despite the paradoxical position of the industry.[97] Brandt describes it as a "two-front offensive". On the one hand the industry continued denying there was anything harmful about their product, while in the meantime the tobacco companies tried to convince the public of the important improvement of their product. Filters had now solved a non-existent problem.[98] "As conditions on the science front deteriorated, the commercial importance of the "promise" of "effective" filtration rose in significance. Health concerns created new marketing opportunities."[99] The tobacco industry would "brilliantly navigate the tension between offering reassurance without fracturing denial."[100]

---

[90] Brandt, as n. 3, 245.

[91] Brandt, as n. 3, 244.

[92] Brandt, as n. 3, 201

[93] Brandt, as n. 3, 244–245.

[94] Teague, Claude. 1953. Survey of Cancer Research with Emphasis upon Possible Carcinogens in Tobacco. 02/02/1953, 23. LTDL. Bates Number: 519198674–519198696. http://legacy.library.ucsf.edu/tid/jyb77a00. Accessed 31 Oct 2014.

[95] Dunn, William, and Johnston, Myron. 1966. Market Potential of a Health Cigarette. 06/1966, 2. LTDL. Bates Number: 3990049246/3990049270. http://legacy.library.ucsf.edu/tid/kzz82i00. Accessed 31 Oct 2014.

[96] Brandt, as n. 3, 245.

[97] Brandt, as n. 3, 247.

[98] Brandt, as n. 3, 261–262.

[99] Brandt, as n. 3, 262.

[100] Brandt, as n. 3, 263.

Meanwhile though, the tobacco companies and their product came under continued and insisting attacks from anti-smoking campaigns. An important blow for the industry came in 1967, when a young New York Lawyer, John F. Banzhaf filed a petition with the Federal Communications Commission (FCC). He argued that according to the legal "fairness doctrine", if there was indeed a tobacco controversy, then television ads for tobacco products should be accompanied by free airtime to explain the possible dangers of smoking.[101] The FCC ruled that broadcasters were required "to devote a significant amount of time to informing [their] listeners of the other side of the matter."[102] Banzhaf himself monitored the air-time, forcing stations to adhere when they fell short. A young lawyer single-handedly had disturbed the tobacco industry, by targeting one of its most important marketing strategies. These imperative messages that accompanied television ads had a notable impact on smoking rates. Consumption of cigarettes dropped for the first time since the Interbellum. Banzhaf's action demonstrated that courts could provide a more sympathetic venue for combatting the tobacco industry. Banzhaf formed one of the first anti-tobacco advocacy organizations, called the Action on Smoking and Health [ASH].[103] In 1969 the industry agreed with the FCC to end all its television advertising. From 1971 onwards, Americans had heard the tobacco jingles on television for the last time. The previous year tobacco companies had been the biggest advertisers on television. Tobacco companies had spent about $230 million a year on television advertising and bought 8 % of all advertising time.[104] Banzhaff's actions brought about the end of the most important manner of marketing for the tobacco industry.

When the 1970s closed, the tobacco industry had shown how special interests could bend regulations and legislation. The prolonging of any FDA jurisdiction continued. Many exemptions on regulation on tobacco products showed the lobbying power of the Tobacco Institute. "The legislation that emerged from Congress during this period testifies to the masterful preparation and strategic command of the tobacco industry", Brandt concludes.[105] But the industry had also suffered a major defeat. The ban on televised marketing had a major impact on tobacco consumption and its sales-techniques. Furthermore, there was another threat on the horizon for the tobacco companies: tobacco litigation. During these trials the industry would not only be accused of a conspiracy against the American public but also of negligence resulting in the deaths of hundreds of thousands of their customers. The tobacco industry would not remain untarnished in the tobacco wars.[106]

---

[101] Brandt, as n. 3, 267–268.

[102] Brandt, as n. 3, 267–268.

[103] Brandt, as n. 3, 269–270.

[104] Brandt, as n. 3, 270.

[105] Brandt, as n. 3, 277.

[106] Brandt, as n. 3, 276–277.

Bibliography

Brandt, Allan. 2007. *The cigarette century: The rise, fall and deadly persistence of a product that defined America*. New York: Basic Books.
Cummings, Michael, Christopher Morley, and Andrew Hyland. 2002. Failed promises of the cigarette industry and its effect on consumer misperceptions about the health risks of smoking. *Tobacco Control* 11: 110–117.
Cummings, Michael, Anthony Brown, and Richard O'Conner. 2007. The cigarette controversy. *Cancer Epidemiology, Biomarkers & Prevention* 16: 1070–1076.
Garland, Joseph. 1953. Cancer of the lung. *New England Journal of Medicine* 249: 465–466.
Garland, Joseph. 1961. The great debate. *New England Journal of Medicine* 264: 1266.
Glantz, Staton, John Slade, Lisa Bero, Peter Hanauer, and Deborah Barnes. 1998. *The cigarette papers*. Berkeley: University of California Press.
Kluger, Richard. 1997. *Ashes to ashes: America's hundred-year cigarette war, the public health, and the unabashed triumph of Philip Morris*. New York: Vintage Books.
Little, Clarence. 1961. An appraisal of the smoking-lung-cancer issue. *New England Journal of Medicine* 264: 1241–1245.
Norr, Roy. 1952. Cancer by the Carton. *Reader's Digest*, December.
Proctor, Robert. 1996. *Cancer wars: How politics shapes what we know and don't know about cancer*. New York: Basic Books.
Proctor, Robert. 2004. The global smoking epidemic: A history and status report. *Clinical Lung Cancer* 5: 371–376.
Wynder, Ernst. 1961. An appraisal of the smoking-lung-cancer issue. *New England Journal of Medicine* 264: 1235–1240.

Chapter 13
Tobacco Litigation

The aggressive posture we have taken regarding depositions and discovery in general continues to make these cases extremely burdensome and expensive for plaintiff's lawyers. ... To paraphrase General Patton, the way we won these cases was not by spending all of our money, but by making that other son of a bitch spend all his.

Michael Jordan, Attorney for R.J. Reynolds

Abstract This chapter examines three waves of tobacco litigation from the 1950s to the present. I especially focus on the role that historians have played as expert judicial witnesses in these cases. Historians testify about whether or not the dangers of smoking were common knowledge in the 1950s, 1960s, 1970s and later and whether there existed a scientific controversy on the subject. Experts have to research all elements that characterize common knowledge and scientific knowledge, and the role the tobacco industry played in its construction. Subsequently, I discuss the legal strategies used by plaintiffs and defendants in tobacco litigation through basic forms of legal game theory. This chapter is also based on the results of my inquiry into the involvement of US historians in tobacco litigation between 1986 and 2014, comprising of 50 historians and 314 cases.

13.1 The First Wave: Cipollone v. Liggett Group

From the 1950s onward, the tobacco industry has been sued by individual plaintiffs. The first case was brought in 1954 when "Ira Lowe, a Saint Louis factory worker, filed a products liability suit against the tobacco industry."[1] By 1964, the year the first Surgeon General's Report on tobacco was published, there had only been 30 lawsuits filed against tobacco companies.[2] Between 1954 and 1994, there had

[1] Miura, Marlo, Daynard, Richard, and Samet, Jonathan. 2006. The Role of Litigation in Tobacco Control. *Salud Pública de México* 48, 125.

[2] Brandt, Allan. 2007. *The Cigarette Century. The Rise, Fall and Deadly Persistence of a Product that Defined America.* New York: Basic Books, 69.

R. Delafontaine, *Historians as Expert Judicial Witnesses in Tobacco Litigation*, Studies in the History of Law and Justice 4, DOI 10.1007/978-3-319-14292-0_13

been 800 lawsuits brought against the industry.[3] During this period, the tobacco companies' legal strategies had been very successful. Their legal tactics were twofold: (1) The tobacco industry claimed there was a scientific controversy on the dangers of smoking, and that although a lot of research had been done, there was no conclusive evidence yet of a causal link between smoking and cancer or respiratory diseases. If there was no causal link, the tobacco companies had not acted in a negligible manner. (2) Secondly, tobacco's legal counsel argued that the plaintiffs knew the dangers of smoking, thereby accepting to endanger their own health when they started smoking.[4] Both strategies were constructed to eliminate the liability of the tobacco companies. During this whole period only two cases resulted in a ruling favouring the plaintiffs and both were reversed on appeal.[5] Not a single case resulted in damages for the plaintiffs.[6]

Cipollone v. Liggett signified a breaking point. The Cipollone case from 1986 found Liggett Group guilty on charges of fraud and conspiracy. Liggett had failed to warn Rose Cipollone about the health risks of smoking and was held responsible in part for her disease, namely, lung cancer, which had been caused by her addiction to smoking. Ms. Cipollone had been diagnosed with lung cancer, to which she had succumbed in 1984. The case was brought by her husband, Antonio Cipollone. After his death their son, Thomas Cipollone, continued the litigation. After several appeals, the US Supreme Court partly reversed and partly affirmed the Cipollone verdict, so the trail had to be retried in part with the requirements set by the Supreme Court. Due to the augmenting costs of 8 years of litigation, Thomas Cipollone withdrew his suit.[7] The Cipollone trial is an excellent example of another legal tactic generally used by the tobacco companies: scorched-earth litigation. Tobacco companies have greater means than any individual plaintiff. By prolonging the trail with motions, depositions, subpoenas, and eventually by appealing as high as the US Supreme Court; the tobacco industry sends a clear message: tobacco litigation will ruin you financially.

Brandt writes that already in the 1950s and 1960s lawyers were controlling the industry's policy. Lawyers set forth the industries strategies to avoid the "potentially disastrous" consequences of liability litigation.[8] "The lawyers were now in control, and litigation anxiety powerfully shaped on-going tobacco strategy", Brandt further

[3]Rutkow, Lainie, Vernick, Jon, and Teret, Stephen. 2007. Public Health Benefits of Recent Litigation Against Tobacco Industry. *Journal of the American Medical Association* 298, 86.

[4]We will discuss the tobacco industry's legal strategies in a following topic. See, Part III, Sect. 13.4. Tobacco Tactics in Court: Legal Game Theory, cfr. infra.

[5]The first is *Pritchard v. Liggett & Myers Tobacco Co.* from 1966 and the second is *Cipollone v. Liggett Group Inc.* from 1986. Cipollone was only partially reversed on appeal by the US Supreme Court, in the end the lawsuit was withdrawn due to exorbitant costs for the individual plaintiff.

[6]Douglas, Clifford, Davis Ronald, and Beasley, John. 2006. Epidemiology of the Third Wave of Tobacco Litigation in the United States, 1994–2005. *Tobacco Control* 15, 9.

[7]For more information on the Cipollone trial see http://tobaccodocuments.org/profiles/litigation/cipollone.html. Accessed 31 Oct 2014.

[8]Brandt, as n. 2, 251–252.

argues.[9] Committees of senior industry lawyers were architects of a legal strategy that maintained that there was a scientific controversy on the health dangers of smoking, while they themselves were constructing the very controversy from within the tobacco industry itself.

Only in the final years of this first wave were historians used as expert witnesses. The first case which made use of a historian was *Dewey v. R.J. Reynolds* from 1986.[10] In *Cipollone v. Liggett Group Inc.*, historians were used to add historical gravitas to the legal strategies of the defence's legal counsel, but also to augment the cost of litigation for the plaintiff. Expert do not come cheap. When the plaintiff does not have the funds to support its own expert witness, the tobacco companies had yet another advantage in court. There have been three historians involved in *Cipollone v. Liggett Group*. (1) Historian John Burnham had already testified in one tobacco-related trial the same year.[11] As a medical historian, John Burnham is one of the few historians who has testified for the industry and has actually researched and published on tobacco history. (2) Historian Fred Carstensen, who had published on Russian economic history and business history in general, was also deposed and later on he testified in court.[12] (3) Kenneth Ludmerer, a medical historian with no research specific on tobacco, started a long career of expert witnessing for the tobacco industry with his deposition in Cipollone.[13]

Brandt concluded that: "[f]ollowing the Cipollone verdict and the failure to secure a pay-out from the tobacco industry in similar suits, the plaintiff's bar viewed tobacco liability litigation with considerable scepticism."[14] Despite the fact that the case had failed for the plaintiff, the Cipollone trial had "a truly historical impact." The verdict had opened access "to some 300,000 internal tobacco industry documents." This opened "a devastating crack in traditional industry defences."[15] For the first time in the history of tobacco litigation the question "who knew what when?", could now also be answered from the perspective of the tobacco companies, thereby enabling the judge to make a judgment on the liability of the tobacco companies based on historical facts. At the time, anti-tobacco activist attorney Richard Daynard said that the documents procured from the Cipollone verdict "were only the tip of the iceberg", but provided "a firm foundation for future plaintiffs to build a convincing case of fraud and conspiracy against the tobacco industry."[16] *Tobacco Control*, a journal devoted to publishing the results of the research on

[9]Brandt, as n. 2, 265.

[10]See Appendix III, Table 7. Involvement of Historians in Tobacco Litigation 1986–2013, cfr. infra.

[11]Namely, *Dewey v. R.J. Reynolds*, See Expert Witness Profile No. 6, John Burnham.

[12]See Expert Witness Profile No. 8, Fred Carstensen.

[13]See Expert Witness Profile No. 30, Kenneth Ludmerer.

[14]Brandt, as n. 2, 403.

[15]Hurt, Richard, Ebbert, Jon, Muggli, Monique, Lockhart, Nikki, and Robertson, Channing. 2012. Open Doorway to Truth: Legacy of the Minnesota Tobacco Trial. *Mayo Clinic Proceedings* 84, 446. & Brandt, as n. 2, 330.

[16]Brant, as n. 2, 330.

secret internal documents of the tobacco industry and tobacco control in general, was first published in 1992. Using the industry's documents, the journal informed the public about the dangers of smoking and the conspiracy of the tobacco industry. Furthermore this research also "formed the basis for public and private lawsuits against the industry in the USA."[17]

The "discovery" of secret tobacco documents knew another high day when in 1995 Professor Staton Glantz of the University of California in San Francisco received "a box containing several thousand pages of documents from the Brown & Williamson Tobacco Corporation."[18] The only return address was that of "Mr. Butts."[19] Brown & Williamson sued the university to have its documents returned, but their request was denied in court.[20] In the following months the documents were published in the *Journal of the American Medical Association* and on the Internet.[21] Glantz published *The Cigarette Papers* in 1996, a book with the results of his research of the secret documents. Everett Koop, US Surgeon General from 1981 until 1989, wrote the foreword and called the book "a vital weapon in the battle against tobacco."[22] Historians began their research of thousands of internal documents and with every note, transcript, record, and memorandum they read, it became clearer that the tobacco industry had committed a fraud against the American public.

Through the early 1990s, tobacco litigation continued with little success for the plaintiffs. The influence of tobacco's internal secret files could not yet be fully measured or used. The secret documents were there but their amount and time-span [more than 60 years of internal documents] took a while to fully examine. So most cases continued to end in a victory for the defence. Typical for almost all plaintiffs was that they started smoking as kids. A typical case from this period of tobacco litigation is the Horton case. Afro-American Nathan Horton from Mississippi, whose wife sued the American Tobacco Company in 1987, had started smoking as a child. He became a two pack smoker when he joined the US Navy and could buy cigarettes at military discount prices. After his military service, he became a carpenter and continued smoking until he was diagnosed with lung cancer in 1986. David Sansing, another historian who was hired by the tobacco companies, was deposed in this case. Sansing specialized in the history of Mississippi.[23]

---

[17]Malone, Ruth, and Warner, Kenneth. 2012. Tobacco Control at Twenty: Reflecting on the Past, Considering the Present and Developing the New Conversations for the Future. *Tobacco Control* 21, 74.

[18]Glantz, Staton, Slade, John, Bero, Lisa, Hanauer, Peter, and Barnes, Deborah. 1998. The Cigarette Papers. Berkeley: University of California Press, XVII.

[19]Brandt, as n. 2, 371.

[20]Brandt, as n. 2, 371–372.

[21]Hurt, Richard, Ebbert, Jon, Muggli, Monique, Lockhart, Nikki, and Robertson, Channing, as n. 15, 446. The documents can be accessed integral via http://publishing.cdlib.org/ucpressebooks/view?docId=ft8489p25j;brand=ucpress. Accessed 31 Oct 2014.

[22]Glantz, Staton, Slade, John, Bero, Lisa, Hanauer, Peter, and Barnes, Deborah, as n. 18, XV.

[23]See Expert Witness Profile No. 42, David Sansing.

Eventually "the Horton case ended in a mistrial; the jury deadlocked."[24] The tobacco industry was accused of "jury tampering, but the charges were never proven."[25] The industry's legal strategies, and extralegal strategies, were still very effective.

The early 1990s saw eight more cases wherein historians were involved.[26] The historians who were hired as experts by the tobacco industry in the first wave were: Stephen Ambrose, James Breeden, John Burnham, Fred Carstensen, Otis Graham, Joan Hoff, Robert Hudson, Kenneth Ludmerer, James Kirby Martin, Michael Parrish, David Sansing, Todd Savitt, and William Stueck.[27] Of these thirteen historians only Burnham had published on tobacco history, or has done since, for that matter.[28] Stephen Ambrose was a military historian who wrote biographies of President Eisenhower. He became famous for his involvement in the making of the HBO mini-series *Band of Brothers*.[29] Joan Hoff also published on American presidents. She has continued to serve as an expert witness for the tobacco companies at least until 2012.[30] Otis Graham was editor of *the Public Historian* and specialized in recent American history, without publishing anything on tobacco.[31] The list goes on in the same logic. Historians who had never done any research on tobacco or the tobacco controversy were testifying under oath about the history of the tobacco industry, smoking, the scientific controversy, and common knowledge about tobacco risks from the 1950s onward.

These historians brought a historical narrative into the courtroom that fitted the legal strategies of the tobacco companies. These experts argued that there was a scientific controversy on the dangers of tobacco smoking, while also arguing that people had known that smoking was unhealthy. None of these historians researched the internal tobacco documents. It is hard to find any legitimate reasons for that choice. By leaving the involvement of the industry out of their historical research, these industry experts failed to meet the requirements of professional historical research. Furthermore, those historians should not have been allowed to testify because how could they possibly testify on the role of the tobacco industry in the cigarette controversy, if they had not researched it? In these final years of the first wave of tobacco litigation the Frye-rule on expert witnessing was still in place.[32]

---

[24]Brandt, as n. 2, 371–372.

[25]Brandt, as n. 2, 371–372. & For more information on *Horton v. American Tobacco Co.* see http://tobaccodocuments.org/profiles/litigation/horton.html. Accessed 31 Oct 2014. For a fictional work on the tobacco industry's jury tampering skills read John Grisham's *The Runaway Jury*.

[26]See Appendix III, Table 7. Involvement of Historians in Tobacco Litigation 1986–2013, cfr. infra.

[27]All expert witness profiles can be found in Appendix I & Appendix II, Table 7. Involvement of Historians in Tobacco Litigation 1986–2013, cfr. infra.

[28]See the systematic overview of the expert witnesses in Appendix II & See Expert Witness Profile No. 6, John Burnham.

[29]See Expert Witness Profile No. 1, Stephen Ambrose.

[30]See Expert Witness Profile No. 30, Joan Hoff.

[31]See Expert Witness Profile No. 17, Otis Graham.

[32]See Part II, Sect. 7.3.6.2. The Frye Standard, cfr. supra.

The tougher regulations of the Daubert-ruling would not preclude these historians from testifying either.[33] Tobacco's legal counsel thus had been successful in selling the courts the idea that their expert historians had done historical research as it was generally accepted, without examining any of the internal tobacco documents. Unopposed by other historians who would have researched all available documents, the industry's version of the history of the cigarette and smoking continued to prevail in court. After the tobacco industry had created a scientific controversy on smoking, tobacco's legal counsel had now constructed their own version of the history of that tobacco controversy with the help of academic historians.

Despite the fact that the industry's legal strategies continued to produce acquittal after acquittal, or maybe just because of that success, the tobacco companies were confronted with an increasing hostile public opinion. Spurred on by public sentiment, government officials toughened up on the tobacco companies. Brandt writes: "[a]s it had done in 1964, the industry took the offensive, expressing outrage and indignation over the charges of nicotine manipulation and the addictiveness of smoking."[34] On the 14th of April 1994, the CEO's of the seven largest US tobacco companies appeared before the Waxman congressional Subcommittee.[35] These hearings were "covered widely in the print and broadcast media."[36] The Waxman hearings were broadcasted live on C-SPAN and CNN. Under oath, the CEO's answered Republican congressman Ron Wyden whether nicotine was addictive or not:

> REP. RON WYDEN: Let me begin my questioning on whether or not nicotine is addictive. Let me ask you first, and I'd like to just go down the row, whether each of you believes that nicotine is not addictive. I heard virtually all of you touch on it. Yes or no, do you believe nicotine is not addictive?
>
> MR. WILLIAM CAMPBELL, Philip Morris:
> I believe nicotine is not addictive, yes.
>
> REP. RON WYDEN: Mr. Johnston?
>
> MR. JAMES JOHNSTON, R.J. Reynolds:
> Mr. Congressman, cigarettes and nicotine clearly do not meet the classic definition of addiction. There is no intoxication.
> REP. RON WYDEN: We'll take that as a "no." Again, time is short. I think that each of you believe that nicotine is not addictive. We would just like to have this for the record.
>
> MR. JOSEPH TADDEO, US Tobacco:
> I don't believe that nicotine or our products are addictive.
> MR. ANDREW TISCH, Lorillard:
> I believe that nicotine is not addictive.

---

[33] See Part II, Sect. 7.3.6.3. The Daubert Standard: Popper & the Judge as Gatekeeper, cfr. supra.

[34] Brandt, as n. 2, 365.

[35] Hurt, Richard, Ebbert, Jon, Muggli, Monique, Lockhart, Nikki, and Robertson, Channing, as n. 15, 446–447.

[36] Brandt, as n. 2, 365.

MR. EDWARD HORRIGAN, Liggett Group:
I believe that nicotine is not addictive.

MR. THOMAS SANDEFUR, Brown & Williamson:
I believe that nicotine is not addictive.

MR. DONALD JOHNSTON, American Tobacco Company:
And I, too, believe that nicotine is not addictive.[37]

The fact that the CEOs were the last seven people on earth to discover that nicotine was addictive caused genuine nationwide outrage. As health advocates described it in a 2006 article: "The image of the seven tobacco CEOs testifying before Congress left an indelible impression on the American public."[38] The scientific controversy-tactic and the call for more research had lost its effectiveness. The strategy was unable to be maintained while every day new documents were unearthed that the tobacco companies knew that smoking was unhealthy and addictive. These final attempts by the seven CEOs to keep the scientific controversy alive, were counterproductive. The tobacco industry's fear to be subjected to harsh litigation and regulation was a very realistic future for the tobacco companies. Yet the seven CEOs had showed one other strategy that made the tobacco companies strong: they were all in it together.[39]

13.2 The Second Wave: Government v. The Tobacco Industry

In the second wave of tobacco litigation, the cases against the tobacco companies were brought by government entities. The individual states and the US federal government had larger financial resources, more experienced legal teams, and greater political power at their disposal than any individual plaintiff ever brought in play against the tobacco companies. The industry's standard legal tactic of scorched-earth litigation had less impact on the government's cases. The timing, as I discussed above, was excellent. Public opinion of the tobacco industry was at an all-time low, thanks to continued publication of internal documents and the declarations of the CEOs on nicotine.

---

[37]Brandt, as n. 2, 366. For more information see http://senate.ucsf.edu/tobacco/executives1994congress.html. Accessed 31 Oct 2014. & http://tobaccodocuments.org/profiles/waxman_henry.html. Accessed 31 Oct 2014.

[38]Henningfield, Jack, Rose, Christine, and Zeller, Mitch. 2006. Tobacco Industry Litigation Position on Addiction: Continued Dependence on Past Views. *Tobacco Control* 15, 27–36.

[39]This is what Sloan et al., called the strength of the oligopolistic structure of the industry. See Sloan, Frank, Trogdon, Justine, and Mathews, Carrie. 2005. Litigation and the Value of Tobacco companies. *Journal of Health Economics* 24, 427–447. See Part III, Sect. 10.2.4. The Oligopolistic Structure of the Tobacco Industry, cfr. supra.

13.2.1 The State Attorney Cases

Since the early 1990s groups of prominent tort lawyers had met to discuss further possibilities in tobacco litigation. Most of them had experience in asbestos tort litigation. The American asbestos industry had been bankrupted through litigation. Furthermore, asbestos litigation had produced "a skilled tort plaintiff's bar."[40] Lawyers like Ron Motley, who was called "the legal nemesis of the asbestos industry", became involved in tobacco litigation.[41] While the internal secret documents of the tobacco companies were unearthed by the thousands, these lawyers considered that it was time for "a massive legal attack."[42]

In Mississippi, an experienced legal team under the leadership of attorney general Michael Moore filed a lawsuit against the tobacco industry on the 23 of May 1994 on behalf of the state of Mississippi. At the press conference Moore explained: "[t]his lawsuit is premised on a simple notion: You caused the health crisis, you pay for it. The free ride is over. It's time these billionaire tobacco companies start paying what they rightfully owe to the Mississippi taxpayers."[43] It was essential for lawyers like Motley and Don Barrett to evade the trap faced by an individual suit. In individual lawsuits, tobacco's legal counsel would argue that the individual had made the choice to smoke. Barrett exclaimed: "The State of Mississippi has never smoked a cigarette."[44] Mississippi made no "choice" to smoke, and so another one of the key legal strategies of the tobacco industry was rendered useless. Other states soon followed Mississippi's example: "Minnesota in August 1994, West Virginia, Florida and Massachusetts in 1995."[45]

By 1997, more than 30 states had "joined the cause."[46] Legal counsel for the plaintiffs filed "motion after motion" in order to obtain the secret documents of the tobacco companies, a legal strategy they had already used in asbestos litigation. In the end they got more than 30 million internal documents.[47] According to Brandt, "considerable evidence" was found that the industry had systematically destroyed evidence of its knowledge of health concerns caused by their product.[48] Despite such attempts, the newly discovered documents proved an important source for legal evidence. As we have seen in the first three chapters which described the history of

---

[40]Alderman, Jess, and Daynard, Richard. 2006. Applying Lessons from Tobacco Litigation to Obesity Lawsuits. *The American Journal of Preventive Medicine* 30, 82.

[41]"Ron Motley's mother had recently died of emphysema-a long and painful death." See Brandt, as n. 2, 409.

[42]Brandt, as n. 2, 409.

[43]Brandt, as n. 2, 413–414.

[44]Brandt, as n. 2, 414.

[45]Brandt, as n. 2, 415.

[46]Brandt, as n. 2, 416.

[47]Brandt, as n. 2, 417.

[48]Brandt, as n. 2, 418.

tobacco and the cigarette controversy, these internal documents showed that tobacco companies had been much more aware of the dangers of their product than they claimed to have been. The secret files demonstrated how tobacco companies had tried their best to convince the general public smoking was not dangerous, against their own knowledge of the contrary.

The tobacco industry was left exceptionally vulnerable from continued revelations of fraud by their own internal documents. An increasingly hostile media assured that damaging documents were brought to the public's attention. Debate was even more augmented when in February 1996 CBS's investigative news program *60 Minutes* broadcasted an episode on Jeffrey Wigand, who had formally been a vice president at the Brown & Williamson Tobacco Company.[49] Wigand had turned on the industry and had been deposed in November 1995 in the lawsuit brought by the State of Mississippi. His deposition was taken by plaintiff's attorney Ron Motley. The deposition had been extremely polemical. Tobacco's legal counsel objected to every question posed by Motley and every answer given by Wigand. The deposition by Wigand and the knowledge he wished to share was of enormous value for the plaintiffs and extremely dangerous for the tobacco industry. Wigand declared that Mr. Sandefur, the CEO of Brown & Williamson, had stated on multiple occasions that the tobacco companies were "in the nicotine delivery business."[50] *60 Minutes* offered an overview of the systematic smear campaign against Wigand organized by the tobacco industry. Wigand and his family suffered greatly under different kinds of harassment. The show itself had been delayed for 6 months out of fear of being subpoenaed by the industry. Eventually the program aired, discrediting the tobacco industry instead of Wigand. Wigand detailed in the interview on *60 Minutes* how the industry adjusted nicotine levels to make cigarettes more addictive. Wigand declared that cigarettes were: "a delivery device for nicotine."[51] On later occasions in court the tobacco companies would argue that "blending tobacco is an art; it's not a nicotine driven science."[52] In 1999 Wigand's story was made into a Hollywood adaptation titled: *The Insider*.[53]

---

[49]Hurt, Richard, Ebbert, Jon, Muggli, Monique, Lockhart, Nikki, and Robertson, Channing, as n. 15, 446.

[50]For Mr. Wigand's deposition see http://www.jeffreywigand.com/pascagoula.php. Accessed 31 Oct 2014.

[51]For more on the *60 Minutes* episode, see http://www.jeffreywigand.com/60minutes.php. Accessed 31 Oct 2014. For the episode itself, see http://www.cbsnews.com/video/watch/?id=7377558n. Accessed 31 Oct 2014.

[52]Cummings, Michael, Brown, Anthony, and Douglas, Christopher. 2006. Consumer Acceptable Risk: How Cigarette Companies Have Responded to Accusations that Their Product are Defective. *Tobacco Control* 15, 85.

[53]Russell Crowe plays Jeffrey Wigand, Al Pacino plays an investigator from *60 Minutes* see http://www.imdb.com/title/tt0140352/?ref_=sr_1. Accessed 31 Oct 2014. *The Insider* was nominated for seven Oscars. Tobacco litigation was also a storyline in the popular television series *The West Wing*, (Season 2, episodes 20–22, 2000). In 2006 another Hollywood movie addressed tobacco's public

Richard Kluger's *Ashes to Ashes: America's Hundred-Year Cigarette War, the Public Health, and the Unabashed Triumph of Philip Morris* published in 1997, narrated in great detail how tobacco companies continued to sell a deadly product and how the industry had succeeded in being permitted to continue to sell a dangerous product.[54] His book won the Pulitzer Prize and contributed to an already heated public debate on the tobacco industry. Public opinion and the media were now eager to see the tobacco companies convicted for, what seemed, the greatest cover-up in American history.

At least in seven of the attorney general suits were historians deposed as expert judicial witnesses for the tobacco industry.[55] In Florida Ambrose, Burns, and Ludmerer were deposed for the industry.[56] By then these three historians had several years of experience in testifying for the defence. Hyman Berman and George Green were deposed and testified in court in the Minnesota trial. Hyman was a professor of history at the University of Minnesota specialized in American Labour history.[57] It would be his only testimony for the tobacco companies. George Green was a colleague of Hyman at the University of Minnesota, he would also only testify this one time. Green is specialized in American business history.[58] In Texas, Otis Graham served as an expert for the industry for a second time, accompanied by John Drobny, an independent consultant. Drobny is the only non-academic who has been identified to have been deposed as a historian in tobacco litigation.[59] In the Mississippi attorney general case, experienced industry-employed experts Ludmerer and Sansing were deposed.[60] Charles Lowery, a professor of History from the University of Mississippi was also deposed. He was specialized in civil rights history.[61] John Ray Skates, a co-worker of Lowery, was also deposed in the same case. He was specialized in the history of Mississippi and the history of the American military struggle with Japan during World War II.[62] Both Lowery and Skates only served as expert witnesses this one time. Experienced experts

campaign relations campaign on the health issues, entitled *Thank You for Smoking*. See http://www.imdb.com/title/tt0427944. Accessed 31 Oct 2014.

[54]Kluger, Richard. 1997. *Ashes to Ashes: America's Hundred-Year Cigarette War, the Public Health, and the Unabashed Triumph of Philip Morris*. New York: Vintage Books, 811.

[55]Appendix III, Table 7. Involvement of Historians in Tobacco Litigation 1986–2013, cfr. infra.

[56]See Expert Witness Profile No. 30, Kenneth Ludmerer. & See Expert Witness Profile No. 1, Stephen Ambrose. & See Expert Witness Profile No. 7, Augustus Burns.

[57]See Expert Witness Profile No. 3, Hyman Berman.

[58]See Expert Witness Profile No. 18, George Green.

[59]Most consultants are active in first stages of the preparation of the expert reports as data finders. See Part II, Sect. 3.3.1. Consulting. & See Expert Witness Profile No. 13, John Drobny.

[60]See Expert Witness Profile No. 42, David Sansing. & See Expert Witness Profile No. 30, Kenneth Ludmerer.

[61]See Expert Witness Profile No. 29, Charles Lowery.

[62]See Expert Witness Profile No. 46, John Ray Skates.

Ludmerer and Parrish were deposed in Washington.[63] Michael Schaller was deposed in Arizona.[64] He is a specialist in the diplomatic relation of the US and East Asia. Wayne Morgan, who studied American culture in the twentieth century, was deposed in Oklahoma.[65]

The industry's legal strategy in most states probably was to construct an expert team of historians combined of, on the one hand local academic historians and on the other, experienced witnesses. It is very probable that there were many more historians involved in the attorney general cases. But since settlement negotiations started in early 1997, the records of the involvement of historians are scarce because in the end only a few were deposed. No historians were recruited by the state attorneys general as expert witnesses. In the end, with only the Mississippi state trial gone to court, no court had ruled, based on historical documents, that the tobacco industry had conspired against the American public. Settling was a valuable strategy for the tobacco companies. The attorneys general got their "victory", and damages were paid. But further tobacco litigation still needed to prove in court that the industry had committed a fraud against the public as long as no judge had ruled on the alleged scientific controversy and the industry's role in its construction.

13.2.2 The Master Settlement Agreement

The tobacco companies knew they were certain to lose some of the state attorney general cases and decided to negotiate a "global settlement agreement."[66] In June of 1997, the tobacco companies agreed to pay $365,5 billion over the next 25 years to the states. The settlement also stipulated that all individual litigation brought against Wigand and other whistle-blowers, and plaintiff's lawyers would be ceased. The tobacco industry also agreed to be regulated by the FDA. In return, the tobacco industry would be protected from class action suits.[67] The Minnesota trial team was awarded the "WHO's Tobacco Free World Award", for their involvement in the litigation against the tobacco companies.[68] Former Minnesota state attorney general Hubert Humphrey III and former assistant attorney general Douglas Blanke wrote that: "[t]hruth matters" and "the real value of truth is in its power to effect change."[69] The cases brought by the state "altered the course of national debates"

[63]See Expert Witness Profile No. 30, Kenneth Ludmerer. & See Expert Witness Profile No. 37, Michael Parrish.

[64]See Expert Witness Profile No. 44, Michael Schaller.

[65]See Expert Witness Profile No. 35, Wayne Morgan.

[66]Brandt, as n. 2, 420.

[67]Brandt, as n. 2, 422.

[68]Blanke, Douglas, and Humphrey III, Hubert. 2006. Putting Truth into Action: Using the Evidence for Justice. *Tobacco Control* 15, 1.

[69]Blanke, Douglas, and Humphrey III, Hubert, as n. 68, 1.

and helped "re-frame the tobacco issue."[70] Not all health advocates were agreeing that the settlement was "the most historic public health achievement in history", as Mississippi attorney general Moore called it.[71] Anti-tobacco advocate Stanton Glantz declared: "The fundamental reality of tobacco is that the way to beat them is to beat them. I have never found a single instance anywhere, anywhere, where a compromise with the industry served the public health."[72] In hindsight, Glantz was not that far off.

A bipartisan bill was prepared in Congress, which proposed serious regulation for the tobacco companies. Under the leadership of Republican senator John McCain from Arizona, a bill was drafted which was called "The McCain bill." The draft included higher taxes on tobacco products, FDA regulation of nicotine and provisions that aimed to regulate and diminish teen smoking.[73] It even augmented the proposals for damages in the "global settlement" from $385 billion to over $500 billion. In 1998, the McCain bill was voted out of the senate subcommittee. The lobbying machine of the tobacco industry in 1997 was sponsored with 23 % more funds when compared with the previous year. The tobacco companies devoted "a record $35.5 million to lobbying." The industry also spent $40 million in radio and television ads in 1998 to represent the bill as "a new tax targeted at working people."[74] The tobacco industry "successfully lobbied to kill the bill on June 17, 1998."[75] The McCain bill was, furthermore, not supported by everyone in the health community. Anti-tobacco advocates like Staton Glantz were critics of the bill, arguing that the tobacco companies could be brought down in court, and settling would only assure the industry's survival.[76] The McCain bill was lost, and with it a great opportunity to regulate the tobacco industry in an unseen manner.

After the collapse of the McCain bill a new settlement had to be negotiated. The failure of the bill and the opposition by parts of the public health community made the state attorneys feel pressured for time and support. Such a "shift in leverage" produced a new settlement which bore little resemblance with the Global Settlement.[77] The new Master Settlement Agreement of 1998 agreed that "five major tobacco companies had to pay $206 billion to 46 states over the next twenty-five years."[78] The four states that had already settled, Florida, Minnesota,

---

[70]Blanke, Douglas, and Humphrey III, Hubert, as n. 68, 1.

[71]Brandt, as n. 2, 422–424.

[72]Brandt, as n. 2, 424.

[73]Brandt, as n. 2, 427.

[74]Brandt, as n. 2, 427–428.

[75]Givel, Michael, and Glantz, Staton. 2004. The "Global Settlement" With the Tobacco Industry. *American Journal of Public Health* 94, 222.

[76]Seffrin, John. 2004. Commentary: The Master Settlement Agreement in Historic Context. *Health Promotion Practice* 5, 18.

[77]Seffrin, as n. 76, 18.

[78]See the whole Master Settlement Agreement at http://publichealthlawcenter.org/sites/default/files/resources/master-settlement-agreement.pdf. Accessed 31 Oct 2014.

Mississippi, and Texas added another $40 billion. The total cost to settle for the tobacco industry was a grand total of $246 billion.[79] Only modest restrictions were put into place on advertising and promotions. Cartoon characters like Joe Camel were prohibited. But in general the marketing restrictions on youngsters and children had largely been removed from the settlement.[80] The global settlement had lost a lot of its power.[81] The proposed FDA regulatory power was dropped along with other provisions on youth smoking.[82] Furthermore, the immunity requirements for class action litigation that were negotiated in the *Global Settlement* remained in place.[83] However, a definitive success of the MSA was that the tobacco companies had agreed to release approximately "seven million documents" totalling "70 million pages of documents and nearly 20,000 other media materials."[84] By 2009, "several hundred peer-reviewed articles had been published" which had researched these sources.[85] The insights gained from such research had significant impact on a national and international level.[86] The MSA of 1998 "left the Marlboro Man in the Saddle", as one observer noted. Health economist Dorothy Rice from the University of California, San Francisco calculated that the cost of treating smoking-related diseases for just 1 year in the state of California was about $8.7 billion. The state had negotiated a settlement in which the tobacco companies agreed to pay the State of California $500 million on a yearly base for the next 25 years. "It's a terrible deal", she concluded.[87]

The Minnesota settlement provisioned the creation of the *Minnesota Partnership for Action Against Tobacco*. The MPAAT was created in 1998 and aimed at "diminishing the human and economic consequences of tobacco use."[88] The organization was funded with damages paid by the tobacco industry. In an article in *Tobacco Control* from 2004, Glantz et al., detail how the industry attacked the foundation in a variety of ways, claiming misuse of funds and conflicts of interest and political expenditures.[89] These accusations from the tobacco industry were

[79]For more information on these settlements see: Hurt, Richard, Ebbert, Jon, Muggli, Monique, Lockhart, Nikki, and Robertson, Channing, as n. 15, 446–448, table 1.

[80]Seffrin, as n. 76, 19.

[81]For a comparative analyses of the two settlements see Givel, Michael, and Glantz, Staton as n. 75, 219–221, 223, table 1–4.

[82]Givel, Michael, and Glantz, Staton as n. 75, 221.

[83]Givel, Michael, and Glantz, Staton as n. 75, 218.

[84]Hurt, Richard, Ebbert, Jon, Muggli, Monique, Lockhart, Nikki, and Robertson, Channing, as n. 15, 446. & Douglas, Clifford, Davis Ronald, and Beasley, John, as n. 6, 10.

[85]Hurt, Richard, Ebbert, Jon, Muggli, Monique, Lockhart, Nikki, and Robertson, Channing, as n. 15, 448.

[86]Givel, Michael, and Glantz, Staton as n. 75, 220.

[87]Brandt, as n. 2, 432.

[88]Ibrahim, Jennifer, Tsoukalas, Theo, and Glantz, Staton. 2004. Public Health Foundations and the Tobacco Industry: Lessons From Minnesota. *Tobacco Control* 13, 228–229.

[89]Ibrahim, Jennifer, Tsoukalas, Theo, and Glantz, Staton, as n. 88, 299–234.

backed up by a new ally of the tobacco companies, the state attorneys general. The attorneys general had found a new source of revenue for the states and were keen on defending that resource. Multiple *amicus briefs* were filed by state attorneys general in support of the tobacco companies in lawsuits concerning the funding of the MPAAT, fearing these expenditures "might jeopardize" the tobacco industry's ability to make payments directly to the states required by the MSA.[90] Brandt came to a similar conclusion: "The industry had secured new allies by providing a steady flow of state revenues. Now state governors and Attorneys General would help the companies fight off litigation."[91] Eventually, many of these tobacco funded programs established by the MSA saw their budgets significantly reduced.[92]

In general, for health advocates, the MSA was "a missed opportunity to make historic change."[93] Despite all the problems with the MSA, the price of a cigarette pack increased. According to Brandt: "[t]he MSA "tax" has itself had a significant impact on youth smoking" and "[i]n the years following the MSA, tobacco sales fell by more than 20 %, reaching a level not seen since 1950."[94] Despite this fall in tobacco sales, the tobacco industry which had been in mortal danger in 1997, entered the new millennium relatively intact ready to sell its product at home and abroad.

13.2.3 *US v. Philip Morris et al.*

In the State of the Union of 1999, President Bill Clinton announced that his administration would initiate civil litigation against the tobacco companies. After the individual states had settled with the tobacco companies, the Department of Justice (DOJ) sought to recover health care costs made by the federal government. The government accused the tobacco companies of having been engaged in "a conspiracy to deny well-established associations between smoking and multiple diseases, the association between second-hand smoke and lung cancer and the addictive nature of nicotine."[95] The tobacco companies were indicted under the *Racketeering Influenced and Corrupt Organizations Act* (RICO). In September 1999, the DOJ brought its case against the tobacco industry (Philip Morris, R.J. Reynolds, Brown & Williams, Lorillard, Liggett, American Tobacco Co., British American Tobacco, the Council for Tobacco Research, and the Tobacco Institute). The DOJ accused the tobacco industry of committing fraud, violation of state

---

[90]Ibrahim, Jennifer, Tsoukalas, Theo, and Glantz, Staton, as n. 88, 231–232, 234.

[91]Brandt, as n. 2, 445.

[92]Givel, Michael, and Glantz, Staton as n. 75, 222.

[93]Seffrin, as n. 76, 19.

[94]Brandt, as n. 2, 434–435, 440.

[95]Rutkow, Lainie, Vernick, Jon, and Teret, Stephen, as n. 3, 87.

consumer protection statutes, marketing, selling of defective and unreasonably dangerous products [strict liability, negligence, and breach of implied warranty], and engagement in a general conspiracy against the American public. The federal government sought to recover federal spending on tobacco-related diseases for "an estimated $280 billion." It was the largest sum ever demanded in a single trial in civil litigation in the history of American law, according to Brandt.[96] Proceedings started in September 2000, the trial itself commenced in September 2004. The whole trial took 99 weeks. The case was appealed on multiple occasions and on various grounds. In 2006, the US Supreme Court denied certiorari.[97] Still legal proceedings continued until November 12th of 2012 when Judge Gladys Kessler reaffirmed her ruling from 2006. In 2006, she had stated that the tobacco companies had lied about the dangers of cigarettes at least since 1964.[98] The tone of her ruling was especially hard for the tobacco industry: "Defendants have marketed and sold their lethal product with zeal, with deception, with a single-minded focus on their financial success, and without regard for the human tragedy or social costs that success exacted."[99] The success of the active evasion by the industry of a condemning verdict, in which the industry was convicted for fraud, had now come to an end by the judgment in *US v. Philip Morris et al.* As we shall discuss in Chap. 14, historians played an important role in this trial as expert witnesses.[100]

13.3 The Third Wave: Engle Progeny Cases

The second wave of tobacco litigation had rendered much of the traditional legal tactics of the tobacco industry obsolete. The scientific controversy tactic had become useless when the internal documents, procured by the Cipollone verdict and the MSA, showed tobacco companies had been aware from early on about the health

[96]For more information on *US v. Philip Morris* et al. see http://tobaccodocuments.org/profiles/litigation/us_vs_pm.html. Accessed 31 Oct 2014. & http://www.justice.gov/civil/cases/tobacco2/index.htm. Accessed 31 Oct 2014. & Brandt, as n. 2, 496. And see Part III, Chap. 14: United States v. Philip Morris et al., cfr. infra.

[97]The Supreme Court only reviews a small number of cases within its jurisdiction. A party can appeal to the Supreme Court to issue a writ of certiorari. The court accepts or denies the certiorari. For more information on this legal term see http://www.law.cornell.edu/wex/certiorari. Accessed 31 Oct 2014.

[98]For an article announcing the final verdict from Reuters http://www.reuters.com/article/2012/11/27/us-usa-tobacco-idUSBRE8AQ18A20121127?fb_action_ids=4497202801467&fb_action_types=og.likes&fb_source=aggregation&fb_aggregation_id=246965925417366. Accessed 31 Oct 2014.

[99]*United States of America v. Philip Morris USA INC.* Final Opinion, 2006, 1683. Consulted via http://www.library.ucsf.edu/sites/all/files/ucsf_assets/FinalOpinion_full_version.pdf. Accessed 31 Oct 2014.

[100]See Part III, Chap. 14: United States v. Philip Morris et al., cfr. infra.

dangers of smoking and the addictiveness of nicotine. Furthermore, due to the decision in *US v. Philip Morris et al.*, consumers could sue the tobacco companies for negligence, backed up by legal precedent. To diminish legal costs consumers joined in class action suits to sue the tobacco industry, creating an unseen number of tobacco-related court cases.[101] The number of historians who were hired as experts for the industry doubled during the period 1999–2013. By 2014 50 historians had testified in tobacco litigation. Only four of them had testified for the plaintiffs, while 46 have been engaged on the defendant's side.[102]

13.3.1 Engle

In the State of Florida on the fourth of May 1999 a class action suit was brought by six smokers with cancer against R.J. Reynolds, Philip Morris, Lorillard, American Tobacco co., Brown & Williamson, Liggett, Brooke Group, Dorsal Tobacco, the Council for Tobacco Research, and the Tobacco Institute.[103] At first the class was defined as "[a]ll United States citizens and residents, and their survivors, who have suffered, presently suffer or who have died from diseases and medical conditions caused by their addiction to cigarettes that contain nicotine."[104] The class was later limited by the court to smokers from Florida because "a nationwide group of more than one million smokers was simply unmanageable." The Engle case was the first smokers' class action ever approved in the US.[105] The Engle trial would become the longest in the history of US civil litigation.[106]

The trial was structured in three phases. Engle I established the general liability, or "common issues affecting all class members", in other words the fraud committed by the tobacco industry. In the second phase the lump sum of $145 billion was awarded to the class, it was "the largest award of its kind in US history."[107] But before the third phase could get started, Engle II was overturned on appeal. The plaintiffs then appealed to the Florida Supreme Court. In its landmark decision of 2006, the majority opinion stated that in every single plaintiff's case, the court had to determine "whether any class members relied on Tobacco's misrepresentations

[101]Class action suits are suits were the plaintiffs have suffered from the same injuries from the defendants and lets those plaintiffs file a case as a group. For more information see http://www.law.cornell.edu/wex/class_action. Accessed 31 Oct 2014.

[102]See Appendix II and Appendix III, cfr. infra.

[103]Rutkow, Lainie, Vernick, Jon, and Teret, Stephen, as n. 3, 87.

[104]General information on Engle see http://tobaccodocuments.org/profiles/litigation/engle.html. Accessed 31 Oct 2014.

[105]Harris, J. B. 2012. Engle v. Liggett: Has Big Tobacco Finally Met Its Match? *The Florida Bar Journal* 86, 16–17.

[106]Brandt, as n. 2, 412. It is still being continued today.

[107]Harris, J. B., as n. 105, 17.

or were injured by Tobacco's conduct."[108] Furthermore, the court found that the entitlement of damages should be considered more closely. There were compensatory damages to which an individual could be entitled, but the court was not sure whether the individuals were entitled to punitive damages from the tobacco companies. The court asked to review the way in which punitive damages were included to the compensation of individuals.[109] The court also addressed the class certification. According to the Florida Supreme Court it was problematic to handle class-wide punitive damages, and at the same time the negligence for every single class member. On those grounds the court decertified the class.[110] The Federal Supreme Court denied certiorari on the first of October 2007.

The decision of the Florida Supreme Court created a "pragmatic solution" in order to try a large number of cases with highly individualized claims. The court determined that each future case would be considered individually. But the court had "affirmed that smoking cigarettes causes numerous diseases and health conditions ... and many forms of cancer" and that "the defendants placed cigarettes on the market that were defective and dangerous ... nicotine in cigarettes is addictive ... the defendants agreed to conceal or omit information regarding the health effects of cigarettes or their addictive nature ... all of the defendants sold or supplied cigarettes that were defective ... and that all of the defendants were negligent."[111] This verdict made the tobacco conspiracy and thus the industry's negligence *res judicata*.[112] Plaintiffs could now, in theory, skip the costly trial period in which the tobacco conspiracy, the addictiveness, and the health dangers of smoking had to be proven.[113]

With the certainty that they did not have to prove the industry's deceptive practices all over again, "more than 8,000 plaintiffs filed individual claims against the tobacco companies."[114] The cases were named the Engle Progeny cases. Bloomberg News reported in March 2013, after the reconfirmation by the Florida Supreme Court of its 2006 decision, that the combined number of cases related to Engle faced by Philip Morris and R.J. Reynolds alone was higher than 8,000. According to its yearly report, Philip Morris is currently involved in 4,800 post-Engle cases. R.J. Reynolds announced in its annual report that the company was currently engaged in

[108] Harris, J. B., as n. 105, 18.

[109] Harris, J. B., as n. 105, 18–19.

[110] Harris, J. B., as n. 105, 19.

[111] Rutkow, Lainie, Vernick, Jon, and Teret, Stephen, as n. 3, 87.

[112] *Res judicata* is a legal term that signifies that certain facts have been judged and cannot be judged again in the same trial. For more information on the legal term of *res judicata* see http://www.law.cornell.edu/wex/res_judicata. Accessed 31 Oct 2014. & Harris, J. B., as n. 105, 19–21.

[113] Rutkow, Lainie, Vernick, Jon, and Teret, Stephen, as n. 3, 88.

[114] Harris, J. B., as n. 105, 21.

Table 13.1 Payouts by the tobacco companies in Engle progeny litigation[a]

Defendants	Compensatory	Punitive	Total
R.J. Reynolds	$46,182,725.63	$103,630,000.00	$149,812,725.63
Philip Morris	$6,511,582.15	$1,590,000.00	$8,101,582.15
Liggett Group	$2,324,194.38	$1,000,000.00	$3,324,194.38
Lorillard	$12,630,088.25	$36,300,000.00	$48,930,088.25

[a]Based on Westlaw court documents

5,750 Engle Progeny cases.[115] Phillip Morris and R.J. Reynolds alone are presently involved in about 10,550 court cases in Florida. I made a schematic overview of the cost of litigation for the tobacco companies in Engle Progeny cases (Table 13.1).

With only 2 % of all Engle Progeny cases brought to trial, the tobacco industry might be confronted with considerable legal cost and the payment of large amounts of damages in the future. In July 2014, a jury in Florida in an Engle Progeny case awarded $23,6 billion in damages to the wife of a smoker who had died of lung cancer. The jury awarded $17 million in compensatory damages, the rest of the $23 billion are punitive damages. Legal counsel for the tobacco companies promised a swift appeal. With thousands of Engle Progeny cases pending trial, tobacco companies' legal counsel will sure go all out to limit the amount of damages awarded in *Robinson v. R.J. Reynolds* to avoid a dangerous precedent.[116] As legal professor from Northeastern University Richard Daynard put it: "There are real risks for the industry here" and "There's presumably nothing about this case that is so special that it could not be replicated in many cases in the future."[117] Although damages are spread over several years and already budgeted into the yearly expenditures of several tobacco companies, several billions of dollars can do serious damage to a company, even to the tobacco industry.[118] The example from the Florida tobacco litigation could inspire other states. Yet, as we shall see, tobacco's lobbying machine has worked hard on avoiding repetition of Engle in other American states by urging for changes in laws on class actions and consumer protection.

Historians continue to play a role in Engle Progeny cases as frequent expert witnesses.[119] Almost all historians serve as witnesses for the defence. They argue

[115]Van Voris, Bob. 2013. Florida Top Court Affirms Ruling Enabling Tobacco Suits. *Bloomberg News*, March 14. http://www.bloomberg.com/news/2013-03-14/florida-top-court-affirms-ruling-enabling-tobacco-suits.html. Accessed 31 Oct 2014.

[116]See the article on the verdict in *The Washington Post:* Palazzolo, Joe. 2014. R.J. Reynolds Loses $23.6 Billion Verdict. *The Washington Post*, July 20. http://online.wsj.com/articles/r-j-reynolds-loses-23-6-billion-verdict-1405898753. Accessed 31 Oct 2014. Historian Robert Proctor was an expert witness for the plaintiffs in this case, see Expert Witness Profile No. 39, Robert Proctor.

[117]Palazzolo, as n. 116.

[118]We will return to this subject in Part III, Sect. 16.2. Litigation as a Solution, cfr. infra.

[119]See Appendix II, Table 2. Active in In re: Engle Progeny Cases, cfr. infra.

that the individual had enough information in order to make an informed adult choice.[120] The "choice" strategy has now become tobacco's main legal strategy. I found only two historians who testified for the plaintiffs in Engle Progeny cases: Robert Proctor and Louis Kyriakoudes.[121] The Engle Progeny cases will take decades more to finalize and historians will continue to play a role, on both sides. This prospect of continued litigation-driven history, forces the historical and legal communities to reflect upon the practice of expert witnessing by historians.

13.3.2 Smaller Cases

Smaller cases; individual, third-party, and class action cases continued through the late 1990s and the 2000s.[122] In February 2005, the *Class Action Fairness Bill*, was signed into law by Republican President George W. Bush. The law moved most class action from state courts to a federal level, thereby considerably augmenting litigation costs. The federal level is also considered "more hostile to class actions than the state courts." Harry Read, then Democratic leader of the US Senate issued a press release after the bill was confirmed which stated: "Yet another real world effect of this bill is to help the tobacco industry avoid accountability."[123] Furthermore, civil liability and punitive damages were "increasingly constrained in the United States, particularly under the industry-friendly Bush Administration."[124]

Despite continued litigation threats, the stock market did not lose its faith in tobacco shares. In an article which researches the influence of litigation on stock prices of tobacco shares, three economists concluded that after the MSA, there was a decline in systematic risk for tobacco stock. The risk was measured by the variance between the returns of a portfolio combined of tobacco shares and that of a diversified [efficient] portfolio.[125] According to their research, "[t]here was no significant change in systematic risk during the litigation period."[126] The restrictions placed on civil liability and on punitive damages by the MSA and further legislation, allowed the tobacco companies to budget their legal costs, thereby ensuring

120 Rutkow, Lainie, Vernick, Jon, and Teret, Stephen, as n. 3, 88.

121 See Expert Witness Profile No. 39, Robert Proctor & See Expert Witness Profile No. 26, Louis Kyriakoudes.

122 For a good overview see: Douglas, Clifford, Davis Ronald, and Beasley, John, as n. 6, 11–14, tables 1–5.

123 Douglas, Clifford, Davis Ronald, and Beasley, John, as n. 6, 14.

124 Mosher, James. 2009. Litigation and Alcohol Policy: Lessons from the US Tobacco Wars. *Addiction* 104, 28.

125 Sloan, Frank, Trogdon, Justine, and Mathews, Carrie, as n. 39, 427–428.

126 Sloan, Frank, Trogdon, Justine, and Mathews, Carrie, as n. 39, 439.

stability and predictability.[127] Furthermore, the "addictive nature of cigarettes" also contributed to the industry's continued market power.[128] According to the study, initial litigation had hurt tobacco, but after the MSA was implemented the risks dropped and tobacco shares remained attractive for buyers.[129] Despite the fact that the tobacco industry was not immediately hit with deadly legal damages, in the long run cases like the Engle Progeny case could have considerable influence on the financial situation of tobacco companies, forcing tobacco companies to raise the prices of their products and so eventually diminish the number of smokers. Selling a hazardous product continues because the legal damages the industry has to pay are nowhere near the profit it makes selling them.

13.4 Tobacco Tactics in Court: Legal Game Theory

In this topic I analyse the legal strategies used by defence counsel in tobacco litigation. To present the industry's tactics, I will use game theory. Game theory is very popular in law and has been used to draft legal policies, especially concerning negligence, and to understand other legal issues.[130] Tort and antitrust legislation is based on the expected strategic behaviour of capitalist companies. ["Game theory is a set of tools and a language for describing and predicting strategic behaviour."][131] Game theory focuses on the interdependence of decision making; worrying about the actions of others makes our own behaviour predictable.[132] I now apply this kind of reasoning to the legal strategies that are used in tobacco litigation.

Tobacco companies have been sued by individuals, in class actions, by third-parties, like insurance companies and unions, and public governments. I will come back to the suits by the states and the federal government because they applied different legal tactics from those cases filed by individuals, third-parties, and in class actions. Individual tobacco victims started to sue tobacco companies from the

---

[127]For a concluding discussion on the economics of tobacco litigation, see Part III, Sect. 16.2. Litigation as a Solution, cfr. infra.

[128]Sloan, Frank, Trogdon, Justine, and Mathews, Carrie, as n. 39, 430. Or as one tobacco spokesman put it in *Thank You for Smoking*: "We sell cigarettes. And there are cool, and available, and addictive. The job is almost done for us." This quote is comparable to the real life quote by Warren Buffet defending his takeover of R.J. Reynolds: "I'll tell you why I like the cigarette business. It costs a penny to make. Sell it for a dollar. It's addictive.", which I mentioned earlier. See Proctor, Robert. 2012. *Golden Holocaust: Origins of the Cigarette Catastrophe and the Case for Abolition.* Berkeley: University of California Press, 42.

[129]Sloan, Frank, Trogdon, Justine, and Mathews, Carrie, as n. 39, 440–441.

[130]Picker, Randal. 1993. *An Introduction to Game Theory and the Law.* Case Lecture Series, The University of Chicago Law School, 25. http://www.law.uchicago.edu/node/1306. Accessed 31 Oct 2014. & Posner, Eric. 2002. *Law and Social Norms.* Cambridge: Harvard University Press, 7.

[131]Picker, as n. 130, 2–3.

[132]The most famous example is The Prisoner's Dilemma. Picker, as n. 130, 4.

1950s onward. Without much success, as we have discussed earlier. The first wave of tobacco litigation revolved around two essential accusations. (1) The first question was whether smoking caused disease. And, as the scientific evidence became undeniable, when did the tobacco companies knew the dangers? The ultimate issue for this question was to determine scientific knowledge. (2) A second element was a personal element. How much did the plaintiff know about the dangers of smoking? Did he or she completely understand what the risk was? Did the plaintiff make a fully informed choice as the defence indicated? The ultimate issue for this question was to determine common knowledge. To answer both of these issues, historians were hired by the industry as expert witnesses to strengthen tobacco's legal strategies with historical arguments. Defence experts explained to the judge and the jury that "there had been a scientific controversy", which had withheld the tobacco companies from formally declaring that their products were dangerous. Meanwhile, these historians maintained that individuals who started smoking were fully aware that smoking was not without its dangers. According to the tobacco industry, smokers made an informed choice to smoke, accepting the risks of the product, whatever they were, and thereby excluding any liability on account of the tobacco companies.

It was extremely important for the tobacco companies that they maintained they were not convinced of the dangers of smoking, otherwise they risked being convicted for negligence. [Negligence: "the failure to exercise the care of an ordinarily prudent and careful man", is a legal theory with an important social function.][133] Consumers are protected by standards that force producers of commodities to adhere to certain minimal rules to prevent that any harm may come to their customers. The socially acceptable levels of precautions taken are variable in time and space but the dominant amount of care is explained in the "Hand Formula", drafted by Judge Learned Hand. He used it in his opinion in *US v. Carroll Towing* from 1947. The Hand Formula defines that in the case that the loss (A) was greater than the cost of prevention (B) then the person who could have prevented the loss acted negligently; (B) is measured in three elements: firstly the magnitude of the loss, secondly the probability of the harm, and thirdly the burden to take precautions.[134] The point where (A) and (B) meet; (C) represents the expected amount of care that should be exercised.[135]

The problem for the tobacco industry is that it sells an inherently deficient and dangerous product. The dilemma is even worse. The harmful characteristics of the cigarette are responsible for its success, nicotine for example. Any augmentation in B has to eliminate nicotine from cigarettes, which would mean people would no longer be addicted to smoking and could stop whenever they wanted. This would

---

[133]Posner, Richard. 1972. A Theory of Negligence. *Journal of Legal Studies* 1, 29–96.

[134]Posner, as n. 133, 32. For more information on the legal term of negligence see http://www.law.cornell.edu/wex/negligence. Accessed 31 Oct 2014.

[135]For a discussion of the Hand rule, see Posner, Richard. 1998. *The Economic Analysis of Law.* New York: Aspen Law and Business.

mean enormous losses for the industry. As long as the industry could deny its negligence, costs might be high for the individual smoker's health, but the tobacco industry could continue to make huge profits through selling a product that is fundamentally harmful. We have seen that tobacco companies have succeeded time after time in evading strict regulation. This regulatory absence lowered the possible cost of negligence litigation even further. "When the cost of accidents is less than the cost of prevention, a rational profit-maximizing enterprise will pay tort judgments to the accident victims rather than incur the larger cost of avoiding liability."[136] This is the fundamental problem in tobacco litigation. As long as the damages for the tobacco companies are "acceptable losses", the industry will continue to produce their deadly product. Tobacco companies try to produce a healthier product, not less addictive. They do this only in small part because of risk of litigation. The dominant reason to make a healthier product is to ensure that their customers live longer. Dead smokers do not smoke.

Former assistant state attorney general Douglas Blanke and former state attorney general of Minnesota Hubert Humphrey III described how tobacco lawyers had created a "trial in a box."[137] In *Boeken v. Philip Morris*, the law firm hired by Philip Morris pre-packaged a standardized set of key documents for tobacco litigation.[138] Tobacco litigation in general, whether it is in the first, second, or third wave, is marked by one general "legal" tactic. It is especially effective against individual plaintiffs: the scorched-earth litigation strategy. This tactic was aimed at outspending individual litigants by order magnitude while vehemently denying any association between their product and diseases.[139] Plaintiffs were simply outbid by the industry, in other words the cost of litigation was pocket change for tobacco companies while it meant a fortune for individuals. Brandt writes: "The industry went to great lengths to ensure that the costs of such suits did not justify the substantial-even overwhelming-financial risks",[140] as we have seen in the Cipollone case, for example. Furthermore, the tobacco industry's lawyers would drag out court cases as long as possible. "The tobacco industry has a long-standing policy of using procedural mechanisms to delay the litigation process, hoping that plaintiffs will die, tire, or simply run out of resources."[141] Scorched-earth litigation; delaying proceedings, refusing to settle, conducting lengthy interviews and depositions, wearing down plaintiffs financially and emotionally, and in a rare case eventually

[136]Posner, as n. 133, 33.

[137]Blanke, Douglas, and Humphrey III, Hubert, as n. 68, 1.

[138]Miura, Marlo, Daynard, Richard, and Samet, Jonathan, as n. 1, 126.

[139]Hurt, Richard, Ebbert, Jon, Muggli, Monique, Lockhart, Nikki, and Robertson, Channing, as n. 15, 446.

[140]Brandt, as n. 2, 403.

[141]Rutkow, Lainie, Vernick, Jon, and Teret, Stephen, as n. 3, 88.

settling because of the underlying philosophy that "a case is never lost if it is never tried", assured win after win in litigation for the tobacco companies.[142]

The first wave of tobacco litigation consisted of a legal strategy based on: one, the argument that there had been a scientific controversy and two, that the individual had made the choice to start smoking. These two main strategies were supplemented with a tactic of numerous depositions, endless motions, and other pre-trial demands. An internal memorandum from Michael Jordan, attorney with R.J. Reynolds, strikingly summarized tobacco's legal strategy: "The aggressive posture we have taken regarding depositions and discovery in general continues to make these cases extremely burdensome and expensive for plaintiff's lawyers . ... To paraphrase General Patton, the way we won these cases was not by spending all of our money, but by making that other son of a bitch spend all his."[143]

This legal strategy was extremely successful. The tactic functioned to a lesser extent in suits brought in the second wave of tobacco litigation by individual states and the Federal government. These government entities were less easily outspent, yet for every lawyer hired by the government, the tobacco industry hired ten. For every million dollars spent by the government, the industry spent ten times as much. Only class action suits and cases brought by third parties like unions and insurance companies would also be able to withstand the financial pressure of legal proceedings against the tobacco companies.[144] But no matter who sued them, the tobacco companies outbid everyone in legal funds. Furthermore, expert historians were part of this legal tactic. Many plaintiff counsels simply could not afford to pay \$150, \$250, \$350, or even \$600 an hour for the expert report, deposition, and testimony of an expert historian. In the 314 cases of tobacco litigation where historians were involved in during the period 1986–2014, only 78 cases saw historians as experts on either sides, or 24.8 % of the total number of cases. In 70.8 % of the cases where only one party had hired expert historians, the tobacco companies had hired the historians. These numbers are staggering and signify a frightening example of one historical narrative simply being outbid by the other in the courtroom.

13.4.1 Game I: The First Wave of Tobacco Litigation

Equipped with the previous knowledge on the general legal tactics of the tobacco companies applied in all three waves, we can now take a look at the following scheme where I use game theory to explain the legal strategies used by plaintiffs and defendants in tobacco litigation of the first wave.

---

142 Alderman, Jess, and Daynard, Richard, as n. 40, 82–83.

143 Douglas, Clifford, Davis Ronald, and Beasley, John, as n. 6, 10.

144 For more information on class action see http://www.law.cornell.edu/wex/class_action. Accessed 31 Oct 2014.

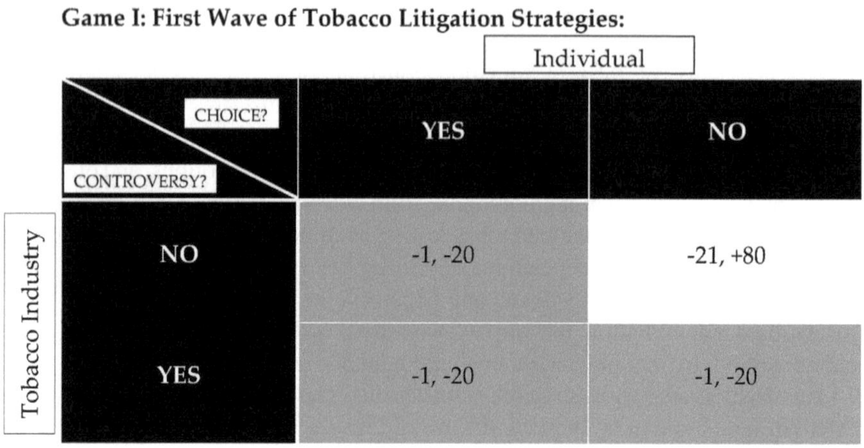

Fig. 13.1 Tobacco litigation strategies of the first wave (The areas coloured in grey signify the instances in which the tobacco industry wins. The white area is the condition upon which the plaintiff wins.)

Tobacco litigation of the first wave confronted two central questions. (1) The court had to rule whether or not there had been a controversy on the causal link between smoking and lung cancer and other diseases. (2) Secondly, the court had to judge whether the individual plaintiff had been able to make an informed choice when he or she started smoking and whether smoking had afterwards become the main cause of his or her disease. Figure 13.1 shows that the only way to win a case for the plaintiffs was to establish two things in court. Firstly, plaintiffs had to prove that the tobacco companies had known how dangerous cigarettes were and consequently, that the industry had not adequately informed the public about the health risks, thus making it impossible for individuals to make an informed choice. The liability question is the second question. If there was no controversy and the tobacco companies had not told their customers about the dangers of their product; then the industry had been negligent. Moreover, then they had committed a fraud against the public. "The industry chose to maintain the strategy it had adopted in 1953: insist that there is no proof that tobacco causes disease; disparage and attack all studies indicating such a relationship; support basic research on cancer largely unrelated to the hypothesis that smoking and cancer are linked; and support research on alternative theories of carcinogenesis. These four principles would continue to guide the industry, which was now firmly under control of its legal counsel."[145] This "no-proof" strategy was very successful.

The industry experts attacked the causal link between smoking and disease on a number of fronts. Tobacco's expert witnesses argued that the scientific research results from epidemiology were fundamentally flawed. Epidemiology could not

[145]Brandt, as n. 2, 231–234.

prove any decisive link between smoking and lung cancer or other respiratory diseases.[146] For example, tobacco experts used tobacco-sponsored research on animals, like mice, to question the results from epidemiological evidence. According to tobacco witnesses, their results in animal models allegedly claimed "there was no increase in lung cancer" with mice exposed to cigarette smoke.[147] The tobacco industry has vigorously opposed the epidemiological approach to tobacco health issues and has attempted to "create a parallel base of published literature supporting claims that the epidemiological findings on second-hand smoke and health reflected bias and not cause" through junk science.[148]

For the tobacco industry much depended on the controversy strategy. The strategy enabled them to evade their civil liability, while also allowing them to continue to sell their product although it was harmful. The numbers on the left of Fig. 13.1. are the costs for the industry; those on the right are the cost for the plaintiff. The cost-ratio is represented as 20 to 1, although the ratio is probably much greater, for the sake of argument, I have opted to remain with these simple representations. The risk of going to trial in this game is enormous for individual litigants. Only in one scenario are they going to be able to claim damages. The abstract costs of litigation presented in this table are low for the industry in three of the four situations. The industry has three possibilities for victory, and that ratio [a chance of 25 % for the individual against a 75 % chance for the tobacco companies] is even much higher in reality where settling is also a positive alternative for the industry.

The most important legal strategy for the tobacco industry is to assure that the question on the tobacco controversy is answered positively by the court or the jury. This is vital for tobacco, for two reasons: first, to ensure that they lose any liability and so cannot be convicted for negligence and fined to pay compensatory damages. If there is no negligence, it does not matter whether the individual was able to make an informed choice or not. Secondly, there can be no legitimate negligence claim if the industry could maintain that there had been a controversy. If there had been no controversy, if the causal evidence had been overwhelming, then the industry had been negligent and had conspired to create the controversy in the first place. Such a ruling would have been devastating for future litigation for the tobacco industry. Therefore, in the second wave of tobacco litigation, tobacco companies tried to postpone a judgment that would explicitly declare that the tobacco industry had created the controversy and had conspired against the public. In order to avoid a negative verdict the tobacco companies were almost always willing to settle.

The plaintiff could be further tarnished by doubting whether smoking was the reason for his or her illness. Lawyers would investigate a plaintiff's personal histories to find argumentation that supported the assertion that other life-style

[146]Francis, John, Shea, Amy, and Samet, Jonathan. 2005. Challenging the Epidemiologic Evidence on Passive Smoking: Tactics of Tobacco Industry Expert Witnesses. *Tobacco Control* 15, 70–74.

[147]Francis, John, Shea, Amy, and Samet, Jonathan, as n. 146, 73.

[148]Francis, John, Shea, Amy, and Samet, Jonathan, as n. 146, 74. As we have seen in Part III: See Sect. 7.1. The Tobacco Controversy: A Careful Construction, cfr. supra.

decisions were the cause of the plaintiff's illness. "In any individual lawsuit, the industry may try to demonstrate that some other factor was a likely cause of the plaintiff's illness or that the plaintiff should bear some or all of the blame."[149] This was yet another reason why tobacco litigation from the plaintiffs' bar perspective was considered a lost cause.

Plaintiff's legal teams were very much aware of the dominant strategy of the tobacco industry in this first wave. Tort lawyers drew from their experience in asbestos litigation, to efficiently attack this dominant tobacco tactic. By filing subpoenas for internal memos and secret documents, the industry's role in creating the tobacco controversy could be discovered step by step. This is why the Cipollone case was so important. It was the first time litigation had procured such an array of internal industry documents.[150] This would serve the plaintiffs in the second wave of tobacco litigation very well.

The first wave had been very successful for the tobacco companies. The oligopolistic structure of the industry provided a coherent and collective legal strategy which ensured acquittal after acquittal. The gentleman's agreement between the tobacco companies envisioned that the controversy and tobacco's role in its construction would remain a well-kept secret. To insure this narrative, tobacco companies hired historians who were willing to testify without reviewing any internal industry document. The success of legal strategies of the tobacco companies in the first wave is explained by two elements: (1) because of the difficulty plaintiffs had with proving that there had been no scientific controversy during the 1950s and 1960s; (2) because of the industry's strategy to "financially and emotionally bankrupt" the plaintiff. The first wave of tobacco litigation meant an unseen evasion of liability by the tobacco industry.[151]

13.4.2 Game II: The Second Wave of Tobacco Litigation

In the 1990s, the tobacco industry saw more and more internal documents and secrets discovered and published. This offered a distinct opportunity to tackle the first legal question: whether there was a kind of scientific controversy. Furthermore, as discussed, the attorneys general cases and the federal case had the advantage that "no state had ever smoked a cigarette." This enabled the states' legal teams to fully concentrate on the controversy question and on the issue of "who knew what and when?" The publications by Richard Kluger and Staton Glantz and the first research results from the internal documents changed the question from whether or not there had been a tobacco controversy to how much did the tobacco companies know and

[149]Rutkow, Lainie, Vernick, Jon, and Teret, Stephen, as n. 3, 88.

[150]See Part III, Sect. 13.1. The First Wave: Cipollone v. Liggett Group, cfr. supra.

[151]Miura, Marlo, Daynard, Richard, and Samet, Jonathan, as n. 1, 125.

Game II: Second Wave of Tobacco Litigation Strategies:

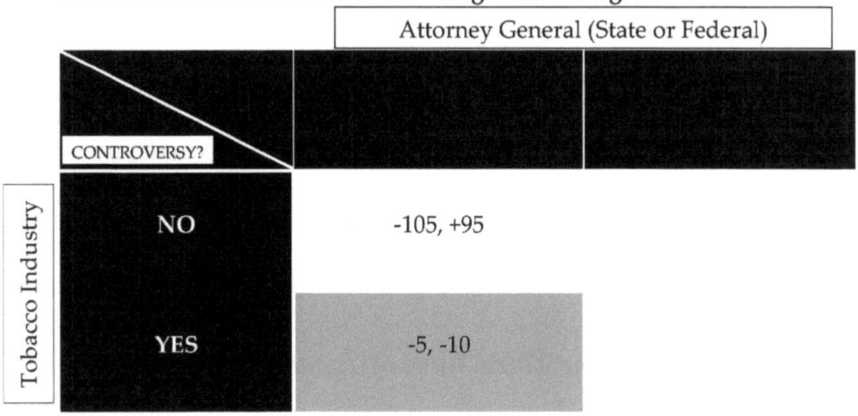

Fig. 13.2 Tobacco litigation strategies of the second wave (The area coloured in grey signifies the instance in which the tobacco industry wins. The white area is the condition upon which the plaintiff wins.)

in how far had they contributed to the construction of the controversy? The second game is thus very different from the first one.

Figure 13.2 shows, because the "choice" question is not relevant in the case of government litigation, there is a 50 % chance of winning for each side. The discrepancy between cost-ratios is also smaller when compared with individual cases. The governments spent less money than the tobacco companies on litigation, yet they were not betting everything they had on it, in contrast to some individual plaintiffs who went to trial against the tobacco companies. The scorched-earth method of the tobacco industry had less effect on the government. The state attorneys general, on the other hand, had to concentrate on the controversy question and the role the tobacco industry had played in its creation. If there had not been a controversy, tobacco had been negligent by continuing to sell their costumers deficient products. Along with continued discoveries about the role the tobacco companies had played in constructing the controversy and confronted with a hostile media, whistle-blowers, and the strategic advantage of the government, the tobacco industry decided to settle. As we have seen, tobacco companies used political tactics to diminish their liability outside the court.[152] The MSA was a weakened version of the Global Settlement. The settlement assured the tobacco companies that the danger from state-initiated litigation would be neutralized. Again the tobacco companies had evaded, by settling, being convicted in court for conspiracy against the public. In the federal case, *US v. Philip Morris et al.*, the tobacco companies would finally be convicted for their conspiracy. The DOJ hired their own historians

[152] See the failure of the Mc Cain bill: Part III, Sect. 13.2.2. The Master Settlement Agreement, cfr. supra.

to face the industry's historians, and so alternative versions of the history of the tobacco controversy were submitted to the court. The court came to an extensive and historical fully informed decision in which Judge Kessler described the tobacco industry's fraud as: "over the course of more than 50 years, Defendants lied, misrepresented, and deceived the American public."[153] The ruling of Judge Kessler has had a major impact on future tobacco litigation. Plaintiffs could now use the verdict of *US v. Philip Morris et al.* to eliminate the controversy question, because it had been proven in federal court that the tobacco companies had committed a fraud against the public.[154]

13.4.3 Game III: The Third Wave of Tobacco Litigation

I add the Engle case to the third wave, although it starts around the same time as the federal case *US v. Philip Morris et al.*. I do this because the litigation done by the government was conducted by very different legal strategies from those used in individual, third-party suits, and class action suits of the first wave. Furthermore the MSA and especially the ruling in *US v. Philip Morris* et al., had distinct consequences for legal strategies in other tobacco-related legal cases. Thanks to the Cipollone case, *the Cigarette Papers* by Staton Glantz, Richard Kluger's *Ashes to Ashes,* the MSA, and many other rulings and settlements, the secret documents of the industry revealed step by step that cigarette companies knew far better than anyone else how dangerous their product was. The tobacco companies had not only produced cigarettes but also a whole heap of scientific and historical doubt. It was now up to historians, lawyers, and health advocates to research the archives. More and more material was put online which allowed fast data searches through millions of documents and pages. Systematically organized with Bates numbering, the databases are suited for research in great depth and detail.

In 1998, US President Bill Clinton issued an executive memorandum that contained guidelines to make the tobacco documents, procured from civil litigation, more accessible. The MSA had procured that the tobacco industry made their documents available online.[155] Yet these databases proved to be difficult to use because of impaired search functions, inconsistencies between the tobacco entities' web sites, and inaccessible images. Furthermore, the tobacco industry web sites

[153]*United States of America v. Philip Morris USA Inc.*, Final Opinion, 2006, 1501. http://www.library.ucsf.edu/sites/all/files/ucsf_assets/FinalOpinion_full_version.pdf. Accessed 31 Oct 2014.

[154]See Part III, Sect. 13.3.1. Engle, cfr. supra.

[155]See for the archives managed by the tobacco industry itself http://tobaccoarchives.com. Accessed 31 Oct 2014. Cummings, Michael, Brown, Anthony, and O'Conner, Richard. 2007. The Cigarette Controversy. *Cancer Epidemiology, Biomarkers & Prevention* 16, 1071.

allowed their managers "to track user searches."[156] In the final version of the MSA the tobacco companies were required to provide all their internal documents that had become available through litigation, in order to create several databases which were more accessible and provided permanent images on the Internet. In 1999, Tobacco Documents Online (TDO) was launched, which made tobacco documents available in a systematic and annotated manner. The TDO confronted researchers with the tobacco industry's internal coding. Philip Morris had used its very own *Dictionary of Tobacco terminology.*[157] The Harvard School of Public Health offers an online *Guide to Deciphering the Internal Codes used by the Tobacco Industry.*[158] In the 1950s, for example, tobacco companies used the word "ZEPHYR" which stood for cancer. Internal documents would discuss studies demonstrating a causal relationship "between ZEPHYR and tobacco smoking." [Zephyr is derived from Greek mythology in which Zephyr is the Greek god of the west wind.][159] Another example is "BORSTAL" a code word for benzpyrene, a polycyclic aromatic hydrocarbon found in cigarette smoke.[160] "FUBYAS" stood for First Usual Brand Young Adult Smokers, and was used by Camel marketing teams in documents with strategies aimed at teenagers.[161] The huge numbers of documents and their encoding made research in the initial period quite challenging.

The TDO did not only encompass the secret industry documents but also the Tobacco Deposition and Trial Testimony Archive project (DATTA). The DATTA provided "millions of pages of transcripts of testimony in tobacco lawsuits" and "deposition and trial exhibits, expert reports, and other litigation documents from law firms, court reporter firms, individual lawyers and witnesses, tobacco company websites and other sources." This all increased already in 2006 to a total of about "820,000 pages of transcripts" which are available on the website.[162] In 2002 the University of California, San Francisco launched an enormous database which combined the internal tobacco industry's documents as well as the DATTA project. The Legacy Tobacco Documents Library (LTDL) is a permanent collection and has served as a research base for over 500 publications across diverse disciplines.[163]

---

[156] Hurt, Richard, Ebbert, Jon, Muggli, Monique, Lockhart, Nikki, and Robertson, Channing, as n. 15, 450.

[157] Cullen, Doris, Wayne, Geoffrey, Connoly, Gregor, and Koh, Howard. 2005. A Guide to Deciphering the Internal Codes Used by the Tobacco Industry. *Tobacco Control* 14, 429.

[158] For the guide see http://legacy.library.ucsf.edu/resources/harvard_monograph.pdf. Accessed 31 Oct 2014.

[159] Proctor, as n. 128, 689.

[160] Proctor, as n. 128, 682.

[161] Proctor, as n. 128, 684.

[162] Davis, Ronald, Douglas, Clifford, and Beasley, John. 2006. The Tobacco Deposition and Trial Testimony Archive (DATTA) Project: Origins, Aims and Methods. *Tobacco Control* 15, 4–6.

[163] Hurt, Richard, Ebbert, Jon, Muggli, Monique, Lockhart, Nikki, and Robertson, Channing, as n. 15, 450.

The LTDL is very user-friendly and enables full-text searching.[164] These publications have served to inform the public about the deceptive practices of the tobacco industry, which in turn furthered "denormalizing smoking as an acceptable behaviour and discrediting the tobacco industry."[165] In subsequent tobacco litigation "the DATTA testimony offered context and connected the dots of seemingly unrelated clues."[166]

For many cases after 1999, the databases have served as fact finding machines to fortify the plaintiff's legal strategies which attacked the idea of a scientific controversy. The databases have been used, furthermore, by historians to prove that individual smokers had no opportunity to fully comprehend the risks they were taking when they started smoking. The databases also offer clear evidence that the tobacco companies had done everything to ensure that individuals were not convinced that smoking was dangerous. Through advertising and the creation of junk science, has the tobacco industry been able to steer public debate away from the scientific conclusion that cigarettes were deadly products. In their book *Merchants of Doubt,* Naomi Oreskes and Erik Conway describe "how a handful of scientists obscured the truth on issues from tobacco smoke to global warming."[167] The comparison they make between the tobacco controversy and the discussions on global warming is very compelling. In both cases a small number of scientists was willing to sell themselves and their craft out to the highest bidder. In return for large remunerations, the scientists produced junk science which could be used by the industry to "scientifically" support the theory that there was no clear causal link between, for example: smoking and disease or between human industrial activity and global warming.[168] If doubt was tobacco's product, scientists supplied it. Proctor argued that expert scientists were hired by the tobacco companies for two reasons: (1) The first reason being "[m]anipulation of knowledge of hazards by tobacco industry, including the manufacture and dissemination of doubt and the hiring of experts to present industry-friendly narratives in court."; (2) the second "[m]anipulation of tobacco chemistry to increase the potency, kick, and addictiveness of tobacco."[169]

In an article from 2012 Brandt called this strategy; a specific strategy developed by the tobacco companies to "unmake" a scientific fact.[170] Proctor wrote a book

[164]The LTDL can be visited here http://legacy.library.ucsf.edu. Accessed 31 Oct 2014.

[165]Hurt, Richard, Ebbert, Jon, Muggli, Monique, Lockhart, Nikki, and Robertson, Channing, as n. 15, 450.

[166]Hurt, Richard, Ebbert, Jon, Muggli, Monique, Lockhart, Nikki, and Robertson, Channing, as n. 15, 446.

[167]Oreskes, Naomi, and Conway, Eric. 2010. *Merchants of Doubt.* New York: Bloomsbury Press.

[168]Another book which addresses this theme is: Michaels, David. 2008. Doubt is Their Product: How Industry's Assault on Science Threatens Your Health. New York: Oxford University Press.

[169]Proctor, as n. 128, 28.

[170]Brandt, Allan. 2012. Inventing Conflicts of Interest: A History of Tobacco Industry Tactics. *American Journal of Public Health* 102, 64.

about the production of ignorance, in which he argued that the argumentations of the tobacco industry were not based on fact but on fiction, and the industry produced ignorance. Proctor coined the study of ignorance with the neologism "Agnotology." "Epistemology is serious business", Proctor wrote.[171] Ignorance is sometimes an active construct, and can be part of a plan, which was the case with the tobacco companies, as we have shown in the previous chapters.[172] In a Foucauldian inspired statement, Proctor argues that: "knowledge is not just power but *danger*."[173] According to Proctor, the tobacco controversy was an active construct to generate ignorance and false knowledge.[174] The tobacco scientists kept on calling for more "objective" research. Industry insiders have called this tactic "strategy objective."[175] Proctor wrote that "[c]igaretteers [tobacco companies] will jump from being Popperian to constructivist as it suits them; they love to argue that no number of experiments can verify a theory, but they also know how to hammer away at the language of a claim until it falls to pieces."[176] Arguments about disease and addiction were rebuffed by the tobacco industry through arguments as "we need more proof", "we need more testing", "we do not subscribe to that definition", "the matter is complex", and "I would not define it as such", etc.. Some tobacco officials went as far as plainly denying any causal relationship between smoking and disease.[177] As explained in an internal memo: "Our consumer I have defined as the mass public, our product as doubt, our message as truth . . . " and in that same memo: "Doubt is our product since it is the best means of competing with the "body of fact" that exists in the mind of the general public."[178]

Tobacco companies soon realized that scientists working directly for tobacco would raise suspicion, so they created "independent" institutes.[179] As Judge Barnes advised the tobacco companies in an internal memo: "an independent approach (research institute) might be smarter, both to eliminate the question of getting

[171]Proctor, Robert, and Schiebinger, Londa. 2008. *Agnotology. The Making & Unmaking of Ignorance.* Palo Alto: Stanford University Press, 1.

[172]Proctor, Robert, and Schiebinger, as n. 171, 9.

[173]Proctor, Robert, and Schiebinger, as n. 171, 10.

[174]Proctor, Robert, and Schiebinger, as n. 171, 11–18.

[175]Edelman, D. 1987. FOTAB ETS-Project: The Overall Plan. 12/03/1987, 14. LTDL. Bates Number: TI02550938/0951. http://legacy.library.ucsf.edu/tid/bau30c00. Accessed 31 Oct 2014.

[176]Proctor, Robert, and Schiebinger, as n. 171, 17. Proctor refers to an tobacco industry scientist of the Academy for Tobacco Studies in the Hollywood motion picture *Thank You For Smoking,* cfr. supra, who could "disprove gravity."

[177]For a list of statements on the causality of smoking and disease see: Cummings, Michael, Brown, Anthony, and O'Conner, Richard, as n. 155, 1073, table 2.

[178]Brown & Williamson. *Smoking and Health Proposal.* s.d., 3–4. LTDL. Bates Number: 690010951–690010959. http://legacy.library.ucsf.edu/tid/zqy56b00. Accessed 31 Oct 2014.

[179]We discussed this earlier in Chap. 12. See Part III, Sect. 12.1. The Tobacco Controversy: A Careful Construction, cfr. supra.

involved in antitrust difficulties and to lend authenticity to the case."[180] Tobacco companies were especially interested in the "disinterest" or objective characteristic usually entitled to science.[181] For years the tobacco industry hired groups of scientists to create the controversy and the documents that fitted their own legal and marketing theory.

Questions on the objectivity of tobacco-sponsored science were raised in the second and third waves of tobacco litigation thanks to the research of the industry's secret documents. Furthermore, plaintiff's lawyers argued that tobacco experts had prepared their research solely in anticipation of litigation, which was a legitimate reason for exclusion under Daubert.[182] As more and more internal documents were researched, the controversy the industry created came boomeranging back to the tobacco companies. A Harvard Economics Professor, Kip Viscusi was excluded from testifying in the Minnesota tobacco trial. The plaintiffs had shown that his research was solely done in anticipation of the trial.[183] Viscusi later stated that he had not been excluded; his testimony was not allowed because of "alleged procedural failings on the part of defence attorneys."[184] Australian professor of public health at the university of Sydney, Simon Chapman, called for "particular vigilance" when confronted with industry sponsored research.[185] Chapman argued for full declaration of any affiliation between the tobacco companies and scientific researchers, "including the duration and financial scale of support."[186] Many expert witnesses have suffered serious loss of their professional credibility due to their research for the tobacco industry.[187] Mark Parascandola, a researcher at the National Cancer Institute, called work done by the scientists and expert hired by the tobacco companies: "quasi-scientific."[188]

According to former attorney general of the state of Minnesota Hubert Humphrey III and former assistant attorney general of the state Minnesota Douglas Blanke: "[f]inding and mobilizing the truths contained in the industry's files and the

---

[180] Hill & Knowlton. 1953. Report of Conversation Between Carl Thompson and Judge Barnes. 31/12/1953, 3. http://tobaccodocuments.org/ness/3796.html. Accessed 31 Oct 2014.

[181] Brandt, as n. 171, 64.

[182] For a discussion on the Daubert rules, see Part II, Sect. 7.3.6.3. The Daubert Standard: Popper & the Judge as Gatekeeper, cfr. supra.

[183] Friedman, Lissy, Daynard, Richard, and Banthin, Christopher. 2005. How Tobacco-Friendly Science Escapes Scrutiny in the Courtroom. *American Journal of Public Health* 95, 16–19.

[184] Viscusi, Kip. 2006. False Claims in Tobacco Litigation Junk Science Article. *American Journal of Public Health* 96, 767.

[185] Chapman, Simon. 2005. Research from tobacco industry affiliated authors: need for particular vigilance. *Tobacco Control* 14, 218.

[186] Chapman, as n. 185, 217–218.

[187] Francis, John, Shea, Amy, and Samet, Jonathan, as n. 146, 75.

[188] Parascandola, Marc. 2005. Science, Industry, and Tobacco Harm Reduction: a Case Study of Tobacco Industry Scientists' Involvement in the National Cancer Institute's Smoking and Health Program, 1964–1980. *Public Health Chronicles* 120, 338.

litigation transcripts should be a top priority."[189] The documents did become very important in tobacco litigation, which also explains why an increasing number of historians were testifying in tobacco cases. In the end, the industry's "very efforts to limit its legal liabilities had augmented those liabilities."[190] However, even with the negligence of the tobacco industry proven in federal court in *US v. Philip Morris et al.*, it remains difficult for the plaintiffs to ensure damages. In Engle Progeny cases for example, plaintiffs still have to prove that they did not make a choice to accept the real dangers of smoking. The tobacco industry seems to have a great deal of confidence in the ability of people to understand the dangers of smoking and to equally be sagacious enough to ignore the propaganda of the industry. The following anecdote illustrates this kind of reasoning very clearly: at a 1996 shareholders' meeting of cigarette manufacturer RJR Nabisco, "a woman in the audience asked the company's chairman Charles Harper whether he would want people smoking around his children and grandchildren. Mr. Harper responded, "If the children don't like to be in as smoky room ... they'll leave." When the woman responded: "An infant cannot leave a room," Mr. Harper answered, "At some point they learn to crawl, okay? And then they begin to walk."[191] In the third wave of tobacco litigation, plaintiffs are still faced with serious challenges and the tobacco industry is not in the habit of giving in.

Figure 13.3 shows that the plaintiffs had a 50 % chance of success. The traditional challenge for individual plaintiffs–the individual choice question–when confronted with tobacco scorched-earth litigation remained. The controversy question does not have to be answered anymore, in theory, because of the verdict in *US v. Philip Morris et al.* The question that remains is the issue of individual responsibility. Individual assessment, responsibility, and judgment had to be weighed against the influence of the scientific controversy on the individual.[192] As we have seen in the Engle cases, this is clearly not an easy argument to make. Only one in twenty of the cases in Engle Progeny have ended with a victory for the plaintiffs.[193] Historians play an important role in these trials. With arguments based on research on advertising, television ads, radio ads, newspapers, magazines, surgeons general's reports and many more, historians try to reconstruct what was considered common knowledge on smoking health hazards. The legal strategy of the defendants stressed that individuals had known that smoking was dangerous referring to multiple subsequent surgeons general's reports from 1964 onward which established smoking as unhealthy. This argument is summarized eloquently by Proctor and can be considered as a legal

[189] Blanke, Douglas, and Humphrey III, Hubert, as n. 68, 2.

[190] Brandt, as n. 2, 234.

[191] Brownell, Kelly, and Warner, Kenneth. 2009. The Perils of Ignoring History: Big Tobacco Played Dirty and Millions Died. How Similar is Big Food? *The Milbank Quarterly* 87, 266.

[192] Brandt, as n. 170, 70.

[193] See Part III, Sect. 13.3.1. Engle, cfr. supra.

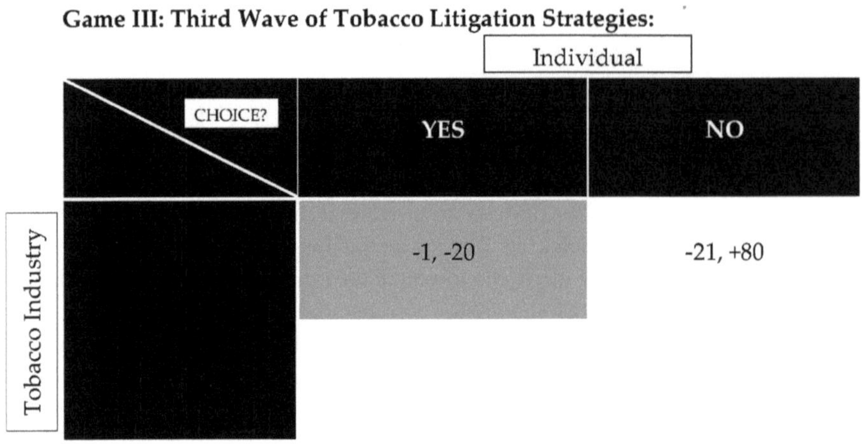

Fig. 13.3 Tobacco litigation strategies of the third wave (The area coloured in grey signifies the instance in which the tobacco industry wins. The white area is the condition upon which the plaintiff wins.)

adage for the tobacco industry's legal strategy in recent litigation: "everyone knew, but no one had ever proven it."[194]

Through the argument of "universal awareness" the tobacco companies again succeeded in eliminating their civil liability and consequentially any claims of negligence. "There is no such thing as a safe cigarette", although manufacturers are investing greatly in research that attempts to realize just that.[195] The tobacco industry has claimed that if the individual smoker did not realize smoking was dangerous, he or she was frankly too stupid to be protected. Rational choice theories which argue that an individual behaves in a reasonable manner and acts through planned behaviour has had a considerable influence on health belief models. Theories of reasoned action present the individual as a rational decision maker instead of a human being who bases his decision on a multi-level choice process. According to health advocates this rational choice model has served corporate interest.[196] The rational choice model is also based on an adult choice, while many smokers start smoking as a child or during puberty, when they are especially vulnerable to addiction.[197] Health advocates argue that there is an "over-reliance on

[194]Proctor, Robert, and Schiebinger, as n. 171, 13.

[195]Cummings, Michael, Brown, Anthony, and Douglas, Christopher, as n. 52, 85. Cummings et al. give an overview of the tobacco industry's defence strategies in several cases: see tables 1–2, 86–87.

[196]Balbach, Edith, Smith, Elizabeth, and Malone, Ruth. 2006. How the Health Belief Model Helps the Tobacco Industry: Individuals, Choice, and 'Information'. *Tobacco Control* 15, 37.

[197]Balbach, Smith, and Malone, as n. 196, 38–39.

individual and interpersonal rational choice models" in the legal argumentation of the tobacco industry.[198]

Another argument the tobacco industry has made in court, is that "tobacco advertising has a relatively weak "share of voice" in the marketing environment and is a weak force in affecting smoking behaviour. Tobacco marketing is "limited in its ability to persuade", according to the industry.[199] By contrast health advocates concluded that: "[a]s the data make clear, and contrary to the claims of the defence witnesses, the tobacco industry has been a major advertiser in the United States and globally", claiming that cigarette advertisements were very successful.[200]

Other tobacco tactics are: arguing that the plaintiff does not have cancer or the disease the plaintiff claims to have, that his or her disease or cancer is not associated with smoking, that in the particular case of the plaintiff smoking is not the cause of the disease, that other cigarette brands are to blame and not that of the defendant, that other risk behaviour is responsible for the disease: such as the plaintiff's overweight, that the plaintiff is genetically prone to develop cancer, or that the plaintiff has a general unhealthy lifestyle, etc..[201] The industry's lawyers have to find only one probable argument that will convince the jury or the judge that the plaintiff's disease is not linked to smoking, and the liability of the tobacco company is neutralized. Defence counsel will always seek to downplay the tobacco risk. Health activists have titled this tactic as: "throwing mud at the wall and hoping some of it will stick."[202] The industry's argumentation always comes down to the conclusion that smoking is simply "a matter of personal choice and willpower." A Philip Morris spokesman testified in Engle that "most people who want to quit smoking can quit."[203] The arguments made by the tobacco industry are multiple but can be rebuffed by simple facts.[204]

The strategies by the plaintiff concentrate on how successful the controversy created by the tobacco industry turned out to be. Tobacco's junk science,[205] the creation of safer filter-cigarettes,[206] tobacco advertising, its use of cartoons and

---

[198]Balbach, Smith, and Malone, as n. 196, 42.

[199]Goldberg, Marvin, Davis, Ronald, and O'Keefe, Anne Marie. 2006. The Role of Tobacco Advertising and Promotion: Themes Employed in Litigation by Tobacco Industry Witnesses. *Tobacco Control* 15, 55–56.

[200]Goldberg, Marvin, Davis, Ronald, and O'Keefe, Anne Marie, as n. 199, 56.

[201]Milberger, Sharon, Davis, Ronald, Douglas, Clifford, Beasley, John, Burns, David, Houston, Thomas, and Shopland, Donald. 2006. Tobacco Manufacturers' Defense Against Plaintiffs' Claims of Cancer Causation: Throwing Mud at the Wall and Hoping Some of it Will Stick. *Tobacco Control* 15, 19–23.

[202]Milberger, Sharon, Davis, Ronald, Douglas, Clifford, Beasley, John, Burns, David, Houston, Thomas, and Shopland, Donald, as n. 201, 17.

[203]Henningfield, Jack, Rose, Christine, and Zeller, Mitch, as n. 38, 27–36.

[204]Goldberg, Marvin, Davis, Ronald, and O'Keefe, Anne Marie, as n. 199, 56.

[205]See Part III, Sect. 12.1. The Tobacco Controversy: A Careful Construction, cfr. supra.

[206]See Part III, as n. 205.

celebrities to attract youngsters,[207] and a decades-long denial of any causal link between smoking and cancer or other diseases are the arguments used by the plaintiffs and their expert historians to prove tobacco's fraud and negligence.[208] To conclude, the argument in court is now whether an individual exactly knew how bad smoking was when he or she took up the habit. The historical issue is thus whether the tobacco industry had been effective in planting doubt in the mind of their costumers that smoking cigarettes was not definitely proven to be a health hazard. The testimony of the expert historian is central to the whole legal strategy of both parties. Only the future can tell how their tactics will fair.

Bibliography

Alderman, Jess, and Richard Daynard. 2006. Applying lessons from tobacco litigation to obesity lawsuits. *The American Journal of Preventive Medicine* 30: 82–88.

Balbach, Edith, Elizabeth Smith, and Ruth Malone. 2006. How the health belief model helps the tobacco industry: Individuals, choice, and 'Information'. *Tobacco Control* 15: 37–43.

Blanke, Douglas, and Hubert Humphrey III. 2006. Putting truth into action: Using the evidence for justice. *Tobacco Control* 15: 1–3.

Brandt, Allan. 2007. *The cigarette century. The rise, fall and deadly persistence of a product that defined America*. New York: Basic Books.

Brandt, Allan. 2012. Inventing conflicts of interest: A history of tobacco industry tactics. *American Journal of Public Health* 102: 63–71.

Brownell, Kelly, and Kenneth Warner. 2009. The perils of ignoring history: Big tobacco played dirty and millions died. How similar is big food? *The Milbank Quarterly* 87: 259–294.

Chapman, Simon. 2005. Research from tobacco industry affiliated authors: Need for particular vigilance. *Tobacco Control* 14: 217–219.

Cullen, Doris, Geoffrey Wayne, Gregor Connoly, and Howard Koh. 2005. A guide to deciphering the internal codes used by the tobacco industry. *Tobacco Control* 14: 429.

Cummings, Michael, Anthony Brown, and Christopher Douglas. 2006. Consumer acceptable risk: How cigarette companies have responded to accusations that their product are defective. *Tobacco Control* 15: 84–89.

Cummings, Michael, Anthony Brown, and Richard O'Conner. 2007. The cigarette controversy. *Cancer Epidemiology, Biomarkers & Prevention* 16: 1070–1076.

Davis, Ronald, Clifford Douglas, and John Beasley. 2006. The tobacco deposition and trial testimony archive (DATTA) project: Origins, aims and methods. *Tobacco Control* 15: 4–8.

Douglas, Clifford, Davis Ronald, and John Beasley. 2006. Epidemiology of the third wave of tobacco litigation in the United States, 1994–2005. *Tobacco Control* 15: 9–16.

Francis, John, Amy Shea, and Jonathan Samet. 2005. Challenging the epidemiologic evidence on passive smoking: Tactics of tobacco industry expert witnesses. *Tobacco Control* 15: 68–78.

Friedman, Lissy, Richard Daynard, and Christopher Banthin. 2005. How tobacco-friendly science escapes scrutiny in the courtroom. *American Journal of Public Health* 95: 16–20.

Givel, Michael, and Staton Glantz. 2004. The "global settlement" with the tobacco industry. *American Journal of Public Health* 94: 218–224.

[207] See Part III, Sect. 10.2.7. Mass-Marketing Techniques, cfr. supra.

[208] For the industry's denial of a causal link between smoking habits and health hazards see Part III, Sect. 11.1. The Discovery of Tobacco Health Hazards, cfr. supra.

Glantz, Staton, John Slade, Lisa Bero, Peter Hanauer, and Deborah Barnes. 1998. *The cigarette papers*. Berkeley: University of California Press.

Goldberg, Marvin, Ronald Davis, and Anne Marie O'Keefe. 2006. The role of tobacco advertising and promotion: Themes employed in litigation by tobacco industry witnesses. *Tobacco Control* 15: 54–67.

Harris, J.B. 2012. Engle v. Liggett: Has big tobacco finally met its match? *The Florida Bar Journal* 86: 16–31.

Henningfield, Jack, Christine Rose, and Mitch Zeller. 2006. Tobacco industry litigation position on addiction: Continued dependence on past views. *Tobacco Control* 15: 27–36.

Hurt, Richard, Jon Ebbert, Monique Muggli, Nikki Lockhart, and Channing Robertson. 2012. Open doorway to truth: Legacy of the Minnesota tobacco trial. *Mayo Clinic Proceedings* 84: 446–456.

Kluger, Richard. 1997. *Ashes to ashes: America's hundred-year cigarette war, the public health, and the unabashed triumph of philip morris*. New York: Vintage Books.

Malone, Ruth, and Kenneth Warner. 2012. Tobacco control at twenty: Reflecting on the past, considering the present and developing the new conversations for the future. *Tobacco Control* 21: 74–76.

Michaels, David. 2008. *Doubt is their product: How industry's assault on science threatens your health*. New York: Oxford University Press.

Milberger, Sharon, Ronald Davis, Clifford Douglas, John Beasley, David Burns, Thomas Houston, and Donald Shopland. 2006. Tobacco manufacturers' defense against plaintiffs' claims of cancer causation: Throwing mud at the wall and hoping some of it will stick. *Tobacco Control* 15: 17–26.

Miura, Marlo, Richard Daynard, and Jonathan Samet. 2006. The role of litigation in tobacco control. *Salud Pública de México* 48: 121–136.

Mosher, James. 2009. Litigation and alcohol policy: Lessons from the US tobacco wars. *Addiction* 104: 27–33.

Oreskes, Naomi, and Eric Conway. 2010. *Merchants of doubt*. New York: Bloomsbury Press.

Palazzolo, Joe. 2014. R.J. Reynolds loses $23.6 billion verdict. *The Washington Post*, July 20.

Parascandola, Mark. 2005. Science, industry, and tobacco harm reduction: A case study of tobacco industry scientists' involvement in the ational Cancer Institute's smoking and health program, 1964–1980. *Public Health Chronicles* 120: 338–349.

Picker, Randal. 1993. *An introduction to game theory and the law*, Cases lecture series. Chicago: The University of Chicago Law School.

Posner, Richard. 1972. A theory of negligence. *Journal of Legal Studies* 1: 29–96.

Posner, Richard. 1998. *The economic analysis of law*. New York: Aspen Law and Business.

Posner, Eric. 2002. *Law and social norms*. Cambridge: Harvard University Press.

Proctor, Robert. 2012. *Golden Holocaust: Origins of the cigarette catastrophe and the case for abolition*. Berkeley: University of California Press.

Proctor, Robert, and Londa Schiebinger. 2008. *Agnotology. The making & unmaking of ignorance*. Palo Alto: Stanford University Press.

Rutkow, Lainie, Jon Vernick, and Stephen Teret. 2007. Public health benefits of recent litigation against tobacco industry. *Journal of the American Medical Association* 298: 86–89.

Seffrin, John. 2004. Commentary: The master settlement agreement in historic context. *Health Promotion Practice* 5: 18–20.

Sloan, Frank, Justine Trogdon, and Carrie Mathews. 2005. Litigation and the value of tobacco companies. *Journal of Health Economics* 24: 427–447.

Van Voris, Bob. 2013. Florida top court affirms ruling enabling tobacco suits. *Bloomberg News*, March 14.

Viscusi, Kip. 2006. False claims in tobacco litigation junk science article. *American Journal of Public Health* 96: 767.

Chapter 14
United States v. Philip Morris et al.

Attorney: (. . .) Did you review any internal tobacco industry documents in your review of the primary literature?
Kenneth Ludmerer: No, I didn't. And this has to do with issues of setting boundaries.

Kenneth Ludmerer (Deposition in US *v. Philip Morris et al.* 2002.)

Abstract In this chapter I discuss the role historians have played as expert judicial witnesses in the US landmark case *US v. Philip Morris et al.* For the first time, multiple tobacco industry experts were opposed by historians hired as expert witnesses by the plaintiff. I have researched the involvement of these historians in *US v. Philip Morris et al.*, in a qualitative manner through a discourse analysis. The chapter goes over the court transcripts of the depositions of all five historians as well as the court testimony by Allan Brandt; that is, a direct-, cross-, and redirect-examination. The chapter ends with an ethical review of the involvement in *US v. Philip Morris et al.* of these five historians through the *Code of Ethics* for historians proposed by the Belgian historian Antoon De Baets.

In this chapter I discuss the role historians have played as expert witnesses in the US landmark case *US v. Philip Morris et al.*[1] In 1999, the DOJ filed a lawsuit against the tobacco companies under the provisions of the *Racketeering Influenced and Corrupt Organizations Act*. Under the RICO act, the DOJ wanted to procure punitive damages from the tobacco industry to recover costs made in the public health sector due to the treatment of tobacco-related diseases. The importance of this case is significant for the involvement of historians in tobacco litigation. For the first time, multiple industry experts would be opposed by historians hired as expert witnesses by the plaintiffs. One of those historians who testified for the plaintiffs was Robert Proctor. He was the first historian ever to testify for the plaintiffs in tobacco litigation. In 1998 he submitted his first expert report in tobacco-related litigation in *Northwest Laborers-Employers Health & Security Trust Fund v. Philip*

[1] I have discussed this case as part of the second wave of tobacco litigation, see Part III, Sect. 13.2.3. US *v. Philip Morris et al.*, cfr. supra.

R. Delafontaine, *Historians as Expert Judicial Witnesses in Tobacco Litigation*, Studies in the History of Law and Justice 4, DOI 10.1007/978-3-319-14292-0_14

Morris.[2] In 1999, he had testified in *Ironworkers v. Philip Morris*.[3] In *US v. Philip Morris et al.*, Proctor was hired by the DOJ along with, and after a long period of convincing, Harvard historian Allan Brandt. The defence procured the services of three veteran industry experts: Peter English, Theodore Wilson, and Kenneth Ludmerer. The case was decided in 2006 when judge Kessler stated in a 1,653-page report that the tobacco industry had conspired against the American public and continued to sell their addictive and deadly product despite their knowledge of serious health hazards. Judge Kessler reaffirmed her judgment in 2012 after it had been appealed by the defence.

Historians played a central role in *US v. Philip Morris et al.* Two expert historians were recruited by the State: Allan M. Brandt and Robert N. Proctor. The latter is a professor of the history of science and professor of pulmonary and critical care medicine at Stanford University. The former is Amalie Moses Kass Professor of the history of medicine at Harvard University. The defence retained the services of historians Kenneth Ludmerer, Peter English, and Theodore Wilson. Both Ludmerer and English were historians as well as practicing physicians. I have researched the involvement of these historians in *US v. Philip Morris et al.* in a qualitative manner. I have analysed the court transcripts of the depositions of all five historians. The records of Brandt's direct examination, cross-examination, and redirect, have also been researched for this chapter.[4] All documents are retrievable on the database *Legacy Tobacco Documents Library* and further from *Tobacco Documents Online,* whose significance and value I discussed in the previous chapter.[5] I furthermore made use of the legal database *Westlaw*. Additionally, I have drawn from the personal account of Brandt's trial experience, which he describes in the epilogue of his book. The epilogue is titled *The Crime of the Century*.[6] Brandt's book, *The Cigarette Century,* was a Pulitzer Prize finalist and gives a privileged and candid look behind the scenes of the trial.[7] Proctor frequently discusses his work as an expert witness in tobacco litigation.[8] In addition, Proctor has published his work on the history of smoking and the tobacco industry in several books, amongst

---

[2]See Expert Witness Profile No. 39, Robert Proctor.

[3]Proctor, Robert. 2000. Expert Witnesses Take the Stand. *Nature* 407, 16. & See Expert Witness Profile No. 39, Robert Proctor.

[4]Brandt was the only historian who testified in *US v. Philip Morris et al.* All five historians were deposed.

[5]The two databases can be accessed via http://legacy.library.ucsf.edu. Accessed 31 Oct 2014. & http://tobaccodocuments.org. Accessed 31 Oct 2014. For more information on the databases see Part III, Sect. 13.4.3. Game III: The Third Wave of Tobacco Litigation, cfr. supra.

[6]Brandt, Allan. 2007. *The Cigarette Century. The Rise, Fall and Deadly Persistence of a Product that Defined America.* New York: Basic Books, 493 ff.

[7]Brandt, as n. 6.

[8]For example in Proctor, Robert. 2006. 'Everyone Knew But No One Had Proof': Tobacco Industry Use of Medical History Expertise in US courts, 1990–2002. *Tobacco Control* 15, 124. He notes at the end of the article: "Competing interests: the author has worked as an expert witness for plaintiffs in tobacco litigation."

which *Golden Holocaust: Origins of the Cigarette Catastrophe and the Case for Abolition.*[9] None of the defendants' historians have published on their experiences in court.

14.1 Brandt's Experience

Brandt was first contacted by attorneys of the defence, who sought answers on the tobacco controversy in the 1950s. Although only contacted by one lawyer for an appointment, Brandt was visited by "four or five" other attorneys at his Harvard office. Brandt writes that his initial answer to their questions was: that there was a scientific controversy, in other words, that there exists no scientific subject without any discussion or scepticism. This answer not surprisingly seemed to please his visitors. Yet when Brandt further elaborated on his answer and explained that the tobacco companies had helped in creating the controversy as a public-relations strategy and that any professional historian who would research the subject could not come to any other conclusion, the lawyers changed their attitude. "I never saw them again", Brandt writes.[10]

Thereafter, Brandt was contacted by the plaintiffs. Richard Daynard and members of the plaintiff legal counsel wished that Brandt aided them in unmasking the "Big Lie" the tobacco industry had conjured up for decades. Brandt was at first sceptic about the changes of success in court. The tobacco companies' legal strategy concentrated on the choice the individual had made to start smoking, allegedly knowing that it was not healthy to smoke. This argument was made in an attempt to eliminate the industry's own negligence, or as Brandt called this strategy, "the industry's traditional blame-the-victim defence." Although Brandt's own research confirmed the tobacco controversy had been created by the industry itself, Brandt declined each request for his expert services. Although sympathizing with the cause of the plaintiffs, he "saw no reason a historian's perspective would carry much weight in the courtroom." Brandt considered the adversarial context of the courtroom to be quite different from that of standard academic debate, and decided to lay out his research in the form of a book, thereby evading being called an "advocate."[11]

---

[9]Proctor, Robert. 2012. *Golden Holocaust: Origins of the Cigarette Catastrophe and the Case for Abolition.* Berkeley: University of California Press.

[10]Brandt, as n. 6, 493–494.

[11]Brandt, as n. 6, 494–495. Brandt's initial reservations are similar to those made by legal scholar Alain Wijffels and other historians who have served as expert witnesses, see Part II, Sect. 3.4. Preliminary Conclusions on the Historian as an Expert Witness in American Courts. & Part II, Chap. 8: A Reassessment of Wijffels' Concept of Forensic History, cfr. supra.

In the 1990s, tobacco litigation was on the rise and the defendants increasingly called historians as expert witnesses. These historians testified on two major questions. The first issue was the scientific debate on the causal link between smoking and disease, whereas the second was about "common knowledge", or in Brandt's words "the argument that, despite the industry denials, everyone knew tobacco was harmful." Brandt read these expert reports with "disgust at the way they radically distorted the historical record." Historians who offered these testimonies had no background in the specific field. Brandt mentions historian Lacy Ford, who specialized in nineteenth-century Southern proslavery radicalism, testifying in tobacco litigation on tobacco science and the mass media in the 1950s.[12]

Brandt was visited for a second time by the plaintiffs, now concerning the cases brought against the industry by the state attorneys. Brandt politely refused again, worrying about the loss of control over his work and "the autonomy that historians so value to assure that their accounts of the past reflect complexity, subtlety, and nuance." In 2002, Brandt was courted by another attorney of the DOJ Tobacco Litigation Team; Stephen Brody. Brody had brought the statements of Peter English and Kenneth Ludmerer with him. Both were historians as well as practicing physicians and had been recruited by the defence to serve as expert witnesses. Brody told Brandt to read the statements of Ludmerer and English before discussing Brandt's potential role as an expert witness further. Brody's tactic proved to be a suitable one to convince Brandt. As Brandt wrote: "I was, quite simply, astounded by their "expert statements."" Both had never published or researched on tobacco. Furthermore, Brandt was "appalled by what they had written. I found their statements to be poorly researched, inaccurate in their historical assessments, and highly selective in the questions they raised." Brandt accepted to participate in *US v. Philip Morris et al.*, as an expert witness for the DOJ.[13]

For the next 2 years Brandt would be concentrating on the central questions of the case. In the first place, Brandt sought to rebut the arguments made by English and Ludmerer about the tobacco controversy and its resolution. Secondly, Brandt examined industry documents to determine "what the industry knew and when it knew it." Instead of being as selective as Ludmerer and English, Brandt sought to be as comprehensive as possible.[14]

In August 2002, Brandt was deposed by defence counsel for 14 hours spread over 2 days. Central to Brandt's argumentation to counter the "no proof" argument of the industry and similar statements by Ludmerer about the experimental standard of epidemiologic findings, was the fact that there was never a "single gold standard for proof of causality in medicine."[15] According to Brandt, the history of medicine showed that different combinations of causal explanations had been legion in the

[12]Brandt, as n. 6, 495. & See Expert Witness Profile No. 16, Lacy Ford.

[13]Brandt, as n. 6, 496–498.

[14]Brandt, as n. 6, 498–499.

[15]Brandt, as n. 6, 500.

medical professions since the nineteenth century. Brandt writes: "I wanted to show that the industry claims of "not proven" were explicitly designed to serve the companies' financial interests with reckless disregard for the health of their patrons and that this approach-"doubt is our product"-cost millions of lives."[16]

Brandt testified on all these critical themes in court. "I understood that my claims would be subject to aggressive and hostile questions from the industry defence counsel", Brandt notes. The night before his cross-examination, he met with JOD attorney Steve Brody to "review questions likely to come up in my cross-examination." At the end of the meeting, Brandt was introduced to the head of the tobacco litigation team, Sharon Eubanks. She asked Brandt whether he understood what he was going to face during cross-examination. Brandt assured her that he realized that "the industry lawyers would try to make me look as bad as possible." "No", she responded. "That's not it. They want to destroy you and leave you in a pool of blood."[17]

The following day the defence attorney, David Bernick, "exhibited contempt and disdain for me and my testimony", Brandt writes. At first, Brandt's qualifications were discussed. The lawyer for the defence, David Bernick, portrayed Brandt as a partisan advocate who sought the prohibition of tobacco. After which, Bernick argued that Brandt's research was one-sided and inadequate. Questions which deserved elaborate answers had to be answered with a simple "yes" or "no". Brandt further reports that he "found my [his] time on the stand highly frustrating" and that "[a]s I [he] had anticipated, the courtroom was not the best forum for me to fully explain my conclusions." The next day, Brandt was subjected to a brief redirect, in which he explained that the practices of the tobacco industry were "well outside the boundaries of American corporate practice."[18]

The trial continued, but the newly appointed members in the DOJ by the Bush administration ordered the Tobacco Trial Team to reduce the government's demands from $280 billion to $10 billion. Moreover, legal strategies by the DOJ were also softened. On the sudden shift in the government's position, Judge Kessler noted: "perhaps it suggests that additional influences have been brought to bear on what the government's case is."[19] Despite the doubtful commitment of the Bush administration to prosecute the case, the defendants were found guilty for violating the racketeering statutes by Judge Kessler in August 2006.[20]

[16]Brandt, as n. 6, 500.

[17]Brandt, as n. 6, 500–501. See also the general discussion on cross-examination: Part II, Sect. 7.3.5.2. Trial Testimony: Direct Examination, Cross-Examination and Redirect Examination, cfr. supra.

[18]Brandt, as n. 6, 501–502.

[19]Brandt, as n. 6, 502–503.

[20]Brandt, as n. 6, 502–503. For a discussion of the final verdict see Part III, Sect. 14.3. The Final Judgment by Judge Kessler, cfr. infra.

14.2 Expert Historians Take the Stand

In what follows I present the results of an inquiry into the arguments used by historians in the case of *US v. Philip Morris et al.*. As mentioned earlier, I have read the depositions and the direct and redirect, and cross-examinations of Brandt. I have made a discourse analysis of these legal texts to determine which arguments these historians have used in court. The idea for this analysis has come from an article by legal scholar David Caudill who discussed "*Sociotechnical*" *Arguments in Scientific Discourse: Expert Depositions in Tobacco Litigation*. Caudill noted that "while one might expect technical arguments to play a central role" in litigation proceedings, "social, historical, economic, or philosophical arguments are coextensive with and constitutive of the 'technical.'"[21] Caudill writes that "social frameworks of explanation are associated with disclosing "bad science", just as naturalistic frameworks of explanation are associated with "good science."[22] Caudill concludes that "scientific expertise in law is a rhetorical and social enterprise, not simply because it takes place in the rhetorical and social context of a legal dispute, but science itself is characterized by these inevitable aspects."[23] For Caudill: "all science (and not just bad science) [sic] is a hybrid of technical and social activities."[24] He came to those conclusions after researching depositions by chemists in tobacco-related trials. In conclusion, in my interpretation of Caudill, he defines sociotechnical arguments as "a combination of technical and extralegal rhetorical strategies."

In this topic, I analysed the involvement of historians as expert witnesses during the fact-finding process and during the trial itself in *US v. Philip Morris et al.*, by these three main questions; (1) Is the historical discipline itself attacked by lawyers? (2) In what manner have the lawyers tried to discredit the expert witness? (3) What kind of arguments are used, technical [historical arguments], formal, legal, or sociotechnical?

I will discuss every expert historian separately, according to the chronological order in which each deposition was taken, which is (1) Proctor, (2) Ludmerer, (3) Brandt, (4) English, and (5) Wilson. Each topic is constructed in the same manner. I start the discussion of each witness with general information on the witness. Thereafter, I analyse his deposition, and in the case of Brandt, also his direct examination, cross-examination, and redirect. Brandt's deposition and testimony are discussed at length because they can be supplemented with his own reflections. The discussions of the depositions are illustrated with direct statements made by the witnesses and the lawyers involved in order to achieve an almost tangible example

---

[21]Caudill, David. 2005. Sociotechnical' Arguments in Scientific Discourse: Expert Depositions in Tobacco Litigation. *The Review of Litigation* 24, 1–2.

[22]Caudill, as n. 21, 4. See my theoretical discussion on this subject Part I, Sect. 3.1.2. The Professionalization of History & Science as The New Intellectual Gold Standard, cfr. supra.

[23]Caudill, as n. 21, 4.

[24]Caudill, as n. 21, 4–5, 54–55.

of the trial experience of an expert witness. All transcripts can be consulted via the LTDL database I discussed earlier.[25] I also used the DATTA project as it offers expert reports [in this case only Proctor's was made available online], exhibits, curricula vitae, direct and cross-examinations, and also redirects.[26] Furthermore, I used the legal database Westlaw. This research makes a full reconstruction of the involvement of historians as expert witnesses in *US v. Philip Morris et al.* possible.

14.2.1 Robert Proctor

Robert Proctor is a professor of the history of science and professor of pulmonary and critical care medicine at Stanford University. He plays a central role in tobacco litigation as a frequent expert witness for the plaintiffs against the tobacco industry.[27] He has specialized in the history of science and medicine during the twentieth century. In *Golden Holocaust: Origins of the Cigarette Catastrophe and the Case for Abolition*, Proctor manifests himself as a major opponent of the commercial production and distribution of cigarettes. The federal case was his third case for the plaintiffs in tobacco litigation. His first case was in *Northwest Laborers-Employers Health & Security Trust Fund v. Philip Morris* from 1998, in which he submitted an expert report. He is currently [fall 2014] active in Engle Progeny cases.[28] Proctor has acknowledged he has made between $1,500,000 and $2,000,000 with his litigation related work. In part because tobacco companies are paying him to do depositions with their legal counsel to find out any weak spots in his research and testimony.[29] Proctor has been active in 93 tobacco-related court cases.[30] Proctor filed an expert report in *US v. Philip Morris et al.*, which is the only report of any of the five historians who testified in this case that is available online.[31] His deposition was the first of all five historians involved.

[25]For my discussion on the database, see Part III, Sect. 13.4.3. Game III: The Third Wave of Tobacco Litigation, cfr. supra.

[26]Davis, Ronald, Douglas, Clifford, and Beasley, John. 2006. The Tobacco Deposition and Trial Testimony Archive (DATTA) Project: Origins, Aims and Methods. *Tobacco Control* 15, 6.

[27]Proctor has been an expert witness in 93 cases, he is by far the historian who participated in the most tobacco ligation. He has always witnessed for the plaintiffs. See Expert Witness Profile No. 39, Robert Proctor.

[28]See Expert Witness Profile No. 39, Robert Proctor.

[29]From personal correspondence with the author.

[30]See Expert Witness Profile No. 39, Robert Proctor.

[31]For Proctor's expert report see: Proctor, Robert. 2004. Tobacco and Health. *Journal of Philosophy, Science & Law*, 4. http://jpsl.org/archives/tobacco-and-health-expert-witness-report-filed-behalf-plaintiffs-united-states-america-plaintiff-v-philip-morris-inc-et-al-defen. Accessed 31 Oct 2014.

14.2.1.1 Deposition

Proctor's deposition was taken on the July 12, 2002 and took 1 day.[32] The deposition started with the agreement on the main rules for the deposition, this is standard practice and is common procedure in all of the depositions discussed here. Douglas Smith, the attorney for the defendant Brown & Williamson Tobacco Company, questioned Proctor. Proctor was asked about the term Agnotology. Proctor had coined the term himself as the study of strategies to create ignorance, a strategy he attributed to the tobacco companies.[33] Smith tried to portray the term as unknown in order to minimize Proctor's intellectual relevance in his field. In order to stress that the idea is an unknown term, Smith asked Proctor to spell the term. Further questioning discredited the term by portraying it as an unpopular term. Proctor had written his book on Agnotology in 1992 and ten years later it had not been used by anyone else.

> *Q. What was that term that you used to refer to*
> *the study of social structures that create doubt or*
> *create ignorance in society?*
> *A. The term I used was agnotology.*
> *Q. And could you spell that please?*
> *A. A-G-N-O-T-O-L-O-G-Y.*
> *Q. And it — I think you testified that you*
> *were the person that came up with that concept of*
> *agnotology?*
> *A. That's correct.*
> *Q. And when did you do that?*
> *A. Probably around ten years ago.*
> *Q. Okay. And since that time, how many*
> *articles have been published on agnotology?*
> *A. I don't know of any that have used that word.*[34]

In the deposition Proctor was also pressed on his use of sources for his expert report. After a discussion on Whiggism, Smith tried to force Proctor to "admit" that he had used a lot of secondary sources instead of primary. As I have already discussed, the court dislikes the use of secondary sources by historians, while favouring the research of primary sources.[35] The rationale behind this preference

[32]Deposition of Robert Neal Proctor, Ph.D., July 12, 2002, United States of America v. Philip Morris Inc. 12/07/2002. LTDL. Bates Number: PROCTORR071202. http://legacy.library.ucsf.edu/tid/bzo11b00. Accessed 31 Oct 2014.

[33]I have discussed Proctor's idea of the study of Agnotology in Part III, Sect. 13.4.3. Game III: The Third Wave of Tobacco Litigation, cfr. supra.

[34]Deposition of Robert Neal Proctor, as n. 32, 373–374. Q = Smith, A = Proctor.

[35]I have discussed this preference by Judges and Lawyers for primary historical sources in Part II, Sect. 3.3.1. Consulting, cfr. supra. & Part II, Sect. 7.4. Preliminary Conclusions on the Historian as an Expert Witness in American Courts, cfr. supra.

is that, according to the legal profession, secondary sources bias the historian, while the study of primary sources offers neutral facts to the historian.[36]

Q. (. . .) I'm sort of curious to see what you
could consider primary and second source for purposes
of the history that you've done here.[37]

Although Proctor acknowledges he uses a lot of secondary sources, he defends his use of secondary sources. Moreover, Proctor seems remarkably at ease. See, for example, his reaction at the beginning of the following segment when Smith is not able to directly follow up on the questions on Whiggism. An explanation for Proctor's self-confidence may be that Proctor has already done several other trials as an expert witness in addition to the two trials he had done for plaintiffs against the tobacco industry.[38]

Q. Well, is it possible that — well, let me
ask a different question than what I was going to ask
you. I'm not a historian by training, so it takes me
a few minutes to gather my thoughts.
A. That's okay.
Q. Well, in your report, you rely — in some
instances you rely on — well, what I guess you would
call primary sources. But in most cases you rely on
secondary sources; is that correct?
A. I don't think that is a fair
characterization. Again, if you — I'm not primarily
relying on what other people have said about the
past. I've tried insofar as possible to rely on
sources that are more primary, though it should be
said that the whole point of this thing, primary
sources and secondary sources is to guarantee
reliability. And sometimes you can rely upon a
secondary source if you think it's trust worthy and if
you have no reason to think that it's not trustworthy.
Q. How do you make the determination whether or
not a secondary source is biased or not?
A. I think that's the art of being a
historian. It's a process of judging contacts, of
judging capability.[39]

Furthermore, Proctor was confronted with questions on funding he had received from government agencies.[40] This line of questioning was an attack meant to question Proctor's impartiality as a scholar. If Proctor's research funding on tobacco

---

[36]This somewhat simplistic view on the historical discipline is addressed in Part III, Sect. 7.4. Preliminary Conclusions on the Historian as an Expert Witness in American Courts, cfr. supra.

[37]Deposition of Robert Neal Proctor, as n. 32, 289–290. Q = Smith.

[38]Proctor, as n. 3, 15–16.

[39]Deposition of Robert Neal Proctor, as n. 32, 286–287. Q = Smith, A = Proctor.

[40]Deposition of Robert Neal Proctor, as n. 32, 490–505. Q = Smith, A = Proctor.

came from federal government agencies, defence counsel could argue that Proctor received extra money from the plaintiffs to construct his witness report. Then Proctor could be accused of advocacy.

Q. So in total, you've received monetary
payments from four different agencies or entities
within the U.S. government?
A. That's correct. Yes. Fortunately, the
national — the government is one of the ways a
scholar can get some funding.
Q. And you're grateful for all the money that
You've been provided from the U.S. government; right?
A. That's true.[41]

The remainder of Proctor's deposition discussed predominantly the sources of his testimony. The defence lawyers seemed keen on knowing if he used primary or secondary sources, but also whether he agreed with the figures on smoking-related diseases cited in those documents. Proctor was often asked if he had a specific document in front of him during the questioning, which was then added to the exhibit list of the deposition. Often, Smith asked Proctor if he could read a certain line from the document, which was followed with a question on Proctor's interpretation of that statement. All of these documents could then be used during the trial itself in the event that Proctor would be put on the stand. Defence lawyers were looking for the sources Proctor had based his witness expert report on, in order to find something by which they could discredit Proctor's expert report. Only in 28 instances was "objection" noted by the plaintiff's attorney during the whole deposition, signifying a less polemic deposition than for example Brandt's deposition.[42] An errata sheet of 16 pages was added to the deposition, which details in length all the mistakes that were typed during the deposition.

I now discuss the three questions central to this qualitative analysis for Proctor's deposition: (1) The historical discipline came under attack because of questions from the defence concerning secondary sources. Defence counsel clearly wanted to state for the record that Proctor was using a lot of secondary sources and that this reliance biased his work. (2) The only time Proctor comes under personal attack is when he is asked about his research funding. (3) The narrative used in this deposition is formal, not legal but technical. In order to avoid answering certain questions, Proctor "has forgotten"[43] or "is uncertain"[44] about a lot of things that seem relevant to his report or testimony. This is an example of a legal strategy which wishes to avoid that certain statements are added to the trial record and can thus be used afterwards against the witness. In this deposition Proctor proves to be very skilled

[41] Deposition of Robert Neal Proctor, as n. 32, 490–491. Q = Smith, A = Proctor.

[42] For Brandt deposition see Part III, Sect. 14.2.3.1. Deposition, cfr. infra.

[43] For an example see Deposition of Robert Neal Proctor, as n. 32, 78.

[44] For an example see Deposition of Robert Neal Proctor, as n. 32, 170.

in handling difficult questions from lawyers, whom he counters with what Caudill described as "sociotechnical" arguments.[45]

14.2.1.2 Robert Proctor's Expert Report

Proctor remains the only historian working in tobacco litigation who has made his expert report public.[46] Brandt, nor any of the expert witnesses' of the defence have done so. It gives us a privileged look at essential parts of the historian's expert testimony. The report itself starts with a general introduction on Proctor's own expertise. The report lists Proctor's opinions and elaborates further on them in a broader historical context. That historical context is based on research of advertisement in print as well as in other forms of media such radio and television ads. Articles of a scientific and non-scientific nature are also researched to discuss the common knowledge aspect of health hazards and smoking. In recent Engle Progeny litigation these journals, newspapers, periodicals and so on will focus on those who were available to the smoker. For instance, for a smoker who lived in Florida, mostly local newspapers will be researched not those from California. In this federal case, Proctor made a much broader analysis. As an expert for the plaintiffs Proctor has also researched a lot of internal industry documents in order to proof the construction of a scientific controversy by the industry. In his report Proctor devotes a lot of attention to the Frank Statement and the false promises the industry made in the statement.[47] Proctor also engages in hypotheses on the rate of smokers that would have not taken up the habit if the industry had come clean from the moment they knew their product had been harmful. Proctor furthermore discusses the expert reports submitted by the experts for the defence. Proctor has considerable problems with the reports submitted by English, Ludmerer, and Wilson. The main issue he has with their reports is that, according to Proctor, they have downplayed the role of the industry in creating common and scientific knowledge on their product. The expert report by Proctor is extremely well-documented and has all the elements of a professional historical paper.

---

[45]See the introduction of this topic, Part III, Sect. 14.2. Experts Historians Take the Stand, cfr. supra.

[46]Proctor, as n. 31. http://jpsl.org/archives/tobacco-and-health-expert-witness-report-filed-behalf-plaintiffs-united-states-america-plaintiff-v-philip-morris-inc-et-al-defen. Accessed 31 Oct 2014.

[47]For a discussion on the Frank Statement, see Part III, Sect. 14.1. The Tobacco Controversy: A Careful Construction, cfr. supra.

14.2.2 *Kenneth Ludmerer*

Ludmerer has degrees in history as well as in medicine. He is professor of the history of American medicine at Duke University. At the time of the trial, he was employed at Washington University. Ludmerer has published multiple books on American health and disease history of the twentieth century. Furthermore, Ludmerer has been president of the American Association of the History of Medicine. He has been one of the first historians to testify for the tobacco industry. In 1990, in Boston he took the stand in *Kotler v. American Tobacco*, an individual plaintiff's case. As we shall see, his deposition in this federal trial unearthed more unknown ties between the tobacco industry and Ludmerer.[48]

14.2.2.1 Deposition

The deposition of Kenneth Ludmerer took 2 days and started at 8 a.m. on the seventh of August 2002.[49] Ludmerer had already been deposed in at least 14 trials as a witness for the tobacco industry and that experience is visible during his deposition.[50] The lawyer for the DOJ is Moltzen. The DOJ's questions were met with counter questions by Ludmerer, which is rather unusual for a deposition. For example, directly from the start Ludmerer asks whether there were different rules for the deposition because it was being taped.[51] His answers were much longer than those given by the other deposed historians in this case. His reactions to the DOJ's questions show the strength of Ludmerer during his deposition. In normal circumstances the tactic of the deposing lawyer is to fatigue and enervate the deposed, in order to let the deposed expert make a mistake. In contrast, in this deposition Ludmerer tries to do the same with opposing counsel at the beginning of the deposition. For example, to the question whether he is an advocate or a historian, Ludmerer gives a two page answer, which is a very long answer in a deposition, since the deposed would normally try to limit his answers as much as possible.[52] But Moltzen, the lawyer from the DOJ doing the deposition, seems to have wanted Ludmerer to feel at ease. After a short recess was taken just before 10 a.m., Moltzen

---

[48] See Expert Witness Profile No. 30, Kenneth Ludmerer.

[49] Deposition of Kenneth Ludmerer, M. D., August 7, 2002, United States of America v. Philip Morris USA Inc., 07/08/2002. LTDL. Bates Number: LUDMERERK080702. http://legacy.library.ucsf.edu/tid/uuo11b00. Accessed 31 Oct 2014. & Continued deposition of Kenneth Ludmerer, M. D., August 8, 2002, United States of America v. Philip Morris USA Inc., 08/08/2012. LTDL. Bates Number: LUDMERERK080802. http://legacy.library.ucsf.edu/tid/xuo11b00. Accessed 31 Oct 2014.

[50] See Expert Witness Profile No. 30, Kenneth Ludmerer.

[51] Deposition of Kenneth Ludmerer, as n. 49, 7.

[52] Deposition of Kenneth Ludmerer, as n. 49, 21–23. See also my discussion on the deposition in Part II, Sect. 7.3.5.1. The Deposition, cfr. supra.

attacked and asked Ludmerer who had written his expert report. Ludmerer admitted without further ado the following:

A. I participated in its preparation. I did not actually draft the report. It was drafted by individuals at one of the firms based on previous testimony, previous conversations, previous depositions. It was sent to me for editing so I read it, approved it, it represents my views. I did not physically compose it.[53]

Moltzen continued his harder line of questioning and asked Ludmerer about his previous testimonies for the tobacco companies. In the 12 years before his deposition in *US v. Philip Morris et al.*, Ludmerer had worked on 14 cases for the tobacco industry. In five he had delivered sworn testimony on the stand, in eight others he had been deposed, and in one other he had delivered an expert report.[54] DOJ lawyer Moltzen asked Ludmerer about his previous work for the defendants.

Q. (. . .) I made up a list, it has been marked as Deposition Exhibit 5. I am doing this because I don't want – this is not a memory game. We don't have to sit here and you try to remember when and where.
A. I appreciate that, thank you.
Q. If this is incorrect, that's fine. It is just as a tool we can use. From the documents that your attorneys sent me, these were the cases over the last four years that you had either been deposed in or had testified at trial. As you look over that list, are there any errors there or are there any additions?
A. We have a camera going, a videotape going so I will try not to be too silent. We have one, two, three, four, five, six, seven, eight, nine, 10, 10 events, four trials, six depositions. That looks about right. It is pretty close.
Q. As we sit here you can't think of any additional cases that you were deposed in over the last four years that come to mind right now?
A. Not that immediately come to mind. This looks right.[55]

Ludmerer forgot some cases. But the next day things got straightened out. A deposition earlier that year had been handed to Moltzen by the defence lawyers in

[53]Deposition of Kenneth Ludmerer, as n. 49, 28. See same subject Continued deposition of Kenneth Ludmerer, as n. 49, at 266. A = Ludmerer.

[54]Twelve years before the trail is the time period from 1990 till 2002. See Expert Witness Report for the 15 cases Ludmerer has worked on: Expert Witness Profile No. 30, Kenneth Ludmerer.

[55]Deposition of Kenneth Ludmerer, as n. 49, 30–31. See the same subject at 60–61, 74–78. Q = Moltzen, A = Ludmerer.

order to make the record complete. The question was no longer how many in the past 4 years, but in his entire career.

Q. So now I believe we have all 14 cases to the best of our knowledge?
A. To the best of our knowledge. That includes the two cases from the early, I call it the early period, and then 12 depositions or trials from 1997 through the present.[56]

The DOJ had helped Ludmerer remember in how many cases he had testified. Still the number was, "to the best of our knowledge." In fact, Ludmerer was still one case short off of the real number of 15 court cases he had been an expert witness in.[57] Ludmerer stayed rather calm under these damaging examinations and said in response to the case he had forgotten the previous day: "If I did not recognize its absence from this list you showed me yesterday, then I apologize."[58] Clearly the witness was not really impressed by the questions of the DOJ. When asked if he had published anything on tobacco, he reacted as follows.

Q. Do any of your publications, the articles or the books, deal directly with tobacco and health?
A. Can I tell you about my other article that was rejected?
Q. Of course you can.
A. I say this because someone stole and plagiarized it.
Q. Go ahead.[59]

Ludmerer changes the question with seemingly no opposition from Moltzen. As in the previous example, Ludmerer seems to be enjoying himself rather than being pressed by the questions of plaintiff's counsel. He is further asked about his medical license, possible disciplinary action, his own medical practice, and again about the fact that he has no publications on the subject of tobacco.[60] Ludmerer is again very confident about his report.

Q. I will ask the question that I didn't let you – that I asked before you had finished your answer. Do any of your publications, the three books or the more than 30 articles, or even the book reviews, deal directly with tobacco and health or smoking and health?
MR. WOODS: Objection.
A. Not directly. Indirectly in the sense that they deal with scientific knowledge and its evolution,

[56]Continued deposition of Kenneth Ludmerer, as n. 49, 280. Q = Moltzen, A = Ludmerer.

[57]So far as I have found.

[58]Continued deposition of Kenneth Ludmerer, as n. 49, 280.

[59]Deposition of Kenneth Ludmerer, as n. 49, 53. See the same subject at Deposition of Kenneth Ludmerer, as n. 49, 148. Q = Moltzen, A = Ludmerer.

[60]Deposition of Kenneth Ludmerer, as n. 49, 51, 52, 53, 59.

and both the concepts and techniques are pertinent to understanding the subject of tobacco and cigarette smoking and health but they were not specific studies of cigarette smoking or health related issues.[61]

Similarly to the other witnesses for the defence, Ludmerer is convinced that smoking is a cause of cancer. He is equally sure that everyone knew those hazards since the Surgeon General's Report of 1964. "That's the common wisdom", he remarks.[62] After some lighter questions, Moltzen also asked questions on Ludmerer's weakest characteristic. An issue which he has in common with all the experts of the defendants, namely, their conscious neglect to research internal documents of the tobacco industry. Those documents form an essential part of any historical research on the question: "When did they know it, and what did they know?"[63] At first Ludmerer tries to evade the questions on the subject.

Q. And did you review any letters or correspondence or memos that weren't in the – that weren't found in some publication or another?
MR. WOODS: Objection.
A. I'm not certain I understand that question. Could you rephrase that please?
Q. There might be some, let's just say internal correspondence in a company that never was meant to be published but for one reason or another might now have found its way into a book about the tobacco industry, let's say. So then I couldn't say to you did you only review literature that was published because that would include those kind of internal memorandums and letters.
MR. WOODS: Objection.
Q. Did you review any published letters and memorandums?
MR. WOODS: Objection.
A. Are you referring from tobacco companies or in general?
Q. In general.
A. I think it would be fair to say that in the review of the secondary literature, everything was secondary, it was published. I don't think anyone looking at that list today would have any doubt that that's secondary literature. Now, any time a historian is doing a book they are going to be primarily quoting documents. So you can read, using our example of President Lincoln, you can

---

[61]Deposition of Kenneth Ludmerer, as n. 49, 59. Mr. Woods served as counsel for Lorrilard. Q = Moltzen, A = Ludmerer.

[62]Deposition of Kenneth Ludmerer, as n. 49, 66.

[63]I discussed the importance of this question in Part III, Sect. 13.4. Tobacco Tactics in Court: Legal Game Theory, cfr. supra.

read a biography of Lincoln and letters will be
quoted in that.[64]

Ludmerer skilfully dodged the question on the neglect of the internal documents of the tobacco companies by bringing up the issues that courts generally have with primary and secondary sources, a subject Moltzen will be inclined to go into. The danger seemed to be adverted thanks to the objection of Mr. Woods, counsel for Lorillard Tobacco Company, and the rhetorical skills of Ludmerer. Yet Moltzen is giving his prey falls hope. Several hours later, Moltzen returns to the subject of the formerly secret files of the tobacco industry.

Q. (. . .) Did you review any internal tobacco industry
documents in your review of the primary
literature?
A. No, I didn't. And this has to do with issues of
setting boundaries. Now that you mention this,
this is something that I would also like to be an
addendum to my response to your earlier question
of how historians do work.[65]

After this small victory for plaintiff's counsel, the rest of first day of the deposition was filled with hours of examining Ludmerer on several footnotes and documents used in his expert report. The following morning Moltzen continued his harder line of questioning and asks Ludmerer about the compensations the tobacco companies paid him for his work, and now Ludmerer seemed more frustrated and his lawyer less ad rem.

Q. How much do you charge per hour for your work?
A. As stated in the disclosure itself, $350 per hour.
Q. In addition to the $350 per hour, do you also have
any kind of daily charge when you are on travel or
do you still charge on an hourly basis?
A. If I'm away overnight, as we were yesterday,
instead of 24 hours I have a $3500 rate if I'm
overnight.[66]

A few questions later Ludmerer is asked how much he has earned in total with his tobacco-related litigation-driven research:

Q. What is the total amount you have earned from
doing the tobacco litigation work to this date?
A. I would say somewhere between 500 and $550,000.
You mean from the very beginning?
Q. From the very beginning.[67]

---

[64]Deposition of Kenneth Ludmerer, as n. 49, 94–95. Q = Moltzen, A = Ludmerer.

[65]Deposition of Kenneth Ludmerer, as n. 49, 241. Q = Moltzen, A = Ludmerer.

[66]Continued deposition of Kenneth Ludmerer, as n. 49, 255. Q = Moltzen, A = Ludmerer.

[67]Continued deposition of Kenneth Ludmerer, as n. 49, 259. Q = Moltzen, A = Ludmerer.

Ludmerer's deposition reads as a kind of satire on historical research. Ludmerer had not reviewed any internal industrial documents, while making enormous amounts of money serving the tobacco companies as an expert witness. Furthermore, he plays games with Moltzen, posing counter-questions to him in turn, asking Moltzen to define words, and sometimes Ludmerer answers in full length, while sometimes limiting his answer to a single word. Clearly Ludmerer has adapted himself quite well to the legal environment and its strategies in a deposition.

Brandt was simply shocked that a man like Ludmerer, with such experience as a licensed physician and a historian of great professional stature, had been willing to offer "such misleading "opinions" on behalf of the industry in such an important litigation."[68] Brandt remarks that Ludmerer has no publications on tobacco history.[69] Ludmerer himself had been a regular witness for the industry since 1990, although he had, as Brandt mentions, never researched any of the industry's internal documents. In 1998, in *Engle v. R.J. Reynolds* Ludmerer had already admitted in court that he had never looked into a single internal document of the tobacco industry.[70] In his book from 2012 Proctor wrote on Ludmerer "How could such a distinguished medical scholar have no opinion on what is arguably the most important medical fact of modernity? We don't have to speculate; the fact is that Ludmerer was simply following the script drafted for him by his handlers."[71] In an article from 2010 by historian Jon Wiener which appeared in *the Nation,* Ludmerer was asked about his deposition in *US v. Philip Morris et al.* Ludmerer declared, "Where is civility in this country? These ad hominem attacks are injurious. I had coronary artery bypass surgery in 2005. I'm sure a lot of the disease came from tension from the comments people made about my testimony. I've never done anything other than serve the public interest." He added: "I was hoping the tobacco industry would lose." Wiener replied: "But then why did he testify for the industry? Ludmerer's answer was: "I considered it honourable to stand up for doing history properly."[72] Consequentially, doing proper history for Ludmerer did not include researching the internal documents of the tobacco industry.

Now I return to the three questions initially asked in this qualitative analysis for Ludmerer's deposition: (1) The historical discipline itself was not attacked by plaintiff's counsel. Although Ludmerer himself tried to bring up the issue on secondary sources, Moltzen did not give the subject much attention. (2) Ludmerer was discredited on several fronts. A first line of questioning by Moltzen discussed the number of times Ludmerer had already testified; the fact that he "forgot" some cases did not elevate his standing as an impartial witness. Furthermore, Ludmerer was examined on the large salary the tobacco companies had paid him for his work

[68] Brandt, as n. 6, 497–498.

[69] See Expert Witness Profile No. 30, Kenneth Ludmerer.

[70] Brandt, as n. 6, 497–498. & Proctor, as n. 9, 476.

[71] Proctor, as n. 9, 477.

[72] Wiener, Jon. 2010. Big Tobacco and the Historians. *The Nation*, February 15. http://www.thenation.com/article/big-tobacco-and-historians. Accessed 31 Oct 2014.

as an expert witness. The idea behind these questions was to present Ludmerer as a hired gun. A last item Ludmerer was pressed on, was the fact that he had not analysed any internal documents of the tobacco industry. This is a very weak point with all the witnesses for the defence. The DOJ Tobacco Litigation Team made ample use of it as we shall see when I discuss the deposition given by Peter English and Theodore Wilson. (3) The discourse in this deposition is a rhetorical game between Moltzen and Ludmerer full off evasive answers and influenced by extralegal factors such as fatigue and irritation with the questions. Ludmerer's testimony is a shocking example of how a historian can fully commit to the tactics of the tobacco industry. The next historian who was to be deposed was the defence's second expert witness; Harvard professor Allan Brandt now faced his tribulations in court.

14.2.3 Allan Brandt

Allan Brandt is a professor of the history of science and Amelie Moses Kass professor of the history of medicine at Harvard. Brandt has published a multitude of major works on the social history of diseases. His most famous work is *The Cigarette Century: The Rise, Fall, and Deadly Persistence of the Product that Defined America* published in 2007. The book resulted from his research before and during the case *US v. Philip Morris et al.* This case is the only instance Brandt has testified as an expert witness.[73] He has not made his expert report available in contrast to Proctor. Brandt's role in the trial seems to have been that of a special expert witness, pivotal to the legal strategies of the DOJ. He was treated accordingly by the defence.

14.2.3.1 Deposition

Brandt's personal account has offered us an intimate look on the landmark case *US v. Philip Morris et al.* Now we turn to the trial transcripts to move on to the official and formal report of his involvement. I begin with his deposition which took place on August 15 and 16, 2002.[74] The plaintiff's attorney, Stephen Brody, was present to assist Brandt during the deposition. Attorney Douglas Smith, counsel for Brown and Williamson, questioned Brandt, while attorney Cindy Gantnier, legal

[73]See Expert Witness Profile No. 4, Allan Brandt.

[74]Deposition of Allan M. Brandt, Ph.D., August 15, 2002, United States of America v. Philip Morris USA Inc., 15/08/2002. LTDL. Bates Number: BRANDTA081502. http://legacy.library.ucsf.edu/tid/elk79a00. Accessed 31 Oct 2014 & Continued deposition of Allan M. Brandt, Ph.D., August 16, 2002, United States of America v. Philip Morris USA Inc., 16/08/2002. LTDL. Bates Number: BRANDTA081602. http://legacy.library.ucsf.edu/tid/dlk79a00. Accessed 31 Oct 2014.

counsel for Philip Morris, joined in via telephone. Smith had also deposed Proctor a month earlier. The deposition started at 8.58 a.m.. A first small discussion originated when Brandt refused to answer how many documents he cites in his reports. Despite multiple questions and rephrasing of those questions, Brandt eventually refused to guess.[75] Thereafter, the defence counsel discussed his reasons for agreeing to become an expert witness for the plaintiff.[76] A more theoretical discussion was opened when the lawyers questioned Brandt on his methods and the already familiar issue of the difference between primary and secondary sources.[77] Furthermore, Brandt was questioned on another major returning theme in all depositions, namely, the question what constitutes common knowledge.[78] Thereafter, Brandt is examined on the history of the tobacco controversy, which is interrupted by the break at 10 a.m., noon, and at 3 p.m..[79] At one moment, Brandt was asked questions about his involvement in the Surgeon General Report of 2000. The following incident clearly shows how historians testifying against the tobacco industry also do not shrink from playing "a legal game." At one instance Smith starts the sentence: "You know that you are under oath", but he is cut short by Brandt, to prevent the record from showing such an intriguing question.

Q. And who did you deal with when you were working on
the 2000 report?
MR. BRODY: Objection.
A. I don't even know. I don't know.
Q. You don't know who you were dealing with?
A. You know, I mean –
MR. BRODY: Objection.
A. You know, I got a letter from somebody, and I
answered it. And I don't know who I– you know,
it wasn't important.
Q. Well, did you have any telephone conversations?
A. No, I had no telephone contact.
Q. You know –
A. It was not extensive review. They have different
levels of peer reviewers in the process, I think,
and people who are really going to address a whole
chapter, and people who are sent a copy for
general review, that kind of thing.[80]

Brandt was also confronted with questions from Smith whether he knew certain persons involved in tobacco litigation. After the 3 p.m. break, Brandt was questioned

[75]Deposition of Allan M. Brandt, as n. 74, 19–21.

[76]Deposition of Allan M. Brandt, as n. 74, 22–30.

[77]Deposition of Allan M. Brandt, as n. 74, 32–54.

[78]Deposition of Allan M. Brandt, as n. 74, 57–58. I discussed the importance of the "common knowledge" issue in Part III, Sect. 13.4.1. Game I: The First Wave of Tobacco Litigation & Part III, Sect. 13.4.2. Game II: The Second Wave of Tobacco Litigation, cfr. supra.

[79]Deposition of Allan M. Brandt, as n. 74, 232.

[80]Deposition of Allan M. Brandt, as n. 74, 97–98. Q = Smith, A = Allan Brandt.

again on his expertise, wherein the defence lawyers tried to find multiple medical fields on which Brandt was not an expert, although, according to the defence's counsel, those fields are in some way related to the scientific controversy: like neurosciences, pharmacology, and the science of nicotine. This line of questioning is shortly intersected with the question "if it's unethical for the tobacco companies to be in the cigarette business?"[81] The question was asked in order to brand Brandt as anti-capitalist. Hereafter, Brandt was asked whether he was an expert in certain fields of which the defence lawyer knew Brandt was not.[82] The questions were aimed at making Brandt feel uncertain and to discredit his expert reports since he had no expertise in scientific fields that played a major role in the tobacco controversy. In general, Brandt does not seem impressed by Smith's questions. For example:

Q. And you've also expressed the view that the medical profession and the public have accepted that smoking – that second-hand smoke is harmful?
A. I wish I had those things that you're reading to me in context, because I think they're general characterizations of something that, you know, you or somebody read; and they don't always seem to me to sharply reflect what I would have written. You know, they don't sound like my language exactly. So, if they are direct quotes, you know, it would be good if they were identified as direct quotations, and I had their sources.
If they're general characterizations of my writing, I sometimes find them, you know, a percentage of degree, you know, shifted. And, so, I'm uncomfortable agreeing with that, Did I write that? You know, by whose characterization am I writing? And if we had direct quotes, then I would say, Yes, that's in the piece. You know, let's read the whole paragraph or whatever it was that really makes it clear.
Q. Well, sitting here today, can you remember if You've written that the medical profession and the public have accepted that second-hand smoke is harmful?
MR. BRODY: Objection.
A. I don't think that's – I don't think that's a quotation from me exactly.[83]

The deposition continued and discussed more of Brandt's articles, the issue of nicotine, and the subject of safe cigarettes.[84] Just before the end of the first day of

[81]Deposition of Allan M. Brandt, as n. 74, 242.

[82]Deposition of Allan M. Brandt, as n. 74, 233–254.

[83]Deposition of Allan M. Brandt, as n. 74, 311. Q = Smith, A = Allan Brandt.

[84]Deposition of Allan M. Brandt, as n. 74, 311–346.

the deposition at 5:50 p.m., Brandt was questioned on the book that he was writing, the contacts he used for this book, and again on his fields of expertise.[85] The next day the debates were reopened with the same lawyers present. The first questions examined Brandt's curriculum vitae with close scrutiny.[86] Concerning the *American Association for the History of Medicine* Mr. Brody, counsel for the plaintiff and Brandt could not resist mocking opposing counsel:

> *Q. And is the American Association for the History of Medicine a prestigious historical organization?*
> *A. I don't know if I would call it prestigious. I would just say that's the organization for this relatively small group of professionals who work in the history of medicine. You know, I don't think that people in the organization feel that they derive considerable prestige from that.*
> *Q. Well –*
> *A. Anyone can join. You'd be welcome to join.*
> *Q. Well, other than the American Association.*
> *MR. BRODY: There goes any prestige.*[87]

The following hours were spent discussing Brandt's expert-witness report, and several of his sources were reviewed and marked as exhibits for possible use in court. Defending council further examined the citations in his witness report.[88] In addition, more questions were posed by Smith related to discussions on plagiarism, causality, and an article of Brandt's that was not provided by the DOJ attorney to the defence.[89] At the end of the deposition, Brandt was asked to state his opinion on the research of his colleagues, other researchers working on the same subject, and that of the other expert witnesses in the trial.[90]

In conclusion on this deposition, I come back to the three questions I posed at the beginning of this chapter: (1) The historical discipline is attacked in Brandt's deposition on the manner by which it finds facts. Defence counsel wanted to make Brandt's research methods seem inadequate for the courtroom. Smith also questioned Brandt on the issue of primary and secondary sources. (2) Brandt's credibility as an expert is undermined by questioning him about whether he is an expert in certain medical fields that are discussed in his report, while demanding yes or no answers from Brandt. This line of questioning by Smith aims to make Brandt feel nervous, since he has to admit over a dozen times that he was no expert

---

[85]Deposition of Allan M. Brandt, as n. 74, 346–353.

[86]Continued deposition of Allan M. Brandt, as n. 74, 363–385.

[87]Continued deposition of Allan M. Brandt, as n. 74, 384. Q = Smith, A = Allan Brandt.

[88]Continued deposition of Allan M. Brandt, as n. 74, 386–583.

[89]Continued deposition of Allan M. Brandt, as n. 74, plagiarism 483–485, causality 530–531, problematic article 540–541.

[90]Continued deposition of Allan M. Brandt, as n. 74, 583–631.

in fields like tobacco toxicology and growing tobacco.[91] (3) The discourse in this deposition was formal. Questioning was seemingly at random, in order to confuse Brandt, who was considered inexperienced in this kind of legal examination. Brandt did his best to keep his nerves and limit his answers, responding often with "yes",[92] "no",[93] "I don't",[94] "I do",[95] and other expletives like "I don't recall" and "I do not remember."[96] Furthermore, Brandt said 1,181 times "you know" as an explicative on record in a 633-page transcript of his deposition. In other words, on almost every page, Brandt is quoted to have said "..., you know ... "once or twice, with only two questions on most pages, that is quite a nervous tick. This rather innocent looking element of the deposition was an extralegal strategy. Brandt is an eloquent man, who has experience in teaching and public speaking. To my knowledge, Brandt shows no sign of this habit in any of his other interviews.[97] It was a rhetorical strategy, designed to prolong answers in order to give Brandt more time to think on his answer and to slow the pace of the deposition. Brandt clearly used sociotechnical arguments to defend his report.[98] Although Brandt had survived his deposition very well, the biggest test of his career as an expert witness awaited him 2 years later during trial testimony. The trial started its second week of proceedings, having started the September 21th 2004, when Allan Brandt was called to testify.

14.2.3.2 Expert Testimony

On September 27th, 2004 at 1 p.m., historian Allan Brandt took the stand in the largest racketeering case the US had ever seen.[99] Brandt was first formally accepted

---

[91] Deposition of Allan M. Brandt, as n. 74, 336.

[92] Deposition of Allan M. Brandt, as n. 74, 237.

[93] Deposition of Allan M. Brandt, as n. 74, 254.

[94] Deposition of Allan M. Brandt, as n. 74, 191.

[95] Deposition of Allan M. Brandt, as n. 74, 231.

[96] Deposition of Allan M. Brandt, as n. 74, 286.

[97] Many interviews with Brandt and presentations by Brandt are available on Youtube. Brandt has also appeared on the popular late night satirical news program *The Daily Show with John Stuart* on June 13, 2007. The interview discussed Brandt's book *The Cigarette Century*; his involvement *in US v. Philip Morris et al.* was not discussed. The interview can be viewed at http://thedailyshow.cc.com/videos/6nceh2/allan-brandt. Accessed 31 Oct 2014.

[98] Brandt used this sociotechnical tactic in his testimony in court albeit to a far lesser extent.

[99] Trial testimony of Allan M. Brandt, Ph.D., September 27, 2004, United States of America v. Philip Morris USA Inc., 27/09/2004. LTDL. Bates Number: BRANDTA092804AM. http://legacy.library.ucsf.edu/tid/clk79a00. Accessed 31 Oct 2014. & Trial testimony of Allan M. Brandt, Ph.D., September 28, 2004 [a.m.], United States of America v. Philip Morris USA Inc., 28/09/2004. LTDL. Bates Number: BRANDTA092804AM. http://legacy.library.ucsf.edu/tid/blk79a00. Accessed 31 Oct 2014. & Trial testimony of Allan M. Brandt, Ph.D., September 28, 2004 [p.m.], United States of America v. Philip Morris USA Inc., 28/09/2004. LTDL. Bates Number: BRANDTA092804PM. http://legacy.library.ucsf.edu/tid/alk79a00. Accessed 31 Oct 2014.

as an expert witness and submitted to direct testimony.[100] Brody, the attorney from the DOJ who had recruited Brandt, questioned him on the development of the hypotheses on the causes of smoking-related diseases and the methodologies used by the field of medicine.[101] The questions produced answers that fitted and stressed the arguments made by the DOJ's legal strategy. Brandt's real on-trial experience came with the cross-examination by attorney David Bernick, representing Brown and Williamson Tobacco Company. Bernick immediately set an aggressive tone with the following interaction between him and Brandt.

> *Q. All of them involve, at this point in time, knowledge of a mechanism in the sense of the identification of a specific infectious agent, correct?*
> *A. Yes, but I think —*
> *Q. I'm sorry, this is cross-examination.*
> *Do they all involve today diseases where we have identified a specific infectious agent?*
> *A. Yes, they all involve diseases with specific infectious agents, but I would distinguish that from saying that those —*
> *Q. Excuse me. I didn't ask you if it was distinguishable, I'm sorry, Dr. Brandt, this is cross-examination, there will be an opportunity for redirect at a certain point of time. It would certainly facilitate the process if you listen to my questions — I know you haven't testified before in trial — and try to focus on answering the question and I'll do my best to be clear.*[102]

By speaking to a Harvard professor like that, Bernic made one thing clear: Brandt had entered Bernic's turf, and Brandt had to play by his rules.[103] In a rather harsh tone, Brandt was questioned on his qualifications as an expert witness. Afterwards, Bernick concluded that Brandt had sacrificed principles of historical research to advocacy.[104] He observed that objectivity was a problem for historians in court.[105] Moreover, Bernick also discussed the actual witness report itself. He examined various subjects and documents, while frequently cutting Brandt off to remind him to limit his answer within the scope of the question. At one instance, Bernick rephrased a question which he had already posed several times. Brody objected to the question, and the court approved his objection, whereupon Bernick rephrased the question in a different manner. Brandt had had enough and could not refrain from a short moment of defiance.

---

[100]Trial testimony of Allan M. Brandt, as n. 99, 640–643.

[101]Trial testimony of Allan M. Brandt, as n. 99, 644–658.

[102]Trial testimony of Allan M. Brandt, as n. 99, 660. Q = Bernick, A = Brandt.

[103]Cfr. the remarks by Wijffels on "the turf" of lawyers and the latters "home turf." See Part II, Chap. 8: A Reassessment of Wijffels' Concept of Forensic History, cfr. infra.

[104]Trial testimony of Allan M. Brandt, as n. 99, 665–673.

[105]Trial testimony of Allan M. Brandt, as n. 99, 671–672. See my discussion on objectivity in the first part of this book, cfr. Part I, Chap. 3: Clio's Modern Paradox Unravelled, cfr. supra.

*Q. All the things that I've talked about — Hueper,
Rosenblatt, the dissension at NCI, Shimkin, Robins' textbook and
Surgeon General Burney's testimony — none of them are quoted in
your direct testimony, are they?
MR. BRODY: Objection, Your Honor. Asked and answered.
We've been through each one of them. Mr. Bernick has asked the
same question each time.
THE COURT: Go ahead. Next question.
BY MR. BERNICK:
Q. None of them — none of those quotes appear or are
discussed in your direct examination, are they?
A. Yeah. You see, I actually used this paper in preparing
my direct testimony, the Shimkin paper. And you know, it's
interesting because you've taken certain quotes out of it, but
here's the question that Shimkin asks in the paper. And I'm
reading from the paper —
THE COURT: Dr. Brandt —
THE WITNESS: Okay. I'm sorry.
THE COURT: Even though this exchange may sound like it's
an academic seminar, it is not supposed to be an academic seminar
and I'm going to try and get us back on track.
Mr. Bernick.
MR. BERNICK: Yes.
THE WITNESS: I apologize.
THE COURT: That's all right.*[106]

The following lines of questioning concerned the scientific controversy during the 1950s and 1960s and discussed epidemiological causality.[107] At 4:30 p.m., the first day of Brandt's cross-examination ended. The following day, Brandt had to face Bernick again for the final hours of cross-examination. Bernick was less enthusiastic than the previous day and after 1 hour of discussing some small details of the expert report, Brandt could take a short recess. In the following hours, Brandt was cross-examined by counsel for Philip Morris, R.J. Reynolds, and Lorillard Tobacco Company, never reaching the same level of tension as in his exchanges with Bernick. Lastly, Brandt was again questioned by Brody for a redirect examination. Brody gave Brandt an excellent opportunity to come to a conclusion on the character of the actions by the tobacco companies:

*Q. Dr. Brandt, yesterday you testified on cross-examination
that you would describe the tobacco industry as "deviant and a
rogue industry." Why do you describe the tobacco industry that
way?
A. I describe them that way, and I realize those are strong
terms, because I think when an industry comes to have a product
that is identified as a major cause of human health — human
disease and sickness, and yet takes the position to denigrate
and try to attack that evidence without really taking it*

[106]Trial testimony of Allan M. Brandt, as n. 99, 717–718. Q = Bernick, A = Brandt.

[107]Trial testimony of Allan M. Brandt, as n. 99, 682–729.

seriously in terms of their commitment to the public, then I don't think that that industry's acting the way I anticipate most businesses operate.
So that, I think, makes the industry deviant and/or rogue and, in other words, outside the boundary of what my expectation would be about an industry whose product — principal product is implicated with such serious disease.[108]

The DOJ used Brandt's historical opinions as a central element of their legal strategy. In their opening statements on September 21st, the plaintiff had presented Brandt as "a leading medical historian from Harvard", who would aid the court in understanding the history of lung cancer and could argue with historical arguments that, around 1950 established scientific procedure had confirmed the link between smoking and lung cancer.[109] Brandt's testimony was thus very damaging for the defence. So, in contrast with the opening statements of the plaintiffs, Bernick's closing statements for the defence tried to discredit Brandt by calling him "the archivist."[110] In addition, Bernick reinterpreted Brandt's testimony to such an extent that the court intervened and recalled what Brandt actually had said.

Mr. Bernick: (. . .)
We took Dr. Brandt, both through the CTR program, the Grant Program, the Contract Program, the SAB Approved Program where the SAB made the judgments, and the companies and their own work and said, all areas of research – I asked him – remember he had those circles of different areas of research that kind of overlapped? I said, "Isn't it true that all areas of research regarding the relationship of smoking and disease were being covered, correct?" "Well, with different emphases, yes." That was the testimony on cross-examination. So where do we –
The Court: That answer "with different emphases", by that phrase, wasn't Dr. Brandt pointing out that CTR was avoiding research on the fundamental issue of what causes cancer?
Mr. Bernick: That's what he said at the outset, but when we took him through the microbiological – that's what was said on the basis of memos that were written by some company scientists in the 1970s, and there were several problems with that.[111]

---

[108]Trial testimony of Allan M. Brandt, as n. 99, 973–974. Q = Brody, A = Brandt. Brandt's answer is not far from determining the ultimate issue of the case; which is whether the tobacco industry has committed a fraud against the American public, yet Brandt arrives at phrasing around the ultimate issue by saying the industry is rogue, which neatly evades offending rule 704 of the FRE. See Part II, Sect. 3.3.6.3. The Daubert Standard: Popper & the Judge as Gatekeeper, cfr. supra.

[109]Plaintiff's Opening Statement, September 21, 2004 [a.m.], United States of America v. Philip Morris USA Inc., 21/09/2004. LTDL. Bates Number: POSDOJ092104AM. http://legacy.library.ucsf.edu/tid/muj79a00. Accessed 31 Oct 2014, 46, 48–49.

[110]Defendants' Closing Statement, June 8, 2005 [a.m.], United States of America v. Philip Morris USA Inc., 08/06/2005. LTDL. Bates Number: DCSDOJ060805AM. http://legacy.library.ucsf.edu/tid/xik79a00. Accessed 31 Oct 2014, 23129.

[111]Defendants' Closing Statement, as n. 110, 23131.

I conclude the topic of Brandt's testimony by turning once more to the three questions posed at the beginning of this qualitative analysis: (1) History was attacked during cross-examination by Bernick, the lawyer for the defence. Bernick argued that it was difficult for historians to remain objective while under oath in the courtroom. None of the industry's expert historians were harmed by this argument, since they had only filed a witness report and had been deposed to answer questions on that report. In other words, the industry's experts had presented facts, while Brandt was testifying a personal opinion or as the argument by Bernick would have formulated it: "a biased judgment."[112] (2) On a personal level Brandt was described as an advocate on a personal crusade against the tobacco industry without the proper qualification to deliver an expert testimony on the subject of the scientific controversy. (3) The cross-examination is a form of legal debate. It is a legal setting which functions by its own rules. If there is one moment in which a historian enters the turf of the legal discipline, then it is as an expert witness during cross-examination. Brandt found out the hard way by Bernick's continuous interruptions, repeated rephrasing of questions, and his restriction of Brandt's answers to just a few words, sometimes even limiting him to "yes" or "no", to prevent the historian from expounding his arguments. Furthermore, the tone in which Brandt was spoken to by Bernick differs greatly from the expected attitude towards a Harvard professor. Bernick was keen on frustrating Brandt. He was successful in one instant, as has come forth from the trail record. Testimony on trial happens in a legal rhetoric atmosphere where it is hard for historians to find the appropriate formulas and be allowed the opportunity to defend their report in a nuanced way.

14.2.3.3 The Trial Experience of Allan Brandt Reviewed

Brandt's trial has shown how historians and their research are put under immense pressure in court. Legal proceedings curtail the ability of historical narrative to present nuanced versions of the past. Depositions are, to a lesser extent than trial testimony, restrictive on historical narrative. In the 633-page deposition, Mr. Brody, assisting counsel for Brandt, said "objection" 602 times. In addition to making the legal figure of objection somewhat obsolete, it signifies the kind of legal discourse that was used by lawyers. Historians were forced into a kind of examination which is different from normal academic debate. Historians have to face the legal tactics of lawyers, which are of a technical and psychological nature. By constantly changing subjects and switching between important and irrelevant questions, the witness is confused, tired out, or enervated. In Brandt's

[112]The idea that historians should only deliver facts to the court and leave the "judgment" of those facts to the court and to the lawyers has been argued by Hannah Arendt concerning the Eichmann trial and by legal scholars Alain Wijffels and Henri Angevin concerning the Papon trial. See for Arendt, Part II, Sect. 6.1.1. Eichmann in Jerusalem, and for Wijffels and Angevin, Part II, Sect. 6. 1.3. Dealing with a Troublesome Past: Vichy in Court, and for a discussion on the argument by Wijffels, Part II, Chap. 8: A Reassessment of Wijffels' Concept of Forensic History, cfr. supra.

case, the latter option was aimed at. In retrospect, the deposition permits more room for contextualisation than the cross-examination. Cross-examination was a harsh experience for Brandt. Constantly switching between questions, demanding "yes" or "no" answers, interrupting answers, reformulating questions over and over again, and ad hominem attacks, are all legal tactics that historians face under cross-examination. The deposition and the trial testimonies are rhetoric events. They fit into larger legal schemes and they mold the historical narratives into legal models of conduct. The discourse used by lawyers is technical in a legal sense, and constantly intertwined with social, economic, philosophical, and historical arguments. As Judge Posner put it, law is about words and it is rhetorical by its own nature.[113] But, considering all these inconveniences, Brandt did an excellent job defending his research even under the harshest attacks by industry lawyers. His success is proven by the fact that the final verdict by Judge Kessler followed many of his arguments.[114]

14.2.4 *Peter English*

Peter English is a physician, a professor of medicine and a professor of history. English has been a practicing physician for 30 years. He has written multiple books on the history of different diseases. English has served in eight tobacco court cases as an expert witness, and in other cases involving asbestos and lead poisoning. As a practicing M.D., English was pressed hard on his reasons for testifying for the tobacco industry vice versa his ethical standards.[115]

14.2.4.1 Deposition

On August 23, 2002, Peter English was deposed by Mr. Kurtin, the lawyer for the plaintiff. Kurtin attacked English straight away, by asking him about the number of sources he had used for his witness report.

> *Q. How many documents would you say that you've reviewed*
> *since February of 2002?*
> *A. I don't have–I don't have the number. But–*
> *Q. Estimated volume, a box, two boxes?*
> *A. Oh, no. I would say much more than one or two boxes.*
> *I would say 20 boxes, maybe more.*[116]

[113]Posner, Richard. 1995. *Overcoming Law.* Cambridge: Harvard University Press, 1995, 498–499.

[114]For the discussion of the final verdict in *US v. Philip Morris et al.*, see Part III, Sect. 14.3. The Final Judgment by Judge Kessler, cfr. infra.

[115]See Expert Witness Profile No. 14, Peter English.

[116]Deposition of Peter Calvin English, M.D., Ph.D., August 23, 2002, United States of America v. Philip Morris USA Inc., 23/08/2002. LTDL. Bates Number: ENGLISHP082302. http://legacy.library.ucsf.edu/tid/qqo11b00. Accessed 31 Oct 2014, 15. A = English.

Furthermore, Kurtin continued his straightforward line of questioning on the salary which English received for his work as an expert witness.

Q. Okay. Dr. English page two of this Expert
Disclosure cover sheet, it states that you are compensated at $350 an hour
in connection with you work on this case?
Q. And can you estimate how much money you have billed
working on this case to date?
A. Between 125 and $130,000.[117]

Kurtin had done his homework and continued to probe English on previous cases and the money he made on them. The total amount English made working for the tobacco industry seemed hard to remember for English.

Q. And do you recall approximately how much you were
compensated for your work on that case?
A. I don't have a specific number.
Q. Was it more than $100,000?
A. Yes. It was more than that.
Q. More than $250,000?
A. Yes. I think that would be right.
Q. Approximately $250,000 or more than that?
A. I think it's–I think it's more than $250,000, yes.
Q. Was it more than $400,000?
A. Probably.
Q. One more. Is it more than $500,000?
A. I don't think so, no.
Q. Is it a fair assessment to say that it was between
400 and $500,000?
A. I don't have a recollection. As I–I don't want to
give you a false degree of specificity here.[118]

Several other cases were discussed but the point of the DOJ was made: Peter English had admitted to have earned several hundreds of thousands of dollars by working as an expert witness for the tobacco companies. Kurtin's next point on which he wanted to discredit English, concerned the preparation that English had done for the trial. English was asked if he thought smoking was healthy and if he would advise his patients to stop smoking. English answered that smoking was bad and that he would consult all his clients to stop smoking. The question important for the case was of course if the health risks had been clear in the 1950s and the 1960s. For English it was "common knowledge" then, despite the controversy, that smoking could not have been healthy. Thereafter Kurtin continued to put English under pressure, with questions about the preparation of his expert report.

Q. Dr. English, why do you testify for the tobacco
industry?
A. Well, as I mentioned a moment ago, 1 smoking and
health I think is the most important public health

---

[117]Deposition of Peter Calvin English, as n. 116, 17. Q = Kurtin, A = English.

[118]Deposition of Peter Calvin English, as n. 116, 32–33. Q = Kurtin, A = English.

story in the 20th century. And I think it's important that there be good history done. And by good history I mean one that, you know, reads all the relevant documents, tries to place events into their appropriate context. And so I think it's a very exciting topic. I think it's a very important topic. And I think that so much of the history is actually being played out in the court room. And I think it–and history is a part of what's going on in the court room and I think it's–I think its very important that the history that's presented in the court room be good solid history using appropriate historical methods.[119]

Especially the phrase "I think it's important that there be good history done. And by good history I mean one that, you know, reads all the relevant documents, tries to place events into their appropriate context" and furthermore the statement that "I think it's very important that the history presented in the courtroom be good solid history using appropriate historical methods", would come back to haunt English. A couple of questions later English was again asked about the documents he used for his witness report.

Q. Okay. So you've studied the public health's response to the smoking and health issue, but you haven't studied the tobacco industry's response to the smoking and health issues?
MR. NARKO: Objection.
A. I have not in any systematic sense studied tobacco Companies' internal responses.
Q. I'm not talking–how about external?
A. And I have not in any systematic sense studied what the Tobacco Institute said publicly.
Q. So the opinions that you've reached about the public health community's response to the smoking and health issue did not factor in industry?
MR. NARKO: Objection.
A. Well, I've certainly–I mean, I know what the public health community was–was thinking. So in that sense I think it's factored in. I certainly have also done very closely what the public opinion polls, so I have a sense of, you know, what the American people were doing. But I have not systematically gone through statements by various aspects of the tobacco industry.
Certainly in reading some of the expert reports I've come across some in this case, in other cases I've come across, but I've not made a systematic research in that regard.
Q. Do you believe it's necessary to conduct a systematic review in order to formulate opinions on smoking and

119 Deposition of Peter Calvin English, as n. 116, 49–50. Q = Kurtin, A = English.

health issues?
A. In my area–let the scientific community and public health community, medical community anew, no, I don't think it's necessary.[120]

The DOJ had forced English in answering questions he rather would not have answered. The defence lawyer tries to refrain him from answering by objecting while their own witness is talking. Yet in that very moment English says he has not systematically studied the tobacco's internal responses, while only a few questions ago he had declared that he had become a witness to ensure good history. Doing good history was defined by English himself as examination of all relevant documents. It is simply astounding that a professor of history comes to court and can be found to have read only half of the documents he should to form an informed opinion on the subject central to his testimony, namely the tobacco controversy.[121] Without studying the internal documents of the tobacco companies, one important historical question cannot be answered: "When did they know?"

I now analyse English's testimony by the three questions I stated at the beginning of this topic: (1) In this deposition the historical discipline is not attacked. (2) English's research was discredited by the DOJ, ironically with the help of English's statements during the same deposition. Furthermore, the believe in his impartiality was harmed because English had made around $500,000 for his work as an expert witness for the industry. (3) The discourse is less rhetoric than in the depositions of Brandt and Ludmerer, although still formal. English also argued in technical and in social arguments. In conclusion, English himself had given his own testimony a vital blow during the deposition. The DOJ's next move was rather obvious considering the rules of expert evidence and the contradicting statements English had made during his deposition.

14.2.4.2 The Motion in Limine to Exclude Expert Testimony of Peter English

In May 2004, the plaintiffs moved to exclude the testimony of Peter English. Plaintiff's legal counsel filed a motion *in limine* in favour of the exclusion of his expert testimony.[122] Their main argument was that the expert report submitted by English was fundamentally flawed because it lacked the research to form an opinion

[120]Deposition of Peter Calvin English, as n. 116, 71–72. Mr. Narko was legal counsel for the defendants. Q = Kurtin, A = English.

[121]Similar statements by English can be found at Deposition of Peter Calvin English, as n. 116, 158, 172, 208, 214–215.

[122]United States' Motion in Limine to Exclude Expert Testimony of Peter C. English, May 5, 2004, United States of America v. Philip Morris USA Inc., 05/05/2004. LTDL. Bates Number: USPMUSMOT0505042. http://legacy.library.ucsf.edu/tid/jrp08h00. Accessed 31 Oct 2014.

on the role the defendants had played in the tobacco controversy. The motion quoted English's deposition several times. English had not studied the defendants' public statements or internal documents. Hence, his research had left a very important perspective out of his report.[123] Furthermore, English had indicted himself by stating on the one hand that he believed that "I think it's important that there be history done. And by good history I mean one that, you know, reads all the relevant documents, tries to place events into their appropriate context", while on the other hand admitting that "I have not systematically gone through statements by various aspects of the tobacco industry."

In reaction the defence filed a motion urging the court not to exclude English as an expert witness. Their arguments were that the plaintiffs overlooked a key part over English's testimony.[124] The plaintiffs replied with a motion in support of their motion *in limine* to exclude the expert testimony of English, in which they used more statements made by English in his deposition, to argue in favour of his exclusion. Especially the "good history" statement of English was now used against himself. English had not read the internal tobacco documents and had thus, by his own definition, not practiced "good history." Furthermore, under rule 702 of the FRE an expert is expected to testify with opinions based on the study of sufficient data and facts.[125] The DOJ concluded that: "[i]n this case, therefore, Dr. English's inadequate factual basis derives directly from his failure to use any method, let alone a "reliable" method, to study Defendants' smoking and health "positions and perspectives."[126] The court's ruling "reluctantly" denied the plaintiff's motion *in limine* to exclude the testimony of English, however, the court noted that the defendants should "seriously consider whether this witness has anything substantial to add to the record."[127] Peter English's report and deposition would thus remain part of the trial and the argumentation of the defence, although after the ruling on the motion, the defence would have done well to head the warning of Judge Kessler.

---

[123] United States' Motion in Limine to Exclude Expert Testimony of Peter C. English, as n. 122, 1–2.

[124] Defendants' Opposition to United States' Motion in Limine to Exclude Expert Testimony of Peter C. English, June 7, 2004. LTDL. United States of America v. Philip Morris USA Inc. Bates Number: USPMDRSP060704. http://legacy.library.ucsf.edu/tid/rap08h00. Accessed 31 Oct 2014.

[125] For rule 702 of the FRE, see Part II, Sect. 3.3.6.3. The Daubert Standard: Popper & the Judge as Gatekeeper, cfr. supra.

[126] United States' Reply in Support of Motion in Limine to Exclude Expert Testimony of Peter C. English, June 22, 2004, United States of America v. Philip Morris USA Inc., 22/06/2004. LTDL. Bates Number: USPMUSRPLY062204. http://legacy.library.ucsf.edu/tid/rap08h00. Accessed 31 Oct 2014, 3.

[127] Order #614 [Re: United States' Motion in Limine to Exclude Expert Testimony of Peter C. English], July 29, 2004, United States of America v. Philip Morris USA Inc., 29/07/2004. LTDL. Bates Number: USPMORDER072904. http://legacy.library.ucsf.edu/tid/bno08h00. Accessed 31 Oct 2014.

14.2.5 *Theodore Wilson*

Theodore Wilson is a professor of history at the University of Kansas. He is a military historian, best known for his work on World War Two and the cold war. Wilson has testified in 11 other tobacco-related cases as an expert witness for the tobacco industry, prior to *US v. Philip Morris et al.*, although he has not researched nor published on the history of tobacco.[128]

14.2.5.1 Deposition

On September 4, 2002, Theodore Wilson was deposed by the DOJ for 2 days. Like all the other depositions in *US v. Philip Morris et al.*, Wilsons's deposition was taped.[129] Jason Laeser was the attorney for the plaintiff. Concerning the videotaping, Wilson was asked to argument verbally because emotions, facial expressions, or hand gestures would not be part of the record.

> *Q. For purposes of the record here today, both with Ms. Blackerby and with the video, it would be appreciated if you could answer verbally and not with a nod of the head or some other type of nonverbal gesture that might not indicate a yes or a no if it's called for.*[130]

In the case of Wilson, who was a military historian, the plaintiff sought to discredit Wilson by making clear that he had not done any historical research on the history of smoking or on the tobacco conspiracy.[131] Wilson acknowledged not having published on the subject, yet he declared that he had taught about the history of tobacco in class.[132] He had no articles, no peer reviewed publications on tobacco, yet he had served as an expert witness for the Tobacco Institute over a period of 6 years.[133] Wilson was asked who he considered an expert on the history of tobacco and how he would define an expert. Apart from the positive effect for the plaintiffs; that Wilson to some degree acknowledged the witnesses of the defence plaintiff as experts, the questions were clearly aimed at tricking Wilson into defining an expert

---

[128] See Expert Witness Profile No. 40, Theodore Wilson.

[129] Deposition of Theodore Allen Wilson, Ph.D., September 4, 2002, United States of America v. Philip Morris USA Inc., 04/09/2002. LTDL. Bates Number: WILSONT090402. http://legacy.library.ucsf.edu/tid/nhp11b00. Accessed 31 Oct 2014. & Continued deposition of Theodore Allen Wilson, Ph.D., September 5, 2002, United States Of America v. Philip Morris USA Inc. LTDL. Bates Number: WILSONT090502. http://legacy.library.ucsf.edu/tid/qhp11b00. Accessed 31 Oct 2014.

[130] Deposition of Theodore Allen Wilson, as n. 129, 5. Q = Laeser.

[131] Deposition of Theodore Allen Wilson, as n. 129, 12–35.

[132] Deposition of Theodore Allen Wilson, as n. 129, 12–15.

[133] Deposition of Theodore Allen Wilson, as n. 129, 18–20, 37.

in such a way that would exclude himself. Wilson was able to keep himself within that definition.[134] After which, Wilson was examined on his earnings while working as an expert witness for the tobacco industry.[135]

Q. How much have you earned based on your work
for the Tobacco industry since 1996?
A. I believe that I haven't, again, done any
kind of precise computation. I believe that it would
be somewhere over– approximating $500,000.[136]

Much unlike English, Wilson is very candid about his earnings as an expert witness. The deposition continued with questions about the preparation of his expert report, and whether he had read any of the other witness reports filed in the case.[137] Wilson was asked questions about possible aid he may have received while writing his expert report.

Q. You typed it yourself?
A. I entered it, word processed it, yes.[138]

Wilson was asked about his methods and standards in constructing the expert witness report.[139] He was also asked after his own smoking habits.[140] Wilson was also asked whether people knew the CEOs in 1994 were lying about the addictiveness of nicotine.

Q. So it's your testimony that
Americans are smart and can see through whatever these
CEOs are saying, basically?
MR. NARKO: Objection.
A. I take – I take as a – as a position that
Americans are rational people, yes, rational beings.[141]

Laeser continued with questions on "common knowledge."

Q. So the man or the woman in
the street would have been aware, regardless of
scientific community, that smoking caused lung cancer,
but the scientists couldn't prove it yet?
MR. NARKO: Objection.
A. The man – As I said before, the man or woman

[134]Deposition of Theodore Allen Wilson, as n. 129, 25–34.

[135]Deposition of Theodore Allen Wilson, as n. 129, 36–40.

[136]Deposition of Theodore Allen Wilson, as n. 129, 39. Q = Laeser, A = Wilson.

[137]Deposition of Theodore Allen Wilson, as n. 129, 40–58.

[138]Deposition of Theodore Allen Wilson, as n. 129, 59. Q = Laeser, A = Wilson.

[139]Deposition of Theodore Allen Wilson, as n. 129, 71–74.

[140]Deposition of Theodore Allen Wilson, as n. 129, 93–94.

[141]Deposition of Theodore Allen Wilson, as n. 129, 100. Q = Laeser, A = Wilson. I discussed the over-reliance on rational choice models in the defence's argumentation in Part III, Sect. 13.4.3. Game III: The Third Wave of Tobacco Litigation, cfr. supra.

in the street, in my opinion, based on the evidence that I've seen, would have been aware that smoking caused diseases of various kinds, and increasingly, that focus would have been lung cancer for that period of time, even though there would have been – there were debates about the issue of provable causation.[142]

Wilson was finding it hard to maintain the tobacco's legal tactic of a scientific controversy. DOJ counsel would often return on the issue of common knowledge of the dangers of tobacco.[143] After hours of revisiting that question, Wilson said that he was not "an expert on the dissemination of information in advertising to groups of Americans."[144] This opened up new possibilities for the DOJ counsel to question Wilson on his views on the difference between awareness and knowledge.[145] After those questions the deposition was adjourned to restart the following morning. Laeser immediately started again with questions about the knowledge of the man and woman in the street and their assumed truth.[146] Just like English, Wilson diminishes the importance of the role of the tobacco industry itself in influencing common knowledge on smoking.

Q. So the tobacco industry, as members of the American public, must have known those very same things?
A. I would assume. I have not interviewed or had any conversation with representatives of the tobacco industry, but I would assume that as Americans, as individuals, members of families, they had the same common sense or accepted the same – at some point accepted the same common sense evaluation of the risks associated with smoking.[147]

Wilson, in a similar way to Ludmerer and English, had neglected to study the internal documents of the tobacco industry "systematically". In conclusion, Wilson said that at least since 1964 the American public had been fully aware of the link between smoking and lung cancer.[148] The DOJ's tactics in this deposition had been to attack Wilson on the ground that he had not discussed internal documents and that he had no publications of research on the subject. As a smoker himself, they questioned him over and over again on the common knowledge which was hard at times to maintain for Wilson during his deposition. The fact that the tobacco

---

142 Deposition of Theodore Allen Wilson, as n. 129, 128. Q = Laeser, A = Wilson.

143 Deposition of Theodore Allen Wilson, as n. 129, 149–150, 176–177, 243.

144 Deposition of Theodore Allen Wilson, as n. 129, 243.

145 Deposition of Theodore Allen Wilson, as n. 129, 255–256, 260.

146 Continued deposition of Theodore Allen Wilson, as n. 129, 267–268, 281–282, 293.

147 Continued deposition of Theodore Allen Wilson, as n. 129, 293. Q = Laeser, A = Wilson.

148 Continued deposition of Theodore Allen Wilson, as n. 129, 339. For the Surgeon General Report of 1964 see Part III, Sect. 11.2. The Reports of the Surgeon General, cfr. supra.

industry hired a historian specializing in military history to defend this critical point of the historical discussion did not add to the credibility of their already one-sided historical legal strategy.

I now discuss the three questions I gave at the beginning of this topic: (1) The historical discipline was not attacked by the DOJ. (2) Wilson's credibility as an expired witness was undermined because of three issues. He was a military historian, he had not researched the internal documents of the industry, and he had made a lot of money of his expert witnessing career. (3) The discourse in this deposition is formal although far less than the previous depositions of Brandt or Ludmerer. In conclusion, because his credibility could be undermined, Wilson did not make a very convincing expert witness.

14.2.6 Conclusions on the Testimony Offered by Historians in US v. Philip Morris

In conclusion to this qualitative study, I summarize the core tactics both legal counsels used in order to neutralize the opposing expert witness. This will be done by looking at the answers I procured after each deposition, namely (1) did opposing counsel undermine the historical discipline, (2) did lawyers try to discredit the expert witness, (3) what kind of discourse was used by the expert historian in these interactions.

1. The DOJ did not question the legitimacy of the discipline of history in order to discredit the reports of opposing experts. As we have seen, Ludmerer even tried to seduce Moltzen, the lawyer representing the plaintiff, into a discussion on primary and secondary sources, in order to escape other questions on the preparation of his report. The idea that historians should only use primary sources was a legal strategy by the defence's counsel. Both Brandt and Proctor were repeatedly examined on this subject. The fact that the DOJ completely ignored this notion that historians should only deliver facts, diminished the legitimacy of the defence's strategy on the subject. Furthermore, history as a discipline was attacked during Brandt's cross-examination. Bernick, who conducted the examination, stated that historians were having trouble remaining objective in the courtroom, implying again that historians should just give facts [as the defence's witnesses had allegedly done], and not opinions.[149]
2. Both parties tried to discredit the professional credibility of the opposing historians through *ad hominem* attacks, although some received less heat than others. The defence left Proctor relatively at ease, only implying that his state-funded

[149] An argument similar to that of Alain Wijffels. See Part II, Chap. 8: A Reassessment of Wijffels' Concept of Forensic History, cfr. supra. On objectivity see Part I, Chap. 3: Clio's Modern Paradox Unravelled, cfr. supra.

research projects meant he had sold his research to the federal state. It was Brandt who really felt what it was like to be on the stand. Bernick accused Brandt of being a biased and inadequate advocate. The defences' strategy was aimed at making Brandt frustrated by interrupting his answers and rephrasing the same questions over and over again. The defence counsel clearly expected, considering Brandt's lack of legal experience, that this would have an effect on Brandt and that could force him to lash out against opposing counsel, which could then be used against him. Brandt withstood these attempts reasonably well, except for one little moment of resistance while on cross-examination, although this did little or no harm to his credibility. The DOJ, on the other hand, focused on three elements to undermine the credibility of Ludmerer, English, and Wilson, which were (1) the fact that all three of them had made around half a million dollars working for the tobacco industry, which the DOJ used to argue that their reports were bought by the industry; (2) the fact that the expert historians for the defence had not practiced "good history" by leaving out of their research all internal documents of the industry, an argument that almost got English's testimony excluded; (3) the fact that the defence's witnesses were no experts in the history of tobacco, as opposed the DOJ's own expert witnesses. This was easily proven as all three had not published anything on tobacco history, and whereas at least Ludmerer and English researched the history of medicine and epidemic disease, Wilson was a military historian.

3. The discourse used by the expert historians from the defence as well as those from the plaintiff's side was sociotechnical, as Caudill described it "social, historical, economic, or philosophical arguments are coextensive with and constitutive or the 'technical.'"[150] According to Caudill, the "scientific expert's "legal" discourse" translates scientific knowledge into "terms that have meaning in law."[151] The legal realm is one of rhetoric's, and when historians enter the courtroom they are forced to participate in a form of debate that is uncommon to them. The debate in the courtroom is not constructed to arrive at new intellectual insights through constructive arguments; on the contrary, the depositions and the trial testimony have one common goal: to establish that one's own version of history is correct while that of the opposition is wrong. To discredit the opposing witness, lawyers and historians engage in what Judge Posner has called "a language game."[152] I have given an ample amount of examples of this legal strategy. Tactics by opposing counsel that attempted to confuse the witness, unnerve him, and fatigue him, were all set up in order to let him make statements that can later be used against him. Especially on cross-examination, Bernick tried to frustrate Brandt. The expert witness himself can also play this game of rhetoric. For example, Ludmerer showed great skill in evading answers, talking

[150]Caudill, as n. 21, 1–2.

[151]Caudill, David. 2002. Scientific Narratives in Law: An Introduction. *Law and Literature* 14, 268.

[152]Posner, Richard. 2009. *Law and Literature*. Cambridge: Harvard University Press, 383–385, 455.

at length about issues that were not asked or relevant to his deposition. Brandt is also a good example. As we have seen, he used very short answers, while stretching out his longer answers with the explicative "..., you know, ...".

After this qualitative analysis of the records of the depositions of the five historians involved in *US v. Philip Morris et al.* and Brandt's testimony in court, I have to concur with Caudill when he stated that "scientific expertise in law is a rhetorical and social enterprise, not simply because it takes place in the rhetorical and social context of a legal dispute, but also because science itself is characterized by these inevitable aspects."[153] In other words and applied to the historical profession, the courtroom forces the historian into the realm of rhetoric's. This not wrong per se, history always uses rhetoric in its argumentation. Although the legal game-element is important in the trial event for expert witnesses, their reports are still under the closest scrutiny by opposing lawyers. Footnotes, sources – primary or secondary–, and methods of research are dissected in search of even the smallest mistake. The expert report forms the heart of the testimony of the historian despite the importance of the legal strategies surrounding it during the trial.

In conclusion, I argue that the court for historians as expert judicial witnesses is a performative and fact-making theatre: (1) *Performative* since lawyers and historians engage in a rhetorical duel. The amount of influence a testimony will have depends on how successfully historians defend their report, factually and rhetorically, using technical as well as socially and philosophically inspired arguments, and rhetorical techniques–(2) *Fact-making*, because the expert reports of the historians and the presented historical facts do matter. If opposing counsel cannot present clearly that the expert has distorted or abused history, the historian's facts stand. It will depend from trial to trial whether the performative element or the fact-making element plays a determinative role. For example, in jury trials the performative element might have a bigger influence than the factual one. In *US v. Philip Morris et al.*, Justitia's set of scales favoured the fact-making element over the performative. Ludmerer, English, and Wilson were successfully portrayed as hired guns of the tobacco companies. Yet, it was the fact that the reports by the defence's experts were historically inferior to those filed by Brandt and Proctor that led Judge Kessler to her condemnation of the tobacco industry. The adversarial system had functioned. Especially the fact that the defence's witnesses had not researched any internal documents of the tobacco companies, records central to the historical research needed to answer the accusations made by the DOJ on the role the tobacco industry had played in creating the tobacco controversy and common knowledge of smokers, destroyed their credibility and the significance of their reports in the eyes of the court. Despite all the theatre in court, professional and reliable history was recognized by the gatekeeper-Judge.[154] It is because of the strength of the exceptionally well-documented and meticulously performed historical researches

[153]Caudill, as n. 151, 286.

[154]For the Judge as a gatekeeper under Daubert see: Part II, Sect. 7.3.6.3. The Daubert Standard: Popper & the Judge as Gatekeeper, cfr. supra.

of both Brandt and Proctor that Judge Kessler followed their argumentations and presented an excruciating historical overview of the crimes of the tobacco industry in her final verdict.

14.3 The Final Judgment by Judge Kessler

On the 17th of August 2006 Gladys Kessler, Judge for the United States District Court for the District of Columbia, produced a final opinion in *US v. Philip Morris* et al.[155] Kessler provided a "Tolkien-length" 1,653-page report which detailed the conspiracy set up by the defendants.[156] Kessler's decision is enormous in scope as well as in legal and historical precision. In general, the court's opinion followed the opinions of both Brandt and Proctor.[157] The verdict is an extensively documented and historically informed opinion that could be considered to be published as a professional historical work.[158] Kessler expressed her conclusions on the case in the following words:

> The extensive, detailed Findings of Fact set forth above, establish – overwhelmingly – that Defendants devised a scheme to defraud and used mailings and wire transmissions for the purpose of furthering it. The purpose of the scheme was to obtain, from smokers and potential smokers, money, i.e., the cost of cigarettes, to fill the coffers of the corporate Defendants. Put more colloquially, and less legalistically, over the course of more than 50 years, Defendants lied, misrepresented, and deceived the American public, including smokers and the young people they avidly sought as "replacement smokers," about the devastating health effects of smoking and environmental tobacco smoke, they suppressed research, they destroyed documents, they manipulated the use of nicotine so as to increase and perpetuate addiction, they distorted the truth about low tar and light cigarettes so as to discourage smokers from quitting, and they abused the legal system in order to achieve their goal – to make money with little, if any, regard for individual illness and suffering, soaring health costs, or the integrity of the legal system.[159]

In addition, she wrote:

> Defendants engaged in a scheme to Defraud Smokers and Potential Smokers. The Government has proven that the Enterprise knowingly and intentionally engaged in a scheme to defraud smokers and potential smokers, for purposes of financial gain, by making false and fraudulent statements, representations, and promises. Defendants participated in the Enterprise's overarching scheme to defraud smokers and potential smokers in order to

---

[155]United States of America v. Philip Morris USA Inc. Final Opinion, 2006. http://www.library.ucsf.edu/sites/all/files/ucsf_assets/FinalOpinion_full_version.pdf. Accessed 31 Oct 2014.

[156]Douglas, Clifford, Davis Ronald, and Beasley, John. 2006. Epidemiology of the Third Wave of Tobacco Litigation in the United States, 1994-2005. *Tobacco Control* 15, 11.

[157]Proctor, as n. 31. http://jpsl.org/archives/tobacco-and-health-expert-witness-report-filed-behalf-plaintiffs-united-states-america-plaintiff-v-philip-morris-inc-et-al-defen. Accessed 31 Oct 2014.

[158]If all the legal technicalities were removed from it.

[159]United States of America v. Philip Morris USA Inc. Final Opinion, as n. 155, 1500–1501.

> maximize their profits by preserving and enhancing the market for cigarettes, to avoid costly liability judgments, to derail attempts to make smoking socially unacceptable, and to sustain the cigarette industry.[160]

Kessler addressed each tactic by the tobacco industry of which the most important were: "Defendants Falsely Denied the Adverse Health Effects of Smoking", "Defendants Falsely Denied that Nicotine and Smoking Are Addictive", "Defendants Falsely Denied that They Manipulated Cigarette Design and Composition so as to Assure Nicotine Delivery Levels Which Create and Sustain Addiction", "Defendants Falsely Represented that Light and Low Tar Cigarettes Deliver Less Nicotine and Tar and, Therefore, Present Fewer Health Risks than Full-Flavour Cigarettes", and "Defendants Falsely Denied that They Market to Youth, and seventhly "Defendants Suppressed Documents, Information, and Research."[161] Moreover, Kessler concluded that the defendants had committed these crimes as "a common unit" and had done with "a common purpose."[162]

The decision highlighted how tobacco industry lawyers had manipulated documents. Epidemiologist Mark Parascandola noted that industry lawyers were closely involved when shaping the role of in-house industry scientific research.[163] The industry's legal counsel had systematically destroyed and concealed information, through the abuse of attorney-client privilege doctrine.[164] Proctor also accused the tobacco companies of having adopted "email deletion policies to avoid leaving such trails (paper or electronic), the theory again being that what you don't know can't hurt you."[165] One article by health advocates Sara Guardino and Richard Daynard called tobacco lawyers "disease vectors."[166] According to Guardino and Daynard, tobacco legal counsel had played a role in "gauging and influencing in house scientists' beliefs", in "vetting scientific research", had engaged in "improper exploitation of attorney-client privilege and work-product protection", and had

---

[160]United States of America v. Philip Morris USA Inc. Final Opinion, as n. 155, 1501.

[161]United States of America v. Philip Morris USA Inc. Final Opinion, as n. 155, 1505–1508–1512–1514–1518–1526.

[162]United States of America v. Philip Morris USA Inc. Final Opinion, as n. 155, 1530–1538. I discussed the unity of the tobacco industry earlier at Part III, Sect. 10.2.4. The Oligopolistic Structure of the Tobacco Industry, cfr. supra.

[163]Parascandola, Marc. 2005. Science, Industry, and Tobacco Harm Reduction: a Case Study of Tobacco Industry Scientists' Involvement in the National Cancer Institute's Smoking and Health Program, 1964–1980. *Public Health Chronicles* 120, 338.

[164]Hurt, Richard, Ebbert, Jon, Muggli, Monique, Lockhart, Nikki, and Robertson, Channing. 2012. Open Doorway to Truth: Legacy of the Minnesota Tobacco Trial. *Mayo Clinic Proceedings* 84, 454. & Proctor, as n. 9, 282–283.

[165]Proctor, Robert, and Schiebinger, Londa. 2008. *Agnotology. The Making & Unmaking of Ignorance.* Palo Alto: Stanford University Press, 25.

[166]Guardino, Sara, and Daynard, Richard. 2007. Tobacco Industry Lawyers as 'Disease vectors'. *Tobacco Control* 16, 224.

played a pivotal role "in document concealment."[167] Judge Kessler also strongly condemned the central role lawyers had played in the crimes of the tobacco industry:

> The evidence is clear that on a significant number of occasions, Defendants did in fact suppress research and destroy documents to protect themselves and the industry. ... By destroying evidence, Defendants make it virtually impossible to know what materials existed prior to their destruction.[168]

Concluding on the role of lawyers in the industry's fraud, she wrote:

> Finally, a word must be said about the role of lawyers in this fifty-year history of deceiving smokers, potential smokers, and the American public about the hazards of smoking and second hand smoke, and the addictiveness of nicotine. At every stage, lawyers played an absolutely central role in the creation and perpetuation of the Enterprise and the implementation of its fraudulent schemes. They devised and coordinated both national and international strategy; they directed scientists as to what research they should and should not undertake; they vetted scientific research papers and reports as well as public relations materials to ensure that the interests of the Enterprise would be protected; they identified "friendly" scientific witnesses, subsidized them with grants from the Center for Tobacco Research and the Center for Indoor Air Research, paid them enormous fees, and often hid the relationship between those witnesses and the industry; and they devised and carried out document destruction policies and took shelter behind baseless assertions of the attorney client privilege.[169]

An aspect that was not addressed by Judge Kessler was the involvement of judges and the tobacco industry. In a 2006 article, tobacco health advocate Lissy Friedman writes about "privately funded judicial seminars" organized by the tobacco industry.[170] Internal industry documents have shown that tobacco companies tried to influence judges through lectures by their experts at prestige seminars. In 1993 Libertad, Inc. was founded as an organization with "a wide international coalition of representatives of commercial, academic and legal circles as well as media and human rights experts [which] has been studying and analysing regulation of commercial speech." The company's sole contributor was Philip Morris.[171] Friedman gives an example of how Ninth Circuit Court of Appeals Judge Alex Kozinski attended two Libertad conferences in 1992 and 1995 at "vacation destinations." Kozinski would later rule in the landmark case *Daubert v. Merrell Dow Pharmaceuticals*, the case that set the precedent for expert witnessing.[172] Some seminar attendees are not even aware of who is sponsoring the lectures at

---

[167] Guardino, Sara, and Daynard, Richard, as n. 166, 224–227.

[168] United States of America v. Philip Morris USA Inc. Final Opinion, as n. 155, 1408.

[169] United States of America v. Philip Morris USA Inc. Final Opinion, as n. 155, 4. I discussed the involvement of lawyers in the general and legal policy of tobacco companies in Part III, Sect. 13.1. The First Wave: Cipollone v. Liggett Group, cfr. supra.

[170] Friedman, Lissy. 2006. Tobacco Industry Use of Judicial Seminars to Influence Rulings in Products Liability Litigation. *Tobacco Control* 15, 120.

[171] Friedman, as n. 170, 122.

[172] Friedman, as n. 170, 122. For a discussion on Daubert in this book see: Part II, Sect. 7.3.6.3. The Daubert Standard: Popper & the Judge as Gatekeeper, cfr. supra.

these conferences.[173] Official response against these biased seminars was minimal. The code of conduct committee from 1980 stated that judges had to decide for themselves if these seminars are appropriate to attend.[174] The tobacco industry is not only putting "dollars into the judges' pockets", there are "planting ideas into their heads", and that is a very powerful combination to withstand even for judges, Friedman observed.[175]

Brandt called Kessler's decision "a model of reasoned historical and legal analysis."[176] Kessler's judgment has been of great importance in recent tobacco litigation. Plaintiffs no longer have to provide, in theory, the evidence to the question; "what did they know and when they know it." In other words, plaintiffs have legal precedent to prove that smoking causes disease and that nicotine is addictive and that the tobacco companies despite their knowledge of those dangers continued to sell and promote their product. The question remains how well the individual was aware of the danger of smoking and whether smoking was the cause of cancer and illness and addictiveness.[177] The decision by Kessler did not demand direct damages from the tobacco industry, but it did order them to acknowledge their deeds on their website and to further inform the American public by means of an advertising campaign of the dangers of smoking.

In retrospect on the trial, Brandt wrote that:

> At times, as I watched the trial unfold, I felt that Eubanks, Brody, and their small team of DOJ career attorneys were all that stood between the tobacco industry and the future global pandemic. If the industry could remove this last major legal obstacle, it would cross over into a new era in which the threat of litigation had been all but removed. If the tobacco companies could win this case, they would have gotten away with the crime of the century. And perhaps they have.[178]

Brandt further elaborates that the tobacco industry has proven "remarkably successful in devising new ways to resist public health regulations and promote its product."[179] "The industry is here to stay", he writes, and history will, according to him, not alter their business practices. But he believes that understanding the history of cigarettes can add an important element "in the process of building societies and cultures that know their dangers and have strategies for their control."[180] For Brandt, *US v. Philip Morris et al.* is "an example of how we might recover a "usable past"

[173] Friedman, as n. 170, 123.

[174] Friedman, as n. 170, 123.

[175] Friedman, as n. 170, 124.

[176] Brandt, as n. 6, 503.

[177] I discussed this subject in Part III, Sect. 13.4.3. Game III: The Third Wave of Tobacco Litigation, cfr. supra.

[178] Brandt, as n. 6, 504.

[179] Brandt, as n. 6, 505.

[180] Brandt, as n. 6, 505.

that serves the public good."[181] Because of the verdict by Judge Kessler, tobacco companies were forced to make another "20,000 other media materials (audiotapes, videotapes, CDs, DVDs, slides, maps, oversized paper materials, microfilm, and external storage devices such as hard drivers) public."[182] These newly acquired documents offered a new opportunity to do even more research on the tobacco conspiracy.

The role historians played in *US v. Philip Morris et al.* has shown that historians face many difficulties when they enter the courtroom. The trial has also shown how some historians are willing to neglect their professional and personal moral responsibilities in exchange for the industry's pay checks. The opinions of all three witnesses for the defence were utterly flawed because they hadn't investigated the internal industry documents, which prevented them from answering one of the central issues of the case: "When did the tobacco industry know smoking was unhealthy?" Furthermore, all three had no publications or had not done any research on the history of tobacco. Wilson was not even a medical historian, but a military historian. The fact that English was almost excluded as a witness, shows how difficult the legal strategy of the defence was to maintain: namely, that their expert witnesses had conducted a full historical research without examining the internal industry's documents. When reading the depositions of the industry's experts, one cannot help but be amazed by the ethical dubious stance taken by Ludmerer, English, and Wilson. Both Ludmerer and Wilson did not testify or work on any court case for the tobacco industry, that we know of, after their depositions in *US v. Philip Morris et al.*[183] English continued to serve as an expert witness for the tobacco companies in the following years in twelve additional cases.[184] The reports of Brandt and Proctor on the other hand, were excellent examples of professional research and well-documented history, the case was very document-intensive, because of the enormous amount of sources analysed by the experts of the plaintiff. In the end, Judge Kessler proved able enough as a gatekeeper to determine whose facts were closest to the truth.

14.4 Confronting Ethics with De Baets

I now analyse the historical research presented in *US v. Philip Morris et al.*, on an ethical level. In this topic I want to determine whether Brandt, Proctor, Ludmerer, Wilson, and English have functioned as professional historians should

[181] Brandt, as n. 6, 505.

[182] Hurt, Richard, Ebbert, Jon, Muggli, Monique, Lockhart, Nikki, and Robertson, Channing, as n. 164, 449.

[183] See Expert Witness Profile No. 30, Kenneth Ludmerer. & See Expert Witness Profile No. 50, Theodore Wilson.

[184] See Expert Witness Profile No. 14, Peter English.

have behaved. In order to reach a more concrete conclusion on their ethics as professional historians, I use the ethical code drafted by Belgian historian Antoon De Baets. De Baets has worked predominantly on censure and ethics in the historical profession. He leads *The Network of Concerned Historians,* which draws attention to the suppression and censuring of historians and their work throughout the world.[185] Inspired by International treaties like the *UNESCO Declaration on Science and the Use of Scientific Knowledge*, the *Universal Declaration of Human Rights*, and the *International Covenant on Civil and Political Rights,* De Baets has proposed an ethical code for historians. The code has twenty articles and describes the rights as well as the duties of historians.[186] Furthermore, in his work of 2009, *Responsible History,* De Baets proposes a definition of the abuse of history. He defines "the abuse of history" as follows: "[t]he abuse of history is its use with intent to deceive."[187] I particularly discuss what the expert witnesses for the defence did, for they have strayed the farthest from the code in contrast to the witnesses of the plaintiffs. I have identified five articles which the historians offended, who worked for the tobacco industry in *US v. Philip Morris et al.,* and which I analyse one by one.

14.4.1 Article 10: Integrity; Historical Truth

Article ten stipulates how historians should maintain their professional integrity when searching for historical truths. I quote from article ten: "[i]t shall be the intent of historians to honestly search for the historical truth" and "[h]istorians shall always oppose the abuse of history."[188] This abuse has been defined by De Baets as the intent to deceive. Ludmerer, English, and Wilson had not reviewed the internal documents of the industry, which had become available through previous settlements and verdicts in tobacco litigation. By making that choice they should have refrained from offering an opinion in court about the common knowledge about the dangers of tobacco within the tobacco companies. The question "what did they know, and when did they know it?", was essential to the case. Ludmerer, English, and Wilson all stated that everybody knew smoking was dangerous, but nobody knew how dangerous, arguing that there was a scientific controversy. By neglecting the secret tobacco records, Ludmerer, English, and Wilson were answering questions on the tobacco controversy, based on insufficient data. This

[185]The Network of Concerned Historians can be accessed via http://www.concernedhistorians.org/content/home.html. Accessed 31 Oct 2014.

[186]For the proposal of the De Baets for a *Code of Ethics for Historians* see http://www.concernedhistorians.org/content_files/file/et/148.pdf. Accessed 31 Oct 2014. See also Appendix IV, cfr. infra.

[187]De Baets, Antoon. 2009. *Responsible History.* New York: Berghahn Books, 14.

[188]De Baets, as n. 186, Appendix IV, article 10.

was the reason why the plaintiffs tried to exclude the testimony of English on the basis of rule 702 of the FRE, since according to the second condition of rule 702, the testimony of the expert witness had to be "based on sufficient facts or data."[189] The fact that they researched the tobacco controversy without examining the tobacco companies' internal archives is the reason why I argue that Ludmerer, English, and Wilson gave up their professional integrity as historians. They literally sold their integrity at rates of $350 or more an hour. Ludmerer, English, and Wilson each made more than half a million dollars while testifying as historians for the tobacco industry.[190]

Undoubtedly Brandt and Proctor have earned substantial sums as well.[191] Yet, these experts did not leave out important sources from their research. Brandt and Proctor had reviewed documents from both within the industry and as well as those from the medical communities and from within the public sphere, such as advertising. As Brandt wrote in his book, he was appalled by the selectiveness in both the reports of Ludmerer and English. He wanted to make a more comprehensive report.[192] The meticulousness and professionalism by which Brandt and Proctor analysed all documentation available is the reason that their historical books are of a very high quality and why Judge Kessler used their testimonies to draft her final opinion on the trial. The two books by Proctor and Brandt, which are the result of litigation-driven history, exemplify how good and even excellent historical research can be done in a controversial legal context.

14.4.2 Article 12: Disclosure of Information & Article 14: Free Debate; Accountability; Universalism

Article 12 of the code discusses the duty to disclose information. Article 14 of the code sets rules on free debate and accountability. I quote from article 12: "[p]ublication of information, and speaking freely about it, is the rule."[193] Article 14 stipulates that "[f]ree and public exchange of ideas is the oxygen of historical scholarship."[194] The experts for the defence have offended both rules. None of them

[189]For the attempts at excluding English's testimony see Part III, Sect. 11.2.3.2. The Exclusion of Peter English's Testimony, cfr. supra & For rule 702 of the FRE, see Part II, Sect. 7.3.6.3. The Daubert Standard: Popper & the Judge as Gatekeeper, cfr. supra.

[190]See Appendix II, Table 6. Remuneration, cfr. infra.

[191]Proctor has confirmed in personal correspondence with the author that he made over $1,500,000 as an expert witness in tobacco litigation. See Expert Witness Profile No. 39, Robert Proctor.

[192]Brandt, as n. 6, 498–499.

[193]De Baets, as n. 186, Appendix IV, article 12.

[194]De Baets, as n. 186, Appendix IV, article 14.

have published on their research on the history of the tobacco industry.[195] There is no disclosure and no transparency about their activities as expert witnesses. The issue would be different if Ludmerer, English, and Wilson had been independent historians who worked on their own as consultants or with a private company, but these are academics who publish [on other subjects], write peer reviews, join in academic and public debates with almost nobody knowing about their work for the tobacco industry. As we will see, this is a phenomenon that seems to be common practice across American Universities.[196] Free and public exchange of ideas, as De Baets writes, is "the oxygen of historical scholarship."[197] If historians use their research in an academic or public context, such as the courtroom, they have to publish that research and let it be peer reviewed. There could be legal restrictions on publication; yet, these restrictions only seem to form a problem for the experts the defence. Expert witnesses for the defence are much more restricted in what they are allowed to publish than those serving the plaintiff's bar. How is that Proctor and Brandt are able to publish monographs on their tobacco research while none of the experts for the defence "can"? It is a conscious choice.

The fact that the experts of the defence did not publish anything on their tobacco research made their testimonies very weak. Wilson was an expert in military history of World War Two and the Cold War, and on top of that he had not published a single article on the history of tobacco. Moreover, English was an M.D. but neither had he done research on the history of tobacco. Only Ludmerer could somewhat argue to have published on the diseases caused by tobacco smoking.[198] In comparison with Proctor and Brandt, the qualifications of the defence experts looked rather pale. That Ludmerer, English, and Wilson were even allowed as expert witnesses shows the relativity of the legal rules of expert evidence set forth in FRE and Daubert. As I discussed in the second part of this book, the second element set forth by the US Supreme Court in Daubert explicitly limited expert testimony to that which had "been subject to peer review and publication."[199] If Judge Kessler had interpreted Daubert as the Supreme Court intended, the defence would not have been left with a single historian as an expert witness.

By contrast, Brandt and Proctor had both done extensive research on tobacco history and had both published their research in peer-reviewed articles and books. Proctor, for example, had been researching Nazi policies on tobacco, but also independent scientific research, and cancer in general.[200] Allan Brandt had published

---

[195] See Expert Witness Profile No. 14, Peter English & See Expert Witness Profile No. 30, Kenneth Ludmerer & See Expert Witness Profile No. 50, Theodore Wilson.

[196] For this transparency problem with expert witnesses see Part III, Sect. 16.3.3. Transparency, cfr. infra.

[197] De Baets, as n. 186, Appendix IV, article 14.

[198] See Expert Witness Profile No. 30, Kenneth Ludmerer.

[199] See Part II, Sect. 7.3.6.3. The Daubert Standard: Popper & the Judge as Gatekeeper, cfr. supra.

[200] See, for example, works such as: Proctor, Robert. 1999. *The Nazi War on Cancer*. New York: Princeton University Press. & Proctor, Robert. 1995. *Cancer Wars: How Politics Shapes What We*

on health history, disease history, and tobacco history.[201] Both Proctor and Brandt openly wrote about their testimonies and work as expert witnesses. Their books serve as an opportunity for their fellow historians to formulate their critiques on Proctor's and Brandt's research and methods. Robert Proctor's website offers a link to one of the expert reports he made as an expert witness.[202] Proctor has furthermore published the expert report he submitted in *US v. Philip Morris et al.* in *The Journal of Philosophy, Science, & Law.*[203] Transparency and publication are factors that indicate how confident historians are about the legitimacy of their research.[204] The fact that on the one hand Ludmerer, English, and Wilson are not openly sharing and defending their tobacco research, and on the other, Brandt as well as Proctor continuously do, seems to reflect the faith they each respectively have in their research.

14.4.3 Article 13: Critical and Objective Method; Independence

The 13th article of the code of ethics proposed by De Baets stipulates that "historians shall adopt a critical attitude and use a method based on; (1) accuracy (transparency;

Know and Don't Know About Cancer. New York: Basic Books. & Proctor, Robert. 1991. *The Purity and Power in Modern Knowledge*. London: Harvard University Press. Proctor's work on Nazi tobacco politics inspired an American Tobacco spokesmen to engage in a reduction ad Hitlerum when they accused health advocate Staton Glantz, among others, of "health fascism." The argument was that only an authoritarian government would limit or abolish the people's right and personal freedom to choose to smoke. The attacks on tobacco companies by health groups were therefore inspired by totalitarian strategies, according to the industry. See for example Proctor, Robert. 2008. On Playing the Nazi Card. *Tobacco Control* 17, 289–290. In the same issue of *Tobacco Control*: Schneider, Nick, and Glantz, Staton. 2008. "Nicotine Nazis Strike Again": a Brief Analysis of the Use of Nazi Rhetoric in Attacking Tobacco Control Advocacy. *Tobacco Control* 17, 291–296.

[201]See, for example, works such as: Brandt, Allan. 1997. *Morality and Health: Interdisciplinary Perspectives.* New York: Routledge. & Brandt, Allan. 1991. Tobacco Liability and Public Health Policy. *Journal of the American Medical Association* 266, 3178–3182. & Brandt, Allan. 1998. Tobacco Epidemiology and the Challenge of Multiple Etiologies. *Journal of the American Medical Association* 279, 969. For more, see Brandt's extensive list of publications in his curriculum vitae at http://www.fas.harvard.edu/~hsdept/bios/brandt.html. Accessed 31 Oct 2014.

[202]See for the website of Robert Proctor http://www.stanford.edu/dept/HPS/proctor.html. Accessed 31 Oct 2014. For the witness report he filed in *Ironworkers v. Philip Morris* see Proctor, Robert. 1998. A Historical Reconstruction of Tobacco and Health in the U. S., 1954–1994. LTDL. Bates Number: 2075493217/3265, 06/11/1998. http://legacy.library.ucsf.edu/tid/vmm56c00. Accessed 31 Oct 2014.

[203]Proctor, as n. 31. http://jpsl.org/archives/tobacco-and-health-expert-witness-report-filed-behalf-plaintiffs-united-states-america-plaintiff-v-philip-morris-inc-et-al-defen. Accessed 31 Oct 2014.

[204]Transparency before publication is another issue because there are risks of copyright infringement and interests of intellectual property at stake. But these should not exclude sharing by experts that they are working as expert witnesses.

respect for evidence and argumentation; control of bias and anachronism; impartiality and objectivity) at the levels of statements of fact and description, and (2) plausibility at the levels of statements of opinion and analysis."[205] The manner in which Ludmerer, English, and Wilson conducted their research for the trial leaves much to be desired. The selectiveness of their investigation, the limits of their research scope, their neglect of industry archives, and their often paradoxical statements on the tobacco controversy are cause for arguing that the historians for the defence offended this article as well. The influence of legal counsel on their argumentation and research cannot be underestimated, even to such an extent that Ludmerer admits that the report he submitted in *US v. Philip Morris et al.* was a "copy-paste" operation done by legal counsel from his previous reports.[206] It would be interesting to analyse these exchanges between the lawyers and the historians at an early stage, yet as I have remarked in part II of this book, lawyers aim to produce no paper trail.[207] In conclusion, the experts for the defence in *US v. Philip Morris et al.* did not investigate the history of tobacco in a sufficiently critical manner that would be expected of a professional historian. As the line of article 13 puts it: "They shall aspire to political, ideological, and intellectual independence and to as much financial independence as possible from government, commissioning entities, and sponsors."

There is little doubt that the DOJ also influenced the reports Proctor and Brandt filed with the court. As I explained before, it is difficult to assess the exact influence counsel had on the expert reports, yet I would argue that the DOJ's influence can in no way be compared to the level of interference and command the legal counsel of the tobacco industry had on the expert reports of Ludmerer, Wilson, and English. Both Proctor and Brandt based themselves on their own research. Brandt, for example, had almost completed his book when he postponed its completion for two years and accepted to become an expert witness for the trial.[208] Brandt's and Proctor's reports were aimed at rebutting the reports of Ludmerer, Wilson, and English, and this seems to be as far as the influence of the DOJ went with Brandt and Proctor.

14.4.4 Article 19: Protection of the Historical Profession

Finally, I argue that Ludmerer, Wilson, and English have violated article 19 of the code of ethics by De Baets. Article 19 lays down the following rule: "[h]istorians shall protect and promote the historical profession and its infrastructure of sources" and that "[t]hey shall also oppose internal threats to the integrity of the profession,

[205]De Baets, as n. 186, Appendix IV, article 14.

[206]See the discussion on Ludmerer's deposition: Part III, Sect. 14.2.4.1. Deposition, cfr. supra.

[207]See Part II, Sect. 7.3.4. The Collaboration with Lawyers, cfr. supra.

[208]Brandt, as n. 6, 498.

that is, the abuse and irresponsible use of history"[209] Through their deeds in court and their willingness to sell history to the tobacco companies, Ludmerer, English, and Wilson supported an image of historians as hired guns, willing to twist the historical facts in the service of the highest bidder. The historical discipline was fortunate to have two historians who were not as easily bought to testify in *US v. Philip Morris et al.* to defend its reputation.

14.4.5 Conclusion

After studying the statements made by Kenneth Ludmerer, Peter English, and Theodore Wilson in their depositions in *US v. Philip Morris et al.,* and after confronting their work in that case with the *Code of Ethics* proposed by De Baets, I conclude that these historians did not act as professional historians when they participated as expert witnesses in the case concerned. Moreover, it is not unreasonable to assume that they were not even advocates because of their ideals but had become "hired guns." In other words Ludmerer, English, and Wilson were in it for the money.[210] It is from examples like these that legal scholars make the argument to forbid the historical discipline to enter into the courtroom.[211] In the defence of the historical craft, I argue that the reports filed by Ludmerer, English, and Wilson were not examples of professional history.[212] However, despite these abuses of history, the adversarial system did work in *US v. Philip Morris et al.* The verdict of Judge Kessler contained a nuanced and reliable historical account, based on the reports of Brandt and Proctor. Historians had defended the history of tobacco and through it the victims of a mass conspiracy committed by the tobacco industry.

Bibliography

Brandt, Allan. 2007. *The cigarette century. The rise, fall and deadly persistence of a product that defined America*. New York: Basic Books.

Caudill, David. 2002. Scientific narratives in law: An introduction. *Law and Literature* 14: 253–274.

[209]De Baets, as n. 186, Appendix IV, article 19.

[210]Based on the qualitative study of their depositions, see Part III, Sect. 14.2. Experts Historians Take the Stand, cfr. supra. Furthermore, I conclude this as a consistent application of De Baets' *Code of Ethics*.

[211]For example, the conclusions of Alain Wijffels on expert witnessing, see Part II, Chap. 8: A Reassessment of Wijffels' Concept of Forensic History, cfr. supra.

[212]Based on the definition of abuse of history by De Baets: "[t]he abuse of history is its use with intent to deceive." In addition, I conclude this on the grounds of the previous ethical discussion of the research conducted by the expert witnesses of the defence.

Caudill, David. 2005. Sociotechnical' arguments in scientific discourse: Expert depositions in tobacco litigation. *The Review of Litigation* 24: 1–56.
Davis, Ronald, Clifford Douglas, and John Beasley. 2006. The tobacco deposition and trial testimony archive (DATTA) project: Origins, aims and methods. *Tobacco Control* 15: 4–8.
De Baets, Antoon. 2009. *Responsible history*. New York: Berghahn Books.
Douglas, Clifford, Davis Ronald, and John Beasley. 2006. Epidemiology of the third wave of tobacco litigation in the United States, 1994–2005. *Tobacco Control* 15: 9–16.
Guardino, Sara, and Richard Daynard. 2007. Tobacco industry lawyers as 'Disease vectors'. *Tobacco Control* 166: 224–228.
Hurt, Richard, Jon Ebbert, Monique Muggli, Nikki Lockhart, and Channing Robertson. 2012. Open doorway to truth: Legacy of the Minnesota tobacco trial. *Mayo Clinic Proceedings* 84: 446–456.
Parascandola, Mark. 2005. Science, industry, and tobacco harm reduction: A case study of tobacco industry scientists' involvement in the National Cancer Institute's smoking and health program, 1964–1980. *Public Health Chronicles* 120: 338–349.
Posner, Richard. 1995. *Overcoming law*. Cambridge: Harvard University Press.
Posner, Richard. 2009. *Law and literature*. Cambridge: Harvard University Press.
Proctor, Robert. 2000. Expert witnesses take the stand. *Nature* 407: 15–16.
Proctor, Robert. 2006. 'Everyone knew but no one had proof': Tobacco industry use of medical history expertise in US courts, 1990–2002. *Tobacco Control* 15: 117–125.
Proctor, Robert. 2008. On playing the Nazi card. *Tobacco Control* 17: 289–290.
Proctor, Robert. 2012. *Golden holocaust: Origins of the cigarette catastrophe and the case for abolition*. Berkeley: University of California Press.
Proctor, Robert. 2004. Tobacco and Health. *Journal of Philosophy, Science & Law* 4.
Proctor, Robert, and Londa Schiebinger. 2008. *Agnotology. The making & unmaking of ignorance*. Palo Alto: Stanford University Press.
Schneider, Nick, and Staton Glantz. 2008. "Nicotine Nazis strike again": A brief analysis of the use of Nazi rhetoric in attacking tobacco control advocacy. *Tobacco Control* 17: 291–296.
Wiener, Jon. 2010. Big tobacco and the historians. *The Nation*, February 15.

Chapter 15
Debates: Reflections in Academic and National Media

Attorney: Have you reviewed any other cigarette industry documents, internal documents, relative to this issue of health and cigarette smoking?
Otis Graham: I may have.

Otis Graham (Deposition in *State of Texas v. American Tobacco Company et al.* 1997.)

Abstract In this chapter, I discuss the debate that historians have had on the role historians as expert judicial witnesses have played in tobacco trials. I examine sources from academic journals such as *Nature, The Lancet, The History News Network,* and *The Chronicle of Higher Education,* while also adding those articles that originate in the regular media like *The Nation, The New York Times,* and *The American Prospect.* In addition, I examined who the protagonists of these debates were and what their arguments were. The debate revolves around already familiar problems of advocacy, objectivity, "hired guns", but also on an attempt by the tobacco industry to censure plaintiffs' experts Proctor and Kyriakoudes in 2009.

15.1 Proctor in *Nature*

In September 2000, Robert Proctor wrote an article in *Nature* entitled: *Expert Witnesses Take The Stand.* As an historian of science, Proctor reported that he had worked on three court cases as an expert witness.[1] Central in each case were two questions: (1) when was it reasonable to know that a product was hazardous, and (2) did the people who sold the product act responsibly, according to the scientific and ethical standards of that time? Proctor wrote that historians of science were especially suitable to demonstrate how "a theory or conviction moved from one community to another, filtered into public consciousness, and was accepted or rejected."[2] Proctor had done three cases of which the first one considered the suit filed by 2,800 women who were forcibly sterilized in Alberta, Canada from the

[1] See Expert Witness Profile No. 39, Robert Proctor.

[2] Proctor, Robert. 2000. Expert Witnesses Take the Stand. *Nature* 407, 15.

R. Delafontaine, *Historians as Expert Judicial Witnesses in Tobacco Litigation*, Studies in the History of Law and Justice 4, DOI 10.1007/978-3-319-14292-0_15

late 1920s until the early 1970s, due to the province's eugenics legislation. The second case Proctor reported was the Vanderbilt case, a class action in which 830 women sued for being fed radioactive iron in a nutrition experiment sponsored by the Rockefeller Foundation, the Atomic Energy Commission, and Vanderbilt University. The third case was *Ironworkers v. Philip Morris* which was tried in 1998. The trial was a class action suit brought on behalf of a pension fund of trade-union workers in Ohio who sought compensation for the costs of health-treatment of tobacco-related illness. Proctor's research delivered proof that although there had been a scientific consensus on the dangers of smoking since the 1950s, the tobacco industry had "maintained that cigarettes were safe", arguing that "further research" was needed, which resulted in "fostering public doubts" on the dangers of their product.[3] Proctor noted that "I was apparently the first historian ever to testify for the plaintiffs in a federal tobacco trial; the tobacco industry, by contrast, has often used historians in its defence, especially to show that knowledge of tobacco hazards was widespread in the 1950s and 1960s."[4]

Proctor acknowledged that he was paid $150 per hour, while he claimed that some of the defence experts were paid "ten times this rate."[5] He stated that such high rates could form a serious treat for the neutrality of the expert. Proctor also addressed the new Daubert standard, and posed the question "how does one determine a historian's rate of error?" According to him, the Daubert rule was unfit for historical evidence in court.[6] Yet, he wrote: "there may come a time when courts will have to decide what kinds of historical expertise are admissible." Proctor proposed to use peer review as a yardstick. History would play an increasingly important role in litigation, he argued, because of its ability to explain to the judge how scientific practices and the perceptions of acceptable risk change over time.[7] Most of Proctor's remarks in this early article would become important issues in the debates on historians in American courts.

15.2 Laura Maggi in *The American Prospect*

Laura Maggi of *The American Prospect* wrote an article in February 2001 titled *Bearing Witness for Tobacco.* She discussed a number of historians who testified for the tobacco companies. Maggi noted that these historians were not known to be experts for the tobacco industry. She noted historians like Stephen Ambrose and

---

[3] Proctor, as n. 2, 16.

[4] Proctor, as n. 2, 16.

[5] Proctor, as n. 2, 16.

[6] For other critical remarks on the Daubert standard see, Part II, Sect. 7.3.6.3. The Daubert Standard: Popper & the Judge as Gatekeeper, cfr. supra.

[7] Proctor, as n. 2, 16.

the "distinguished medical historian" Kenneth Ludmerer.[8] Maggi quoted Ambrose in a deposition from 1997 in the attorney-general trial brought by the state of Florida against the tobacco industry.[9] He was asked "why he was testifying for the defendants." Ambrose replied: "For compensation." The attorney followed up, "So the reason you have agreed to provide the services is for the money?" The answer? "Yes."[10] On Ludmerer, she noted that he had not published on the history of tobacco.[11] She further described the legal tactics of the tobacco industry, on which she noted the reaction of Allan Brandt: "[i]t is a very narrow view of what a sophisticated historian would call common knowledge."[12] Moreover, Maggi reported an article from 1998 written by researchers from the Gallup organization that criticized "the biased selection of polls by historians in tobacco trials, noting they consistently picked polls that give an inflated sense of the public's awareness of health risks from smoking."[13] The Gallup paper focused on testimony given for the tobacco industry by Lacy Ford, a professor of history specialized in the history of the American South. Gallop accused Ford of selecting polls that supported the industry's argument that the hazards of smoking were common knowledge, while leaving out those polls which had different results.[14]

Maggi stated that Ambrose refused to comment on his activities in service for tobacco companies. Ford made it clear in a phone interview that "he had made it a policy not to talk about the substance of his testimony."[15] In her conclusion, Maggi noted that "[t]he tobacco industry pays generously and gets its money's worth." In addition, she wrote that "[w]hat's disconcerting is that plenty of independent scholars, when paid enough money, are evidently willing to lend their names to an enterprise that is responsible for hundreds of thousands of smoking deaths annually, and to what would be dubious scholarship in any other context."[16]

This article is a good example of how questions on the tobacco experts rose only after the practice had been active for a couple of years. By the time of Maggi's article, Ambrose had served in three cases as an expert for the tobacco companies, Ford had been active in at least seven court cases, and Ludmerer in no less than twelve cases.[17] The secrecy with which these practices were conducted

---

[8]Maggi, Laura. 2001. Bearing Witness for Tobacco. *The American Prospect*, November 9. http://prospect.org/article/bearing-witness-tobacco. Accessed 31 Oct 2014, 1. See Expert Witness Profile No. 1, Stephen Ambrose. & See Expert Witness Profile No. 30, Kenneth Ludmerer.

[9]For my discussion on these trials see Part III, Sect. 13.2.1. The State Attorney Cases, cfr. supra.

[10]Maggi, as n. 8, 3.

[11]Maggi, as n. 8, 4.

[12]Maggi, as n. 8, 3.

[13]Maggi, as n. 8, 3.

[14]Maggi, as n. 8, 3. See Expert Witness Profile No. 16, Lacy Ford.

[15]Maggi, as n. 8, 3.

[16]Maggi, as n. 8, 5.

[17]See Expert Witness Profile No. 30, Kenneth Ludmerer.

left them unnoticed and unpublished. Moreover, I would argue that experts like Ford, Ludmerer, and Ambrose failed to let their research be reviewed by their peers, which is an essential part of the historical enterprise. We can only speculate whether *The New York Times* had read Maggi's article, when it stated in 2002 that Stephen Ambrose was "the most prolific, the most commercially successful and the most academically accomplished of a new group of blockbuster historians", referring to his work on the Second World War and his work as a producer on the award-winning television series *Band of Brothers.*[18] The fact that expert witnesses like Ambrose, Ludmerer, and Ford have not published on tobacco and on their litigation-related research and, furthermore, refuse to comment on their involvement seems self-explanatory for the pride they take in their research on tobacco.

15.3 Patricia Cohen in *The New York Times*

In 2003, *The New York Times* published an article titled *History for Hire in Industry Lawsuits.* The author, Patricia Cohen, wrote that it had become important to question the role of medical historians as expert witnesses in lawsuits. She quoted Proctor on the subject: "[t]he historical profession has really not been prepared for this" and "[w]e don't have disclosure rules for publications, we haven't had discussions about the ethics of whether to testify or not to testify."[19] She also quoted John Burnham, an historian who has served as a consultant for a multitude of companies, including tobacco, lead, soda, and asbestos industries, when he declared that "everyone has a financial interest." Furthermore, Burnham said that "[h]istorians can maintain their integrity no matter whose side they're on", adding that "[e]ven large corporations are entitled to justice." The article was fully documented with many quotes from Proctor on tobacco and Agnotology,[20] the news briefs from the AHA written by Martin and Neuenschwander, and referred to the work done by Rosner and Markowitz in lead cases.[21] Cohen summarizes the state of the debate on historians as expert witness at the time, without reaching conclusions of her own. The article of Cohen clearly demonstrated that by 2003, there was within and outside of the historical community a debate about whether historians should serve as expert witnesses, especially those involved with the tobacco industry.[22]

---

[18]Kirpatrick, David. 2002. As Historian's Fame Grows, So Do Questions on Methods. *The New York Times,* January 11. http://www.nytimes.com/2002/01/11/us/as-historian-s-fame-grows-so-do-questions-on-methods.html?pagewanted=all&src=pm. Accessed 31 Oct 2014.

[19]Cohen, Patricia. 2003. History for Hire In Industry Lawsuits. *The New York Times,* June 14. http://www.nytimes.com/2003/06/14/arts/history-for-hire-in-industry-lawsuits.html?pagewanted=all&src=pm. Accessed 31 Oct 2014.

[20]For more information on the study of Agnotology, see Part III, Sect. 13.4.3. Game III: The Third Wave of Tobacco Litigation, cfr. supra.

[21]For Rosner and Markowitz, see my discussion in Part II, Sect. 6.2.3. Toxic Tort Litigation: Lead Paint Toxic Tort Litigation, cfr. supra.

[22]Cohen, as n. 19.

15.4 David Rothman in the *Bulletin of the History of Medicine*

That same year, the *Bulletin of the History of Medicine* published an article by David Rothman, director of *the Center for the Study of Science and Medicine* at the Columbia College of Physicians and Surgeons, who himself had himself served as an expert witness in the Vanderbilt case, in which Proctor had also been an expert. Rothman gave a short historical introduction to the practice of expert witnessing by historians, mentioning among others *Brown v. Board of Education*, the Sears case, Native Peoples trials, and tobacco trials but also European examples like Eichmann, Papon, and Lippstadt.[23] Rothman examined the question whether the standards of the historical craft would be "inevitable compromised" when historians served as expert witnesses.[24] After discussing two cases of expert witnessing by historians and his own experiences, Rothman was relatively positive about historians taking the stand. Arguing that it was "far too simplistic" to interpret what happened in the courtroom as a practice where historians were "too committed to their side of the case to remain objective." Furthermore, Rothman also used the "tu quoque-argument", which we saw earlier with public historians, to argue that "[h]istorians are no less "objective" in the courtroom than they are in the lecture hall or in print."[25] Somewhat divergent from his own argumentation, Rothman stated that "[t]o enter the courtroom is do many things, but is not to do history."[26] Yet his final conclusion was that "[s]ome judges, and perhaps some colleagues as well, may prefer to think of expert witnesses as purely neutral and without personal commitment to the outcome. Such a stance, however, is not only unrealistic but also misguided. Advocacy has its place, and it can be promoted without compromising the craft."[27]

This last conclusion is more consistent with Rothman's reasoning when we take into account his previous argumentation that there were two reasons for historians to enter the courtroom. A first reason was that everyone deserves their day in court and needs to be defended in the best possible manner, and if need be also by historical facts presented by historians. The second reason, Rothman wrote, is that historians in the courtroom serve to aid justice.[28] Rothman was apparently unsure about his view on the practice of historians as expert witnesses, since he arrives at opposing conclusions. The following year, in a reaction to an article of Proctor in *The Lancet* that interpreted Rothman's article as an argument in favour of historians serving as experts in court, Rothman argued that his article should be interpreted otherwise. He declared that he had written that it was possible for expert witnesses to serve the trier of fact without compromising their professional integrity, but he insisted

---

[23]Rothman, David. 2003. Serving Clio and Client: The Historian as Expert Witness. *Bulletin of the History of Medicine* 77, 26–31.

[24]Rothman, as n. 23, 31.

[25]Rothman, as n. 23, 44. For the "tu quoque-argument", see Part I, Sect. 3.1.4. Descending the Ivory Tower, cfr. supra.

[26]Rothman, as n. 23, 44.

[27]Rothman, as n. 23, 44.

[28]Rothman, as n. 23, 44.

at length that "historians working for the defence or for the plaintiffs are not acting as true historians."[29] At the end of his reply, he repeated that, according to him, "[h]istorians working for the defence or for the plaintiffs are doing many things, but they are not acting as historians."[30] Of course, many articles that cite Rothman stick with the first conclusion as a catchy phrase to offer a conclusion.[31] I find Rothman's argument somewhat problematic. If historians are not practicing history in the courtroom, what are they doing then? If they can maintain their professional integrity, how can they at the same time not follow the standards of their craft, two elements which are, to me, inseparable from each other.

15.5 Proctor in *The Lancet*

In 2004, Proctor wrote an article, suggestively titled *Should Medical Historians Be Working for the Tobacco Industry*, which got significant response from the historical and medical community in the US. Proctor stated that: "[t]he industry is now hiring historians to assist in its defence, mainly by having its experts narrow their focus of attention to only those topics that show the industry in a favourable light."[32] He discussed the litigation-driven work done by Ludmerer, English, and Wilson, whose testimonies for the tobacco industry he knew from the case *US v. Philip Morris et al.*. Proctor added that Ludmerer, English, and Wilson did "not have a lot of peer reviewed expertise." Furthermore, he mentioned Elizabeth Cobbs Hoffman and Jon Harkness as experts for the tobacco industry, remarking that the latter had only published on the history of clinical medical ethics and the former on American foreign relations.[33] Quoting from Ludmerer's deposition in *US v. Philip Morris et al.*, Proctor had no problem to discredit Ludmerer's litigation-driven work.[34] He lists Allan Brandt, Louis Kyriakoudes, and himself as the only historians who testified against the tobacco companies.[35] For Proctor the question whether historians who are publishing tobacco-funded research can do this without disclosing the source of their funding presented itself consequently. As an answer

[29]Rothman, David. 2004. Medical Historians and the Tobacco Industry. *The Lancet* 364, 839.

[30]Rothman, as n. 28, 839.

[31]Cohen, as n. 19.

[32]Proctor, Robert. 2004. Should Medical Historians Be Working for the Tobacco Industry? *The Lancet* 363, 1174.

[33]See Expert Witness Profile No. 10, Elizabeth Cobbs Hoffman. & See Expert Witness Profile No. 20, Jon Harkness.

[34]See for example the quote "I did not draft the original report. It was drafted for me to save me time ... it reflects my views.", see Part III, Sect. 14.2.2.1. Deposition, cfr. supra.

[35]Proctor, as n. 32, 1175. See Expert Witness Profile No. 4, Allan Brandt. & See Expert Witness Profile No. 26, Louis Kyriakoudes & See Expert Witness Profile No. 39, Robert Proctor.

he referred to the *American Medical Association* who in 1996 adopted a "policy, urging scientific journals to reject for publication research funded by the tobacco industry."[36]

Proctor's attacks on expert witnesses on the payroll of tobacco provoked a reaction from John Burnham, a medical historian at Ohio State University, who had worked in two cases as an expert witness for the tobacco companies.[37] His response called Proctor's article "misleading." Furthermore, he wrote that Proctor "is making fundamental criticisms of the legal system" because he, according to Burnham, suggested that "a scholar could be manipulated in his or her opinion by counsel."[38] For me, Proctor did not make a fundamental critique of the legal system by stating that experts were influenced in their opinion by legal counsel. In his author's reply, Proctor elaborated on Burnham's critique and rephrased his previous statement to the following: that "the bias [of the experts of the tobacco companies] is largely in the form of the framing (or delimitation) of the kinds of questions defence experts are asked to investigate."[39] Proctor concludes his arguments with three statements, namely that (1) "[a]ccording to the WTO and other scholars, cigarettes now cause about 5 million annual premature deaths every year", that (2) the tobacco industry has succeeded in evading paying damages in litigation since the 1950s in all but two cases, and (3) that "[s]cholars who assist in the defence of the industry-e.g., by arguing that the industry's response to publicity of harms was 'both timely and appropriate'-would perhaps do well to ponder some of these numbers."[40] David Rothman's reaction on Proctor's article has already been discussed.[41] The following years the debate slumbered despite continued tobacco litigation and the increasing involvement of expert witnesses in those cases.

15.6 The Tobacco Companies v. Robert Proctor

By 2009, the Engle Progeny cases were starting to multiply and historians were involved on both sides of the court.[42] The defence had several historians in its service, whereas the plaintiffs were limited in their choice to only two historians: Robert Proctor and Louis Kyriakoudes. In 2009, Proctor was working on more than

[36]Proctor, as n. 32, 1175.

[37]See Expert Witness Profile No. 6, John Burnham.

[38]Burnham, John. 2004. Medical Historians and the Tobacco Industry. *The Lancet* 364, 838.

[39]Proctor, Robert. 2004. Medical Historians and the Tobacco Industry, Author's Reply. *The Lancet* 364, 838.

[40]Proctor, as n. 39, 838.

[41]See Part III, Sect. 15.4. David Rothman in the Bulletin of Historical Medicine, cfr. supra.

[42]See Part III, Sect. 13.3.1. Engle, cfr. supra.

ten Engle Progeny cases.[43] Proctor had proven himself not only a noted opponent of the tobacco industry in the courtroom but also a very vocal one in academic and public debate. The industry, annoyed by the raising number of Engle Progeny cases and Proctor's continued involvement, decided to attack Proctor personally.

In November 2009, the *Chronicle of Higher Education* reported: *Big Tobacco Strikes Back at Historian in Court.*[44] The issue revolved around the fact that Proctor was accused of influencing students who did research for the tobacco companies and furthermore of threatening them with publishing their names. Under the subtitle *Getting Burned for Putting the Heat on Tobacco*, Peter Schmidt details the chronology of the story. In April 2008, Gregg Michel, professor of history at the University of Texas, asked Matthew Gallman, professor of history at the University of Florida, to post notice on campus for graduate students to research on tobacco. In May, Michel, who served for the tobacco industry as an expert witness in multiple cases, recruited four students and identified them in a deposition.[45] The transcript was then given by lawyers of the plaintiffs to Kyriakoudes, who was an expert witness in the same case. Kyriakoudes then forwarded the deposition to Robert Proctor.[46]

A week later Proctor e-mailed Ms. Smocovitis, a professor of history at the University of Florida, on the subject that "graduate students in the history department have been working quite intensively for the tobacco industry." She was shocked and wanted more background explanation. Proctor wrote her that "[i]n my view this is historical practice, and I would be very interested to know if the advisers of these students know what they have been doing." Smocovitis talked to Gallman, and allegedly declared she feared that Proctor might publish the identities of the students. One of the graduate students e-mailed Michel, after a conversation with her department's chairman, relaying that she feared that their names would be published by Proctor. Proctor and Smocovitis continued to send e-mails, in which Proctor urged her to reveal on the next faculty meeting that students were secretly working for the tobacco industry. Proctor wrote her that "the majority of your faculty will do the right thing." Smocovitis did not raise the subject at the next faculty meeting.[47]

In July 2009, lawyers from "Liggett Group, Lorillard Tobacco Company, Philip Morris USA, and R.J. Reynolds Tobacco Company" deposed Proctor to interview him on his involvement with the Florida Students. His e-mail exchanges with Smocovitis and Kyriakoudes were subpoenaed. Kyriakoudes himself was also deposed. In September, Proctor was again deposed in order to gain information on more documents. Smocovitis was deposed in October. Afterwards Proctor was

---

[43]See Expert Witness Profile No. 26, Louis Kyriakoudes & See Expert Witness Profile No. 41, Robert Proctor.

[44]Schmidt, Peter. 2009. Big Tobacco Strikes Back at Historian in Court. *The Chronicle of Higher Education* 56, November 13.

[45]See Expert Witness Profile No. 34, Gregg Michel.

[46]Schmidt, as n. 44.

[47]Schmidt, as n. 44.

accused of witness tampering, in a motion filed by lawyers of R.J. Reynolds. The motion furthermore asked the court to exclude Proctor's testimony in a pending Engle Progeny case: *Koballa v. R.J. Reynolds*. Two weeks later, Proctor was again accused of witness tempering in a motion filed in another Engle Progeny case.[48]

Two days after Proctor had been accused for the second time of witness tampering, *History Network News* published the motion of the plaintiffs in *Koballa v. R.J. Reynolds* to prevent the exclusion of Proctor's testimony from the trial. Legal counsel at R.J. Reynolds had also subpoenaed the manuscript of his unpublished book, *Golden Holocaust.*[49] Proctor's manuscript was protected by academic privilege, journalist's privilege, and the right of privacy. If the court ruled that Proctor had to give up his manuscript, it would set a dangerous precedent, which would scare off many sincere expert witnesses, plaintiffs' counsel argued. As a conclusion, the plaintiff's lawyers wrote: "[p]laintiffs pray that the Court will issue an order protecting Dr. Proctor from being compelled to produce the Manuscript for Defendant."[50] Ann Arvin, dean of research at Stanford University, submitted in the name of Stanford University an *Amicus Curiae* brief in support of the plaintiff's motion for a protective order.[51] Proctor defended himself in an affidavit that urged the court not to give R.J. Reynolds an unfinished manuscript which nobody else had read, which could possibly damage his professional credibility and standing.[52] An article on the subject authored by Sam Kean was published in *Science* in November 2009. The article quoted industry-lawyer Grossman, who said: "[w]hen you become a paid expert witness, your notes, your correspondence with other people become available" and furthermore argued that "they're needed in order to conduct an effective cross-examination."[53] According to the author of the article, such requests "for unpublished scientific research is unusual but not unprecedented." An article dating back to February 2002 in *BMJ* reported that "nine major US universities are preparing to go to court to contest a demand by US tobacco manufacturers that they turn over documents going back 50 years relating to research on smoking by faculty members."[54] These attacks on Proctor's freedom of academic research are part of a

[48]Schmidt, as n. 44.

[49]Kaney, Jonathan. 2008. Plaintiffs' Motion for Reconsideration of Order Overruling Objections to Subpoena and for Protective Order Concerning Unpublished Manuscript. *George Mason University's History News Network*, October 12. http://hnn.us/articles/118209.html. Accessed 31 Oct 2014.

[50]Kaney, as n. 49.

[51]Arvin, A. 2009. Amicus Curiae Brief from Stanford University in Koballa v. R. J. Reynolds. *George Mason University's History News Network*, October 12. http://hnn.us/Pics2009/proctor/Stanford.html. Link has been removed.

[52]Proctor, Robert. 2008. Affidavit of Dr. Robert Proctor in Support of Plaintiffs' Motion for Protective Order. *George Mason University's History News Network*, October 12. http://hnn.us/articles/118210.html#comment. Accessed 31 Oct 2014.

[53]Kean, Sam. 2009. Court Orders Stanford Expert to Surrender Manuscript. *Science* 326, 780–781.

[54]Marwick, Charles. 2002. Academics Face Court Clash with Tobacco Giants. *British Medical Journal* 324, 257.

legal strategy by the tobacco industry and their legal counsel to discourage historians to serve as experts for the plaintiffs.

Eventually, the court ordered Proctor to hand over the e-mails on the students at the University of Florida. According to historian Jon Wiener, "nothing improper was found."[55] The subpoena for Proctor's manuscript was refused by the Florida court on the grounds that it "would violate his academic freedom, his privacy rights and his freedom of speech."[56] By the time Wiener's article was published in March 2010, Proctor had been accused of witness tampering and witness intimidation, he had furthermore been subpoenaed for his unfinished manuscript, and R.J. Reynolds had tried to bar him from further testifying in Engle Progeny cases. Proctor had spent sixteen hours under oath with twelve lawyers hired by the tobacco industry and had lost over $25,000 in legal costs.[57] According to Proctor, the tobacco companies had spent more than a million dollars on deposing him and subpoenaing his e-mails. Proctor brought the harassment by subpoena-incidents to the attention of Antoon De Baets, the chairman of *The Network of Concerned Historians*.[58] Jon Wiener concludes that historian Robert Proctor was the victim of a "campaign of harassment and intimidation."[59]

This strategy does not seem to be limited to Proctor. Kyriakoudes declared in Wiener's article that he had been deposed "at least seven or eight times" by tobacco's legal counsel.[60] Tobacco's legal strategy aimed at making witnessing for the plaintiffs an even more time-consuming activity, which involves risks for their own financial situation and research. Kyriakoudes told Wiener: "I've cut back a lot of what I've been doing" and goes on to state that "[t]hey hit me pretty hard, making it difficult to do my research. So I've pulled out of cases. I cut back to one or two trials a year. Harassment is effective."[61] Kyriakoudes has been active as a witness in twelve cases in 2009, six in 2010, five in 2011, two in 2012, and five in 2013.[62] Proctor has served in an increasing number of cases. In the period 2009–2013, Proctor has served in 62 cases, almost all involving Engle Progeny litigation.[63] So in hindsight, the industry's strategy against Proctor and Kyriakoudes had only minor consequences for them, or only strengthened their conviction.

---

[55]Wiener, Jon. 2010. Big Tobacco and the Historians. *The Nation*, February 15. http://www.thenation.com/article/big-tobacco-and-historians. Accessed 31 Oct 2014.

[56]Wiener, as n. 55.

[57]Wiener, as n. 55. & Arvin, as n. 51.

[58]*The Network of Concerned Historians* lists the motion by the tobacco companies to access the manuscript of Proctor's unpublished book see http://www.concernedhistorians.org/content/le.html. Accessed 31 Oct 2014.

[59]Wiener, as n. 55.

[60]Wiener, as n. 55.

[61]Wiener, as n. 55.

[62]See Expert Witness Profile No. 26, Louis Kyriakoudes.

[63]See Expert Witness Profile No. 39, Robert Proctor.

Jon Wiener's article raised questions about historians who worked as expert witnesses for the tobacco companies. Why were these expert paid so much? Why did they decline to be interviewed or refuse to openly address their involvement and with research for the tobacco companies? In addition, Wiener argued that the experts who were witnessing for the tobacco industry were part of the defence's very successful legal strategy. Individuals were already having trouble paying lawyers, let alone expert witnesses.[64] The division of the Engle class action into thousands of individual cases meant that tobacco industry could use its most favoured legal strategy which had served them well for over 50 years: "a scorched-earth litigation policy. They [the tobacco companies] would never give up. Never settle. If they ever lost a case, they would appeal. Forever. That's the way it still is. The message to the plaintiffs' bar is clear: don't screw with us, or you'll be sorry. We will break you financially."[65] Wiener had himself declined an invitation from historian and expert witness for the tobacco industry Michael Schaller to work as an expert witness.[66] Schaller had praised the work as a "lucrative consulting opportunity."[67]

Such all-out attacks on the tobacco industry and their experts could and would not go unanswered. The first historian to react was Matthew Gallman, who had been contacted by Gregg Michel to recruit graduate students to do research on tobacco documents. Gallman argued that the students were not hired in some scheme by the tobacco companies. According to Gallman, "[t]he students were only doing the most basic low-paid research and were not engaging in any sort of advocacy." Furthermore, he wrote that "Proctor was a bit of a zealot and [that] it was entirely unclear what he might do with the information."[68] Gallman testified that the chair of the department spoke to one of the students assuring that she worked "within university guidelines. The student contacted Michel, who called the lawyers." "They smelled a rat", Gallman wrote.[69] Gallman quoted an article from *The Gainesville Sun*, which wrote about the same case. The judge who tried the case against Proctor for harassing the students, concluded, according to the article, that the undertaking by Proctor "represents the lowest of the low in terms of a professor of such high standing. To advance your own cause at the expense of graduate students trying to get through college strikes this court as appalling."[70] Gallman

[64]I discussed tobacco's legal strategies in Part III, Sect. 13.4. Tobacco Tactics in Court: Legal Game Theory, cfr. supra.

[65]Wiener, as n. 55.

[66]See Expert Witness Profile No. 44, Michael Schaller.

[67]Wiener, as n. 55.

[68]Gallman, Matt. 2010. Re 'Big Tobacco and the Historians'. *The Nation*, March 9. http://www.thenation.com/article/re-big-tobacco-and-historians. Accessed 31 Oct 2014.

[69]Gallman, as n. 68.

[70]Crabbe, Nathan. 2009. UF Students Caught in Middle of Tobacco Case's Controversy. *The Gainsville Sun*, December 8. http://www.gainesville.com/article/20091208/ARTICLES/912081008?p=1&tc=pg. Accessed 31 Oct 2014. At my request Crabbe was not able to produce the verdict from which he quoted in his piece. Personal e-mail conversation is with the author.

found it "mysteriously" that Wiener "failed" to quote *the Gainesville Sun* article.[71] Jon Wiener's reply corrects Gallman on a couple of points and defines some parts of Gallman's letter as "gossip." According to Wiener, Proctor's intentions were "good." Wiener further noted that the tobacco industry continues to blame individual smokers, despite the fact that their own conspiracy has been proven in court. In his defence to the accusations formulated by Matthew Gallman, namely that Wiener did not provide a "balanced portrait" of the conflict, Jon Wiener pleaded "guilty."[72]

John Burnham, professor of history at Ohio State University and an expert witness for the tobacco industry in two cases, also wrote a reply on the article by Jon Wiener.[73] In Burnham's article, titled *In Defense of Historians as Expert Witnesses: A Rebuttal to Jon Wiener,* he accused Wiener of using one of the tactics of McCarthyism, namely to "name names."[74] He called it "damaging" tactics not only for reputations but also for careers. According to Burnham, "the seed of doubt has been sown", even if the named person defends himself afterwards. In addition, he called the basis of the article of Wiener a "tissue of assumptions." For Burnham, Wiener was writing not as a historian but as a journalist.[75] He also accused Wiener of making unreasonable demands when he argued that historians who are expert witnesses should stand up and defend themselves. Burnham explained that experts, himself amongst them, often do not have the permission to publish on their role in litigation. Burnham writes that "[t]he demand that those historians who have worked for one side or the other stand up and be counted is therefore not legally possible, and to condemn silence on this point is ridiculous."[76] I will return on this argument later in Chap. 16.[77]

Another reaction to Wiener's article came from Alan Blum, professor of Medicine at the University of Alabama and Director of *The University of Alabama Center for the Study of Tobacco and Society*. Blum is a known critic of the tobacco industry. He writes that he is "sceptical of Jon Wiener's hagiography of anti-Big Tobacco Stanford University historian Robert Proctor." Moreover, he writes that Wiener failed to produce figures on the money Proctor made himself. According to Blum, Proctor "admits to having pocketed" $480,000 himself. For Blum, "[t]here are few heroes in this issue, and Robert Proctor –profiting financially from his industry–bashing and at the same time impugning the motives of other historians

---

[71]Gallman, as n. 68.

[72]Wiener, Jon. 2010. Re 'Big Tobacco and the Historians', Wiener Replies. *The Nation*, March 9. http://www.thenation.com/article/re-big-tobacco-and-historians. Accessed Oct 31 2014.

[73]See Expert Witness Profile No. 6, John Burnham.

[74]Burnham, John. 2010. In Defense of Historians as expert Witnesses: A Rebuttal to Jon Wiener. *George Mason University's History News Network*, April 1. http://hnn.us/articles/124924.html. Accessed 31 Oct 2014.

[75]Burnham, as n. 74.

[76]Burnham, as n. 74.

[77]See Part III, Sect. 16.3.3. Transparency, cfr. infra.

who interpret things differently–is definitely not one of them, in spite of Jon Wiener's biased and incompletely researched efforts in his behalf."[78]

The last reaction came from tobacco industry lawyer Theodore Grossman. Grossman called Wiener's article "a journalistic lapse." Grossman also finds it "stupefying" that Wiener had not consulted the court's opinion on Proctor's conduct concerning the four graduate students. Grossman claimed that "Proctor had engaged in an unsuccessful cover-up", when he tried to delete the concerned e-mails from his computer. On Kyriakoudes, Grossman noted that he withdrew from a case when "an e-mail was discovered advising Proctor to change and falsify testimony."[79] Wiener's final reply identified Grossman as one of the industry's top lawyers who had won several high profile cases. He acknowledged that judge Parsons called Proctor's actions "the lowest of the low", but he further quotes the same Judge Parsons, declaring that "the court has never had the opportunity to meet Dr. Proctor" and "there was no evidentiary hearing in which Proctor could have appeared or offered a defence." Furthermore, Wiener noted that Judge Parsons refused to bar Proctor from testifying, despite his actions, implying that if the charges had been proven, Proctor would have been barred. Proctor and Smocovitis continue to deny that Proctor intended to publish the identities of the graduate students.[80]

15.7 Polemic Debates

A common feature of the entire debate is the swiftness by which the discussions fall into the trap of *ad hominem* argumentation and personal quarrels. That personal gain, market value as an expert witness, and professional standing are at risk, explain the polemic nature of these discussions. Even the issue involving the legal harassment of Proctor and Kyriakoudes was not discussed at length in professional or public media. I argue that the problem is again transparency. Proctor and Kyriakoudes are active voices in the debate, reachable for comments and explanation, in contrast to almost all the witnesses employed by the tobacco companies. John Burnham, an expert for the defence, has also been willing to discuss this topic. More than 95 % of the protagonists on the issue are absent from the debate. By doing so, they succeed in creating the idea that expert witnessing in tobacco litigation is only an insignificant practice and concerns only a very small number of historians. Moreover, the outcries from Proctor and other historians on

[78] Blum, Alan. 2010. A Dissenting view of Robert Proctor by a fellow Anti-Smoking Advocate. *George Mason University's History News Network*, April 25. http://hnn.us/node/125505. Accessed 31 Oct 2014.

[79] Grossman, Theodore. 2010. "Smoking Gun ..." *The Nation*, April 19. http://www.thenation.com/article/letters-337. Accessed 31 Oct 2014.

[80] Wiener, Jon. 2010. Smoking Gun ... Wiener Replies. *The Nation*, April 19. http://www.thenation.com/article/letters-337. Accessed 31 Oct 2014.

the abuse of history in the legal strategies of the tobacco industry are drowned by accusations which are thrown back and forth between discussants. I am amazed how limited the debate is, confined to a selected few insiders, who have to quote almost all their sources from personal conversations and e-mails, because all but one of the defence's experts is willing to publish or comment on the subject. It is very probable, that the tobacco industry has no objections to the current state of the academic and public debate on the involvement of historians as expert witnesses for the tobacco industry. If historians were to hold a debate on a more theoretical level, historians could have very important and meaningful discussions on the practice of litigation-driven history without getting dragged into settling personal scores.

The lack of debate in recent years is also notable despite the overall increased involvement of historians in Engle Progeny cases. In 2012, historians David Hollinger, professor of history at Berkeley and former president of the Organization of American Historians, and Paul Sutter, professor of history at the university of Colorado tried to bring experts together to have a session at the American Historical Association's annual meeting of January 2013 devoted to expert witnessing in tobacco litigation. The session would discuss Proctor's book *Golden Holocaust* but also other aspects of tobacco litigation. The chairs aimed to bring experts together from both litigating parties. Hollinger declared that: "Paul [Sutter] made contact with several, and I with several others, sometimes by e-mail, sometimes by phone, during the early months of 2012. All of the people we asked either did not respond at all, or declined to be part of the session. The ones who responded but declined included James Kirby Martin, Jeff Norrell, Michael Schaller, Lisa Cobbs Hoffman, Otis Graham, and Kenneth Ludmerer. Some just said no politely and left it at that. Several others said no, and added negative comments about Proctor, saying that they had no respect for him, and did not want to give his work professional respectability by engaging it. I have no record of any response from Lacy Ford and Michael Parrish, but I know they were among the people we wrote to."[81] Sutter contributed that he "approached a handful of historians who had testified on the industry side, as I really wanted it to be a meaningful debate on the issue, but none of them would agree to join the session. Some simply begged off politely while others felt as if such a session would only devolve into a condemnation of their activities. Some expressed discomfort with Proctor's book being a focus, since he had been such an outspoken and strident critic of historians who had worked on the industry's side."[82]

Eventually the session was reoriented to a session on a variety of issues of scientific controversy. All the experts who worked for the defence had refused to enter public debate. At the 2014 annual meeting of the Organization of American Historians, there was one session devoted to litigation-driven history: "State of the Field: Disease in the Courtroom." Again, only the plaintiff's bar was represented. Kyriakoudes and historian David Rosner, who had been an expert in lead-paint cases, were panel members. To conclude this chapter on the debate of expert

[81]From personal correspondence with David Hollinger.

[82]From personal correspondence with Paul Sutter.

witnesses in tobacco litigation: there are two experts who are keeping that debate alive and they both testify for the plaintiff's side. I have to add that John Burnham, as an expert for the defence, has been very open on his involvement and has also contributed to the debate, albeit not in way as Kyriakoudes and Proctor have.

Bibliography

Blum, Alan. 2010. A dissenting view of Robert Proctor by a fellow anti-smoking advocate. *George Mason University History New Network*, April 25.

Burnham, John. 2004. Medical historians and the tobacco industry. *The Lancet* 364: 838.

Burnham, John. 2010. In Defense of historians as expert witnesses: A rebuttal to Jon Wiener. *George Mason University's History News Network*, April 1.

Charles, Marwick. 2002. Academics face court clash with tobacco giants. *British Medical Journal* 324: 257.

Cohen, Patricia. 2003. History for Hire in industry lawsuits. *The New York Times*, June 14.

Crabbe, Nathan. 2009. UF students caught in middle of tobacco case's controversy. *The Gainsville Sun*, December 8.

Grossman, Theodore. 2010. Smoking gun ... *George Mason University's History News Network*, April 19.

Kaney, Jonathan. 2008. Plaintiffs' motion for reconsideration of order overruling objections to subpoena and for protective order concerning unpublished manuscript. *George Mason University's History News Network*, October 12.

Kean, Sam. 2009. Court orders Stanford expert to surrender manuscript. *Science* 326: 780–781.

Kirpatrick, David. 2002. As historian's fame grows, so do questions on methods. *The New York Times*, January 11.

Maggi, Laura. 2001. Bearing witness for tobacco. *The American Prospect*, November 9.

Proctor, Robert. 2000. Expert witnesses take the stand. *Nature* 407: 15–16.

Proctor, Robert. 2004a. Medical historians and the tobacco industry, author's reply. *The Lancet* 364: 838.

Proctor, Robert. 2004b. Should medical historians be working for the tobacco industry? *The Lancet* 363: 1174–1175.

Proctor, Robert. 2008. Affidavit of Dr. Robert Proctor in support of Plaintiffs' motion for protective order. *George Mason University History New Network*, October 12.

Rothman, David. 2003. Serving Clio and client: The historian as expert witness. *Bulletin of the History of Medicine* 77: 25–44.

Rothman, David. 2004. Medical historians and the tobacco industry. *The Lancet* 364: 839.

Schmidt, Peter. 2009. Big tobacco strikes back at historian in court. *The Chronicle of Higher Education*, November 13.

Wiener, Jon. 2010a. Big tobacco and the historians. *The Nation*, February 15.

Wiener, Jon. 2010d. Re 'Big tobacco and the historians'. *The Nation*, March 9.

Wiener, Jon. 2010c. Smoking gun ... Wiener replies. *The Nation*, April 19.

Chapter 16
Historians in Tobacco Litigation, a Conclusion

Science sans conscience n'est que ruine de l'âme.
Science without conscience is but the ruin of the soul.

François Rabelais

Abstract This chapter offers a conclusion on the role historians have played in tobacco litigation in the US. It discusses the current tobacco epidemic based on material from the WHO. The chapter further examines the strength of litigation to force the tobacco industry to change its habits. I also discuss the role of historians as an expert judicial witnesses in tobacco litigation as a controversial legal practice in general and on three specific points: advocacy, ethics, and transparency. For this chapter, I drew from my qualitative as well as quantitative analyses on the involvement of historians as expert judicial witnesses in tobacco litigation.

16.1 The Framework Convention on Tobacco Control

When Dr. Gro Harlem Brundtland became director of the World Health Organization (WHO) in 1998, she stated that "the tobacco epidemic should be tackled by an international collective and that the WHO should take a leadership role."[1] The tobacco epidemic caused death and destruction not only in the form of cancer and disease, but also through fire accidents from burning cigarettes and massive agricultural deforestation.[2] In addition, more and more harmful additives were discovered in cigarettes. An opinion from Proctor published in *The New York Times*, narrated how smokers were "puffing on polonium", and hundreds of other toxic chemicals.[3]

---

[1]Shibuya, Kenji, Ciecierski, Christina, Guidon Emmanuel, Bettcher, Douglas, Evans, David, and Murray, Christopher. 2011. WHO Framework Convention on Tobacco Control: Development of an Evidence Based Global Public Health Treaty. *British Medical Journal* 327, 154.

[2]Proctor, Robert. 2004. The Global Smoking Epidemic: A History and Status Report. *Clinical Lung Cancer* 5, 371.

[3]Proctor, Robert. 2006. Puffing on Polonium. *The New York Times,* December 1. http://www.nytimes.com/2006/12/01/opinion/01proctor.html?_r=0. Accessed 31 Oct 2014.

R. Delafontaine, *Historians as Expert Judicial Witnesses in Tobacco Litigation*,
Studies in the History of Law and Justice 4, DOI 10.1007/978-3-319-14292-0_16

Yet smokers, and non-smokers for that matter, remain remarkably unaware of the dangers of cigarette smoking. In a study from 2011 published in *Tobacco Control,* researchers probed 239 adult smokers on their knowledge about smoking. They concluded that: "As a whole, the study sample showed important deficits in knowledge and beliefs about smoking.[4] For example, nearly half of the study population (48 %) either agreed or strongly agreed with the statement "nicotine is only a minor factor whether a person can stop smoking."[5] This deficient knowledge about smoking is yet another example of the industry's capacity to determine the public image of its product. Under the subtitle *A question of Priorities*, two American anti-tobacco advocates wrote in 2009 that: "[t]oday 50 Americans will be murdered; 89 will take their own lives; 40 will succumb to HIV/AIDS; and 112 will die from motor vehicle injuries. This sums to 291 deaths, compared to the 1,200 people who will die as a result of their smoking."[6]

"Almost 6,000,000,000,000 cigarettes are smoked every year", according to Proctor, which is "enough to make a continuous chain from the earth to the sun and back, with enough left over for a couple of round trips to Mars."[7] The cost in human terms of smoking those cigarettes can be presented in a couple of disturbing numbers which the WHO publishes in their fact-sheet on tobacco:

> 1) Tobacco kills up to half of its users.
> 2) Tobacco kills nearly 6 million people each year. More than five million of those deaths are the result of direct tobacco use while more than 600 000 are the result of non-smokers being exposed to second-hand smoke. Unless urgent action is taken, the annual death toll could rise to more than eight million by 2030.
> 3) Nearly 80 % of the world's one billion smokers live in low- and middle-income countries. Consumption of tobacco products is increasing globally, though it is decreasing in some high-income and upper middle-income countries.
> 4) Tobacco caused 100 million deaths in the 20th century. If current trends continue, it may cause one billion deaths in the 21st century.[8]

The WHO has not sat idly by, but has issued the first-ever global health treaty: *The Framework Convention on Tobacco Control* (FCTC), which has now been

---

[4]Smith, Philip, Bansal-Travers, Maansi, O'Connor, Richard, Brown, Anthony, Banthin, Chris, Guardino-Colket, Sara, and Cummings, Michael. 2011. Correcting Over 50 Years of Tobacco Industry Misinformation. *The American Journal of Preventive Medicine* 40, 691, 694–696.

[5]Smith, Philip, Bansal-Travers, Maansi, O'Connor, Richard, Brown, Anthony, Banthin, Chris, Guardino-Colket, Sara, and Cummings, Michael, as n. 4, 694.

[6]Brownell, Kelly, and Warner, Kenneth. 2009. The Perils of Ignoring History: Big Tobacco Played Dirty and Millions Died. How Similar is Big Food? *The Milbank Quarterly* 87, 284. Dr. Brundtland has lent her name to the famous Brundtland commission on climate change and sustainable development.

[7]Proctor, Robert. 2012. *Golden Holocaust: Origins of the Cigarette Catastrophe and the Case for Abolition.* Berkeley: University of California Press.

[8]The WHO fact-sheet on tobacco can be found at http://www.who.int/mediacentre/factsheets/fs339/en/index.html. Accessed 31 Oct 2014. For more statistics on the mortal consequences of smoking see http://www.tobaccoatlas.org/topic/smokings-death-toll/. Accessed 31 Oct 2014.

signed and ratified by 168 countries worldwide.[9] These countries committed to higher cigarette prices, abolition of most tobacco advertising, and global cooperation in combatting cigarette smuggling.[10] The drafting and acceptance of the convention happened under strong opposition of the US delegation to the WHO, and even today the United States Congress has yet to ratify the FCTC.[11] Health advocates described the FCTC as "a landmark step towards global cooperative actions against health threats."[12] Despite all the efforts by the WHO and anti-tobacco advocates, "[t]obacco continues to aggressively promote their deadly product."[13] Proctor writes that "[t]he value of a life to a cigarette maker is about $10,000."[14] According to the *World Lung Foundation* that number is only $6,000.[15] Whatever the number, the tobacco industry continues to sell its dangerous products. For Proctor "[t]he cigarette is the deadliest artefact in the history of human civilization."[16]

16.2 Litigation as a Solution

Health advocates have increasingly argued in favour of tobacco litigation as a means to counter the tobacco industry. For Alderman and Daynard, two anti-tobacco advocates, litigation is an important tool in public health policy.[17] Daynard lists seven positive results of tobacco litigation[18]: (1) millions of internal documents

---

[9]Malone, Ruth, and Warner, Kenneth. 2012. Tobacco Control at Twenty: Reflecting on the Past, Considering the Present and Developing the New Conversations for the Future. *Tobacco Control* 21, 74. For the number of countries who have ratified the FCTC see https://treaties.un.org/pages/ViewDetails.aspx?src=TREATY&mtdsg_no=IX-4&chapter=9&lang=en. Accessed on 31 Oct 2014. For the FCTC itself see http://www.who.int/fctc/text_download/en/. Accessed 31 Oct 2014.

[10]Brownell, Kelly, and Warner, Kenneth, as n. 6, 275.

[11]See https://treaties.un.org/pages/ViewDetails.aspx?src=TREATY&mtdsg_no=IX-4&chapter=9&lang=en. Accessed on 31 Oct 2014.

[12]Shibuya, Kenji, Ciecierski, Christina, Guidon Emmanuel, Bettcher, Douglas, Evans, David, and Murray, Christopher, as n. 1, 157.

[13]Malone, Ruth, and Warner, Kenneth, as n. 9,74.

[14]Proctor, Robert. 2011. The History of the Discovery of the Cigarette-Lung Cancer Link: Evidentiary Traditions, Corporate Denial, Global Toll. *Tobacco Control*, 21, 87. & Proctor, as. 7, 9.

[15]See *the Tobacco Atlas* informational video clip at this website created by *the World Lung Foundation*, http://www.tobaccoatlas.org. Accessed 31 Oct 2014.

[16]Proctor, as n. 14, 89.

[17]Alderman, Jess, and Daynard, Richard. 2006. Applying Lessons from Tobacco Litigation to Obesity Lawsuits. *The American Journal of Preventive Medicine* 30, 83.

[18]Daynard, Richard. 2003. Why Tobacco Litigation? *Tobacco Control* 12, 1.

were obtained,[19] (2) research publications of those internal documents diminished the legitimacy of the tobacco industry,[20] (3) the tobacco companies were forced to admit smoking is bad for health on their websites,[21] (4) victims of tobacco-related diseases received damages,[22] (5) tobacco control programs were instituted,[23] (6) an example for other tort litigation concerning guns, lead paint, and fast foods,[24] (7) augmented public interest.[25] The WHO also recognized the value of tobacco litigation when it rewarded the Minnesota trial team with the *WHO's Tobacco Free World Award.*[26]

Daynard offers an interesting sixth argument: that consumers of other defect products can be inspired by tobacco litigation to sue the companies responsible for their illness.[27] Alderman came to similar conclusions: just as the plaintiff's lawyers in tobacco litigation had matured their strategies in asbestos litigation; tobacco cases may inspire other categories of lawsuits to protect public health.[28] Those categories were, inter alia, obesity lawsuits and alcohol-related litigation.[29] Big food was, according to Brownell and Warner, two public health researchers, "an organized and politically powerful industry", similar to the tobacco industry.[30] According to Brownell and Warner, ignoring tobacco's history was a serious peril for other public health policies.[31]

An additional and eighth argument in favour of tobacco litigation in the US is the example it sets for other countries.[32] According to Finnish political scientist Heikki Hiilamo, tobacco litigation is under way in Argentina, Australia, Brazil, Columbia,

---

[19]See Part III, Sect. 13.1. The First Wave: Cipollone v. Liggett Group, cfr. supra. & Part III, Sect. 13.2.2. The Master Settlement Agreement. & Part III, Sect. 4.4.3. Game III: The Third Wave of Tobacco Litigation, cfr. supra.

[20]See Part III, Sect. 13.2. The Second Wave: Government v. The Tobacco Industry, cfr. supra.

[21]See Part III, Sect. 14.3. The Final Judgment by Judge Kessler, cfr. supra.

[22]See Part III, Sect. 13.3.1. Engle, cfr. supra.

[23]See Part III, Sect. 13.2.2. The Master Settlement Agreement, cfr. supra.

[24]Cfr. infra in this topic.

[25]See Part III, Sect. 13.1. The First Wave: Cipollone v. Liggett Group. & Part III, Sect. 13.2. The Second Wave: Government v. The Tobacco Industry, cfr. supra.

[26]See Part III, Sect. 13.2.2. The Master Settlement Agreement, cfr. supra.

[27]Daynard, Richard, as n. 18, 1.

[28]Alderman, Jess, and Daynard, Richard, as n. 17, 85.

[29]Alderman, Jess, and Daynard, Richard, as n. 17, 82–88. & Mosher, James. 2009. Litigation and Alcohol Policy: Lessons from the US Tobacco Wars. *Addiction* 104, 27–33.

[30]Brownell, Kelly, and Warner, Kenneth, as n. 6, 263. For more on the structure of the tobacco industry see Part III, Sect. 10.2.4. The Oligopolistic Structure of the Tobacco Industry, cfr. supra.

[31]Brownell, Kelly, and Warner, Kenneth, as n. 6, 286.

[32]Hiilamo, Heikki. 2007. The Impact of Strategic Funding by the Tobacco Industry of Medical Expert Witnesses Appearing for the Defense in the Aho Finnish Product Liability Case. *Addiction* 102, 979–988.

Finland, India, Israel, Japan, The United Kingdom, Turkey, and Uganda.[33] Heikki's article describes how the tobacco industry is starting to recruit medical expert witnesses in Europe for tobacco litigation, demonstrating in detail how European researchers are getting research funding in exchange for their testimony.[34] Legal counsel of the defence used similar legal strategies as in US litigation.[35]

In an article from 2006, Vernick and other anti-tobacco advocates argued that litigation results from Engle and *US v. Philip Morris et al.* represented "a substantial future threat to the industry and a corresponding potential benefit for the public's health."[36] As we have discussed, the third wave of tobacco litigation in the US holds great opportunity's to put the tobacco industry under pressure in court, although the tobacco companies are doing everything in their power to diminish the legal possibilities for doing so. *The Class Action Fairness Bill of 2005*, which makes class action suits harder for plaintiffs to litigate, is a clear example of the industry's influence in Washington.[37] The tobacco industry is pushing hard for legal reforms because litigation in Engle-related cases is hurting them. With 164 of 8,000 cases tried, tobacco companies have paid over 200 million dollars in damages in Engle Progeny cases.[38] The tobacco industry shows remarkable resilience from these payouts. Tobacco companies are budgeting the cost of litigation in order to reassure stockholders that tobacco litigation is kept under control.[39] In their annual report, Altria Group Inc., the company that controls Philip Morris, stated that "[f]or the years ended [sic] December 31, 2012, 2011 and 2010, product liability defence costs for PM USA [Philip Morris], were $228 million, $272 million and $259 million, respectively."[40] In contrast, Altria made $1,27 billion in the second quarter of 2013, and is thus projecting a profit totalling $5 billion for the fiscal year 2013.[41] Although

[33]Miura, Marlo, Daynard, Richard, and Samet, Jonathan. 2006. The Role of Litigation in Tobacco Control. *Salud Pública de México* 48, 131–135.

[34]Hiilamo, Heikki, as n. 32, 981–985.

[35]Hiilamo, Heikki, as n. 32, 981 & 983.

[36]Rutkow, Lainie, Vernick, Jon, and Teret, Stephen. 2007. Public Health Benefits of Recent Litigation Against Tobacco Industry. *Journal of the American Medical Association* 298, 87.

[37]See the remark of Democratic US Senator Harry Reid on the Class Action Fairness Bill, Part III, Sect. 13.3.2. Smaller Cases, cfr. supra.

[38]For more on the damages awarded in Engle Progeny cases, see Part III, Sect. 13.3.1. Engle, cfr. supra.

[39]This strategy is discussed in Part III, Sect. 13.3.2. Smaller Cases, cfr. supra. See also the article by Sloan et al.: Sloan, Frank, Trogdon, Justine, and Mathews, Carrie. 2005. Litigation and the Value of Tobacco companies. *Journal of Health Economics* 24, 427–447.

[40]Altria Annual Report, Fiscal Year 2012, 31. http://investor.altria.com/phoenix.zhtml?src=leftnav&c=80855&p=irol-financialreview. Accessed 31 Oct 2014.

[41]For a discussion on the financial results of Altria of the second quarter of 2013 see s.n. 2013. Altria Improves Forecast for Year as Profit Rises 3 %. *The New York Times,* July 27. http://www.nytimes.com/2013/07/24/business/altria-posts-3-increase-in-profit-and-improves-forecast.html. Accessed 31 Oct 2014. For the Press Release of Altria, see http://investor.altria.com/phoenix.zhtml?c=80855&p=irol-newsArticle&ID=1839894&highlight. Accessed 31 Oct 2014.

litigation costs are higher than a decade ago, they are far from bankrupting the industry, as had happened with the asbestos industry.[42] In their report on the second fiscal quarter that ended in June 2013, Altria announced that: "Altria Group, Inc. and its subsidiaries have achieved substantial success in managing litigation."[43] The tobacco industry is a capitalistic enterprise which will continue to sell its harmful product as long as regulation does not force it to change its product. In other words, and as Judge Posner described it in his article on negligence from 1972: "When the cost of accidents is less than the cost of prevention, a rational profit-maximizing enterprise will pay tort judgments to the accident victims rather than incur the larger cost of avoiding liability."[44]

16.3 The Role of Historians in Tobacco Litigation

British historian Virginia Berridge gave a lecture in 2000 at the London School of Hygiene and Tropical Medicine entitled *History in Public Health: Who Needs It?*. She argued that: "[h]istory can offer insight into public-health policy (....) to open up issues and to ask broad questions that no-one else does."[45] Berridge, who herself has published on the history of tobacco, offered such an insight when she argued that there were "clear parallels between the story of opium at the end of the nineteenth century, its growing cultural and legal isolation, and that of tobacco and smoking at the end of the twentieth century, which seems to be going through a similar process."[46] Furthermore, she stated that when confronted with presentism and interdisciplinary work, historians were encouraged to question their own methodologies. Although, according to Berridge, presentism "sends a shiver down many historians' spines", the interdisciplinary work between the discipline of history and the public health movement offered "analytical tools, both sides need and could benefit from."[47] Erich Haberer had similarly argued in favour of the interdisciplinary cooperation between lawyers and historians as established in the Ludwigsburg paradigm.[48] In tobacco litigation, historians, lawyers, and the

---

[42]See Part III, Sect. 13.2.1. The State Attorney Cases, cfr. supra.

[43]Quarterly Report of the Fiscal Period that ended June 30, 2013, 22. http://www.altria.com/Documents/Altria_10Q_Filed07242013.pdf. Accessed 31 Oct 2014.

[44]Posner, Richard. 1972. A Theory of Negligence. *Journal of Legal Studies* 1, 33. For my discussion on negligence in tobacco litigation see, Part III, Sect. 13.1. The First Wave: Cipollone v. Liggett Group, cfr. supra.

[45]Berridge, Virginia. 2012. History in Public Health: Who Needs It? *The Lancet* 356, 1923.

[46]Berridge, Virginia, as n. 45, 1923.

[47]Berridge, Virginia, as n. 45, 1923.

[48]See Part II, Sect. 6.1.2. The Frankfurt-Auschwitz Trials and the Ludwigsburg Paradigm, cfr. supra. & Part II, Sect. 6.1.4. Conclusions on the Post-War Judgment of History in Court, cfr. supra.

health community have successfully worked together to come to a very reliable and outstanding historical account of the history of the cigarette and its industry.

Since 1986, 50 historians have testified in tobacco litigation. They have presented the history of the tobacco industry and their product, as expert witnesses in court. A summarized version of their testimony was presented in the first chapters of this third part of the book. Chapter 10 discussed the rise of the cigarette by means of seven developments which explain the rise of the cigarette; namely, flue curing, matches, mechanization of production, the oligopolistic structure of the tobacco industry, World War I, taxation, and mass-marketing. Thereafter, in Chap. 11, I analysed the discovery by the scientific community of the health hazards related to smoking. While studies that showed that smoking was dangerous had been met with scepticism by scientists in the 1930s and 1940s, the causal connection between disease and smoking had become accepted by the scientific community in early the 1950s. When the Surgeon General Report of 1964 was presented, the scientific community was not the target that needed convincing, the general public was.[49] The public needed convincing because tobacco companies had continued to maintain that its product was not unhealthy, through public messages as for example *The Frank Statement* from 1954. As we have seen in chapters 11 and 12, the industry reacted fast and decisively to save its product. The tobacco industry developed three compatible strategies: (1) they hired scientists to create a scientific controversy on the health risks of smoking[50]; (2) the tobacco companies evaded regulation through effective lobbying[51]; (3) the tobacco industry continued to aggressively promote their product as desirable and hazardless through mass-marketing.[52]

This historical overview was based on historical research of advertising materials, like ads in newspapers, ads in magazines, television ads, product placement in movies, and much more. Intriguingly, while the most important resource for expert witnesses on the history of the cigarette and its industry should have been the internal tobacco documents, in *US v. Philip Morris et al.*, only the historians on the plaintiff's side had researched them.[53] Furthermore, only five historians of the

[49]Tobbaco's most important litigation tactic of the first two waves was to equate "scientific" and "common knowledge" on the tobacco subject. See Part III, Sect. 13.4.1. Game I: The First Wave of Tobacco Litigation. & Part III, Sect. 13.4.2. Game II: The Second Wave of Tobacco Litigation, cfr. supra.

[50]The creation of the TIRC and the demands for more definitive proof and more research were all part of this strategy. See Part III, Sect. 12.1. The Tobacco Controversy: A Careful Construction, cfr. supra.

[51]Especially the Tobacco Institute had prevented oversight from the FDA or effective regulation on a Federal level. See Part III, Sect. 11.2. The Reports of the Surgeon General, cfr. infra.

[52]The meeting of Hill & Knowlton and the CEO's in December 1953 in the Plaza Hotel in New York laid the basis for an marketing strategy that succeeded in the following decades to define and control the popular image of the cigarette as an attractive product. Advertising through all possible media especially targeted young "replacement smokers." See Part III, Sect. 12.1. The Tobacco Controversy: A Careful Construction, cfr. supra.

[53]See Part III, Sect. 14.4.3. Article 13: Critical and Objective Method; Independence, cfr. supra.

50 experts are publishing or have published or researched and are researching on the history of smoking and the tobacco industry.[54] This and other damaging facts were uncovered during the depositions of Ludmerer, English, and Wilson.[55] Historians have served the tobacco companies in their three-part legal strategy: (1) by arguing that there was a scientific controversy on the health hazards of tobacco, (2) by claiming that consumers were well aware of the dangers of smoking and made an informed choice, (3) by augmenting the cost of litigation in the tradition of tobacco's scorched-earth tactic.[56] Hereafter, I analyse three related issues for historians in tobacco litigation, namely, advocacy, ethics, and transparency. Although these problems are intertwined I will, for the sake of argument, treat them separately.

16.3.1 Advocacy

Public history and especially expert witnesses have been accused on multiple occasions of advocacy, the argument being that historians will sell themselves and history as hired guns.[57] In the case of tobacco litigation the argument of advocacy is a plausibility. We have discussed multiple examples of historians who have made tens of thousands and even hundreds of thousands of dollars as expert witnesses, working for the plaintiff or for the defence.[58]

As mentioned before, Proctor has made over $1,500,000 as an expert witness.[59] In his article in *Nature* from 2000, he had declared that he made $150 an hour.[60] Michael Schaller from the University of Arizona has made over $1,500,000.[61] Robert Norrell from the University of Tennessee has received over $1,000,000 in compensation.[62] Peter English stated in his deposition in *US v. Philip Morris et al.*, that he charged $350 an hour. English also declared in that same deposition that he had made "approximately" $400,000–500,000 as an expert witness for the

[54]See Appendix II, Table 5. Published on the History of Smoking and the Tobacco Industry, cfr. infra.

[55]See Part III, Sect. 14.2. Experts Historians Take the Stand, cfr. supra.

[56]See Part III, Chap. 12: The Tobacco Industry and its Tactics, cfr. supra.

[57]See Part I, Sect. 3.1.4. Descending the Ivory Tower, cfr. supra & Part II, Sect. 7.4. Preliminary Conclusions on the Historian as an Expert Witness in American Courts & Part III, Chap. 15: Debates: Reflections in Academic and National Media, cfr. supra.

[58]For an overview of the remunerations historians as expert witnesses get see Appendix II, Table 6. Remuneration, cfr. infra.

[59]From personal correspondence with the author.

[60]Proctor, Robert. 2000. Expert Witnesses Take the Stand. *Nature* 407, 16.

[61]See Expert Witness Profile No. 36, Michael Schaller, cfr. infra. See deposition of Michael Schaller, August 22, 2012, *Graham v. R.J. Reynolds*. Westlaw reference: 2012 WL 4107339.

[62]See Expert Witness Profile No. 44, Robert Norrell, cfr. infra. See deposition of Robert Norrell, August 22, 2012, *Larrabee v. R.J. Reynolds*. Westlaw reference: 2012 WL 4107355.

tobacco companies.[63] In the same trial, Kenneth Ludmerer acknowledged that he made $350 an hour and an extra $3500 when he had to stay overnight. He had made $500,000–550,000 in his career as an expert witness for the tobacco companies.[64] Stephen Ambrose reported to Laura Maggi of *The American Prospect* that he had made $25,000 in *Covert v. Liggett Group* [1994].[65] Jon Harkness, historian now turned patent lawyer, has also made around half a million dollars for his work for the tobacco industry; $300,000 for testifying and another $200,000 for research.[66] Robert Wilson, who was also deposed in *US v. Philip Morris et al.*, declared that he had made "approximately" $500,000 as an expert for the tobacco industry.[67] Historians are charging rates ranging from $100, $200, $300, and $400, to $600 an hour. The lower figures are for research hours, while the higher ones are charged for hours spent on depositions and testimonies. These numbers are immensely high and it is very likely that experts will be influenced by them.[68] Some historians make more from their litigation-driven research than from their regular salary as a tenured professor. For example, Peter English acknowledged in his deposition in *US v. Philip Morris* that he got over 50 % of his income from tobacco-related research for legal firms.[69] When historians receive these lucrative payments can these endanger professional ethics? When a professor represents an industry and a university, does (s)he not leverage his university's reputation for objectivity for the benefit of an interested party?

---

[63]For the analysis of English's deposition see Part III, Sect. 14.2.4.1. Deposition, cfr. supra. See Expert Witness Profile No. 14, Peter English.

[64]For the analysis of Ludmerer's deposition see Part III, Sect. 14.2.2.1. Deposition, cfr. supra. See Expert Witness Profile No. 30, Kenneth Ludmerer.

[65]Maggi, Laura. 2001. Bearing Witness for Tobacco. *The American Prospect*, November 9. http://prospect.org/article/bearing-witness-tobacco. Accessed 31 Oct 2014, 3. See Expert Witness Profile No. 1, Stephen Ambrose.

[66]Proctor, as n. 7, 475.

[67]See Part III, Sect. 14.2.4.1. Deposition, cfr. supra.

[68]Another champion in tobacco-related earning as an expert witness, is Harvard Professor Donald Rubin. He testified in the Minnesota Attorney General trial in defence of the tobacco industry. Rubin charged $1,000 an hour for consulting, and $1,250 an hour for testimony in 1997. Later he raised the amount to $1,250 an hour, and $1,600 an hour. Rubin made $1,5 million to $2 million during 1997 and 2002 from his work as an expert witness. Neither his website, nor curriculum vitae, nor his short biography mention his involvement in tobacco litigation in any way. See http://www.stat.harvard.edu/faculty_page.php?page=rubin.html. Accessed 31 Oct 2014. http://www.stat.harvard.edu/Faculty_Content/Rubin-cv.pdf. Accessed 31 Oct 2014. & http://www.stat.harvard.edu/Faculty_Content/Rubin-short-bio.pdf. Accessed 31 Oct 2014. He has published one article [which is thus not mentioned on the above websites] where he states that: "I am defending the importance of honest and competent statistics, that is all." See Rubin, Donald. 2002. The Ethics of Consulting for the Tobacco Industry. *Statistical Methods in Medical Research* 11, 373–374, 378.

[69]See Expert Witness Profile No. 14, Peter English. & Deposition of Peter Calvin English, M.D., Ph.D., August 23, 2002, United States of America v. Philip Morris USA Inc., 23/08/2002. LTDL. Bates Number: ENGLISHP082302. http://legacy.library.ucsf.edu/tid/qqo11b00. Accessed 31 Oct 2014, 32.

Some experts working for the defence have argued that they are not working for the tobacco industry but for independent legal firms and that they do not receive salaries from the tobacco industry itself.[70] For example John Burnham, himself an expert for the defence, has argued that his duty was to assists outside counsel as a consultant. He just worked on the question what evidence there was out there that was relevant to the case. He argues he did not work as an expert witness. I do not agree with Burnham, in so far that I argue that there is a clear difference between a consultant and an expert witness.

What is a consultant? I do not study historians working as consultants. Because their work is untraceable without corporation of either the historian or the legal firm, which in case of tobacco litigation is non-existing with most actors involved. Furthermore, legal firms let historians working as consultants sign confidentiality agreements and their work is in no way public record, as it is completely secluded from pre-trail fact finding activities. Wijffels argues in favour of historians limiting their involvement in litigation to the pre-trail period. I, by contrast, am completely opposed to this idea, because there is no way of knowing what these historians have done, as it is a private agreement. Which is perfectly fine with me, except when academic historians, who not only have a private interest but also bear social responsibilities, hide behind the façade of the consultant. The matter is different for private historians, who have a company, or work solely as a consultant. No institution is paying them, they have a business to run. Yet, a professor should keep a higher cause in mind, namely, the broader public interest. In addition, if historians work as consultants do they not have an obligation to enable their peers to review them and to be open about their work? Peer review is essential for good scholarship, and I believe that scholars have the responsibility to share their research, something consultants in general do not do. Furthermore, should consultants not know which litigating party will use their research or in which manner? Should historians or other scholars working as consultants not continue to ask broader questions that go beyond the requests put before them by legal counsel? Is that not the duty of a historian, whether working as a consultant or an expert?

Burnham wrote me: "My duty was to assist outside counsel. Their duty was to defend certain business firms in specific cases, not to make a social statement." I think the jobs of lawyers and historians are sometimes similar when they are looking for evidence. Yet the "duty" (as Burnham described it) is quite different for a historian, as a scholar, from that of a lawyer. A lawyer will want to know everything about a case. After which, the lawyer will select the facts which suit him best, because it is his duty to win the case. A historian, and certainly a scholar, has no such duty. On the contrary, a historian should always keep a more moral and social stance on his work. As a scholar and historian, one must surely go beyond "aiding

[70]See Burnham, John. 2004. Medical Historians and the Tobacco Industry. *The Lancet* 364, 838. & Burnham, John. 2010. In Defense of Historians as expert Witnesses: A Rebuttal to Jon Wiener. *George Mason University's History News Network*, April 1. http://hnn.us/articles/124924.html. Accessed 31 Oct 2014. & Personal correspondence with John Burnham.

outside counsel." A contract makes an expert assist outside counsel. The expert made a choice to work for them. So consultants should consider the pro's and con's before singing. How is it that the choice to work as a consultant eliminates the most basic standards of professional research expected from a scholar and a historian?

What is an expert witness? I only research the involvement of historians as expert witnesses, for practical reasons I explained above. Judicial records are publicly available and, furthermore, the expert has to publicly align himself with a party. And it does not matter who is paying whom. There is a legal connection between a litigating party and a witness that far outweighs the contract between the expert and outside counsel. In the case of an expert witness, even more so. A normal witness–an eyewitness–is held to report the facts as he or she witnessed them. An expert witness testifies an opinion in court in order to aid the trier of fact. Experts are allowed to give an opinionated testimony because of their expert knowledge and study. The experts are allowed to communicate their opinion on their speciality to aid lay people–judge and/or jury–so that they too can understand the matter at hand, which is of great importance to the trier of fact. This difference is stated clearly in the FRE 702–705, the ruling in *Frye v. United States*; and *Daubert v. Merell Dow Pharmaceuticals;* and *Kumho Tire Co. v. Carmichael*. So according to caselaw and evidence rules, Burnham has clearly worked as an expert witness in *Dewey v. R.J. Reynolds* 1986, and in *Cipollone v. R.J. Reynolds* also in 1986, and not as a consultant.[71]

So when a party in the adversarial process of litigation starts the search for an expert witness, they invite a historian. They will invite someone who is sympathetic to their cause, to their story, to their interpretation of events, to their legal strategy. That is the duty of legal counsel. The experts are invited. They make the choice to testify under oath, to be deposed under oath, to write an expert report for their party. He or she has a choice. An expert, as an expert witness opposed to what an eyewitness does, renders an opinion based on expert knowledge. The expert gives a version of history that is sympathetic to the cause of the litigating party for whom the expert testifies–not out of bias but because the expert has formed that opinion through years of research. The clash of different opinions that follows, is the nature of the adversarial process, so that through the confrontation of opposing opinions (on law, on the facts, on history) the judge or the jury will find a road, mostly in the middle between both arguments, where justice lies. No party will thus choose an expert witness whose opinion is hostile towards their own arguments. Again there is nothing wrong with that, assuming that the experts have formed their opinions through years of research and discussions with his or her peers, and not because of recently acquired funds through a litigating party or their legal representatives.

So I disagree with Burnham that expert witnesses do not testify for the tobacco industry, which legally, they, without doubt, do. When a witness is called into court or for a deposition, the witness is called as the plaintiff's or the defence's witness. Experts are sworn in as either the plaintiff's or defence's witness. An expert witness,

[71]See Expert Witness Profile No. 6, John Burnham.

in a legal sense, is directly linked to the litigating party who calls him. Who legally pays the witnesses for their time, does not matter.

Burnham's argument that everyone deserves legal representation is of course valid. "Corporations are people", in that sense that they have a legal personality. Which is the same in Europe, and to my knowledge, is an almost universal principle. Everyone deserves legal representation and the ability to use experts when needed. Legal representation and equal arms in an equal-level playing field are fundamental legal rights for everyone. To be clear, I do not, as Proctor has argued, support the idea that historians should refrain from testifying for the tobacco industry. Although, their choice to testify should be based on the firm belief, rooted in their research, that the opinion they render is the truth. Which is, I argue based on my research, a sentiment almost completely absent with most historians working for the defence. Considering that most have never researched anything on the history of smoking and the tobacco industry. That is also why I argue that most historians working for the defence "are in it for the money."

In defence of these experts: historians who chose to become expert witnesses take risks. They put their professional careers, as well as their professional and personal reputations on the line.[72] Furthermore, expert witnesses conduct lengthy researches and go through much effort to make every footnote fit in their witness report.[73] In addition, historians working as expert witnesses go through the stressful and unfamiliar tribulations of the courtroom. Depositions and testimony in court, certainly cross-examination, are activities that deserve appropriate compensation. Moreover, considering that prices are set by the ratio between supply and demand, historians also use the fact that they have expert knowledge on a certain subject and that litigators only have a limited choice of candidates. In conclusion: these high salaries are on the one hand understandable because of the special kind of service historians as experts witnesses deliver and, on the other, economic reasoning also explains the high figures to a certain extent. Whatever the reasons, these high numbers will and do affect the research and the expert. In the following topic I discuss whether, according to the *Code of Ethics* proposed by De Baets, historians who have served as expert witnesses in tobacco litigation have done so ethically?

16.3.2 Ethics

As discussed in topic *5.4. Confronting Ethics with De Baets,* the role Ludmerer, English, and Wilson have played in *US v. Philip Morris et al.*, did not conform to the code drafted by De Baets. An ethical code may ensure that the expert

[72]See Part II, Chap. 8: A Reassessment of Wijffels' Concept of Forensic History, cfr. supra.

[73]See Part II, Sect. 7.3.3. Preparing the Witness Report, cfr. supra.

historian tells the truth and avoids that he engages in advocacy.[74] Historians can manipulate historical knowledge by changing, leaving out, minimalizing, switching and distorting historical information. De Baets defines the abuse of history as "[t]he abuse of history is its use with intent to deceive."[75] He believes that there is a difference between the abuse and irresponsible use of history.[76] He defines the irresponsible use of history as "[t]he irresponsible use of history is either its deceptive or its negligent use."[77] There is a difference of intent between the two.

On the subject of sanctioning certain abuse, De Baets sees many possibilities but is confronted with a dilemma. What type of punishment should be imposed: a symbolic, professional, or legal one? The dilemma De Baets is confronted with is that if we choose to punish historians, there is a threat that this will endanger innovative research and historiography. Punishing means risking, on the one hand historical monopoly of one master-narrative and, on the other hand, oblivion for certain parts of history. Punishment conjures up disturbing images of unjustified repression of historians. While when, we refrain from acting upon abuse of history, this calls for repetition of abuse and destruction of legitimate memory.[78] Instead of punishments, De Baets argues for prevention and professional duty. Prevention is achieved by teaching and raising awareness with students about acknowledging intellectual debts. Another form of prevention lies in the element of personal reputation. Many historians cannot risk to be completely discredited in court; for what historians do in court influences their own intellectual standing and that of their works. Secondly, historians in all their academic and public responsibilities have the duty to oppose a known abuse in their field. They should refuse to cooperate with such ventures and denounce its products. Historians have a professional duty of accountability.[79] The ethical code De Baets proposes, addresses, and theoretically conceptualizes subjects as the right to information, academic freedom, the right to truth and the obligation for historians to be critical, truthful, moral, and to disclose information.[80]

Conceptualizing ethics has been a predominantly American affair and is directly connected to the rise of public history. Many historians, academics, and to a lesser extent public historians worried about the possibility that public historians would become hired guns. There was a suspicion that historians would lower themselves

---

[74]Evans, Richard. 2002. History, Memory, and the Law: the Historian as Expert Witness. *History and Theory* 41, 330.

[75]De Baets, Antoon. 2009. Responsible History. New York: Berghahn Books, 14.

[76]De Baets, as n. 75, 2.

[77]De Baets, as n. 75, 14.

[78]De Baets, as n. 75, 35–38.

[79]De Baets, as n. 75, 37–38.

[80]De Baets, as n. 75, 173. Or via http://www.concernedhistorians.org/content_files/file/et/148.pdf. Accessed 31 Oct 2014.

to "Sell history?"[81] When public historians formed the NCPH and *the Public Historian* commenced publishing, there were no ethical guidelines, except for those of each individual university, but these are general, non-specific guidelines, for all academics, and not just for historians.[82] Historians who were looking for work in the public or private sector were thus confronted with employers who had certain expectations from their newly acquired employees. These were sometimes troublesome and the reluctance and inability of public historians to stand up to these demands has formed the basis on which some academic historians have uttered criticism against the whole public history movement. The need to be able to turn to a guidebook of ethical standards was urgent.[83] Historian Karamanski gives a good introduction to the first codes of professional ethics. He finds them with the oral history association in 1968, the American Association of Museum in 1978 and the society of American Archivists in 1980.[84] The first real code was made by *the Californian Committee for the Promotion of History* (CCPH) in 1984. It is a formal declaration of professional standards for conduct of public historians. They are minimal standards, but at least they offer a basic start for an ethical code. It had the goal to assist both public historians and their clients in carrying out their professional responsibilities in better mutual understanding.[85] By registering with the CCPH, historians accepted the code of ethics. The CCPH supervised historians who were registered with them and vouched for their conduct with employers. Codes like these strengthen the possibility of the historian to adhere to ethics in the private market.[86] The NCPH finally issued an ethical code in 1985.[87] The American Historical Association (AHA) and the Organization of American Historians (OAH) soon followed with their ethical guidelines clearly inspired on the NCPH's standards.[88] Because of these guidelines, firms who hire historians know what to expect from them and "to what extent their project is conform to them [the

[81]Shallat, Todd. 1978. We Who Would Sell History? *The Public Historian* 1, 81–82.

[82]For more on Public History see Part I, Sect. 3.1.4. Descending the Ivory Tower, cfr. supra.

[83]Tobey, Ronald. 1986. The Public Historian as Advocate: Is Special Attention to Professional Ethics Necessary? *The Public Historian* 8, 27–30.

[84]Karamanski, Theodore. 1986. Ethics and Public History. *The Public Historian* 8, 6.

[85]Williams, James. 1986. Standards of Professional Conduct in California. *The Public Historian* 8, 57–59. The code can be found via http://www.concernedhistorians.org/content_files/file/ET/183.pdf. Accessed via 31 Oct 2014.

[86]Karamanski, as n. 84, 7.

[87]The latest version of 2007 that replaced the one from 1985 can be found at http://ncph.org/cms/about/bylaws-and-ethics/#Code of Ethics & Prof Conduct. Accessed on 31 Oct 2014.

[88]The code by the AHA can be accessed via http://www.historians.org/jobs-and-professional-development/statements-and-standards-of-the-profession/statement-on-standards-of-professional-conduct. Accessed 31 Oct 2014. The code by the OAH can be accessed via http://www.oah.org/about/reports/reports-statements/professional-integrity-and-the-oah/. Accessed 31 Oct 2014.

guidelines]."[89] Public history forces historians to go beyond their normal comfort zone and think practical and critical to make history work.

Codes like the one drafted by De Baets build a bridge between academic and public historians.[90] It helps increase the credibility of historians.[91] "By championing honesty as a historical virtue over the more celebrated but hard-to-obtain value of objectivity, . . . ", historians regain legitimacy through their methods and reliability of research, rather than through a God-given positivist objectivity.[92] Furthermore, by making historical practice more concrete and making theory more easily accessible to clients and lawyers, the historian is better understood in court.

As we have seen through evaluating the actions of Ludmerer, English, and Wilson in the *US v. Philip Morris et al.* trial with the ethical code of Antoon De Baets, historians for the defence had used history for personal gain.[93] Kyriakoudes argues in an article from 2006 that all the historians who serve as expert witnesses for the tobacco industry ignore the secret documents by the industry.[94] The TDO, DATTA, and LTDL databases are left untouched in order to minimize the influence of tobacco advertising on the common knowledge issue and also to limit the role of the tobacco companies in creating the tobacco controversy.[95] This neglect of the industry's internal archives lets tobacco's legal counsel continue its "solid wall of denial"-strategy, however unreal it had become.[96] Satirically Kyriakoudes remarks that "[f]rom the testimony of industry historians, one would never understand how it came to be that anyone ever smoked", since according to the Ludmerer, English, and Wilson, and other historians in the service of the defence "everybody knew" the mortal health hazards of smoking.[97] Moreover, Kyriakoudes argues that historians in the service of the tobacco industry draw from a common body of research conducted by the industry's legal counsel in support of its litigation efforts, and not from their own research. This research performed by the historians on the payroll of the tobacco companies "fails to meet basic professional standards of scholarship", according to Kyriakoudes.[98]

---

[89] Ryant, Carl. 1986. The Public Historian and Business History: A Question of Ethics. *The Public Historian* 8, 33–34, 37.

[90] Hurtado, Albert. 1986. Historians and Their Employers: A Perspective on Professional Ethics. *The Public Historian* 8, 51.

[91] Hordes, Stanley. 1986. Does He Who Plays the Piper Call the Tune? Historians, Ethics, and the Community. *The Public Historian* 8, 56.

[92] Karamanski, as n. 84, 12.

[93] See Part I, Sect. 3.1.5. Conclusions on Clio's Modern Paradox, cfr. supra.

[94] Kyriakoudes, Louis. 2006. Historians' Testimony on 'Common Knowledge' of the Risks of Tobacco Use: a Review and Analysis of Experts Testifying on Behalf of Cigarette Manufacturers in Civil Litigation. *Tobacco Control* 15, 111.

[95] Kyriakoudes, as n. 94, 112.

[96] Malone, Ruth. 2009. Standing With Those Who Seek Justice. *Tobacco Control* 18, 337.

[97] Kyriakoudes, as n. 94, 114.

[98] Kyriakoudes, as n. 94, 114.

The qualitative inquiry into the trial records in *US v. Philip Morris et al.*, revealed that the historians' actions in court are in the "grey area of professional ethics", as physician and expert witness Jess Alderman called his tobacco trial experience.[99] The advocacy by the defence's historians has been amply proven, but also Proctor and Brandt showed clear signs of advocacy. The courtroom forces historians to leave their nuanced answers behind and defend their version of history with the fervour of an advocate. I argue that this is not wrong, when that opinion is based on solid historical research. To determine whether historians are basing their opinions on reliable research, we need a code of ethics like the one drafted by the De Baets.[100] In conclusion of the issue of ethics, I quote Brandt from the end of his book:

> *It seems to me that United States v. Philip Morris is an example of how we might recover a "usable past" that serves the public good. And it is equally critical that this past not be purchased and subverted by the interest of the industry. At one time, I worried that serving as an expert witness might be perceived as compromising the integrity and persuasiveness of this book. I have put this concern to rest. Historians are hardly exempt from the common duty to contribute to public life and civil society. It seems to me now, after the hopes and disappointments of the courtroom battle, that we [historians] have a role to play in determining the future of the tobacco pandemic. If we occasionally cross the boundary between analysis and advocacy, so be it. The stakes are high, and there is much work yet to do.*[101]

16.3.3 Transparency

The most important apparent conclusion from my quantitative research on the involvement of historians in tobacco litigation was to ascertain that of the fifty historians who were deposed or testified, filed affidavits, were deposed, and filed witness expert reports in tobacco litigation since 1986, only a few publicly discuss their involvement as an expert witness in tobacco litigation. Few historians involved declare publically that he or she has been witnessing for or against the tobacco companies in court, while continuing to write peer reviews, publish, and engage in academic and public debate, without anyone knowing that this historian is receiving money from the tobacco industry. I do not consider it problematic that historians are paid for their work as an expert witness; I argue that the lack of transparency makes it problematic, because whether the numbers are big or small, in some sense funding determines research. This issue is not limited to the discipline of history; funding plays a role in all intellectual activity. In addition, I have already argued

---

[99] Alderman, Jess. 2007. Ethical Implications of Physician Involvement in Lawsuits on Behalf of the Tobacco Industry. *Journal of Law, Medicine & Ethics* 35, 697.

[100] Alderman also called for ethical codes for litigation-driven research and testimony. Alderman, as n. 99, 692.

[101] Brandt, Allan. 2007. *The Cigarette Century. The Rise, Fall and Deadly Persistence of a Product that Defined America.* New York: Basic Books, 505.

that the fact that the historian is defending his historical opinion is not a problem as long as his opinion is based on solid research.[102] My solution is founded on procuring transparency through the use of ethical codes by universities, historical organizations, and consulting companies to ensure some level of professional conduct.

In reaction to Jon Wiener's article from 2009 in *The Nation*, in which he fervently defended Proctor against the accusations by the tobacco industry, John Burnham, as an expert historian himself for the tobacco industry, defended expert witnesses who were unwilling to discuss their work for the tobacco companies.[103] Burnham writes that "[t]he demand that those historians who have worked for one side or the other stand up and be counted is therefore not legally possible, and to condemn silence on this point is ridiculous."[104]

This argument made by Burnham is erroneous. Confidentiality agreements are agreements. Agreements are by choice. Historians agree to work under those rules. Signing that contract is a choice. In other words, how is that historians working for the plaintiffs have not been obligated to remain silent on their litigation-driven research and have published a lot of it, and experts for the defence have not? Again we come back to the argument I made earlier, when professors of history trade their professional reputation and that of their universities in addition to their expert knowledge for remuneration, these experts should be held accountable for their litigation-driven research by their peers. Yes, there are exceptions wherein, because of the rare nature of the crime or facts of the case, the judge through court orders or the law, implements certain boundaries on disclosure of case-related material, but the other restrictions that we are confronted with in tobacco litigation are established via contractual agreement. And that is fully up to the historians, nobody is forcing their hand. For example, when Richard Abrams, of the University of California, Berkeley, specialized in the history of government-business relations, was contacted by lawyers of the tobacco industry with a proposal to witness for the industry in court, he asked whether he could see the industry's archives. The lawyers replied "you can't see our archive, but we'll send you stuff." Abrams reports that he thereupon respectfully declined their offer.[105]

If historians would be bound by minimal standards, I argue, more historians would be inclined to say "no" to the tobacco industry's demands and big pay checks, in fear of their reputation and maybe their positions at their universities. The counterargument would be that the tobacco industry will simply raise its payments to lure historians. My only rebuttal to that is my hope that there will be enough

[102]For this argument see Part II, Chap. 8: A Reassessment of Wijffels' Concept of Forensic History, cfr. supra.

[103]See for the discussion on Wiener's article, Part III, Sect. 15.6. The Tobacco Companies v. Robert Proctor, cfr. supra.

[104]Burnham, as n. 70.

[105]Wiener, Jon. 2010. Re 'Big Tobacco and the Historians', Wiener Replies. *The Nation*, March 9. http://www.thenation.com/article/re-big-tobacco-and-historians. Accessed Oct 31 2014.

strength within the historical community to collectively refuse to work under such circumstances. For I do not argue that the industry does not deserve the services of an expert historian, I argue that the limitations defence counsel places upon those historians produces abuse and distortion of historical fact.[106] In contrast to Burnham, and this is the central point of my argument, if historians refuse to work under the circumstances proposed by tobacco's legal counsel, among those the promise that their work will be confidential, they give defence counsel two options: Either (1) to let lawyers present historical arguments in court while faced with real historians on the opposing side who have much more experience in historical research and have far more historical credibility with the judge and the jury, thus damaging their overall legal strategy, or (2) to accept the rules set forth by ethical codes to let historians research in relative independence.

I would not demand the same high standards from independent historians or consulting firms, in the end they are free to do whatever they like; however all but one of all the historians involved in tobacco litigation was an independent. 98 % of the historians involved are academics; not only do they represent their Faculties and Universities, but they also represent the historical discipline.[107] It is, in part, because of the abuses of history like those by Ludmerer, English, and Wilson that the historical discipline can be portrayed in court as well as in the media as a profession that will not hesitate to sell its integrity and history itself to the highest bidder. When titles like *History for Hire in Industry Lawsuits* appear in *The New York Times,* they do enormous damage to the social legitimacy of the discipline of history.[108] Individual historians as well as the historical community as a whole bear responsibility to counter these practices and accusations.

There have been attempts to make the involvement of historians in tobacco litigation more transparent. A wiki existed on the involvement of historians in litigation in the USA. It was created by Bill Childs, a former law professor at Western New England University School of Law in 2011, but the project was abandoned when Childs returned to private practice and has been untended since.[109] The tobacco section of the wiki was somewhat "messy", because of the project's cancellation.[110] Furthermore, certain pages have been removed by anonymous wiki-users. For example, the profile of Kenneth Ludmerer, detailing his work for the

[106]Argument based on the definition of abuse of history by De Baets and the discussion in Part III, Sect. 14.4. Confronting Ethics with De Baets, cfr. supra.

[107]See Appendix I for an overview.

[108]Cohen, Patricia. 2003. History for Hire In Industry Lawsuits. *The New York Times,* June 14. http://www.nytimes.com/2003/06/14/arts/history-for-hire-in-industry-lawsuits.html?pagewanted=all&src=pm. Accessed 31 Oct 2014.

[109]Childs returned to his private practice. For the wiki see http://masstort.org/mediawiki/index.php?title=Main_Page. Accessed 31 Oct 2014. The wiki has been offline for quite some time. Prof. Childs has written me that the website had come under attack of digital viruses and Trojan horses.

[110]For the overview of tobacco litigation see http://masstort.org/mediawiki/index.php?title=Category:Tobacco. Accessed 31 Oct 2014. Same remark as above.

tobacco industry was removed on August 20, 2012.[111] The TDO website had already reported in 2007 that Philip Morris used computer programs to scan information from Wikipedia on content related to tobacco companies. When the information is considered harmful, they edit that content.[112] Considering the historical record of the tobacco industry, such practices do not come as much of a surprise.[113] Subsequently, the wiki has been entirely removed in the fall of 2013. Childs has confirmed that his site had to be taken down because of an overload of "spambots" and "some sort of computer virus."[114]

There are examples of good transparency displayed by expert witnesses, but almost all are witnesses who have testified against the tobacco industry. For example, after his testimony in the Minnesota attorney general's suit, professor of medicine and M.D., Jonathan Samet, reported in *Tobacco Control*: "I am writing to describe my experience as an expert, covering my decision to participate, the preparatory work for the trail, and the presentation of testimony in the courtroom."[115] The six-page-long article described the trial experience of Samet. If all expert witnesses wrote a similar article after their litigation-driven work, peer review and reflection would be possible.

Bibliography

Alderman, Jess. 2007. Ethical implications of physician involvement in lawsuits on behalf of the tobacco industry. *Journal of Law, Medicine & Ethics* 35: 692–698.

Alderman, Jess, and Richard Daynard. 2006. Applying lessons from tobacco litigation to obesity lawsuits. *The American Journal of Preventive Medicine* 30: 82–88.

Berridge, Virginia. 2012. History in public health: Who needs it? *The Lancet* 356: 1923–1925.

Blum, Alan. 2010. A dissenting view of Robert Proctor by a fellow anti-smoking advocate. *George Mason University History New Network*, April 25.

Brandt, Allan. 2007. *The cigarette century. The rise, fall and deadly persistence of a product that defined America*. New York: Basic Books.

Brownell, Kelly, and Kenneth Warner. 2009. The perils of ignoring history: Big tobacco played dirty and millions died. How similar is big food? *The Milbank Quarterly* 87: 259–294.

Burnham, John. 2004. Medical historians and the tobacco industry. *The Lancet* 364: 838.

Burnham, John. 2010. In Defense of historians as expert witnesses: A rebuttal to Jon Wiener. *George Mason University's History News Network*, April 1.

[111] The page stated: "Kenneth Ludmerer. This page has been deleted. The deletion and move log for the page are provided below for reference.00:14, 20 August 2012 Delete page script (Talk | contribs) deleted "Kenneth Ludmerer." See http://masstort.org/mediawiki/index.php?title=Kenneth_Ludmerer. Accessed 31 Oct 2014.

[112] See the article at http://archive.tobacco.org/resources/general/wikiscanner.html. Accessed 31 Oct 2014.

[113] I can only hope that my attempt at an overview is left in peace. See http://www.thejudgeandthehistorian.ugent.be. Accessed 31 Oct 2014.

[114] Personal correspondence with Mr. Childs.

[115] Samet, Jonathan. 1999. Reflections in the Minnesota Tobacco Lawsuit. *Tobacco Control* 8, 101.

Cohen, Patricia. 2003. History for hire in industry lawsuits. *The New York Times*, June 14.
Daynard, Richard. 2003. Why tobacco litigation? *Tobacco Control* 12: 1–2.
De Baets, Antoon. 2009. *Responsible history*. New York: Berghahn Books.
Evans, Richard. 2002. History, memory, and the law: The historian as expert witness. *History and Theory* 41: 326–345.
Hiilamo, Heikki. 2007. The impact of strategic funding by the tobacco industry of medical expert witnesses appearing for the defense in the Aho Finnish product liability case. *Addiction* 102: 979–988.
Horder, Stanley. 1986. Does he who plays the piper call the tune? Historians, ethics, and the community. *The Public Historian* 8: 53–56.
Hurtado, Albert. 1986. Historians and their employers: A perspective on professional ethics. *The Public Historian* 8: 46–51.
Karamanski, Theodore. 1986. Ethics and public history. *The Public Historian* 8: 5–12.
Maggi, Laura. 2001. Bearing witness for tobacco. *The American Prospect*, November 9.
Malone, Ruth. 2009. Standing with those who seek justice. *Tobacco Control* 18: 337.
Malone, Ruth, and Kenneth Warner. 2012. Tobacco control at twenty: Reflecting on the past, considering the present and developing the new conversations for the future. *Tobacco Control* 21: 74–76.
Miura, Marlo, Richard Daynard, and Jonathan Samet. 2006. The role of litigation in tobacco control. *Salud Pública de México* 48: 121–136.
Mosher, James. 2009. Litigation and alcohol policy: Lessons from the US Tobacco Wars. *Addiction* 104: 27–33.
Posner, Richard. 1972. A theory of negligence. *Journal of Legal Studies* 1: 29–96.
Proctor, Robert. 2000. Expert witnesses take the stand. *Nature* 407: 15–16.
Proctor, Robert. 2004. The global smoking epidemic: A history and status report. *Clinical Lung Cancer* 5: 371–376.
Proctor, Robert. 2006. Puffing on polonium. *The New York Times*, December 1.
Proctor, Robert. 2011. The history of the discovery of the cigarette-lung cancer link: Evidentiary traditions, corporate denial, global toll. *Tobacco Control* 21: 7–91.
Proctor, Robert. 2012. *Golden holocaust: Origins of the cigarette catastrophe and the case for abolition*. Berkeley: University of California Press.
Rubin, Donald. 2002. The ethics of consulting for the tobacco industry. *Statistical Methods in Medical Research* 11: 373–380.
Rutkow, Lainie, Jon Vernick, and Stephen Teret. 2007. Public health benefits of recent litigation against tobacco industry. *Journal of the American Medical Association* 298: 86–89.
Ryant, Carl. 1986. The public historian and business history: A question of ethics. *The Public Historian* 8: 31–38.
Samet, Jonathan. 1999. Reflections in the Minnesota tobacco lawsuit. *Tobacco Control* 8: 101–105.
Shallat, Todd. 1978. We who would sell history? *The Public Historian* 1: 81–82.
Shibuya, Kenji, Christina Ciecierski, Guidon Emmanuel, Douglas Bettcher, David Evans, and Christopher Murray. 2011. WHO framework convention on tobacco control: Development of an evidence based global public health treaty. *British Medical Journal* 327: 154–157.
Sloan, Frank, Justine Trogdon, and Carrie Mathews. 2005. Litigation and the value of tobacco companies. *Journal of Health Economics* 24: 427–447.
Smith, Philip, Maansi Bansal-Travers, Richard O'Connor, Anthony Brown, Chris Banthin, Sara Guardino-Colket, and Michael Cummings. 2011. Correcting over 50 years of tobacco industry misinformation. *The American Journal of Preventive Medicine* 40: 694–696.
Tobey, Ronald. 1986. The public historian as advocate: Is special attention to professional ethics necessary? *The Public Historian* 8: 21–30.
Wiener, Jon. 2010. Big tobacco and the historians. *The Nation*, February 15.
Williams, James. 1986. Standards of professional conduct in California. *The Public Historian* 8: 57–59.

Chapter 17
Final Conclusion on the Involvement of Historians in Tobacco Litigation

Never doubt that a small group of thoughtful, committed citizens can change the world. Indeed, it is the only thing that ever has.

Margaret Mead

Abstract This chapter gives a final conclusion on the role historians have played in tobacco litigation based on qualitative and quantitative inquiries the book has presented in previous chapters. Although experts for the defence are not following professional historical ethics, experts for the plaintiff are showing that litigation-driven history can produce solid historical research.

In an article from 2004, Proctor listed 29 historians who had witnessed for the tobacco industry.[1] Two years later Proctor and Kyriakoudes compiled a list of 36 historians who were working for tobacco companies as expert witnesses.[2] By 2008, that number had risen to 40.[3] In his book from 2012, Proctor listed 48 historians who had testified for the defence.[4] I have made a list with 50 experts based on my quantitative research of the involvement of historians in tobacco litigation.[5] I have left out three names from Proctor's list, because in one case I did not consider the person to be a historian, and in the two other instances I did not find any trial records to prove their involvement. While on the other hand, I have added five historians in addition to Proctor's list; on the one hand, the historians who have testified for the

[1]Proctor, Robert. 2004. Should Medical Historians Be Working for the Tobacco Industry? *The Lancet* 363, 1174.

[2]Proctor, Robert. 2006. 'Everyone Knew But No One Had Proof': Tobacco Industry Use of Medical History Expertise in US courts, 1990–2002. *Tobacco Control* 15, 122.

[3]Proctor, Robert. 2008. Plaintiffs' Motion for Reconsideration of Order Overruling Objections to Subpoena and for Protective Order Concerning Unpublished Manuscript. *George Mason University's History News Network*, October 12. http://hnn.us/articles/118209.html. Accessed 31 Oct 2014.

[4]Proctor, Robert. 2012. *Golden Holocaust: Origins of the Cigarette Catastrophe and the Case for Abolition.* Berkeley: University of California Press, 460–463.

[5]See Appendix I list for the expert witness profiles and Appendix II for an overview, cfr. infra.

R. Delafontaine, *Historians as Expert Judicial Witnesses in Tobacco Litigation*, Studies in the History of Law and Justice 4, DOI 10.1007/978-3-319-14292-0_17

plaintiffs, Brandt, Díaz-Hernández, Kyriakoudes, and Proctor, and on the other, I have added one historian to the list of the defendants' witnesses.

Furthermore, the number of cases in which historians were involved is higher in the list which I have compiled than compared to previous lists. Especially in recent years, with the Engle Progeny cases well underway, historians are testifying at a higher rate than ever before.[6] Between 1986 and 2014, 50 historians were active in 314 cases.[7] I found that the phenomenon of repeat players is also taking shape with historians as expert witnesses.[8] Of the 50 historians involved, 22 have served in only one or two cases, while 17 other experts have engaged in ten or more cases respectively. Historians like Proctor (93 cases), Kyriakoudes (66 cases), Michael Schaller (36 cases), Joan Hoff (31 cases), Robert Norrell (28 cases), Randy Roberts (25 cases), James Kirby Martin (23 cases), Terry Parssinen (22 cases), Elizabeth Cobbs Hoffman (21 cases), William Stueck (20 cases), Lacy Ford (19 cases), Michael Parrish (17 cases), Peter English (15 cases), and Kenneth Ludmerer (15 cases) have all become experts at expert witnessing.[9] The high number of cases attended by Proctor and Kyriakoudes is obvious, as they are the only historians willing to continue to testify against the tobacco companies in court, despite the harassing campaign that has been conducted by the tobacco industry against both historians.[10] The number of experts working for the defence is probably much higher. Table 17.1 presents the number of cases historians participated in on a yearly basis.

As this chart demonstrates, there are two clear spikes of increased involvement. The first started around 1997–1998 when historians were recruited in the state attorney general trials by legal firms working for the tobacco industry. A second spike began in 2008, and continues to this day, when the Supreme Court of Florida ruled that plaintiffs had to sue as individuals, not as members of a class. This resulted in more than 8,000 individual cases. Up until now, sixteen different historians – fourteen for the defence and two for the plaintiff – have been active as expert witnesses in Engle Progeny cases.[11]

---

[6]See Appendix III, cfr. infra.

[7]As far as I have found, it is very probable that the tobacco industry has recruited even more historians in American Universities.

[8]I discussed specialized lawyers for tobacco as repeat players earlier. See Part II, Sect. 7.3.2. Recruitment of the Expert Witness, cfr. supra.

[9]See Expert Witness Profile No. 41, Robert Proctor; Expert Witness Profile No. 26, Louis Kyriakoudes; Expert Witness Profile No. 44 Michael Schaller; Expert Witness Profile No. 23 Joan Hoff; Expert Witness Profile No. 36 Robert Norrell; Expert Witness Profile No. 31 James Kirby Martin; Expert Witness Profile No. 48 William Stueck; Expert Witness Profile No. 16 Lacy Ford; Expert Witness Profile No. 30, Kenneth Ludmerer. See also Appendix II, Table 4. Number of Cases, cfr. infra.

[10]See Part III, Sect. 15.6. The Tobacco Companies v. Robert Proctor, cfr. supra.

[11]For the different waves in tobacco litigation see: Part III, Chap. 13: Tobacco Litigation, cfr. supra. See Appendix II, Table 2. Active in In re: Engle Progeny Cases, cfr. infra.

Table 17.1 Involvement of historians in tobacco litigation from 1986 to 2013

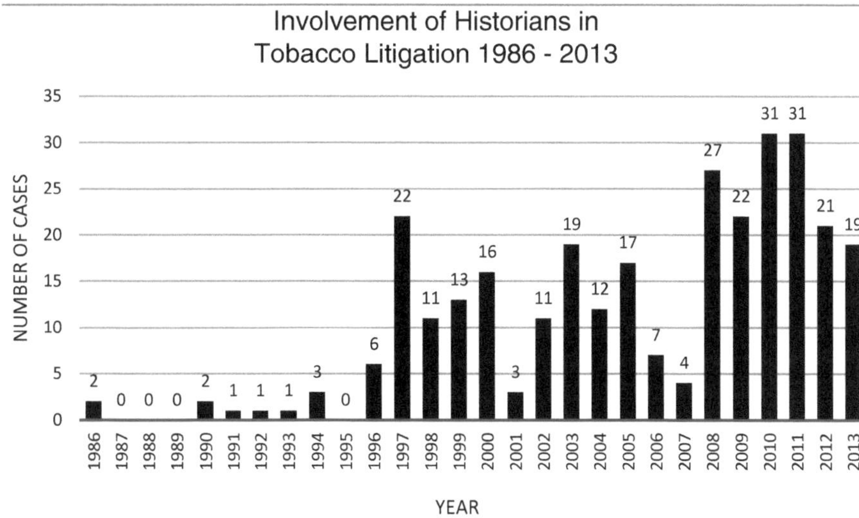

See Appendix III, Table 7. Involvement of Historians in Tobacco Litigation 1986–2013, cfr. infra

Of those who testified for the defence, only two historians, John Burnham, and Jon Harkness have published something on the history of smoking albeit not extensive nor on the core issues treated in court. Harkness wrote one article on public health on smoking during the Eisenhower and Kennedy administrations.[12] In other words, 4 % of the historians testifying for the tobacco industry have published on tobacco before their testimony, or afterwards. Another disturbing figure, which I have discussed in the previous chapter, is the limited number of historians offering information on their involvement in tobacco litigation on their website or in academic debate. It is in the spirit of and with the conviction that there is a need for more transparency that I have put my overview of these 50 expert witnesses online, free to visit for anyone interested.[13]

Although the overall numbers are shocking and alarming, especially when it comes to transparency, I am confident that with the right ethical tools, for instance the code drafted by De Baets and the consequent applications of those codes by

[12]See Appendix II, cfr. infra. & See Expert Witness Profile No. 6, John Burnham.

[13]Every single historian has his or her own expert witness profile, which lists his or her name, website, degree, focus of research, most important publications, number of cases, and a shortlist of those cases, detailing the name of the case, the year and the manner of involvement by the historian. Furthermore, the profile offers a short description of the historian and his or her work, and if available statements he or she has made about their work in tobacco litigation as an expert judicial witness. I hope the website may add to further debate on the involvement of historians in tobacco litigation. See all the witness profiles online at http://www.thejudgeandthehistorian.ugent.be. Accessed 31 Oct 2014. Disclosure: website made and maintained by the author. All experts involved have been contacted and have been provided with their expert witness profile.

universities and historical organizations, much can be done to prevent extreme examples of historical distortion, and, hopefully, to attract other historians to defend their historical reports in court in a more professional manner.

As I have detailed, through qualitative and quantitative research of the involvement of historians in tobacco litigation, historians and litigation-driven history have played and are playing an important role in tobacco litigation. Through historical research and the publication of the results of their research, historians have come to a better understanding of the manner in which a product that kills 1,200 people a day in the US alone could remain so popular and even become the quintessential American product. Historians have also played a role in public debate about cigarettes. Every time more secret documents were recovered and researched the American public became more hostile towards the tobacco industry. Litigation-driven history stands with the premise that professional historical practice and method may offer historical insights into contemporary policy and cultural change.[14] By providing the history of the tobacco industry and its tactics, historians assured that Judge Kessler was able to make a historically informed verdict in *US v. Philip Morris et al.*, that condemned the tobacco industry for the fraud these companies perpetrated against the American public. Judge Kessler's verdict is a testimony to the legacy of the critical role which Brandt and Proctor have played in holding the tobacco industry accountable. David Armitage, from Harvard, and Jo Guldi, from Brown University, have made an argument for a more engaged historical profession.[15] The article praises the work of both Brandt and Proctor for their research in the field of public health. Proctor's work has been singled out by the White House, which invited him to attend the celebration of the 50th anniversary of the 1964 Surgeon General's report on smoking.[16]

Brandt, Díaz-Hernández, Kyriakoudes, and Proctor, although not innocent from a degree of advocacy of their own, have defended the history of tobacco and the historical discipline. In *US v. Philip Morris et al.*, Brandt and Proctor prevented a coup on history organized by a small number of historians who were willing to sell history and their professional integrity to the tobacco industry. In individual cases of the third wave of tobacco litigation, plaintiffs' expert witnesses, Proctor and Kyriakoudes, continue to testify for those individuals and families who face "the industry's armies of well-paid lawyers and their investigators and consultants, who leave no stone unturned in excavating the personal pasts of plaintiffs and trying to excoriate them in court."[17]

---

[14]Brandt makes a similar argument in his book. Brandt, Allan. 2007. *The Cigarette Century. The Rise, Fall and Deadly Persistence of a Product that Defined America.* New York: Basic Books, 15.

[15]Article is in press, see http://scholar.harvard.edu/files/armitage/files/rld_annales_revised_0.pdf. Accessed 31 Oct 2014.

[16]See http://history.stanford.edu/news/professor-robert-proctor-senior-scientific-reviewer-50th-anniversary-surgeon-generals-report. Accessed 31 Oct 2014.

[17]Malone, Ruth. 2009. Standing With Those Who Seek Justice. *Tobacco Control* 18, 337. For example, the son of Rose Cipollone who had succumbed to lung cancer because of her addiction

One of the lessons from the involvement of historians as expert witnesses in tobacco litigation is the power that comes from a few historians who are willing to stand up against the abuse of history by their colleagues who serve in a greater scheme of the tobacco industry. The engagement by Brandt and Proctor, through hard-won but professional and ethical historical research has been able to destroy the quasi-historical versions of the history of the cigarette Ludmerer, English, and Wilson brought to court in *US v. Philip Morris et al.* In the end, the few have withstood the many, and their shields were historical facts.

Bibliography

Brandt, Allan. 2007. *The cigarette century: The rise, fall and deadly persistence of a product that defined America*. New York: Basic Books.

Malone, Ruth. 2009. Standing with those who seek justice. *Tobacco Control* 18: 337.

Proctor, Robert. 2004. Should medical historians be working for the tobacco industry? *The Lancet* 363: 1174–1175.

Proctor, Robert. 2006. 'Everyone knew but no one had proof': Tobacco industry use of medical history expertise in US courts, 1990–2002. *Tobacco Control* 15: 117–125.

Proctor, Robert. 2008. Plaintiffs' motion for reconsideration of order overruling objections to subpoena and for protective order concerning unpublished manuscript. *George Mason University's History News Network*, October 12.

Proctor, Robert. 2012. *Golden holocaust: Origins of the cigarette catastrophe and the case for abolition*. Berkeley: University of California Press.

---

to smoking; Thomas Cipollone continued litigation against the tobacco industry all the way to the US Supreme Court even after his father, Antonio Cipollone, had also died.

Chapter 18
Final Conclusion

> *Every once in a while, every once in a while, there's a day with an absolute right and an absolute wrong, but those days almost always include body counts.*
>
> President Bartlett (Aaron Sorkin's The West Wing)

Abstract This final chapter offers a conclusion to my research on forensic history which I have presented in this book. I reviewed *Clio's Modern Paradox* in forensic history. Furthermore, I discussed the European and American experiences with historians serving as expert witnesses. From these theoretical and practical issues on historians working as expert judicial witnesses I have come to a number of conclusions on the controversial involvement of historians in tobacco litigation as expert judicial witnesses. To end, I discuss the courtroom as a performative and fact-making theatre for historians and I define my concept of the forensification of history.

I set out to research forensic history. In order to achieve this ambitious goal, I have made a systematic and interdisciplinary analysis of the interaction between history and law when historians enter the courtroom as expert witnesses. Although history and law had been interrelated since the time of the ancient Greeks and Romans, historians were and are not welcomed in court by the legal profession. Despite the fact that historians have been called upon to testify in court as expert judicial witnesses at an exponential rate in transnational justice tribunals, post-World War II trials, post-Holocaust trials, Holocaust denial trials, indigenous peoples trials in Commonwealth countries, and in civil litigation in the United States, forensic history remains a controversial activity for a historian to engage in.

The first part of my research has provided me with a theoretical framework to portray the litigation discussed in parts II and III of this book on. The theoretical discussion addressed the low level of legitimacy the historical discipline has in the public sphere in contrast with the past, which is very much alive in our society. I called this relationship: Clio's Modern Paradox. I argued that historians had to look critically at their own discipline to explain the discrepancy in social appraisal between the historical discipline and the past. I have identified three elements which, I argue, account for the problems which history is facing in court: namely (1) the quest undertaken by historians to turn their discipline into a science;

R. Delafontaine, *Historians as Expert Judicial Witnesses in Tobacco Litigation*,
Studies in the History of Law and Justice 4, DOI 10.1007/978-3-319-14292-0_18

(2) the dangers posed by postmodern relativism; and (3) a lack of theoretical conceptualization. These are three elements within the historical discipline which undermine its legitimacy to present historical facts. Historians are having trouble abandoning the idea of positivist objectivity. We have seen that it is still used as a selling-point in historical consulting. This notion that historians can simply find and state "the facts" is hopelessly antiquated and should be abandoned in favour of a new form of objectivity. This does not mean historians have to run to the other side of the theoretical field and join postmodern relativism, which would cut the band between historical fact and historical narrative. I have argued that a good proposal for a form of intersubjective objectivity can be found somewhere in the middle of those extreme positions, neither presenting it as a given nor as impossible to attain. Inspired by practical standards from the study of law, I have proposed an intersubjective form of objectivity which is achieved through peer review as well as publication of research and primary sources enabling source checking by their fellow historians. Although, I have not argued in favour of a "Code of Historical Conduct", which would offer a dogmatic view on the historical practice, constructed from imperatives without any nuance, I have argued that the historical discipline is in need of a basic ethical guides which lists the very basic requirements which historians and historical research have to fulfil. It is with great reluctance and reservation that such a code should be constructed, yet I argue that the historical discipline can only prosper by adhering to an ethical code. Collective theoretical conceptualization and effective adherence by the majority of the historical discipline, for example to the code proposed by Antoon De Baets, offers clarity and reliability, and thus legitimacy in the eyes of employers, clients, lawyers, judges, and perhaps the general public. Forensic history in the form of litigation-driven history, confronts historians in a tangible manner with the most basic problems of the historical discipline, namely funding, advocacy, ethics, transparency, and thorough and reliable historical research. Historians involved in litigation-driven history, public as well as academic, should take the time to discuss and critically reflect upon their practices, in order to overcome *Clio's Modern Paradox* and make Clio's entrance into the chambers of Justitia a more accepted practice.

The second part of the book addressed three waves in which historians have been active as expert witnesses. From my European perspective, I have addressed the post-World War II and the post-Holocaust trials in Israel, Germany, and France. Except for the Ludwigsburg paradigm and the relative success of the Irving-trial, the European experience with expert witnessing has been generally negative. History has been abused predominantly in the interest of political convictions to rewrite history on trial. Furthermore, I have also examined American civil litigation in which historians are called to testify. The practical guide to expert witnessing has given an overview of the consecutive steps that are taken before and on trial by an expert witness. This practical guide offered a manner to concretize expert witnessing and demonstrate the meaning of what it means to "serve" as an expert witness, how they are recruited, how expert historians and consulting firms construct witness reports, in what way experts cooperate with lawyers, and what it means to be deposed or appear on the stand. It showed expert witnessing at work on a practical level. Furthermore, I have examined under which rules of evidence an expert opinion is given in the American legal system. The Daubert rule represents a simplified definition of the Popperian concept of science. Its demand for a verifiable theory with a retrievable error-rate is not suited to review historical expert opinion. In my view, the court should distinguish between different kinds of knowledge that are presented in court. Concerning the historical discipline, Daubert's other condition of peer review, should be stressed in favour of the others.

By contrasting the American and European experiences of expert witnessing, I reassessed Alain Wijffels' idea of a forensic form of history from his editorial *History in Court,* published in 2001. Wijffels argued that historians should remain active in the preparation of historical arguments used in court but that they should not enter "the turf" [as he called it] of lawyers and judges, because the legal environment forces history into a legal straightjacket which historians would do well to avoid. Essentially, Wijffels argued in favour of historians as fact-delivers which lawyers and the court can use as they please, or in the words of the Latin adage: *da mihi facta, dabo tibi ius.* In contrast, I have argued that witnessing is an essential part of forensic history, since witnessing in court is a public affair which is open to close scrutiny by opposing counsel, the historical community, and the general public. Any historian willing to risk their professional reputation on the stand to defend the version of history that he believes is the most truthful will make sure his historical research cannot be discredited. This risk results in the fact that some of the historical research carried out in litigation-driven history offers examples of the best historical works that the discipline has to offer. The counterargument to Wijffels' proposal is that it is a self-fulfilling prophecy, limiting the historians' involvement to the grey areas of consulting with little or no paper trial, sets the door wide open for advocacy and historical distortion.

In the third part of the book I have aimed to go beyond a level of anecdote and generalizations based on one particular trial experience, which is apparent in a lot of historiographical literature on expert witnessing. I have presented a systematic overview of one subject of American civil litigation, namely, tobacco litigation. I have systematically analysed this category by means of four basic characteristics: (1) what did historians testify on?, (2) when did they testify; in other words, in which trials?, (3) how did they testify?, and (4) who did the testifying? These elements of the involvement of historians in tobacco litigation were analysed by means a qualitative and a quantitative analysis. The qualitative analysis researched the on-trial experience of five historians in the landmark case *US v. Philip Morris et al.* from 2002. In the qualitative analysis, I examined in how far the legal straightjacket has an influence on the narrative and the historical facts presented by the historian. As a conclusion, I have argued that the courtroom was a performative and fact-making theatre. The quantitative analysis has procured the expert witness profiles of 50 historians who have been involved in 314 cases of tobacco litigation from 1986 to October 2014. This analysis has allowed me to systematically research their involvement, and to discover that the biggest problem with the involvement of historians in tobacco litigation is a complete lack of transparency. In order to revive the debate on expert witnessing in tobacco litigation by historians, I have published the profiles of those 50 historians online, so that their peers can know when reading their other scholarly work what the author's conflicting interests are.[1] I furthermore hope that the publication of these expert profiles will increase debate on the involvement of historians in tobacco litigation as expert judicial witnesses.

In conclusion, I address two points: (1) my argument that the court is a performative and fact-making theatre, and (2) a formulation of the concept of the forensification of history.

1. After the qualitative analysis of the civil landmark case *US v. Philip Morris et al.* and with the practical guide to expert witnessing in mind, I have concluded that the courtroom is a performative and fact-making theatre. The courtroom is a performative drama. Historians engage in a rhetorical duel with lawyers, which differs greatly from standard academic debate. As we have seen, opposing counsel submits historians to all kinds of rhetorical techniques with one goal only: to completely destroy and discredit the credibility and the validity of the expert witness himself and of his expert report. Historians themselves do not shrink from engaging in rhetorical jousting with lawyers by means of those very same rhetorical techniques.

   Legally and extralegally, the courtroom influences the historian's discourse, but does it change the research of the historian in a factual manner? I have concluded, that the demands by the court of historians serving as expert witnesses does not limit solid historical research, in fact on the contrary; it enhances it. Historians who openly testify in court put their professional reputations and research at stake, and in anticipation of the meticulous research by opposing counsel and the opposing expert witnesses' report, they will make sure, as I have discussed in the practical guide to expert witnessing, that every footnote and every source is double-checked and that every argument the expert makes can be proven with multiple primary and secondary sources. In other words, under ideal circumstances, the adversarial context of the American courtroom produces the best historical research in the form of reliable and extremely well-documented historical reports.

   The fact-making aspect of the courtroom lies in the reception by the judge or the jury of such a report. The reception of historical arguments is determined by a whole array of aspects; especially when historians were able to defend themselves and their opinions against the attacks by lawyers, and when being judged through personal experience, preferences, and preconditions that exist independently from historians and their reports with the judge or the jury members.[2] The decision for historians whether to lay Clio onto the scales of

[1]See all the expert witness profiles online at http://www.thejudgeandthehistorian.ugent.be. Accessed 31 Oct 2014. Disclosure: website created and maintained by the author.

[2]See the statement by Supreme Court Justice Anthony Kennedy which I quoted at the beginning of part I of this book for an eloquent translation of this argument.

Justitia is a personal choice which should not be made lightly.[3] History will always be judged in court, whether or not historians are present. It is up to the individual historian to decide whether they want to be there when history is being presented, used, and judged, or whether they just want to leave the historical facts in the hands of lawyers and judges, or stay in their ivory tower to avoid any stain of advocacy or social reality to keep von Ranke's ghost company.[4] Historians should not shrink from public scrutiny because their historical facts are not a 100 % completely proven although well beyond a reasonable doubt. Professional historical research can provide facts that are beyond a reasonable doubt. As the British eighteenth-century philosopher Joseph Butler remarked: "Probability is the guide of life."[5]

2. "The forensification of history is an international phenomenon in which historians-and this is key – testify with an opinion in court as expert judicial witnesses on a historical matter on which they have expert [which is understood as having extensively researched and published on the subject] knowledge."[6] Although more and more historians are involved around the globe in transnational justice, post-World War II, post-Holocaust trials, indigenous peoples trials, and in American civil litigation, litigation-driven history remains controversial. The forensification of history is connected with issues of advocacy, the loss of positivist objectivity, the fact that history is judged in a definitive manner, where the historians' arguments can be used by the judge, the reluctance to testify when a person's fate hangs in the balance, the legal straightjacket, and problems with transparency. In discussing these problems, I have often thought about the remark Michel Foucault made in his classic work *Surveiller et Punir*, where he stated that: "The lyricism of marginality may find inspiration in the image of the 'outlaw', the great social nomad, who prowls on the confines of a docile, frightened order."[7] Foucault argues that there lies great social strength in a marginal movement, for it forces traditional institutions to reflect upon themselves and find a way to incorporate and appease the demands of the marginal movement in order to silence its critical voice. I argue that this marginal role is the significant influence that the forensification of history has on the historical profession and it should be worn as a badge of honour. By challenging traditional ideas and practices, litigation-driven history and the whole movement

---

[3]It is the ambition of the author that the reader, by going through an overview filled with examples and practical experience-like descriptions, will reflect upon the question whether he or she would be willing to take the risk to defend his or her research on the stand as an expert witness.

[4]As George Orwell remarked: 'History is a palimpsest', it is up to historians to decide if they want to be there when a new version is inscribed on the parchment. I quoted Orwell at the beginning of the second part of the book.

[5]Butler, Joseph. 1740. *The Analogy of Religion.* Third edition. London: John & Paul Knapton.

[6]This is my definition of "the forensification of history", based on the research presented in this book.

[7]Foucault, Michel. 1975. *Surveiller et punir: naissance de la prison.* Paris: Gallimard.

of public history challenges the institutionalized form of the historical disciplines in the academy. If academic and public historians are willing to reflect on their historical activities, on a meta-level and a practical level, then litigation-driven history may influence the overall direction of the historical discipline in a way that overcomes Clio's Modern Paradox.

Historian Caroline Fink, wrote an article entitled: *A New Historian?,* in which she argues that: "We need historians who represent voices of fairness, meticulousness and scrupulousness, able to set research agendas, analyse and interpret documents and identify untruths, but who also admit the remaining gaps in our knowledge."[8] The forensification of history procures research funding that otherwise would not have been there, it procures secret industry documents for further historical research, and it can elevate the relevance and legitimacy of the historical discipline. Moreover, if historians use rhetoric to defend their legitimate opinion based on professional historical research, critics should look beyond the theatres of the court and look at the facts historians bring to court. My analysis of the involvement of historians in tobacco litigation has shown that a minority of historians through their abuse of history can undermine the historical discipline if it remains unquestioned by their colleagues. However, the lesson from the involvement of historians as expert witnesses in tobacco litigation is that such abuse of history can be countered and even rebuffed by an even smaller group of historians willing to risk their reputations and research in court in order to defend the historical discipline through truthful historical research.

To conclude: there are six major problems with historians working as expert witnesses in tobacco litigation: (1) Experts hired by the defence are not experts on the history of tobacco. (2) Historians working for defence counsel do not use neutral methods to select their sources. Their sources are selected by legal counsel. In addition they disregard pertinent secondary and primary sources, namely the internal industry documents. (3) Historians working for the defence have not published on the history of tobacco, smoking, the cigarette, or it's industry. (4) All experts, those working for the plaintiff as well as those working for the defence are receiving large salaries. (5) Expert witnesses for the defence operate under a veil of secrecy. (6) Overall, there is little debate on the subject.

The expert witnesses for the defence have not published their research on tobacco, and none of their work is corroborated by peer review while funded by litigating parties or law firms. This modus operandi presents a considerable danger for the public image of academic impartiality generally attributed to the historical profession. Advocacy is not a sin, and in some cases it can be a virtue. Yet we owe it to history, the public, and our profession to more actively discuss where we draw the line. A majority of the historians involved in tobacco litigation have vouched for scholarship of a doubtful nature without peer review. In addition, these historians have refused by and large to comment on their activities. Historians, the legal profession, and the public have a right to know who is testifying as an

[8]Fink, Carole. 2005. A New Historian? *Contemporary European History* 14, 147.

expert witness. When experts are hired not because of their knowledge but for their position, justice is not served. When historians and their research are shrouded in mystery, open debate is impossible.

In an increasingly litigious society, historical arguments will continue to play an important role in court. The legal and historical discipline should discuss the role of historians in court. Do historians have an obligation to enter the courtroom? And if so, should historians refrain from providing witness testimony? Should they limit their involvement, agreeing to serving only as a consultant? Or should historians serve as expert witnesses to protect and defend historical truths in court? Do the Daubert standard and the Federal Rules of Evidence for expert witnesses provide sufficient legal provisions to keep junk scholarship out of American courts? What should the role of the experts' institutions be? Are universities obliged to submit the work of their experts to any kind of oversight? Is it the responsibility of the AHA, the OAH, or the NCPH to expand their ethical guidelines? Do expert historians need specific research standards on litigation-driven history? In short, does the social responsibility of the historical profession stop at the doors of the courtroom, or do we cross the doorstep and take the stand? And when historians embark upon such an interdisciplinary adventure, in which manner should Clio best heed Justitia's call?

The forensification of history is a new form of practicing history. It combines the classic form of rigid historical research and a controversial legal practice. The forensification of history is here to stay and allows historians to be active and critical voices in matters that matter to the people who pay their tenures. The forensification of history challenges us as historians and legal scholars to think critically on the historical and legal profession, its research methods, its ethical responsibility, and its goals. I argue in favour of the forensification of history and the majority of its practitioners. After this conclusion, I place a five-point manifest, inspired by Gilissen's ten-point proposal from 1960, that addresses the basic principles that can aid in ensuring that the worst distortions and abuses disappear from forensic history.[9] In a preliminary conclusion of my attempt at researching *forensic history*, I would argue that the right tools are available, and as historians know, we can only let time pass, and let history judge those who pick them up.

Bibliography

Butler, Joseph. 1740. *The analogy of religion*. London: John & Paul Knapton.

Carole, Fink. 2005. A new historian? *Contemporary European History* 14: 135–147.

Foucault, Michel. 1975. *Surveiller et punir: naissance de la prison*. Paris: Gallimard.

Gilissen, John. 1960. La responsabilité civile et pénale de l'historien. *Revue Belge de Philologie et d'Histoire* 38: 1005–1039.

[9]Gilissen, John. 1960. La responsabilité civile et pénale de l'historien. Second Part. *Revue Belge de Philologie et d'Histoire* 38, 1038–1039.

Five General Principles on Forensic History

1. ***A Duty to Respect the Standards of Professional Historical Research.***
Historians should maintain standards of professional historical research while involved in litigation-driven history. These standards are of an intersubjective nature, in other words they are recognized by the historians' peers.

2. ***A Duty to Work in an Interdisciplinary Manner.***
Historians should work together with lawyers in a constructive spirit that will bring about better understanding of each other's disciplines. Better understanding will set more realistic expectations with the legal profession from historical expert witnesses and consultants when lawyers demand facts that fit their legal strategies.

3. ***A Duty to Research all Possible Sources.***
Litigation-driven history threatens the historian's obligation to research *all* legally accessible sources on their subject. When lawyers come to historians for historical expertise, historians should set strong preconditions on their cooperation. Historians should not let their historical scope nor research of available sources be limited by legal strategies. Historians sit at the bargaining end of the table and should exploit that advantage by demanding that they are allowed to research on their own terms.

4. ***A Duty to Adhere to a Code of Ethics.***
Historians have to adhere to an ethical code which is actively promoted and enforced by universities and historical organizations. Above all, transparency in litigation-driven history should be maintained by obliging expert witnesses to publish litigation-driven research in order to maintain an objectivity of an intersubjective nature with historians working as expert judicial witnesses and their work through peer review. Advocacy does not impair a historian from being ethical, as long as it is there in the open for all to see.

5. ***A Right to Refuse.***
Participating in the courtroom is a personal choice to which no historian can be forced.

R. Delafontaine, *Historians as Expert Judicial Witnesses in Tobacco Litigation*,
Studies in the History of Law and Justice 4, DOI 10.1007/978-3-319-14292-0

Appendices

Appendix I: Expert Witness Profiles

Historians as Expert Witnesses in Tobacco Litigation

Expert witness profile number	First name	Last name
0	Standard expert witness profile	
1	Stephen	Ambrose
2	Jonathan	Bean
3	Hyman	Berman
4	Allan	Brandt
5	James	Breeden
6	John	Burnham
7	Augustus	Burns
8	Fred	Carstensen
9	Michael	Chesson
10	Elizabeth	Cobbs Hoffman
11	Luis	Díaz-Hernández
12	Thomas	DiBacco
13	John	Drobny
14	Peter	English
15	Frederick	Fausz
16	Lacy	Ford
17	Otis	Graham Jr.
18	George	Green
19	Janette	Greenwood
20	Jon	Harkness
21	Paul	Harvey
22	James	Hilty

(continued)

R. Delafontaine, *Historians as Expert Judicial Witnesses in Tobacco Litigation*,
Studies in the History of Law and Justice 4, DOI 10.1007/978-3-319-14292-0

Expert witness profile number	First name	Last name
23	Joan	Hoff
24	Robert	Hudson
25	Jacob	Judd
26	Louis	Kyriakoudes
27	Timothy	Lenoir
28	Kenneth	Lipartito
29	Charles	Lowery
30	Kenneth	Ludmerer
31	James	Martin
32	Luis	Martinez-Fernandez
33	Glenn	May
34	Gregg	Michel
35	Wayne	Morgan
36	Robert	Norrell
37	Michael	Parrish
38	Terry	Parssinen
39	Robert	Proctor
40	Randy	Roberts
41	Mark	Rose
42	David	Sansing
43	Todd	Savitt
44	Michael	Schaller
45	James	Sharp
46	John	Skates
47	John	Snetsinger
48	William	Stueck
49	Joseph	Tulchin
50	Theodore	Wilson

0. Standard Expert Witness Profile

Name	First name – Last name
Professional occupation	X
Institution	X
Website	A website maintained by the university which employs the expert witness or a personal website.
Short description	Maximal 1,000 words on the historian and his professional research and litigation-related issues, based on his or her own website, secondary sources from historians, legal scholars, and the public media, and furthermore, documentation from database research in TOD, DATTA, LTDL, and Westlaw.
Education	X
Major fields	X
Major publications	X
Number of cases	X

Case	Year	Manner of involvement
1. Plaintiff v. Defence	Ranging from 1986–2014	Designated
		Affidavit
		Expert report submitted
		Deposition
		Direct examination or testimony
		Cross-examination
		Redirect examination
		Or any combination of the above.

Standard Citation offered: Delafontaine, Ramses. 2015. [FIRST NAME SECOND NAME Expert Witness Profile.] In *Historians as Expert Judicial Witnesses In Tobacco Litigation: A Controversial Legal Practice.* Springer, [PAGE].

1. Stephen Ambrose

Name	Stephen Ambrose (Deceased)
Professional occupation	Professor of History
Institution	University of New Orleans
Website	http://www.achievement.org/autodoc/page/amb0pro-1
	http://www.nationalww2museum.org/about-the-museum/about-the-founder.html
Short description	Stephen Ambrose was professor of history at the University of New Orleans. Ambrose wrote more than 30 books, primarily on World War II and President Eisenhower. His work *Band of Brothers* was made into a television miniseries for which he won a Primetime Emmy as one of the producers. As a historian, he appeared on American national television on several occasions to discuss different presidencies and World War II. Ten months prior to his death, *the New York Times* wrote that Ambrose had become: "the most prolific, the most commercially successful and the most academically accomplished of a new group of blockbuster historians."[1] Despite his fame or because of it, Ambrose's work came under close scrutiny and questions of plagiarism arose. In the years after his death, Ambrose's work has in some instances been confirmed as plagiarism.[2] In addition, his interviews with President Eisenhower are estimated to be far fewer in number than Ambrose had us believe.[3] Ambrose founded The National WWII Museum in New Orleans. His involvement in the museum can also be linked to his work for the tobacco industry. In April of 1995, Ambrose sent two letters to employees of Philip Morris asking for funding for the National D-Day Museum, now the National World War Two museum. Ambrose sent the letters as Chairman of the Board of the national D-Day Museum. The subject of Ambrose's letters were the alleged promises of Philip Morris's executives for funding for the newly established museum. In response to his letters, Bring Murray, an executive at Philip Morris responded that even if those promises were made, those executives who made those promises did not have the authority to make them. After due deliberation, no such funds could be made available at Philip Morris at that time.[4] Ambrose had testified for the tobacco industry in *Covert v. Liggett Group* only the year before. Some months later it seems that the industry's recruiters were not willing to redeem all of their promises. Yet, Ambrose continued his work for the tobacco companies. In 1997, Ambrose was deposed in the Attorney General's case *Florida v. American Tobacco*. He was furthermore designated in *Haines v. Liggett Group* that same year. On April 28, 1999 the board of directors of Philip Morris Companies Inc. assembled in Richmond, Virginia for their pre-annual dinner meeting. Geoffrey Bible, CEO of Philip Morris at the time, introduced the evening's guest speaker: national famed historian Stephen Ambrose. After Ambrose's speech, Bible promised "a grant to the National D-Day Museum."[5] To celebrate their 10th anniversary, the museum published a list with the founding contributors. Philip Morris Companies Inc. is among those early beneficiaries.[6]

(continued)

	Ambrose has been reported by several sources to have testified for the tobacco industry.[7] He received $25,000 for the work he did as an expert witness in *Covert v. Liggett Group*. Laura Maggi quotes Ambrose under cross-examination whether he was working as an expert witness for the money: "Yes.", he answered honestly.[8] Ambrose died, as a smoker, of lung cancer at the age of 66 in 2002.[9]
Education	Ph.D.
Major fields	World War Two and biographer of U.S. Presidents Dwight D. Eisenhower and Richard Nixon
Major publications	Dwight D. Eisenhower (1991), Band of Brothers (1992), D-Day (1994)
Number of cases	3

Case[10]	Year	Manner of involvement
1. Covert v. Liggett Group	1994	Testimony
2. Florida v. American Tobacco	1997	Deposition
3. Haines v. Liggett Group	1997	Designated

[1]Kirkpatrick, David. 2002. As Historian's Fame Grows, So Do Questions on Methods. *The New York Times,* January 11. http://www.nytimes.com/2002/01/11/us/as-historian-s-fame-grows-so-do-questions-on-methods.html?pagewanted=all&src=pm. Accessed 31 Oct 2014.

[2]Kirkpatrick, as n. 1.

[3]Rayner, Richard. 2010. Channelling Ike. *The New Yorker,* April 26. http://www.newyorker.com/talk/2010/04/26/100426ta_talk_rayner. Accessed 31 Oct 2014.

[4]Murray, Bring. 1995. *Letter to Stephen Ambrose.* 20/04/1995, 3. LTDL. Bates Number: 2045756873/6875. http://legacy.library.ucsf.edu/tid/lks57d00. Accessed 31 Oct 2014.

[5]s.n. 1999. *Suggested Remarks by Geoffrey C. Bible Chairman of the Board and CEO Philip Morris Companies Inc.: Introduction of Stephen E. Ambrose at the Dinner for the Board of Directors and Guests.* 28/04/1999, 4. LTDL. Bates Number: 2077407403/7406. http://legacy.library.ucsf.edu/tid/zhq80c00. Accessed 31 Oct 2014.

[6]s.n. 2010. *Annual-report National World War Two Museum,* 16. http://www.nationalww2museum.org/about-the-museum/www.nationalww2museum.org/about-the-museum/2010-annual-report.pdf. Accessed 31 Oct 2014.

[7]Martin, Jonathan. 2003. Historians at the Gate: Accommodating Expert Historical Testimony in Federal Courts. *The New York University Law Review* 78, 1518–1519, 1539–1540. & Proctor, Robert. 2012. *Golden Holocaust: Origins of the Cigarette Catastrophe and the Case for Abolition.* Berkeley: University of California Press, 460.

[8]Maggi, Laura. 2001. Bearing Witness for Tobacco. *The American Prospect*, November 9. http://prospect.org/article/bearing-witness-tobacco. Accessed 31 Oct 2014.

[9]Wiener, Jon. 2010. Big Tobacco and the Historians. *The Nation*, February 15. http://www.thenation.com/article/big-tobacco-and-historians. Accessed 31 Oct 2014.

[10]Information on the cases is based on Proctor, Robert. 2012. *Golden Holocaust: Origins of the Cigarette Catastrophe and the Case for Abolition.* Berkeley: University of California Press, 460. & The following online databases: http://legacy.library.ucsf.edu, http://tobaccodocuments.org, http://lawschool.courtroomview.com/experts, & Westlaw.

2. *Jonathan Bean*

Name	Jonathan Bean
Professional occupation	Research Fellow – Professor of History
Institution	The Independent Institute – Southern Illinois University
Website	http://cola.siu.edu/history/faculty-and-staff/faculty/bean.php
	http://www.independent.org/aboutus/person_detail.asp?id=840
	http://i-history.blogspot.be/
Short description	Jonathan Bean is a Research Fellow at the Independent Institute and a Professor of History at Southern Illinois University. He has written multiple books and articles. As a consultant, he has worked for the Japanese government. Furthermore, Bean testified before the US Senate on corruption in government contracting. His website states that he has "served as an expert witness in two landmark court cases", without describing or naming these cases.[1] He is a former senior editor for *H-Business,* an on-line journal for business historians. Bean has two active blogs which are cited above. Bean writes on his Westlaw expert-witness profile that he has worked as a consultant for the defence in *US v. Philip Morris*.
Education	Ph.D.
Major fields	Racial minorities, American business and government, civil rights, Ohio history, digital history
Major publications	Race and Liberty in America (2009), Big Government and Affirmative Action: The Scandalous History of the Small Business Administration (2001), Beyond the Broker State: Federal Policies Toward Small Business, 1936–1961 (1996)
Number of cases	2

Case[2]	Year	Manner of involvement
1. Schwab v. Philip Morris	2004–2006	Designated
2. St. Louis v. American Tobacco	2004–2008	Deposition

[1]This litigation work is not described any further, so I do not regard this phrase as a formal and open acknowledgment of Bean's expert services for the tobacco industry.

[2]Information on the cases is based on Proctor, Robert. 2012. *Golden Holocaust: Origins of the Cigarette Catastrophe and the Case for Abolition.* Berkeley: University of California Press, 460. & The following online databases: http://legacy.library.ucsf.edu, http://tobaccodocuments.org, http://lawschool.courtroomview.com/experts, & Westlaw.

3. *Hyman Berman*

Name	Hyman Berman
Professional occupation	Professor Emeritus of History
Institution	University of Minnesota
Website	http://cla.umn.edu/about/directory/profile/berma001
Short description	Hyman Berman is a professor emeritus at the Department of History, University of Minnesota. He taught courses on Minnesota history and US labour history. Berman has published mainly on American labour history.
Education	Ph.D.
Major fields	The twentieth century, American labour and radicalism, Minnesota history, Minnesotan immigrants, the Jewish labour movement, Twin Cities, U.S. labour history
Major publications	Labour in America (1962), A Cursory view of the Jewish Labour Movement: A History Survey (1963)
Number of cases	1

Case[1]	Year	Manner of involvement
1. Minnesota v. Philip Morris	1997–1998	Deposition and testimony

[1]Information on the cases is based on Proctor, Robert. 2012. *Golden Holocaust: Origins of the Cigarette Catastrophe and the Case for Abolition.* Berkeley: University of California Press, 460. & The following online databases: http://legacy.library.ucsf.edu, http://tobaccodocuments.org, http://lawschool.courtroomview.com/experts, & Westlaw.

4. Allan Brandt

Name	Allan Brandt
Professional occupation	Professor of the History of Science
	Amalie Moses Kass Professor of the History of Medicine
Institution	Harvard University
Website	http://www.fas.harvard.edu/~hsdept/bios/brandt.html
	http://www.cigarettecentury.com/
Short description	Allan M. Brandt is the Amalie Moses Kass Professor of the History of Medicine and Professor of the History of Science at Harvard University. He holds a joint appointment with the Faculty of Arts and Sciences and Harvard Medical School. Brandt served as Dean of the Graduate School of Arts and Sciences from 2008 to 2012. His work focuses on social and ethical aspects of health, disease, medical practices, and global health in the twentieth century. Brandt is the author of No Magic Bullet: A Social History of Venereal Disease in the United States since 1880 (1987); and is co-editor of Morality and Health (1997). He has written on the social history of epidemic disease; the history of public health and health policy; and the history of human experimentation among other topics. His book on the social and cultural history of cigarette smoking in the U.S., The Cigarette Century: The Rise, Fall, and Deadly Persistence of the Product that Defined America, remains up to this day an authority on the history of cigarettes and the tobacco industry in the US. The book received the Bancroft Prize from Columbia University in 2008 and the Welch Medal from the American Association for the History of Medicine in 2011. The link to the website of the book is cited above. Brandt has testified only in one case: The landmark case *US v. Philip Morris et al.,* on behalf of the Department of Justice. Brandt's testimony was central to the DOJ's argumentation that the tobacco industry had lied and conspired against the American Public for decades. The final verdict by Judge Kessler drew heavily from Brandt's testimony. His experiences before and during the trail are also depicted in *The Cigarette Century*.
Education	Ph.D.
Major fields	Social and ethical aspects of health, disease, and medical practices in the twentieth century United States, history of tobacco
Major publications	No Magic Bullet: A Social History of Venereal Disease in the United States since 1880 (1987), The Cigarette Century: The Rise, Fall, and Deadly Persistence of the Product That Defined America (2007)
Number of cases	1

Case[1]	Year	Manner of involvement
1. United States v. Philip Morris et al.	1999–2006	Deposition and cross-examination

[1]The following online databases: http://legacy.library.ucsf.edu, http://tobaccodocuments.org, http://lawschool.courtroomview.com/experts, & Westlaw.

5. James Breeden

Name	James O. Breeden
Professional occupation	Professor Emeritus of History
Institution	Southern Methodist University
Website	http://www.lib.utexas.edu/taro/smu/00109/smu-00109.html
Short description	James O. Breeden worked as a professor emeritus of American history at Southern Methodist University from 1969 until 2004. Breeden taught history of medicine courses at the University of Washington in the late 1960s before coming to SMU. Breeden's area of historical focus was the American South, in particular antebellum Southern history. During his 35 year tenure at SMU, he taught the American history survey course; an undergraduate class in historiography; and Southern history courses, including the development of science and medicine in the region. He wrote and edited several books on these subjects. Breeden retired in 2004.
Education	Ph.D.
Major fields	Racial minorities, American business and government, civil rights, Ohio history
Major publications	Advice Among Masters: The Ideal in Slave Management in the Old South (1980), Medicine in the West (1982), and Long Ride in Texas: The Explorations of John Leonard Riddell (1994)
Number of cases	1

Case[1]	Year	Manner of involvement
1. Allgood v. R.J. Reynolds	1994	Expert report submitted

[1]Information on the cases is based on Proctor, Robert. 2012. *Golden Holocaust: Origins of the Cigarette Catastrophe and the Case for Abolition.* Berkeley: University of California Press, 460. & The following online databases: http://legacy.library.ucsf.edu, http://tobaccodocuments.org, http://lawschool.courtroomview.com/experts, & Westlaw.

6. John Burnham

Name	John Burnham
Professional occupation	Professor of History
Institution	Ohio State University
Website	http://history.osu.edu/directory/Burnham2
Short description	Professor Burnham specializes in the history of medicine and American social history. His particular interest is the history of psychiatry. His recent books include *How Superstition Won and Science Lost: Paths into American Culture: Psychology, Medicine, and Morals* (1988), *Bad Habits: Drinking, Smoking, Taking Drugs, Gambling, Sexual Misbehaviour, and Swearing in American History* (1993), and *What Is Medical History? (2005).* Burnham is presently studying the impact of Freud on the Western world, and also the deinstitutionalization of mental patients in the 1950s. Professor Burnham has taught at Stanford University. He has served as President of the American Association for the History of Medicine and has held many other offices in scholarly organizations both in the United States and abroad, and he is a Fellow of the American Association for the Advancement of Science. Burnham has been a vocal supporter of those historians who are willing to testify for the tobacco industry. *The Lancet* of 2004 debated the role of historians in tobacco trials. Historian and expert witness Robert Proctor had written an article that condemned historians who testified for the tobacco companies. Burnham wrote a short reply to defend the historians who were working with tobacco companies.[1] In 2010, Burnham also wrote a reaction to historian Jon Wiener's article in *the Nation* on the same subject. Burnham defended historians who served as expert witnesses for the tobacco industry.[2] Claiming that "everyone has a financial interest."[3] Burnham has also served in a number of other court cases as a consultant for asbestos, lead, and soda companies.[4] Proctor noted in his article from 2006 on historians as expert witnesses in tobacco-related litigation that Burnham functioned as a recruiter of new expert historians for the legal firms defending the tobacco industry.[5] Burnham is one of the few historians who has served as an expert witness for the tobacco industry who had done research on the history of tobacco previous to his litigation work. Burnham is also the only expert working for the defence who is willing to discuss his work as an expert witness in tobacco litigation at length in public or with his peers.
Education	Ph.D.
Major fields	History of medicine, American social history, American history, US history to 1877
Major publications	Bad Habits: Drinking, Smoking, Taking Drugs, Gambling, Sexual Misbehaviour, and Swearing in American History (1993), American Physicians and Tobacco Use: Two Surgeons General, 1929 and 1964. In: *Bull. Hist. Med.*, Vol. 63, No. 1, 1989, pp. 1–31., How Superstition Won and Science Lost: Popularizing Science and Health in the United States (1987)
Number of cases	2

Case[6]	Year	Manner of involvement
1. Dewey v. R.J. Reynolds	1986	Designated
2. Cipollone v. Liggett Group	1986–1991	Designated

[1]For the debate in *The Lancet* see: Proctor, Robert. 2004. Should Medical Historians Be Working for the Tobacco Industry? *The Lancet* 363, 1174–1175. & Proctor, Robert. 2004. Medical Historians and the Tobacco Industry, Author's Reply. *The Lancet* 364, 838. & Burnham, John. 2004. Medical Historians and the Tobacco Industry. *The Lancet* 364, 838.

[2]For the debate in *The Nation* see: Wiener, Jon. 2010. Big Tobacco and the Historians. *The Nation*, February 15. http://www.thenation.com/article/big-tobacco-and-historians. Accessed 31 Oct 2014. & Wiener, Jon. 2010. Re 'Big Tobacco and the Historians', Wiener Replies. *The Nation*, March 9. http://www.thenation.com/article/re-big-tobacco-and-historians. Accessed Oct 31 2014. & Wiener, Jon. 2010. Smoking Gun ... Wiener Replies. *The Nation*, April 19. http://www.thenation.com/article/letters-337. Accessed 31 Oct 2014. & Burnham, John. 2010. In Defense of Historians as expert Witnesses: A Rebuttal to Jon Wiener. *George Mason University's History News Network*, April 1. http://hnn.us/articles/124924.html. Accessed 31 Oct 2014.

[3]Cohen, Patricia. 2003. History for Hire In Industry Lawsuits. *The New York Times*, June 14. http://www.nytimes.com/2003/06/14/arts/history-for-hire-in-industry-lawsuits.html?pagewanted=all&src=pm. Accessed 31 Oct 2014.

[4]Cohen, as n. 3.

[5]Proctor, Robert. 2006. 'Everyone Knew But No One Had Proof': Tobacco Industry Use of Medical History Expertise in US courts, 1990–2002. *Tobacco Control* 15, 121.

[6]Information on the cases is based on Proctor, Robert. 2012. *Golden Holocaust: Origins of the Cigarette Catastrophe and the Case for Abolition.* Berkeley: University of California Press, 460. & The following online databases: http://legacy.library.ucsf.edu, http://tobaccodocuments.org, http://lawschool.courtroomview.com/experts, & Westlaw.

7. Augustus Burns III

Name	Augustus M. Burns (Deceased)
Professional occupation	Professor of History
Institution	University of Florida
Website	http://tobaccodocuments.org/profiles/people/burns_augustus.html
Short description	A lecture series has been organized annually since 2000 to recognize Burns' contributions. Guest speakers on the first memorial lecture included historian Stephen Ambrose, who has also testified as an expert for the tobacco industry.[1] Burns was deposed in two cases. In his deposition in *Engle v. R.J. Reynolds*, Burns acknowledged that he made $100 an hour for his litigation-driven work.[2] In *Florida v. American Tobacco*, Burns was also questioned on his remuneration: *"Q. What does it add up to, do you know, in terms of compensation to you over this period of time?* *A. $75,000, $80,000.* *Q. What is your annual salary there at the university?* *A. $52,000 a year."*[3] In 2 years Burns got paid by the tobacco companies for his work as an expert witness amounting to 80 % of his normal salary that he received from his university.
Education	Ph.D.
Major fields	Racial history in the South
Major publications	Graduate Education for Blacks in North Carolina, 1930–1951 (1980), Frank Porter Graham and the 1950 Senate Race in North Carolina (1990)
Number of cases	2

Case[4]	Year	Manner of involvement
1. Florida v. American Tobacco	1997	Deposition
2. Engle v. R.J. Reynolds	1998	Deposition

[1]Consulted via http://www.clas.ufl.edu/events/news/Articles%201996-2004/200003-atc.html. Accessed 31 Oct 2014.

[2]See deposition of Augustus Burns, November 6, 1998, *Engle v. R.J. Reynolds*. Westlaw reference: 1998 WL 35273084.

[3]See deposition of Augustus Burns, May 9, 1997, *Florida v. R.J. Reynolds*. Westlaw reference: 1997 WL 34665268.

[4]Information on the cases is based on Proctor, Robert. 2012. *Golden Holocaust: Origins of the Cigarette Catastrophe and the Case for Abolition.* Berkeley: University of California Press, 460. & The following online databases: http://legacy.library.ucsf.edu, http://tobaccodocuments.org, http://lawschool.courtroomview.com/experts, & Westlaw.

8. Fred Carstensen

Name	Fred V. Carstensen
Professional occupation	Professor of Economics
Institution	University of Connecticut
Website	http://ccea.uconn.edu/ccea_staff.htm
	http://ideas.repec.org/e/pca81.html
Short description	Carstensen is an economic historian who focuses on political issues concerning economic history. He has served as an expert witness in the landmark case *Cipollone v. Liggett*. In his deposition for Cipollone, he acknowledged having made $85,000 with his work as an expert witness for the tobacco industry.[1] Under cross-examination he was forced to admit that he had not fully investigated the impact of tobacco advertising and product placement in movies on the common knowledge of health hazards connected with cigarette smoking. Carstensen argued that it was impossible not to be fully aware of the dangers of smoking. He based his arguments on articles from popular newspapers and magazines which discussed tobacco related issues. The plaintiff's counsel was able to prove and make Carstensen acknowledge during cross-testimony that those articles on smoking made up for less than one percent of all the articles published in these magazines.[2] This made it very hard for the defence to maintain that everyone had been fully aware of the issue because of the relative small number of these articles and without even considering the influence of tobacco publicity and disinformation distributed by the tobacco companies.[3] Despite his problematic testimony, Carstensen has continued to offer the opinion that common knowledge on the risks of smoking was widespread. He has, furthermore, argued that experts who have testified on behave of smokers agree with the statement that smokers were fully aware of the dangers from the 1930s onward.[4] In addition, Carstensen maintains that the verdicts in favour of the plaintiffs in tobacco litigation are the result of a changed legal standard in product-liability litigation. According to Carstensen, the awareness-argument has been removed as valuable evidence and has no influence anymore on the verdict.[5] The fact that many cases in recent tobacco litigation are lost by the plaintiffs because they started smoking despite their knowledge of the dangers for example, in ongoing Engle Progeny cases, proves that the legal standard of awareness in product-liability cases has not been abandoned as Carstensen would have us believe. On the contrary, the "personal choice" argument or "awareness" argument remains a key legal defence strategy used by the tobacco industry's legal counsel.
Education	Ph.D.
Major fields	Business history, poverty in Connecticut, Russian economic history
Major publications	American Enterprise in Foreign Markets: Singer and International Harvester in Imperial Russia (1984)
Number of cases	2

Case[6]	Year	Manner of involvement
1. Cipollone v. Liggett Group	1986–1991	Deposition and testimony
2. Gerrity v. Lorillard	2005	Deposition

[1]Cross-examination of Fred Carstensen, April 7, 1998, *Cipollone v. Liggett Group*. LTDL. Bates Number: CARSTENSENF040788PM. http://legacy.library.ucsf.edu/tid/yat07a00. Accessed 31 Oct 2014, 7592 ff.

[2]Brandt, Allan. 2007. *The Cigarette Century. The Rise, Fall and Deadly Persistence of a Product that Defined America.* New York: Basic Books, 342.

[3]Cross-examination of Fred Carstensen, as n. 1, 7713 ff.

[4]Personal correspondence with prof. Carstensen.

[5]Personal correspondence with prof. Carstensen.

[6]Information on the cases is based on Proctor, Robert. 2012. *Golden Holocaust: Origins of the Cigarette Catastrophe and the Case for Abolition.* Berkeley: University of California Press, 460. & The following online databases: http://legacy.library.ucsf.edu, http://tobaccodocuments.org, http://lawschool.courtroomview.com/experts, & Westlaw. This profile is furthermore completed with information from personal correspondence with prof. Carstensen.

9. Michael Chesson

Name	Michael Chesson
Professional occupation	Professor Emeritus of History
Institution	American College of History and Legal Studies, former University of Massachusetts-Boston
Website	http://www.michaelchesson.com/?page_id=8
Short description	Michael Chesson is founding professor at the American College of History and Legal Studies. Chesson was also professor of history at the University of Massachusetts at Boston. He has published several books on the American Civil War. He has been active in only one tobacco-related case.
Education	Ph.D.
Major fields	American civil war
Major publications	Exile in Richmond: The Confederate Journal of Henri Garidel (2001), The Journal of a Civil War Surgeon (2003)
Number of cases	1

Case[1]	Year	Manner of involvement
1. Longden v. Philip Morris	2003	Affidavit

[1]Information on the cases is based on Proctor, Robert. 2012. *Golden Holocaust: Origins of the Cigarette Catastrophe and the Case for Abolition.* Berkeley: University of California Press, 460. & The following online databases: http://legacy.library.ucsf.edu, http://tobaccodocuments.org, http://lawschool.courtroomview.com/experts, & Westlaw.

10. Elizabeth Cobss Hoffman

Name	Elizabeth Cobbs Hoffman
Professional occupation	Dwight Stanford Chair in U.S. Foreign Relations
Institution	San Diego State University
Website	http://www-rohan.sdsu.edu/~histweb/faculty_and_staff/faculty_bios/e_cobbs-hoffman.htm
	http://elizabethcobbshoffman.com/
Short description	Elizabeth Cobbs Hoffman is the Dwight E. Stanford Chair in US Foreign Relations at San Diego State University. She is a historian and novelist, and the author of several books. Professor Cobbs Hoffman currently writes articles for both scholarly and popular journals, and has served on the editorial boards of Diplomatic History and the Encyclopedia of American Foreign Relations. She recently served two terms as a member of the Historical Advisory Committee to the US Department of State. Cobbs Hoffman has also been a member of the jury for the Pulitzer Prize in History. Her research interests include US, European, Third World, and Latin American history. In 2012–2013, Professor Cobbs Hoffman held her third fellowship at Stanford's Hoover Institution for War, Revolution, and Peace, where she just completed a new history of American foreign relations from 1776 to the present. Currently, Cobbs Hoffman is an active expert witness in *In re: Engle Progeny cases* as a witness for the defence. In a deposition pertaining to *Rodehaver v. R.J. Reynolds* Cobbs Hoffman declared she had made $616,000 as an expert witness for the tobacco industry.[1]
Education	Ph.D.
Major fields	Diplomacy, international politics, American foreign relations
Major publications	The Rich Neighbour Policy: Rockefeller and Kaiser in Brazil (1992), All You Need is Love: The Peace Corps and the Spirit of the 1960s' (1998), Broken Promises: A Novel of the Civil War (2003), American Umpire (2013)
Number of cases	21

Case[2]	Year	Manner of Involvement
1. Boeken v. Philip Morris	2001–2003	Deposition and testimony
2. Brown v. American Tobacco[3]	2002–2004	Deposition
3. Bradley v. R.J. Reynolds	2008–2012	Deposition
4. Evers v. R.J. Reynolds	2008–2013	Cross-examination
5. Kirkland v. R.J. Reynolds	2008–2011	Designated
6. Long v. R.J. Reynolds	2008	Designated
7. Wyerick v. R.J. Reynolds	2008	Designated
8. Patterson v. R.J. Reynolds	2009	Deposition
9. In re: Engle Progeny cases[4]	2009–2014	Testimony

(continued)

Case[2]	Year	Manner of Involvement
10. Rohr v. R.J. Reynolds	2010	Cross-examination
11. Smith v. R.J. Reynolds	2010–2012	Testimony
12. Aycock v. R.J. Reynolds	2011	Designated
13. Gollihue v. R.J. Reynolds	2011	Deposition
14. Narushka v. R.J. Reynolds	2011–2012	Deposition
15. Pickett v. R.J. Reynolds	2011–2012	Testimony
16. Rodehaver v. R.J. Reynolds	2011–2012	Testimony
17. Rudy v. R.J. Reynolds	2011–2012	Testimony
18. Soffer v. R.J. Reynolds	2011	Testimony
19. Weick v. Philip Morris	2011	Cross-examination
20. Hill v. R.J. Reynolds	2012	Deposition
21. Anderson v. R.J. Reynolds	2013–2014	Cross-examination

[1]See testimony of Elizabeth Cobbs Hoffman, June 7, 2012, *Rodehaver v. R.J. Reynolds*. Westlaw reference: 2012 WL 3541153.

[2]Information on the cases is based on Proctor, Robert. 2012. *Golden Holocaust: Origins of the Cigarette Catastrophe and the Case for Abolition*. Berkeley: University of California Press, 460. & The following online databases: http://legacy.library.ucsf.edu, http://tobaccodocuments.org, http://lawschool.courtroomview.com/experts, & Westlaw. In personal communication with the author prof. Cobbs Hoffman stated she had already commented sufficiently on the subject on other instances.

[3]Relates to In re: Tobacco Cases II.

[4]Cobbs Hoffman was deposed pertaining to multiple Engle Progeny cases. Most Engle Progeny cases Cobbs Hoffman is involved in have been tried in court. Yet the Martin and Waggoner suits, for which she was deposed under In re: Engle Progeny cases have not gone to trial. See Proctor, as n. 2, 460.

11. Luis Díaz-Hernández

Name	Luis Díaz-Hernández
Professional occupation	Professor of History
Institution	Pontifical Catholic University in Ponce, Puerto Rico
Website	http://www.expertwitnessprofiler.com/Luis+Diaz-Hernandez/73419
Short description	Prof. Díaz-Hernández has been a witness for the plaintiffs in tobacco-related litigation. He teaches at the Pontifical Catholic University in Ponce, Puerto Rico, since 1975. He has written and published mainly on the history of Puerto Rico. His witness report can be ordered via a website.[1] He has written reports for tobacco litigation in Puerto Rico for the plaintiffs. Díaz-Hernández acknowledged during a deposition in *Alvarez v. R.J. Reynolds* that he charged $275 an hour for his tobacco related litigation work.[2] In *Valle-Ortiz v. R.J. Reynolds* his testimony was successfully challenged by the defence under the Daubert standard.[3]
Education	Ph.D.
Major fields	History of Puerto Rico
Major publications	Documentos para el estudio de la historia de Puerto Rico, 1868–1900 (1981), Catálogo de temblores y terremotos de Puerto Rico (1983)
Number of cases	8

Case[4]	Year	Manner of involvement
1. Rivera v. R.J. Reynolds	2003–2005	Testimony
2. Alvarez v. R.J. Reynolds	2004–2005	Deposition
3. Caraballo-Rodriguez v. R.J. Reynolds	2005	Testimony
4. De Jesus v. R.J. Reynolds	2005	Expert report submitted
5. Nieves-Rodriguez v. R.J. Reynolds	2005	Testimony
6. Ortega v. Philip Morris	2005	Testimony
7. Ramos v. Philip Morris	2005	Expert report submitted
8. Valle-Ortiz v. R.J. Reynolds	2005	Testimony inadmissible

[1] See http://www.expertwitnessprofiler.com/Luis+Diaz-Hernandez/73419. Accessed 31 Oct 2014.

[2] Deposition of Luis Díaz-Hernández, September 21, 2004, *Alvarez v. R.J. Reynolds*. Westlaw reference: 2004 WL 5487028.

[3] Defendant's Motion to Strike the New Expert Report of Dr. Luis E. Diaz, August 4, 2005, *Valle-Ortiz v. R.J. Reynolds*. Westlaw Number: 2005 WL 6141299.

[4] Compiled with following online databases: http://legacy.library.ucsf.edu, http://tobaccodocuments.org, http://lawschool.courtroomview.com/experts, & Westlaw.

12. Thomas DiBacco

Name	Thomas DiBacco
Professional occupation	Professor Emeritus and Consultant
Institution	The Kogod School of Business of the American University
Website	http://www.friendsofbusinesshistory.com/ThomasDiBacco.pdf
Short description	Thomas V. DiBacco has had a distinguished career in teaching and as a consultant working for governmental and private organizations. He is the author of numerous books and articles in scholarly journals and newspapers. He retired from teaching in 1999. In a deposition taken during *Katz v. R.J. Reynolds* DiBacco acknowledged that he had made $380,000 with tobacco-related litigation-work since 1995.[1]
Education	Ph.D.
Major fields	US history, US social history, and history of business, technology, and the economy
Major publications	History of the United States (1991–1997), Made in the USA: The History of American Business (1987, 2003)
Number of cases	6

Case[2]	Year	Manner of involvement
1. Engle v. R.J. Reynolds	1997–1999	Deposition and testimony
2. Blue Cross v. Philip Morris	2000–2001	Deposition
3. Eastman v. Brown and Williamson	2003–2007	Deposition and testimony
4. Ferlanti v. Liggett Group	2009	Cross-examination
5. Katz v. R.J. Reynolds	2010–2011	Deposition and testimony
6. Blitch v. R.J. Reynolds	2011	Testimony

[1]Deposition of Thomas DiBacco, October 8, 2010, *Katz v. R.J. Reynolds*. Westlaw reference: 2010 WL 3537162.

[2]Information on the cases is based on Proctor, Robert. 2012. *Golden Holocaust: Origins of the Cigarette Catastrophe and the Case for Abolition*. Berkeley: University of California Press, 460. & The following online databases: http://legacy.library.ucsf.edu, http://tobaccodocuments.org, http://lawschool.courtroomview.com/experts, & Westlaw.

13. John Drobny

Name	John Drobny
Professional occupation	Consultant
Institution	
Website	http://tobaccodocuments.org/profiles/people/drobny_john.html
Short description	Mr. Drobny is a managed care specialist and is currently President of IHG, Inc. His areas of expertise include Texas medicaid design and history, Texas and national demographics and population compositions, case mix, Medicaid and health care financing, and the Texas medicaid insurance arrangement.[1] During deposition in *Texas v. American Tobacco*, Drobny stated that he charged $250 an hour for his services as an expert witness. He furthermore said he had been paid $41,000 for his work in the case.[2]
Education	n/a
Major fields	History of Texas
Major publications	n/a
Number of cases	1

Case[3]	Year	Manner of involvement
1. Texas v. American Tobacco	1997	Deposition

[1]I list Mr. Drobny as a historian because the court accepted him as such. Deposition of John Drobny, 13/08/1997. LTDL. Bates Number: DROBNYJ08193. http://legacy.library.ucsf.edu/tid/jgk79a00. Accessed 31 Oct 2014.

[2]Deposition of John Drobny, August 13, 1997, *Texas v. American Tobacco.* Westlaw reference: 1997 WL 34668149.

[3]Information on the cases is based on Proctor, Robert. 2012. *Golden Holocaust: Origins of the Cigarette Catastrophe and the Case for Abolition.* Berkeley: University of California Press, 460. & The following online databases: http://legacy.library.ucsf.edu, http://tobaccodocuments.org, http://lawschool.courtroomview.com/experts, & Westlaw.

14. Peter English

Name	Peter Calvin English
Professional occupation	Professor Emeritus of History
	Professor Emeritus of Pediatrics
Institution	Duke University
Website	http://fds.duke.edu/db/aas/history/penglish
Short description	Peter English, MD, Ph.D. is professor of history and professor of paediatrics. For 30 years, until 2005, he was also a primary care paediatrician. He has written three books on the history of medicine, covering topics including pneumonia, diphtheria, and rheumatic fever. His interests in medical history have led to his focus on teaching about epidemic diseases and public health. Professor English is a member of the Board of Directors of the Josiah Charles Trent Memorial Foundation. He is currently writing a book titled: "Resistance to Antibiotics: A History." English has served as an expert historian in many tobacco related cases, but also in litigation involving child poisoning by lead paint and in multiple asbestos cases.[1] In *US v. Philip Morris et al.* English admitted to only have read the documents that were given to him by counsel representing the tobacco companies in preparation of his testimony[2], despite having done several hundreds of hours of research at a rate of $250 an hour.[3] By 2005 English's hourly rate as an expert witness had risen to $350 an hour, as English himself stated in affidavits submitted in multiple tobacco cases.[4] English has made at least $800,000 during his litigation-related work for the tobacco industry. During his deposition in *US v. Philip Morris et al.*, English acknowledged he made more from his tobacco litigation-driven work than from his academic salary.[5]
Education	Ph.D.
Major fields	Epidemic diseases and public health
Major publications	Rheumatic Fever. A Biological, Epidemiological, and Medical History of Rheumatic Fever in America and Britain from the eighteenth to the nineteenth century (1999), Old Paint: A Medical History of Childhood Lead-Paint Poisoning in the United States to 1980 (2001)
Number of cases	15

Case[6]	Year	Manner of involvement
1. Haines v. Liggett	1992	Designated
2. United States v. Philips Morris	1999–2006	Deposition
3. Blue Cross v. Philip Morris	2000–2001	Testimony
4. Brown v. American Tobacco	2002–2004	Deposition
5. Bullock v. Philip Morris	2002	Deposition
6. Miles v. Philip Morris	2002	Expert report submitted
7. Schwab v. Philip Morris	2004–2006	Expert report submitted
8. St. Louis v. American Tobacco	2004–2008	Deposition
9. Benedict v. Altria Group	2005	Affidavit
10. Craft v. Philip Morris	2005–2010	Deposition
11. Huntsberry v. R.J. Reynolds	2005	Expert report submitted
12. Clinton v. Altria Group	2006–2012	Expert report submitted
13. Cleary v. Philip Morris	2009	Expert report submitted
14. Donovan v. Philip Morris	2009–2011	Expert report submitted
15. In re: Light Cigarettes	2010	Affidavit

[1]Cohen, Patricia. 2003. History for Hire In Industry Lawsuits. *The New York Times,* June 14. http://www.nytimes.com/2003/06/14/arts/history-for-hire-in-industry-lawsuits.html?pagewanted=all&src=pm. Accessed 31 Oct 2014. & Deposition of Peter Calvin English, M.D., Ph.D., August 23, 2002, United States of America v. Philip Morris USA Inc., 23/08/2002. LTDL. Bates Number: ENGLISHP082302. http://legacy.library.ucsf.edu/tid/qqo11b00. Accessed 31 Oct 2014.

[2]Proctor, Robert. 2004. Should Medical Historians Be Working for the Tobacco Industry? *The Lancet* 363, 1175.

[3]Proctor, Robert. 2006. 'Everyone Knew But No One Had Proof': Tobacco Industry Use of Medical History Expertise in US courts, 1990–2002. *Tobacco Control* 15, 123. & Deposition of Peter Calvin English, as n. 1, 32.

[4]See for example: Affidavit of Peter English, December 12, 2005, *Benedict v. Altria Group.* Westlaw reference: 2005 WL 4044682.

[5]Deposition of Peter Calvin English, as n. 1, 45–46. & Proctor, as n. 3.

[6]Information on the cases is based on Proctor, Robert. 2012. *Golden Holocaust: Origins of the Cigarette Catastrophe and the Case for Abolition.* Berkeley: University of California Press, 460. & The following online databases: http://legacy.library.ucsf.edu, http://tobaccodocuments.org, http://lawschool.courtroomview.com/experts, & Westlaw.

15. Frederick Fausz

Name	Frederick Fausz
Professional occupation	Professor of History
Institution	University of Missouri
Website	http://www.umsl.edu/~umslhistory/faculty/fausz.html
Short description	Professor Fausz is a professor of American History at the University of Missouri. He has produced many articles and books on the history of indigenous peoples of America, Colonial America, and the history of the Mississippi Valley. In his affidavit for White Fausz noted that: "public awareness of the dangers of smoking (including its addictive nature) was so widespread since the 1950s "a thoughtful and prudent person would have had to consciously ignore prominent warnings in deciding to begin smoking cigarettes . . . "; thereby directly referring to the legal liability standard of a thoughtful and prudent person.[1]
Education	Ph.D.
Major fields	American Indians, colonial America, fur trade, Lewis & Clark expedition and era, French creole culture in the Mississippi valley
Major publications	Monument School of the People: A Sesquicentennial History of St. Mary's College of Maryland, 1840–1990 (1990), The Day Kikotan Became Hampton: England's First Indian War, 1609–1614 (2010), Founding St. Louis: First City of the New West (2011)
Number of cases	2

Case[2]	Year	Manner of involvement
1. White v. R.J. Reynolds	2000	Affidavit
2. Waterhouse v. R.J. Reynolds	2005–2006	Affidavit

[1] See 109 F. Supp. 2d 432, 432.
[2] Compiled with the following online databases: http://legacy.library.ucsf.edu, http://tobaccodocuments.org, http://lawschool.courtroomview.com/experts, & Westlaw.

16. Lacy Ford

Name	Lacy Ford
Professional occupation	Professor of Southern History
Institution	University of South Carolina
Website	http://artsandsciences.sc.edu/hist/lacy-k-ford-jr
	http://artsandsciences.sc.edu/hist/sites/sc.edu.hist/files/vitae/Ford.pdf
Short description	Lacy Ford is specialized in the history of the American South and especially in the history of slavery. He has served in several tobacco-related court cases as an expert witness for the tobacco industry. Laura Maggi writes that Ford declared during a phone interview for *The American Prospect* that "he had made it a policy not to talk about the substance of his testimony."[1] Ford also declined to comment on Jon Wiener's article in *The Nation.*[2] He, furthermore, declined to give further information for an article in *The Wall Street Journal.*[3] Ford's testimony in tobacco litigation was questioned by the Gallup Organization who accused Ford of consistently picking polls that gave an inflated sense of the public's awareness of health risks from smoking.[4] Ford received a letter from Frank Newport, editor-in-chief at the Gallup Organization, which read as follows: "Presenting selective data or distorting the meaning of individual Gallup poll questions out of context violates the purpose and the spirit in which these surveys were originally written."[5] Lawyers for R.J. Reynolds "fired back a testy five-page letter accusing the Gallup organization of limiting free discussion by scholars and questioning whether the polling group is in league with plaintiff's attorneys."[6] The selectiveness by which industry experts make use of polling date is a common strategy for the industry's witnesses, yet a peculiar standard for a "highly respected historian."[7] Allan Brandt notes in his book *The Cigarette Century* that: "Lacy Ford, a well-known historian of early nineteenth-century southern proslavery radicalism, testified on behalf of the industry about public knowledge of tobacco science and the mass media in the 1950s, a subject and a period on which he had published no research at all."[8]
Education	Ph.D.
Major fields	Nineteenth and twentieth century United States, The American South and political thought
Major publications	Origins of Southern Radicalism: The South Carolina Upcountry, 1800–1860 (1988), Blackwell Companion to the Civil War and Reconstruction (2005), Deliver Us From Evil: The Slavery Question in the Old South (2009)
Number of cases	19

Case[9]	Year	Manner of involvement
1. Engle v. R.J. Reynolds	1997–1999	Deposition and testimony
2. Karbiwnyk v. R.J. Reynolds	1997	Deposition and testimony
3. Keegan v. R.J. Reynolds	1997	Designated
4. Raulerson v. R.J. Reynolds	1997	Testimony
5. In re: Tobacco Litigation	2000	Deposition
6. Jones v. R.J. Reynolds	2000	Testimony
7. Little v. Brown & Williamson	2000	Deposition and testimony
8. Sheppard v. R.J. Reynolds	2000–2004	Expert report submitted
9. Kenyon v. R.J. Reynolds	2001	Testimony
10. Allen v. R.J. Reynolds	2002–2003	Testimony
11. Blankenship v. R.J. Reynolds	2004–2008	Deposition and testimony
12. St Louis v. American Tobacco	2004	Designated
13. Huntsberry v. R.J. Reynolds	2005	Expert Report Submitted
14. Vandenburg v. R.J. Reynolds	2005	Expert Report Submitted
15. In re: Engle Progeny Cases[10]	2009–2014	Testimony
16. Sherman v. R.J. Reynolds	2009	Testimony
17. Cohen v. R.J. Reynolds	2010–2013	Cross-examination
18. Koballa v. Philip Morris	2010	Cross-examination
19. Hargroves v. R.J. Reynolds	2011	Cross-examination

[1]Maggi, Laura. 2001. Bearing Witness for Tobacco. *The American Prospect*, November 9. http://prospect.org/article/bearing-witness-tobacco. Accessed 31 Oct 2014.

[2]Wiener, Jon. 2010. Big Tobacco and the Historians. *The Nation*, February 15. http://www.thenation.com/article/big-tobacco-and-historians. Accessed 31 Oct 2014.

[3]Milo, Geyelin. 1997. How RJR Won its Latest Tobacco Case. *The Wall Street Journal,* May 7. http://tobaccodocuments.org/youth/CnLgNON19980000.Ar.html. Accessed 31 Oct 2014.

[4]Maggi, as n. 1. & Kyriakoudes, Louis. 2006. Historians' Testimony on 'Common Knowledge' of the Risks of Tobacco Use: a Review and Analysis of Experts Testifying on Behalf of Cigarette Manufacturers in Civil Litigation. *Tobacco Control* 15, 111. See furthermore the report from Gallup: Saad, Lydia, and O'Brien, Steve. 1998. *The Tobacco Industry Summons Polls to the Witness Stand: A Review on Public Opinion on the Risks of Smoking.* Princeton: The Gallop Organization. LTDL. Bates Number: LGSRNON19980515.CF. http://legacy.library.ucsf.edu/tid/fos76b00. Accessed 31 Oct 2014. & Milo, as n. 3.

[5]Milo, as n. 3.

[6]Milo, as n. 3.

[7]Martin, Jonathan. 2003. Historians at the Gate: Accommodating Expert Historical Testimony in Federal Courts. *The New York University Law Review* 78, 1540.

[8]Brandt, Allan. 2007. *The Cigarette Century. The Rise, Fall and Deadly Persistence of a Product that Defined America.* New York: Basic Books, 495.

[9]Information on the cases is based on Proctor, Robert. 2012. *Golden Holocaust: Origins of the Cigarette Catastrophe and the Case for Abolition.* Berkeley: University of California Press, 460. & The following online databases: http://legacy.library.ucsf.edu, http://tobaccodocuments.org, http://lawschool.courtroomview.com/experts, & Westlaw.

[10]Proctor reports Ford was deposed in multiple Engle Progeny Cases (2008–2014). See Proctor, as n. 9, 460.

17. Otis Graham Jr.

Name	Otis L. Graham Jr.
Professional occupation	Professor Emeritus of History
Institution	University of North Carolina
Website	http://www.history.ucsb.edu/people/person.php?account_id=107
Short description	Graham taught at the University of North Carolina. He is the author and editor of nineteen books and numerous articles on the history of the United States, especially on American reform movements, political economy, environment, and immigration. He has been named a Guggenheim Fellow, a Fellow at the Woodrow Wilson Centre for Scholars, the National Endowment for the Humanities, and the Centre for Advanced Study and Behavioural Sciences, and received the Robert Kelley Memorial Award from the National Council on Public History. He has served as the editor of the journal *The Public Historian* for eight years. He continues his involvement with *The Public Historian* as a senior editor. Graham has been active in four trials over a time period spanning more than fifteen years. In a deposition given for *Schwartz v. Liggett Group,* Graham declared he charged $125 an hour for his litigation-driven work.[1] In his 2006-article on historians as expert witnesses, Proctor states that Graham is a recruiter of other expert historians for tobacco-related litigation in service of legal firms who defend the tobacco industry.[2]
Education	Ph.D.
Major fields	Recent US history
Major publications	Unguarded Gates: a History of America's Immigration Crisis (2004)
Number of cases	4

Case[3]	Year	Manner of involvement
1. Kotler v. American Tobacco	1990	Testimony
2. Texas v. American Tobacco	1997	Deposition
3. Schwartz v. Liggett Group	2003–2006	Deposition
4. Davis v. Liggett Group	2004	Testimony

[1]Deposition of Otis Graham, December 18, 2003, *Schwartz v. Liggett Group*. Westlaw reference: 2003 WL 25967718.

[2]Proctor, Robert. 2006. 'Everyone Knew But No One Had Proof': Tobacco Industry Use of Medical History Expertise in US courts, 1990–2002. *Tobacco Control* 15, 121.

[3]Information on the cases is based on Proctor, Robert. 2012. *Golden Holocaust: Origins of the Cigarette Catastrophe and the Case for Abolition.* Berkeley: University of California Press, 461. & The following online databases: http://legacy.library.ucsf.edu, http://tobaccodocuments.org, http://lawschool.courtroomview.com/experts, & Westlaw.

18. George Green

Name	George Green
Professional occupation	Professor of American Economic History
Institution	University of Minnesota
Website	http://cla.umn.edu/about/directory/profile/green007
Short description	George Green is professor of history at the University of Minnesota. He specializes in American business history. Green testified for the defence solely in the case brought by state attorney general Hubert Humphrey III of Minnesota against the tobacco industry seeking damages for smoking-related health care costs in the state of Minnesota.
Education	Ph.D.
Major fields	History of the medical science in the twentieth century in American context
Major publications	Finance and Economic Development in the Old South: Louisiana Banking, 1804–1861 (1972), American Business History (1981), The Business of Wellness: The Health Insurance Industry's Response to Public Health Campaigns, 1960–1990 (1999)
Number of cases	1

Case[1]	Year	Manner of involvement
1. Minnesota v. Philip Morris	1997	Deposition and testimony

[1]Information on the cases is based on Proctor, Robert. 2012. *Golden Holocaust: Origins of the Cigarette Catastrophe and the Case for Abolition.* Berkeley: University of California Press, 461. & The following online databases: http://legacy.library.ucsf.edu, http://tobaccodocuments.org, http://lawschool.courtroomview.com/experts, & Westlaw.

19. Janette Greenwood

Name	Janette Greenwood
Professional occupation	Professor of History
Institution	Clark University
Website	http://www.clarku.edu/faculty/facultybio.cfm?id=322
Short description	Greenwood teaches a variety of courses in American history at Clark University; including American race and ethnicity, history of the South, Reconstruction, and the Gilded Age. She is the author of *First Fruits of Freedom: The Migration of Former Slaves and Their Search for Equality in Worcester, Massachusetts, 1862–1900*, University of North Carolina Press, 2010, which examines the Civil War-era migration of former slaves to central Massachusetts. Her first book, *Bittersweet Legacy* explores the emergence and interaction of the black and white middle class in a New South city. Greenwood has been active in Engle Progeny cases.
Education	Ph.D.
Major fields	Race and ethnic relations and women's studies
Major publications	Bittersweet Legacy: The Black and White "Better Classes" in Charlotte, North Carolina, 1850–1910 (1994), The Gilded Age: A History in Documents (2000), First Fruits of Freedom: The Migration of Former Slaves and Their Search for Equality in Worcester, Massachusetts, 1862–1900 (2010)
Number of cases	5

Case[1]	Year	Manner of involvement
1. Craft v. Philip Morris[2]	2005–2010	Deposition
2. Donovan v. Philip Morris	2006–2011	Designated
3. Cohen v. R.J. Reynolds	2010–2013	Deposition
4. In re: Light Cigarettes	2010	Designated
5. Ciccone v. R.J. Reynolds	2011	Cross-examination

[1]Information on the cases is based on Proctor, Robert. 2012. *Golden Holocaust: Origins of the Cigarette Catastrophe and the Case for Abolition.* Berkeley: University of California Press, 461. & The following online databases: http://legacy.library.ucsf.edu, http://tobaccodocuments.org, http://lawschool.courtroomview.com/experts, & Westlaw.

[2]Engle Progeny case also pertaining to Stone, Larsen, and Alper-Pressman.

20. Jon Harkness

Name	Jon Harkness
Professional occupation	Patent Attorney (Former Professor of History of Medicine)
Institution	Former University of Minnesota
Website	http://www.med.umn.edu/history/ppl/fac/
	http://www.geiserlaw.com/jon-m-harkness
Short description	Jon Harkness has largely left his career as a historian of medicine to become a patent attorney at Geiser Law, a Minnesota based law-firm specializing in patent law. Jon Harkness has served for 7 years (1992–1999) as managing editor of *Isis*, the official journal of the *History of Science Society*, during which time he also testified for the tobacco industry.[1] Jon Harkness has made around half a million dollars for his work for the tobacco industry; $300,000 for testifying and another $200,000 for research.[2] He charged $150 an hour for his litigation-related work.[3] While at Cornell, he taught survey courses in the history of medicine in that university's Department of Science and Technology Studies. In the mid-1990s (1994–1995), he also served as a consultant to President Clinton's Advisory Committee on Human Radiation Experiments. His research focussed on the history of medical science in the twentieth century, largely in an American context. He is especially interested in the history of human experimentation and the development of chronic disease epidemiology. Harkness has published an article on the policy issues facing the Public Health Service during the Eisenhower and Kennedy administrations.[4] At the beginning of this article Harkness discloses that he has received funding from the tobacco industry for litigation-related work. He did not receive funding for the article in question and the article has been peer reviewed.[5] Brandt remarks in a footnote on the article of Harkness; stating that like other industry experts, Harkness does not explore the role the tobacco industry played in shaping the PHS's policies, and thus leaving out an important historical factor.[6]
Education	Ph.D.
Major fields	History of the medical science in the twentieth century in American context
Major publications	Research behind Bars: A History of Nontherapeutic Research on American Prisoners (1996), "Laying Ethical Foundations for Clinical Research," Bulletin of the World Health Organization, Vol. 79, 2001, pp. 365–366
Number of cases	3[7]

Case[8]	Year	Manner of involvement
1. Boerner v. Brown & Williamson	2000–2003	Testimony
2. Frankson v. Brown & Williamson	2003–2007	Affidavit
3. Rose v. American Toacco	2003–2007	Designated

[1]Proctor, Robert. 2006. 'Everyone Knew But No One Had Proof': Tobacco Industry Use of Medical History Expertise in US courts, 1990–2002. *Tobacco Control* 15, 121.

[2]Proctor, Robert. 2012. *Golden Holocaust: Origins of the Cigarette Catastrophe and the Case for Abolition.* Berkeley: University of California Press, 475. & Testimony of Jon Harkness, May 15, 2003, Boerner v. Brown & Williamson. Westlaw reference: 2003 WL 25744676.

[3]Testimony of Jon Harkness, as n. 2.

[4]Harkness, Jon. 2006. The U.S. Public Health Service and Smoking in the 1950s: The Tale of Two More Statements. *Journal of The History of Medicine and Allied Sciences* 62, 171–212.

[5]Harkness, as n. 4, 171.

[6]See note 20 of Chap. 7 in Brandt, Allan. 2007. *The Cigarette Century. The Rise, Fall and Deadly Persistence of a Product that Defined America.* New York: Basic Books, 535–536.

[7]Harkness has been named in multiple cases as a possible witness.

[8]Information on the cases is based on Proctor, Robert. 2012. *Golden Holocaust: Origins of the Cigarette Catastrophe and the Case for Abolition.* Berkeley: University of California Press, 461. & The following online databases: http://legacy.library.ucsf.edu, http://tobaccodocuments.org, http://lawschool.courtroomview.com/experts, & Westlaw. Further compiled through personal correspondence with Mr. Harkness.

21. Paul Harvey

Name	Paul Harvey
Professional occupation	Professor of History
Institution	University of Colorado
Website	http://www.uccs.edu/history/paul-harvey.html http://paulharvey.org/
Short description	Paul Harvey researches, writes, and teaches in the field of American history from the sixteenth century to the present. His particular interests include Southern history, American religious history, popular culture, war and society, and the history of American music. Harvey is the creator of the professional scholarly blog *Religion in American History*. He is a contributor to the online journal *Religion Dispatches*. He also serves on the Board of Editors for the *Journal of Southern History and American Nineteenth Century History* as well as *Religion Compass*. In an expert report Harvey submitted in 2007 pertaining to *Alexander v. Philip Morris* he disclosed he charged $250 an hour for his litigation-driven research on tobacco.[1]
Education	Ph.D.
Major fields	History and religion in the American South
Major publications	Redeeming the South: Religious Cultures and Racial Identities Among Southern Baptists, 1865–1925 (1997), Freedom's Coming: Religious Cultures and the Shaping of the South from the Civil War through the Civil Rights Era (2005)
Number of cases	4

Case[2]	Year	Manner of involvement
1. Coolidge v. Philip Morris	2004–2005	Deposition
2. Alexander v. R.J. Reynolds	2007–2012	Expert report submitted
3. Evans v. Lorillard	2010	Affidavit
4. Koballa v. R.J. Reynolds	2010–2011	Designated

[1]See expert report of Paul Harvey, August 7, 2007, *Alexander v. Philip Morris*. Westlaw reference: 2007 WL 6114298.

[2]Information on the cases is based on Proctor, Robert. 2012. *Golden Holocaust: Origins of the Cigarette Catastrophe and the Case for Abolition*. Berkeley: University of California Press, 461. & The following online databases: http://legacy.library.ucsf.edu, http://tobaccodocuments.org, http://lawschool.courtroomview.com/experts, & Westlaw.

22. *James Hilty*

Name	James W. Hilty
Professional occupation	Professor Emeritus of History
Institution	Temple University Ambler
Website	http://www.cla.temple.edu/history/faculty/
Short description	Hilty was dean of Temple University Ambler Campus and a professor of history. He is now retired. James Hilty is an expert on the history of American politics, specializing in the history of the presidency. In *Carter v. Philip Morris*, Hilty declared on cross-examination that he charged $150 an hour for his expert work and that he had been paid $75,000 for this case while also acknowledging he was working on other cases for the defence.[1]
Education	Ph.D.
Major fields	US public history, history of higher education, and history of American politics, specializing in the history of the presidency
Major publications	Robert Kennedy: Brother Protector (1998); "The Kennedy Administration," in Presidential Administration Profiles, (1999); "John Fitzgerald Kennedy" and "Robert Francis Kennedy," Historic World Leaders (1994)
Number of cases	2

Case[2]	Year	Manner of involvement
1. Carter v. Philip Morris	1999–2003	Cross-examination
2. Viguers v. Philip Morris	2002–2004	Affidavit

[1]Cross-examination of James Hilty, 1999, *Carter v. Philip Morris*. Westlaw reference: 1999 WL 35025578.

[2]Information on the cases is based on Proctor, Robert. 2012. *Golden Holocaust: Origins of the Cigarette Catastrophe and the Case for Abolition.* Berkeley: University of California Press, 461. & The following online databases: http://legacy.library.ucsf.edu, http://tobaccodocuments.org, http://lawschool.courtroomview.com/experts, & Westlaw.

23. *Joan Hoff*

Name	Joan Hoff
Professional occupation	Professor of History
Institution	University of Montana
Website	http://www.montana.edu/wwwhi/joan_hoff.html
Short description	Joan Hoff is research professor of history at the Montana State University. She has published mainly on US presidents. Hoff has been active as an expert witness in tobacco litigation from 1996 to 2012. She has been very active in Engle Progeny cases in Florida. Hoff has served as an expert witness for the tobacco industry in 31 cases. In a deposition taken in 2012 in New York on Park Avenue relating to *Narushka v. R.J. Reynolds*, Hoff acknowledged she had made around $325,000 with her tobacco related work.[1]
Education	Ph.D.
Major fields	Legal status US women and Presidents
Major publications	Faustian Diplomacy: From Woodrow Wilson to George W. Bush (2008), Too Little, Too Late: Changes in the Legal Status of U.S. Women (2000), The Nixon Presidency (1996)
Number of cases	31

Case[2]	Year	Manner of involvement
1. Rogers v. R.J. Reynolds	1996	Testimony
2. Dunn v. R.J. Reynolds	1997–1998	Deposition and testimony
3. Whiteley v. Raybestos-Manhattan	1999–2000	Deposition and testimony
4. Conely v. R.J. Reynolds	2000	Designated
5. Tompkin v. American Brands	2001	Deposition and testimony
6. Bradley v. R.J. Reynolds	2008-2012	Deposition
6. Douglas v. Philip Morris	2008	Designated
8. Grant v. R.J. Reynolds	2008–2009	Designated
9. Putney v. R.J. Reynolds	2008–2010	Direct and cross-examination
10. Raley v. R.J. Reynolds	2008	Designated
11. Sottosanti v. R.J. Reynolds	2008	Designated
12. Tullo v. R.J. Reynolds	2008–2010	Deposition
13. Wyerick v. R.J. Reynolds	2008	Designated
14. Barbanell v. R. J. Reynolds	2009–2014	Deposition and cross-examination
15. In re: Engle Progeny cases[3]	2009–2014	Deposition
16. Pagliarello v. R.J. Reynolds	2009	Designated
17. Rivera v. Philip Morris	2009	Affidavit
18. Gafney v. R.J. Reynolds	2010	Deposition
19. Smith v. R.J. Reynolds	2010–2012	Deposition
20. Buchanan v. R.J. Reynolds	2011	Deposition
21. Folks v. R.J. Reynolds	2011	Designated
22. Narushka v. R.J. Reynolds	2011–2012	Deposition
23. Rodehaver v. R.J. Reynolds	2011–2012	Deposition

(continued)

Case[2]	Year	Manner of involvement
24. Rudy v. R.J. Reynolds	2011–2012	Testimony
25. Larrabee v. R.J. Reynolds	2012	Deposition
26. Giddens v. R.J. Reynolds	2012	Testimony
27. Graham v. R.J. Reynolds	2012	Deposition
28. Hill v. R.J. Reynolds	2012	Testimony
29. Reider v. R.J. Reynolds	2012	Testimony
30. Vanblarcom v. R.J. Reynolds	2012	Testimony
31. Wilder v. R.J. Reynolds	2012	Deposition

[1]Deposition of Joan Hoff, May 24, 2012, *Narushka v. R.J. Reynolds*. Westlaw reference: 2012 WL 3450343.

[2]Information on the cases is based on Proctor, Robert. 2012. *Golden Holocaust: Origins of the Cigarette Catastrophe and the Case for Abolition*. Berkeley: University of California Press, 461. & The following online databases: http://legacy.library.ucsf.edu, http://tobaccodocuments.org, http://lawschool.courtroomview.com/experts, & Westlaw. In Engle Progeny Cases many depositions and testimonies are reused in other cases instead of solely in the case where the actual testimony was given for the first time. I list these cases separately because in each one the deposition or testimony was submitted as important evidence and thereby it influenced the court and the jury.

[3]In re: Engle Progeny Cases pertaining to Barnabanell, Tate, Rodehaver, Smith, Narushka, Brinson, Miller, Brown, Wilder, Bradley, and Rudy.

24. Robert Hudson

Name	Robert Hudson (deceased)
Professional occupation	Former Chairman of the History of Medicine Department
Institution	University of Kansas
Website	http://www.kumc.edu/school-of-medicine/history-and-philosophy-of-medicine/about-us.html
Short description	Professor Hudson was chairman of the History of Medicine Department at the University of Kansas from 1966 to 1994. Hudson participated in only one tobacco-related trial. He was contacted by John Burnham, another expert witness for the tobacco companies.[1] Hudson made around $92,000 for his tobacco-related work in litigation.[2]
Education	Ph.D.
Major fields	History of medicine
Major publications	Disease and its control: The shaping of modern thought (1987)
Number of cases	1

Case[3]	Year	Manner of involvement
1. Allgood v. R.J. Reynolds	1994	Deposition

[1]Proctor, Robert. 2006. 'Everyone Knew But No One Had Proof': Tobacco Industry Use of Medical History Expertise in US courts, 1990–2002. *Tobacco Control* 15, 121.

[2]Deposition of Robert Hudson, M.D., Ph.D., March 14, 1994, *Allgood v. R.J. Reynolds*, 14/03/1994. LTDL. Bates Number: HUDSONR031494. http://legacy.library.ucsf.edu/tid/obr07a00. 31 Oct 2014, 136–137.

[3]Information on the cases is based on Proctor, Robert. 2012. *Golden Holocaust: Origins of the Cigarette Catastrophe and the Case for Abolition.* Berkeley: University of California Press, 461. & The following online databases: http://legacy.library.ucsf.edu, http://tobaccodocuments.org, http://lawschool.courtroomview.com/experts, & Westlaw.

25. Jacob Judd

Name	Jacob Judd
Professional occupation	Professor Emeritus of History
Institution	Lehman College
Website	http://digital-connect.lehman.edu/media/lehman-college-oral-history-project_jacob-judd
Short description	Jacob Judd is professor emeritus of history at Herbert H. Lehman College. He retired in 1998. The link above is an interview with Jacob Judd for an oral history project conducted by Lehman College.
Education	Ph.D.
Major fields	Colonial America, New York history
Major publications	Colonial America: A Basic History (1998)
Number of cases	3

Case[1]	Year	Manner of involvement
1. Rose v. American Tobacco	2003–2007	Testimony
2. Standish v. American Tobacco	2003	Expert report submitted
3. Tomasino v. American Tobacco	2003	Affidavit

[1]Information on the cases is based on Proctor, Robert. 2012. *Golden Holocaust: Origins of the Cigarette Catastrophe and the Case for Abolition.* Berkeley: University of California Press, 461. & The following online databases: http://legacy.library.ucsf.edu, http://tobaccodocuments.org, http://lawschool.courtroomview.com/experts, & Westlaw.

26. Louis Kyriakoudes

Name	Louis M. Kyriakoudes
Professional occupation	Professor
Institution	University of Southern Mississippi
Website	http://www.usm.edu/history/faculty/louis-kyriakoudes
Short description	As a specialist in the social and economic history of the nineteenth and twentieth century United States, Kyriakoudes has published works such as *The Social Origins of the Urban South: Race, Gender and Migration in Nashville and Middle Tennessee, 1890–1930* (University of North Carolina Press, 2003). He has authored articles in *The Alabama Review*, *Agricultural History*, *Social Science History*, *Southern Cultures*, and *Tobacco Control* as well as in various edited collections and encyclopaedias. He is currently working on two projects: (1) a history of cigarette use in the twentieth century and (2) a study of the demography of rural poverty in the American South in the nineteenth and twentieth centuries. Kyriakoudes is the director of the Center for Oral History and Cultural Heritage at the University of Southern Mississippi. In an article in *the Nation* from 2010, Kyriakoudes explains he has been harassed by the tobacco industry. Kyriakoudes declared in Wiener's article that he had been deposed "at least seven or eight times" by tobacco's legal counsel.[1] Tobacco's legal strategy seems to be to make witnessing for the plaintiffs an even more time-consuming activity, which involves risks for their own financial situation and research. Kyriakoudes told Wiener: "I've cut back a lot of what I've been doing" and "They hit me pretty hard, making it difficult to do my research. So I've pulled out of cases. I cut back to one or two trials a year. Harassment is effective."[2] In 2009, Kyriakoudes was involved in 12 tobacco related court cases. The following years that number dropped considerably. He worked on six cases in 2010 and on five in 2011 with similar lower numbers for 2012 and 2013. Kyriakoudes has been active as an expert witness from 2000 onward and has been involved in 66 cases. His hourly rate for testimony was $400 in 2010.[3] In 2013 Kyriakoudes declared he charged $450 an hour for his research as an expert judicial witness.[4] Kyriakoudes has been a prominent expert witness in tobacco litigation. In 2006 he published an article in tobacco control on the subject of historical testimony in tobacco related court cases.[5] Kyriakoudes has been the research team leader in 2003 on "Public Understanding of the Risks of Tobacco Use and Passive Smoking" and "Tobacco Deposition and Trial Transcript Research Project" with Ronald Davis, M.D. as the principal investigator. The project is funded by the National Cancer Institute and the American Legacy

(continued)

	Foundation to the Michigan Public Health Institute, and the Center for Tobacco Use Prevention and Research. His current research is titled: "Why We Smoke? Culture, History, and the North American Origins of the Global Tobacco Epidemic." Kyriakoudes has, furthermore, given multiple lectures on his involvement in tobacco litigation and his research on the subject. For example, in 2013, Kyriakoudes gave a lecture entitled "Disputed Science, the Tobacco Industry, the Press, and the Public" at the Eighth World Conference of Science Journalists in Helsinki, Finland.
Education	Ph.D.
Major fields	Nineteenth & twentieth century US economic history, US urban history, social history of the American South
Major publications	The Social Origins of the Urban South: Race, Gender and Migration in Nashville, and Middle Tennessee, 1890–1930. (2003), Historians Testimony on 'Common Knowledge' of the Risks of Tobacco Use: A Review and Analysis of Experts Testifying on Behalf of Cigarette Manufacturers in Civil Litigation. (2006), The Grand Ole Opry and Big Tobacco: Radio Transcripts from the Files of the R. J. Reynolds Tobacco Company, 1948 to 1959. (2006); Selling Which South? Economic Change in Rural and Small-Town North Carolina in an Era of Globalization, 1940–2007 (2007)
Number of Cases	66

Case[6]	Year	Manner of involvement
1. Boerner v. Brown & Williamson Tobacco	2000–2003	Deposition and testimony
2. Cannon v. Brown & Willison Tobacco	2000	Affidavit
3. Allen v. R.J. Reynolds	2002–2003	Designated
4. Campbell v. R.J. Reynolds	2002–2013	Testimony
5. Eiser v. Brown & Williamson[7]	2002–2005	Testimony Precluded
6. Landers v. R.J. Reynolds	2002	Deposition and Testimony
7. Eastman v. Brown & Williamson Tobacco	2003	Testimony
8. Frankson v. Brown & Williamson Tobacco	2003–2007	Testimony
9. Hall v. R.J. Reynolds	2003	Designated
10. Reller v. Philip Morris	2003–2005	Deposition
11. Rose v. The American Tobacco	2003–2007	Affidavit
12. Rosol v. R.J. Reyolds	2003	Deposition
13. Standish v. The American Tobacco	2003	Affidavit
14. Tomasino v. American Tobacco	2003	Affidavit
15. Arnitz v. Philip Morris	2004	Deposition and testimony
16. Coolidge v. Philip Morris	2004–2005	Deposition and testimony
17. Gadelata v. Lorillard Tobacco	2004	Testimony
18. Mash v. Brown & Williamson	2004	Deposition
19. Moore v. R.J. Reynolds	2004	Deposition
20. Beckum v. Philip Morris	2005–2006	Deposition and testimony

(continued)

Case[6]	Year	Manner of involvement
21. Gerrity v. R.J. Reynolds	2005	Deposition
22. Hargroves v. Philip Morris	2005	Designated
23. Rosen v. Brown & Williasmon Tobacco	2005	Testimony
24. Ertman v. R.J. Reynolds	2007	Deposition
25. Ferlanti v. Liggett Group, Inc. et al.	2007–2009	Cross-examination
26. Dorn v. R.J. Reynolds	2008	Designated
27. Evers v. R.J. Reynolds	2008–2013	Deposition
28. Grant v. R.J. Reynolds	2008–2009	Designated
29. Hess v. R.J. Reynolds	2008–2009	Deposition and testimony
30. Kalyvas v. Philip Morris	2008–2009	Precluded[8]
31. Loyd v. R.J. Reynolds	2008	Designated
32. Martin v. R.J. Reynolds	2008–2009	Deposition and testimony
33. Putney v. R.J. Reynolds	2008–2010	Deposition
34. Rodriguez v. R.J. Reynolds	2008	Designated
35. Tullo v. R.J. Reynolds	2008–2011	Designated
36. Barbanell v. R.J. Reynolds	2009–2014	Deposition and testimony
37. Bifolck v. Philip Morris	2009–2012	Deposition
38. Buonomo v. R.J. Reynolds	2009	Deposition
39. Clay v. R.J. Reynolds	2009	Deposition
40. Grossman v. R.J. Reynolds	2009–2013	Deposition
41. Hall v. R.J. Reynolds	2009–2010	Deposition and testimony
42. In re: Engle Progeny Cases[9]	2009–2014	Deposition
43. Izzarelli v. R.J. Reynolds	2009–2010	Deposition
44. Kaplan v. Philip Morris	2009	Deposition
45. Koballa v. R.J. Reynolds	2009–2010	Deposition
46. Sherman v. R.J. Reynolds	2009	Cross-examination
47. Willis v. Philip Morris	2009	Deposition
48. Alexander v. R.J. Reynolds	2010–2012	Deposition and testimony
49. Castleman v. R.J. Reynolds	2010	Deposition
50. Haldeman v. R.J. Reynolds	2010–2013	Deposition and testimony
51. Jones v. Philip Morris	2010	Designated
52. Katz v. R.J. Reynolds	2010–2011	Deposition
53. Rohr v. R.J. Reynolds	2010	Deposition and testimony
54. Calloway v. Philip Morris	2011	Deposition
55. Ciccone v. R.J. Reynolds	2011	Cross-examination
56. Jewett v. R.J. Reynolds	2011	Deposition and testimony
57. Marotta v. R.J. Reynolds	2011–2013	Deposition
58. Weick v. Philip Morris	2011	Deposition and testimony
59. Frailey v. R.J. Reynolds	2012	Deposition and testimony

(continued)

Case[6]	Year	Manner of involvement
60. Hiott v. R.J. Reynolds	2012	Deposition and testimony
61. Bowden v. R.J. Reynolds	2013–2014	Deposition
62. Deshaies v. R.J. Reynolds	2013	Affidavit
63. Elkins v. R.J. Reynolds	2013	Affidavit
64. Hartford v. R.J. Reynolds	2013	Testimony
65. Meeker v. R.J. Reynolds	2013	Deposition and testimony
66. Morse v. R.J. Reynolds	2014	Testimony

[1] Wiener, Jon. 2010. Re 'Big Tobacco and the Historians', Wiener Replies. *The Nation*, March 9. http://www.thenation.com/article/re-big-tobacco-and-historians. Accessed Oct 31 2014.

[2] Wiener, as n. 1.

[3] See affidavit of Luis Kyriakoudes, December 8, 2010, *Jones v. Philip Morris*. Westlaw reference: 2010 WL 9551992.

[4] See affidavit of Luis Kyriakoudes, December 2, 2013, *Hartford v. R.J. Reynolds*. Westlaw reference: 2013 WL 8505972.

[5] Kyriakoudes, Louis. 2006. Historians' Testimony on 'Common Knowledge' of the Risks of Tobacco Use: a Review and Analysis of Experts Testifying on Behalf of Cigarette Manufacturers in Civil Litigation. *Tobacco Control* 15, 107–116.

[6] Compiled with following online databases: http://legacy.library.ucsf.edu, http://tobaccodocuments.org, http://lawschool.courtroomview.com/experts, & Westlaw. This profile is furthermore completed with information from personal correspondence with Mr. Kyriakoudes. In Engle Progeny Cases many depositions and testimonies are reused in other cases instead of solely in the case where the actual testimony was given for the first time. I list these cases separately because in each one the deposition or testimony was submitted as important evidence and thereby it influenced the court and the jury.

[7] The Court properly precluded Dr. Louis Kryiakoudes from presenting testimony because Plaintiff intended to introduce through Dr. Kyriakoudes the testimony the Court had ruled Dr. Cummings could not give. This was impermissible insofar as it would have resulted in the circumvention of a court order and the introduction of evidence previously ruled inadmissible. In addition, no abuse of discretion occurred here because the Plaintiff failed to identify Dr. Kryiakoudes in a timely fashion so as to give the Defendants sufficient time to prepare a defence to his testimony. Moreover, in setting forth the gist of the doctor's testimony during the discovery, the Plaintiff failed to provide a clear picture of what she intended to elicit from the doctor, thereby impeding the Defendants in their preparation of a defence. See, *Eiser v. Brown & Williamson Tobacco Corp*. Westlaw reference: 2006 WL 933394.

[8] Dr. Kyriakoudes was not allowed to give a deposition or testimony in this case because the plaintiff had been a member of the Greek public for most of his live; considering that Dr. Kyriakoudes was going to testify on the misinformation concerning smoking and health that Defendants allegedly disseminated to the American public, the court precluded Kyriakoudes as a witness. See *Kalyvas v. Philip Morris*, 2008 WL 6333456.

[9] Pertaining to Currao, Desbaies, Elkins, Harford, Jolley, Lydick, Marrazzo, Meeker, and Mogell.

27. Timothy Lenoir

Name	Timothy Lenoir
Professional occupation	Professor of History
Institution	Duke University
Website	http://jenkins.duke.edu/tim.php
	http://jenkins.duke.edu/publications.php
Short description	Tim Lenoir is the Kimberly J. Jenkins Chair for New Technologies in Society at Duke University. He has published several books and articles on the history of biomedical science from the nineteenth century to the present. His more recent work has focused on the introduction of computers into biomedical research from the early 1960s to the present, particularly the development of computer graphics, medical visualization technology, the development of virtual reality and its applications in surgery and other fields. Lenoir has also been engaged in constructing online digital libraries for a number of projects, including an archive on the history of Silicon Valley.
Education	Ph.D.
Major fields	The history of biomedical science
Major publications	Makeover: Writing the Body into the Posthuman Technoscape (2002)
Number of cases	1

Case[1]	Year	Manner of involvement
1. Tune v. Philip Morris	2002	Expert report and testimony

[1]Information on the cases is based on Proctor, Robert. 2012. *Golden Holocaust: Origins of the Cigarette Catastrophe and the Case for Abolition.* Berkeley: University of California Press, 461. The following online databases: http://legacy.library.ucsf.edu, http://tobaccodocuments.org, http://lawschool.courtroomview.com/experts, & Westlaw.

28. Kenneth Lipartito

Name	Kenneth Lipartito
Professional occupation	Professor of History
Institution	Florida International University
Website	http://phonebook.fiu.edu/id/Kenneth.Lipartito@fiu.edu/
	http://www2.fiu.edu/~lipark/cv.pdf
Short description	Professor Lipartito's areas of specialization are economic and business history and the history of technology. Most of his research has been on the history of the United States in the twentieth century, although he also engages in comparative work on Europe and maintains a strong interest in the Atlantic world. His work covers business history, the history of the global economy, political economy, the history of technology, as well as Atlantic civilization and twentieth century America. In a deposition taken on 04/04/2012 Lipartito stated that: *"Q. None of your university service is tobacco-related? A. No."*[1]
Education	Ph.D.
Major fields	Economic history, business history, history of technology
Major publications	A History of Kennedy Space Center. University Press of Florida (2007), Corporate Responsibility: The American Experience (2012)
Number of cases	3

Case[2]	Year	Manner of involvement
1. Evers v. R.J. Reynolds	2008–2013	Designated
2. In re: Engle Progeny Cases[3]	2009–2014	Deposition
3. Willis v. R.J. Reynolds	2009	Deposition

[1]Deposition of Kenneth Lipartito, PhD, April 4, 2012, in Engle Progeny cases; Pertains to Carolyn Hiott, as Personal Representative of the Estate of Kenneth Hiott; Volume 1. LTDL. Bates Number: LIPARTITOK20120404. http://legacy.library.ucsf.edu/tid/zev20j00. Accessed 31 Oct 2014. Q = Janine Pollack attorney for the plaintiff, A = Kenneth Lipartito expert witness for the defendants.

[2]Information on the cases is based on Proctor, Robert. 2012. *Golden Holocaust: Origins of the Cigarette Catastrophe and the Case for Abolition.* Berkeley: University of California Press, 461. & The following online databases: http://legacy.library.ucsf.edu, http://tobaccodocuments.org, http://lawschool.courtroomview.com/experts, & Westlaw.

[3]Pertaining to Hiott.

29. Charles Lowery

Name	Charles Lowery
Professional occupation	Professor Emeritus of History
Institution	Mississippi State University
Website	http://www.history.msstate.edu/people/charles-d-lowery
Short description	Charles Lowery is professor emeritus of Mississippi State University. Lowery was only deposed once for the defence, namely in the State Attorney case in Mississippi.
Education	Ph.D.
Major fields	Civil rights history
Major publications	The Greenwood Encyclopedia of African American Civil Rights [Two Volumes]: From Emancipation to the Twenty-First Century (2003)
Number of cases	1

Case[1]	Year	Manner of involvement
1. In re: Mississippi Tobacco Litigation	1997	Deposition

[1]Information on the cases is based on Proctor, Robert. 2012. *Golden Holocaust: Origins of the Cigarette Catastrophe and the Case for Abolition.* Berkeley: University of California Press, 461. & The following online databases: http://legacy.library.ucsf.edu, http://tobaccodocuments.org, http://lawschool.courtroomview.com/experts, & Westlaw.

30. Kenneth Ludmerer

Name	Kenneth M. Ludmerer
Professional occupation	Mabel Dorn Reeder Distinguished Professor in the History of Medicine
Institution	Washington University
Website	http://history.artsci.wustl.edu/ludmerer
Short description	Kenneth Ludmerer is professor of the history of American Medicine. In Proctor's *'Should Medical Historians be Working for the Tobacco Industry'* Ludmerer was mentioned as follows: "Historians of medicine last year [2003] were shocked to learn that Kenneth Ludmerer, president of the American Association for the History of Medicine, has been quietly working as an expert witness for the tobacco industry since the late 1980s."[1] In a deposition relating to his work as an expert witness in *US v. Philip Morris Inc. et al.*, the landmark federal case against the tobacco industry, Ludmerer acknowledged he had earned over half a million dollars through his tobacco related work. *"Q. What is the total amount you have earned from doing the tobacco litigation work to this date?* *A. I would say somewhere between 500 and $550,000. You mean from the very beginning?* *Q. From the very beginning.* *A. Correct."*[2] In the same deposition he acknowledges that he has not researched the industry's internal documents.[3] Ludmerer has worked on 15 separate trials over 12 years, always for the defence. Ludmerer has also been active in asbestos litigation.[4]
Education	Ph.D.
Major fields	The history of American medicine
Major publications	Time to Heal: American Medical Education from the Turn of the Century to the Era of Managed Care (1999), Learning to Heal: The Development of American Medical Education (1985), Genetics and American Society: A Historical Appraisal (1972)
Number of cases	15

Case[5]	Year	Manner of involvement
1. Cipollone v. Liggett Group	1986–1991	Deposition
2. Kotler v. American Tobacco	1990	Testimony
3. Unkel v. Liggett Group	1994	Expert report submitted
4. Engle v. R.J. Reynolds	1997–1998	Deposition
5. Florida v. American Tobacco	1997	Deposition
6. In re: Mississippi Tobacco Litigation	1997	Deposition
7. Washington v. American Tobacco	1998	Deposition
8. US v. Philip Morris et al.	1999–2006	Expert report and deposition
9. Williams v. Philip Morris	1999	Testimony
10. Anderson v. American Tobacco	2000	Testimony
11. Apostolou v. American Tobacco	2000	Testimony
12. Blankenship v. Philip Morris	2000–2004	Deposition
13. Scott v. American Tobacco	2000–2001	Deposition
14. Boeken v. Philip Morris	2001	Testimony
15. Tompkin v. American Tobacco	2001–2003	Deposition

[1]Proctor, Robert. 2004. Should Medical Historians Be Working for the Tobacco Industry? *The Lancet* 363, 1174.

[2]Deposition of Kenneth Ludmerer, M.D., August 8, 2002, *US v Philip Morris et al.* LTDL. Bates Number: LUDMERERK080802. http://legacy.library.ucsf.edu/tid/xuo11b00. Accessed 31 Oct 2014. Q = Moltzen attorney for the plaintiff, A = Ludmerer expert witness for the defence.

[3]Deposition of Kenneth Ludmerer, M.D., August 8, 2002, *US v Philip Morris et al.* LTDL. Bates Number: LUDMERERK080802. http://legacy.library.ucsf.edu/tid/xuo11b00. Accessed 31 Oct 2014.

[4]For example: *Harvey v. ABB Lummus Global Inc.* 2002.

[5]Information on the cases is based on Proctor, Robert. 2012. *Golden Holocaust: Origins of the Cigarette Catastrophe and the Case for Abolition.* Berkeley: University of California Press, 461. & The following online databases: http://legacy.library.ucsf.edu, http://tobaccodocuments.org, http://lawschool.courtroomview.com/experts, & Westlaw.

31. James Kirby Martin

Name	James Kirby Martin
Professional occupation	Professor of History
Institution	University of Houston
Website	http://www.uh.edu/class/history/faculty-and-staff/martin_j/index.php
Short description	Martin is a nationally recognized scholar of Early American history, especially the era of the American Revolution, and he is also well known for his writings on various aspects of American military and social history. He received his B.A. degree from Hiram College and then earned his M.A. and Ph.D. degrees from the University of Wisconsin. He began his teaching career at Rutgers University, where he earned the rank of Professor of History and also served for a period as Vice President for Academic Affairs. In 1980, he moved to the University of Houston, having accepted the assignment of serving as Department Chair of History with the mandate to foster the development of a cutting- edge program fully devoted to excellence in teaching and the production of high quality scholarship. He has done consulting with some of the nation's most eminent law firms in regard to the history of various consumer products, including alcohol and tobacco. Martin's teaching interests include *Early American history through the Revolution, American military history through the Civil War, aspects of World War II, and Medicine and Health in the American Experience*, especially in relation to the history of drinking, smoking, and hard drugs. Martin has been involved in 23 tobacco-related court cases for the defence, especially in Engle Progeny cases. In a deposition in 1999 pertaining to *National Asbestos Workers Medical Fund v. Philip Morris* Martin declared he charged $120 an hour for his expert witness work.[1] A decade later he stated in an expert report submitted in *Richardson v. R.J. Reynolds* that he billed $225 an hour for his litigation-driven research.[2] In a deposition from 2012 relating to an Engle Progeny cases Martin acknowledged he had made around $800,000 in seven years [2005–2012] through his work for tobacco litigation.[3]
Education	Ph.D.
Major fields	Early American history, American revolution, American military history and social history
Major publications	Forgotten Allies: The Oneida Indians and the American Revolution (2006), Benedict Arnold, Revolutionary Hero: An American Warrior Reconsidered (1997), Drinking in America: A History 1620–1980 (1987)
Number of cases	23

Case[4]	Year	Manner of involvement
1. Burton v. R.J. Reynolds	1996	Expert report and deposition
2. Richardson v. R.J. Reynolds	1996	Affidavit
3. Ironworkers v. Philip Morris	1998–1999	Deposition and testimony
4. Bergeron v. Philip Morris	1999	Affidavit
5. Klein v. R.J. Reynolds	1999	Testimony
6. National Asbestos Workers Medical Fund v. Philip Morris	1999	Deposition
7. Blue Cross and Blue Shield of New Jersey v. Philip Morris	2000	Deposition
8. Falise v. American Tobacco	2000–2001	Deposition and testimony
9. Tompkin v. R.J. Reynolds	2000	Deposition
10. Pearson v. R.J. Reynolds	2006	Designated
11. Mcivor v. Philip Morris	2008	Designated
12. Viswat v. R.J. Reynolds	2008	Designated
13. In re: Engle Progeny Cases	2009–2014	Deposition
14. Oliva v. R.J. Reynolds	2010	Deposition and testimony
15. Richardson v. R.J. Reynolds	2010	Affidavit & expert report
16. Vasko v. R.J. Reynolds	2010	Testimony
17. Reese v. R.J. Reynolds	2011	Deposition and testimony
18. Giddens v. R.J. Reynolds	2012	Expert report and deposition
19. Graham v. R.J. Reynolds	2012	Expert report submitted
20. Hoppes v. R.J. Reynolds	2012	Expert report submitted
21. Larrabee v. R.J. Reynolds	2012	Expert report and deposition
22. Reider v. R.J. Reynolds	2012	Deposition
23. Vanblarcom v. R.J. Reynolds	2012	Testimony

[1]See deposition of James Kirby Martin, September 29, 1999, *National Asbestos Workers Medical Fund v. Philip Morris*. Westlaw reference: 1999 WL 34749162.

[2]See expert witness report of James Kirby Martin, February 17, 2010, *Giddens v. R.J. Reynolds*. Westlaw reference: 2012 WL 4107324.

[3]See deposition of James Kirby Martin, August 22, 2012, *In re: Engle Progeny Cases*. Westlaw reference: 2012 WL 4107353.

[4]Information on the cases is based on Proctor, Robert. 2012. *Golden Holocaust: Origins of the Cigarette Catastrophe and the Case for Abolition*. Berkeley: University of California Press, 461. & The following online databases: http://legacy.library.ucsf.edu, http://tobaccodocuments.org, http://lawschool.courtroomview.com/experts, & Westlaw. In Engle Progeny Cases many depositions and testimonies are reused in other cases instead of solely in the case where the actual testimony was given for the first time. I list these cases separately because in each one the deposition or testimony was submitted as important evidence and thereby it influenced the court and the jury.

32. Luis Martinez-Fernandez

Name	Luis Martinez-Fernandez
Professional occupation	Professor of History
Institution	The University of Central Florida
Website	http://history.cah.ucf.edu/staff.php?id=308
Short description	Martinez-Fernandez is professor of history at the University of Central Florida. He has recently finished a survey history of the Cuban Revolution; working on a general history of early colonial Cuba. He has been an expert witness for the defence in Puerto Rican tobacco-related court cases. Later he became active in Engle Progeny cases in Florida. Martinez-Fernandez has disclosed in multiple court-related declarations how much he charges per hour for his litigation-driven work. In 2003, in *Rivera v. R.J. Reynolds* he declared that he charged $125 an hour. He also stated that he had worked 600 hours on his expert report and an extra 30 hours for issues relating specifically to Rivera.[1] One year later Martinez-Fernandez was deposed in *Alvarez v. R.J. Reynolds*. In this deposition he declared that he charged depending on the work: $200 to $275 an hour for his litigation research.[2] The following year, Martinez-Fernandez testified that he made $150 an hour. He furthermore acknowledged that he had done 670 hours of litigation-driven research.[3] So by Martinez-Fernandez' most conservative hourly rate, he has made in excess of $83,750.
Education	Ph.D.
Major fields	Puerto Rican and Hispanic Caribbean Studies Latin America, the Caribbean, Cuba and Puerto Rico Latinos in the United States
Major publications	Frontiers, Plantations, and Walled Cities: Essays on Society, Culture, and Politics in the Hispanic Caribbean, 1800–1945 (2010), Encyclopedia of Cuba: People, History, Culture. (2003), Protestantism and Political Conflict in the Nineteenth-Century Hispanic Caribbean. (2002)
Number of cases	14

Case[4]	Year	Manner of involvement
1. Eli Rogelio Fiqueroa Cruz v. R.J. Reynolds	2002	Testimony
2. Cruz-Vargas v. R.J. Reynolds	2003	Testimony
3. Rivera v. R.J. Reynolds	2003–2005	Expert report submitted
4. Alvarez v. R.J. Reynolds	2004–2005	Deposition
5. Araballoz v. R.J. Reynolds	2005	Deposition
6. Ramos v. Philip Morris	2005	Expert report submitted
7. Nieves-Rodriguez v. R.J. Reynolds	2005	Testimony
8. Valle-Ortiz v. R.J. Reynolds	2005	Testimony
9. Winell v. R.J. Reynolds	2008–2009	Deposition
10. Brown vs. R.J. Reynolds	2009–2013	Testimony
11. In re: Engle Progeny Cases[5]	2009–2014	Deposition
12. Talenfeld v. R.J. Reynolds	2010	Testimony
13. Ojeda v. Philip Morris	2011	Testimony
14. Larkin v. R.J. Reynolds	2012	Cross-examination

[1]See affidavit of Luis Martinez-Fernandez, *Rivera v. R.J. Reynolds.* Westlaw reference: 2003 WL 25625479.

[2]See deposition of Luis Martinez-Fernandez, September 21, 2004, *Alvarez v. R.J. Reynolds.* Westlaw reference: 2004 WL 5487028.

[3]See affidavit of Luis Martinez-Fernandez, June 14, 2005, *Valle-Ortiz v. R.J. Reynolds.* Westlaw reference: 2005 WL 6772401.

[4]Information on the cases is based on Proctor, Robert. 2012. *Golden Holocaust: Origins of the Cigarette Catastrophe and the Case for Abolition.* Berkeley: University of California Press, 462. The following online databases: http://legacy.library.ucsf.edu, http://tobaccodocuments.org, http://lawschool.courtroomview.com/experts, & Westlaw. In Engle Progeny Cases many depositions and testimonies are reused in other cases instead of solely in the case where the actual testimony was given for the first time. I list these cases separately because in each one the deposition or testimony was submitted as important evidence and thereby it influenced the court and the jury.

[5]Pertaining to Cohen and Rodriguez.

33. Glenn May

Name	Glenn May
Professional occupation	Professor of History
Institution	University of Oregon
Website	http://history.uoregon.edu/faculty/profiles/index.php?name=gmay
Short description	Glenn May is professor of history at the University of Oregon specializing in Southeast Asian history, history of US foreign relations, and Chicano history. His online available *curriculum vitae* does not mention his tobacco-related litigation work. In a deposition taking for *Williams v. Philip Morris,* a case from 1999, May acknowledged that he made $120 an hour. He worked 70 hours a month on his litigation-driven work. Upon questioning by plaintiff's counsel, May stated that he had not made in excess of $80,000 a year on any other project before in his career.[1]
Education	Ph.D.
Major fields	Southeast Asian History U.S. foreign relations Chicano history (focus Philippines)
Major publications	Inventing a Hero: The Posthumous Re-Creation of Andres Bonifacio (1996), Battle for Batangas: A Philippine Province at War (1991), A Past Recovered: Essays on Philippine History and Historiography (1987)
Number of cases	3

Case[2]	Year	Manner of involvement
1. Branch v. Philip Morris	1999	Testimony
2. Schwarz v. Philip Morris	1999–2002	Testimony
3. Williams v. Phillip Morris	1999	Deposition

[1]See testimony of Glenn May, March 12, 1999, *Williams v. Philip Morris.* Westlaw reference: 1999 WL 34874961.

[2]Information on the cases is based on Proctor, Robert. 2012. *Golden Holocaust: Origins of the Cigarette Catastrophe and the Case for Abolition.* Berkeley: University of California Press, 462. & The following online databases: http://legacy.library.ucsf.edu, http://tobaccodocuments.org, http://lawschool.courtroomview.com/experts, & Westlaw.

34. Gregg Michel

Name	Gregg Michel
Professional occupation	Associate Professor of History
Institution	University of Texas at San Antonio
Website	http://colfa.utsa.edu/history/faculty/michel
Short description	Gregg Michel, Associate Professor of History, received a B.A. from the University of Chicago and an M.A. and Ph.D. from the University of Virginia. Michel's scholarly work focuses on movements for social change in post-World War II America, particularly in the 1960s South. He has published several articles and delivered numerous papers on this topic. His book, *Struggle for a Better South: The Southern Student Organizing Committee, 1964–1969*, examines the turbulent history of the bending progressive white student organizations in the 1960s South. Gregg Michel has been active in 11 tobacco-related cases, always for the defence. He has been almost solely involved in Engle Progeny cases. In a deposition pertaining to Engle Progeny cases Michel acknowledged he had made over $180,000 with tobacco related litigation work. Michel disclosed he made $200 an hour. He, furthermore, confirmed that his work for the tobacco industry currently made up for over half of his total income.[1] In 2010 in *Webb v. R.J. Reynolds* Michel was again deposed on the compensations he received for his tobacco-related work. His hourly rate was still $200 an hour. In addition, he stated he had made over $220,000 with his litigation-driven research for the tobacco industry.[2] Two years later Michel declared during cross-examination that he charged $225 an hour for his services as an expert witness.[3]
Education	Ph.D.
Major fields	Social change in post-World War II America, particularly in the 1960s, South African-American history, history of the civil rights movement
Major publications	Better South: The Southern Student Organizing Committee, 1964–1969 (2004)
Number of cases	11

Case[4]	Year	Manner of involvement
1. Blasco v. R.J. Reynolds	2009–2013	Deposition
2. In re: Engle Progeny Cases[5]	2009–2014	Deposition
3. Jacobson v. R.J. Reynolds	2009	Deposition
4. Webb v. R.J. Reynolds	2010	Deposition and cross-examination
5. Cox v. R. J. Reynolds	2011	Deposition and cross-examination
6. Katz v. R.J. Reynolds	2011	Deposition
7. Frailey v. R. J. Reynolds	2012	Testimony
8. Schlenther v. R. J. Reynolds	2012	Testimony
9. Walker v. R.J. Reynolds	2012	Cross-examination
10. Brown-Hildegard v. R.J. Reynolds	2013	Deposition
11. Bryant v. R.J. Reynolds	2014	Testimony

[1]See deposition of Gregg Michel, *In Re: Engle Progeny Cases*. Westlaw reference: 2010 WL 6511222.

[2]See deposition of Gregg Michel, October 15, 2010, *Webb v. R.J. Reynolds*. Westlaw reference: 2010 WL 6546731.

[3]See cross-examination of Gregg Michel, May 17, 2012, Walker v. R.J. Reynolds. Westlaw reference: 2012 WL 9510404.

[4]Information on the cases is based on Proctor, Robert. 2012. *Golden Holocaust: Origins of the Cigarette Catastrophe and the Case for Abolition*. Berkeley: University of California Press, 462. & The following online databases: http://legacy.library.ucsf.edu, http://tobaccodocuments.org, http://lawschool.courtroomview.com/experts, & Westlaw. In Engle Progeny Cases many depositions and testimonies are reused in other cases instead of solely in the case where the actual testimony was given for the first time. I list these cases separately because in each one the deposition or testimony was submitted as important evidence and thereby it influenced the court and the jury.

[5]Pertaining to Campbell and Walden.

35. Wayne Morgan

Name	Wayne Morgan (Deceased)
Professional occupation	Professor Emeritus of History
Institution	University of Oklahoma
Website	http://history.ou.edu/ou-mourns-the-loss-of-wayne-morgan
Short description	Morgan was professor emeritus of the University of Oklahoma. He earned his bachelor's degree in history from Arizona State University, a master's from Claremont College and a Ph.D. from UCLA. He established, together with his wife, the Anne Hodges and H. Wayne Morgan Fellowship to facilitate the travel and research of graduate students in history. He has predominantly researched the history of American culture. He retired from UO in 1999 as George Lynn Cross Research Professor Emeritus. He passed away 29 January, 2014. Morgan has been involved in only one tobacco related court case: namely, the state attorney general case in Oklahoma.
Education	Ph.D.
Major fields	American cultural history, history of Oklahoma
Major publications	William McKinley and His America (2004), Drugs in America: A Social History, 1800–1980 (1994), Kenyon Cox 1856 1919: A Life in American Art (1994)
Number of cases	1

Case[1]	Year	Manner of involvement
1. Oklahoma v. R.J. Reynolds	1998	Deposition and testimony

[1]Information on the cases is based on Proctor, Robert. 2012. *Golden Holocaust: Origins of the Cigarette Catastrophe and the Case for Abolition.* Berkeley: University of California Press, 462. & The following online databases: http://legacy.library.ucsf.edu, http://tobaccodocuments.org, http://lawschool.courtroomview.com/experts, & Westlaw.

36. Robert Norrell

Name	Robert Norrell
Professional occupation	Professor of History
Institution	University of Tennessee
Website	http://history.utk.edu/peopletwo/robert-j-norrell/
Short description	Robert Norrell is a professor of history at the University of Tennessee. He has lectured in several American and European universities. In addition, he has published prize-winning books on the racial history of the American South. Norrell has been an expert witness for the defence in 28 tobacco related court cases, especially in Engle Progeny cases. In a deposition taken in *Karney v. Brown and Williamson* in 1998 Norrell declared that he charged $100 an hour for his litigation-driven work.[1] Two years later that rate was still the same,[2] but by 2010 Norrell's hourly rate had changed to $225,[3] and 2 years later to $250.[4] Norrell acknowledged in testimony given in Engle Progeny that he has charged tobacco companies for one million dollars, or $55,000 yearly during the period 1994–2012.[5]
Education	Ph.D.
Major fields	History of American race relations
Major publications	Reaping the Whirlwind: The Civil Rights Movement in Tuskegee (1986), The House I Live In: Race in the American Century (2005), Up from History: The Life of Booker T. Washington (2011)
Number of cases	28

Case[6]	Year	Manner of involvement
1. Konkle v. R.J. Reynolds	1997	Deposition and testimony
2. Marks v. R.J. Reynolds	1997	Testimony
3. Karney v. Brown and Williamson	1998–1999	Deposition and testimony
4. Newcomb v. R.J. Reynolds	1999	Testimony
5. Seaborn v. R. J. Reynolds	2000	Deposition
6. Scott v. American Tobacco	2000–2001	Deposition and testimony
7. Campbell v. R.J. Reynolds	2002–2013	Testimony
8. Sachs v. Lorillard	2003	Affidavit
9. Waterhouse v. R.J. Reynolds	2005–2006	Affidavit
10. Martin v. R.J. Reynolds	2008–2009	Deposition and testimony
11. Staggs v. R.J. Reynolds	2008	Designated
12. Hill v. R.J. Reynolds	2009	Testimony

(continued)

Case[6]	Year	Manner of involvement
13. In re: Engle Progeny Cases[7]	2009–2014	Deposition and testimony
14. Chamberlain v. R.J. Reynolds	2010–2013	Testimony
15. Piendle v. R.J. Reynolds	2010	Deposition and testimony
16. Smith v. R.J. Reynolds	2010–2012	Testimony
17. Narushka v. R.J. Reynolds	2011–2012	Testimony
18. Rodehaver v. R.J. Reynolds	2011–2012	Testimony
19. Rudy v. R.J. Reynolds	2011–2012	Testimony
20. Vanblarcom v. R.J. Reynolds	2011–2012	Testimony
21. Brinson v. R.J. Reynolds	2012	Expert report submitted
22. Giddens v. R.J. Reynolds	2012	Testimony
23. Graham v. R.J. Reynolds	2012	Deposition
24. Hill v. R.J. Reynolds	2012	Expert report submitted
25. Larrabee v. R.J. Reynolds	2012	Deposition
26. Reider v. R.J. Reynolds	2012	Testimony
27. Searcy v. R.J. Reynolds	2012	Expert report submitted
28. Wilder v. R.J. Reynolds	2012	Expert report submitted

[1]See deposition of Robert Norrell, December 9, 1998, *Karney v. Brown and Williamson*. Westlaw reference: 1998 WL 35271781.

[2]See deposition of Robert Norrell, August 17, 2000, *Seaborn v. R.J. Reynolds*. Westlaw reference: 2000 WL 35651535.

[3]See deposition of Robert Norrell, July 28, 2010, *Piendle v. R.J. Reynolds*. Westlaw reference: 2010 WL 6568264.

[4]See affidavit of Robert Norrell, April 17, 2012, *Hill v. R.J. Reynolds*. Westlaw reference: 2012 WL 4062302.

[5]See deposition of Robert Norrell, June 7, 2012, *Narushka v. R.J. Reynolds*. Westlaw reference: 2012 WL 3450341.

[6]Information on the cases is based on Proctor, Robert. 2012. *Golden Holocaust: Origins of the Cigarette Catastrophe and the Case for Abolition*. Berkeley: University of California Press, 462. & The following online databases: http://legacy.library.ucsf.edu, http://tobaccodocuments.org, http://lawschool.courtroomview.com/experts, & Westlaw. In Engle Progeny Cases many depositions and testimonies are reused in other cases instead of solely in the case where the actual testimony was given for the first time. I list these cases separately because in each one the deposition or testimony was submitted as important evidence and thereby it influenced the court and the jury.

[7]Pertaining to Allen, Clay, Ward, and Warrick.

37. Michael Parrish

Name	Michael Parrish
Professional occupation	Professor of History
Institution	University of California of San Diego
Website	http://historyweb.ucsd.edu/people/faculty/parrish.html
Short description	Michael Parrish joined the UCSD Department of History in 1968 and served as department chairman during the early 1990s. He received his BA degree from the University of California, Riverside in 1964 and his Ph.D. from Yale University in 1968. He teaches courses on the history of American law and American politics and culture since the Civil War. Parrish has been involved in 17 court cases related to tobacco issues spread over more than a decade. In 1998, Parrish declared during a deposition in *Henley v. Philip Morris* that he charged $125 an hour for his litigation-driven research on tobacco.[1] In 2004 that rate had gone up to $225 an hour.[2] The affidavit Parrish submitted in *Izzarelli v. R.J. Reynolds* in 2009 stated that his hourly rate for research was $175, for a deposition $300, and for testimony $400.[3]
Education	Ph.D.
Major fields	The history of American law and American politics and culture since the Civil War
Name	Michael Parrish
Major publications	Anxious Decades: America in Prosperity and Depression, 1921–1941 (1992), Felix Frankfurtur and His Times: The Reform Years (1982)
Number of cases	17

Case[4]	Year	Manner of involvement
1. Hoskins v. R.J. Reynolds	1996	Affidavit
2. Small v. Lorillard	1996	Affidavit
3. Stewart-Lomanitz v. Brown & Williamson	1996	Affidavit
4. Arch v. American Tobacco	1997	Affidavit
5. Barnes v. American Tobacco	1997	Deposition
6. Frosina v. Philip Morris	1997	Deposition
7. Henley v. Philip Morris	1998–1999	Deposition and testimony
8. Tabb v. Philip Morris	1998	Affidavit
9. Washington v. American Tobacco	1998	Deposition
10. Boerner v. Brown and Williamson	2000–2003	Deposition

(continued)

Case[4]	Year	Manner of involvement
11. Sounders v. Philip Morris	2002	Affidavit
12. Bowyer v. Philip Morris	2003	Affidavit
13. Miele v. American Tobacco	2003	Testimony
14. Reynolds v. Philip Morris	2003	Affidavit
15. Kimball v. R.J. Reynolds	2004	Deposition
16. Logan v. Brown and Williamson	2004	Affidavit
17. Izzarelli v. R.J. Reynolds	2009	Affidavit

[1]See deposition of Michael Parrish, December 29, 1998, *Henley v. Philip Morris*. Westlaw reference: 1998 WL 35262559.

[2]See affidavit of Michael Parrish, October 1, 2004, *Logan v. Brown and Williamson*. Westlaw reference: 2004 WL 5660651.

[3]See affidavit of Michael Parrish, December 29, 2014, *Izzarelli v. R.J. Reynolds*. Westlaw reference: 2009 WL 2995399.

[4]Information on the cases is based on Proctor, Robert. 2012. *Golden Holocaust: Origins of the Cigarette Catastrophe and the Case for Abolition*. Berkeley: University of California Press, 462. & The following online databases: http://legacy.library.ucsf.edu, http://tobaccodocuments.org, http://lawschool.courtroomview.com/experts, & Westlaw.

38. Terry Parssinen

Name	Terry Parssinen
Professional occupation	Professor of History
Institution	University of Tampa
Website	http://www.ut.edu/TerryParssinen/
Short description	Parssinen has published *Secret Passions, Secret Remedies: Narcotic Drugs and British Society, 1820–1930,*and *Webs of Smoke: Smugglers, Warlords, Spies and the History of the International Drug Trade.* Using memoirs and recently discovered documents, Parssinen has published the first-ever book on the little-known plot that collapsed following the Munich conference of 1938: *The Oster Conspiracy of 1938: The Unknown Story of the Military Plot to Kill Hitler and Avert World War II.* In a deposition taken for *Sulcer v. R.J. Reynolds* in September 2010 Parssinen declared that he charged $135 an hour for his research on tobacco-related issues. He furthermore stated that he had made around $360,000 with litigation-driven work for the tobacco companies.[1] One year later, in a deposition pertaining to *McCray v. R.J. Reynolds* Parssinen disclosed he had made $450,000 as an expert judicial witness for the tobacco industry.[2] The following year Parssinen acknowledged in an expert report submitted in *Rodehaver v. R.J. Reynolds* that his hourly rate for research was $135, and that for testimony $200.[3]
Education	Ph.D.
Major fields	History of the middle ages The second world war Narcotic drugs in modern society
Major publications	Secret Passions, Secret Remedies: Narcotic Drugs and British Society, 1820–1930 (1984), Webs of Smoke: Smugglers, Warlords, Spies and the History of the International Drug Trade (2002), The Oster Conspiracy of 1938: The Unknown Story of the Military Plot to Kill Hitler and Avert World War II (2004)
Number of cases	22

Case[4]	Year	Manner of involvement
1. Arnitz v. Philip Morris	2004	Testimony
2. Pearson v. R.J. Reynolds	2006	Designated
3. Boss v. R.J. Reynolds	2008	Designated
4. Kirkland v. R.J. Reynolds	2008–2011	Designated
5. Long v. R.J. Reynolds	2008	Designated
6. Mcivor v. Philip Morris	2008	Designated
7. Staggs v. R.J. Reynolds	2008	Designated
8. In re: Engle Progency cases[5]	2009–2014	Deposition
9. Smith v. R.J. Reynolds	2010–2012	Deposition
10. Sulcer v. R.J. Reynolds	2010	Deposition
11. Jewett v. R.J. Reynolds	2011	Testimony
12. McCray v. R.J. Reynolds	2011	Deposition
13. Narushka v. R.J. Reynolds	2011–2012	Deposition
14. Rodehaver	2011–2012	Expert report submitted
15. Rudy v. R.J. Reynolds	2011–2012	Deposition
16. Vanblarcom v. R.J. Reynolds	2011–2012	Deposition
17. Giddens v. R.J. Reynolds	2012	Deposition
18. Graham v. R.J. Reynolds	2012	Deposition
19. Hill v. R.J. Reynolds	2012	Deposition
20. Larrabee v. R.J. Reynolds	2012	Deposition
21. Reider v. R.J. Reynolds	2012	Deposition
22. Wilder v. R.J. Reynolds	2012	Expert report submitted

[1] See deposition of Terry Parssinen, September 8, 2010, *Sulcer v. R.J. Reynolds*. Westlaw reference: 2010 WL 9926701.

[2] See deposition of Terry Parssinen, September 26, 2011, *McCray v. R.J. Reynolds*. Westlaw reference: 2011 WL 8741848.

[3] See expert report of Terry Parssinen, June 21, 2012, *Rodehaver v. R.J. Reynolds*. Westlaw reference: 2012 WL 3541162.

[4] Information on the cases is based on Proctor, Robert. 2012. *Golden Holocaust: Origins of the Cigarette Catastrophe and the Case for Abolition*. Berkeley: University of California Press, 462. The following online databases: http://legacy.library.ucsf.edu, http://tobaccodocuments.org, http://lawschool.courtroomview.com/experts, & Westlaw.

[5] Pertaining to Brwon, Campbell, Gray, Hatziyannakis, Naugle, Mccray, and Sulcer.

39. Robert Proctor

Name	Robert N. Proctor
Professional occupation	Professor of History
Institution	Stanford University
Website	http://www.stanford.edu/dept/HPS/proctor.html
Short description	Robert Proctor is Professor of the History of Science and Professor of Pulmonary and Critical Care Medicine at Stanford. He has testified as an expert witness regarding negligence claims made by smokers against tobacco companies. Tobacco companies have made many efforts to prevent Proctor from testifying in these cases. He has argued that the tobacco industry, relying heavily on historians, has created a new "science", which he terms "agnotology", for the creation of doubt and ignorance about its actions in the past. Proctor has surpassed any other historian in the number of cases he has served in as an expert witness: that number is 93. In a deposition pertaining to *Rosol v. R.J. Reynolds* from 2003 Proctor stated that he charged $350 an hour for tobacco-related research.[1] The following year Proctor disclosed during a deposition for *Ferlanti v. Liggett Group* that he charged $500 an hour for research and $600 for depositions and testimony.[2] In 2010 he acknowledged that he had made $600,000 dollar as an expert witness for the plaintiffs in tobacco litigation. Proctor added that he was paid $4,800 by the tobacco industry for or each deposition he did.[3] Later that same year Proctor declared he had made $700,000 as an expert judicial witness in tobacco litigation. He also pointed out that a lot of that amount has come from the 25 times he has been deposed and thus has been paid a retainer of $4,800 per deposition by the tobacco companies.[4] In a deposition given in 2012 concerning *Reider v. R.J. Reynolds* Proctor stated that he had made around $1.5-$1.6 million as an expert witness in tobacco litigation. He claimed that he made approximately $100,000 a year as an expert for 16 years. That was the equivalent of 40 % of his total income, Proctor furthermore declared.[5] Proctor has acknowledged that he has made between 1.5 and 2 million dollars with his tobacco-related litigation work. He further notes that his remuneration to a considerable extent comes from depositions he gets paid to do by the tobacco companies to enable legal counsel for the tobacco companies to question him.[6] Proctor has been the victim of intimidation by the tobacco industry who tried to exclude him for further testifying in Engle Progeny cases and subpoenaed his unfinished manuscript of *Golden Holocaust* in 2009.[7] The book is, together with *The Cigarette Century* by Allan Brandt, an epic work on the history of tobacco and its deadly product.[8] Proctor has been a very active voice in the debate on the involvement of historians in tobacco litigation with articles on the subject in *Nature*,[9] *The Lancet*,[10] and *Tobacco Control*.[11]

(continued)

	Proctor has been active in over 90 court cases. His research and heavy involvement in tobacco related litigation, not in the least in the federal case *US v. Philip Morris et al.*, has recently been acknowledged when Proctor was invited to attend the celebratory events at the White House remembering the 50th anniversary of the Surgeon General Report on Smoking from 1964.
Education	Ph.D.
Major fields	Professor Proctor specializes in the history of twentieth century science, technology, medicine, and tobacco
Major publications	Proctor R. N., Cancer Wars: How Politics Shapes What We Know and Don't Know About Cancer. New York, Basic Books, 1996, p. 356. Proctor R. N., The Nazi War on Cancer. Princeton, New York, Princeton University Press, 1999, p. 380. Proctor R. N., "Expert witnesses take the stand." In: Nature, Vol. 407, 2000, pp. 15–16. Proctor R. N., "Should Medical Historians Be Working for the Tobacco Industry?" In: The Lancet, Vol. 363, 2004, pp. 1174–1175. Proctor R. N., "'Everyone Knew But No One Had Proof': Tobacco Industry Use of Medical History Expertise in US courts, 1990–2002." In: Tobacco Control, Vol. 15, 2006, pp. 117–125. Proctor R. N. & Schiebinger L. (eds.), Agnotology. The Making & Unmaking of Ignorance., Palo Alto, California, Stanford University Press, 2008, p. 312. Proctor R. N., Golden Holocaust: Origins of the Cigarette Catastrophe and the Case for Abolition. Berkeley and Los Angeles California, University of California Press, 2012, p. 752.
Number of cases	93

Case[12]	Year	Manner of involvement
1. Ironworkers v. Phillip Morris	1998–1999	Expert report submitted
2. Northwest Laborers-Employers Health & Security Trust Fund v. Philip Morris	1998	Expert report submitted
3. United States v. Philip Morris	1999–2006	Expert report and deposition
4. Campbell v. R.J. Reynolds	2002–2013	Deposition and testimony
5. Frankson v. Brown & Williamson Tobacco	2003–2004	Testimony
6. Rose v. American Tobacco	2003–2007	Designated
7. Rosol v. R.J. Reynolds	2003	Deposition
8. St. Louis v. American Tobacco	2004–2008	Deposition

(continued)

Case[12]	Year	Manner of involvement
9. Schwab v. Philip Morris	2004–2006	Deposition and testimony
10. McLaughlin v. Philip Morris	2005	Expert report submitted
11. Ferlanti v. Liggett Group	2007–2009	Deposition and testimony
12. Avant v. R.J. Reynolds	2008–2012	Deposition
13. Ballard v. R.J. Reynolds	2008–2012	Affidavit and testimony
14. Bradley v. R.J. Reynolds	2008–2012	Deposition
15. Brown v. R.J. Reynolds	2008–2013	Deposition and testimony
16. Dorn v. R.J. Reynolds	2008	Designated
17. Evers v. R.J. Reynolds	2008–2013	Designated
18. Grant v. R.J. Reynolds	2008–2009	Designated
19. Hess v. R.J. Reynolds	2008–2009	Deposition and cross-examination
20. Kalyvas v. R.J. Reynolds	2008–2009	Precluded[13]
21. Kirkland v. R.J. Reynolds	2008–2011	Testimony
22. Loyd v. R.J. Reynolds	2008	Designated
23. Martin v. R.J. Reynolds	2008–2009	Deposition
24. Putney v. R.J. Reynolds	2008–2010	Deposition
25. Raley v. R.J. Reynolds	2008	Designated
26. Sottosanti v. R.J. Reynolds	2008	Designated
27. Staggs v. R.J. Reynolds	2008	Designated
28. Stalley v. R.J. Reynolds	2008	Designated
29. Tullo v. R.J. Reynolds	2008–2011	Affidavit
30. Barbanell v. R.J. Reynolds	2009–2014	Deposition and testimony
31. Blasco v. R.J. Reynolds	2009–2013	Testimony
32. Bullock v. Philip Morris	2009	Affidavit
33. Grossman v. R.J. Reynolds	2009–2013	Testimony
34. Hall v. R.J. Reynolds	2009–2011	Testimony
35. Hetzner v. R.J. Reynolds	2009–2010	Deposition
36. In re: Engle Progeny cases[14]	2009–2014	Deposition and testimony
37. Izzarelli v. R.J. Reynolds	2009–2010	Expert report submitted
38. Jacobson v. R.J. Reynolds	2009–2012	Testimony
39. Koballa v. R.J. Reynolds	2009–2010	Deposition and testimony
40. Sherman v. R.J. Reynolds	2009	Testimony
41. Townsend v. R.J. Reynolds	2009–2010	Deposition
42. Alexander v. Philip Morris	2010	Deposition
43. Andy Allen v. R.J. Reynolds	2010–2011	Deposition and testimony
44. Chamberlain v. R.J. Reynolds	2010–2012	Deposition and testimony
45. Cohen v. R.J. Reynolds	2010–2013	Deposition and testimony
46. Coleman Alexander v. Philip Morris	2010–2012	Deposition and testimony
47. Evans v. R.J. Reynolds	2010	Affidavit

(continued)

Case[12]	Year	Manner of involvement
48. Frazier v. Philip Morris	2010	Deposition and testimony
49. Mack v. R.J. Reynolds	2010	Deposition
50. McEniry v. R.J. Reynolds	2010	Deposition
51. Oliva v. R.J. Reynolds	2010–2011	Deposition and testimony
52. Perez v. R.J. Reynolds	2010	Deposition
53. Rubio v. R.J. Reynolds	2010	Designated
54. Scott v. R.J. Reynolds	2010–2012	Deposition and testimony
55. Smith v. R.J. Reynolds	2010–2012	Deposition and testimony
56. Tate v. Philip Morris	2010	Deposition and testimony
57. Warrick v. R.J. Reynolds	2010	Deposition and testimony
58. Bowman v. R.J. Reynolds	2011	Deposition and testimony
59. In re: Tobacco Litigation	2011–2013	Deposition and testimony
60. Junious v. R.J. Reynolds	2011	Deposition and testimony
61. Marotta v. R.J. Reynolds	2011–2013	Deposition and testimony
62. Miller v. Lorillard	2011	Designated
63. Reese v. R.J. Reynolds	2011	Deposition and testimony
64. Sury v. R.J. Reynolds	2011	Deposition and testimony
65. Vanblarcom v. R.J. Reynolds	2011–2012	Designated
66. Collaway v. R.J. Reynolds	2012	Deposition and testimony
67. Giddens v. R.J. Reynolds	2012	Deposition
68. Graham v. R.J. Reynolds	2012	Deposition
69. Larkin v. R.J. Reynolds	2012	Deposition and testimony
70. Larrabee v. R.J. Reynolds	2012	Deposition
71. Proud v. R.J. Reynolds	2012	Deposition
72. Reider v. R.J. Reynolds	2012	Deposition
73. Sikes v. R.J. Reynolds	2012–2013	Testimony
74. Williams v. R.J. Reynolds	2012	Testimony
75. Banks v. R.J. Reynolds	2013–2014	Testimony
76. Crawford v. R.J. Reynolds	2013	Testimony
77. Dombney v. R.J. Reynolds	2013	Testimony
78. Ellis v. R.J. Reynolds	2013–2014	Testimony
79. Ruffo v. R.J. Reynolds	2013	Deposition and testimony
80. Skolnic v. R.J. Reynolds	2013	Deposition and testimony
81. Spolzino v. R.J. Reynolds	2013	Deposition and testimony
82. Thibault v. R.J. Reynolds	2013	Deposition and testimony
83. Weinstein v. R.J. Reynolds	2013	Deposition and testimony
84. Baum v. R.J. Reynolds	2014	Testimony
85. Clayton v. R.J. Reynolds	2014	Testimony
86. Cuculino v. Philip Morris	2014	Testimony
87. Gonzalez v. Philip Morris	2014	Testimony
88. Hubbird v. R.J. Reynolds	2014	Testimony
89. Irmi v. R.J. Reynolds	2014	Testimony

(continued)

Case[12]	Year	Manner of involvement
90. Lourie v. R.J. Reynolds	2014	Testimony
91. Robinson v. Philip Morris	2014	Testimony
92. Wendel v. R.J. Reynolds	2014	Testimony
93. Wilcox v. R.J. Reynolds	2014	Testimony

[1]See deposition of Robert Proctor, December 2, 2003, *Rosol v. R.J. Reynolds*. Westlaw reference: 2003 WL 25885108.

[2]See deposition of Robert Proctor, December 13, 2007, *Ferlanti v. Liggett Group*. Westlaw reference: 2007 WL 7010907.

[3]See deposition of Robert Proctor, March 8, 2010, *Mack v. R.J. Reynolds*. Westlaw reference: 2010 WL 5647593.

[4]See testimony of Robert Proctor, September 20, 2010, *In re: Engle Progeny Cases*. Westlaw reference: 2010 WL 5647599.

[5]See deposition of Robert Proctor, August 22, 2012, *Reider v. R.J. Reynolds*. Westlaw reference: 2012 WL 4050497.

[6]From personal correspondence with the author.

[7]Schmidt, Peter. 2009. Big Tobacco Strikes Back at Historian in Court. The Chronicle of Higher Education 56, November 13. For the polemic discussion that followed afterwards in *The Nation* of Jon Wiener's article on the subject see Wiener, Jon. 2010. Big Tobacco and the Historians. *The Nation*, February 15. http://www.thenation.com/article/big-tobacco-and-historians. Accessed 31 Oct 2014.

[8]The following link is an interview with prof. Proctor on C-SPAN, discussing his book. See http://www.c-span.org/video/?312354-5/book-discussion-golden-holocaust. Accessed 31 Oct 2014.

[9]Proctor, Robert. 2000. Expert Witnesses Take the Stand. *Nature* 407, 15–16.

[10]Proctor, Robert. 2004. Should Medical Historians Be Working for the Tobacco Industry? *The Lancet* 363, 1174–1175.

[11]Proctor, Robert. 2006. 'Everyone Knew But No One Had Proof': Tobacco Industry Use of Medical History Expertise in US courts, 1990–2002. *Tobacco Control* 15, 117–125.

[12]The following online databases: http://legacy.library.ucsf.edu, http://tobaccodocuments.org, http://lawschool.courtroomview.com/experts, & Westlaw. This profile is furthermore completed with information gathered from personal correspondence with Prof. Proctor. In Engle Progeny Cases many depositions and testimonies are reused in other cases instead of solely in the case where the actual testimony was given for the first time. I list these cases separately because in each one the deposition or testimony was submitted as important evidence and thereby it influenced the court and the jury.

[13]Dr. Proctor was not allowed to give a deposition or testimony in this case because the plaintiff had been a member of the Greek public for most of his live; considering that Dr. Proctor was going to testify on the misinformation concerning smoking and health that Defendants allegedly disseminated to the American public, the court precluded Proctor as a witness. See *Kalyvas v. Philip Morris*, 2008 WL 6333456.

[14]Pertaining to Avant, Barbanell, Brown, Buonomo, Cohen, Gavan, Hess, Giddens, Kaufmann, Kaplan, Larrabee, Lopez, Naugle, Proud, Reider, Scott, Stephens, Sury, Sherman, Scarcy, Tucci, Vanblarcom, and Warrick.

40. Randy Roberts

Name	Randy W. Roberts
Professional occupation	Professor of History
Institution	Purdue University
Website	https://www.cla.purdue.edu/history/directory/?p=Randy_Roberts
	https://www.cla.purdue.edu/history/documents/Publications/PublRoberts_10-11.pdf
Short description	Roberts is professor of History at Purdue University in Indiana. Roberts has been active as an expert witness for the defence in 25 tobacco-related court cases. Roberts has acknowledged in 2010 during a deposition pertaining to *In re: Engle Progeny cases* that he had made around $500,000, charging $300 hourly for his tobacco-related litigation-driven work.[1] In testimony given in court by Roberts in that same case in 2012 he stated that he had made over $900,000 as an expert witness for the tobacco industry.[2]
Education	Ph.D.
Major fields	Modern American history, mass culture
Major publications	A Team for America: The Army-Navy Game That Rallied a Nation. (2011), Joe Louis: Hard Times Man. (2010), A Line in the Sand: The Alamo in Blood and Memory. (2000)
Number of cases	25

Case[3]	Year	Manner of involvement
1. Bradley v. R.J. Reynolds	2008–2011	Deposition
2. Cleary v. R.J. Reynolds	2009	Affidavit
3. Hetzner v. R.J. Reynolds	2009–2010	Deposition
4. In re: Engle Progeny Cases	2009–2014	Deposition and testimony
5. Allen v. R.J. Reynolds	2010	Deposition
6. Budnick v. R.J. Reynolds	2010	Cross-examination
7. Haldeman v. R.J. Reynolds	2010–2013	Deposition and testimony
8. Smith v. R.J. Reynolds	2010–2012	Testimony
9. Walden v. R.J. Reynolds	2010	Designated
10. Baker v. R.J. Reynolds	2011	Designated
11. Denton v. R.J. Reynolds	2011	Expert report submitted
12. In re: Tobacco Litigation	2011–2013	Testimony
13. Miller v. Lorillard	2011	Cross-examination
14. Mrozek v. R.J. Reynolds	2011	Testimony
15. Narushka v. R.J. Reynolds	2011–2012	Testimony
16. Rodehaver v. R.J. Reynolds	2011–2012	Testimony

(continued)

Case[3]	Year	Manner of involvement
17. Rudy v. R.J. Reynolds	2011–2012	Testimony
18. Giddens v. R.J. Reynolds	2012	Deposition
19. Graham v. R.J. Reynolds	2012	Deposition
20. Hill v. R.J. Reynolds	2012	Deposition
21. Larrabee v. R.J. Reynolds	2012	Deposition
22. Reider v. R.J. Reynolds	2012	Deposition
23. Wilder v. R.J. Reynolds	2012	Expert report submitted
24. Elkins v. R.J. Reynolds	2013	Expert report submitted
25. Meeker v. R.J. Reynolds	2013	Expert report submitted

[1]See deposition of Randy Roberts, July 15, 2010, *In re: Engle Progeny* Cases. Westlaw reference: 2010 WL 6546729.

[2]See testimony of Randy Roberts, June 7, 2012, *In re: Engle Progeny Cases*. Westlaw reference: 2012 WL 3450319.

[3]Information on the cases is based on Proctor, Robert. 2012. *Golden Holocaust: Origins of the Cigarette Catastrophe and the Case for Abolition*. Berkeley: University of California Press, 462. & The following online databases: http://legacy.library.ucsf.edu, http://tobaccodocuments.org, http://lawschool.courtroomview.com/experts, & Westlaw. In Engle Progeny Cases many depositions and testimonies are reused in other cases instead of solely in the case where the actual testimony was given for the first time. I list these cases separately because in each one the deposition or testimony was submitted as important evidence and thereby it influenced the court and the jury.

41. Mark Rose

Name	Mark Rose
Professional occupation	Professor of History
Institution	Florida Atlantic University
Website	http://www.fau.edu/history/rose.php
Short description	Mark Rose studies and teaches the social and policy bases of American life in the twentieth century. He is the author of more than thirty articles in such journals as *the Journal of Urban History*, *Technology and Culture*, *the Journal of Policy History*, and *the Journal of Planning History*. Rose is active in several professional associations. Since 2000, he has held elected and appointed positions in the Business History Conference, the Organization of American Historians, the Society for American City and Regional Planning History, and the Urban History Association. Rose was also a member of the Editorial Board of *the Journal of Urban History*. In 2008–2009, Rose had the honour to serve as president of the Business History Conference. For his research in *Jackson v. Brown and Williamson* Rose charged $125 an hour.[1]
Education	Ph.D.
Major fields	History of transportation
Major publications	Interstate: Express Highway Politics, 1941–1956 (1979), The Best Transportation System in the World: Railroads, Trucks, Airlines and American Public Policy in the Twentieth Century (2006)
Number of cases	2

Case[2]	Year	Manner of involvement
1. Jackson v. Brown and Williamson	1997	Affidavit
2. Brown v. Liggett Group	2003	Designated

[1]See affidavit of Mark Rose, March 27, 1997, *Jackson v. Brown and Williamson*. Bates Number: 2084299416–2084299420. See http://legacy.library.ucsf.edu/tid/iso00i00, accessed on 31/10/2014.

[2]Information on the cases is based on Proctor, Robert. 2012. *Golden Holocaust: Origins of the Cigarette Catastrophe and the Case for Abolition*. Berkeley: University of California Press, 462. & The following online databases: http://legacy.library.ucsf.edu, http://tobaccodocuments.org, http://lawschool.courtroomview.com/experts, & Westlaw.

42. David Sansing

Name	David Sansing
Professional occupation	Professor Emeritus of History
Institution	University of Mississippi
Website	http://history.olemiss.edu/2011/11/18/emeritus-faculty/
Short description	David Sansing is professor emeritus of the University of Mississippi. Sansing has been an expert witness for the defence in seven tobacco-related cases, although during cross-examination in *Boerner v. Brown and Williamson* in 2003 Sansing acknowledged that he had also been involved in Schuts and Walton and a number of other tobacco-suits that had never gone to trial. In addition, he declared that he had made over $500,000 as an expert judicial witness in tobacco litigation.[1] Sansing stated in a deposition taken for *Horton v. American Tobacco* that he charged the tobacco companies $125 an hour for tobacco related work.[2] By 2003 his hourly rate had more than doubled to $300.[3]
Education	Ph.D.
Major fields	History of the state of Mississippi, history of higher education in Mississippi, history of the University of Mississippi
Major publications	The University of Mississippi: A Sesquicentennial History (1999), Making Haste Slowly: The Troubled History of Higher Education in Mississippi (2008)
Number of cases	7

Case[4]	Year	Manner of involvement
1. Horton v. American Tobacco	1990	Deposition and testimony
2. Ierardi v. Lorillard	1991	Expert report submitted
3. Wilks v. American Tobacco	1993	Deposition and testimony
4. Grinnell v. American Tobacco	1997	Deposition and testimony
5. In re: Mississippi Tobacco Litigation	1997	Deposition
6. Carter v. Philip Morris	1999–2003	Deposition and testimony
7. Boerner v. Brown and Williamson	2003	Cross-examination

[1]See cross-examination of David Sansing, May 19, 2003, *Boerner v. Brown and Williamson*. Westlaw reference: 2003 WL 25737063.

[2]See deposition of David Sansing, August 15, 1990, *Horton v. American Tobacco*. Westlaw reference: 1990 WL 10544591.

[3]See cross-examination of David Sansing, May 19, 2003, *Boerner v. Brown and Williamson*. Westlaw reference: 2003 WL 25737063.

[4]Information on the cases is based on Proctor, Robert. 2012. *Golden Holocaust: Origins of the Cigarette Catastrophe and the Case for Abolition.* Berkeley: University of California Press, 462. & The following online databases: http://legacy.library.ucsf.edu, http://tobaccodocuments.org, http://lawschool.courtroomview.com/experts, & Westlaw.

43. Todd Savitt

Name	Todd Savitt
Professional occupation	Professor of History
Institution	East Carolina University
Website	http://www.ecu.edu/cs-dhs/medhum/savitt.cfm
Short description	Todd Savitt is a historian of medicine with a particular interest in African-American medical history. He received his BA from Colgate University (1965), attended the University of Rochester School of Medicine (1965–1968), and earned his MA (1970) and Ph.D. (1975) in history from the University of Virginia. After teaching at the University of Florida College of Medicine (1976–1982) he joined the Department of Bioethics and Interdisciplinary Studies at The Brody School of Medicine, East Carolina University where he teaches history of medicine, literature and medicine, social and cultural issues in medical practice, and medical ethics. Savitt is also Assistant Dean for Diversity at BSOM (since January 2011).
Education	Ph.D.
Major fields	African-American medical history, medical history of the American South and West
Major publications	Medicine and Slavery: The Diseases and Health Care of Blacks in Antebellum Virginia (2002), Race and Medicine in Nineteenth- and Early-Twentieth-Century America (2007)
Number of cases	1

Case[1]	Year	Manner of involvement
1. Ierardi v. Lorillard	1991	Expert report submitted

[1]Information on the cases is based on Proctor, Robert. 2012. *Golden Holocaust: Origins of the Cigarette Catastrophe and the Case for Abolition.* Berkeley: University of California Press, 463. & The following online databases: http://legacy.library.ucsf.edu, http://tobaccodocuments.org, http://lawschool.courtroomview.com/experts, & Westlaw.

44. Michael Schaller

Name	Michael Schaller
Professional occupation	Professor of History
Institution	University of Arizona
Website	http://history.arizona.edu/user/180
Short description	Michael Schaller is Regents Professor of History at the University of Arizona. He works predominantly on the history of America's foreign relations. Schaller has been an active expert witness for the defence in tobacco litigation. In more than 15 years, Schaller has participated in 36 court cases relating to tobacco issues. In an affidavit submitted for *Caronia v. Philip Morris* in 2007 Schaller stated that he charged $225 an hour for his litigation-driven research on tobacco.[1] He furthermore acknowledged during a deposition taken for *Grill v. Philip Morris* in 2010 that he made approximately $100,000 a year as an expert judicial witness for the tobacco industry. In addition, Schaller disclosed he had started working for the tobacco companies in 1995 and had made $1.3 million dollars in total as an expert.[2] In 2012, Schaller was deposed on the salaries he has made as an expert witness. He acknowledged having made around 1.5 to 1.6 million dollars. According to the same deposition, he started working for the tobacco industry in 1995.[3] He has not published any historical research on tobacco.
Education	Ph.D.
Major fields	United States foreign policy/diplomatic history, United States since 1865, United States – East Asian relations
Major publications	The US Crusade in China, 1938–1945 (1979), The Republican Ascendancy: American Politics, 1968–2001 (2002), Right Turn: American Life in the Reagan-Bush Era (2007)
Number of Cases	36

Case[4]	Year	Manner of involvement
1. Mulholland v. Philip Morris	1997	Deposition
2. Arizona v. American Tobacco	1998	Designated
3. Selcer v. R.J. Reynolds	1998	Deposition and testimony
4. Sweeney v. Philip Morris	1999	Designated
5. Apostolou v. Philip Morris	2000	Testimony
6. Simon v. Philip Morris	2000	Designated
7. Boeken v. Philip Morris	2001–2003	Designated
8. Bullock v. Philip Morris	2002	Expert report submitted
9. Frankson v. Brown and Williamson	2003–2007	Testimony
10. Lucier v. R.J. Reynolds	2003	Testimony

(continued)

Case[4]	Year	Manner of involvement
11. Reller v. Philip Morris	2003–2005	Testimony
12. Rose v. American Tobacco	2003–2007	Designated
13. Schwab v. Philip Morris	2004–2006	Affidavit
14. Benedict v. Altria Group	2005	Expert report submitted
15. Ortega v. Philip Morris	2005	Affidavit
16. Caronia v. Philip Morris	2006–2010	Expert report submitted
17. Mulholland v. Altria Group	2006	Expert report submitted
18. Grill v. Philip Morris	2007–2010	Deposition and testimony
19. Bradley v. R.J. Reynolds	2008–2012	Deposition and testimony
20. Hess v. R.J. Reynolds	2008–2009	Cross-examination
21. Bifolck v. Philip Morris	2009–2012	Deposition
22. Grossman v. R.J. Reynolds	2009–2013	Cross-examination
23. In re: Engle Progeny Cases[5]	2009–2014	Deposition and testimony
24. Smith v. R.J. Reynolds	2010–2012	Testimony
25. Aycock v. R.J. Reynolds	2011–2013	Deposition and testimony
26. Hallgren v. R.J. Reynolds	2011	Deposition
27. Narushka v. R.J. Reynolds	2011–2012	Deposition and testimony
28. Rodehaver v. R.J. Reynolds	2011–2012	Testimony
29. Rudy v. R.J. Reynolds	2011–2012	Deposition and testimony
30. Vanblarcom v. R.J. Reynolds	2011–2012	Deposition
31. Giddens v. R.J. Reynolds	2012	Expert report submitted
32. Graham v. R.J. Reynolds	2012	Deposition
33. Hill v. R.J. Reynolds	2012	Deposition and testimony
34. Larrabee v. R.J. Reynolds	2012	Deposition
35. Reider v. R.J. Reynolds	2012	Deposition
36. Kemp v. R.J. Reynolds	2013	Deposition

[1]See affidavit of Michael Schaller, June 14, 2007, *Caronia v. Philip Morris*. Westlaw reference: 2007 WL 5334145.

[2]See deposition of Michael Schaller, March 26, 2010, *Grill v. Philip Morris*. Westlaw reference: 2010 WL 5691836.

[3]See deposition of Michael Schaller, August 22, 2012, *Graham v. R.J. Reynolds*. Westlaw reference: 2012 WL 4107339.

[4]Information on the cases is based on Proctor, Robert. 2012. *Golden Holocaust: Origins of the Cigarette Catastrophe and the Case for Abolition*. Berkeley: University of California Press, 463. The following online databases: http://legacy.library.ucsf.edu, http://tobaccodocuments.org, http://lawschool.courtroomview.com/experts, & Westlaw. In Engle Progeny Cases many depositions and testimonies are reused in other cases instead of solely in the case where the actual testimony was given for the first time. I list these cases separately because in each one the deposition or testimony was submitted as important evidence and thereby it influenced the court and the jury.

[5]Pertaining to Aycock, Blundell, Denton, Duke, Gollihue, Grossman, Hess, McCray, Picket, Rix, Starling, Waggoner, and Walker.

45. James Sharp

Name	James Roger Sharp
Professional occupation	Professor Emeritus of History
Institution	Maxwell School of Syracuse University
Website	http://www.maxwell.syr.edu/faculty.aspx?id=6442451545
Short description	James Roger Sharp is professor emeritus of history at Maxwell School of Syracuse University. Sharp has been an expert judicial witness in seven tobacco-related court cases. In testimony given in *Mehlman v. Philip Morris* in 2001 Sharp declared he charged $150 an hour for his research on tobacco. He furthermore stated that he had earned $100,000 in research and under questioning acknowledged that he would earn another $30,000 for the work he had done on *Mehlman*.[1]
Education	Ph.D.
Major fields	American political history, early national and middle period, 1789–1860
Major publications	American Politics in the Early Republic: The New Nation in Crisis. (1995), American Legislative Leaders in the West, 1911–1994. (1997)
Number of cases	7

Case[2]	Year	Manner of involvement
1. Anderson v. American Tobacco	2000	Deposition and testimony
2. Mehlman v. Philip Morris	2000–2001	Deposition and testimony
3. Clinton v. Altria Group	2006	Designated
4. Clinton v. Brown and Williamson	2006	Expert report submitted
5. Grill v. Philip Morris	2007–2010	Designated
6. Hall v. R.J. Reynolds	2009–2011	Deposition
7. Townsend v. R.J. Reynolds	2009–2010	Deposition and testimony

[1] See testimony of Roger Sharp, May 3, 2001, *Mehlman v. Philip Morris*. Westlaw reference: 2001 WL 36139650.

[2] Information on the cases is based on Proctor, Robert. 2012. *Golden Holocaust: Origins of the Cigarette Catastrophe and the Case for Abolition*. Berkeley: University of California Press, 463. & The following online databases: http://legacy.library.ucsf.edu, http://tobaccodocuments.org, http://lawschool.courtroomview.com/experts, & Westlaw.

46. John Skates

Name	John Skates
Professional occupation	Professor Emeritus of History
Institution	University of Southern Mississippi
Website	http://www.lib.usm.edu/legacy/archives/m130.htm
Short description	John Skates is professor emeritus of history of the University of Southern Mississippi. He was only once deposed in a tobacco related court case; namely in the attorney general case in Mississippi.
Education	Ph.D.
Major fields	The history of the invasion of Japan and the history of Mississippi
Major publications	A History of the Mississippi Supreme Court, 1817–1948 (1973), The Invasion of Japan: Alternative to the Bomb (1994), Discovering Mississippi: A Mississippi Studies Textbook (1995)
Number of cases	1

Case[1]	Year	Manner of involvement
1. In re: Mississippi Tobacco Litigation	1997	Deposition

[1]Information on the cases is based on Proctor, Robert. 2012. *Golden Holocaust: Origins of the Cigarette Catastrophe and the Case for Abolition.* Berkeley: University of California Press, 463. & The following online databases: http://legacy.library.ucsf.edu, http://tobaccodocuments.org, http://lawschool.courtroomview.com/experts, & Westlaw.

47. John Snetsinger

Name	John Snetsinger
Professional occupation	Professor Emeritus of History
Institution	California Polytechnic State University
Website	http://www.cla.calpoly.edu/hist_snetsinger.html
Short description	Snetsinger is professor emeritus of the history department of California Polytechnic State University. He has only been involved in one tobacco related-case for the defence, namely, in *Bullock v. Philip Morris* in 2002. In the deposition he gave in that case Snetsinger acknowledged he had made over $100,000 as an expert judicial witness working for the tobacco industry. He furthermore declared that he had been first contacted to work on tobacco litigation by Allen Pervis, a lawyer from the firm Johsen, Tyler & Pervis. Michael Schaller, another expert historian working for the tobacco companies had recommended Snetsinger to Pervis.[1]
Education	Ph.D.
Major fields	US history, modern world history, US foreign relations, Jewish history
Major publications	Truman, the Jewish Vote and the Creation of Israel (1974), Irreconcilable Differences? The Waning of the American Jewish Love Affair with Israel. (2002)
Number of cases	1

Case[2]	Year	Manner of involvement
1. Bullock v. Philip Morris	2002	Deposition

[1]See deposition of John Snetsinger, April 23, 2002, *Bullock v. Philip Morris*. Westlaw reference: 2002 WL 34425562.

[2]Information on the cases is based on Proctor, Robert. 2012. *Golden Holocaust: Origins of the Cigarette Catastrophe and the Case for Abolition.* Berkeley: University of California Press, 463. & The following online databases: http://legacy.library.ucsf.edu, http://tobaccodocuments.org, http://lawschool.courtroomview.com/experts, & Westlaw.

48. William Stueck

Name	William Stueck
Professional occupation	Professor Emeritus of History
Institution	University of Georgia
Website	http://history.uga.edu/directory/william-w-stueck
Short description	William Stueck is professor emeritus of history of the University of Georgia. He has predominantly published on American political history. He has been hired by the legal firms King & Spalding LLP and Jones Day LLP, Chadbourne & Parke LLP, and Dinsmore & Shohl to offer consultation and expert witness testimony on the public awareness of the health risks of cigarette smoking. Stueck has been active as an expert witness for the defence in 20 cases during the period 2001–2013. Stueck has been involved in recent Engle Progeny cases in Florida. In 2004 he declared in a deposition taken for *Gault v. Brown and Williamson* that he charged $200 hourly for his work as an expert judicial witness.[1] In a deposition pertaining to *Alexander v. Philip Morris* from 2010, Stueck also acknowledged he charged $200 an hour for his research.[2]
Education	Ph.D.
Major fields	United States diplomatic history, Cold War, US-Korean relations, although not having published on the subject Stueck adds history of tobacco use and health in US to his major fields.
Major publications	The Korean War (1997), Rethinking the Korean War: A New Diplomatic and Strategic History (2004), The Korean War in World History (2004), Globalization and the American South (2005)
Number of cases	20

Case[3]	Year	Manner of involvement
1. Eiser v. Brown and Williamson	2002–2005	Affidavit
2. Gault v. Brown and Williamson	2004	Deposition
3. Mash v. Brown and Williamson	2004	Deposition and testimony
4. Bagshaw v. R.J. Reynolds	2006	Designated
5. Harford v. R.J. Reynolds	2008	Expert report submitted
6. In re: Engle Progeny Cases	2009–2014	Expert report submitted
7. Alexander v. Philip Morris	2010–2012	Deposition and testimony
8. Smith v. R.J. Reynolds	2010–2012	Cross-examination
9. Duke v. R.J. Reynolds	2011	Deposition
10. Huish v. R.J. Reynolds	2011	Cross-examination
11. Vanblarcom v. R.J. Reynolds	2011	Testimony
12. Graham v. R.J. Reynolds	2012	Deposition
13. Larrabee v. R.J. Reynolds	2012	Deposition

(continued)

Case[3]	Year	Manner of involvement
14. Linda Cumbess v. R.J. Reynolds	2012	Cross-examination
15. Proud v. R.J. Reynolds	2012	Expert report submitted
16. Reider v. R.J. Reynolds	2012	Testimony
17. Banks v. R.J. Reynolds	2013	Deposition
18. Ellis v. R.J. Reynolds	2013–2014	Deposition
19. Hausner v. R.J. Reynolds	2013	Testimony
20. Milledge v. R.J. Reynolds	2013	Deposition

[1]See deposition of William Stueck, January 30, 2004, *Gault v. Brown and Williamson*. Westlaw reference: 2004 WL 3737107.

[2]See deposition of William Stueck, June 16, 2010, *Alexander v. Philip Morris*. Westlaw reference: 2010 WL 6568237.

[3]Information on the cases is based on Proctor, Robert. 2012. *Golden Holocaust: Origins of the Cigarette Catastrophe and the Case for Abolition*. Berkeley: University of California Press, 463. & The following online databases: http://legacy.library.ucsf.edu, http://tobaccodocuments.org, http://lawschool.courtroomview.com/experts, & Westlaw. This profile is furthermore completed with information from personal correspondence with Mr. Stueck. In Engle Progeny Cases many depositions and testimonies are reused in other cases instead of solely in the case where the actual testimony was given for the first time. I list these cases separately because in each one the deposition or testimony was submitted as important evidence and thereby it influenced the court and the jury.

49. Joseph Tulchin

Name	Joseph S. Tulchin
Professional occupation	Visiting Fellow at Harvard
Institution	The Mexico and Central America Program at Harvard University's David Rockefeller Center for Latin American Studies
Website	http://www.joetulchin.com/
	http://geopolitical-info.com/en/expert/dr_joseph_s_tulchin
Short description	Joe Tulchin is a Latin Americanist. He is a widely published research scholar and a successful teacher. He spent 25 years teaching—first at Yale and then at the University of North Carolina at Chapel Hill —and then for 16 years directed a program of public policy research on Latin America, as part of the Woodrow Wilson International Center for Scholars. He has been active in only one tobacco-related trial: *Widdick v. Brown and Williamson.* Under cross-examination in that case Tulchin declared that he had billed the tobacco companies for $90,000. He charged $250 an hour for his work as an expert judicial witness.[1]
Education	Ph.D.
Major fields	US foreign policy, inter-American relations, contemporary Latin America, social science research methodology
Major publications	Citizenship in Latin America (2007), New Voices in the Study of Democracy in Latin America (2008), The Strategic Culture of Chile (2010)
Number of cases	1

Case[2]	Year	Manner of involvement
1. Widdick v. Brown & Williamson	1998	Cross-examination

[1]See cross-examination of Joseph Tulchin, June 1, 1998, *Widdick v. Brown and Williamson.* Westlaw reference: 1998 WL 35262237.

[2]Information on the cases is based on Proctor, Robert. 2012. *Golden Holocaust: Origins of the Cigarette Catastrophe and the Case for Abolition.* Berkeley: University of California Press, 463. & The following online databases: http://legacy.library.ucsf.edu, http://tobaccodocuments.org, http://lawschool.courtroomview.com/experts, & Westlaw.

50. Theodore Wilson

Name	Theodore Wilson
Professional occupation	Professor of History
Institution	University of Kansas
Website	http://gmp.ku.edu/ted-wilson
Short description	Theodore Wilson is a military historian at the University of Kansas in Lawrence. He is a history professor and is the Assistant Chair and Director of Graduate Studies. He has directed approximately 40 M.A. theses and 30 Ph.D. dissertations, mostly treating aspects of US foreign relations and the American military experience. His current research embraces Anglo-American cultural interaction during World War II, the US Army and the early Cold War, and a long-gestating biography of Henry A. Wallace. In an affidavit submitted for *Insolia v. Philip Morris* he disclosed that he had made $320,000 working for the tobacco industry as an expert historian.[1] In his deposition in the landmark case *US v. Philip Morris et al.*, in 2002, Wilson stated that he had made approximately $500,000 as an expert judicial witness for the tobacco industry.[2]
Education	Ph.D.
Major fields	Twentieth-century US political, military, and diplomatic history, Anglo-American cultural interaction during World War II, US Army and the early Cold War
Major publications	D-Day Modern War Studies (1994), Victory in Europe 1945: From World War to Cold War (2000), Presidents Diplomats and Other Mortals (2007), Coalition Warfare: A Guide to the Issues (Contemporary Military, Strategic, and Security Issues) (2013)
Number of cases	12

Case[3]	Year	Manner of involvement
1. Barnes v. American Tobacco	1997	Deposition
2. Emis v. American Tobacco	1997	Affidavit
3. Insolia v. Philip Morris	1997-1999	Expert report submitted
4. Mason v. American Tobacco	1997	Affidavit
5. Walls v. American Tobacco	1997	Affidavit
6. Smith v. Brown & Williamson	1998–1999	Deposition
7. Clay v. Philip Morris	1999	Deposition
8. Thompson v. American Tobacco	1999	Affidavit

(continued)

Case[3]	Year	Manner of involvement
9. US v. Philip Morris	1999–2006	Expert report and deposition
10. Blankenship v. Philip Morris	2000–2004	Deposition
11. In re: Tobacco Litigation	2000	Deposition
12. Miles v. Philip Morris	2002	Deposition

[1]Affidavit of Theodore Wilson, 1997, *Insolia v. Philip Morris*. Westlaw reference: 1997 WL 33833947.

[2]Deposition of Theodore Wilson, September 4, 2002, *US v. Philip Morris et al*. LTDL. Bates Number: WILSONT090402. http://legacy.library.ucsf.edu/tid/nhp11b00. Accessed 31 Oct 2014, 39.

[3]Information on the cases is based on Proctor, Robert. 2012. *Golden Holocaust: Origins of the Cigarette Catastrophe and the Case for Abolition*. Berkeley: University of California Press, 463. & The following online databases: http://legacy.library.ucsf.edu, http://tobaccodocuments.org, http://lawschool.courtroomview.com/experts, & Westlaw.

Appendix II: Historians Who Have Testified as an Expert Witness in Tobacco Litigation

Table 1. Deceased.
Table 2. Active in In re: Engle Progeny Cases.
Table 3. Institution.
Table 4. Number of Cases.
Table 5. Published on the History of Smoking and the Tobacco Industry.
Table 6. Remuneration.

Table 1 Deceased

Number	First name	Last name	Deceased
1	Stephen	Ambrose	Yes
2	Jonathan	Bean	No
3	Hyman	Berman	No
4	Allan	Brandt	No
5	James	Breeden	No
6	John	Burnham	No
7	Augustus	Burns	Yes
8	Fred	Carstensen	No
9	Michael	Chesson	No
10	Elizabeth	Cobbs Hoffman	No
11	Luis	Díaz-Hernández	No
12	Thomas	DiBacco	No
13	John	Drobny	No
14	Peter	English	No
15	Frederick	Fausz	No
16	Lacy	Ford	No
17	Otis	Graham Jr.	No
18	George	Green	No
19	Janette	Greenwood	No
20	Jon	Harkness	No
21	Paul	Harvey	No
22	James	Hilty	No
23	Joan	Hoff	No
24	Robert	Hudson	Yes
25	Jacob	Judd	No
26	Louis	Kyriakoudes	No
27	Timothy	Lenoir	No
28	Kenneth	Lipartito	No
29	Charles	Lowery	No
30	Kenneth	Ludmerer	No
31	James	Kirby Martin	No
32	Luis	Martinez-Fernandez	No
33	Glenn	May	No
34	Gregg	Michel	No
35	Wayne	Morgan	Yes
36	Robert	Norrell	No
37	Michael	Parrish	No
38	Terry	Parssinen	No
39	Robert	Proctor	No
40	Randy	Roberts	No

(continued)

Table 1 (continued)

Number	First name	Last name	Deceased
41	Mark	Rose	No
42	David	Sansing	No
43	Todd	Savitt	No
44	Michael	Schaller	No
45	James	Sharp	No
46	John	Skates	No
47	John	Snetsinger	No
48	William	Stueck	No
49	Joseph	Tulchin	No
50	Theodore	Wilson	No

Table 2 Active in In re: Engle progeny cases

Number	First name	Last name	Active in In re: Engle Progeny Cases
1	Stephen	Ambrose	No
2	Jonathan	Bean	No
3	Hyman	Berman	No
4	Allan	Brandt	No
5	James	Breeden	No
6	John	Burnham	No
7	Augustus	Burns	No
8	Fred	Carstensen	No
9	Michael	Chesson	No
10	Elizabeth	Cobbs Hoffman	Yes
11	Luis	Díaz-Hernández	No
12	Thomas	DiBacco	No
13	John	Drobny	No
14	Peter	English	No
15	Frederick	Fausz	No
16	Lacy	Ford	Yes
17	Otis	Graham Jr.	No
18	George	Green	No
19	Janette	Greenwood	Yes
20	Jon	Harkness	No
21	Paul	Harvey	No
22	James	Hilty	No
23	Joan	Hoff	Yes
24	Robert	Hudson	No
25	Jacob	Judd	No
26	Louis	Kyriakoudes	Yes
27	Timothy	Lenoir	No
28	Kenneth	Lipartito	Yes
29	Charles	Lowery	No
30	Kenneth	Ludmerer	No
31	James	Kirby Martin	Yes
32	Luis	Martinez-Fernandez	Yes
33	Glenn	May	No
34	Gregg	Michel	Yes
35	Wayne	Morgan	No
36	Robert	Norrell	Yes
37	Michael	Parrish	No
38	Terry	Parssinen	Yes
39	Robert	Proctor	Yes
40	Randy	Roberts	Yes

(continued)

Table 2 (continued)

Number	First name	Last name	Active in In re: Engle Progeny Cases
41	Mark	Rose	No
42	David	Sansing	No
43	Todd	Savitt	No
44	Michael	Schaller	Yes
45	James	Sharp	No
46	John	Skates	No
47	John	Snetsinger	No
48	William	Stueck	Yes
49	Joseph	Tulchin	No
50	Theodore	Wilson	No

Table 3 Institution

Number	First name	Last name	University
1	Stephen	Ambrose	University of New Orleans
2	Jonathan	Bean	Southern Illinois University
3	Hyman	Berman	University of Minnesota
4	Allan	Brandt	Harvard University
5	James	Breeden	Southern Methodist University
6	John	Burnham	Ohio State University
7	Augustus	Burns	University of Florida
8	Fred	Carstensen	University Connecticut
9	Michael	Chesson	University of Massachusetts-Boston
10	Elizabeth	Cobbs Hoffman	San Diego State University
11	Luis	Díaz-Hernández	Pontifical Catholic University in Ponce, Puerto Rico
12	Thomas	DiBacco	The Kogod School of Business of the American University
13	John	Drobny	n/a
14	Peter	English	Duke University
15	Frederick	Fausz	University of Missouri
16	Lacy	Ford	University of South Carolina
17	Otis	Graham Jr.	University of North Carolina
18	George	Green	University of Minnesota
19	Janette	Greenwood	Clark University
20	Jon	Harkness	University of Minnesota
21	Paul	Harvey	University of Colorado
22	James	Hilty	Temple University Ambler
23	Joan	Hoff	University of Montana
24	Robert	Hudson	University of Kansas
25	Jacob	Judd	Lehman College
26	Louis	Kyriakoudes	University of Southern Mississippi
27	Timothy	Lenoir	Duke University
28	Kenneth	Lipartito	Florida International University
29	Charles	Lowery	Mississippi State University
30	Kenneth	Ludmerer	Washington University
31	James	Kirby Martin	University of Houston
32	Luis	Martinez-Fernandez	University of Central Florida
33	Glenn	May	University of Oregon
34	Gregg	Michel	University of Texas
35	Wayne	Morgan	University of Oklahoma
36	Robert	Norrell	University of Tennessee
37	Michael	Parrish	University of California of San Diego
38	Terry	Parssinen	University of Tampa
39	Robert	Proctor	Stanford University
40	Randy	Roberts	Purdue University

(continued)

Table 3 (continued)

Number	First name	Last name	University
41	Mark	Rose	Florida Atlantic University
42	David	Sansing	University of Mississippi
43	Todd	Savitt	East Carolina University
44	Michael	Schaller	University of Arizona
45	James	Sharp	Maxwell School of Syracuse University
46	John	Skates	University of Southern Mississippi
47	John	Snetsinger	California Polytechnic State University
48	William	Stueck	University of Georgia
49	Joseph	Tulchin	Harvard University
50	Theodore	Wilson	University of Kansas

Table 4 Number of cases

Number	First name	Last name	Number of cases
1	Stephen	Ambrose	3
2	Jonathan	Bean	2
3	Hyman	Berman	1
4	Allan	Brandt	1
5	James	Breeden	1
6	John	Burnham	2
7	Augustus	Burns	2
8	Fred	Carstensen	2
9	Michael	Chesson	1
10	Elizabeth	Cobbs Hoffman	21
11	Luis	Díaz-Hernández	8
12	Thomas	DiBacco	6
13	John	Drobny	1
14	Peter	English	15
15	Frederick	Fausz	2
16	Lacy	Ford	19
17	Otis	Graham Jr.	4
18	George	Green	1
19	Janette	Greenwood	5
20	Jon	Harkness	3
21	Paul	Harvey	4
22	James	Hilty	2
23	Joan	Hoff	31
24	Robert	Hudson	1
25	Jacob	Judd	3
26	Louis	Kyriakoudes	66
27	Timothy	Lenoir	1
28	Kenneth	Lipartito	3
29	Charles	Lowery	1
30	Kenneth	Ludmerer	15
31	James	Kirby Martin	23
32	Luis	Martinez-Fernandez	14
33	Glenn	May	3
34	Gregg	Michel	11
35	Wayne	Morgan	1
36	Robert	Norrell	28
37	Michael	Parrish	17
38	Terry	Parssinen	22
39	Robert	Proctor	93

(continued)

Table 4 (continued)

Number	First name	Last name	Number of cases
40	Randy	Roberts	25
41	Mark	Rose	2
42	David	Sansing	7
43	Todd	Savitt	1
44	Michael	Schaller	36
45	James	Sharp	7
46	John	Skates	1
47	John	Snetsinger	1
48	William	Stueck	20
49	Joseph	Tulchin	1
50	Theodore	Wilson	12

Table 5 Published on the history of smoking and the tobacco industry

Number	First name	Last name	Published
1	Stephen	Ambrose	No
2	Jonathan	Bean	No
3	Hyman	Berman	No
4	Allan	Brandt	Yes
5	James	Breeden	No
6	John	Burnham	Yes
7	Augustus	Burns	No
8	Fred	Carstensen	No
9	Michael	Chesson	No
10	Elizabeth	Cobbs Hoffman	No
11	Luis	Díaz-Hernández	No
12	Thomas	DiBacco	No
13	John	Drobny	No
14	Peter	English	No
15	Frederick	Fausz	No
16	Lacy	Ford	No
17	Otis	Graham Jr.	No
18	George	Green	No
19	Janette	Greenwood	No
20	Jon	Harkness	Yes
21	Paul	Harvey	No
22	James	Hilty	No
23	Joan	Hoff	No
24	Robert	Hudson	No
25	Jacob	Judd	No
26	Louis	Kyriakoudes	Yes
27	Timothy	Lenoir	No
28	Kenneth	Lipartito	No
29	Charles	Lowery	No
30	Kenneth	Ludmerer	No
31	James	Kirby Martin	No
32	Luis	Martinez-Fernandez	No
33	Glenn	May	No
34	Gregg	Michel	No
35	Wayne	Morgan	No
36	Robert	Norrell	No
37	Michael	Parrish	No
38	Terry	Parssinen	No
39	Robert	Proctor	Yes
40	Randy	Roberts	No

(continued)

Table 5 (continued)

Number	First name	Last name	Published
41	Mark	Rose	No
42	David	Sansing	No
43	Todd	Savitt	No
44	Michael	Schaller	No
45	James	Sharp	No
46	John	Skates	No
47	John	Snetsinger	No
48	William	Stueck	No
49	Joseph	Tulchin	No
50	Theodore	Wilson	No

Table 6 Remuneration

Number	First name	Last name	Remuneration
1	Stephen	Ambrose	$25,000 (For one case)
2	Jonathan	Bean	
3	Hyman	Berman	
4	Allan	Brandt	
5	James	Breeden	
6	John	Burnham	
7	Augustus	Burns	$80,000
8	Fred	Carstensen	$85,000
9	Michael	Chesson	
10	Elizabeth	Cobbs Hoffman	$616,000
11	Luis	Díaz-Hernández	
12	Thomas	DiBacco	$380,000
13	John	Drobny	$41,000 (For one case)
14	Peter	English	$800,000
15	Frederick	Fausz	
16	Lacy	Ford	
17	Otis	Graham Jr.	
18	George	Green	
19	Janette	Greenwood	
20	Jon	Harkness	$500,000
21	Paul	Harvey	
22	James	Hilty	$75,000 (For one case)
23	Joan	Hoff	$325,000
24	Robert	Hudson	$92,000 (For one case)
25	Jacob	Judd	
26	Louis	Kyriakoudes	
27	Timothy	Lenoir	
28	Kenneth	Lipartito	
29	Charles	Lowery	
30	Kenneth	Ludmerer	$550,000
31	James	Kirby Martin	$800,000
32	Luis	Martinez-Fernandez	$83,750
33	Glenn	May	$80,000
34	Gregg	Michel	$220,000
35	Wayne	Morgan	
36	Robert	Norrell	$1,000,000
37	Michael	Parrish	
38	Terry	Parssinen	$450,000
39	Robert	Proctor	$1,500,000–$2,000,000
40	Randy	Roberts	$900,000

(continued)

Table 6 (continued)

Number	First name	Last name	Remuneration
41	Mark	Rose	
42	David	Sansing	$500,000
43	Todd	Savitt	
44	Michael	Schaller	$1,500,000–1,600,000
45	James	Sharp	$130,000
46	John	Skates	
47	John	Snetsinger	
48	William	Stueck	
49	Joseph	Tulchin	$90,000
50	Theodore	Wilson	$500,000

Appendix III: Timetable Involvement Historians as Expert Witnesses in Tobacco Cases

Table 7 Involvement of historians in tobacco litigation 1986–2013

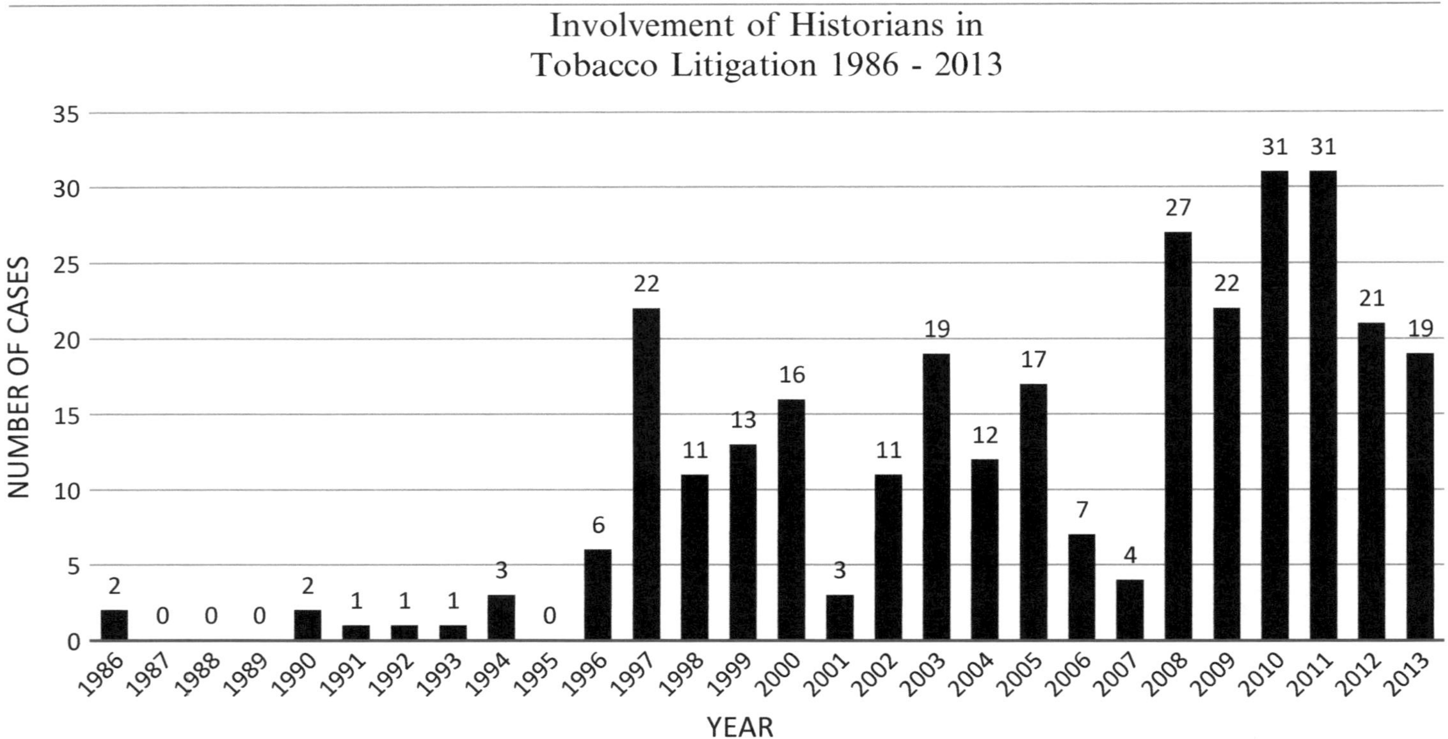

Table 8 Involvement of historians in tobacco litigation 1986–2014

Number	Year	Case	Historian	Involvement
1	1986	Dewey v. R.J. Reynolds	Burnham	Designated
2	1986–1991	Cipollone v. Liggett Group	Burnham	Designated
			Carstensen	Deposition and testimony
			Ludmerer	Deposition
3	1990	Horton v. American Tobacco	Sansing	Deposition and testimony
4	1990	Kotler v. American Tobacco	Graham	Testimony
			Ludmerer	Testimony
5	1991	Ierardi v. Lorillard	Sansing	Expert report submitted
			Savitt	Expert report submitted
6	1992	Haines v. Liggett Group	English	Designated
7	1993	Wilks v. American Tobacco	Sansing	Deposition and testimony
8	1994	Allgood v. R.J. Reynolds	Breeden	Expert report submitted
			Hudson	Deposition
9	1994	Covert v. Liggett Group	Ambrose	Testimony
10	1994	Unkel v. Liggett Group	Ludmerer	Expert report submitted
11	1996	Burton v. R.J. Reynolds	Martin	Deposition
12	1996	Hoskins v. R.J. Reynolds	Parrish	Affidavit
13	1996	Richardson v. R.J. Reynolds	Martin	Affidavit
14	1996	Rogers v. R.J. Reynolds	Hoff	Testimony
15	1996	Small v. Lorillard	Parrish	Affidavit
16	1996	Stewart-Lomanitz v. Brown & Williamson	Parrish	Affidavit
17	1997	Arch v. American Tobacco	Parrish	Affidavit
18	1997	Barnes v. American Tobacco	Parrish	Deposition
			Wilson	Deposition
19	1997–1998	Dunn v. R.J. Reynolds	Hoff	Deposition and testimony
20	1997	Emis v. American Tobacco	Wilson	Affidavit
21	1997–1999	Engle v. R.J. Reynolds	Burns	Deposition
			DiBacco	Deposition and testimony
			Ford	Deposition and testimony
			Ludmerer	Deposition
22	1997	Florida v. American Tobacco	Ambrose	Deposition
			Burns	Deposition
			Ludmerer	Deposition

(continued)

Table 8 (continued)

Number	Year	Case	Historian	Involvement
23	1997	Frosina v. Philip Morris	Parrish	Deposition
24	1997	Grinnell v. American Tobacco	Sansing	Deposition and testimony
25	1997	Haines v. Liggett Group	Ambrose	Designated
26	1997	In re: Mississippi Tobacco Litigation	Lowery	Deposition
			Ludmerer	Deposition
			Sansing	Deposition
			Skates	Deposition
27	1997–1999	Insolia v. Philip Morris	Wilson	Expert report submitted
28	1997	Jackson v. Brown and Williamson	Rose	Affidavit
29	1997	Karbiwnyk v. R.J. Reynolds	Ford	Deposition and testimony
30	1997	Keegan v. R.J. Reynolds	Ford	Designated
31	1997	Konkle v. R.J. Reynolds	Norrell	Deposition and testimony
32	1997	Marks v. R.J. Reynolds	Norrell	Testimony
33	1997	Mason v. American Tobacco	Wilson	Affidavit
34	1997–1998	Minnesota v. Philip Morris	Berman	Deposition and testimony
			Green	Deposition and testimony
35	1997	Mulholland v. Philip Morris	Schaller	Deposition
36	1997	Raulerson v. R.J. Reynolds	Ford	Testimony
37	1997	Texas v. American Tobacco	Drobny	Deposition
			Graham	Deposition
38	1997	Walls v. American Tobacco	Wilson	Affidavit
39	1998	Arizona v. American Tobacco	Schaller	Designated
40	1998	Henley v. Philip Morris	Parrish	Deposition and testimony
41	1998–1999	Ironworkers v. Philip Morris	Martin	Deposition and testimony
			Proctor	Expert report submitted
42	1998–1999	Karney v. Brown and Williamson	Norrell	Deposition and testimony
43	1998	Northwest Laborers v. Philip Morris	Proctor	Expert report submitted
44	1998	Oklahoma v. R.J. Reynolds	Morgan	Deposition and testimony
45	1998	Selcer v. R.J. Reynolds	Schaller	Deposition and testimony

(continued)

Table 8 (continued)

Number	Year	Case	Historian	Involvement
46	1998–1999	Smith v. Brown and Williamson	Wilson	Deposition
47	1998	Tabb v. Philip Morris	Parrish	Affidavit
48	1998	Washington v. American Tobacco	Ludmerer	Deposition
			Parrish	Deposition
49	1998	Widdick v. Brown and Williamson	Tulchin	Cross-examination
50	1999	Bergeron v. Philip Morris	Martin	Affidavit
51	1999	Branch v. Philip Morris	May	Testimony
52	1999–2003	Carter v. Philip Morris	Hilty	Cross-examination
			Sansing	Deposition and testimony
53	1999	Clay v. Philip Morris	Wilson	Deposition
54	1999	Klein v. R.J. Reynods	Martin	Testimony
55	1999	National Asbestos v. Philip Morris	Martin	Deposition
56	1999	Newcomb v. R.J. Reynolds	Norrell	Testimony
57	1999–2002	Schwarz v. Philip Morris	May	Testimony
58	1999	Sweeney v. Philip Morris	Schaller	Designated
59	1999	Thompson v. American Tobacco	Wilson	Affidavit
60	1999–2006	US v. Philip Morris et al.	Brandt	Deposition and cross-examination
			English	Expert report and deposition
			Ludmerer	Expert report and deposition
			Proctor	Expert report and deposition
			Wilson	Expert report and deposition
61	1999–2000	Whitely v. Raybestos-Manhattan	Hoff	Deposition and testimony
62	1999	Williams v. Philip Morris	Ludmerer	Testimony
			May	Deposition
63	2000	Anderson v. American Tobacco	Ludmerer	Testimony
			Sharp	Deposition and testimony
64	2000	Apostolou v. American Tobacco	Ludmerer	Testimony
			Schaller	Testimony
65	2000–2004	Blankenship v. R.J. Reynolds	Ford	Deposition and testimony
			Ludmerer	Deposition
			Wilson	Deposition

(continued)

Table 8 (continued)

Number	Year	Case	Historian	Involvement
66	2000–2001	Blue Cross v. Philip Morris	DiBacco	Deposition
			English	Testimony
			Martin	Deposition
67	2000–2003	Boerner v. Brown and Williamson	Harkness	Testimony
			Kyriakoudes	Deposition and testimony
			Parrish	Deposition
			Sansing	Cross-examination
68	2000	Cannon v. Brown and Williamson	Kyriakoudes	Affidavit
69	2000	Conely v. R.J. Reynolds	Hoff	Designated
70	2000	Falise v. American Tobacco	Martin	Deposition and testimony
71	2000	In re: Tobacco Litigation	Ford	Deposition
			Wilson	Deposition
72	2000	Jones v. R.J. Reynolds	Ford	Testimony
73	2000	Little v. Brown and Williamson	Ford	Deposition and testimony
74	2000–2001	Mehlman v. Philip Morris	Sharp	Deposition and testimony
75	2000	Seaborn v. R.J. Reynolds	Norrell	Deposition
76	2000–2001	Scott v. American Tobacco	Ludmerer	Deposition
			Norrell	Deposition and testimony
77	2000	Simon v. Philip Morris	Schaller	Designated
78	2000	White v. R.J. Reynolds	Fausz	Affidavit
79	2001–2003	Boeken v. Philip Morris	Cobbs Hoffman	Deposition and testimony
			Ludmerer	Testimony
			Schaller	Designated
80	2001	Kenyon v. R.J. Reynolds	Ford	Testimony
81	2001	Tompkin v. R.J. Reynolds	Hoff	Deposition and testimony
			Ludmerer	Deposition
			Martin	Deposition
82	2002–2003	Allen v. R.J. Reynolds	Ford	Testimony
			Kyriakoudes	Designated
83	2002–2004	Brown v. American Tobacco	Cobbs Hoffman	Deposition
			English	Deposition

(continued)

Table 8 (continued)

Number	Year	Case	Historian	Involvement
84	2002	Bullock v. Philip Morris	English	Deposition
			Schaller	Expert report submitted
			Snetsinger	Deposition
85	2002–2013	Campbell, Sr. v. R.J. Reynolds	Kyriakoudes	Testimony
			Norrell	Testimony
			Proctor	Deposition and testimony
86	2002	Cruz v. R.J. Reynolds	Martinez-Fernandez	Testimony
87	2002–2005	Eiser v. Brown and Williamson	Kyriakoudes	Testimony precluded
			Stueck	Affidavit
88	2002	Landers v. R.J. Reynolds	Kyriakoudes	Deposition and testimony
89	2002	Miles v. Philip Morris	English	Expert report submitted
			Wilson	Deposition
90	2002	Sounders v. Philip Morris	Parrish	Affidavit
91	2002	Tune v. Philip Morris	Lenoir	Testimony
92	2002–2004	Viguers v. Philip Morris	Hilty	Affidavit
93	2003	Bowyer v. Philip Morris	Parrish	Affidavit
94	2003	Brown v. Liggett Group	Rose	Designated
95	2003	Cruz-Vargas	Martinez-Fernandez	Testimony
96	2003	Eastman v. Brown and Williamson	DiBacco	Deposition and testimony
			Kyriakoudes	Testimony
97	2003–2007	Frankson v. Brown and Williamson	Harkness	Affidavit
			Kyriakoudes	Testimony
			Proctor	Testimony
			Schaller	Testimony
98	2003	Hall v. R.J. Reynolds	Kyriakoudes	Designated
99	2003	Longden v. Philip Morris	Chesson	Affidavit
100	2003	Lucier v. R.J. Reynolds	Schaller	Testimony
101	2003	Miele v. American Tobacco	Parrish	Testimony
102	2003–2005	Reller v. Philip Morris	Kyriakoudes	Deposition
			Schaller	Testimony
103	2003	Reynolds v. Philip Morris	Parrish	Affidavit
104	2003–2005	Rivera v. R.J. Reynolds	Díaz-Hernández	Testimony
			Martinez-Fernandez	Expert report submitted

(continued)

Table 8 (continued)

Number	Year	Case	Historian	Involvement
105	2003–2007	Rose v. American Tobacco	Harkness	Designated
			Judd	Testimony
			Kyriakoudes	Affidavit
			Proctor	Designated
			Schaller	Designated
106	2003	Rosol v. R.J. Reynolds	Kyriakoudes	Deposition
			Proctor	Deposition
107	2003	Sachs v. Lorillard	Norrell	Affidavit
108	2003–2006	Schwartz v. Liggett Group	Graham	Deposition
109	2003	Sheppard v. R.J. Reynolds	Ford	Affidavit and expert report
110	2003	Standish v. American Tobacco	Judd	Expert report submitted
			Kyriakoudes	Affidavit
111	2003	Tomasino v. American Tobacco	Judd	Affidavit
			Kyriakoudes	Affidavit
112	2004–2005	Alvarez v. R.J. Reynolds	Díaz-Hernández	Deposition
			Martinez-Fernandez	Designated
113	2004	Arnitz v. Philip Morris	Kyriakoudes	Deposition and testimony
			Parssinen	Testimony
114	2004–2005	Coolidge v. Philip Morris	Harvey	Deposition
			Kyriakoudes	Deposition and testimony
115	2004	Davis v. Liggett Group	Graham	Testimony
116	2004	Gadelata v. Lorillard	Kyriakoudes	Testimony
117	2004	Gault v. Brown and Williamson	Stueck	Deposition
118	2004	Kimball v. R.J. Reynolds	Parrish	Deposition
119	2004	Logan v. Brown and Williamson	Parrish	Affidavit
120	2004	Mash v. Brown and Williamson	Kyriakoudes	Deposition
			Stueck	Deposition and testimony
121	2004	Moore v. R.J. Reynolds	Kyriakoudes	Deposition
122	2004–2006	Schwab v. Philip Morris	Bean	Designated
			English	Expert report submitted
			Proctor	Deposition and testimony
			Schaller	Affidavit

(continued)

Table 8 (continued)

Number	Year	Case	Historian	Involvement
123	2004–2008	St. Louis v. American Tobacco	Bean	Deposition
			English	Deposition
			Ford	Designated
			Proctor	Deposition
124	2005	Araballoz v. R.J. Reynolds	Martinez-Fernandez	Deposition
125	2005–2006	Beckum v. Philip Morris	Kyriakoudes	Deposition and testimony
126	2005	Benedict v. Altria Group	English	Affidavit
			Schaller	Expert report submitted
127	2005	Caraballo-Rodriguez v. R.J. Reynolds	Díaz-Hernández	Testimony
128	2005–2010	Craft v. Philip Morris	English	Deposition
			Greenwood	Expert report and deposition
129	2005	De Jesus v. R.J. Reynolds	Díaz-Hernández	Expert report submitted
130	2005	Gerrity v. Lorillard	Carstensen	Deposition
			Kyriakoudes	Deposition
131	2005	Hargroves v. Philip Morris	Kyriakoudes	Designated
132	2005	Huntsberry v. R.J. Reynolds	English	Expert report submitted
			Ford	Expert report submitted
133	2005	Nieves-Rodriguez v. R.J. Reynolds	Díaz-Hernández	Testimony
			Martinez-Fernandez	Testimony
134	2005	McLaughlin v. Philip Morris	Proctor	Expert report submitted
135	2005	Ortega v. Philip Morris	Díaz-Hernández	Testimony
			Schaller	Affidavit
136	2005	Ramos v. Philip Morris	Díaz-Hernández	Testimony
			Martinez-Fernandez	Expert report submitted
137	2005	Rosen v. Brown and Williamson	Kyriakoudes	Testimony
138	2005	Valle-Ortiz v. R.J. Reynolds	Díaz-Hernández	Testimony inadmissible
			Martinez-Fernandez	Testimony
139	2005	Vandenburg v. R.J. Reynolds	Ford	Expert report

(continued)

Table 8 (continued)

Number	Year	Case	Historian	Involvement
140	2005–2006	Waterhouse v. R.J. Reynolds	Fausz	Affidavit
			Norrell	Affidavit
141	2006	Bagshaw v. R.J. Reynolds	Stueck	Designated
142	2006–2010	Caronia v. Philip Morris	Schaller	Expert report submitted
143	2006–2012	Clinton v. Altria Group	English	Expert report submitted
			Sharp	Designated
144	2006	Clinton v. Brown and Williamson	Sharp	Expert report submitted
145	2006–2011	Donovan v. Philip Morris	English	Expert report submitted
			Greenwood	Expert report submitted
146	2006	Mulholland v. Altria Group	Schaller	Expert report submitted
147	2006	Pearson v. R.J. Reynolds	Martin	Designated
			Parssinen	Designated
148	2007–2012	Alexander v. R.J. Reynolds	Harvey	Expert report submitted
			Kyriakoudes	Deposition and testimony
			Proctor	Deposition
			Stueck	Deposition and testimony
149	2007	Ertman v. R.J. Reynolds	Kyriakoudes	Deposition
150	2007–2009	Ferlanti v. Liggett Group	DiBacco	Cross-examination
			Kyriakoudes	Cross-examination
			Proctor	Deposition and testimony
151	2007–2010	Grill v. Philip Morris	Schaller	Deposition and testimony
			Sharp	Designated
152	2008–2012	Avant v. R.J. Reynolds	Proctor	Deposition
153	2008–2012	Ballard v. R.J. Reynolds	Proctor	Affidavit and testimony
154	2008	Boss v. R.J. Reynolds	Parssinen	Designated
155	2008–2012	Bradley v. R.J. Reynolds	Cobbs Hoffman	Deposition
			Hoff	Deposition
			Proctor	Deposition
			Roberts	Deposition
			Schaller	Deposition and testimony

(continued)

Table 8 (continued)

Number	Year	Case	Historian	Involvement
156	2008–2013	Brown v. R.J. Reynolds	Martinez-Fernandez	Testimony
			Proctor	Deposition and testimony
157	2008	Dorn v. R.J. Reynolds	Kyriakoudes	Designated
			Proctor	Designated
158	2008	Douglas v. Philip Morris	Hoff	Designated
159	2008–2013	Evers v. R.J. Reynolds	Cobbs Hoffman	Cross-examination
			Kyriakoudes	Deposition
			Lipartito	Designated
			Proctor	Designated
160	2008–2009	Grant v. R.J. Reynolds	Hoff	Designated
			Kyriakoudes	Designated
			Proctor	Designated
161	2008	Harford v. R.J. Reynolds	Stueck	Expert report submitted
162	2008–2009	Hess v. R.J. Reynolds	Kyriakoudes	Testimony and deposition
			Proctor	Cross-examination
			Schaller	Cross-examination
163	2008–2009	Kalyvas v. Philip Morris	Kyriakoudes	Precluded
			Proctor	Affidavit
164	2008–2011	Kirkland v. R.J. Reynolds	Cobbs Hoffman	Designated
			Parssinen	Designated
			Proctor	Testimony
165	2008	Long v. R.J. Reynolds	Cobbs Hoffman	Designated
			Parssinen	Designated
166	2008	Loyd v. R.J. Reynolds	Kyriakoudes	Designated
			Proctor	Designated
167	2008–2009	Martin v. R.J. Reynolds	Kyriakoudes	Deposition and testimony
			Norrell	Deposition and testimony
			Proctor	Deposition
168	2008	Mcivor v. Philip Morris	Martin	Designated
			Parssinen	Designated
169	2008–2010	Putney v. R.J. Reynolds	Hoff	Direct and cross-examination
			Kyriakoudes	Deposition
			Proctor	Deposition

(continued)

Table 8 (continued)

Number	Year	Case	Historian	Involvement
170	2008	Raley v. R.J. Reynolds	Hoff	Designated
			Proctor	Designated
171	2008	Rodriguez v. R.J. Reynolds	Kyriakoudes	Designated
			Proctor	Designated
172	2008	Sottosanti v. R.J. Reynolds	Hoff	Designated
			Proctor	Designated
173	2008	Staggs v. R.J. Reynolds	Norrell	Designated
			Parssinen	Designated
174	2008	Stalley v. R.J. Reynolds	Proctor	Designated
175	2008–2011	Tullo v. R.J. Reynolds	Hoff	Deposition
			Kyriakoudes	Designated
			Proctor	Affidavit
176	2008	Viswat v. R.J. Reynolds	Martin	Designated
177	2008	Winell v. R.J. Reynolds	Martinez-Fernandez	Deposition
178	2008	Wyerick v. R.J. Reynolds	Cobbs Hoffman	Designated
			Hoff	Designated
179	2009–2014	Barbanell v. R.J. Reynolds	Hoff	Deposition and cross-examination
			Kyriakoudes	Deposition and testimony
			Proctor	Deposition and testimony
180	2009–2012	Bifolck v. Philip Morris	Kyriakoudes	Deposition
			Schaller	Deposition
181	2009–2013	Blasco v. R.J. Reynolds	Michel	Deposition
			Proctor	Testimony
182	2009	Bullock v. Philip Morris	Proctor	Affidavit
183	2009	Buonomo v. R.J. Reynolds	Kyriakoudes	Deposition
184	2009	Clay v. R.J. Reynolds	Kyriakoudes	Deposition
185	2009	Cleary v. Philip Morris	English	Expert report submitted
			Roberts	Affidavit
186	2009	Patterson v. R.J. Reynolds	Cobbs Hoffman	Deposition
187	2009–2013	Grossman v. R.J. Reynolds	Kyriakoudes	Deposition
			Proctor	Testimony
			Schaller	Cross-examination
188	2009–2010	Hall v. R.J. Reynolds	Kyriakoudes	Deposition and testimony
			Proctor	Testimony
			Sharp	Deposition

(continued)

Table 8 (continued)

Number	Year	Case	Historian	Involvement
189	2009–2010	Hetzner v. R.J. Reynolds	Proctor	Deposition
			Roberts	Deposition
190	2009	Hill v. R.J. Reynolds	Norrell	Testimony
191	2009–2014	In re: Engle Progeny cases	Cobbs Hoffman	Testimony
			Ford	Testimony
			Hoff	Deposition
			Kyriakoudes	Deposition
			Lipartito	Deposition
			Martin	Deposition
			Martinez-Fernandez	Deposition
			Michel	Deposition
			Norrell	Deposition and testimony
			Parssinen	Deposition
			Proctor	Deposition and testimony
			Roberts	Deposition and testimony
			Schaller	Deposition and testimony
			Stueck	Expert report submitted
192	2009–2010	Izzarelli v. R.J. Reynolds	Kyriakoudes	Deposition
			Parrish	Affidavit
			Proctor	Expert report submitted
193	2009–2012	Jacobson v. R.J. Reynolds	Michel	Deposition
			Proctor	Testimony
194	2009	Kaplan v. R.J. Reynolds	Kyriakoudes	Deposition
195	2009–2010	Koballa v. R.J. Reynolds	Kyriakoudes	Deposition
			Proctor	Deposition and testimony
196	2009	Pagliarello v. R.J. Reynolds	Hoff	Designated
197	2009	Rivera v. R.J. Reynolds	Hoff	Affidavit
198	2009	Sherman v. R.J. Reynolds	Ford	Testimony
			Kyriakoudes	Cross-examination
			Proctor	Testimony
199	2009–2010	Townsend v. R.J. Reynolds	Proctor	Deposition
			Sharp	Deposition and testimony
200	2009	Willis v. Philip Morris	Kyriakoudes	Deposition
			Lipartito	Deposition

(continued)

Table 8 (continued)

Number	Year	Case	Historian	Involvement
201	2010–2011	Andy Allen v. R.J. Reynolds	Proctor	Deposition and testimony
			Roberts	Deposition
202	2010	Budnick v. R.J. Reynolds	Roberts	Cross-examination
203	2010	Castleman v. R.J. Reynolds	Kyriakoudes	Deposition
204	2010–2013	Chamberlain v. R.J. Reynolds	Norrell	Testimony
			Proctor	Deposition and testimony
205	2010–2013	Cohen v. R.J. Reynolds	Ford	Cross-examination
			Greenwood	Deposition
			Proctor	Deposition and testimony
206	2010–2012	Coleman Alexander v. R.J. Reynolds	Proctor	Deposition and testimony
207	2010	Evans v. R.J. Reynolds	Proctor	Designated
208	2010	Frazier v. Philip Morris	Proctor	Deposition and testimony
209	2010	Gafney v. R.J. Reynolds	Hoff	Deposition
210	2010–2013	Haldeman v. R.J. Reynolds	Kyriakoudes	Deposition and testimony
			Roberts	Deposition
211	2010	In re: Light Cigarettes	English	Designated
			Greenwood	Designated
212	2010	Jones v. Philip Morris	Kyriakoudes	Designated
213	2010–2011	Katz v. R.J. Reynolds	DiBacco	Deposition and testimony
			Kyriakoudes	Deposition
			Michel	Deposition
214	2010–2011	Koballa v. Philip Morris	Ford	Cross-examination
			Harvey	Designated
215	2010	Mack v. R.J. Reynolds	Proctor	Deposition
216	2010	McEniry v. R.J. Reynolds	Proctor	Deposition
217	2010–2011	Oliva v. R.J. Reynolds	Martin	Deposition and testimony
			Proctor	Deposition and testimony
218	2010	Perez v. R.J. Reynolds	Proctor	Deposition
219	2010	Piendle v. R.J. Reynolds	Norrell	Deposition and testimony
220	2010	Richardson v. R.J. Reynolds	Martin	Testimony
221	2010	Rohr v. R.J. Reynolds	Cobbs Hoffman	Cross-examination
			Kyriakoudes	Deposition and testimony

(continued)

Table 8 (continued)

Number	Year	Case	Historian	Involvement
222	2010	Rubio v. R.J. Reynolds	Proctor	Designated
223	2010–2012	Scott v. R.J. Reynolds	Proctor	Deposition and testimony
224	2010–2012	Smith v. R.J. Reynolds	Cobbs Hoffman	
			Hoff	Deposition
			Norrell	Testimony
			Parssinen	Deposition
			Proctor	Deposition and testimony
			Roberts	Testimony
			Schaller	Testimony
			Stueck	Cross-examination
225	2010	Sulcer v. R.J. Reynolds	Parssinen	Deposition
226	2010	Talenfeld v. R.J. Reynolds	Martinez-Fernandez	Testimony
227	2010	Tate v. R.J. Reynolds	Proctor	Deposition and testimony
228	2010	Vasko v. R.J. Reynolds	Martin	Testimony
229	2010	Walden v. R.J. Reynolds	Roberts	Designated
230	2010	Warrick v. R.J. Reynolds	Proctor	Deposition and testimony
231	2010	Webb v. R.J. Reynolds	Michel	Cross-examination
232	2011	Aycock v. R.J. Reynolds	Cobbs Hoffman	Designated
			Schaller	Deposition and testimony
233	2011	Baker v. R.J. Reynolds	Roberts	Designated
234	2011	Blitch v. R.J. Reynolds	DiBacco	Testimony
235	2011	Bowman v. R.J. Reynolds	Proctor	Deposition and testimony
236	2011	Buchanan v. R.J. Reynolds	Hoff	Deposition
237	2011	Calloway v. Philip Morris	Kyriakoudes	Deposition
238	2011	Ciccone v. R.J. Reynolds	Greenwood	Cross-examination
			Kyriakoudes	Cross-examination
239	2011	Cox v. R.J. Reynolds	Michel	Deposition and cross-examination
240	2011	Denton v. R.J. Reynolds	Roberts	Expert report submitted
241	2011	Duke v. R.J. Reynolds	Stueck	Deposition
242	2011	Folks v. R.J. Reynolds	Hoff	Designated
243	2011	Gollihue v. R.J. Reynolds	Cobbs Hoffman	Deposition
244	2011	Hargroves v. R.J. Reynolds	Ford	Cross-examination

(continued)

Table 8 (continued)

Number	Year	Case	Historian	Involvement
245	2011	Hallgren v. R.J. Reynolds	Schaller	Deposition
246	2011	Huish v. R.J. Reynolds	Stueck	Cross-examination
247	2011–2013	In re: Tobacco Litigation	Proctor	Deposition and testimony
			Roberts	Testimony
248	2011	Jewett v. R.J. Reynolds	Kyriakoudes	Deposition and testimony
			Parssinen	Testimony
249	2011	Junious v. R.J. Reynolds	Proctor	Deposition and testimony
250	2011–2013	Marotta v. R.J. Reynolds	Kyriakoudes	Deposition
			Proctor	Deposition and testimony
251	2011	McCray v. R.J. Reynolds	Parssinen	Deposition
252	2011	Miller v. R.J. Reynolds	Proctor	Designated
			Roberts	Cross-examination
253	2011	Mrozek v. R.J. Reynolds	Roberts	Testimony
254	2011–2012	Narushka v. R.J. Reynolds	Cobbs Hoffman	Deposition
			Hoff	Deposition
			Norrell	Testimony
			Parssinen	Deposition
			Roberts	Testimony
			Schaller	Deposition and testimony
255	2011	Ojeda v. R.J. Reynolds	Martinez-Fernandez	Testimony
256	2012	Pickett v. R.J. Reynolds	Cobbs Hoffman	Testimony
257	2011	Reese v. R.J. Reynolds	Martin	Deposition and testimony
			Proctor	Deposition and testimony
258	2011–2012	Rodehaver v. R.J. Reynolds	Cobbs Hoffman	Testimony
			Hoff	Deposition
			Norrell	Testimony
			Parssinen	Expert report submitted
			Roberts	Testimony
			Schaller	Testimony

(continued)

Table 8 (continued)

Number	Year	Case	Historian	Involvement
259	2011–2012	Rudy v. R.J. Reynolds	Cobbs Hoffman	Testimony
			Hoff	Testimony
			Norrell	Testimony
			Parssinen	Deposition
			Roberts	Testimony
			Schaller	Deposition and testimony
260	2011	Soffer v. R.J. Reynolds	Cobbs Hoffman	Testimony
261	2011	Sury v. R.J. Reynolds	Proctor	Deposition and testimony
262	2011–2012	Vanblarcom v. R.J. Reynolds	Hoff	Testimony
			Martin	Testimony
			Norrell	Testimony
			Parssinen	Deposition
			Proctor	Designated
			Schaller	Deposition
			Stueck	Testimony
263	2011	Weick v. Philip Morris	Cobbs Hoffman	Cross-examination
			Kyriakoudes	Deposition and testimony
264	2012	Alexander v. Lorrilord	Proctor	Testimony
265	2012	Brinson v. R.J. Reynolds	Norrell	Expert report submitted
266	2012	Collaway v. R.J. Reynolds	Proctor	Deposition and testimony
267	2012	Linda Cumbness v. R.J. Reynolds	Stueck	Cross-examination
268	2012	Frailey v. R.J. Reynolds	Kyriakoudes	Deposition and testimony
			Michel	Testimony
269	2012	Giddens v. R.J. Reynolds	Hoff	Testimony
			Martin	Expert report and deposition
			Norrell	Testimony
			Parssinen	Deposition
			Proctor	Deposition
			Roberts	Deposition
			Schaller	Expert report submitted

(continued)

Table 8 (continued)

Number	Year	Case	Historian	Involvement
270	2012	Graham v. R.J. Reynolds	Hoff	Deposition
			Martin	Expert report submitted
			Norrell	Deposition
			Parssinen	Deposition
			Proctor	Deposition
			Roberts	Deposition
			Schaller	Deposition
			Stueck	Deposition
271	2012	Hill v. R.J. Reynolds	Hoff	Testimony
			Norrell	Expert report submitted
			Parssinen	Deposition
			Roberts	Deposition
			Schaller	Deposition and testimony
272	2012	Hiot v. R.J. Reynolds	Kyriakoudes	Deposition and testimony
273	2012	Hoppes v. R.J. Reynolds	Martin	Expert report submitted
274	2012	Larkin v. R.J. Reynolds	Martinez-Fernandez	Direct and cross-examination
			Proctor	Deposition and testimony
275	2012	Larrabee v. R.J. Reynolds	Hoff	Deposition
			Martin	Deposition
			Norrell	Deposition
			Parssinen	Deposition
			Proctor	Deposition
			Roberts	Deposition
			Schaller	Deposition
			Stueck	Deposition
276	2012	Proud v. R.J. Reynolds	Proctor	Deposition and expert report
			Stueck	Expert report submitted
277	2012	Reider v. R.J. Reynolds	Hoff	Testimony
			Martin	Deposition
			Norrell	Testimony
			Parssinen	Deposition
			Proctor	Deposition
			Roberts	Deposition
			Schaller	Deposition
			Stueck	Testimony

(continued)

Table 8 (continued)

Number	Year	Case	Historian	Involvement
278	2012	Schlenther v. R.J. Reynolds	Michel	Testimony
279	2012	Searcy v. R.J. Reynolds	Norrell	Expert report submitted
280	2012–2013	Sikes v. R.J. Reynolds	Proctor	Deposition and testimony
281	2012	Walker v. R.J. Reynolds	Michel	Cross-examination
282	2012	Wilder v. R.J. Reynolds	Hoff	Deposition
			Norrell	Expert report submitted
			Parssinen	Expert report submitted
			Roberts	Expert report submitted
283	2012	Williams v. R.J. Reynolds	Proctor	Testimony
284	2013–2014	Anderson v. R.J. Reynolds	Cobbs Hoffman	Cross-examination
285	2013–2014	Banks v. R.J. Reynolds	Proctor	Testimony
			Stueck	Deposition
286	2013–2014	Bowden v. R.J. Reynolds	Kyriakoudes	Deposition
287	2013	Brown-Hildgegard v. R.J. Reynolds	Michel	Deposition
288	2013	Crawford v. R.J. Reynolds	Proctor	Testimony
289	2013	Dombney v. R.J. Reynolds	Proctor	Testimony
290	2013	Deshaies v. R.J. Reynolds	Kyriakoudes	Affidavit
291	2013–2014	Ellis v. R.J. Reynolds	Proctor	Testimony
			Stueck	Deposition
292	2013	Elkins v. R.J. Reynolds	Kyriakoudes	Affidavit
			Roberts	Expert report submitted
293	2013	Hartford v. R.J. Reynolds	Kyriakoudes	Testimony
294	2013	Hausner v. R.J. Reynolds	Stueck	Testimony
295	2013	Kemp v. R.J. Reynolds	Schaller	Deposition
296	2013	Meeker v. R.J. Reynolds	Kyriakoudes	Deposition and testimony
			Roberts	Expert report submitted
297	2013	Milledge v. R.J. Reynolds	Stueck	Deposition
298	2013	Ruffo v. R.J. Reynolds	Proctor	Deposition and testimony
299	2013	Skolnic v. R.J. Reynolds	Proctor	Deposition and testimony
300	2013	Spolzino v. R.J. Reynolds	Proctor	Deposition and testimony

(continued)

Table 8 (continued)

Number	Year	Case	Historian	Involvement
301	2013	Thibault v. R.J. Reynolds	Proctor	Deposition and testimony
302	2013	Weinstein v. R.J. Reynolds	Proctor	Deposition and testimony
303	2014	Baum v. R.J. Reynolds	Proctor	Testimony
304	2014	Bryant v. R.J. Reynolds	Michel	Testimony
305	2014	Clayton v. R.J. Reynolds	Proctor	Testimony
306	2014	Cuculino v. Philip Morris	Proctor	Testimony
307	2014	Gonzalez v. Philip Morris	Proctor	Testimony
308	2014	Hubbird v. R.J. Reynolds	Proctor	Testimony
309	2014	Irmi v. R.J. Reynolds	Proctor	Testimony
310	2014	Lourie v. R.J. Reynolds	Proctor	Testimony
311	2014	Morse v. R.J. Reynolds	Kyriakoudes	Testimony
312	2014	Robinson v. R.J. Reynolds	Proctor	Testimony
313	2014	Wendel v. R.J. Reynolds	Proctor	Testimony
314	2014	Wilcox v. R.J. Reynolds	Proctor	Testimony

Table 9 Historians in tobacco litigation 1986–2014 and Westlaw reference

Number	Year	Case	Historian	WESTLAW
1	1986	Dewey v. R.J. Reynolds	Burnham	
2	1986–1991	Cipollone v. Liggett Group	Burnham	
			Carstensen	1988 WL 1531597
			Ludmerer	1991 WL 11685904
3	1990	Horton v. American Tobacco	Sansing	1990 WL 10544591
4	1990	Kotler v. American Tobacco	Graham	1990 WL 10550099
			Ludmerer	
5	1991	Ierardi v. Lorillard	Sansing	
			Savitt	
6	1992	Haines v. Liggett Group	English	
7	1993	Wilks v. American Tobacco	Sansing	1993 WL 13634677
8	1994	Allgood v. R.J. Reynolds	Breeden	
			Hudson	
9	1994	Covert v. Liggett Group	Ambrose	1994 WL 16776197
10	1994	Unkel v. Liggett Group	Ludmerer	
11	1996	Hoskins v. R.J. Reynolds	Parrish	1996 WL 34569153
12	1996	Burton v. R.J. Reynolds	Martin	
13	1996	Richardson v. R.J. Reynolds	Martin	
14	1996	Rogers v. R.J. Reynolds	Hoff	1996 WL 34439304
15	1996	Small v. Lorillard	Parrish	
16	1996	Stewart-Lomanitz v. Brown & Williamson	Parrish	1996 WL 34476785
17	1997	Arch v. American Tobacco	Parrish	1997 WL 34719230
18	1997	Barnes v. American Tobacco	Parrish	
			Wilson	
19	1997–1998	Dunn v. R.J. Reynolds	Hoff	1997 WL 34662989
20	1997	Emis v. American Tobacco	Wilson	1997 WL 34623858
21	1997–1999	Engle v. R.J. Reynolds	Burns	1998 WL 35273084
			DiBacco	1999 WL 34965597
			Ford	
			Ludmerer	1998 WL 35271772
22	1997	Florida v. American Tobacco	Ambrose	
			Burns	1997 WL 34665268
			Ludmerer	
23	1997	Frosina v. Philip Morris	Parrish	
24	1997	Grinnell v. American Tobacco	Sansing	
25	1997	Haines v. Liggett Group	Ambrose	

(continued)

Table 9 (continued)

Number	Year	Case	Historian	Westlaw
26	1997	In re: Mississippi Tobacco Litigation	Lowery	1997 WL 34672117
			Ludmerer	1997 WL 34663497
			Sansing	1997 WL 34668157
			Skates	1997 WL 34665106
27	1997–1999	Insolia v. Philip Morris	Wilson	1997 WL 33833947
28	1997	Jackson v. Brown and Williamson	Rose	
29	1997	Karbiwnyk v. R.J. Reynolds	Ford	
30	1997	Keegan v. R.J. Reynolds	Ford	
31	1997	Konkle v. R.J. Reynolds	Norrell	
32	1997	Marks v. R.J. Reynolds	Norrell	
33	1997	Mason v. American Tobacco	Wilson	
34	1997–1998	Minnesota v. Philip Morris	Berman	1998 WL 35261056
			Green	
35	1997	Mulholland v. Philip Morris	Schaller	
36	1997	Raulerson v. R.J. Reynolds	Ford	1997 WL 34662800
37	1997	Texas v. American Tobacco	Drobny	1997 WL 34668149
			Graham	1997 WL 34662921
38	1997	Walls v. American Tobacco	Wilson	
39	1998	Arizona v. American Tobacco	Schaller	
40	1998	Henley v. Philip Morris	Parrish	1998 WL 35262559
41	1998–1999	Ironworkers v. Philip Morris	Martin	
			Proctor	1999 WL 34874898
42	1998–1999	Karney v. Brown and Williamson	Norrell	1998 WL 35271781
43	1998	Northwest Laborers v. Philip Morris	Proctor	1998 WL 35169453
44	1998	Oklahoma v. R.J. Reynolds	Morgan	
45	1998	Selcer v. R.J. Reynolds	Schaller	
46	1998–1999	Smith v. Brown and Williamson	Wilson	1998 WL 35159200
47	1998	Tabb v. Philip Morris	Parrish	
48	1998	Washington v. American Tobacco	Ludmerer	1998 WL 35271782
			Parrish	
49	1998	Widdick v. Brown and Williamson	Tulchin	1998 WL 35262237
50	1999	Bergeron v. Philip Morris	Martin	1999 WL 34768671
51	1999	Branch v. Philip Morris	May	1999 WL 34790390
52	1999–2003	Carter v. Philip Morris	Hilty	1999 WL 35025578
			Sansing	
53	1999	Clay v. Philip Morris	Wilson	1999 WL 34965744

(continued)

Table 9 (continued)

Number	Year	Case	Historian	Westlaw
54	1999	Klein v. R.J. Reynods	Martin	1999 WL 34874677
55	1999	National Asbestos v. Philip Morris	Martin	1999 WL 34749162
56	1999	Newcomb v. R.J. Reynolds	Norrell	1999 WL 34875701
57	1999–2002	Schwarz v. Philip Morris	May	2002 WL 33931262
58	1999	Sweeney v. Philip Morris	Schaller	
59	1999	Thompson v. American Tobacco	Wilson	
60	1999–2006	US v. Philip Morris et al.	Brandt	2004 WL 5582805
			English	2002 WL 33936304
			Ludmerer	2002 WL 34428170
			Proctor	2002 WL 34428084
			Wilson	2002 WL 34428168
61	1999–2000	Whitely v. Raybestos-Manhattan	Hoff	2000 WL 36152077
62	1999	Williams v. Philip Morris	Ludmerer	1999 WL 34876134
			May	1999 WL 34874961
63	2000	Anderson v. American Tobacco	Ludmerer	2000 WL 35640858
			Sharp	
64	2000	Apostolou v. American Tobacco	Ludmerer	
			Schaller	
65	2000–2004	Blankenship v. R.J. Reynolds	Ford	
			Ludmerer	
			Wilson	
66	2000–2001	Blue Cross v. Philip Morris	DiBacco	2000 WL 1805359
			English	2001 WL 36142306
			Martin	2000 WL 35431986
67	2000–2003	Boerner v. Brown and Williamson	Harkness	2003 WL 25744676
			Kyriakoudes	2003 WL 24241513
			Parrish	
			Sansing	2003 WL 25737063
68	2000	Cannon v. Brown and Williamson	Kyriakoudes	
69	2000	Conely v. R.J. Reynolds	Hoff	2000 WL 35764820
70	2000	Falise v. American Tobacco	Martin	2000 WL 35639702
71	2000	In re: Tobacco Litigation	Ford	2000 WL 35717504
			Wilson	2000 WL 35643137
72	2000	Jones v. R.J. Reynolds	Ford	2000 WL 35640855
73	2000	Little v. Brown and Williamson	Ford	

(continued)

Table 9 (continued)

Number	Year	Case	Historian	Westlaw
74	2000–2001	Mehlman v. Philip Morris	Sharp	2001 WL 36139650
75	2000	Seaborn v. R.J. Reynolds	Norrell	2000 WL 35651535
76	2000–2001	Scott v. American Tobacco	Ludmerer	
			Norrell	2001 WL 36142942
77	2000	Simon v. Philip Morris	Schaller	
78	2000	White v. R.J. Reynolds	Fausz	
79	2001–2003	Boeken v. Philip Morris	Cobbs Hoffman	2001 WL 36136755
			Ludmerer	2001 WL 34919799
			Schaller	2001 WL 34920020
80	2001	Kenyon v. R.J. Reynolds	Ford	2001 WL 36140110
81	2001	Tompkin v. R.J. Reynolds	Hoff	2001 WL 36139900
			Ludmerer	
			Martin	
82	2002–2003	Allen v. R.J. Reynolds	Ford	2003 WL 25744686
			Kyriakoudes	2003 WL 25608275
83	2002–2004	Brown v. American Tobacco	Cobbs Hoffman	
			English	
84	2002	Bullock v. Philip Morris	English	
			Schaller	2002 WL 34457416
			Snetsinger	2002 WL 34425562
85	2002–2013	Campbell, Sr. v. R.J. Reynolds	Kyriakoudes	2009 WL 9081298
			Norrell	2009 WL 9071902
			Proctor	2009 WL 9071903
86	2002	Cruz v. R.J. Reynolds	Martinez-Fernandez	
87	2002–2005	Eiser v. Brown and Williamson	Kyriakoudes	2005 WL 5006212
			Stueck	
88	2002	Landers v. R.J. Reynolds	Kyriakoudes	
89	2002	Miles v. Philip Morris	English	
			Wilson	
90	2002	Sounders v. Philip Morris	Parrish	
91	2002	Tune v. Philip Morris	Lenoir	
92	2002–2004	Viguers v. Philip Morris	Hilty	2004 WL 3437694
93	2003	Bowyer v. Philip Morris	Parrish	2003 WL 68057
94	2003	Brown v. Liggett Group	Rose	
95	2003	Cruz-Vargas	Martinez-Fernandez	2003 WL 25562887
96	2003	Eastman v. Brown and Williamson	DiBacco	2003 WL 25744617
			Kyriakoudes	2003 WL 26465922

(continued)

Table 9 (continued)

Number	Year	Case	Historian	Westlaw
97	2003–2007	Frankson v. Brown and Williamson	Harkness	2003 WL 25700384
			Kyriakoudes	2004 WL 203073
			Proctor	2003 WL 25745940
			Schaller	
98	2003	Hall v. R.J. Reynolds	Kyriakoudes	2003 WL 23176451
99	2003	Longden v. Philip Morris	Chesson	
100	2003	Lucier v. R.J. Reynolds	Schaller	2003 WL 25745483
101	2003	Miele v. American Tobacco	Parrish	2003 WL 23318497
102	2003–2005	Reller v. Philip Morris	Kyriakoudes	
			Schaller	2003 WL 25741421
103	2003	Reynolds v. Philip Morris	Parrish	2003 WL 21213277
104	2003–2005	Rivera v. R.J. Reynolds	Díaz-Hernández	2005 WL 6443784
			Martinez-Fernandez	2003 WL 25625479
105	2003–2007	Rose v. American Tobacco	Harkness	2005 WL 6357418
			Judd	2003 WL 25751646
			Kyriakoudes	2005 WL 6413564
			Proctor	2005 WL 1817523
			Schaller	2007 WL 7500766
106	2003	Rosol v. R.J. Reynolds	Kyriakoudes	2003 WL 25809849
			Proctor	2003 WL 25885108
107	2003	Sachs v. Lorillard	Norrell	
108	2003–2006	Schwartz v. Liggett Group	Graham	2003 WL 25967718
109	2003	Sheppard v. R.J. Reynolds	Ford	2003 WL 24241583
110	2003	Standish v. American Tobacco	Judd	2003 WL 25587152
			Kyriakoudes	2003 WL 25581573
111	2003	Tomasino v. American Tobacco	Judd	2003 WL 25500915
			Kyriakoudes	2003 WL 25500929
112	2004–2005	Alvarez v. R.J. Reynolds	Díaz-Hernández	2004 WL 5487028
			Martinez-Fernandez	
113	2004	Arnitz v. Philip Morris	Kyriakoudes	
			Parssinen	2004 WL 4182142
114	2004–2005	Coolidge v. Philip Morris	Harvey	2005 WL 2170737
			Kyriakoudes	2005 WL 2170737
115	2004	Davis v. Liggett Group	Graham	2004 WL 5919934
116	2004	Gadelata v. Lorillard	Kyriakoudes	
117	2004	Gault v. Brown and Williamson	Stueck	2004 WL 3737107

(continued)

Table 9 (continued)

Number	Year	Case	Historian	Westlaw
118	2004	Kimball v. R.J. Reynolds	Parrish	2004 WL 3651942
119	2004	Logan v. Brown and Williamson	Parrish	2004 WL 5660651
120	2004	Mash v. Brown and Williamson	Kyriakoudes	2004 WL 5580439
			Stueck	2004 WL 5537103
121	2004	Moore v. R.J. Reynolds	Kyriakoudes	
122	2004–2006	Schwab v. Philip Morris	Bean	
			English	2005 WL 4858723
			Proctor	2005 WL 3292588
			Schaller	2005 WL 4858727
123	2004–2008	St. Louis v. American Tobacco	Bean	
			English	
			Ford	
			Proctor	2004 WL 5792169
124	2005	Araballoz v. R.J. Reynolds	Martinez-Fernandez	
125	2005–2006	Beckum v. Philip Morris	Kyriakoudes	2006 WL 162644
126	2005	Benedict v. Altria Group	English	2005 WL 4044682
			Schaller	2005 WL 4044684
127	2005	Caraballo-Rodriguez v. R.J. Reynolds	Díaz-Hernández	2005 WL 6768286
128	2005–2010	Craft v. Philip Morris	English	
			Greenwood	
129	2005	De Jesus v. R.J. Reynolds	Díaz-Hernández	2005 WL 6443783
130	2005	Gerrity v. Lorillard	Carstensen	
			Kyriakoudes	
131	2005	Hargroves v. Philip Morris	Kyriakoudes	2005 WL 6357284
132	2005	Huntsberry v. R.J. Reynolds	English	2005 WL 6800087
			Ford	2005 WL 6800086
133	2005	Nieves-Rodriguez v. R.J. Reynolds	Díaz-Hernández	2005 WL 6459137
			Martinez-Fernandez	2005 WL 2346910
134	2005	McLaughlin v. Philip Morris	Proctor	2005 WL 4858749
135	2005	Ortega v. Philip Morris	Díaz-Hernández	2005 WL 6443792
			Schaller	2005 WL 6443790
136	2005	Ramos v. Philip Morris	Díaz-Hernández	2005 WL 6319422
			Martinez-Fernandez	2005 WL 6443776

(continued)

Table 9 (continued)

Number	Year	Case	Historian	Westlaw
137	2005	Rosen v. Brown and Williamson	Kyriakoudes	
138	2005	Valle-Ortiz v. R.J. Reynolds	Díaz-Hernández	2005 WL 5775635
			Martinez-Fernandez	2005 WL 6772401
139	2005	Vandenburg v. R.J. Reynolds	Ford	2006 WL 755716
140	2005–2006	Waterhouse v. R.J. Reynolds	Fausz	
			Norrell	
141	2006	Bagshaw v. R.J. Reynolds	Stueck	2006 WL 6862948
142	2006–2010	Caronia v. Philip Morris	Schaller	2007 WL 5334145
143	2006–2012	Clinton v. Altria Group	English	2012 WL 8963687
			Sharp	2006 WL 6364033
144	2006	Clinton v. Brown and Williamson	Sharp	2006 WL 3540460
145	2006–2011	Donovan v. Philip Morris	Greenwood	2006 WL 5877270
			English	2011 WL 9154963
146	2006	Mulholland v. Altria Group	Schaller	2006 WL 6849497
147	2006	Pearson v. R.J. Reynolds	Martin	2006 WL 6375476
148	2007–2012	Alexander v. R.J. Reynolds	Harvey	2007 WL 6114298
			Kyriakoudes	2010 WL 6511228
			Proctor	2012 WL 10864387
			Stueck	2010 WL 6568237
149	2007	Ertman v. R.J. Reynolds	Kyriakoudes	
150	2007–2009	Ferlanti v. Liggett Group	DiBacco	2009 WL 1133709
			Kyriakoudes	
			Proctor	2007 WL 7010907
151	2007–2010	Grill v. Philip Morris	Schaller	2010 WL 5691836
			Sharp	2007 WL 7553702
152	2008–2012	Avant v. R.J. Reynolds	Proctor	2008 WL 8910990
153	2008–2012	Ballard v. R.J. Reynolds	Proctor	2008 WL 9009539
154	2008	Boss v. R.J. Reynolds	Parssinen	2008 WL 8727185
155	2008–2012	Bradley v. R.J. Reynolds	Cobbs Hoffman	2012 WL 4766472
			Hoff	2012 WL 3919800
			Proctor	2010 WL 9433238
			Roberts	2011 WL 9157991
			Schaller	2012 WL 4766470
156	2008–2013	Brown v. R.J. Reynolds	Martinez-Fernandez	2009 WL 2058215
			Proctor	2008 WL 6708815
157	2008	Dorn v. R.J. Reynolds	Kyriakoudes	
			Proctor	2008 WL 8716592

(continued)

Table 9 (continued)

Number	Year	Case	Historian	Westlaw
158	2008	Douglas v. Philip Morris	Hoff	2008 WL 8727190
159	2008–2013	Evers v. R.J. Reynolds	Cobbs Hoffman	2008 WL 7042863
			Kyriakoudes	2008 WL 7042870
			Lipartito	
			Proctor	2008 WL 7042857
160	2008–2009	Grant v. R.J. Reynolds	Hoff	2009 WL 8539859
			Kyriakoudes	2009 WL 2608534
			Proctor	2008 WL 8716581
161	2008	Harford v. R.J. Reynolds	Stueck	
162	2008–2009	Hess v. R.J. Reynolds	Kyriakoudes	
			Proctor	2009 WL 6725867
			Schaller	2009 WL 641616
163	2008–2009	Kalyvas v. Philip Morris	Kyriakoudes	2009 WL 1702161
			Proctor	2008 WL 6333456
164	2008–2011	Kirkland v. R.J. Reynolds	Cobbs Hoffman	2008 WL 8716593
			Parssinen	2008 WL 8716602
			Proctor	
165	2008	Long v. R.J. Reynolds	Cobbs Hoffman	2008 WL 7071486
			Parssinen	2008 WL 7071495
166	2008	Loyd v. R.J. Reynolds	Kyriakoudes	
			Proctor	2008 WL 7042857
167	2008–2009	Martin v. R.J. Reynolds	Kyriakoudes	2008 WL 6725867
			Norrell	2009 WL 2599268
			Proctor	2008 WL 8987818
168	2008	Mcivor v. Philip Morris	Martin	2008 WL 7003840
169	2008–2010	Putney v. R.J. Reynolds	Hoff	
			Kyriakoudes	2009 WL 6748790
			Proctor	2009 WL 6748791
170	2008	Raley v. R.J. Reynolds	Hoff	2008 WL 8727085
			Proctor	2008 WL 8716625
171	2008	Rodriguez v. R.J. Reynolds	Kyriakoudes	2008 WL 7042768
			Proctor	
172	2008	Sottosanti v. R.J. Reynolds	Hoff	2008 WL 8727053
			Proctor	2008 WL 6988345
173	2008	Staggs v. R.J. Reynolds	Norrell	2008 WL 6898644
			Proctor	2008 WL 6898626
174	2008	Stalley v. R.J. Reynolds	Proctor	2008 WL 6988345
175	2008–2011	Tullo v. R.J. Reynolds	Hoff	2010 WL 9594605
			Kyriakoudes	2008 WL 9492568
			Proctor	2011 WL 11057051
176	2008	Viswat v. R.J. Reynolds	Martin	2008 WL 6988333

(continued)

Table 9 (continued)

Number	Year	Case	Historian	Westlaw
177	2008–2009	Winell Rodriguez v. R.J. Reynolds	Martinez-Fernandez	2009 WL 5172335
178	2008	Wyerick v. R.J. Reynolds	Cobbs Hoffman	2008 WL 6722400
			Hoff	2008 WL 8727058
179	2009–2014	Barbanell v. R.J. Reynolds	Hoff	2009 WL 3023465
			Kyriakoudes	2009 WL 3155298
			Proctor	2009 WL 3480454
180	2009–2012	Bifolck v. Philip Morris	Kyriakoudes	2012 WL 3262450
			Schaller	2010 WL 8815841
181	2009–2013	Blasco v. R.J. Reynolds	Michel	2009 WL 9568677
			Proctor	2013 WL 8434150
182	2009	Bullock v. Philip Morris	Proctor	2009 WL 1850669
183	2009	Buonomo v. R.J. Reynolds	Kyriakoudes	2009 WL 6748789
184	2009	Clay v. R.J. Reynolds	Kyriakoudes	2009 WL 9096704
185	2009	Cleary v. R.J. Reynolds	English	2009 WL 8394913
			Roberts	2009 WL 8394908
186	2009	Patterson v. R.J. Reynolds	Cobbs Hoffman	2009 WL 6666232
187	2009–2013	Grossman v. R.J. Reynolds	Kyriakoudes	
			Proctor	
			Schaller	
188	2009–2011	Hall v. R.J. Reynolds	Kyriakoudes	
			Proctor	2009 WL 8730874
			Sharp	2010 WL 5893762
189	2009–2010	Hetzner v. R.J. Reynolds	Proctor	
			Roberts	
190	2009	Hill v. R.J. Reynolds	Norrell	2012 WL 3758222
191	2009–2014	In re: Engle Progeny cases	Cobbs Hoffman	2012 WL 3450317
			Ford	2010 WL 6568235
			Hoff	2012 WL 3234144
			Kyriakoudes	2009 WL 3334249
			Lipartito	
			Martin	2012 WL 5882553
			Martinez-Fernandez	2010 WL 6546722
			Michel	2010 WL 6511222
			Norrell	2012 WL 3234144
			Parssinen	2012 WL 4324526
			Proctor	2009 WL 7363532
			Roberts	2012 WL 3450319
			Schaller	2011 WL 8883344
			Stueck	2011 WL 7141436

(continued)

Table 9 (continued)

Number	Year	Case	Historian	Westlaw
192	2009–2010	Izzarelli v. R.J. Reynolds	Kyriakoudes	2010 WL 3000717
			Parrish	2009 WL 2995399
			Proctor	2010 WL 1227876
193	2009–2012	Jacobson v. R.J. Reynolds	Michel	2009 WL 9170771
			Proctor	2012 WL 9510817
194	2009	Kaplan v. R.J. Reynolds	Kyriakoudes	
195	2009–2010	Koballa v. R.J. Reynolds	Kyriakoudes	
			Proctor	
196	2009	Pagliarello v. R.J. Reynolds	Hoff	2009 WL 8539890
197	2009	Rivera v. R.J. Reynolds	Hoff	2007 WL 1549197
198	2009	Sherman v. R.J. Reynolds	Ford	2009 WL 1895991
			Kyriakoudes	
			Proctor	2009 WL 7419886
199	2009–2010	Townsend v. R.J. Reynolds	Proctor	
			Sharp	2010 WL 9933078
200	2009	Willis v. Philip Morris	Kyriakoudes	
			Lipartito	
201	2010–2011	Andy Allen v. R.J. Reynolds	Proctor	
			Roberts	2009 WL 4101020
202	2010	Budnick v. R.J. Reynolds	Roberts	
203	2010	Castleman v. R.J. Reynolds	Kyriakoudes	
204	2010–2013	Chamberlain v. R.J. Reynolds	Norrell	2013 WL 6143298
			Proctor	2012 WL 9510412
205	2010–2013	Cohen v. R.J. Reynolds	Ford	2010 WL 1924415
			Greenwood	2010 WL 1924419
			Proctor	2010 WL 1347299
206	2010–2012	Coleman Alexander v. R.J. Reynolds	Proctor	2012 WL 10864387
207	2010	Evans v. R.J. Reynolds	Proctor	2010 WL 5183980
208	2010	Frazier v. Philip Morris	Proctor	
209	2010	Gafney v. R.J. Reynolds	Hoff	
210	2010–2013	Haldeman v. R.J. Reynolds	Kyriakoudes	
			Roberts	
211	2010	In re: Light Cigarettes	English	2010 WL 4624054
			Greenwood	2010 WL 3358299
212	2010	Jones v. Philip Morris	Kyriakoudes	2010 WL 9551992
213	2010–2011	Katz v. R.J. Reynolds	DiBacco	2010 WL 6537162
			Kyriakoudes	2010 WL 6537151
			Michel	
214	2010–2011	Koballa v. Philip Morris	Ford	
			Harvey	

(continued)

Table 9 (continued)

Number	Year	Case	Historian	Westlaw
215	2010	Mack v. R.J. Reynolds	Proctor	2010 WL 5647593
216	2010	McEniry v. R.J. Reynolds	Proctor	
217	2010–2011	Oliva v. R.J. Reynolds	Martin	
			Proctor	2011 WL 1562180
218	2010	Perez v. R.J. Reynolds	Proctor	2010 WL 5647595
219	2010	Piendle v. R.J. Reynolds	Norrell	2010 WL 6568264
220	2010	Richardson v. R.J. Reynolds	Martin	2010 WL 8983426
221	2010	Rohr v. R.J. Reynolds	Cobbs Hoffman	2010 WL 4718967
			Kyriakoudes	2010 WL 4718967
222	2010	Rubio v. R.J. Reynolds	Proctor	2010 WL 3411698
223	2010–2012	Scott v. R.J. Reynolds	Proctor	2010 WL 8942491
224	2010–2012	Smith v. R.J. Reynolds	Cobbs Hoffman	2012 WL 3450322
			Hoff	2012 WL 3450323
			Norrell	2012 WL 3450321
			Parssinen	2011 WL 8741858
			Proctor	
			Roberts	2012 WL 3450324
			Schaller	2012 WL 3811900
			Stueck	
225	2010	Sulcer v. R.J. Reynolds	Parssinen	2010 WL 9926701
226	2010	Talenfeld v. R.J. Reynolds	Martinez-Fernandez	
227	2010	Tate v. R.J. Reynolds	Proctor	2010 WL 5086744
228	2010	Vasko v. R.J. Reynolds	Martin	
229	2010	Walden v. R.J. Reynolds	Roberts	
230	2010	Warrick v. R.J. Reynolds	Proctor	2010 WL 5647599
231	2010	Webb v. R.J. Reynolds	Michel	2010 WL 6546731
232	2011	Aycock v. R.J. Reynolds	Schaller	2012 WL 1930699
233	2011	Baker v. R.J. Reynolds	Roberts	2011 WL 9694833
234	2011	Blitch v. R.J. Reynolds	DiBacco	
235	2011	Bowman v. R.J. Reynolds	Proctor	
236	2011	Buchanan v. R.J. Reynolds	Hoff	
237	2011	Calloway v. Philip Morris	Kyriakoudes	
238	2011	Ciccone v. R.J. Reynolds	Greenwood	
			Kyriakoudes	
239	2011	Cox v. R.J. Reynolds	Michel	2011 WL 7780710
240	2011	Denton v. R.J. Reynolds	Roberts	2001 WL 7092757
241	2011	Duke v. R.J. Reynolds	Stueck	2011 WL 9521363
242	2011	Folks v. R.J. Reynolds	Hoff	2011 WL 6866844
243	2011	Gollihue v. R.J. Reynolds	Cobbs Hoffman	2012 WL 680654
244	2011	Hargroves v. R.J. Reynolds	Ford	
245	2011	Hallgren v. R.J. Reynolds	Schaller	
246	2011	Huish v. R.J. Reynolds	Stueck	2011 WL 1495581

(continued)

Table 9 (continued)

Number	Year	Case	Historian	Westlaw
247	2011–2013	In re: Tobacco Litigation	Proctor	
			Roberts	
248	2011	Jewett v. R.J. Reynolds	Kyriakoudes	
			Parssinen	
249	2011	Junious v. R.J. Reynolds	Proctor	
250	2011–2013	Marotta v. R.J. Reynolds	Kyriakoudes	
			Proctor	
251	2011	McCray v. R.J. Reynolds	Parssinen	2011 WL 8741848
252	2011	Miller v. R.J. Reynolds	Proctor	2011 WL 7120976
			Roberts	2011 WL 1193909
253	2011	Mrozek v. R.J. Reynolds	Roberts	2011 WL 1811652
254	2011–2012	Narushka v. R.J. Reynolds	Cobbs Hoffman	2012 WL 3811918
			Hoff	2012 WL 3450343
			Norrell	2012 WL 3450341
			Parssinen	2011 WL 8741880
			Roberts	2012 WL 3450344
			Schaller	2012 WL 3811914
255	2011	Ojeda v. R.J. Reynolds	Martinez-Fernandez	
256	2011–2012	Pickett v. R.J. Reynolds	Cobbs Hoffman	2011 WL 7141442
257	2011	Reese v. R.J. Reynolds	Martin	
			Proctor	
258	2011–2012	Rodehaver v. R.J. Reynolds	Cobbs Hoffman	2012 WL 3541153
			Hoff	2012 WL 3541158
			Norrell	2012 WL 3541161
			Parssinen	2012 WL 3541162
			Roberts	2012 WL 3451155
			Schaller	2011 WL 8946591
259	2011–2012	Rudy v. R.J. Reynolds	Cobbs Hoffman	2012 WL 4062258
			Hoff	2012 WL 4062273
			Norrell	2012 WL 4062276
			Parssinen	2011 WL 9025223
			Roberts	2012 WL 4062261
			Schaller	2012 WL 4810586
260	2011	Soffer v. R.J. Reynolds	Cobbs Hoffman	
261	2011	Sury v. R.J. Reynolds	Proctor	2011 WL 9523065
262	2011–2012	Vanblarcom v. R.J. Reynolds	Hoff	2012 WL 4062245
			Martin	2012 WL 0062242
			Norrell	2012 WL 4062244
			Parssinen	2012 WL 4062247
			Proctor	2012 WL 6185891
			Schaller	2012 WL 4062241
			Stueck	2011 WL 9025219

(continued)

Table 9 (continued)

Number	Year	Case	Historian	Westlaw
263	2011	Weick v. Philip Morris	Cobbs Hoffman	
			Kyriakoudes	
264	2012	Alexander v. Lorrilord	Proctor	
265	2012	Brinson v. R.J. Reynolds	Norrell	2012 WL 3450330
266	2012	Collaway v. R.J. Reynolds	Proctor	
267	2012	Linda Cumbness v. R.J. Reynolds	Stueck	
268	2012	Frailey v. R.J. Reynolds	Kyriakoudes	
			Michel	
269	2012	Giddens v. R.J. Reynolds	Hoff	2012 WL 4107326
			Martin	2012 WL 4107324
			Norrell	2012 WL 4107355
			Parssinen	2012 WL 4107328
			Proctor	2012 WL 4107331
			Schaller	2012 WL 4107323
270	2012	Graham v. R.J. Reynolds	Hoff	2012 WL 4107336
			Martin	2012 WL 4107332
			Norrell	2012 WL 4107325
			Parssinen	2012 WL 4107338
			Proctor	2012 WL 4107341
			Roberts	2012 WL 4107337
			Schaller	2012 WL 4107339
			Stueck	2012 WL 4107334
271	2012	Hill v. R.J. Reynolds	Cobbs Hoffman	2012 WL 4062298
			Hoff	2012 WL 4062280
			Norrell	2012 WL 4062302
			Parssinen	2012 WL 4810736
			Roberts	2012 WL 4062304
			Schaller	2012 WL 4810698
272	2012	Hiot v. R.J. Reynolds	Kyriakoudes	
273	2012	Hoppes v. R.J. Reynolds	Martin	
274	2012	Larkin v. R.J. Reynolds	Martinez-Fernandez	
			Proctor	
275	2012	Larrabee v. R.J. Reynolds	Hoff	2012 WL 4107356
			Martin	2012 WL 4107353
			Norrell	2012 WL 4107355
			Parssinen	2012 WL 4107358
			Proctor	2012 WL 4107366
			Roberts	2012 WL 4107357
			Schaller	2012 WL 4107359
			Stueck	2012 WL 4107354

(continued)

Table 9 (continued)

Number	Year	Case	Historian	Westlaw
276	2012	Proud v. R.J. Reynolds	Proctor	2012 WL 4107287
			Stueck	2012 WL 4324532
277	2012	Reider v. R.J. Reynolds	Hoff	2012 WL 4050494
			Martin	2012 WL 4050491
			Norrell	2012 WL 4050493
			Parssinen	2012 WL 4050496
			Proctor	2012 WL 4050500
			Roberts	2012 WL 4050495
			Schaller	2012 WL 4050497
			Stueck	2012 WL 4050492
278	2012	Schlenther v. R.J. Reynolds	Michel	
279	2012	Searcy v. R.J. Reynolds	Norrell	2012 WL 4324530
280	2012–2013	Sikes v. R.J. Reynolds	Proctor	
281	2012	Walker v. R.J. Reynolds	Michel	2012 WL 9510404
282	2012	Wilder v. R.J. Reynolds	Hoff	2012 WL 3450334
			Norrell	2012 WL 3450337
			Parssinen	2012 WL 3450338
			Roberts	2012 WL 3450339
283	2012	Williams v. R.J. Reynolds	Proctor	
284	2013–2014	Anderson v. R.J. Reynolds	Cobbs Hoffman	
285	2013–2014	Banks v. R.J. Reynolds	Proctor	
			Stueck	
286	2013–2014	Bowden v. R.J. Reynolds	Kyriakoudes	
287	2013	Brown-Hildgegard v. R.J. Reynolds	Michel	
288	2013	Crawford v. R.J. Reynolds	Proctor	2013 WL 6711230
289	2013	Dombney v. R.J. Reynolds	Proctor	
290	2013	Deshaies v. R.J. Reynolds	Kyriakoudes	2013 WL 8505967
291	2013–2014	Ellis v. R.J. Reynolds	Proctor	
			Stueck	
292	2013	Elkins v. R.J. Reynolds	Kyriakoudes	2013 WL 8505970
293	2013	Hartford v. R.J. Reynolds	Kyriakoudes	2013 WL 8505972
294	2013	Hausner v. R.J. Reynolds	Stueck	
295	2013	Kemp v. R.J. Reynolds	Schaller	
296	2013	Meeker v. R.J. Reynolds	Kyriakoudes	2013 WL 8743141
297	2013	Milledge v. R.J. Reynolds	Stueck	
298	2013	Ruffo v. R.J. Reynolds	Proctor	2013 WL 6047827
299	2013	Skolnic v. R.J. Reynolds	Proctor	
300	2013	Spolzino v. R.J. Reynolds	Proctor	
301	2013	Thibault v. R.J. Reynolds	Proctor	
302	2013	Weinstein v. R.J. Reynolds	Proctor	

(continued)

Table 9 (continued)

Number	Year	Case	Historian	Westlaw
303	2014	Baum v. R.J. Reynolds	Proctor	
304	2014	Bryant v. R.J. Reynolds	Michel	
305	2014	Clayton v. R.J. Reynolds	Proctor	
306	2014	Cuculino v. Philip Morris	Proctor	2014 WL 673387
307	2014	Gonzalez v. Philip Morris	Proctor	
308	2014	Hubbird v. R.J. Reynolds	Proctor	
309	2014	Irmi v. R.J. Reynolds	Proctor	
310	2014	Lourie v. R.J. Reynolds	Proctor	
311	2014	Morse v. R.J. Reynolds	Proctor	
312	2014	Robinson v. R.J. Reynolds	Proctor	
313	2014	Wendel v. R.J. Reynolds	Proctor	
314	2014	Wilcox v. R.J. Reynolds	Proctor	

Appendix IV: A Code of Ethics for Historians, by Antoon De Baets

A Code of Ethics for Historians (Proposal)

Extract from Antoon De Baets, *Responsible History* (New York and Oxford: Berghahn, 2009), 188–196.

Introduction

Article 1: Scope

This code is intended for academic historians (further abbreviated as "historians.") Its use is recommended for other professional and nonprofessional historians. It is also a tool for the general public wanting to be informed about the standards of the historical profession. It constitutes a set of principles about the historians' rights and duties and expresses a vision on its four irreducible values: freedom and integrity (of historians), respect (for those they study), and the careful and methodically determined and executed search for historical truth (as the result of the interactions between historians and others).

The code flows from the UNESCO *Recommendation Concerning the Status of Higher-Education Teaching Personnel* (1997), Article 22(k): "[H]igher education institutions should be accountable for . . . the creation, through the collegial process and/or through negotiation with organizations representing higher-education teaching personnel, consistent with the principles of academic freedom and freedom of speech, of statements or codes of ethics to guide higher education personnel in their teaching, scholarship, research and extension work," and from the *Constitution* of the International Committee of Historical Sciences (2005), Article 1: "It shall defend freedom of thought and expression in the field of historical research and teaching, and is opposed to the misuse of history and shall use every means at its disposal to ensure the ethical professional conduct of its members."

Article 2: Implementation

Historians shall use, discuss, and promote this code at congresses and during their research and teaching. It must be interpreted as a whole; nothing in it may be explained on the basis of arguments that are contrary to its spirit. Complaints about breaches of the code, when supported with evidence, merit investigation by a representative, authoritative, and independent body of historians, which, if necessary, takes the advice of experts.

Core Tasks

Article 3: Research; Teaching

Historians have two equal and connected core tasks: the search for historical truth (historical research) and its transmission (publishing and history teaching).

Universal Rights

Article 4: Freedom of Information and Expression; Peaceful Assembly; Intellectual Property

Historians' rights are based on the *Universal Declaration of Human Rights* (1948) and the international covenants derived from it. Particularly important are Article 19(1) and 19(2) of the *International Covenant on Civil and Political Rights* that protect the freedom of information necessary for historical research and the freedom of expression necessary for publishing and the teaching of history. Article 19 stipulates that: "(1) Everyone shall have the right to hold opinions without interference; (2) Everyone shall have the right to freedom of expression; this right shall include freedom to seek, receive and impart information and ideas of all kinds, regardless of frontiers, either orally, in writing or in print, in the form of art, or through any other media of his choice." In addition, Article 21 of the *Covenant* states that historians have the right to organize meetings and form professional associations. Equally important is Article 15(1)(c) of the *International Covenant on Economic, Social and Cultural Rights* that protects the intellectual property of historians. It stipulates that, "States Parties to the present Covenant recognize the right of everyone . . . to benefit from the protection of the moral and material interests resulting from any scientific . . . production of which he is the author."

Duty-Dependent Rights

Article 5: Academic Freedom; Autonomy; International Contacts

Duty-dependent rights can be claimed and exercised only while historians discharge their duties. While historians discharge their duties inside or outside of academe, Articles 15(2), 15(3), and 15(4) of the *International Covenant on Economic, Social and Cultural Rights* (1966) are applicable, in particular that "the States Parties to the present Covenant" will take steps "necessary for the conservation, the development and the diffusion of science and culture," that these states "undertake to respect the freedom indispensable for scientific research," and "recognize the benefits to be derived from the encouragement and development of international contacts and cooperation in the scientific and cultural fields." These articles imply that historians are entitled to academic freedom, including the right to organize themselves autonomously. Paragraph 27 of the UNESCO *Recommendation* defines academic freedom as follows: "[T]he right [of higher-education teaching personnel], without constriction by prescribed doctrine, to freedom of teaching and discussion, freedom in carrying out research and disseminating and publishing the results thereof, freedom to express freely their opinion about the institution or system in which they work, freedom from institutional censorship and freedom to participate in professional or representative academic bodies." This academic freedom also extends to expressions and activities in the public sphere if those are unambiguously performed as part of the academic work. Historians are allowed to exchange information at an international level, which includes the right to travel for scientific purposes. The tasks of historians demand long-term commitments and, therefore, the academic freedom of historians is best protected by a system of tenure.

Article 6: Choice of Topics

Historians have the right to choose and design their research topics and their curricula of teaching topics without political or other nonscientific interference.

Article 7: Selection of Information

Historians have the right to work on the basis of equitable laws on copyright, freedom of information, archives, secrecy and privacy and defamation. They are entitled to demand that archival selection criteria (that is, criteria to preserve or destroy records) are not politically inspired and take due account of the historical interest; that maximal, free, and equal access to information is the rule and that restrictions are exceptional and only for purposes prescribed by law and necessary in a democratic society. It should be possible to contest any restriction through a procedure independent of the executive branch.

Duties in General

Article 8: Complementarity

In their capacity as human beings, citizens, professionals, and academics, historians have general duties stipulated in international instruments. To these general duties, their specific duties are complementary. Historians have specific duties because they obtain expert knowledge about the past. In order to discharge these specific duties, they should have the rights described above. If these rights are lacking in whole or in part, historians shall still attempt to discharge their specific duties to the best of their ability. Furthermore, they shall discuss conflicts between general and specific duties (in particular, between their duties as loyal citizens and those as critical scholars) at congresses and during their research and teaching, and balance them in the spirit of this code.

Duties Regarding Subjects of Study

Article 9: Respect

Aware of the universal rights of the living and the universal duties to the dead, historians shall respect the dignity of the living and the dead they study. The *International Covenant on Civil and Political Rights* (1966) is applicable, in particular Article 17(1): "No one shall be subjected to arbitrary or unlawful interference with his privacy, family, home or correspondence, nor to unlawful attacks on his honour and reputation," and Article 19(3): "[The right to freedom of expression] may . . . be subject to certain restrictions, but these shall only be such as are provided by law and are necessary: (a) for respect of the rights or reputations of others; (b) for the protection of national security or of public order. . ., or of public health or morals."

Duties Regarding Work

Article 10: Integrity; Historical Truth

Integrity is the moral foundation of the historians' work. It shall be the intent of historians to honestly search for the historical truth, even if they are aware that their knowledge is provisional and fallible, and even if there are limits to that search as stipulated in Article 9 ("Respect"). Historians shall always oppose the abuse of history (its use with intent to deceive) and the irresponsible use of history (either its deceptive or negligent use).

Article 11: Access to Information

When accessing information, historical and otherwise, historians shall respect: (1) embargoes provided by the laws on freedom of information and on archives, (2) the informed consent principle governing interviews, and (3) pledges of confidentiality. Historians accessing confidential information on individuals, private institutions, or the government under certain conditions—conditions such as: monopolistic access; privileged access; selective access; approval of research design; oath of secrecy about the information during and/or after research; anonymization of information or its sources (informants, witnesses, and respondents); manuscript approval; pre-publication review and clearance by third parties; partial or total or temporary publication ban—shall fairly balance, in the spirit of this code, the benefit in terms of the estimated information surplus against the harm for all parties involved in terms of unequal access, biased information, or nonidentifiability of persons. Historians have a right to nondisclosure of sources of confidential information, but given their scholarly duties of transparency and accountability, they should balance any nondisclosure against disclosure with a presumption in favor of disclosure.

Article 12: Disclosure of Information

The disclosure of information is governed by Articles 10 and 11, and restricted by Article 9. Publication of information, and speaking freely about it, is the rule; confidentiality is the exception. As part of their right to silence—itself an integral part of the universal right to free expression—historians have the right, after balancing the individual against the public interest, not to disclose historical facts harming the privacy and reputation of persons, either living or dead. The balancing test takes place as follows: in privacy cases, the interests in disclosure and secrecy are of equal importance; in reputation cases there is, in principle, a presumption in favor of disclosure.

Article 13: Critical and Objective Method; Independence

Historians shall adopt a critical attitude and use a method based on: (1) accuracy (transparency; respect for evidence and argumentation; control of bias and anachronism; impartiality and objectivity) at the levels of statements of fact and description, and (2) plausibility at the levels of statements of opinion and analysis. Historians shall be candid about their perspective on the past and disclose the names of institutions or persons from whom they are dependent. They shall aspire to political, ideological, and intellectual independence and to as much financial independence as possible from government, commissioning entities, and sponsors.

Article 14: Free Debate; Accountability; Universalism

Free and public exchange of ideas is the oxygen of historical scholarship. Historians shall publish and disseminate their corroborated research findings as much as possible. Reports with a secret or confidential character shall be kept to a minimum. Peer review shall be carried out objectively and impartially; it shall be anonymous only when absolutely necessary. Peers with a conflict or harmony of interests, real or perceived, with the historians under review, shall abstain from reviewing them. Historians shall check their findings in a free and public debate among informed and verifying colleagues, students, and third parties. They shall be tolerant of divergent informed and *bona fide* opinions of mainstream historians and their opponents. Their orientation shall be universalistic in that their research shall not be audience-relative but shall allow, in principle, worldwide verification.

Article 15: Moral Evaluations

Historians shall be sensitive to their implicit moral evaluations. As part of their right to silence, historians have an absolute right not to mention their own explicit moral evaluations about the past. However, they shall be allowed to make such explicit moral evaluations on their subjects of study, on the condition that these have sufficient factual basis, are prudent and fair, and are a contribution to the public debate about history. In such evaluations, historians shall at all times clearly distinguish the values of contemporaries of the epoch studied, those of themselves, and those embodied in universal human rights standards. Although historians are not obliged to make statements about responsibility and guilt of historical actors or to draw moral lessons from the past, in cases of imprescriptible crimes, such as genocide, crimes against humanity, and war crimes, they shall try, to the best of their ability, to indicate the range of well-founded evaluations.

Duties Regarding Society at Large

Article 16: The Right to History

The first duty of historians regarding society—understood as their local, national, and global community—is the discharge of the other duties mentioned in this code. Article 13(1) of the *International Covenant on Economic, Social and Cultural Rights* stipulates that "The States Parties. . . agree that education shall be directed to the full development of the human personality" and its Articles 15(1)(a) and 15(1)(b) recognize the right of every one "to take part in cultural life," and "to enjoy the benefits of scientific progress and its applications." Therefore, historians shall attempt to answer important historical questions asked by their society to the best of their ability. They shall further the historical awareness of their society and facilitate its right to history, provided that such promotion corresponds to the spirit of this code. When performing activities in the public forum, historians shall avoid every ambiguity as to whether they operate with professional or scholarly authority. Historians shall help enhance the quality of history teaching in primary and secondary education, including the contents of history curricula and history textbooks.

Article 17: The Right to Memory

Memories are opinions and, as such, they are protected by Article 19(1) of the *International Covenant on Civil and Political Rights.* Holding opinions, and by extension memories, permits no exception or restriction. Every individual has a right to memory. The right to have memories implies the right not to be forced by others to have specific memories. No duty to remember can be imposed on others. Expressing opinions, and by extension memories, is subject to the restrictions of Article 19(3) of the *International Covenant on Civil and Political Rights* (quoted above). Although historians should reject the duty to remember and although individually they have the freedom to choose their research and teaching topics, they form a global professional community that, when perceived as such, has the collective duty, in principle, to study and teach the past in its entirety, including suppressed, generally forgotten, or controversial historical issues.

Article 18: Democracy

Historians shall support democracy because a democratic society—a society that recognizes and respects the human rights set forth in the *Universal Declaration of Human Rights*—is a necessary condition for a sound historiography. Conversely, a sound historiography reflects and strengthens the democratic society.

Duties Regarding the Historical Profession

Article 19: Protection

Historians shall protect and promote the historical profession and its infrastructure of sources. They shall oppose external threats to the autonomy of the profession. They shall also oppose internal threats to the integrity of the profession, that is, the abuse and irresponsible use of history mentioned in Articles 1, 2 and 10, the unfair treatment of colleagues and students, and inequality under equal conditions.

Article 20: Solidarity

Historians shall treat colleagues and history students with respect and sympathy. They shall work for the rights of all members of the profession worldwide. They shall show solidarity with colleagues and history students whose rights are violated.

Index

R. Delafontaine, *Historians as Expert Judicial Witnesses in Tobacco Litigation*, Studies in the History of Law and Justice 4, DOI 10.1007/978-3-319-14292-0

C

D

E

F

MIX
Papier aus verantwortungsvollen Quellen
Paper from responsible sources
FSC® C105338

If you have any concerns about our products,
you can contact us on
ProductSafety@springernature.com

In case Publisher is established outside the EU,
the EU authorized representative is:
Springer Nature Customer Service Center GmbH
Europaplatz 3, 69115 Heidelberg, Germany

Printed by Libri Plureos GmbH
in Hamburg, Germany